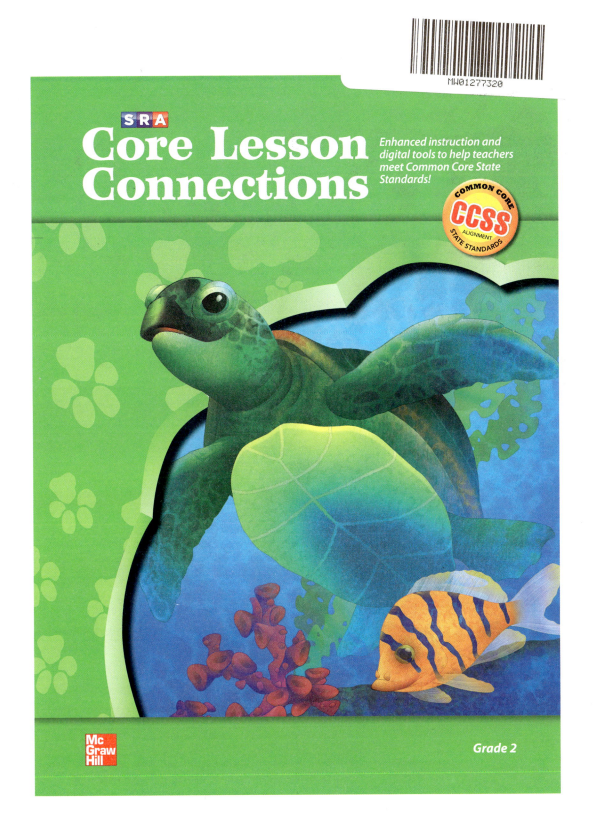

Nancy E. Marchand-Martella, Ph.D.
Ronald C. Martella, Ph.D.
Angela M. Przychodzin, M.Ed.
Susan Hornor, M.Ed.
Lisa Warner, M.Ed.

Bothell, WA • Chicago, IL • Columbus, OH • New York, NY

MHEonline.com

 Education

Copyright © 2013 The McGraw-Hill Companies, Inc.

All rights reserved. No part of this publication may be reproduced or distributed in any form or by any means, or stored in a database or retrieval system, without the prior written consent of The McGraw-Hill Companies, Inc., including, but not limited to, network storage or transmission, or broadcast for distance learning.

Permission is granted to reproduce the material contained on pages A3–A15 on the condition that such material be reproduced only for classroom use; be provided to students, teachers, or families without charge; and be used solely in conjunction with *SRA Reading Mastery Signature Edition*.

Send all inquiries to:
McGraw-Hill Education
8787 Orion Place
Columbus, OH 43240

ISBN: 978-0-02-128249-4
MHID: 0-02-128249-8

Printed in the United States of America.

2 3 4 5 6 7 8 9 RMN 17 16 15 14 13

Table of Contents

GRADE 2

Overview of SRA *Core Lesson Connections*............................ **cc1**

Summary of Skills **cc7**

Scope and Sequence of SRA *Core Lesson Connections* **cc9**

Lesson 1 1	Lesson 44........................136
Lesson 2........................... 4	**Lesson 45** 139
Lesson 3 7	Lesson 46........................142
Lesson 4........................... 9	**Lesson 47** 146
Lesson 5 12	Lesson 48........................150
Lesson 6..........................15	**Lesson 49** 153
Lesson 7 18	Lesson 50........................157
Lesson 8..........................21	**Lesson 51** 161
Lesson 9 24	Lesson 52........................164
Lesson 10.........................27	**Lesson 53** 166
Lesson 11 31	Lesson 54........................169
Lesson 12.........................34	**Lesson 55** 172
Lesson 13 37	Lesson 56........................175
Lesson 14.........................40	**Lesson 57** 178
Lesson 15 43	Lesson 58........................181
Lesson 16.........................46	**Lesson 59** 184
Lesson 17 49	Lesson 60........................187
Lesson 18.........................52	**Lesson 61** 191
Lesson 19 55	Lesson 62........................194
Lesson 20.........................58	**Lesson 63** 197
Lesson 21 61	Lesson 64........................201
Lesson 22.........................64	**Lesson 65** 204
Lesson 23 67	Lesson 66........................206
Lesson 24.........................70	**Lesson 67** 209
Lesson 25 73	Lesson 68........................212
Lesson 26.........................76	**Lesson 69** 215
Lesson 27 79	Lesson 70........................218
Lesson 28.........................82	**Lesson 71** 221
Lesson 29 85	Lesson 72........................224
Lesson 30.........................87	**Lesson 73** 227
Lesson 31 91	Lesson 74........................230
Lesson 32.........................95	**Lesson 75** 234
Lesson 33 99	Lesson 76........................237
Lesson 34........................102	**Lesson 77** 240
Lesson 35 106	Lesson 78........................243
Lesson 36........................109	**Lesson 79** 247
Lesson 37 113	Lesson 80........................251
Lesson 38........................116	**Lesson 81** 255
Lesson 39 120	Lesson 82........................258
Lesson 40........................123	**Lesson 83** 261
Lesson 41 127	Lesson 84........................264
Lesson 42........................130	**Lesson 85** 267
Lesson 43 133	Lesson 86........................270

Table of Contents (cont.)

GRADE 2

Lesson 87	273		**Lesson 117**	372
Lesson 88	277		Lesson 118	375
Lesson 89	280		**Lesson 119**	378
Lesson 90	283		Lesson 120	381
Lesson 91	287		**Lesson 121**	385
Lesson 92	290		Lesson 122	388
Lesson 93	293		**Lesson 123**	391
Lesson 94	297		Lesson 124	394
Lesson 95	301		**Lesson 125**	396
Lesson 96	304		Lesson 126	399
Lesson 97	307		**Lesson 127**	402
Lesson 98	310		Lesson 128	405
Lesson 99	313		**Lesson 129**	408
Lesson 100	317		Lesson 130	411
Lesson 101	321		**Lesson 131**	415
Lesson 102	324		Lesson 132	419
Lesson 103	327		**Lesson 133**	422
Lesson 104	330		Lesson 134	425
Lesson 105	333		**Lesson 135**	427
Lesson 106	336		Lesson 136	430
Lesson 107	339		**Lesson 137**	432
Lesson 108	343		Lesson 138	435
Lesson 109	346		**Lesson 139**	438
Lesson 110	349		Lesson 140	441
Lesson 111	353		**Lesson 141**	445
Lesson 112	357		Lesson 142	447
Lesson 113	360		**Lesson 143**	450
Lesson 114	363		Lesson 144	453
Lesson 115	366		**Lesson 145**	456
Lesson 116	369			

Appendix A Blackline Masters

Appendix B: Differentiated Instruction

Appendix C: Levels of Support

Appendix D: Professional Development

Appendix E: Fluency/Paired Reading Guidelines

Appendix F: Scope and Sequence of *Reading Mastery Signature Edition,* Grade 2

Appendix G: Correlation to the Common Core State Standards

SRA Reading Mastery

Signature Edition

Your Master Plan for
Core Comprehensive Reading

The comprehensive program that helps at-risk students succeed

- Validated by extensive and exhaustive research
- Proven to work in a wide range of classrooms, schools, and districts
- Systematic, explicit instruction for heightened academic achievement

SRA

A Core Comprehension Solution

Welcome to **Reading Mastery Signature Edition**! It's a comprehensive solution that is flexible enough to serve as your intervention program, in addition to your core program, or combine all strands to work together as a complete program. **Reading Mastery Signature Edition** is research-based and field-tested, and it meets rigorous Common Core State Standards.

How Reading, Language Arts, and Literature work together

Three strands address Reading, Oral Language/Language Arts, and Literature

- Activities within each strand reflect clearly stated goals and objectives
- Skills and processes are clearly linked within, as well as across, each strand
- Each strand can be targeted for use as an intervention program, in addition to the core program, or combined for use as a comprehensive stand-alone reading program

Reading Strand

- Addresses all five essential components of reading as identified by Reading First: phonemic awareness, phonics and word analysis, fluency, vocabulary, and comprehension
- Provides spelling instruction to enable students to make the connection between decoding and spelling patterns
- Develops student decoding and word recognition skills that transfer to other subject areas

Oral Language/Language Arts Strand

- Teaches the oral language skills necessary to understand what is spoken, written, and read in the classroom
- Helps students to communicate ideas and information effectively
- Develops the ability to use writing strategies and writing processes successfully

Literature Strand

- Supports the reading strand with a wide variety of literary forms and text structures
- Provides multiple opportunities for students to work with useful and important words
- Gives ample opportunity for each student to read at his or her independent level

What makes *Reading Mastery Signature Edition* unique is how:

- Information is presented
- Assignments are structured
- Understanding is tested

Strategy-based instruction allows students to learn new information in a more efficient way:

- Complex tasks are analyzed and broken into component parts
- Each part is taught in a logical progression
- The amount of new information is controlled and connected to prior learning
- Ample practice opportunities ensure mastery

Intensive, explicit, systematic instruction helps students use skills and processes with a high rate of success, because:

- Whatever is presented is **taught**, clearly and directly
- Whatever is taught is actively **practiced**, multiple times
- Whatever is practiced is **linked and applied** to new learning

Fully aligned materials help you guide students through the learning cycle and promote independent learning through:

- Highly detailed lessons
- Consistent teacher-friendly instructional routines
- Frequent teacher-student interactions
- Deliberate and carefully scaffolded teaching
- Specific correction techniques
- Cumulative review and application of skills

Continuous informal tests and curriculum-based assessments help:

- Monitor and report student, class, and district progress.
- Determine areas that need attention
- Guide placement and movement through the program

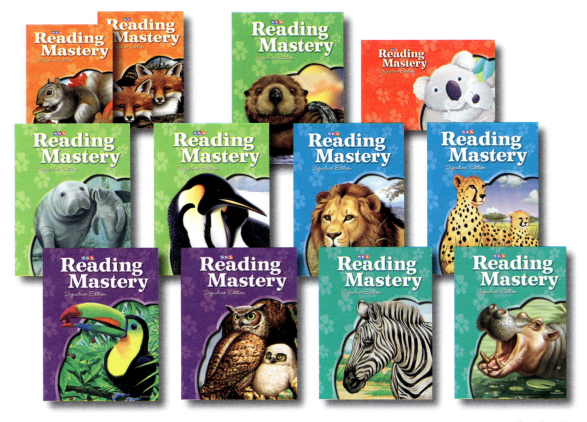

Reading Strand

Give students the keys to success

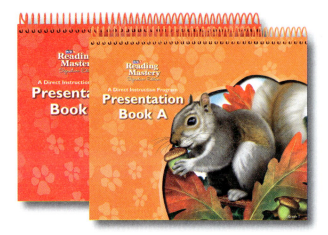

Grades K and 1

Designed to teach students skills needed to become **accurate and fluent readers**:

- Decoding is taught explicitly and systematically
- There are numerous opportunities for building fluency, allowing students to focus on the meaning of the text
- Comprehension instruction begins early to teach students how to infer, predict, and conclude

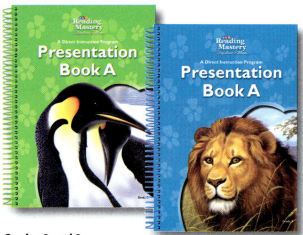

Grades 2 and 3

Continue to emphasize accurate and fluent decoding. The primary focus of these levels is to teach students how to **"read to learn."** Students are taught:

- The skills necessary to read, comprehend, and learn from informational text
- Background information needed for content area reading through information passages
- The background information that becomes the basis from which students make inferences as they read

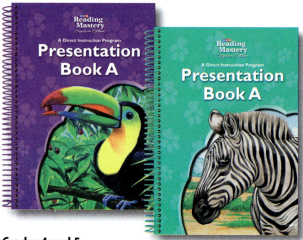

Grades 4 and 5

The focus is **literature**:

- Students are taught to analyze and interpret literature
- Students read classic and contemporary novels, short stories, poems, myths, folktales, biographies, and factual articles
- They learn new comprehension skills for interpreting all these different types of literature
- The reading selections are reinforced with literary analysis, reasoning strategies, and extended daily writing

Grades K–5

Spelling is explicitly taught at all levels to (Grades K–5):

- Engage beginning readers in activities at the phoneme and morphemic level
- Help older students identify known word parts
- Reduce confusion about words that are pronounced the same and provide a basis for using the appropriate word in context

A **Curriculum-Based Assessment and Fluency Handbook** combines with in-program mastery tests to provide a complete system for guiding student instruction. Use it to:

- Ensure students are properly placed in the program
- Measure student achievement within the program
- Identify skills students have mastered
- Present remedial exercises to students who are experiencing difficulty

Exactly the **right components**

Reading Mastery Signature Edition Core Components (Reading Strand)	K	1	2	3	4	5
Student Materials						
Storybook(s)	√	√				
Textbooks			√	√	√	√
Workbooks	√	√	√	√	√	√
Test Books	√	√	√	√	√	√
Teacher Materials						
Presentation Books	√	√	√	√	√	√
Teacher's Guide	√	√	√	√	√	√
Teacher's Takehome Book or Answer Key	√	√	√	√	√	√
Spelling Book	√	√	√	√	√	√
Curriculum-Based Assessment Handbook	√	√	√	√	√	
Skills Profile Folder	√	√				
Audio CD	√					

Reading Mastery Signature Edition Tools to Differentiate Instruction (Reading Strand)	K	1	2	3	4	5
Library of Independent Readers	√	√				
Seatwork	√	√				
Activities Across the Curriculum			√	√	√	√
Practice and Review Activities	√	√	√	√	√	√

Language Arts Strand

Oral language skills are an essential part of learning to read. The early grades of **Reading Mastery Signature Edition** teach oral language skills necessary to understand what is spoken, written, and read in the classroom.

Starting at **Grade K**, students learn the important background information, vocabulary, and thinking skills they need to achieve high levels of comprehension. Students:

- Learn vocabulary words commonly used in school
- Engage in talking and answering questions
- Use different sentence forms and structures
- Acquire important information and concepts

As they progress into **Grade 1**, specific activities are added to integrate language arts with other important reading skills including:

- Continued vocabulary development
- Instruction that focuses on elements of story grammar
- Sentence construction
- Cooperative story writing

Grades 2–5 provide the structure and challenging materials that allow students to communicate effectively in writing and critique the writing of others. Students learn to:

- Write stories with a clear beginning, middle, and end
- Maintain focus on a single idea and develop supporting details
- Edit for standard conventions of grammar, usage, and mechanics
- Analyze persuasive text for misleading claims, faulty or inadequate arguments, and contradictory statements
- Develop skills related to real-world tasks—recall and summarize information presented orally, write directions, and take notes

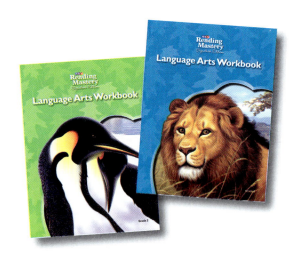

Core Components (Language Strand)	K	1	2	3	4	5
Student Materials						
Textbooks			√	√	√	√
Workbooks	√	√	√	√		
Teacher Materials						
Presentation Books	√	√	√	√	√	√
Teacher's Guide	√	√	√	√	√	√
Teacher's Take-Home Book or Answer Key	√	√	√	√	√	√
Skills Profile Folder	√					

Literature Strand

Learning to read opens new doors for students

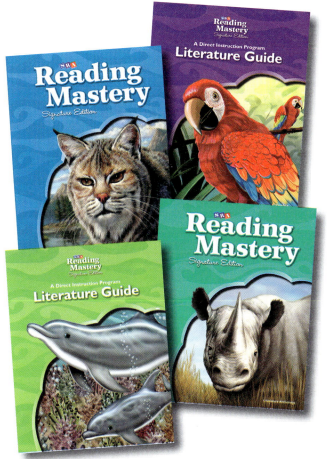

Literature Collection and Guide (Grades K and 1) expand on skills students are learning in *Reading Mastery Signature Edition*. The program:

- Develops their ability to listen attentively and demonstrate understanding
- Sharpens their understanding of story grammar and structure

Anthology and Guide (Grades 2–5) enrich students' experience with novels, poetry, and plays that complement the content and themes of the *Reading Mastery Signature Edition* Textbooks by featuring:

- Classics such as *The Bracelet; Thank You, Ma'am; The Velveteen Rabbit; Stone Soup;* and *The Story of Daedalus and Icarus*
- Insight into elements of story structure and literary strategies so students can discuss and write about the meanings of these selections

Literature Strand						
	K	1	2	3	4	5
Literature Guide	√	√	√	√	√	√
Collection	√	√				
Anthology			√	√	√	√

Literature

Robust vocabulary instruction tied closely to comprehension

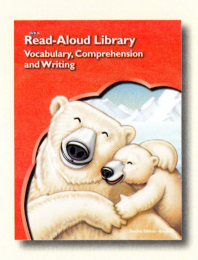

For **Grades K and 1**, daily reading with an emphasis on word meaning expands students' vocabulary into the world of mature speakers and provides:

- Lessons that offer direct teaching of Tier 2 words, enabling students to become more precise and descriptive with their language

- Numerous encounters with target words over time helps students to incorporate them into their speaking vocabulary

- Varied activities for students to interact with words in a variety of situations to deepen understanding

- Thirty high-quality books at each level including: folk tales, fairy tales, legends, poetry, as well as social studies and science expository works

From the introduction of new vocabulary to the informal assessment of understanding, the lesson plans expand oral language by encouraging conversation about the book.

Day 1: Students are introduced to the book and learn the key elements of a book such as title, author, and illustrator.

- They make predictions about what will happen in the story and share those predictions with their classmates.
- They formulate questions they may have about the story or the book.
- The story is read aloud to students with minimal interruptions.
- Target vocabulary words and their meanings are introduced within the context of how they are used in the story.

Day 2: The lesson begins with the story being read aloud by the teacher and discussed.

- Students become actively involved in responding to the story and constructing meaning.
- They are prompted to use target words throughout the discussion.
- Target vocabulary is reviewed.

Day 3: Students participate in varied activities using the new vocabulary words in and beyond the context of the story. Activities include:

- Retelling the story
- Playing word games
- Completing an activity sheet

Additional tools that teachers have used with Reading Mastery Signature Edition

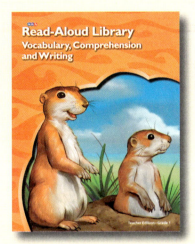
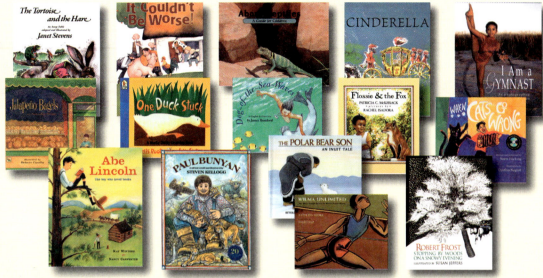

Day 4: Literary analysis and cumulative review are provided in the fourth day of instruction.

- Students play a verbal game that uses all of the new words in addition to words that have been taught in earlier lessons.
- Students also learn songs that help them recall the literary elements and patterns.

Day 5: On the last day students retell the story to a partner.

- An assessment is administered to measure students' mastery of the new vocabulary as well as review items.
- Students are allowed to choose a book they would like the teacher to read to them as a reward.
- Students are taught the routine for the learning center they will work in the following week. Students can practice new and previously learned vocabulary in the Super Words Center.

Reading Strand

Library of Independent Readers
Entertaining, trade-style books written in the special *Reading Mastery Signature Edition* alphabet, one library each for **Grades K and 1**.

Activities Across the Curriculum
Encourage students in **Grades 2–5** to use reading, reference, and writing skills through activities that support science, social studies, math, and language arts.

Seatwork
Provide fun and rewarding reinforcement for students in **Grades K and 1**, that is closely correlated with lessons in *Reading Mastery Signature Edition*.

Additional tools that teachers have used with Reading Mastery Signature Edition

Practicing Standardized Test Formats help students understand test formats and learn test-taking skills by providing:

- Concepts to address important test content as well as instructional standards
- Short, daily activities familiarize students with questions and formats they will encounter on the most recent forms
- Help for students so they perform at their optimal levels and obtain scores that more accurately reflect the student's achievement

Research Assistant
Grades 2–5

Presents a systematic process for the collection, processing, and presentation of information. Helps students:

- Generate ideas for a search
- Use appropriate resources to obtain information
- Present informational reports that include main ideas and relevant details with visual supports

Interactive Student Review

Practice and Review Activities
Grades K–5

Practice Software offers engaging, interactive review to help students master key skills through:

- Brief, frequent practice activities and games
- Direct links to daily lessons
- Monitoring of student progress and performance

Practice Decodable Takehome Books
Grades K and 1

Offers short, decodable stories for students to read independently:

- Provides additional opportunities for students to apply the skills and vocabulary they've learned
- Are available as Blackline Masters or 4-color pages to fold and staple into books each student can keep and read
- Can be taken home and shared with families

11

Common Core Connection Kit

Proven lesson instruction

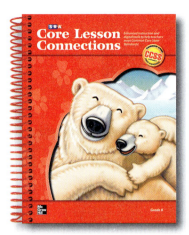

Core Lesson Connections
Grades K–5

Strategic, targeted instruction that supports and enhances the core reading program, including:

- Brief, 20-minute activities aligned to specific program lessons
- Explicit instruction with modeling, guided practice, and independent practice to develop word-learning and comprehension strategies
- An instructional model designed to be presented in conjunction with each program lesson

What you'll find:

Phonological and phonemic awareness
Grades K and 1

Develops through a wide variety of activities including:

- Word segmentation
- Rhyme recognition and production
- Syllable blending, segmentation, and deletion
- Onset-rime segmentation and blending
- Phoneme isolation (initial, medial, and final)
- Phoneme identification, segmentation, and blending

Vocabulary Instruction boosts the acquisition of word-learning strategies and contextual practice through:

- Daily instruction of specific words found in the core program
- Opportunities for students to develop, use, and apply word knowledge
- Word awareness through vocabulary journaling and practice activities
- Vocabulary notebook with word practice and study strategies

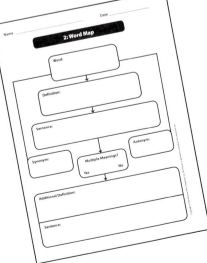

Comprehension Strategies are applied across lessons so students understand their usefulness while learning:

- Before-, during-, and after-reading strategies
- Bloom's Taxonomy level questions
- Narrative and expository text strategies
- Story grammar and story retell
- Graphic organizers
- Main idea and summarizing
- Comprehension monitoring
- Deep processing of text

Fluency Building through increased repetitions use core program stories and partner reading for:

- Emphasis on prosody and reading for meaning
- Effective partner reading
- Charting and decision making for maximum benefit

In addition, the following resources help you enhance learning for all students by providing:

- A **Scope and Sequence** chart to assist you in planning, conducting, and assessing instruction
- **Differentiated Instruction** with suggestions to boost the academic success for approaching mastery, at mastery, and ELL students
- **Professional Development** discusses how you can help students select appropriate material to read for personal pleasure and supplies tips/strategies to help students who struggle with reading fluency
- **Correlation** to the Common Core State Standards to help you keep students on target for meeting standards.

New tools help you promote student engagement and extend learning

Dynamic Digital Resources
Powered by McGraw-Hill ConnectED

Interactive Whiteboard Activities
Deliver key concepts and skills with academic vocabulary practice, graphic organizers, critical writing, and more

SRA 2 Inform
Online Progress Monitoring
Collect data, monitor performance, and administer reports to inform instruction

eInquiry
Helps students solve problems through writing, presenting, preparing reflection tasks, and completing assessments

Research Projects
Allow students to collaborate on common topics and systematically collect, process, and present information

Online Professional Development via the Teaching Tutor
Access on-demand routine formats for topics such as optimal pacing, classroom arrangement, daily lesson characteristics, error corrections, and achieving mastery

Professional Development Videos

eInquiry

SRA 2 Inform

Three strands
work together to form a
core comprehensive program

- Reading, Language Arts, and Literature integrated into a coherent instructional design
- Content focused on the five essential components of reading and aligned with Common Core State Standards
- Explicit instructional strategies for efficient, effective learning
- Student materials that support what you are teaching in daily lessons
- Frequent assessments that track student progress

Andersen Ross/Media Bakery

SRA Core Lesson Connections

GRADE 2

Introduction

What is SRA Core Lesson Connections?

SRA Core Lesson Connections provides targeted instruction that is related to the skills and information presented in the Reading Strand of the **Reading Mastery Signature Edition** program. Used in conjunction with **Reading Mastery Signature Edition,** *Core Lesson Connections* offers strategic support to master the Common Core State Standards for English Language Arts. Each lesson links with the core daily lesson. Explicit instruction through modeling, guided practice, and independent practice helps students meet the rigorous vocabulary, writing, and comprehension strands of the Common Core State Standards.

Core Lesson Connections uses the same teacher-script conventions that appear in **Reading Mastery Signature Edition.** These conventions include what the teacher says, what the teacher does, and what the correct students' responses should be. As with **Reading Mastery,** the teacher calls for group responses, uses clear signals, and employs specific correction procedures. Additionally, teachers deliver key concepts and skills with academic vocabulary practice, graphic organizers, critical writing, and more through interactive whiteboard activities.

How do you use Core Lesson Connections?

There are 145 lessons in Grade 2 *Core Lesson Connections,* aligned with Grade 2 of **Reading Mastery.** Each lesson requires approximately 20 minutes.

The **Reading Mastery Signature Edition** lesson should always take priority when scheduling instruction. The *Core Lesson Connections* activities are designed to enhance and extend the learning of the **Reading Mastery** lesson. Each lesson corresponds with the **Reading Mastery Signature Edition** lesson—for example, Lesson 11 of *Core Lesson Connections* corresponds with Lesson 11 of **Reading Mastery Signature Edition**— Reading Strand.

Some activities are important to conduct **before, during,** or **after** the **Reading Mastery Signature Edition** program lesson. These activities are specifically identified in the *Core Lesson Connections.* The following suggestions are noted:

- Provide a reading center to display books being read so that students can enjoy them again during free time.
- Choose narrative and informational texts that are appropriate for students in your class. You may want to refer to Appendix B of the Common Core State Standards for a list of exemplar texts for read-aloud selections for specific grade levels. Otherwise, you may choose from your own classroom or school library.
- Review vocabulary words found in context in *Textbooks A, B,* and *C.*
- Use partner reading with the story of the day to build fluency after the lesson.

Core Lesson Connections lessons are divided into major parts or strands. For example, Comprehension Strategies is an important part of the *Core Lesson Connections* for Level 2 and appears as Part B. Each part includes:

- Suggested instructional minutes (top left-hand column),
- Instructional materials for the teacher and student (left-hand column),
- What the teacher does (black type, right-hand column),
- What the teacher says (blue type, right-hand column), and
- What the students say/do (black italic type, right-hand column).

Overview of SRA Lesson Connections **cc1**

Here's an example from Lesson 111.

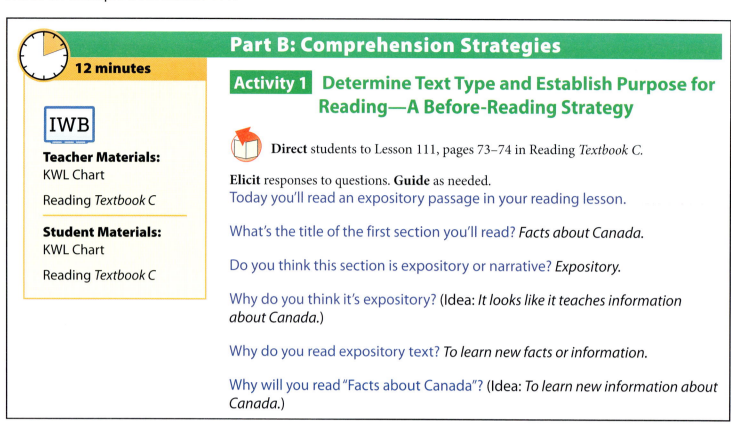

Lessons correspond to and enhance instruction found in the **Reading Mastery Signature Edition** program. The lesson example shown above and found in Lesson 111 of the *Core Lesson Connections* presents a before-reading strategy to help students focus on determining text type and establishing a purpose for reading the "Facts about Canada" passage. *Core Lesson Connections* enhances rather than supplants the **Reading Mastery** program.

What Major Parts Compose Core Lesson Connections?

There are four major parts of *Core Lesson Connections* for Level 2. These include: **vocabulary instruction, comprehension strategies, fluency building, and writing.** Explicit instruction for each of these major parts is based on best practices in reading research (see recommendations provided by Armbruster, Lehr, & Osborn, 2003; Carnine, Silbert, Kame'enui, & Tarver, 2010; National Institute of Child Health & Human Development [NICHD], 2000; Snow, Burns, & Griffin, 1998; and Vaughn & Linan-Thompson, 2004). Skills taught and examples for each part follow.

Vocabulary Instruction

Overview

- Daily instruction of specific words found in basic program
- Explicit instruction with modeling, guided practice, and independent practice
- Opportunities for students to develop, use, and apply word knowledge over time, within context, and in different contexts
- Development of word awareness through the use of word learning strategies, vocabulary journaling, and practice activities that are engaging, encourage deep processing, and connect word meaning to prior knowledge
- Vocabulary notebook with word practice and study strategies

Skills Taught

- Deriving specific word meaning with contextual practice
- Using a vocabulary notebook
- Acquisition and use of vocabulary including shades of meaning

Comprehension Strategies

Overview

- Daily focus on comprehension strategies applied across lessons so students understand their usefulness
- Explicit instruction with modeling, guided practice, and independent practice
- Stories/passages linked to basic program
- Reading for understanding and constructing meaning from text
- Readers' theatre with dialogue linked to basic program
- Modeled think-alouds to enhance comprehension through metacognition
- Note-taking to enhance understanding
- Independent strategic learning, engagement, and deep processing of text

Skills Taught

- Narrative and informational text strategies
- Before-, during-, and after-reading strategies
- Bloom's Taxonomy extension activities (Pair-Share format) with focus on Level 3 (Apply Knowledge)
- Making connections
- Story grammar
- Reading for purpose
- Predictions
- Story retell
- Graphic organizers
- Activating background knowledge
- Strategy generation
- Compare/contrast for analyzing text
- Cause and effect for analyzing text
- KWL
- Summarizing
- Comprehension monitoring
- Connections through writing

Overview of SRA Lesson Connections **cc3**

Fluency Building

Overview

- Daily focus on oral reading fluency
- Increased repetitions using basic program stories and partner reading
- Emphasis on prosody and reading for meaning
- Charting and decision making for maximum benefit

Skills Taught

- Reading with prosody
- Reading with improved fluency
- Reading effectively with a partner

Writing/Language Arts

Overview

- Opportunities to make connections between text selections and writing
- Gain mastery of essential conventions

Skills Taught

- Writing with purpose and connection to text
- Conventions of standard English
- Collaborating effectively with a partner
- Draw evidence and knowledge from the text

What Other Components Compose Core Lesson Connections?

Core Lesson Connections includes eight other important sections.

First, a **summary of skills** and **scope and sequence chart** are provided. These charts provide an overview of the skills taught in the program by major part. In a quick glance, teachers can see what skills are taught for each lesson of the program as well as the span of lessons that cover a specific skill.

Second, **graphic organizers** are used to carefully scaffold instruction for comprehension, writing, and phonemic awareness. These organizers also appear as interactive whiteboard activities online via McGraw-Hill's *ConnectED*. Teachers can write on, save, and print the organizers. Interactive whiteboard activities increase student engagement and improve understanding.

Third, **differentiated instruction** appears in *Core Lesson Connections* to help teachers enhance learning for **all** students. Instructional tips provide teachers and parents (called "home connection") with important suggestions to enhance academic success for approaching mastery, at mastery, and ELL students. Teacher and parent tips align with assessments found in the ***Reading Mastery*** program.

cc4   *Overview of SRA Lesson Connections*

Here is an example from Appendix B.

Test	Tips for Teachers	Home Connections
Fluency Checkout (Lesson 15) **Approaching Mastery**	• See guidelines for students who do not read within error or time limit for Lesson 15 on page 85 in *Presentation Book A*. • Review finger placement and tracking for sentence reading. • Have adult model reading story; have student read story until firm. • Use paired reading.	• Provide word flash cards for students to take home for additional practice. • Have an adult model reading story; have students listen and track during story reading; have students read story; have an adult review difficult words following story reading.
At Mastery	• See guidelines for students who read within error and time limit for Lesson 15 on page 85 in *Presentation Book A*. • Partner with "approaching mastery" or ELL student and model reading story; have student read story.	
ELL	• See "Tips for Teachers" for "approaching mastery" and "at mastery" students. • Use sentence strips to practice reading sentences in story. • Show realia or other visuals of objects and concepts.	• See "Home Connections" for "approaching mastery" and "at mastery" students. • Provide audiotape of story; have students listen and track during story reading; then students read aloud with tape while tracking; then students read aloud and track independently; have an adult review difficult words following independent story reading. • Encourage an adult to help students identify realia and other visuals illustrating meaning of sentences in story.

Fourth, teachers can access tips to help ensure maximum access for students with intellectual disabilities. These suggestions are linked to the ***Reading Mastery*** content and provide guidance for three **levels of support** to allow all students the opportunity to access learning with the program materials.

Fifth, teachers can increase their knowledge about fluency building and reading level determination through a **professional development** section. This section provides the latest research on fluency and how to include fluency building through effective instructional activities. Strategies for students who struggle with fluency are also provided.

Sixth, explicit instructional activities for **fluency/paired reading** give teachers the necessary scaffolding to incorporate fluency into the daily lesson. These guidelines incorporate modeling, guided practice, and independent practice so that students read text quickly, accurately, and with expression.

Seventh, a **five-day lesson planning chart** is provided in Appendix F. This chart shows a "week at a glance," illustrating all major parts of the program and specific skills taught within these parts in groups of five lessons. This chart assists teachers in planning, conducting, and assessing instruction.

Finally, a **correlation to the Common Core State Standards** for English Language Arts is presented. The correlation notes the standards for the specified grade level with detailed notations of how the content of ***Reading Mastery Signature Edition*** supports the standard.

Overview of SRA Lesson Connections **cc5**

References

Armbruster, B., Lehr, F., & Osborn, J. (2003). *Put reading first: The research building blocks of reading instruction: Grades K-3* (2nd ed.). Washington, DC: Center for the Improvement of Early Reading Achievement, National Institute for Literacy, U.S. Department of Education.

Carnine, D. W., Silbert, J., Kame'enui, E. J., & Tarver, S. G. (2010). *Direct Instruction reading* (5th ed.). Upper Saddle River, NJ: Pearson Education.

National Institute of Child Health and Human Development [NICHD]. (2000). *Report of the National Reading Panel. Teaching children to read: An evidence-based assessment of the scientific research literature on reading and its implications for reading instruction: Reports of the subgroups* (NIH Publication NO. 00-4754). Washington, DC: U.S. Government Printing Office.

Snow, C., Burns, M., & Griffin, P.(eds.). (1998). *Preventing reading difficulties in young children.* Washington, DC: National Academy Press.

Vaughn, S., & Linan-Thompson, S. (2004). *Research-based methods of reading instruction: Grades K-3.* Alexandria, VA: ASCD.

Summary of Skills

GRADE 2

A. Vocabulary Instruction

1. Explicit Instruction (1–145)
2. Word Learning Strategies (1–145)
3. Review/Knowledge Check (2–145)
4. Vocabulary Notebook (11–145)
5. Aquisition and Use (5, 10, 15, 20, 25, 30, 35, 40, 45, 50, 55, 60, 65, 70, 75, 80, 85, 90, 95, 100, 105, 110, 115, 120, 125, 130, 135, 140, 145)

B. Comprehension Strategies

1. Explicit Instruction (1–145)
2. Narrative Text (1–4, 6–9, 11–14, 16–19, 21–24, 26–30, 31–34, 36–40, 42–44, 46, 47, 49, 51–54, 56–59, 61–63, 66, 67, 69– 74, 76–79, 81–84, 91–94, 96–99, 101–104, 106–109, 116–119, 121–124, 128, 131–134, 136–139, 141, 144)
3. Expository Text (1–4, 6, 9, 18, 19, 24, 31–34, 36–38, 41–44, 46–48, 51, 53, 54, 57, 62–64, 66, 68, 74, 83, 84, 86–89, 94, 97, 103, 108, 111–114, 116, 117, 123, 126–129, 132, 138, 139, 142–144)
4. Before Reading Strategies (1–4, 6, 18, 24, 31, 32, 36, 38, 41, 43, 47, 53, 57, 62–64, 66–68, 71–74, 76–78, 81, 83, 86, 92, 97, 98, 101, 103, 106, 111, 113, 116, 119, 121, 122, 126, 128, 132, 134, 137, 142, 144)
5. Story Grammar (2–19, 21–24, 26–30, 38–40, 46, 49, 56, 58, 59, 61, 63, 69, 70, 74, 76–79, 81, 91–94, 96–99, 104, 115, 121, 124, 131, 133, 134, 136, 141)
6. Graphic Organizers (2–17, 19–50, 53–55, 58–60, 63–66, 68–108, 110–115, 117, 119–127, 129–130, 132, 135–138, 140–143, 145)
7. After Reading Strategies (2–4, 6–9, 11–14, 17, 19, 21–24, 26–29, 33, 34, 37, 39, 42, 44, 46, 48, 49, 54, 58, 59, 61, 63, 64, 66, 68, 69, 72–74, 76–79, 82–84, 87–89, 91–94, 96–99, 101–104, 106–109, 112, 114, 117, 118, 121–124, 127, 129, 131, 133, 136, 138, 139, 141, 143)
8. Bloom's Taxonomy Extension Activities (every 5th lesson through 145)
9. During Reading Strategies (7–9, 11–14, 16–19, 21, 31–34, 36–38, 42–44, 46–49, 51–54, 56–59, 67, 74, 91–94, 96–99, 101–103, 106, 109, 118, 119, 121–123, 129, 132–134, 137, 139)
10. Comprehension Monitoring (7–9, 11–14, 16–19, 21, 31–34, 36–38, 51–54, 56–59, 67, 102, 103, 118, 121, 123, 132, 134, 137, 139)
11. Story Retell (11–14, 16, 17, 19, 21–24, 26–29, 39, 58, 59, 69, 74, 76–78, 96, 97, 101, 104, 124, 131, 136, 141)
12. Predictions (71–74, 76–79, 81–84, 92, 93, 101, 106, 107, 111, 113, 121–124, 126, 134, 136–138, 142)
13. KWL (31–34, 36, 37, 41–44, 46–48, 53, 54, 62, 63, 74, 83, 84, 86–89, 101, 111–114, 117, 124, 126, 127, 134, 136, 137, 142, 143)

Summary of Skills **cc7**

14. Activate Background Knowledge (31, 36, 41, 43, 47, 53, 57, 62–64, 66–68, 71–73, 86, 97, 101, 103, 111, 113, 119, 126, 128, 132, 134, 137, 142)
15. Make Connections (31, 36, 41, 43, 47, 53, 62, 64, 66–68, 71–74, 81, 82, 86, 97–99, 101–104, 106–109, 111, 113, 116–119, 124, 126, 128, 132, 136, 139, 142)
16. Question Generation (32, 36, 42–44, 46–49, 53, 65, 74, 86, 101, 109, 111–114, 117, 122, 126, 127, 129, 133, 139, 142, 143)
17. Summarizing (37, 76–79, 83, 84, 87–89, 91–94, 98, 99, 101, 112, 114, 121, 124, 133, 136)
18. Compare/Contrast (46, 49, 50, 63, 64, 66, 68, 74, 79, 81, 82, 98, 99, 101, 107, 108, 116, 117, 124, 129, 136, 138)
19. Cause and Effect (91–101, 106, 119, 124, 132, 136)
20. Strategy Generation (101, 102, 109, 111–114, 124, 126, 127, 134, 136, 137, 139, 142, 143)

C. Fluency Building (1–145)

D. Writing/Language Arts

1. Write and Use Parts of Speech and Conventions (10, 20, 30, 40, 50, 60, 70, 80, 90, 100, 110, 120, 130, 140)

Scope and Sequence
of SRA Core Lesson Connections

Scope and Sequence (1-70)

Skills	1 – 5	6-10	11-15	16-20	21-25
VOCABULARY INSTRUCTION					
Explicit Instruction	√	√	√	√	√
Word Learning Strategies	√	√	√	√	√
Review/Knowledge Check	•	√	√	√	√
Vocabulary Notebook			√	√	√
Vocabulary Acquisition and Use	•	•	•	•	•
COMPREHENSION STRATEGIES					
Explicit Instruction	√	√	√	√	√
Narrative Text	•	•	•	•	•
Expository Text	•	•		•	•
Before Reading Strategies	•	•		•	•
Story Grammar	•	√	√	•	•
Graphic Organizers	•	√	√	•	√
After Reading Strategies	•	•	•	•	•
Bloom's Taxonomy Extension Activities	•	•	•	•	•
During Reading Strategies		•	•	•	•
Comprehension Monitoring		•		•	•
Story Retell				•	•
Predictions					
KWL					
Activate Background Knowledge					
Make Connections					
Question Generation					
Summarizing					
Compare/Contrast					
Cause and Effect					
Strategy Generation					
FLUENCY BUILDING	√	√	√	√	√
WRITING/LANGUAGE ARTS					
Use Parts of Speech and Conventions		•		•	

Key
√ = skill in every lesson
• = skill in some of the lessons

GRADE 2

26-30	31-35	36-40	41-45	46-50	51-55	56-60	61-65	66-70
√	√	√	√	√	√	√	√	√
√	√	√	√	√	√	√	√	√
√	√	√	√	√	√	√	√	√
√	√	√	√	√	√	√	√	√
•	•	•	•	•	•	•	•	•
√	√	√	√	√	√	√	√	√
√		√						•
	•	•	•	•	•	•	•	•
	•	•	•	•	•	•	•	•
√		•		•		•	•	•
√	√	√	√	√	•	•	•	•
•	•	•	•	•	•	•	•	•
	•	•	•	•	•	•	•	•
	•	•	•	•	•	•	•	•
•	•	•		•	•	•		•
•		•				•		•
	•	•	•	•	•		•	
	•	•	•	•	•	•	•	•
	•	•	•	•	•	•	•	•
	•	•	•	•	•		•	
		•						
				•			•	•
√	√	√	√	√	√	√	√	√
•		•		•		•		•

Scope and Sequence **cc11**

Scope and Sequence (71-145)

Skills	71 – 75	76-80	81-85	86-90	91-95	96-100
VOCABULARY INSTRUCTION						
Explicit Instruction	√	√	√	√	√	√
Word Learning Strategies	√	√	√	√	√	√
Review/Knowledge Check	√	√	√	√	√	√
Vocabulary Notebook	√	√	√	√	√	√
Vocabulary Acquisition and Use	•	•	•	•	•	•
COMPREHENSION STRATEGIES						
Explicit Instruction	√	√	√	√	√	√
Narrative Text	•	•	•		•	•
Expository Text	•		•	•	•	•
Before Reading Strategies	•	•	•	•	•	•
Story Grammar	•	•	•		•	•
Graphic Organizers	√	√	√	√	√	√
After Reading Strategies	•	•	•	•	•	•
Bloom's Taxonomy Extension Activities	•	•	•	•	•	•
During Reading Strategies	•				•	•
Comprehension Monitoring						
Story Retell	•	•				•
Predictions	•	•	•		•	
KWL	•		•	•		
Activate Background Knowledge	•			•		•
Make Connections	•		•	•		•
Question Generation	•			•		
Summarizing		•	•	•	•	•
Compare/Contrast	•	•	•			•
Cause and Effect					√	√
Strategy Generation						
FLUENCY BUILDING	√	√	√	√	√	√
WRITING/LANGUAGE ARTS						
Use Parts of Speech and Conventions		•		•		•

Key
√ = skill in every lesson
• = skill in some of the lessons

cc12   *Scope and Sequence*

GRADE 2

101-105	106-110	111-115	116-120	121-125	126-130	131-135	136-140	141-145
√	√	√	√	√	√	√	√	√
√	√	√	√	√	√	√	√	√
√	√	√	√	√	√	√	√	√
√	√	√	√	√	√	√	√	√
•	•	•	•	•	•	•	•	•
√	√	√	√	√	√	√	√	√
•	•	•	•	•	•	•	•	•
•	•	•	•	•	•	•	•	•
•	•	•	•	•	•	•	•	•
•		•		•	•	•	•	•
√	•	√	•	√	•	•	•	•
•	•	•	•	•	•	•	•	•
•	•	•		•	•	•	•	•
•	•			•	•	•	•	•
•			•	•	•	•	•	
•			•		•	•	•		•
•	•	•	•	•	•	•	•	•
•		•	•	•	•	•	•	•
•		•		•	•	•	•	•
•		•	•	•	•	•	•	•
•	•	•	•	•	•	•	•	•
•	•	•		•	•	•		•
•		•	•	•	•	•	•	•
•	•		•	•	•	•	•	•
√	√	√	√	√	√	√	√	
	•		•		•		•	

Scope and Sequence   **cc13**

Lessons

Lesson 1

> **Materials**
> **Teacher:** Reading *Textbook A*
> **Student:** Reading *Textbook A*

8 minutes

Teacher Materials:
Reading *Textbook A*

Student Materials:
Reading *Textbook A*

Part A: Vocabulary Development

Activity 1 Overview of Vocabulary Development

Today you'll start learning important skills to help you understand what you read. The first skill you'll work on is learning vocabulary words. Vocabulary words are all the words that make up our language. Learning new vocabulary words will help you unlock the meaning of what you read. New vocabulary words will also help you in speaking and writing.

Activity 2 Learn New Vocabulary Word

Elicit responses to questions. **Guide** as needed.
Today you'll learn a new vocabulary word. **Examine. Examine** means "to look at carefully." What does **examine** mean? *To look at carefully.*

Another way to say "to look at carefully" is **examine.** What's another way to say "to look at carefully"? *Examine.*
Discuss examples of when students would <u>examine</u> something.

Tom saw three boxes in the room. His brother told him a rule about the boxes. Tom had **to look at** the boxes **carefully** to see which one had the frog in it. He had to **examine** the boxes.

What's another way to say "to look at carefully"? *Examine.*

Tell me a sentence using the word **examine.** (Student responses.)
Discuss sentence.

 Review vocabulary word in appropriate context in Reading *Textbook A.*

Lesson 1 1

Part B: Comprehension Strategies

12 minutes

Teacher Materials:
Reading *Textbook A*

Student Materials:
Reading *Textbook A*

Activity 1 Overview—Importance of Comprehension

Elicit response to question. **Guide** as needed.
Today we'll talk about the importance of comprehension. **Comprehension** means understanding what you read. What does **comprehension** mean? *Understanding what you read.*

If you read something and you don't understand it, you really aren't reading. One of the reasons you read is to understand what you read. You read for many reasons. You read to learn new information. You read for fun and enjoyment. You read to follow directions for how to do something. You read for school assignments. When you understand what you read, you have good comprehension.

Discuss why reading is important.

Discuss what kinds of reading students enjoy doing.

Activity 2 Determine Text Type—A Before-Reading Strategy

Elicit responses to questions. **Guide** as needed.
Today you'll read two types of text. The first type of text is called **expository text.** Expository text is written to teach you new information or facts about something. Why do you read expository text? *To learn new information or facts about something.*

It's important to know **when** you're reading expository text so you know **why** you're reading. What kind of text are you reading when you're reading to learn new facts or information? *Expository text.*

All About Sharks is expository because the text gives you facts about sharks. The purpose of the text is to teach you new information about sharks.
Elicit second example of expository text from students.

A second type of text is called **narrative text.** It's important to know **when** you're reading narrative text so you know **why** you're reading. Narrative text tells you a story. What does narrative text tell you? *A story.*

Narrative texts or stories are fun to read. You'll often read narrative texts for fun. Narrative texts might include new facts or information that you did not know before, but the main purpose of narrative text is to tell you a story. What kind of text are you reading when you read a story? *Narrative text.*

The Little Red Hen is narrative because the text tells you a story about the Little Red Hen and her adventures. The story is fun to read.
Elicit second example of narrative text from students.

You'll read expository and narrative text almost every day. When you know what kind of text you're reading, it helps you understand why you're reading. You'll have better comprehension if you can figure out what kind of text you're reading before you read.

Read each example. **Elicit** responses to questions. **Discuss** what makes each example expository or narrative text. **Guide** as needed.
Say **expository** or **narrative** for each of the following examples of text.

1. "Living Things" tells rules and information about living things. *Expository.*

2. "The Tiger and the Frog" tells a story about Tom, his brother, and his brother's pets. *Narrative.*

3. "Make-Believe Animals" explains the difference between real animals and make-believe animals. *Expository.*

4. "Trees" tells facts and information about trees. *Expository.*

5. "Bob and Don Find Moops" tells about boys named Bob and Don who find make-believe animals. *Narrative.*

6. "Don Washes the White Spot" tells about a boy named Don who wanted a blue coat. *Narrative.*

5 minutes

Student Materials:
Reading *Textbook A*

Part C: Fluency Building

(See Appendix E for Fluency/Paired Reading Guidelines.)

 Conduct after the lesson using the story of the day.

Activity 1 Partner Reading

It's time for partner reading.

Model partner reading. **Direct** students to assigned partners. **Monitor** partner reading.

Lesson 1   **3**

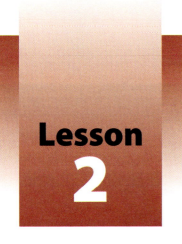

Lesson 2

Materials
Teacher: 1-Narrative Story Map; Reading *Textbook A*
Student: Reading *Textbook A*

Part A: Vocabulary Development

8 minutes

Teacher Materials:
Reading *Textbook A*

Student Materials:
Reading *Textbook A*

Activity 1 Learn New Vocabulary Word

Elicit responses to questions. **Guide** as needed.

Today you'll learn a new vocabulary word. **Path. Path** means "walkway." What does **path** mean? *Walkway.*

Another word for "walkway" is **path.** What's another word for "walkway"? *Path.*

Bob and Don want to go looking for moops in the forest. To get around the forest, they must follow a **walkway.** The **path** goes through the forest. **Discuss** examples of a path students have used.

What's another word for **walkway?** *Path.*

Activity 2 Review Vocabulary Word

Elicit responses to questions. **Guide** as needed.

What's another way to say "to look at carefully"? *Examine.*

Tell me a sentence using the word **examine.** *(Student responses.)*
Discuss sentence.

  Review vocabulary words in appropriate context in Reading *Textbook A*.

Part B: Comprehension Strategies

12 minutes

Teacher Materials:
Narrative Story Map

Reading *Textbook A*

Student Materials:
Reading *Textbook A*

Activity 1 Narrative Story Map: Identify Title, Characters, and Setting—An After-Reading Strategy

  Direct students to Lesson 1, page 4 of Reading *Textbook A*.

Elicit response to question. **Guide** as needed.
In the last lesson, you read "The Tiger and the Frog."

What kind of text was it? *Narrative text.*

Why do you read narrative text? *(Idea: To read the story for fun.)*

Show Narrative Story Map.

Today I'll show you how to use a Narrative Story Map to help you organize your thinking about narrative texts so you understand and remember what you read.

Point to the title, characters, and setting on Narrative Story Map as they are discussed.
All stories have titles, characters, and a setting. The **title** is the **name** that the author gave to the story and tells what the story is about. What's the title of this story? *The Tiger and the Frog.*

The **characters** are the important **people, animals, or objects** that do things in the story. What are characters? (Idea: *The important people, animals, or objects that do things in the story.)*

The **setting** tells **where** and **when** the story happens. What does the setting tell? *Where and when the story happens.*

Model think-aloud for the title, characters, and setting. **Write** the title, characters, and setting on Narrative Story Map.
I'll show you how to fill out the title, characters, and setting on my Narrative Story Map. You'll learn about the Problems and Events in later lessons.

Sample Wording for Think-Aloud

I'll look at the title for the story and copy the title in the box labeled "Title."

Next I'll identify the characters. I know the characters are the important people, animals, or objects that do things in a story. So I can look over the story and remember that the characters in this story are Tom and Tom's brother. The title also tells me that the tiger and the frog are characters. I want to think about who the most important or main characters are. As I look at the story and think about it, I remember that the story is mostly about Tom. The title shows me that the tiger and the frog are important so I'll write "Tom, tiger, and frog" in the box for characters.

The next part to figure out is the setting. I know the setting tells when and where a story happens. I need to look carefully at the story and figure out when the story happens. In the fourth sentence, I see the words "One day." That tells me when. I'll write "one day" in the box for setting by the word "When."

In the third paragraph I see the words "he went into the room with boxes." That tells a place or where. So I know that this story took place in a room with boxes. I'll write a "room with boxes" by the word "Where" in the setting box.

Lesson 2   **5**

Activity 2 — Determine Text Type and Establish Purpose for Reading—A Before-Reading Strategy

Elicit responses to questions. **Guide** as needed.

Today you'll read both narrative and expository text in your reading lesson. The title of the first section is "Make-Believe Animals." This section of text tells the difference between real and make-believe animals. What type of text is "Make-Believe Animals"—expository or narrative? *Expository.*

Why do you read expository text? *To learn new facts or information.*

What will you try to do when you read "Make-Believe Animals"? *(Idea: Learn new information about make-believe animals.)*

The title of the second section you'll read is "Bob and Don Find Moops." This section tells about boys named Bob and Don who find make-believe animals.

What type of text is "Bob and Don Find Moops"—expository or narrative? *Narrative.*

What does narrative text tell you? *A story.*

Why will you read "Bob and Don Find Moops?" *(Idea: To read the story for fun).*

5 minutes

Student Materials:
Reading *Textbook A*

Part C: Fluency Building

(See Appendix E for Fluency/Paired Reading Guidelines.)

 Conduct after the lesson using the story of the day.

Activity 1 — Partner Reading

It's time for partner reading.

Model partner reading. **Direct** students to assigned partners. **Monitor** partner reading.

6   Lesson 2

Lesson 3

> **Materials**
> **Teacher:** 1-Narrative Story Map; Reading *Textbook A*
> **Student:** Reading *Textbook A*

8 minutes

Teacher Materials:
Reading *Textbook A*

Student Materials:
Reading *Textbook A*

Part A: Vocabulary Development

Activity 1 Learn New Vocabulary Word

Elicit responses to questions. **Guide** as needed.
Today you'll learn a new vocabulary word. **Fact. Fact** means "something that is true." What does **fact** mean? *Something that is true.*

Another way to say "something that is true" is **fact.** What's another way to say "something that is true"? *Fact.*

Trees grow when the weather gets warmer; this is **something** we know **that is true.** It's a **fact** that the roots of a tree take in the water for the tree to live. **Discuss** examples of things that are <u>facts</u>.

What's another way to say "something that is true"? *Fact.*

Activity 2 Review Vocabulary Word

Elicit responses to questions. **Guide** as needed.
What's another word for **walkway?** *Path.*

Tell me a sentence using the word **path.** (Student responses.)
Discuss sentence.

 Review vocabulary words in appropriate context in Reading *Textbook A*.

12 minutes

Teacher Materials:
Narrative Story Map
Reading *Textbook A*

Student Materials:
Reading *Textbook A*

Part B: Comprehension Strategies

Activity 1 Narrative Story Map: Identify Title, Characters, Setting—An After-Reading Strategy

 Direct students to Lesson 2, page 8 of Reading *Textbook A*.

Elicit responses to questions. **Guide** as needed.
In the last lesson, you read "Bob and Don Find Moops."

What kind of text was it? *Narrative text.*

Why do you read narrative text? *(Idea: To read a story for fun.)*

Lesson 3

Show Narrative Story Map.
Today we'll use a Narrative Story Map to help you organize your thinking about narrative texts so you understand and remember what you read.
Point to the title, characters, and setting on 1-Narrative Story Map as they are discussed.
All stories have titles, characters, and a setting. The title is the name that the author gave. What is the title of this story? *Bob and Don Find Moops.*

The characters are the important people, animals, or objects that do things in the story. What are characters? *(Idea: The important people, animals, or objects that do things in the story.)*

The setting tells where and when the story happens. What does the setting tell? *Where and when the story happens.*

I'll show you how to fill out the title, characters, and setting on my Narrative Story Map. The title is "Bob and Don Find Moops." The most important or main characters are Bob, Don, and the moops. The setting is "a strange forest" for where and "one day" for when.
Model how to fill in the title, characters, and setting on 1-Narrative Story Map.
Write the title, characters and setting on 1-Narrative Story Map.

Activity 2 Determine Text Type and Establish Purpose for Reading—A Before-Reading Strategy

Elicit responses to questions. **Guide** as needed.
Today you'll read both narrative and expository text in your lesson. The title of the first section is "Trees." This section of text tells facts about trees. What type of text is "Trees"—expository or narrative? *Expository.*

Why do you read expository text? *To learn new facts or information.*

What will you try to do when you read, "Trees"? *(Idea: Learn about trees.)*

The title of the second section you'll read is "Don Washes the White Spot." This section tells about a boy named Don who wants a blue coat.
What type of text is "Don Washes the White Spot"—expository or narrative? *Narrative.*

What does narrative text tell you? *A story.*

Why will you read "Don Washes the White Spot"? *(Idea: For fun.)*

Part C: Fluency Building

5 minutes

Student Materials:
Reading *Textbook A*

(See Appendix E for Fluency/Paired Reading Guidelines.)

 Conduct after the lesson using the story of the day.

Activity 1 Partner Reading

It's time for partner reading.

Model partner reading. **Direct** students to assigned partners. **Monitor** partner reading.

Lesson 4

> **Materials**
> **Teacher:** 1-Narrative Story Map; Reading *Textbook A*
> **Student:** Copy of 1-Narrative Story Map; Reading *Textbook A*

8 minutes

Teacher Materials:
Reading *Textbook A*

Student Materials:
Reading *Textbook A*

Part A: Vocabulary Development

Activity 1 — Learn New Vocabulary Word

Elicit responses to questions. **Guide** as needed.
Today you'll learn a new vocabulary word. **Ripe. Ripe** means "ready to be eaten." What does **ripe** mean? *Ready to be eaten.*

Another way to say "ready to be eaten" is **ripe.** What's another way to say "ready to be eaten"? *Ripe.*

When apples are **ready to be eaten,** they should be picked from the tree. The apples are usually **ripe** and ready to be picked in the fall.
Discuss things that get ripe.

What's another way to say "ready to be eaten"? *Ripe.*

Activity 2 — Review Vocabulary Word

Elicit responses to questions. **Guide** as needed.
What's another way to say "something that is true"? *Fact.*

Tell me a sentence using the word **fact.** (Student responses.)
Discuss sentence.

 Review vocabulary word in appropriate context in Reading *Textbook A*.

12 minutes

Teacher Materials:
Narrative Story Map

Reading *Textbook A*

Student Materials:
Narrative Story Map

Reading *Textbook A*

Part B: Comprehension Strategies

Activity 1 — Narrative Story Map: Identify Title, Characters, and Setting—An After-Reading Strategy

 Direct students to Lesson 3, page 16 of Reading *Textbook A*.

Elicit responses to questions. Guide as needed.
In the last lesson, you read "Don Washes the White Spot."

What kind of text was it? *Narrative text.*

Why do you read narrative text? *(Idea: To read the story for fun.)*

Lesson 4   9

Show Narrative Story Map.
Today you'll use a Narrative Story Map to help you organize your thinking about narrative texts so you understand and remember what you read.

All stories have titles, characters, and a setting. Touch the line labeled *Title* on your Narrative Story Map. The title of the story is "Don Washes the White Spot." What's the title of the story? *"Don Washes the White Spot."*

Guide students as you both write the title on Narrative Story Map.
Write the title on the line for title on your Narrative Story Map.

Touch the box for *Characters* on your Narrative Story Map. The characters are the important people, animals, or objects that do things in the story. What are characters? *(*Idea: *The important people, animals, or objects that do things in the story.)*

Guide students as you both write the characters on Narrative Story Map.
In this story, the characters are Don and the wise old man. Who are the characters in the story? *Don and the wise old man.*

Write their names in the box for characters.

Touch the box for *Setting* on your Narrative Story Map. The setting tells where and when the story happens. What does the setting tell? *Where and when the story happens.*

Guide students as you both write the setting on Narrative Story Map.
In this story, the story takes place in the strange forest. Touch the word "Where" in the *Setting* box. Where does the story take place? *In the strange forest.*

Write "the strange forest" next to the word "where."

Touch the word "When" in the *Setting* box. This story does not really tell us when the story happens, so we will leave this part blank.

Activity 2   Determine Text Type and Establish Purpose for Reading—A Before-Reading Strategy

Elicit responses to questions. Guide as needed.
Today you'll read both narrative and expository text in your reading lesson. The title of the first section is "Apple Trees." This section of text tells facts about apple trees. What type of text is "Apple Trees"—expository or narrative? *Expository.*

Why do you read expository text? *To learn new facts or information.*

What will you try to do when you read "Apple Trees"? *(*Idea: *Learn new information about apple trees.)*

The title of the second section you'll read is "The Little Apple Tree." This section tells about an apple tree named Tina who lived in a forest of tall trees.

10   *Lesson 4*

What type of text is "The Little Apple Tree"—expository or narrative? *Narrative.*

What does narrative text tell you? *A story.*
Why will you read "The Little Apple Tree"? (Idea: *To read the story for fun.*)

Part C: Fluency Building

5 minutes

Student Materials:
Reading *Textbook A*

(See Appendix E for Fluency/Paired Reading Guidelines.)

 Conduct after the lesson using the story of the day.

Activity 1 Partner Reading

It's time for partner reading.

Direct students to assigned partners. **Monitor** partner reading.

Lesson 4

Lesson 5

> **Materials**
> **Teacher:** Reading *Textbook A*, 2-Vocabulary Acquisition and Use
> **Student:** Drawing paper; Reading *Textbook A*, Copy of 2-Vocabulary Acquisition and Use

8 minutes

Teacher Materials:
Reading *Textbook A*

Vocabulary Acquisition and Use

Student Materials:
Reading *Textbook A*

Vocabulary Acquisition and Use

Part A: Vocabulary Development

Activity 1 Cumulative Vocabulary Review

Elicit responses to questions. **Guide** as needed. **Review** vocabulary words as needed.

Directions: Listen and tell me whether I use our vocabulary words the right way or the wrong way. If I use the word the right way, say **"yes."** If I use the word the wrong way, say **"no."** Then we'll talk about each word.

1. Sally's little brother skinned his knee so she decided to take care of it. She needed to **examine** the cut to see whether there was any dirt in it.

   Did I use the word examine the right way? *Yes.*

   How do you know? *(Student responses.)*

2. Marla and Jessica had a hard time walking through the woods. They saw a **path** and began to walk on it. It was much easier.

   Did I use the word **path** the right way? *Yes.*

   How do you know? *(Student responses.)*

3. Jason told his mother that he did not break her new vase. He did break the vase. He told her a **fact.**

   Did I use the word **fact** the right way? *No.*

   How do you know? *(Student responses.)*

4. The farmer told us the apples were not ready to eat. He said they were **ripe.**

   Did I use the word **ripe** the right way? *No.*

   How do you know? *(Student responses.)*

 Review vocabulary words in appropriate context in Reading *Textbook A*.

Activity 2 | Vocabulary Acquisition and Use

Display Vocabulary Acquisition and Use. **Have** students work with a neighbor to complete Vocabulary Acquisition and Use.

Today's vocabulary words are ____ and ____ [and ____ and ____].
Vocabulary words: **examine** and **look; ripe** and **ready**
Write the words on the lines provided. Then write the words in the boxes based on whether you think each word is less/smaller or more/larger than the other word. Below the boxes, write why you think word 1 is less/smaller and word 2 is more/larger than word 1.

Repeat for words 3 and 4. **Have** students share what they wrote. **Discuss** examples of how these words might be used.

Part B: Comprehension Strategies

12 minutes

Teacher Materials:
Reading *Textbook A*

Student Materials:
Drawing paper

Reading *Textbook A*

Display directions for activity.

 Direct students to Lesson 4, page 22 of Reading *Textbook A*.

Directions: Discuss who is the most important or main character in "The Little Apple Tree." Draw a picture to illustrate what the main character looks like during each of the four seasons.

Activity 1 | Pair-Share Activity—Apply Knowledge (Level 3 of Bloom's Taxonomy)

You'll do an activity called Pair-Share to show some things you have learned in the last four lessons. The directions are on the board. I'll read them to you.

Discuss the steps in Pair-Share.

Now I'll show you how to work with your partner in a Pair-Share activity. In the Pair section, you and your partner will talk about what to do and then you'll do it. In the Share section, you and your partner will share your work with the class.

Model think-aloud for pair process using a student as your partner.

Sample Wording for Think-Aloud

First my partner and I will talk about who the most important or main character is. (Elicit from partner who the most important or main character is.) I agree with my partner that the most important or main character is Tina, the apple tree. Now we'll look at the directions to see what to do. Oh, we have to draw Tina in four seasons. The four seasons are winter, spring, summer, and fall. I need to think of what an apple tree looks like during each season. I'll talk to my partner about who will do each part. (Elicit from partner which parts he/she will draw.) Great! Now we're ready to begin drawing. My partner will draw Tina in winter and spring and I'll draw Tina in summer and fall.

Lesson 5

Assign partners. **Provide** drawing paper.

Guide students as they determine most important or main character—Tina, the apple tree; the drawings should show what Tina looks like in each season.

You'll have 5 minutes to do the Pair part of this activity. Draw quick sketches so you'll finish on time.

Step 2 is to Share your work with the class. I'll call on pairs of students to share their work with the rest of the class.

Call on as many students to share as time allows.

5 minutes

Student Materials:
Reading *Textbook A*

Part C: Fluency Building

(See Appendix E for Fluency/Paired Reading Guidelines.)

 Conduct after the lesson using the story of the day.

Activity 1 Partner Reading

It's time for partner reading.

Direct students to assigned partners. **Monitor** partner reading.

14   Lesson 5

Lesson 6

Materials
Teacher: 1-Narrative Story Map; Reading *Textbook A*
Student: Copy of 1-Narrative Story Map; Reading *Textbook A*

Part A: Vocabulary Development

8 minutes

Teacher Materials:
Reading *Textbook A*

Student Materials:
Reading *Textbook A*

Activity 1 Learn New Vocabulary Word

Elicit responses to questions. **Guide** as needed.
Today, you'll learn a new vocabulary word. **Huge. Huge** means "big." What does **huge** mean? *Big.*

Another word for "big" is **huge.** What's another word for **big?** *Huge.*

Tina was an apple tree. She was smaller than the other trees. The other trees in the forest were **big**. Those trees were **huge.**

Discuss things that are huge.

What's another word for **big?** *Huge.*

Activity 2 Review Vocabulary Word

Elicit responses to questions. **Guide** as needed.
What's another way to say "ready to be eaten"? *Ripe.*

Tell me a sentence using the word **ripe.** (Student responses.)
Discuss sentence.

 Review vocabulary word in appropriate context in Reading *Textbook A*.

Part B: Comprehension Strategies

12 minutes

Teacher Materials:
Narrative Story Map
Reading *Textbook A*

Student Materials:
Narrative Story Map
Reading *Textbook A*

Activity 1 Narrative Story Map: Identify Title, Characters, and Setting—An After-Reading Strategy

 Direct students to Lesson 5, page 29 of Reading *Textbook A*.

Elicit response to question. Guide as needed.
In the last lesson, you read "Campers Come into the Forest."

What kind of text is it? *Narrative text.*

Why do you read narrative text? (Idea: *To read the story for fun.*)

Lesson 6   15

Show Narrative Story Map.

Today you'll use a Narrative Story Map to help you organize your thinking about narrative texts so you understand and remember what you read.

What are the first three things you write when you fill out a Narrative Story Map? *(Idea: Titles, characters, and a setting.)*

Touch the line labeled *Title* on your Narrative Story Map. What's the title of the story? *"Campers Come into the Forest."*

Let's write the title of the story on your Narrative Story Map.
Guide students as you both write the title on Narrative Story Map.

Touch the box for Characters on your Narrative Story Map. The characters are the important people, animals, or objects that do things in the story. What are characters? *(Idea: The important people, animals, or objects that do things in the story.)*
Guide students as you both write the characters on Narrative Story Map.

Who are the characters in the story? *(Idea: Tina, the big trees, and the campers.)*

Write their names in the box for characters.

Touch the box for *Setting* on your Narrative Story Map. The setting tells where and when the story happens. What does the setting tell? *Where and when the story happens.*
Guide students as you both write the setting (where and when) on Narrative Story Map.

Touch the word "Where" in the *Setting* box. Where does the story take place? *The forest.*

Write it in the *Setting* box.

Touch the word "When" in the *Setting* box. When does the story take place? *One fall day.*

Write it in the *Setting* box.

You'll learn about Problems and Events in later lessons.

Activity 2 Determine Text Type and Establish Purpose for Reading—A Before-Reading Strategy

Elicit responses to questions. **Guide** as needed.

Today you'll read both narrative and expository text in your lesson. The title of the first section is "Camels and Pigs." Is this section expository or narrative? *Expository.*

Why do you think it's expository? *(Idea: It looks like it teaches information about pigs and camels.)*

Why do you read expository text? *To learn new facts or information.*

16   *Lesson 6*

Why will you read "Camels and Pigs"? *(Idea: To learn new information about camels and pigs.)*

The title of the second section you'll read is "Tina Is Happy." Look at this section of text. Is it expository or narrative? *Narrative.*

Why do you think it's narrative? *(Idea: The title and the pictures seem to tell a story.)*

What kind of text tells a story? *A narrative text.*

Why will you read "Tina Is Happy"? *(Idea: To read the story for fun.)*

5 minutes

Student Materials:
Reading *Textbook A*

Part C: Fluency Building

(See Appendix E for Fluency/Paired Reading Guidelines.)

 Conduct after the lesson using the story of the day.

Activity 1 Partner Reading

It's time for partner reading.

Direct students to assigned partners. **Monitor** partner reading.

Lesson 6

Lesson 7

Materials
Teacher: 1-Narrative Story Map; Reading *Textbook A*
Student: Copy of 1-Narrative Story Map; Reading *Textbook A*

8 minutes

Teacher Materials:
Reading *Textbook A*

Student Materials:
Reading *Textbook A*

Part A: Vocabulary Development

Activity 1 Learn New Vocabulary Word

Elicit responses to questions. **Guide** as needed.
Today you'll learn a new vocabulary word. **Store. Store** means "to keep something for later use." What does **store** mean? *To keep something for later use.*

Another way to say "keep something for later use" is **store.** What's another way to say "keep something for later use"? *Store.*

Camels can go a very long time without drinking water. Camels are able to **keep** water **for later use.** Most animals cannot **store** water like camels can. **Discuss** things that you store.

What's another way to say "to keep something for later use"? *Store.*

Activity 2 Review Vocabulary Word

Elicit responses to questions. **Guide** as needed.
What's another word for **big?** *Huge.*

Tell me a sentence using the word **huge.** (Student responses.)
Discuss sentence.

 Review vocabulary word in appropriate context in Reading *Textbook A*.

18   Lesson 7

12 minutes

Teacher Materials:
Narrative Story Map

Reading *Textbook A*

Student Materials:
Narrative Story Map

Reading *Textbook A*

Part B: Comprehension Strategies

Activity 1 Narrative Story Map: Identify Title, Characters, and Setting—An After-Reading Strategy

 Direct students to Lesson 6, page 34 of Reading *Textbook A*.

Elicit responses to questions. Guide as needed.
In the last lesson, you read "Tina Is Happy."

What kind of text is it? *Narrative text.*

Why do you read narrative text? *(Idea: To read the story for fun.)*

Show Narrative Story Map.

Today you'll use a Narrative Story Map to help you organize your thinking about narrative texts so you understand and remember what you read.

What are the first three things you write when you fill out a Narrative Story Map? *(Idea: Titles, characters, and setting.)*

Guide students as they write the title on Narrative Story Map.
Touch the line labeled *Title* on your Narrative Story Map. What's the title of the story? *"Tina Is Happy."*

Write the title on your Narrative Story Map.

Guide students they write the characters on 1-Narrative Story Map.
Touch the box for *Characters* on your Narrative Story Map. The characters are the important people, animals, or objects that do things in the story. What are characters? *(Idea: The important people, animals, or objects that do things in the story.)*

Who are the characters in the story? *(Idea: Tina, the big trees, and the campers.)*

Write the names of the characters on your Narrative Story Map.

Guide students as they write the setting on Narrative Story Map.
Touch the box for *Setting* on your Narrative Story Map. The setting tells where and when the story happens. What does the setting tell? *Where and when the story happens.*

Touch the word "Where" in the *Setting* box on your Narrative Story Map. Where does the story take place? *The forest.*

Write where the story takes place in the *Setting* box.

Touch the word "When" in the *Setting* box. This story does not really tell when the story happens. You can leave that part blank. Can you make a guess about when the story happens? *(Idea: It might be summer because that is when people go camping.)*

You'll learn about Problems and Events in later lessons.

Lesson 7   **19**

Activity 2 | Comprehension Monitoring: Read Narrative Text with Prosody—A During-Reading Strategy

 Direct students to Lesson 6, page 34 of Reading *Textbook A*.

Today I'll read the narrative story "Tina Is Happy." If you pause at the end of each sentence, you can understand what you read better. Listen to me stop at the end of each sentence and take a small breath. Follow along in the book as I read.

Read title and first page of Lesson 6, page 34 of Reading *Textbook A* with prosody, attending to the punctuation.

Elicit responses to questions. **Guide** as needed.

What were the trees afraid of? *A forest fire.*

What did the big trees want Tina to do? (Idea: *Drop apples on the campers.*)

Now I'll read the story without stopping at the end of each sentence. See whether you can tell the difference. See whether it's easier or harder to understand the story. Follow along as I read.
Read second page without prosody, running sentences together in a monotone voice.

Discuss how your last reading sounded and whether you could understand the story well.

Reread second page and last page with prosody, attending to punctuation.

Which way sounds better—when you stop at the end of the sentences or when you don't? (Idea: *When you stop at the end of the sentences.*)

Which way helps you understand the story better—when you stop at the end of the sentences or when you don't? (Idea: *When you stop at the end of the sentences.*)

Remember when you read, you'll understand the story better if you take a small breath at the end of each sentence.

Part C: Fluency Building

5 minutes

Student Materials:
Reading *Textbook A*

(See Appendix E for Fluency/Paired Reading Guidelines.)

 Conduct after the lesson using the story of the day.

Activity 1 | Partner Reading

It's time for partner reading.

Direct students to assigned partners. **Monitor** partner reading.

20   Lesson 7

Lesson 8

Materials

Teacher: 1-Narrative Story Map; Reading *Textbook A*
Student: Copy of 1-Narrative Story Map for each set of partners; Reading *Textbook A*

Part A: Vocabulary Development

8 minutes

Teacher Materials:
Reading *Textbook A*

Student Materials:
Reading *Textbook A*

Activity 1 Learn New Vocabulary Word

Elicit responses to questions. **Guide** as needed.
Today you'll learn a new vocabulary word. **Trade. Trade** means "to give and get things." What does **trade** mean? *To give and get things.*

Another way to say "to give and get things" is **trade.** What's another way to say "to give and get things"? *Trade.*

The camel and pig are two very different animals. So when the camel agreed **to give** up his hump and **get** a pig nose, he was not happy. When you **trade** it should be for something you want.

Discuss things that people trade.

What's another way to say **to give and get things?** *Trade.*

Activity 2 Review Vocabulary Word

Elicit responses to questions. **Guide** as needed.
What's another way to say "to keep something for later use"? *Store.*

Tell me a sentence using the word store. (Student responses.)
Discuss sentence.

  Review vocabulary words in appropriate context in Reading *Textbook A*.

Lesson 8   21

Teacher Materials:
Narrative Story Map

Reading *Textbook A*

Student Materials:
Narrative Story Map

Reading *Textbook A*

Part B: Comprehension Strategies

Activity 1 Narrative Story Map: Identify Title, Characters, and Setting—An After-Reading Strategy

 Direct students to Lesson 7, page 41 of Reading *Textbook A*.

Elicit responses to questions. **Guide** as needed.
In the last lesson, you read "The Camel and the Pig."

What kind of text is it? *Narrative text.*

Why do you read narrative text? *(Idea: To read the story for fun.)*

Show 1-Narrative Story Map.
Today you'll work with a partner to fill out the first three sections of your Narrative Story Map. Why do you use a Narrative Story Map? *(Idea: To help you organize your thinking about narrative texts so you understand and remember what you read.)*

What are the first three things you write when you fill out a Narrative Story Map? *(Idea: Titles, characters, and setting.)*

Touch the line labeled "Title" on your Narrative Story Map. Work with your partner to write the title on the line.
Monitor students as they write the title on Narrative Story Map.

Touch the box for characters on your Narrative Story Map. What are characters? *(Idea: The important people, animals, or objects that do things in the story.)*

Work with your partner to decide who the important characters are in the story, and write their names in the box for characters.
Monitor students as they write the characters on Narrative Story Map.

Touch the box for setting on your Narrative Story Map. What does the setting tell? *Where and when the story happens.*

Monitor students as they write the setting on Narrative Story Map.
Today it's very tough to figure out the setting. The best clues for the setting come from the picture. Also look at the end of the story for some clues. Work with your partner and see whether you can figure out where the story takes place. Write your idea in the box for *Setting*.

Touch the word "When" in the *Setting* box. This story does not really tell when the story happens. You can leave that part blank. However, you might want to talk with your partner and see whether you can make a guess about when the story happens from the picture. If you make a guess, write it in the box for *Setting*.

22 *Lesson 8*

Now let's check what you wrote on your Narrative Story Map. *(Ideas: Title—"The Camel and the Pig;" Characters—a camel and a pig; Setting—Where: a field or a garden with a fence, When: One day because the picture does not show night.*

Discuss the title, characters, and setting and why answers might be different.

We will learn about Problems and Events in later lessons.

Activity 2 Comprehension Monitoring: Read Narrative Text with Prosody—A During-Reading Strategy

 Direct students to Lesson 7, page 41 of Reading *Textbook A*.

Today I'll read the beginning of "The Camel and the Pig." I'll stop at the end of each sentence and take a little breath. If I do that, I'll understand the story better. Follow along in your book as I read.
Model reading first page with prosody.

Now you'll read the first page with me, and we'll take a little breath after each sentence. Watch for the punctuation or end marks.

 Monitor students to ensure they read along in Reading *Textbook A*.

Guide as needed.

Assign student partners. **Monitor** student reading. **Guide** as needed.
Your turn to read half of the next page to your partner. Then your partner can read to the end. Be careful to take a small breath after each sentence. Check your partner to make sure he or she reads the right way. Remember, the punctuation tells you where to take a small breath. When you read the right way, it improves your comprehension.

Part C: Fluency Building

5 minutes

Student Materials:
Reading *Textbook A*

(See Appendix E for Fluency/Paired Reading Guidelines.)

 Conduct after the lesson using the story of the day.

Activity 1 Partner Reading

It's time for partner reading.

Direct students to assigned partners. **Monitor** partner reading.

Lesson 8 **23**

Lesson 9

Materials
Teacher: 1-Narrative Story Map; Reading *Textbook A*
Student: Copy of 1-Narrative Story Map; Reading *Textbook A*

Part A: Vocabulary Development

8 minutes

Teacher Materials:
Reading *Textbook A*

Student Materials:
Reading *Textbook A*

Activity 1 Learn New Vocabulary Word

Elicit responses to questions. **Guide** as needed.
Today you'll learn a new vocabulary word. **Member. Member** means "someone who belongs to a group." What does **member** mean? *Someone who belongs to a group.*

Another way to say "someone who belongs to a group" is **member.** What's another way to say "someone who belongs to a group"? *Member.*

Joe **belongs to a group** that includes pencils, pens, and brushes, just to name a few things. As a **member**, his job is to make pictures.
Discuss examples of <u>members</u>.

What's another way to say "someone who belongs to a group"? *Member.*

Activity 2 Review Vocabulary Word

Elicit responses to questions. **Guide** as needed.
What's another way to say "to give and get things"? *Trade.*

Tell me a sentence using the word **trade.** (Student responses.)
Discuss sentence.

 Review vocabulary words in appropriate context in Reading *Textbook A*.

24   Lesson 9

12 minutes

Teacher Materials:
Narrative Story Map

Reading *Textbook A*

Student Materials:
Narrative Story Map

Reading *Textbook A*

Part B: Comprehension Strategies

Activity 1 Narrative Story Map: Identify Title, Characters, and Setting—An After-Reading Strategy

 Direct students to Lesson 8, page 46 of Reading *Textbook A*.

Elicit response to question. **Guide** as needed.

In the last lesson, you read "The Camel and the Pig Trade Parts."

What kind of text is it? *Narrative text.*

Why do you read narrative text? *(Idea: To read the story for fun.)*

Show 1-Narrative Story Map.
Today you'll work by yourself to fill out the first three sections of your Narrative Story Map. Why do you use a Narrative Story Map? *(Idea: To help you organize your thinking about narrative texts so you understand and remember what you read.)*

What are the first three things you write when you fill out a Narrative Story Map? *(Idea: Title, characters, and setting.)*

Touch the line labeled *Title* on your Narrative Story Map. Write the title on the line.
Monitor students as they write the title on 1-Narrative Story Map.

Touch the box for *Characters* on your Narrative Story Map. What are characters in a story? *(Idea: The important people, animals, or objects that do things in the story.)*

Write the names of the characters in the box.
Monitor students as they write the characters on Narrative Story Map.

Touch the box for *Setting* on your Narrative Story Map. What does the setting tell? *Where and when the story happens.*

Write where the story takes place in the box for setting.
Monitor students as they write the setting on Narrative Story Map.

This story does not tell when the story takes place so leave that part blank.

Discuss the title, characters, and setting and why answers might be different.
Now let's check what you wrote on your Narrative Story Map. *(Ideas: Title—"The Camel and the Pig Trade Parts;" Characters—a camel and a pig; Setting—Where: a field or a garden with a fence, When: leave blank.)*

We'll learn about Problems and Events in later lessons.

Activity 2 Comprehension Monitoring: Read Expository Text with Prosody—A During-Reading Strategy

 Direct students to Lesson 7, page 39–40 of Reading *Textbook A*.

Elicit response to question. **Guide** as needed.
Today I'll read "More Facts about Camels." Notice that I am reading about facts so this is expository text.

Why do you read expository text? *To learn new information.*

I need to read expository text by pausing after each sentence the same way I do when I read narrative texts. Follow along in your textbook as I read. I'll read the story the right way some of the time by stopping and taking a small breath after each sentence. When I pause after each sentence, it's easier to understand what I read.

But I'll try to trick you sometimes by reading the wrong way. When I read the wrong way say, "STOP."

Read pages 39-40, alternating between reading with prosody and then reading in a monotone voice and disregarding punctuation. **Guide** as needed.

Why do we read and pause at the end of the sentence? *(Idea: So it's easier to understand.)*

Remember, it helps you have better comprehension of both narrative and expository text if you read the text the right way.

Part C: Fluency Building

5 minutes

Student Materials:
Reading *Textbook A*

(See Appendix E for Fluency/Paired Reading Guidelines.)

 Conduct after the lesson using the story of the day.

Activity 1 Partner Reading

It's time for partner reading.

Direct students to assigned partners. **Monitor** partner reading.

Lesson 10

Materials

Teacher: Reading *Textbook A,* 2-Vocabulary Acquisition and Use, Writing Prompts, 3-My Writing Checklist

Student: Drawing paper; Reading *Textbook A,* Copy of 2-Vocabulary Acquisition and Use, Copy of 3-My Writing Checklist, Lined paper

8 minutes

Teacher Materials:
Reading *Textbook A*

Vocabulary Acquisition and Use

Student Materials:
Reading *Textbook A*

Vocabulary Acquisition and Use

Part A: Vocabulary Development

Activity 1 Cumulative Vocabulary Review

Elicit responses to questions. **Guide** as needed. **Review** vocabulary words as needed.
Directions: Listen and tell me whether I use our vocabulary words the right way or the wrong way. If I use the word the right way, say **"yes."** If I use the word the wrong way, say **"no."** Then we'll talk about each word.

1. Julia's father had to **examine** her finger closely to see her paper cut.

   Did I use the word **examine** the right way? *Yes.*

   How do you know? (Student responses.)

2. Tim and John made a **path** in the snow from their front door to their mailbox.

   Did I use the word **path** the right way? *Yes.*

   How do you know? (Student responses.)

3. It's a **fact** that all flowers are red.

   Did I use the word **fact** the right way? *No.*

   How do you know? (Student responses.)

4. Joe did not eat his ice cream because it was not **ripe.**

   Did I use the word **ripe** the right way? *No.*

   How do you know? (Student responses.)

5. Elephants are **huge** animals.

   Did I use the word **huge** the right way? *Yes.*

   How do you know? (Student responses.)

Lesson 10   27

6. Kathy bought four cans of tomatoes even though she only needed two for dinner. She would **store** the extra cans for later.

   Did I use the word store the right way? *Yes.*

   How do you know? (Student responses.)

7. Emily gave her teddy bear to Josh. Josh did not give her anything. She thought it was a good **trade.**

   Did I use the word **trade** the right way? *No.*

   How do you know? (Student responses.)

8. Lewis and Danny just met at school and became best friends. Each was a **member** of the same family.

   Did I use the word **member** correctly? No.

   How do you know? (Student responses.)

 Review vocabulary words in appropriate context in Reading *Textbook A.*

Activity 2 Vocabulary Acquisition and Use

Display Vocabulary Acquisition and Use. **Have** students work with a neighbor to complete Vocabulary Acquisition and Use.
Today's vocabulary words are ____ and ____ [and _____ and ____].
Vocabulary words: **huge** and **big; trade** and **give**
Write the words on the lines provided. Then write the words in the boxes based on whether you think each word is less/smaller or more/larger than the other word. Below the boxes, write why you think word 1 is less/smaller and word 2 is more/larger than word 1.
Repeat for words 3 and 4. **Have** students share what they wrote. **Discuss** examples of how these words might be used.

12 minutes

Teacher Materials:
Reading *Textbook A*

Student Materials:
Drawing paper

Reading *Textbook A*

Part B: Comprehension Strategies

Display directions for the activity.

 Direct students to Lesson 8, page 46 of Reading *Textbook A*.

Directions: Discuss who or what the most important or main characters were in "The Camel and the Pig Trade Parts." Show how you could change the story to have two different animals that could trade body parts.

Activity 1 Pair-Share Activity—Apply Knowledge (Level 3 of Bloom's Taxonomy)

You'll do an activity to show some things you have learned in the last four lessons. The directions are on the board. I'll read them to you.

Discuss the steps in Pair-Share. **Assign** partners. **Provide** drawing paper.
Step 1 is the Pair part of the activity. You'll talk to your partner to decide the most important or main characters in "The Camel and the Pig Trade Parts." Then you'll think together about two different animals that could trade parts. Think about what parts they would trade and decide who'll draw each animal. Then do the drawings. You have 6 minutes to do this activity. First talk and decide what to do and then do the activity. Draw quick sketches so you're done on time.

Guide students as they determine most important or main characters—the camel and the pig; the drawings should show two different animals with traded body parts.

Step 2 is to Share. I'll call on pairs of students to share their work with the rest of the class.
Call on as many students to share as time allows.

5 minutes

Student Materials:
Reading *Textbook A*

Part C: Fluency Building

 Conduct after the lesson, using the story of the day.

Activity 1 Partner Reading

It's time for partner reading.
Direct students to the story of the day. **Assign** student partners as Partner 1 and Partner 2. **Monitor** partner reading. **Guide** as needed.

Lesson 10

10 minutes

Teacher Materials:
Writing Prompts

My Writing Checklist

Student Materials:
Lined Paper

My Writing Checklist

Part D: Writing/Language Arts

Activity 1 Write and Use Parts of Speech and Conventions

Time to write using a writing prompt based on the stories we've been reading.

Assign student partners. **Distribute** lined paper to students. **Display** writing prompts and have students choose one to write about or assign a writing prompt of your choice. **Review** parts of speech and punctuation as well as the writing checklist with students. **Tell** students to write one to two paragraphs (minimum of four sentences per paragraph) on their own to answer the writing prompt. **Tell** them to use their writing checklist (first column labeled "Did I use them?") to ensure they include important parts of speech or punctuation in their writing. **Tell** students which parts of speech or punctuation to focus on, if you wish. **Model** what it means to answer a writing prompt and to use the writing checklist during and after the writing process, as needed. **Monitor** and guide students as needed. **Model** what it means to have a neighbor look over his or her neighbor's writing and to complete the writing checklist (second column labeled "Did my neighbor use them?"), as needed. **Have** students share what they wrote as time permits.

Writing Prompt 1	*Writing Prompt 2*	*Writing Prompt 3*
Develop your own make-believe animal and tell me about it.	If you owned a moop, what problems might you have?	Describe one thing you could do while camping in a forest.

30   *Lesson 10*

Lesson 11

Materials
Teacher: 4-Vocabulary Notebook, 5-Narrative Story Map; Reading *Textbook A*
Student: Vocabulary notebook; Reading *Textbook A*

8 minutes

Teacher Materials:
Vocabulary Notebook

Reading *Textbook A*

Student Materials:
Vocabulary notebook

Reading *Textbook A*

Part A: Vocabulary Development

Activity 1 Learn New Vocabulary Word and Start Vocabulary Notebook

Elicit responses to questions. **Guide** as needed.
Today you'll learn a new vocabulary word. **Ruler. Ruler** means "a flat stick for measuring." What does **ruler** mean? *A flat stick for measuring.*
Discuss things that are measured with a ruler.

Another way to say "a flat stick for measuring" is **ruler.** What's another way to say "a flat stick for measuring"? *Ruler.*

Joe wanted to make a change with his job. Joe wanted to become **a flat stick for measuring.** Even though Joe was round, he got a job as a **ruler.**

What's another way to say "a flat stick for measuring"? *Ruler.*

Today you'll start a vocabulary notebook. You'll keep track of new vocabulary words you learn in this program. I'll show you how to write your vocabulary word and its definition in your vocabulary notebook. Then you'll write your word and its definition in your notebook.

Display Vocabulary Notebook.
Divide notebook into two columns: Write "Word" in the left column and "Definition" in the right column.

Model writing ruler and its definition in vocabulary notebook. **Guide** students as they write ruler and its definition.

Activity 2 Review Vocabulary Word

Elicit responses to questions. **Guide** as needed.
What's another way to say "someone who belongs to a group"? *Member.*

Tell me a sentence using the word **member**. (Student responses.)
Discuss sentence.

 Review vocabulary words in appropriate context in Reading *Textbook A*.

Lesson 11   31

12 minutes

Teacher Materials:
Narrative Story Map

Reading *Textbook A*

Student Materials:
Reading *Textbook A*

Part B: Comprehension Strategies

Activity 1 Narrative Story Map: Identify Title, Characters, and Setting—An After-Reading Strategy

 Direct students to Lesson 9, page 52–54 of Reading *Textbook A*.

Elicit responses to questions. **Guide** as needed.
You'll work by yourself to fill out the first three sections of your Narrative Story Map.

Show Narrative Story Map.

What are the first three things you write when you fill out a Narrative Story Map? *(Idea: Title, characters, and setting.)*

Write the title, important characters, and setting on your Narrative Story Map.
Guide as students write the title, characters, and setting.

Discuss the title, characters, and setting.
What did you write on your Narrative Story Map? *(Ideas: Title—"Joe Williams Wants a New Job;" Main Characters—Joe, the felt-tipped pen; Setting—Where: apartment (desk), When: all day.)*
Write answers on Narrative Story Map.

Activity 2 Narrative Story Map: Identify Events—An After-Reading Strategy

Continue filling out Narrative Story Map. **Model** think-aloud for finding Events.
Next you'll learn how to fill in the *Events* part of the Narrative Story Map.
Listen as I show you how I figure out the **beginning, middle,** and **end** of the story for the *Events* section of the Narrative Story Map.
Model writing simple sentences to tell beginning—Joe works to make pictures; middle—Joe is tired of his job; end—Joe is sad because he only works as a felt-tipped pen.

> **Sample Wording for Think-Aloud**
>
> I look at the story and try to remember the things that happened in the story. I want to write a sentence in each part of the *Events* section of the Narrative Story Map that tells the beginning, the middle, and the end of this chapter in the Joe Williams story.
>
> In the *Beginning* box I want to write something about the beginning of the story. I remember that Joe works to make pictures, so I'll write that idea in the box.
>
> In the *Middle* box, I will write about how Joe is tired of his job. He wants to do a different job.
>
> In the *End* box, I'll write that Joe is sad because he can't think of a job to do except be a felt-tipped pen.
>
> This is the end of the chapter and my Narrative Story Map is finished for this chapter. There is another chapter about Joe that tells what happens next.

When I'm finished writing about the events that happened at the beginning, middle, and end of the chapter, I can use my Narrative Story Map to remember what happened in the chapter and retell this part of the story. You'll practice retelling stories in later lessons.

Activity 3 Comprehension Monitoring: Read Narrative Text with Prosody—A During-Reading Strategy

 Direct students to Lesson 9, page 54 of Reading *Textbook A*.

Today I'll read the end of "Joe Williams Wants a New Job." I'll stop at the end of each sentence and take a little breath. Notice that when I get to a question mark, my voice goes up a little to ask the question. Follow along in your book as I read.

Model reading the page with prosody.

 Monitor students to ensure they read along in Reading *Textbook A*.

Now you'll read page 54 with me, and we'll take a little breath after each sentence. Watch for the punctuation or end marks and remember to make your voice go up when you see the question mark.
Monitor students to make sure they are reading with prosody as they read with you.
Guide as needed.
When you read the right way, it improves your comprehension.

Part C: Fluency Building

5 minutes

Student Materials:
Reading *Textbook A*

 Conduct after the lesson, using the story of the day.

Activity 1 Partner Reading

It's time for partner reading.
Direct students to the story of the day. **Assign** student partners as Partner 1 and Partner 2. **Monitor** partner reading. **Guide** as needed.

Lesson 11

Lesson 12

Materials
Teacher: 4-Vocabulary Notebook; Reading *Textbook A*, 5-Narrative Story Map
Student: Vocabulary notebook; Reading *Textbook A*

8 minutes

Teacher Materials:
Vocabulary Notebook
Reading *Textbook A*

Student Materials:
Vocabulary notebook
Reading *Textbook A*

Part A: Vocabulary Development

Activity 1 Learn New Vocabulary Word

Elicit responses to questions. **Guide** as needed.
Today you'll learn a new vocabulary word. **Formed. Formed** means "started."
What does **formed** mean? *Started.*

Another word for "started" is **formed**. What's another word for "started"? *Formed.*

Aunt Fanny had a lot of fleas. She **started** a circus in 1993 using fleas for her acts. The circus was **formed** in 1993.

Discuss examples of things that have been formed.

What's another word for "started"? *Formed.*

Display Vocabulary Notebook. **Model** as needed. **Direct** students to write formed and its definition in their vocabulary notebook. **Guide** as needed.
Write **formed** and what it means in your vocabulary notebook.

Activity 2 Review Vocabulary Word

Elicit responses to questions. **Guide** as needed.
What's another way to say "a flat stick for measuring"? *Ruler.*

Tell me a sentence using the word **ruler**. (Student responses.)
Discuss sentence.

 Review vocabulary words in appropriate context in Reading *Textbook A*.

34   Lesson 12

12 minutes

Teacher Materials:
Narrative Story Map

Reading *Textbook A*

Student Materials:
Reading *Textbook A*

Part B: Comprehension Strategies

Activity 1 Narrative Story Map: Identify Title, Characters, and Setting—An After-Reading Strategy

 Direct students to Lesson 11, pages 61–63 of Reading *Textbook A*.

Elicit responses to questions. **Guide** as needed.
You'll work by yourself to fill out the first three sections of your Narrative Story Map.

Show Narrative Story Map.

What are the first three things you write when you fill out a Narrative Story Map? *(Idea: Title, characters, and setting.)*

Write the title, important characters, and setting on your Narrative Story Map.
Guide as students write the title, characters, and setting.

Discuss the title, characters, and setting. **Write** answers on 5-Narrative Story Map.
What did you write on your Narrative Story Map? *(Ideas: Title—"Joe Williams Gets a New Job;" Main Characters—Joe, the felt-tipped pen and Mary, his wife; Setting—Where: apartment (desk), When: each night.)*

Activity 2 Narrative Story Map: Identify Events—An After-Reading Strategy

Continue filling out Narrative Story Map.
Next you'll learn how to fill in the *Events* part of the Narrative Story Map. Listen as I show you how I figure out the beginning, middle, and end of this chapter of the Joe story for the *Events* part of the Narrative Story Map.
Model finding Events.

Model writing simple sentences for Events. Suggested sentences: Beginning—Joe has an idea for a new job; Middle—Mary draws lines on Joe; End—Joe works as a round ruler. When I'm finished writing about the events that happened at the beginning, middle, and end of the chapter, I can use the Narrative Story Map to remember what happened in the chapter and retell this part of the story. You'll practice retelling stories in later lessons.

Activity 3 Comprehension Monitoring: Read Narrative Text with Prosody—A During-Reading Strategy

 Direct students to Lesson 11, page 61 of Reading *Textbook A*.

Today I'll read the first page of "Joe Williams Gets a New Job." I'll stop at the end of each sentence and take a little breath. Notice that when I get to a question mark, my voice goes up a little to ask the question. Follow along in your book as I read.
Model reading the page with prosody.

 Monitor students to ensure they read along in Reading *Textbook A*.

Lesson 12   **35**

Assign partners.

Now it's your turn to read the page the right way to a partner. Be sure to take a breath or a little pause at the end of each sentence and remember to make your voice go up a little when you get to a question mark. After you read the right way, have your partner read the page the right way. Check each other to make sure you do it correctly.

Monitor students to make sure they are reading with prosody as they read with a partner. **Guide** as needed.

When you read the right way, it improves your comprehension.

Part C: Fluency Building

5 minutes

Student Materials:
Reading *Textbook A*

  Conduct after the lesson, using the story of the day.

Activity 1 Partner Reading

It's time for partner reading.

Direct students to the story of the day. **Assign** student partners as Partner 1 and Partner 2. **Monitor** partner reading. **Guide** as needed.

36   Lesson 12

Lesson 13

Materials
Teacher: 5-Narrative Story Map: Reading *Textbook A*
Student: Vocabulary notebook: Copy of 5-Narrative Story Map; Reading *Textbook A*

8 minutes

Teacher Materials:
Reading *Textbook A*

Student Materials:
Vocabulary notebook
Reading *Textbook A*

Part A: Vocabulary Development

Activity 1 — Learn New Vocabulary Word

Elicit responses to questions. **Guide** as needed.
Today you'll learn a new vocabulary word. **Packed. Packed** means "full." What does **packed** mean? *Full.*

Another word for "full" is **packed.** What's another word for "full"? *Packed.*

The area set aside for people to watch Aunt Fanny's circus was **full**. Although it was **packed,** the fleas would not perform their acts.

Discuss examples of things that are packed.

What's another word for "full"? *Packed.*

Direct students to write packed and its definition in their vocabulary notebook. **Guide** as needed.
Write **packed** and what it means in your vocabulary notebook.

Activity 2 — Review Vocabulary Word

Elicit responses to questions. **Guide** as needed.
What's another word for "started"? *Formed.*

Tell me a sentence using the word **formed.** (Student responses.)
Discuss sentence.

 Review vocabulary words in appropriate context in Reading *Textbook A*.

Lesson 13   37

Part B: Comprehension Strategies

12 minutes

Teacher Materials:
Narrative Story Map

Reading *Textbook A*

Student Materials:
Narrative Story Map

Reading *Textbook A*

Activity 1 Narrative Story Map: Identify Title, Characters, and Setting—An After-Reading Strategy

 Direct students to Lesson 12, pages 68–70 of Reading *Textbook A*.

Elicit responses to questions. **Guide** as needed.
You'll work by yourself to fill out the first three sections of your Narrative Story Map.

Show Narrative Story Map.

What are the first three things you write when you fill out a Narrative Story Map? *(Idea: Title, characters, and setting.)*
Guide as students write the title, characters, and setting.

What's a **title**? *(Idea: Words written by the author to tell what a story is about.)*

What are **characters**? *(Idea: The most important people, animals, or objects that do things in a story.)*

What's a **setting**? *(Idea: When and where the story takes place.)*

Guide as students write the title, characters, and setting.
Write the title, important or main characters, and setting on your Narrative Story Map.

Discuss the title, characters, and setting. **Write** answers on Narrative Story Map.
What did you write on your Narrative Story Map? *(Ideas: Title—"Aunt Fanny's Flea Circus;" Main Characters—Aunt Fanny, Carl Goodscratch, Martha Jumpjump, Henry Ouch; Setting—Where: flea circus, When: 1993 and 1999.)*

Activity 2 Narrative Story Map: Identify Events—An After-Reading Strategy

Continue filling out Narrative Story Map. **Elicit** responses to questions. **Guide** as needed.
Next you'll fill out the *Events* part of the Narrative Story Map. Let's figure out what to put in each of the boxes for *Events*.

Guide students as they think about events at the beginning, middle, and end of the story. **Discuss** events.
What events happened at the beginning of the chapter? (Student responses.)

Model writing simple sentences for Events: Beginning—Aunt Fanny has a flea circus; Middle—Aunt Fanny and the fleas fight; End—Fleas decide things must change.
Monitor as students copy sentences in their Events boxes.
I noticed that the beginning of the chapter told about Aunt Fanny and her flea circus. So let's write that for the first event.

What events happened in the middle of the chapter? (Student responses.)

38 Lesson 13

The middle of the chapter tells that Aunt Fanny and the fleas began to fight because Aunt Fanny kept all the money and had good food and a good place to live, while the fleas ate dry bread and lived in a small box. Let's write about Aunt Fanny and the fleas fighting for the middle.

Finally, what events happened at the end of the chapter? (Student responses.)

At the end of the chapter, the fleas decide that things must change so let's write that event for the *Ending*.

When you review your story map, you can remember a lot about the chapter. You'll be able to use your Narrative Story Map to retell the chapter. You'll practice retelling stories in later lessons.

Activity 3 Comprehension Monitoring: Read Narrative Text with Prosody—A During-Reading Strategy

Direct students to Lesson 12, page 68 of Reading *Textbook A*.

Today I'll read the first page of "Aunt Fanny's Flea Circus." I'll stop at the end of each sentence and take a little breath. Notice that if I get to a question mark, my voice goes up a little to ask the question. Follow along in your book as I read.
Model reading page with prosody.

Monitor students to ensure they read along in Reading *Textbook A*.

Assign partners.
Now it's your turn to read the page the right way to a partner. Be sure to take a breath or a little pause at the end of each sentence and remember to make your voice go up a little when you get to a question mark. After you read the right way, have your partner read the page the right way. Check each other to make sure you do it correctly.

Monitor students to make sure they are reading with prosody as they read with a partner. **Guide** as needed.

When you read the right way, it improves your comprehension.

Part C: Fluency Building

5 minutes

Student Materials:
Reading *Textbook A*

Conduct after the lesson, using the story of the day.

Activity 1 Partner Reading

It's time for partner reading.
Direct students to the story of the day. **Assign** student partners as Partner 1 and Partner 2. **Monitor** partner reading. **Guide** as needed.

Lesson 13

Lesson 14

Materials
Teacher: 5-Narrative Story Map; Reading *Textbook A*
Student: Vocabulary notebook; Copy of 5-Narrative Story Map; Reading *Textbook A*

8 minutes

Part A: Vocabulary Development

Teacher Materials:
Reading *Textbook A*

Student Materials:
Vocabulary notebook
Reading *Textbook A*

Activity 1 Learn New Vocabulary Word

Elicit responses to questions. **Guide** as needed.
Today you'll learn a new vocabulary word. **Crowd. Crowd** means "a large number of people." What does **crowd** mean? *A large number of people.*

Another way to say "a large number of people" is **crowd.** What's another way to say "a large number of people"? *Crowd.*

A large number of people were expecting to see a really good show. The **crowd** was not happy when the fleas didn't do their acts.

Discuss examples of where there might be a crowd.

What's another way to say "a large number of people"? *Crowd.*

Direct students to write crowd and its definition in their vocabulary notebook. **Guide** as needed.
Write **crowd** and what it means in your vocabulary notebook.

Activity 2 Review Vocabulary Word

Elicit responses to questions. **Guide** as needed.
What's another word for "full"? *Packed.*

Tell me a sentence using the word **packed.** (Student responses.)
Discuss sentence.

 Review vocabulary words in appropriate context in Reading *Textbook A*.

40   Lesson 14

12 minutes

Teacher Materials:
Narrative Story Map

Reading *Textbook A*

Student Materials:
Narrative Story Map

Reading *Textbook A*

Part B: Comprehension Strategies

Activity 1 Narrative Story Map: Identify Title, Characters, and Setting—An After-Reading Strategy

 Direct students to Lesson 13, pages 75–76 of Reading *Textbook A*.

Elicit responses to questions. **Guide** as needed.
You'll work by yourself to fill out the first three sections of your Narrative Story Map.

Show Narrative Story Map.

What's a narrative text? *A story.*

Narratives have a title, characters, and settings.

What are the first three things you write when you fill out a Narrative Story Map? *(Idea: Title, characters, and setting.)*

Guide as students write the title, characters, and setting.
Write the title, important characters, and setting on your Narrative Story Map.

Discuss the title, characters, and setting. **Write** answers on 5-Narrative Story Map.
What did you write on your Narrative Story Map? *(Ideas: Title—"The Fleas Surprise Aunt Fanny;" Main Characters—Aunt Fanny, Carl Goodscratch, Martha Jumpjump, Henry Ouch; Setting—Where: flea circus, When: the next day or during the show.*

Activity 2 Narrative Story Map: Identify Events—An After-Reading Strategy

Continue filling out Narrative Story Map.
Narratives have a beginning, middle and an end. When you fill out the Events part of the Narrative Story Map, you're thinking about the beginning, middle and end of this chapter. Let's figure out what to put in each of the boxes for Events.

Guide students to think about events at the beginning, middle, and end of the story.
What events happened at the beginning of the chapter? (Student responses.)

Model writing simple sentences for Events. Suggested sentences: Beginning—Fleas were not happy; Middle—Fleas tried to get Aunt Fanny to change; End—The fleas did not do their acts in the circus. **Monitor** students as they copy sentences in their Events boxes.
I think that at the beginning of the chapter, the fleas were not happy with Aunt Fanny, so let's write that idea for the beginning event.

What events happened in the middle of the chapter? (Student responses.)

Lesson 14 **41**

I think that in the middle of the story, the fleas tried to get Aunt Fanny to change and give them a better home, better food and more money, so let's write that for the middle event.

Finally, what events happened at the end of the chapter? (Student responses.)

I think at the end of the story the fleas decided to not do their acts in the circus to try to make Aunt Fanny change so let's write that in the box for the end event.

When you review your narrative story map, you can remember a lot about the chapter. You'll use your Narrative Story Map to retell the chapter. You'll practice retelling stories in later lessons.

Activity 3 Comprehension Monitoring: Read Narrative Text with Prosody—A During-Reading Strategy

 Direct students to Lesson 13, page 75 of Reading *Textbook A*.

Today I'll read the first half of the page of "The Fleas Surprise Aunt Fanny." I'll stop at the end of each sentence and take a little breath. Notice that if I get to a question mark, my voice goes up a little to ask the question. Follow along in your book as I read.

Model reading page with prosody. **Monitor** students to ensure they read along in *Textbook A*.

Assign student partners.
Now it's your turn to read the rest of the page the right way to a partner. Be sure to take a breath or a little pause at the end of each sentence and remember to make your voice go up a little when you get to a question mark. After you read the right way, have your partner read the rest of the page the right way. Check each other to make sure you do it correctly.
Monitor students to make sure they are reading with prosody as they read with a partner. **Guide** as needed.

When you read the right way, it improves your comprehension.

Part C: Fluency Building

5 minutes

Student Materials:
Reading *Textbook A*

 Conduct after the lesson, using the story of the day.

Activity 1 Partner Reading

It's time for partner reading.
Direct students to the story of the day. **Assign** student partners as Partner 1 and Partner 2. **Monitor** partner reading. **Guide** as needed.

42   Lesson 14

Lesson 15

Materials

Teacher: 4-Vocabulary Notebook, Reading *Textbook A*, 2-Vocabulary Acquisition and Use

Student: Vocabulary notebook; drawing paper; Reading *Textbook A*, Copy of 2-Vocabulary Acquisition and Use

8 minutes

Teacher Materials:
Vocabulary Notebook
Reading *Textbook A*
Vocabulary Acquisition and Use

Student Materials:
Vocabulary notebook
Reading *Textbook A*
Vocabulary Acquisition and Use

Part A: Vocabulary Development

Activity 1 Vocabulary Notebook Review

Today you'll learn to study from your vocabulary notebook. Studying your words and what they mean will help you know your words even better. You'll look at the four words we studied this week. Watch as I study **ruler.**

Display Vocabulary Notebook. **Write** ruler and its meaning and model think-aloud for studying the word and its meaning.

Sample Wording for Think-Aloud

Ruler is "a flat stick for measuring." First, I cover what the word means with my hand. I cover **a flat stick for measuring** with my hand like this. Then I think of what it means. Ruler means . . . "a flat stick for measuring." I remove my hand and check to see if I'm right. I am. Now I cover the word with my hand. I cover **ruler** and read what it means—"a flat stick for measuring." The word that means "a flat stick for measuring" is **ruler.** I remove my hand and check to see whether I'm right. I am. It's **ruler.** Now I read both the word and its meaning. I say, **ruler** means "a flat stick for measuring." I'm finished studying this word.

Guide students through all words.
You'll study each word this way to learn your vocabulary words at a high level.

Activity 2 Cumulative Vocabulary Review

Elicit responses to questions. **Guide** as needed. **Review** vocabulary words as needed.

Directions: Listen and tell me whether I use our vocabulary words the right way or the wrong way. If I use the word the right way, say **"yes."** If I use the word the wrong way, say **"no."** Then we'll talk about each word.

1. Jana's teacher asked her to take out her **ruler** and measure the length of her desk.

   Did I use the word **ruler** the right way? *Yes.*

   How do you know? (Student responses.)

Lesson 15 43

2. There was a big **crowd** at the championship football game.

   Did I use the word **crowd** the right way? *Yes.*

   How do you know? (Student responses.)

3. Joe could sit wherever he wanted because the theater was **packed.**

   Did I use the word **packed** the right way? *No.*

   How do you know? (Student responses.)

4. Della **formed** a car for her family.

   Did I use the word **formed** the right way? *No.*

   How do you know? (Student responses.)

 Review vocabulary words in appropriate context in Reading *Textbook A*.

Activity 3 Vocabulary Acquisition and Use

Display Vocabulary Acquisition and Use. **Have** students work with a neighbor to complete Vocabulary Acquisition and Use.
Today's vocabulary words are _____ and _____ [and _____ and _____].
Vocabulary words: **formed** and **started; packed** and **full**
Write the words on the lines provided. Then write the words in the boxes based on whether you think each word is less/smaller or more/larger than the other word. Below the boxes, write why you think word 1 is less/smaller and word 2 is more/larger than word 1.
Repeat for words 3 and 4. **Have** students share what they wrote. **Discuss** examples of how these words might be used.

Part B: Comprehension Strategies

12 minutes

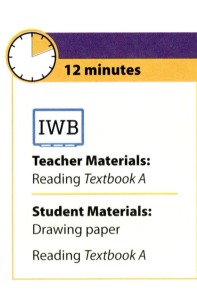

Teacher Materials:
Reading *Textbook A*

Student Materials:
Drawing paper

Reading *Textbook A*

Display directions for activity. **Direct** students to Lesson 14, pages 79–80 of Reading *Textbook A*.
Directions: Explain who the character was that did the high dive and why he didn't want to do his dive. Illustrate what the dive looked like to the crowd at the circus when he performed his act.

Activity 1 Pair-Share Activity—Apply Knowledge (Level 3 of Bloom's Taxonomy)

You'll do an activity called Pair-Share to show some things you have learned in the last four lessons. The directions are on the board. I will read them to you.

Discuss the steps in Pair-Share. **Assign** partners. **Provide** drawing paper.
Step 1 is the Pair part of the activity. You'll talk to your partner to agree on who did the high dive in "Aunt Fanny Changes Her Ways" and why he did not want to do the dive. Then you'll think about what that dive looked like. Make a picture of the dive to show what the crowd saw at the circus. Decide who'll do what part of the drawing. You have 6 minutes to complete the job. Draw quick sketches so you're done on time.

Guide students to answers: Character—Henry Ouch; the drawings should show Henry turning 5 times, making 7 loops, and no splash.

Step 2 is to Share. I'll call on pairs of students to share their work with the rest of the class.
Call on as many students to share as time allows.

5 minutes

Student Materials:
Reading *Textbook A*

Part C: Fluency Building

 Conduct after the lesson, using the story of the day.

Activity 1 Partner Reading

It's time for partner reading.

Direct students to the story of the day. **Assign** student partners as Partner 1 and Partner 2. **Monitor** partner reading. **Guide** as needed.

Lesson 15 **45**

Lesson 16

Materials

Teacher: 5-Narrative Story Map; Reading *Textbook A*

Student: Vocabulary notebook; Copy of 5-Narrative Story Map; Copy of Lesson 14 for each student group; 4 colors of highlighter for each student group; Reading *Textbook A*

Part A: Vocabulary Development

8 minutes

Teacher Materials:
Reading *Textbook A*

Student Materials:
Vocabulary notebook
Reading *Textbook A*

Activity 1 Learn New Vocabulary Word

Elicit responses to questions. **Guide** as needed.
Today you'll learn a new vocabulary word. **Suddenly. Suddenly** means "happening quickly." What does **suddenly** mean? *Happening quickly.*

Another way to say "happening quickly" is **suddenly.** What's another way to say "happening quickly"? *Suddenly.*

A hunter noticed something **happening quickly**. He saw a rock moving **suddenly.**

Discuss examples of things that happen suddenly.

What's another way to say "happening quickly"? *Suddenly.*

Write **suddenly** and what it means in your vocabulary notebook.

Direct students to write suddenly and its definition in their vocabulary notebook. **Guide** as needed.

Activity 2 Review Vocabulary Word

Elicit responses to questions. **Guide** as needed.

What's another way to say "a large number of people"? *Crowd.*

Tell me a sentence using the word **crowd.** Student response.
Discuss sentence.

 Review vocabulary words in appropriate context in Reading *Textbook A*.

46 Lesson 16

12 minutes

Teacher Materials:
Narrative Story Map

Reading *Textbook A*

Student Materials:
Narrative Story Map

Copy of Lesson 14 for each student group

4 colors of highlighter for each student group

Reading *Textbook A*

Part B: Comprehension Strategies

Activity 1 Narrative Story Map: Identify Title, Characters, Setting, and Events—An After-Reading Strategy

 Direct students to Lesson 15, pages 85–87 in Reading *Textbook A*.

Elicit responses to questions. **Guide** as needed.
You'll work by yourself to fill out the first three sections of your Narrative Story Map. Narratives have a title, characters, and settings.

Show Narrative Story Map.

Write the title, important characters, and setting on your Narrative Story Map.

Monitor as students write the title, characters, and setting. **Discuss** the title, characters, and setting. **Write** answers on Narrative Story Map.
What did you write on your Narrative Story Map? *(Ideas: Title—"Goad the Toad;" Main Character—Goad the toad; Setting—Where: Four Mile Lake, When: once.)*

Narratives have a beginning, middle and an end. Let's figure out what to put in each of the boxes for Events.

Elicit responses for events at the beginning, middle, and end of chapter. **Guide** as needed.

Write best response on Narrative Story Map. Suggested sentences: Beginning—Goad was a big, smart, fast toad; Middle—Goad was not fast in the water; End—Hunters wanted to catch Goad for a circus or zoo to get rich.

Monitor as students copy sentences in their Events boxes.

What events happened at the beginning of the chapter? **(Student responses.)**

Copy the sentence I wrote in your Narrative Story Map in the box for *Beginning*.

What events happened in the middle of the chapter? **(Student responses.)**

Copy the sentence I wrote in your Narrative Story Map in the box for *Middle*.

Finally, what events happened at the end of the chapter? **(Student responses.)**

Copy the sentence I wrote in your Narrative Story Map in the box for *End*.

When you review your story map, you can remember a lot about the chapter. You'll be able to use your Narrative Story Map to retell the chapter. You'll practice retelling stories in later lessons.

Lesson 16

Activity 2 — Comprehension Monitoring: Reading Dialogue with Prosody—A During-Reading Strategy

Provide photocopy of Lesson 14, pages 79–80 in Reading *Textbook A*, for each student group. **Show** what quotation marks look like on the board.

In order to read with better comprehension, it is important to pay attention to the punctuation marks in a story. **Quotation marks** are punctuation marks that show that a character is talking in a story. The words characters say in narratives are called **dialogue**. Often, narratives have lots of dialogue. Sometimes the dialogue can get confusing. We will practice paying attention to the quotation marks and reading the story in a way that will help us understand which character is saying the words.

Dialogue is marked with quotation marks. How's dialogue marked in stories? *(Idea: With quotation marks or talking marks.)*

What's dialogue? *(Idea: The words characters say in the story.)*

This is the story "Aunt Fanny Changes Her Ways." I'll show you how I mark the dialogue with a highlighter so that I see the words really well.

Model marking dialogue between the quotation marks with different colors according to who is speaking. Mark the rest of the words for the narrator.

I want you to mark the dialogue for the characters. One color will be for the words that Aunt Fanny says. Mark what Carl Goodscratch says with another color. Mark the words from the crowd with a third color. Then you need a narrator to read all the parts not in quotation marks, so those words should be in a fourth color.

Group students in groups of 4. **Provide** copies of story for students to mark the dialogue.

Have students mark dialogue with highlighters—4 colors needed. **Monitor** groups as they mark story.

Your turn to read the story with four people. Try to read with expression. Decide who'll read which part. The colors will help you know when it's your turn. Take turns and try to make the dialogue interesting.

Monitor groups as they practice dialogue.

When you read dialogue and pay attention to the quotation marks, you will better understand what you read.

Encourage students to perform parts of the dialogue in front of the class, after practice.

Part C: Fluency Building

5 minutes

Student Materials:
Reading *Textbook A*

Conduct after the lesson, using the story of the day.

Activity 1 — Partner Reading

It's time for partner reading.

Direct students to the story of the day. **Assign** student partners as Partner 1 and Partner 2. **Monitor** partner reading. **Guide** as needed.

48 Lesson 16

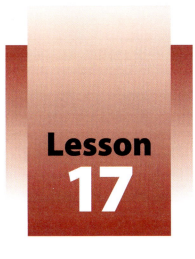

Lesson 17

Materials
Teacher: 5-Narrative Story Map; Reading *Textbook A*
Student: Vocabulary notebook; Copy of 5-Narrative Story Map for each student pair; Reading *Textbook A*

8 minutes

Teacher Materials:
Reading *Textbook A*

Student Materials:
Vocabulary notebook
Reading *Textbook A*

Part A: Vocabulary Development

Activity 1 Prefix Introduction

Elicit response to question. **Guide** as needed.
Today you'll learn about a **prefix**. A **prefix** is a "word part added to the beginning of a word that changes the word's meaning." What do we call a "word part added to the beginning of a word that changes the word's meaning"? *Prefix.*

Activity 2 Learn New Prefix

Elicit responses to questions. **Guide** as needed.
Today you'll learn a new prefix. **Un-. Un-** means "not." What does **un-** mean? *Not.*

The prefix that means "not" is **un-.** What's the prefix that means "not"? *Un-.*

Unfair. **Un**fair means **not** fair. **Un**buttoned. **Un**buttoned means **not** buttoned. **Un**lucky. What does **un**lucky mean? *Not lucky.*

So when we add the prefix **un-** to the beginning of words, we change what they mean. Believable. Adding **un-** to believable makes it **un**believable. What does **un**believable mean? *Not believable.*

What prefix means "not"? *Un-.*

Tell me an **un-** word. (Student responses.)
Discuss response.

Direct students to write the prefix <u>un-</u> and its definition in their vocabulary notebook. **Guide** as needed.
Write the prefix **un-** and its meaning in your vocabulary notebook.

Activity 3 Review Vocabulary Word

Elicit responses to questions. **Guide** as needed.
What's another way to say "happening quickly"? *Suddenly.*

Tell me a sentence using the word **suddenly.** (Student responses.)
Discuss sentence.

 Review vocabulary words in appropriate context in Reading *Textbook A*.

Lesson 17   49

12 minutes

Teacher Materials:
Narrative Story Map

Reading *Textbook A*

Student Materials:
Narrative Story Map

Reading *Textbook A*

Part B: Comprehension Strategies

Activity 1 Narrative Story Map: Identify Title, Characters, Setting, and Events—An After-Reading Strategy

 Direct students to Lesson 16, pages 91–92 in Reading *Textbook A*.

Elicit response to question. **Guide** as needed. **Show** Narrative Story Map.

You'll work with a partner to fill out the first three sections of your Narrative Story Map.

Narratives have a title, characters, and settings.

Write the title, important characters, and setting on your Narrative Story Map.

Monitor as students write the title, characters, and setting. **Discuss** the title, characters, and setting. **Write** answers on Narrative Story Map.
What did you write on your Narrative Story Map? *(Ideas: Title—"Goad Uses Her First Trick;" Main Character—Goad the toad; Setting—Where: Four Mile Lake and Toadsville, When: in the evening.)*

Narratives have a beginning, middle, and an end. Work with your partner to write a sentence for each of the boxes for Events.

Monitor as student s complete sentences for Events.

Discuss responses on Narrative Story Map. Suggested sentences: Beginning—Hunters liked to tell about trying to catch Goad; Middle—Hunters tried to catch Goad with a net; End—Goad escaped by acting like a rock.

When you review your story map, you can remember a lot about the chapter. You'll be able to use your Narrative Story Map to retell the chapter. You'll practice retelling stories in later lessons.

Activity 2 Comprehension Monitoring: Read Narrative Text with Prosody—A During-Reading Strategy

 Direct students to Lesson 16, page 92 in Reading *Textbook A*.

Today I'll read the last page of "Goad Uses Her First Trick." I'll stop at the end of each sentence and take a little breath. Notice that if I get to a question mark, my voice goes up a little to ask the question. If I come to quotation marks, I will read the words with expression. Follow along in your book as I read.
Model reading page with prosody.

50 *Lesson 17*

Monitor students to ensure they read along in *Reading Textbook A*.

Assign student partners.

Now it's your turn to read the page the right way to a partner. Be sure to take a breath or a little pause at the end of each sentence and remember to make your voice go up a little if you get to a question mark. Remember to pay attention to dialogue if you find it. After you read the right way, have your partner read the page the right way. Check each other to make sure you do it correctly.

Monitor students to make sure they are reading with prosody as they read with a partner. **Guide** as needed.

When you read the right way, it improves your comprehension.

5 minutes

Student Materials:
Reading *Textbook A*

Part C: Fluency Building

 Conduct after the lesson, using the story of the day.

Activity 1 Partner Reading

It's time for partner reading.

Direct students to the story of the day. **Assign** student partners as Partner 1 and Partner 2. **Monitor** partner reading. **Guide** as needed.

Lesson 17

Lesson 18

Materials
Teacher: Reading *Textbook A*
Student: Vocabulary notebook; Reading *Textbook A*

Part A: Vocabulary Development

8 minutes

Teacher Materials:
Reading *Textbook A*

Student Materials:
Vocabulary notebook
Reading *Textbook A*

Activity 1 Learn New Vocabulary Word

Elicit responses to questions. **Guide** as needed.
Today you'll learn a new vocabulary word. **Gulp. Gulp** means "swallow quickly." What does **gulp** mean? *Swallow quickly.*

Another way to say "swallow quickly" is **gulp.** What's another way to say "swallow quickly"? *Gulp.*

Goad must have been hungry because she wanted to **swallow** many of the blue flies **quickly.** She ate most of the flies with one big **gulp.**

Discuss examples of things that someone might gulp.

What's another way to say "swallow quickly"? *Gulp.*

Direct students to write gulp and its definition in their vocabulary notebook. **Guide** as needed.
Write **gulp** and what it means in your vocabulary notebook.

Activity 2 Review Vocabulary Word

Elicit responses to questions. **Guide** as needed.
What prefix means "not"? *Un-.*

Tell me a sentence using a word with the prefix **un-.** (Student responses.) **Discuss** sentence.

 Review vocabulary words in appropriate context in Reading *Textbook A*.

52   Lesson 18

12 minutes

Teacher Materials:
Reading *Textbook A*

Student Materials:
Reading *Textbook A*

Part B: Comprehension Strategies

Activity 1 — Determine Text Type and Establish a Purpose for Reading—A Before-Reading Strategy

 Direct students to Lesson 18, pages 103–106 in Reading *Textbook A*.

Elicit responses to questions. **Guide** as needed.
Today you'll read both narrative and expository text in your reading lesson.

What's the title of the first section you'll read? *Facts about Moles.*
Do you think this section is expository or narrative? *Expository.*

Why do you think it is expository? *(Idea: It looks like it teaches information about moles.)*

Why do you read expository text? *To learn new facts or information.*

Why will you read "Facts about Moles"? *(Idea: To learn new information about moles.)*

What's the title of the next section you'll read? *The Opposite Direction.*

Do you think this section is expository or narrative? *Expository.*

Why do you think it is expository? *(Idea: It looks like new information or facts to learn.)*

What's the title of the next section you'll read? *"Goad's Four Tricks."*

Do you think this section is expository or narrative? *Narrative.*

Why do you think it's narrative? *(Idea: It looks like more of the Goad story.)*

Why is it important to figure out what kind of text you're reading before you read it? *(Idea: Knowing what kind of text you are reading helps you understand if you are reading to learn or reading a story. Then you can understand what you are reading better.)*

Activity 2 — Comprehension Monitoring: Read Expository Text with Prosody—A During-Reading Strategy

 Direct students to Lesson 17, page 96 in Reading *Textbook A*.

Today I'll read "How Toads Catch Flies." This is expository text, but I'll do the same thing as when I read narrative text. I'll stop at the end of each sentence and take a little breath. Notice that if I get to a question mark, my voice goes up a little. If I come to quotation marks, I will read the words with expression. Follow along as I read.
Model reading page with prosody.

Lesson 18   **53**

Monitor students to ensure they read along in Reading *Textbook A*.

Assign student partners.
Now it's your turn to read the page the right way to a partner. Be sure to take a breath at the end of each sentence and remember to make your voice go up a little if you get to a question mark. Remember to pay attention to dialogue. After you read the right way, have your partner read the right way. Check each other.

Monitor students to make sure they are reading with prosody as they read with a partner. **Guide** as needed.
When you read the right way, it improves your comprehension.

Part C: Fluency Building

5 minutes

Student Materials:
Reading *Textbook A*

 Conduct after the lesson, using the story of the day.

Activity 1 Partner Reading

It's time for partner reading.
Direct students to the story of the day. **Assign** student partners as Partner 1 and Partner 2. **Monitor** partner reading. **Guide** as needed.

54 *Lesson 18*

Lesson 19

Materials
Teacher: 5-Narrative Story Map; Reading *Textbook A*
Student: Vocabulary notebook; Copy of 5-Narrative Story Map; Reading *Textbook A*

8 minutes

Teacher Materials:
Reading *Textbook A*

Student Materials:
Vocabulary notebook
Reading *Textbook A*

Part A: Vocabulary Development

Activity 1 Learn New Vocabulary Word

Elicit responses to questions. **Guide** as needed.
Today you'll learn a new vocabulary word. **Trained. Trained** means "taught how to do something." What does **trained** mean? *Taught how to do something.*

Another way to say "taught how to do something" is **trained.** What's another way to say "taught how to do something"? *Trained.*

There were many hunters who had been **taught how to do something,** like how to catch Goad. But even the **trained** hunters did not have any luck catching her.

Discuss examples of ways people or animals are trained.

What's another way to say "taught how to do something"? *Trained.*

Direct students to write trained and its definition in their vocabulary notebook. **Guide** as needed.
Write **trained** and what it means in your vocabulary notebook.

Activity 2 Review Vocabulary Word

Elicit responses to questions. **Guide** as needed.
What's another way to say "swallow quickly"? *Gulp.*

Tell me a sentence using the word **gulp.** (Student responses.)
Discuss sentence.

 Review vocabulary words in appropriate context in Reading *Textbook A*.

Lesson 19 55

12 minutes

Teacher Materials:
Narrative Story Map

Reading *Textbook A*

Student Materials:
Narrative Story Map

Reading *Textbook A*

Part B: Comprehension Strategies

Activity 1 — Narrative Story Map: Identify Title, Characters, Setting, and Events—An After-Reading Strategy

 Direct students to Lesson 18, pages 104–106 in Reading *Textbook A*.

Elicit responses to questions. **Guide** as needed.
You'll work by yourself to fill out the first three sections of your Narrative Story Map.

Show Narrative Story Map.

Narratives have a title, characters, and settings.

Write the title, important characters, and setting on your Narrative Story Map.

Monitor as students write the title, characters, and setting. **Discuss** the title, characters, and setting. **Write** answers on Narrative Story Map.
What did you write on your Narrative Story Map? *(Ideas: Title—"Goad's Four Tricks;" Main Character—Goad the toad; Setting—Where: the story does not tell but we know Four Mile Lake from the previous chapters, When: the story does not tell; you can leave blank or guess "during the day" from the picture.)*

Narratives have a beginning, middle, and an end. Work by yourself to write a sentence for each of the boxes for Events.

Monitor as students complete sentence for Events.

Discuss responses on Narrative Story Map. Suggested sentences: Beginning—Goad escaped from 400 traps by using tricks; Middle—A hunter tried a steel trap to catch Goad; End—Goad got trapped by the steel trap.

When you review your story map, you can remember a lot about the chapter. You'll be able to use your Narrative Story Map to retell the chapter. You'll practice retelling stories in later lessons.

Activity 2 — Comprehension Monitoring: Read Expository Text with Prosody—A During-Reading Strategy

 Direct students to Lesson 18, pages 103–104 in Reading *Textbook A*.

Assign student partners. **Elicit** responses to questions. **Guide** as needed.
Today it's your turn to read the expository passage "The Opposite Direction" the right way to a partner. Be sure to take a breath or a little pause at the end of each sentence and remember to make your voice go up a little if you get to a question mark. Remember to pay attention to dialogue if you find it. After you read the right way, have your partner read the page the right way. Check each other to make sure you do it correctly.

Monitor students to make sure they are reading with prosody as they read with a partner. **Guide** as needed.

Why is it important to read the right way? *(Idea: It improves your comprehension.)*

56 *Lesson 19*

5 minutes

Student Materials:
Reading *Textbook A*

Part C: Fluency Building

 Conduct after the lesson, using the story of the day.

Activity 1 Partner Reading

It's time for partner reading.

Direct students to the story of the day. **Assign** student partners as Partner 1 and Partner 2. **Monitor** partner reading. **Guide** as needed.

Lesson 19   **57**

Lesson 20

Materials

Teacher: Reading *Textbook A*, 2-Vocabulary Acquisition and Use, Writing Prompts, 3-My Writing Checklist

Student: Vocabulary notebook; drawing paper; Reading *Textbook A*, Copy of 2-Vocabulary Acquisition and Use, Copy of 3-My Writing Checklist, Lined paper

Part A: Vocabulary Development

8 minutes

Teacher Materials:
Reading *Textbook A*

Vocabulary Acquisition and Use

Student Materials:
Vocabulary Notebook

Reading *Textbook A*

Vocabulary Acquisition and Use

Activity 1 Vocabulary Notebook Review

Model how to study 2 words. **Guide** students as they study all words.
Today you'll study from your vocabulary notebook. Studying your words and what they mean will help you know your words even better. You'll study the eight words we studied over the past two weeks.

Activity 2 Cumulative Vocabulary Review

Elicit responses to questions. **Guide** as needed.
Directions: Listen and tell me whether I use our vocabulary words the right way or the wrong way. If I use the word the right way, say **"yes."** If I use the word the wrong way, say **"no."** Then we'll talk about each word.

1. A **crowd** gathered around to see the puppies that were for sale.

   Did I use the word **crowd** the right way? *Yes.*

   How do you know? (Student responses.)

2. The car **suddenly** came to a stop.

   Did I use the word **suddenly** the right way? *Yes.*

   How do you know? (Student responses.)

3. Sue used a **ruler** to stir the cookie batter.

   Did I use the word **ruler** the right way? *No.*

   How do you know? (Student responses.)

4. Jack **trained** his cat to use the litter box.

   Did I use the word **trained** the right way? *Yes.*

   How do you know? (Student responses.)

5. He put his jacket on and **unzipped** it.

   Did I use the word **unzipped** correctly? *No.*

   How do you know? (Student responses.)

6. The gym was **packed** for the basketball game.

   Did I use the word **packed** the right way? *Yes.*

   How do you know? (Student responses.)

7. Lisa **formed** her dirty clothes.

   Did I use the word **formed** the right way? *No.*

   How do you know? (Student responses.)

8. Mae used a big **gulp** of shampoo to wash her hair.

   Did I use the word **gulp** the right way? *No.*

   How do you know? (Student responses.)

Review vocabulary words as needed.

 Review vocabulary words in appropriate context in Reading *Textbook A*.

Activity 3 Vocabulary Acquisition and Use

Display Vocabulary Acquisition and Use. **Have** students work with a neighbor to complete Vocabulary Acquisition and Use.
Today's vocabulary words are ____ and ____ [and _____ and ____].
Vocabulary words: **trained** and **taught; gulp** and **swallow**
Write the words on the lines provided. Then write the words in the boxes based on whether you think each word is less/smaller or more/larger than the other word. Below the boxes, write why you think word 1 is less/smaller and word 2 is more/larger than word 1.
Repeat for words 3 and 4. **Have** students share what they wrote. **Discuss** examples of how these words might be used.

Part B: Comprehensive Strategies

12 minutes

Teacher Materials:
Reading *Textbook A*

Student Materials:
Drawing paper

Reading *Textbook A*

Display directions for the activity.
Directions: Discuss the kinds of traps from which Goad has escaped. Solve the problem that the hunters are having catching Goad by drawing a trap from which you think she could not escape. Explain why she'll not escape from your trap.

Activity 1 Pair-Share Activity—Apply Knowledge (Level 3 of Bloom's Taxonomy)

 Direct students to Lessons 15–19, pages 85–115 in Reading *Textbook A*.

You'll do an activity called **Pair-Share** to show some things you have learned in the last four lessons. The directions are on the board. I'll read them to you.

Discuss the steps in Pair-Share. **Assign** partners. **Provide** drawing paper.
Step 1 is the **Pair** part of the activity. You'll talk to your partner about the kinds of traps and the tricks Goad has used to escape from traps. Think of a new kind of trap so she can't escape and then draw it. Decide who'll do what part of the drawing. Be ready to explain why Goad won't be able to escape from your trap. You have 7 minutes to complete the job. Draw quick sketches so you are done on time.
Guide students to discuss traps, draw a new trap, and explain how the trap works and why Goad would not be able to escape.

Call on as many students to share as time allows.
Step 2 is to Share. I'll call on pairs of students to share their work with the rest of the class.

Part C: Fluency Building

5 minutes

Student Materials:
Reading *Textbook A*

 Conduct after the lesson, using the story of the day.

Activity 1 Partner Reading

It's time for partner reading.
Direct students to the story of the day. **Assign** student partners as Partner 1 and Partner 2. **Monitor** partner reading. **Guide** as needed.

Part D: Writing/Language Arts

5 minutes

Teacher Materials:
Writing Prompts

My Writing Checklist

Student Materials:
Lined Paper

My Writing Checklist

Activity 1 Write and Use Parts of Speech and Conventions

Time to write using a writing prompt based on the stories we've been reading.
Assign student partners. **Distribute** lined paper to students. **Display** writing prompts and have students choose one to write about or assign a writing prompt of your choice. **Review** parts of speech and punctuation as well as the writing checklist with students. **Tell** students to write one to two paragraphs (minimum of four sentences per paragraph) on their own to answer the writing prompt. **Tell** them to use their writing checklist (first column labeled "Did I use them?") to ensure they include important parts of speech or punctuation in their writing. **Tell** students which parts of speech or punctuation to focus on, if you wish. **Model** what it means to answer a writing prompt and to use the writing checklist during and after the writing process, as needed. **Monitor** and guide students as needed. **Model** what it means to have a neighbor look over his or her neighbor's writing and to complete the writing checklist (second column labeled "Did my neighbor use them?"), as needed. **Have** students share what they wrote as time permits.

Writing Prompt 1	Writing Prompt 2	Writing Prompt 3
Would you rather be a felt-tipped pen or a pencil? Why?	Would you want to have a flea circus? Why or why not?	Would you rather be a frog or a toad? Why?

60 Lesson 20

Lesson 21

Materials
Teacher: 5-Narrative Story Map; Reading *Textbook A*
Student: Vocabulary Notebook, Reading *Textbook A*

Part A: Vocabulary Development

8 minutes

Teacher Materials:
Reading *Textbook A*

Student Materials:
Reading *Textbook A*
Vocabulary Notebook

Activity 1 Learn New Vocabulary Word

Elicit responses to questions. **Guide** as needed.
Today you'll learn a new vocabulary word. **Bother. Bother** means "cause trouble." What does **bother** mean? *Cause trouble.*

Another way to say "cause trouble" is **bother.** What's another way to say "cause trouble"? *Bother.*

When there is a fire in the forest, the animals do not **cause trouble** for one another. They just try and get far away from the fire. The animals don't **bother** each other because they just want to get away.

Discuss examples of things that <u>bother</u> people.

What's another way to say **cause trouble?** *Bother.*

Direct students to write <u>bother</u> and its definition in their vocabulary notebook.
Guide as needed.
Write **bother** and what it means in your vocabulary notebook.

Activity 2 Review Vocabulary Word

Elicit responses to questions. **Guide** as needed.
What's another way to say "taught how to do something"? *Trained.*

Tell me a sentence using the word **trained.** (Student responses.)
Discuss sentence.

   Review vocabulary words in their appropriate context in Reading *Textbook A*.

Lesson 21   **61**

12 minutes

Teacher Materials:
Narrative Story Map

Reading *Textbook A*

Student Materials:
Reading *Textbook A*

Part B: Comprehension Strategies

Activity 1 Narrative Story Map: Identify Title, Characters, Setting, and Events—An After-Reading Strategy

 Direct students to Lesson 19, pages 112–114 in Reading *Textbook A*.

Elicit responses to questions. **Guide** as needed.
Narratives have a title, characters, setting, and events.

Show Narrative Story Map.

Monitor students as they write the title, characters, setting, and events.
Write the title, important characters, setting, and events on your Narrative Story Map.

Discuss answers for the title, characters, setting, and events. **Write** answers on Narrative Story Map.
What did you write on your Narrative Story Map? (Ideas: *Title—"The Brown Family Comes to Catch Goad;" Main Character—Goad the toad; Setting—Where: Four Mile Lake and Toadsville, When: Last summer; Beginning—Goad blew the steel trap away; Middle—People tried to catch Goad swimming; End—The Brown family came to town to try to catch Goad.*)

Activity 2 Narrative Story Map: Identify Problem—An After-Reading Strategy

The last part of the Narrative Story Map is the **problem.** All narratives have a problem. The **problem** is the **thing in the story that goes wrong.** The problem makes me want to read more of the story to find out what happens. Sometimes it is hard to figure out the problem.

Model think-aloud for identifying problem. **Write** problem on Narrative Story Map. Suggested sentence: Goad is so slow in the water that the hunters might catch her.
I'll show you how I figure out the problem in a story or chapter.

> **Sample Wording for Think-Aloud**
>
> When I want to figure out the **problem** in a narrative, I have to figure out **what is going wrong in the story.** "The Brown Family Comes to Catch Goad" has a **problem.** I need to think about **what is going wrong.** I know that in the past chapter, many hunters have tried to catch Goad. But Goad is too smart, fast, and big to get caught. She has escaped from 400 traps. Then I notice that Goad is not fast in the water. All the hunters want to catch Goad while she is swimming because she is slow in the water. That part makes me want to read more to find out what happens. So I think that is the **problem.** If Goad is not careful, she'll get caught when she is swimming. She might get caught by the Brown family.

Now that I've filled all the sections on my Narrative Story Map, I'm ready to retell this chapter of Goad. I can remember all the parts. You'll practice retelling stories in later lessons.

62 *Lesson 21*

Activity 3 Comprehension Monitoring: Read Narrative Text with Prosody—A During-Reading Strategy

 Direct students to Lesson 19, page 112 in Reading *Textbook A*.

Elicit responses to questions. **Guide** as needed.
Today it's your turn to read the first page of "The Brown Family Comes to Catch Goad" the right way to a partner.

What should you do when you come to a period? (Idea: *Take a small breath or pause.*)

What should you do when you come to a question mark? (Idea: *Make your voice go up a little.*)

What should you do if you come to quotation marks? (Idea: *Read with expression.*)

Assign student partners.
After you read the right way, have your partner read the page the right way. Check each other to make sure you do it correctly.
Monitor students to make sure they are reading with prosody as they read with to a partner. **Guide** as needed.

Why is it important to read the right way? (Idea: *It improves your comprehension.*)

---

5 minutes

Student Materials:
Reading *Textbook A*

Part C: Fluency Building

 Conduct after the lesson, using the story of the day.

Activity 1 Partner Reading

It's time for partner reading.
Direct students to the story of the day. **Assign** student partners as Partner 1 and Partner 2. **Monitor** partner reading. **Guide** as needed.

Lesson 21 **63**

Lesson 22

Materials
Teacher: 5-Narrative Story Map, 6-Narrative Story Map; Reading *Textbook A*
Student: Vocabulary notebook; Copy of 5-Narrative Story Map; Reading *Textbook A*

8 minutes

Teacher Materials:
Reading *Textbook A*

Student Materials:
Vocabulary notebook
Reading *Textbook A*

Part A: Vocabulary Development

Activity 1 Learn New Vocabulary Word

Elicit responses to questions. **Guide** as needed.
Today you'll learn a new vocabulary word. **Orders. Orders** means "directions."
What does **orders** mean? *Directions.*

Another word for "directions" is **orders.** What's another word for "directions"? *Orders.*

The Brown family was running around yelling at each other. But it was Grandmother Brown who was giving out the **directions.** She yelled the loudest, giving everyone their **orders.**

Discuss examples of orders that are given.

What's another word for "directions"? *Orders.*

Direct students to write orders and its definition in their vocabulary notebook.
Guide as needed.
Write **orders** and what it means in your vocabulary notebook.

Activity 2 Review Vocabulary Word

Elicit responses to questions. **Guide** as needed.
What's another way to say "cause trouble"? *Bother.*

Tell me a sentence using the word **bother.** (Student responses.)
Discuss sentence.

 Review vocabulary words in their appropriate context in Reading *Textbook A*.

12 minutes

Teacher Materials:
Narrative Story Map

Reading Textbook A

Student Materials:
Narrative Story Map

Reading Textbook A

Part B: Comprehension Strategies

Activity 1 Narrative Story Map: Identify Title, Characters, Setting, and Events—An After-Reading Strategy

 Direct students to Lesson 21, pages 123–125 in Reading *Textbook A*.

Elicit responses to questions. **Guide** as needed.
Narratives have a title, characters, setting, and events.

Show Narrative Story Map (you will not write on this screen).

Monitor students as they write the title, characters, setting, and events.
Write the title, important characters, setting, and events on your Narrative Story Map.

Discuss answers for the title, characters, setting, and events. **Write** answers on the Narrative Story Map so that you can complete the map in the next activity.
What did you write on your Narrative Story Map? (Ideas: *Title—"The Browns Make Up a Plan;" Main Character—Goad the toad; Setting—Where: Four Mile Lake and Toadsville, When: Last summer; Beginning—The Browns came to town to catch Goad; Middle—They gave Goad the impression the hills were on fire; End—Goad hopped down the hill into the water.*)

Activity 2 Narrative Story Map: Identify Problem—An After-Reading Strategy

 Direct students to Lesson 21, pages 123–125 in Reading *Textbook A*.

You're learning how to figure out the problem in narratives. All narratives have a problem. The **problem** is the **thing in the story that goes wrong.** The problem is what makes you want to read more to find out what happens. Sometimes it is hard to figure out the problem.

Show Narrative Story Map pointing out where to fill out the problem. Note the difference from Narrative Story Map.
I'll show you how I figure out the problem in a story or chapter.
I read the story carefully until I can figure what is going wrong in the story or what the problem is that has to be solved.

Model identifying problem and write it on the map. Suggested problem: Browns are tricking Goad into thinking there is a fire so she is headed to the water where she will be slow enough to catch.

When you think of what is going wrong in the story, you'll be able to figure out the problem.

Lesson 22   **65**

Activity 3 Use Narrative Story Map: Retell the Story—An After-Reading Strategy

Show Narrative Story Map (completed in Activities 1 and 2). **Model** think-aloud for retelling narrative story.

I have completed my Narrative Story Map, and now I can use it to help me while I retell the story. When I retell the story, I want to be sure to tell about the title, the characters, the setting, the problem, and the events that happened in the right order. Watch me as I use the map to retell the story.

Sample Wording for Think-Aloud

The title of the story is "The Browns Make Up a Plan." The Browns came to Four Mile Lake to try to catch Goad. (I told the title, characters, and setting in those sentences). They want to get her in the water where she will be easy to catch. (I told the problem in that sentence). First the Browns made a plan. They gave Goad the impression the hills were on fire. So Goad jumped down the hill and into the water. (I told the events of the story in those sentences.)

Retelling the story helps you remember all the parts of the story.

Part C: Fluency Building

5 minutes

Student Materials:
Reading *Textbook A*

 Conduct after the lesson, using the story of the day.

Activity 1 Partner Reading

It's time for partner reading.
Direct students to the story of the day. **Assign** student partners as Partner 1 and Partner 2. **Monitor** partner reading. **Guide** as needed.

Lesson 23

Materials
Teacher: 6-Narrative Story Map; Reading *Textbook A*
Student: Vocabulary notebook; Reading *Textbook A*

8 minutes

Teacher Materials:
Reading *Textbook A*

Student Materials:
Vocabulary notebook

Reading Textbook A

Part A: Vocabulary Development

Activity 1 Learn New Vocabulary Word

Elicit responses to questions. **Guide** as needed.
Today you'll learn a new vocabulary word. **Outsmarted. Outsmarted** means "to do better than someone else." What does **outsmarted** mean? *To do better than someone else.*

Another way to say "to do better than someone else" is **outsmarted.** What's another way to say "to do better than someone else"? *Outsmarted.*

Goad seemed to always have ways **to do** things **better than someone else.** Goad **outsmarted** the entire Brown family when she let out a big wind and went flying backward.

Discuss examples of ways people are outsmarted.

What's another way to say "to do things better than someone else"? *Outsmarted.*

Direct students to write outsmarted and its definition in their vocabulary notebook. **Guide** as needed.
Write **outsmarted** and what it means in your vocabulary notebook.

Activity 2 Review Vocabulary Word

Elicit responses to questions. **Guide** as needed.
What's another word for "directions"? *Orders.*

Tell me a sentence using the word **orders.** (Student responses.)
Discuss sentence.

 Review vocabulary words in their appropriate context in Reading *Textbook A*.

Lesson 23 **67**

Part B: Comprehension Strategies

12 minutes

Teacher Materials:
Narrative Story Map

Reading Textbook A

Student Materials:
Reading Textbook A

Activity 1 Narrative Story Map: Identify Title, Characters, Setting, and Events—An After-Reading Strategy

 Direct students to Lesson 22, pages 130–132 in Reading *Textbook A*.

Elicit responses to questions. **Guide** as needed.
Narratives have a title, characters, setting, a problem, and events.

Complete Narrative Story Map as you discuss answers for the title, characters, setting and events. (Fill out the problem in next activity.) Ideas: Title—"Goad in the Water"; Main Character—Goad the toad; Setting—Where: Four Mile Lake, When: Last summer; Beginning—The Browns tried to catch Goad in the water; Middle—Goad filled up with air; End—Goad went flying away from the Browns.
Let's fill out my Narrative Story Map as we figure out the parts together. We'll figure out the problem in a few minutes.

Activity 2 Narrative Story Map: Identify Problem—An After-Reading Strategy

 Direct students to Lesson 22, pages 130–132 in Reading *Textbook A*.

Elicit responses to questions. **Guide** as needed.
You're learning how to figure out the problem in narratives. All narratives have a problem. The **problem** is the **thing in the story that goes wrong.** The problem makes you want to read more.

How do you figure out what the problem is in a narrative? (Idea: *Think about what is going wrong or what problem has to be solved.*)

Discuss ideas to identify the problem. Suggested problem: Goad is in the water and the Browns are about to catch her. **Complete** Narrative Story (begun in Activity 1) by filling out the problem.
Let's see whether we can work together to figure out the problem in the chapter. Let's look at, "Goad in the Water" and see whether we can identify what is going wrong in this chapter.

When you think of what part is going wrong in the story that makes you want to read more, you'll be able to figure out the problem.

Lesson 23

Activity 3 Use Narrative Story Map: Retell the Story—An After-Reading Strategy

Show Narrative Story Map (completed in Activities 1 and 2).

I have completed my Narrative Story Map and now I can use it to help me while I retell the story. I want to be sure to tell about the title, the characters, the setting, the problem, and the events that happened in the right order. Watch me as I use the map to retell the story.

Model retelling narrative story by using Narrative Story Map completed in Activities 1 and 2.

Retelling the story helps you remember all the parts of the story.

Part C: Fluency Building

5 minutes

Student Materials:
Reading *Textbook A*

 Conduct after the lesson, using the story of the day.

Activity 1 Partner Reading

It's time for partner reading.

Direct students to the story of the day. **Assign** student partners as Partner 1 and Partner 2. **Monitor** partner reading. **Guide** as needed.

Lesson 23   **69**

Lesson 24

Materials

Teacher: 6-Narrative Story Map; Reading *Textbook A*; Copy of recorded problem from Lesson 23
Student: Vocabulary notebook; Reading *Textbook A*

 8 minutes

Teacher Materials:
Reading *Textbook A*

Student Materials:
Vocabulary notebook

Reading *Textbook A*

Part A: Vocabulary Development

Activity 1 Learn New Vocabulary Word

Elicit responses to questions. **Guide** as needed.
Today you'll learn a new vocabulary word. **Pant. Pant** means "breathe quickly." What does **pant** mean? *Breathe quickly.*

Another way to say "breathe quickly" is **pant.** What's another way to say "breathe quickly"? *Pant.*

Whenever Jack went out running he would start to **breathe quickly.** He could hardly talk to his sister because he would have to **pant** between words.

Discuss examples of things people do that make them pant.

What's another way to say "breathe quickly"? *Pant.*

Direct students to write pant and its definition in their vocabulary notebook. **Guide** as needed.
Write **pant** and what it means in your vocabulary notebook.

Activity 2 Review Vocabulary Word

Elicit responses to questions. **Guide** as needed.
What's another way to say "to do better than someone else"? *Outsmarted.*

Tell me a sentence using the word **outsmarted.** (Student response.)
Discuss sentence.

 Review vocabulary words in their appropriate context in Reading *Textbook A*.

70 Lesson 24

12 minutes

Teacher Materials:
Narrative Story Map

Reading *Textbook A*

Copy of recorded problem from Lesson 23

Student Materials:
Reading *Textbook A*

Part B: Comprehension Strategies

Activity 1 Skim Text to Find Answers—A Before- or After-Reading Strategy

 Direct students to Lesson 23, pages 135–136 in Reading *Textbook A*.

Elicit responses to questions. **Guide** as needed.

Today you'll learn how to skim text to find answers to questions. Skimming text is when you look at the title, the pictures, and the words of the text the fast way to find answers. You can skim expository text or narrative text. You can skim before or after you read carefully. Skimming text is a very useful skill to help you find answers to questions in text.

Model think-aloud for skimming text.

Sample Wording for Think-Aloud

I'm going to skim "Facts about Miles" to see whether I can figure out if this text is **narrative** or **expository.** First I look at the title. The title says the word "facts" which is a clue to me that this is **expository.** Next my eyes go down the list of facts. That is another clue that this is **expository.** Finally I look at the picture, and I see a map and some labels. Sometimes there are maps in narrative text, but usually maps and labels are found in **expository** text. So I think that skimming the passage has helped me understand that this text is **expository.**

What do you do when you skim text? (**Idea:** *Read text, title, and pictures the fast way.*)

Why do you skim text? (**Idea:** *To find answers to questions.*)

Does skimming work for both narrative and expository text? *Yes.*

Activity 2 Narrative Story Map: Identify Title, Characters, Setting, and Events—An After-Reading Strategy

 Direct students to Lesson 23, pages 136–138 in Reading *Textbook A*.

Narratives have a title, characters, setting, a problem, and events.

Complete the 6-Narrative Story Map as you discuss answers for the title, characters, setting, and events. (Fill out problem in next activity.) Ideas: Title—"A Big Picnic;" Main Character—Goad the toad; Setting—Where: Four Mile Lake, When: last summer; Beginning—The Browns knew that Goad had outsmarted them by flying away; Middle—They started to laugh; End—They decided to have a picnic.
Let's fill out my Narrative Story Map as we figure out the parts together. We'll figure out the problem in a few minutes.

Lesson 24

Activity 3 Narrative Story Map: Identify Problem—An After-Reading Strategy

 Direct students to Lesson 23, pages 136–138 in Reading *Textbook A*.

Elicit responses to questions. **Guide** as needed.
You're learning how to figure out the problem in narratives. All narratives have a problem. The problem is the thing in the story that goes wrong. The problem makes you want to read more.

How do you figure out what the problem is in a narrative? (Idea: *Think about what is going wrong or what problem has to be solved.*)

Discuss ideas to identify the problem. Suggested problem: The Browns didn't catch Goad. **Complete** Narrative Story Map (begun in Activity 2) by filling out the Problem box.
Let's see whether we can work together to figure out the problem in the chapter. Let's look at "A Big Picnic" and see whether we can identify what is going wrong in this chapter.

When you think of what part is going wrong in the story that makes you want to read more, you'll be able to figure out the problem.

Activity 4 Use Narrative Story Map: Retell the Story—An After-Reading Strategy

Show Narrative Story Map (completed in Activities 2 and 3).
We have completed the Narrative Story Map and now we can use it to help us while we retell the story. When we retell the story, we want to be sure to tell about the title, the characters, the setting, the problem, and the events that happened in the right order. Let's use the map to help us retell the story.
Guide retelling a narrative story by using Narrative Story Map completed in Activities 1 and 2.

What was the title? *A Big Picnic.*

Tell about the characters and the setting in a sentence. (Student responses.)

Tell the problem in a sentence. (Student responses.)

Tell the events in the story. (Student responses.)

Retelling the story helps you remember all the parts of the story.

Part C: Fluency Building

5 minutes

Student Materials:
Reading *Textbook A*

 Conduct after the lesson, using the story of the day.

Activity 1 Partner Reading

It's time for partner reading.
Direct students to the story of the day. **Assign** student partners as Partner 1 and Partner 2. **Monitor** partner reading. **Guide** as needed.

72 Lesson 24

Lesson 25

> **Materials**
> **Teacher:** Reading *Textbook A*, 2-Vocabulary Acquisition and Use
> **Student:** Vocabulary notebook; lined paper; Reading *Textbook A*, Copy of 2-Vocabulary Acquisition and Use

8 minutes

Teacher Materials:
Reading *Textbook A*

Vocabulary Acquisition and Use

Student Materials:
Vocabulary notebook

Reading *Textbook A*

Vocabulary Acquisition and Use

Part A: Vocabulary Development

Activity 1 Vocabulary Notebook Review

Guide students through all words.
Today you'll study from your vocabulary notebook. Studying your words and what they mean will help you know your words even better. You'll look at the four words we studied this week.

Activity 2 Cumulative Vocabulary Review

Elicit responses to questions. **Guide** as needed.
Directions: Listen and tell me whether I use our vocabulary words the right way or the wrong way. If I use the word the right way, say **"yes."** If I use the word the wrong way, say **"no."** Then we'll talk about each word.

1. Mr. Lowhurst gave **orders** to the children to not ride their bikes in the middle of the street.

   Did I use the word **orders** the right way? *Yes.*

   How do you know? (Student responses.)

2. When you are not tired, you will **pant.**

   Did I use the word **pant** the right way? *No.*

   How do you know? (Student responses.)

3. Mario **outsmarted** his brother and got to his grandmother's house first by taking a shortcut.

   Did I use the word **outsmarted** the right way? *Yes.*

   How do you know? (Student responses.)

4. Lance's father asked him to always **bother** him while he was on the phone.

   Did I use the word **bother** the right way? *No.*

   How do you know? (Student responses.)

Review vocabulary words as needed.

 Review vocabulary words in their appropriate context in *Reading Textbook A*.

Lesson 25   73

Activity 3 Vocabulary Acquisition and Use

Display Vocabulary Acquisition and Use. **Have** students work with a neighbor to complete Vocabulary Acquisition and Use.

Today's vocabulary words are ____ and ____ [and ____ and ____].
Vocabulary words: **pant** and **breathe**; **outsmarted** and **outwitted**
Write the words on the lines provided. Then write the words in the boxes based on whether you think each word is less/smaller or more/larger than the other word. Below the boxes, write why you think word 1 is less/smaller and word 2 is more/larger than word 1.

Repeat for words 3 and 4. **Have** students share what they wrote. **Discuss** examples of how these words might be used.

Part B: Comprehension Strategies

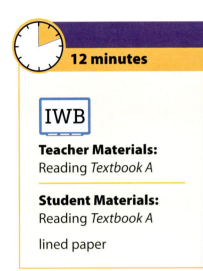

12 minutes

Teacher Materials:
Reading *Textbook A*

Student Materials:
Reading *Textbook A*
lined paper

Display directions for activity.

 Direct students to Lessons 15–23, pages 85–138 of Reading *Textbook A*.

Directions: Discuss the traps that Goad escaped from and how she escaped. Draw and complete a chart to show what kinds of traps were used on Goad and to tell how she escaped.

Activity 1 Pair-Share Activity—Apply Knowledge (Level 3 of Bloom's Taxonomy)

Discuss the steps in Pair-Share.
You'll do an activity called Pair-Share to show some things you have learned in previous lessons. The directions are on the board. I'll read them to you.

Assign partners. **Provide** lined paper.
Step 1 is the Pair part of the activity. You'll talk to your partner, skim Lessons 15–23, and discuss what kinds of traps Goad escaped from and how she escaped. Then complete the chart to show the kinds of traps and how she escaped. You have 7 minutes to complete the job. Draw the chart quickly and fill it in so you're done on time.

Kind of Trap	How Goad Escaped

74   Lesson 25

Guide students to answers:

Kind of Trap	How Goad Escaped
Net trap	Acted like a rock
Food trap	Dug under trap
Steel trap	Blew it away
Water trap	Fill up with air and sailed away

Call on as many students to share as time allows.
Step 2 is to Share. I'll call on pairs of students to share their work with the rest of the class.

Part C: Fluency Building

5 minutes

Student Materials:
Reading *Textbook A*

 Conduct after the lesson, using the story of the day.

Activity 1 Partner Reading

It's time for partner reading.
Direct students to the story of the day. **Assign** student partners as Partner 1 and Partner 2. **Monitor** partner reading. **Guide** as needed.

Lesson 25

Lesson 26

> **Materials**
> **Teacher:** 6-Narrative Story Map; Reading *Textbook A*
> **Student:** Vocabulary notebook; Reading *Textbook A*

Part A: Vocabulary Development

8 minutes

Teacher Materials:
Reading *Textbook A*

Student Materials:
Vocabulary notebook

Reading *Textbook A*

Activity 1 Learn New Vocabulary Word

Elicit responses to questions. **Guide** as needed.
Today you'll learn a new vocabulary word. **Greetings. Greetings** means "saying hello." What does **greetings** mean? *Saying hello.*

Another way for "saying hello" is **greetings.** What's another way for "saying hello"? *Greetings.*

The little man made the ant run away. By **saying hello** to Nancy, he got her to turn around and look at him. The little man's first word to Nancy was **"greetings."**

Discuss examples of when someone says greetings.

What's another way for "saying hello"? *Greetings.*

Direct students to write greetings and its definition in their vocabulary notebook.
Guide as needed.
Write **greetings** and what it means in your vocabulary notebook.

Activity 2 Review Vocabulary Word

Elicit responses to questions. **Guide** as needed.
What's another way to say "breathe quickly"? *Pant.*

Tell me a sentence using the word **pant.** (Student responses.)
Discuss sentence.

  Review vocabulary words in their appropriate context in Reading *Textbook A*.

76   Lesson 26

12 minutes

Teacher Materials:
Narrative Story Map

Reading *Textbook A*

Student Materials:
Reading *Textbook A*

Part B: Comprehension Strategies

Activity 1 Narrative Story Map: Identify Title, Characters, Setting, and Events—An After-Reading Strategy

 Direct students to Lesson 25, pages 152–155 in Reading *Textbook A*.

Narratives have a title, characters, setting, a problem, and events.

Complete Narrative Story Map as you discuss answers for the title, characters, setting, and events.
Let's fill out my Narrative Story Map as we discuss the parts together.
We will figure out the problem in a few minutes.

Activity 2 Narrative Story Map: Identify Problem—An After-Reading Strategy

 Direct students to Lesson 25, pages 152–155 in Reading *Textbook A*.

Elicit responses to questions. **Guide** as needed.
You're learning how to figure out the problem in narratives. All narratives have a problem. The problem makes you want to read more to find out what happens.

What's a **problem** in a narrative? (Idea: *The thing that goes wrong or the problem that has to be solved.*)

How do you figure out what the problem is in a narrative? (Idea: *Think about what is going wrong or what problem has to be solved.*)

Discuss ideas to identify the problem. Suggested problem: Nancy does not want to grow up *or* Nancy is spoiled. **Complete** Narrative Story (started in Activity 1) by filling out the problem.
Let's see whether we can work together to figure out the problem in the chapter. Let's skim "Nancy Wants to Stay Little" and see whether we can identify what's going wrong in this chapter.

When you think of what's going wrong in the story, you can figure out the problem.

Activity 3 Use Narrative Story Map: Retell the Story—An After-Reading Strategy

Show 6-Narrative Story Map (completed in Activities 1 and 2).
We've completed the Narrative Story Map and now we can use it to help us while we retell the story. When we retell the story, we want to be sure to tell about the title, the characters, the setting, the problem, and the events that happened in the right order. Let's use the Narrative Story Map to help us retell the story.

Lesson 26

Guide retelling narrative story by using Narrative Story Map completed in Activities 1 and 2.

What was the title? *"Nancy Wants to Stay Little."*

Tell about the characters and the setting in a sentence. (Student responses.)

Tell about the problem in a sentence. (Student responses.)

Tell the events in the story. (Student responses.)

Retell the whole story. (Student responses.)

Retelling the story helps you remember all the parts of the story.

5 minutes

Student Materials:
Reading *Textbook A*

Part C: Fluency Building

 Conduct after the lesson, using the story of the day.

Activity 1 Partner Reading

It's time for partner reading.

Direct **students to the story of the day.** Assign **student partners as Partner 1 and Partner 2.** Monitor **partner reading.** Guide **as needed.**

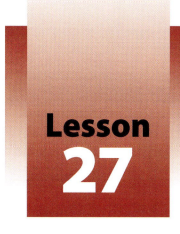

Lesson 27

Materials
Teacher: 6-Narrative Story Map; Reading *Textbook A;* Copy of problem from Lesson 26
Student: Vocabulary notebook; Reading *Textbook A*

8 minutes

Teacher Materials:
Reading *Textbook A*

Student Materials:
Vocabulary notebook
Reading *Textbook A*

Part A: Vocabulary Development

Activity 1 Learn New Vocabulary Word

Elicit responses to questions. **Guide** as needed.
Today you'll learn a new vocabulary word. **Miniature. Miniature** means "tiny." What does **miniature** mean? *Tiny.*

Another word for "tiny" is **miniature.** What's another word for **tiny?** *Miniature.*

Nancy could walk right under the door without opening it because she was so **tiny.** Nancy was **miniature** so everything else was huge.

Discuss examples of things that are miniature.

What's another word for "tiny"? *Miniature.*

Direct students to write miniature and its definition in their vocabulary notebook. **Guide** as needed.
Write **miniature** and what it means in your vocabulary notebook.

Activity 2 Review Vocabulary Word

Elicit responses to questions. **Guide** as needed.
What's another word for "saying hello"? *Greetings.*

Tell me a sentence using the word **greetings.** (Student responses.)
Discuss sentence.

 Review vocabulary words in their appropriate context in Reading *Textbook A.*

Lesson 27   79

12 minutes

Teacher Materials:
Narrative Story Map

Reading *Textbook A*

Copy of problem from Lesson 26

Student Materials:
Reading *Textbook A*

Part B: Comprehension Strategies

Activity 1 Narrative Story Map: Identify Title, Characters, Setting, and Events—An After-Reading Strategy

 Direct students to Lesson 26, pages 158–160 in Reading *Textbook A*.

Narratives have a title, characters, setting, a problem, and events.

Complete Narrative Story Map as you discuss answers for the title, characters, setting, and events.
Let's fill out my Narrative Story Map as we figure out the parts together.
We'll figure out the problem in a few minutes.

Activity 2 Narrative Story Map: Identify Problem—An After-Reading Strategy

 Direct students to Lesson 26, pages 158–160 in Reading *Textbook A*.

Elicit responses to questions. **Guide** as needed.
You're learning how to figure out the problem in narratives. All narratives have a problem. The problem makes you want to read more.

What's a **problem** in a narrative? (Idea: *The thing that goes wrong or the problem that has to be solved.*)

How do you figure out what the problem is in a narrative? (Idea: *Think about what is going wrong or what problem has to be solved.*)

Assign student partners. **Monitor** student partners as they skim text to locate the problem.

Work with a partner and see whether you can work together to figure out the problem in the chapter. Skim "A Green Man Visits Nancy" and see whether you can identify what is going wrong in this chapter. When you have an idea for the problem, raise your hand.

Discuss ideas to identify the problem. Suggested problem: The Green Man makes Nancy so tiny that she is smaller than an ant. Now she is in danger.

Complete the Narrative Story Map (started in Activity 1) by filling out the problem.

When you think of what's going wrong in the story, you can figure out the problem.

Activity 3 — Use Narrative Story Map: Retell the Story—An After-Reading Strategy

Show Narrative Story Map (completed in Activities 1 and 2).
We have completed the Narrative Story Map and now we can use it to help us while we retell the story. When we retell the story, we want to be sure to tell about the title, the characters, the setting, the problem, and the events that happened in the right order. Let's use the map to help us retell the story.

Assign student partners. **Guide** retelling a narrative story to a partner by using Narrative Story Map (completed in Activities 1 and 2).
Work with your partner to retell the story from the Narrative Story Map we filled out together. You can each take a turn retelling the story to each other.

Retelling the story helps you remember all the parts of the story.

Part C: Fluency Building

5 minutes

Student Materials:
Reading *Textbook A*

 Conduct after the lesson, using the story of the day.

Activity 1 — Partner Reading

It's time for partner reading.
Direct students to the story of the day. **Assign** student partners as Partner 1 and Partner 2. **Monitor** partner reading. **Guide** as needed.

Lesson 28

Materials
Teacher: 6-Narrative Story Map; Reading *Textbook A*
Student: Vocabulary notebook; Copy of 6-Narrative Story Map for each student pair; Reading *Textbook A*

Part A: Vocabulary Development

 8 minutes

Teacher Materials:
Reading *Textbook A*

Student Materials:
Vocabulary notebook
Reading *Textbook A*

Activity 1 Learn New Vocabulary Word

Elicit responses to questions. **Guide** as needed.
Today you'll learn a new vocabulary word. **Crumb. Crumb** means "a small piece of food." What does **crumb** mean? *A small piece of food.*

Another way to say "a small piece of food" is **crumb.** What's another way to say "a small piece of food"? *Crumb.*

Nancy was walking through her carpet when she noticed **a small piece of food.** She had found a **crumb.**

Discuss examples of a crumb.

What's another way to say "a small piece of food"? *Crumb.*

Direct students to write crumb and its definition in their vocabulary notebook. **Guide** as needed.
Write **crumb** and what it means in your vocabulary notebook.

Activity 2 Review Vocabulary Word

Elicit responses to questions. **Guide** as needed.
What's another word for "tiny"? *Miniature.*

Tell me a sentence using the word **miniature.** (Student responses.)
Discuss sentence.

 Review vocabulary words in their appropriate context in Reading *Textbook A*.

82 *Lesson 28*

12 minutes

Teacher Materials:
Narrative Story Map

Reading *Textbook A*

Student Materials:
Narrative Story Map

Reading *Textbook A*

Part B: Comprehension Strategies

Activity 1 Narrative Story Map: Identify Title, Characters, Setting, Events, and Problem—An After-Reading Strategy

 Direct students to Lesson 27, pages 163–165 in Reading *Textbook A*.

Elicit responses to questions. **Guide** as needed. **Assign** student partners.
Narratives have a title, characters, settings, a problem, and events. Skim "Nancy Is Still Tiny," and then work with your partner to fill in the title, important characters, setting, problem, and events on your Narrative Story Map.

Monitor student pairs as they write the title, characters, setting, problem, and events. **Discuss** answers for the title, characters, setting, problem, and events. **Write** answers on Narrative Story Map.

What did you write on your Narrative Story Map? (Ideas: *Title*—"Nancy Is Still Tiny;" *Main Character*—Nancy; *Setting*—Where: Nancy's house and Nancy's dollhouse, When: Chapter does not say, so leave blank; *Problem*—Nancy is so tiny she can't do anything; *Beginning*—Nancy went to her room; *Middle*—Nancy took a nap; *End*—Nancy woke up because her mother was telling a police officer that she was gone.)

Activity 2 Use Narrative Story Map: Retell the Story—An After-Reading Strategy

Show the Narrative Story Map completed in Activity 1.
You have completed the Narrative Story Map and now you can use it to help you retell the story. When you retell the story, you want to be sure to tell about the title, the characters, the setting, the problem, and the events that happened in the right order. Use your Narrative Story Map to help you retell the story.

Assign student partners. **Monitor** student partners as they retell the narrative story to a partner by using Narrative Story Map they completed in Activity 1.
Retell the story to your partner from your Narrative Story Map. Then your partner can take a turn retelling the story to you.

Retelling the story helps you remember all the parts of the story.

5 minutes

Student Materials:
Reading *Textbook A*

Part C: Fluency Building

 Conduct after the lesson, using the story of the day.

Activity 1 Partner Reading

It's time for partner reading.
Direct students to the story of the day. **Assign** student partners as Partner 1 and Partner 2. **Monitor** partner reading. **Guide** as needed.

Lesson 29

Materials
Teacher: 6-Narrative Story Map; Reading *Textbook A*
Student: Vocabulary notebook; Copy of 6-Narrative Story Map; Reading *Textbook A*

Part A: Vocabulary Development

8 minutes

Teacher Materials:
Reading *Textbook A*

Student Materials:
Vocabulary notebook
Reading *Textbook A*

Activity 1 Learn New Vocabulary Word

Elicit responses to questions. **Guide** as needed.
Today you'll learn a new vocabulary word. **Moist. Moist** means "a little bit wet." What does **moist** mean? *A little bit wet.*

Another way to say "a little bit wet" is **moist.** What's another way to say "a little bit wet"? *Moist.*

Nancy was very thirsty. She knew since she was so small she only needed to find something a **little bit wet.** She thought if the lawn was **moist** she could get a drink.

Discuss things that are moist.

What's another way to say "a little bit wet"? *Moist.*

Direct students to write moist and its definition in their vocabulary notebook.
Guide as needed.
Write **moist** and what it means in your vocabulary notebook.

Activity 2 Review Vocabulary Word

Elicit responses to questions. **Guide** as needed.
What's another way to say "a small piece of food"? *Crumb.*

Tell me a sentence using the word **crumb.** (Student responses.)
Discuss sentence.

  Review vocabulary words in their appropriate context in Reading *Textbook A*.

Lesson 29   **85**

Part B: Comprehension Strategies

12 minutes

Teacher Materials:
Narrative Story Map

Reading *Textbook A*

Student Materials:
Narrative Story Map

Reading *Textbook A*

Activity 1 Narrative Story Map: Identify Title, Characters, Setting, Events, and Problem—An After-Reading Strategy

 Direct students to Lesson 28, pages 168–170 in Reading *Textbook A*.

Elicit responses to questions. **Guide** as needed.
Narratives have a title, characters, settings, a problem, and events.
Skim "Nancy Finds Something to Eat" and then work by yourself to fill in the title, important characters, setting, problem, and events on your Narrative Story Map.

Monitor students as they write the title, characters, setting, problem, and events. **Discuss** answers for the title, characters, setting, problem, and events. **Write** answers on the Narrative Story Map.

What did you write on your Narrative Story Map? (Ideas: *Title—"Nancy Finds Something to Eat;" Main Character—Nancy; Setting—Where: Nancy's house and Nancy's dollhouse, When: Chapter does not say, so leave blank; Problem—Nancy is hungry and thirsty; Beginning—Nancy tried to follow her mother, but she was too little; Middle—Nancy ate a cookie crumb; End—Nancy was very thirsty.*)

Activity 2 Use Narrative Story Map: Retell the Story—An After-Reading Strategy

Show the Narrative Story Map completed in Activity 1.
You have completed the Narrative Story Map and now you can use it to help you retell the story. When you retell the story, you want to be sure to tell about the title, the characters, the setting, the problem, and the events that happened in the right order. Use your Narrative Story Map to help you retell the story.

Assign student partners. **Monitor** student partners as they retell the narrative story to a partner by using Narrative Story Map they completed in Activity 1.
Retell the story to your partner from your Narrative Story Map. Then your partner can take a turn retelling the story to you.

Retelling the story helps you remember all the parts of the story.

Part C: Fluency Building

5 minutes

Student Materials:
Reading *Textbook A*

 Conduct after the lesson, using the story of the day.

Activity 1 Partner Reading

It's time for partner reading.
Direct students to the story of the day. **Assign** student partners as Partner 1 and Partner 2. **Monitor** partner reading. **Guide** as needed.

86 Lesson 29

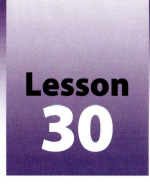

Lesson 30

Materials

Teacher: Selection of narrative picture books for student partners, 2-Vocabulary Acquisition and Use, Writing Prompts, 3-My Writing Checklist

Student: Vocabulary notebook; Copy of 2-Vocabulary Acquisition and Use, 1 picture book for each student pair; 6-Narrative Story Map, Copy of 3-My Writing Checklist, Lined paper

8 minutes

Teacher Materials:
Reading *Textbook A*

Vocabulary Acquisition and Use

Student Materials:
Vocabulary Notebook

Reading *Textbook A*

Vocabulary Acquisition and Use

Part A: Vocabulary Development

Activity 1 Vocabulary Notebook Review

Guide students as they study all vocabulary words.
Today you'll study from your vocabulary notebook. Studying your words and what they mean will help you know your words even better. You'll study the eight words we studied over the past two weeks.

Activity 2 Cumulative Vocabulary Review

Elicit responses to questions. **Guide** as needed.
Directions: Listen and tell me whether I use our vocabulary words the right way or the wrong way. If I use the word the right way, say **"yes."** If I use the word the wrong way, say **"no."** Then we'll talk about each word.

1. When Joshua was leaving, he said **"Greetings."**

   Did I use the word **greetings** the right way? *No.*

   How do you know? (Student responses.)

2. The camp director gave everyone **orders** so the campers would know where they were supposed to go.

   Did I use the word **orders** the right way? *Yes.*

   How do you know? (Student responses.)

3. The player **outsmarted** the other team by stealing a base.

   Did I use the word **outsmarted** the right way? *Yes.*

   How do you know? (Student responses.)

4. For Julie's birthday, she got a **miniature** car that looks like the car she wants when she gets older.

   Did I use the word **miniature** the right way? *Yes.*

   How do you know? (Student responses.)

5. Melissa was very hungry so her mother gave her a **crumb** for breakfast.

Lesson 30   87

Did I use the word **crumb** the right way? *No.*

How do you know? (Student responses.)

6. Randall liked playing at Ted's house because Ted had a younger sister who would always **bother** them.

   Did I use the word **bother** the right way? *No.*

   How do you know? (Student responses.)

7. Taylor would **pant** when he sat on the couch and relaxed.

   Did I use the word **pant** the right way? *No.*

   How do you know? (Student responses.)

8. At the squirt-gun fight, everyone got soaked. Tina got only a little bit wet. Her bathing suit was **moist.**

   Did I use the word **moist** the right way? *Yes.*

   How do you know? (Student responses.)

Review vocabulary words as needed.

 Review vocabulary words in their appropriate context in Reading *Textbook A*.

Activity 3 Vocabulary Acquisition and Use

Display Vocabulary Acquisition and Use. **Have** students work with a neighbor to complete Vocabulary Acquisition and Use.
Today's vocabulary words are ____ and ____ [and ____ and ____].
Vocabulary words: **miniature** and **tiny**; **moist** and **wet**
Write the words on the lines provided. Then write the words in the boxes based on whether you think each word is less/smaller or more/larger than the other word. Below the boxes, write why you think word 1 is less/smaller and word 2 is more/larger than word 1.

Repeat for words 3 and 4. **Have** students share what they wrote. **Discuss** examples of how these words might be used.

12 minutes

Teacher Materials:
Selection of narrative picture books for student partners

Student Materials:
1 picture book for each student pair

Narrative Story Map

Part B: Comprehension Strategies

Display directions for the activity.
Directions: Explain what parts are found in all narrative stories. (**Hint:** they are listed on your Narrative Story Map.) Show your understanding of these parts of a narrative by choosing an easy picture book and completing a Narrative Story Map. Remember, you'll get clues to write on your chart from pictures in the picture books.

Activity 1 Pair-Share Activity—Apply Knowledge (Level 3 of Bloom's Taxonomy)

Discuss the steps in Pair-Share.
You'll do an activity called Pair-Share to show some things you have learned in previous lessons. The directions are on the board. I'll read them to you.

Assign partners. **Direct** students to choose a picture book. **Provide** a copy of Narrative Story Map to each pair of students.
Step 1 is the **Pair** part of the activity. Discuss with your partner all the parts you find in a narrative book. Then choose a picture book, look at the pictures, and read your book. Complete the Narrative Story Map for your picture book. You have 10 minutes to complete the job. Read and write quickly so you finish on time.
Guide students as needed as they complete the Narrative Story Map.

Call on as many students to share as time allows. **Find** additional time in the day for students to report on their books.
Step 2 is to **Share.** I'll call on pairs of students to share their work with the rest of the class.

5 minutes

Student Materials:
Reading *Textbook A*

Part C: Fluency Building

Conduct after the lesson, using the story of the day.

Activity 1 Partner Reading

It's time for partner reading.
Direct students to the story of the day. **Assign** student partners as Partner 1 and Partner 2. **Monitor** partner reading. **Guide** as needed.

Lesson 30 **89**

Part D: Writing/Language Arts

Activity 1 — Write and Use Parts of Speech and Conventions

10 minutes

Teacher Materials:
Writing Prompts
My Writing Checklist

Student Materials:
Lined Paper
My Writing Checklist

Time to write using a writing prompt based on the stories we've been reading.

Assign student partners. **Distribute** lined paper to students. **Display** writing prompts and have students choose one to write about or assign a writing prompt of your choice. **Review** parts of speech and punctuation as well as the writing checklist with students. **Tell** students to write one to two paragraphs (minimum of four sentences per paragraph) on their own to answer the writing prompt. **Tell** them to use their writing checklist (first column labeled "Did I use them?") to ensure they include important parts of speech or punctuation in their writing. **Tell** students which parts of speech or punctuation to focus on, if you wish. **Model** what it means to answer a writing prompt and to use the writing checklist during and after the writing process, as needed. **Monitor** and guide students as needed. **Model** what it means to have a neighbor look over his or her neighbor's writing and to complete the writing checklist (second column labeled "Did my neighbor use them?"), as needed. **Have** students share what they wrote as time permits.

Writing Prompt 1	Writing Prompt 2	Writing Prompt 3
Would you like a giant toad as a pet? Why?	Think of a close friend or brother or sister. What does he or she do better than you, and what do you do better than him or her?	Would you rather be little or big? Why?

90   Lesson 30

Lesson 31

> **Materials**
> **Teacher:** 7-KWL Chart; Reading *Textbook A*
> **Student:** Vocabulary notebook; Reading *Textbook A*

8 minutes

Teacher Materials:
Reading *Textbook A*

Student Materials:
Vocabulary notebook

Reading *Textbook A*

Part A: Vocabulary Development

Activity 1 Learn New Vocabulary Word

Elicit responses to questions. **Guide** as needed.
Today you'll learn a new vocabulary word. **Dents. Dents** mean "small holes on something." What does **dents** mean? *Small holes on something.*

Another way to say "small holes on something" is **dents.** What's another way to say "small holes on something"? *Dents.*

Water spiders weigh very little. When they walk on things, they only make **small holes on something.** They do not go all the way through so they just make **dents.**

Discuss things that have <u>dents</u>.

What's another way to say "small holes on something"? *Dents.*

Direct students to write <u>dents</u> and its definition in their vocabulary notebook.
Guide as needed.
Write **dents** and what it means in your vocabulary notebook.

Activity 2 Review Vocabulary Word

Elicit responses to questions. **Guide** as needed.
What's another way to say "a little bit wet"? *Moist.*

Tell me a sentence using the word **moist.** (Student responses.)
Discuss sentence.

 Review vocabulary words in appropriate context in Reading *Textbook A*.

Lesson 31 **91**

12 minutes

Teacher Materials:
KWL Chart

Reading *Textbook A*

Student Materials:
Reading *Textbook A*

Part B: Comprehension Strategies

Activity 1 KWL Chart: Topic and What I Know—A Before-Reading Strategy

Elicit responses to questions. **Guide** as needed.
Your brain is full of information. That information is organized in your brain so that you can remember it. Everything you know in your brain is called **background knowledge.** What do you call everything you know in your brain? *Background knowledge.*

It's a good idea to think about everything you know about a topic before you read a new story. Then you can connect what you know to the new information that you learn when you read. When you do this, you're activating your background knowledge.

What do you do when you activate your background knowledge? (Idea: *Think about what you already know.*)

You'll be reading a passage about grams in future lessons. Before you read, it's a great idea to think about what you know already about grams. Then you'll be able to connect what you know to what you learn. That will make it easier for you to understand or remember the new information you learn.

Show 7-KWL Chart.
The new map we're going to use is called a **KWL chart.** You use a KWL chart when you read **expository text.** It helps you organize and remember what you read. This chart will help you think about what you know, what you want to know, and what you learn from expository text. A KWL chart helps you organize your thinking about expository text.

Why do you use a KWL chart? (Idea: *To organize thinking about expository text.*)

The first box we write in is the *Topic* box. **A topic** is what the text is mostly about.

What's **a topic?** *What the text is mostly about.*

Write topic on KWL Chart.
We'll read about grams so I'll write that in the *Topic* box.

Model think-aloud to activate background knowledge for What I Know section of the KWL Chart. **Write** what you know about grams on chart.
Now I'll show you how I activate my background knowledge about grams for the "What I Know" section of the KWL chart.

92 Lesson 31

> **Sample Wording for Think-Aloud**
>
> I'm going to read about grams in this expository text. So I'm going to look in my brain and think about **what I know.**
>
> I think I've seen grams on packages in the grocery store. I'll write that on my chart.
>
> I think grams are small things. I'll write that on my chart.
>
> I think that grams might measure things. I'll write that on my chart.

Save the KWL Chart for Lesson 32.
When you connect what you already know with the text, you'll be building more background knowledge in your brain and you'll be smarter.

Activity 2 Comprehension Monitoring: Reread Narrative Text—A During-Reading Strategy

Direct students to Lesson 29, pages 174–176 in Reading *Textbook A*.

Elicit responses to questions. **Guide** as needed.
Comprehension means "understanding what you read." Sometimes when you read, you get confused and you don't understand the meaning of what you're reading. While you read, you should always ask yourself, "Does this make sense?" A great strategy to use when reading doesn't make sense is to reread the part that didn't make sense. It's called **rereading.**

What's the strategy called? *Rereading.*

I'll show you how I reread a part of the story when something does not make sense.
Model think-aloud for rereading strategy for narrative text.

> **Sample Wording for Think-Aloud**
>
> I'm reading "Nancy Tries to Get Some Water." As I read, I come to the part that says that tiny animals don't get hurt if they fall from a high place. I'm confused. I thought all things got hurt if they fall from a high place. I'll **reread** the sentence from the beginning and see whether I can understand the idea. (Reread sentence.) Oh, I didn't know that. If I keep reading, I find out that the story gives some examples of tiny animals not getting hurt if they fall from high places. I get it.

Rereading is a great strategy to use any time you have a problem understanding what you read.

What's this strategy called? *Rereading.*

What question should you be asking yourself all the time when you read? (Idea: *Does this make sense?*)

When should you use rereading as a strategy? (Idea: *Whenever I don't understand what I am reading.*)

Part C: Fluency Building

 Conduct after the lesson, using the story of the day.

Student Materials:
Reading *Textbook A*

Activity 1 Partner Reading

It's time for partner reading.

Direct students to the story of the day. **Assign** student partners as Partner 1 and Partner 2. **Monitor** partner reading. **Guide** as needed.

Lesson 32

Materials

Teacher: 7-KWL Chart (partially completed in Lesson 31); Reading *Textbook A*
Student: Vocabulary notebook; Reading *Textbook A*

8 minutes

Teacher Materials:
Reading *Textbook A*

Student Materials:
Vocabulary notebook

Reading *Textbook A*

Part A: Vocabulary Development

Activity 1 Learn New Vocabulary Word

Elicit responses to questions. **Guide** as needed.
Today you'll learn a new vocabulary word. **Wondered. Wondered** means "wanted to know something." What does **wondered** mean? *Wanted to know something.*

Another way to say "wanted to know something" is **wondered.** What's another way to say "wanted to know something"? *Wondered.*

Nancy **wanted to know something.** She wanted to know how she could still be hungry after eating a crumb. She **wondered** about this because since she was so small the crumb should have filled her up.

Discuss things that people have wondered about.

What's another way to say "wanted to know something"? *Wondered.*

Direct students to write wondered and its definition in their vocabulary notebook. **Guide** as needed.
Write **wondered** and what it means in your vocabulary notebook.

Activity 2 Review Vocabulary Word

Elicit responses to questions. **Guide** as needed.
What's another way to say "small holes on something"? *Dents.*

Tell me a sentence using the word **dents.** (Student responses.)
Discuss sentence.

 Review vocabulary words in their appropriate context in Reading *Textbook A*.

Lesson 32   **95**

Part B: Comprehension Strategies

12 minutes

Teacher Materials:
KWL Chart (partially completed in Lesson 31)

Reading *Textbook A*

Student Materials:
Reading *Textbook A*

Activity 1 KWL Chart: What I Wonder—A Before-Reading Strategy

Show KWL Chart (partially completed in Lesson 31).
Today you'll learn how to fill in the next section of your KWL chart. This section is called "What I Wonder." When you wonder about things, you ask questions. Asking questions gets you interested in what you're going to learn—it makes you think about what you're going to read. You'll write the questions you have about the topic in this section of the chart.

What will you write in this section of the chart? (Ideas: *Questions you have, what you wonder about.*)

I'll show you how I think of questions for the "What I Wonder" section of the KWL chart.
Model think-aloud to generate questions for "What I Wonder" section of the KWL Chart. **Write** questions on chart.

> **Sample Wording for Think-Aloud**
>
> When I think about the topic **grams,** I need to think of some questions to help me learn about this topic.
>
> I know that **questions** start with words like **who, when, where, why, what,** and **how.** Those are good words to use when I try to think of questions.
>
> I am not really sure what a gram is. So I wonder: What's a gram? I'll write that on my chart.
>
> I'm not sure **what size** a gram is. I wonder: What size is a gram? I'll write that on my chart.
>
> I wonder: **What's** a gram used **for?** I'll write that on my chart.
>
> I wonder: **When** do you use a gram? I'll write that on my chart.
>
> I wonder: **Who** uses grams? I'll write that on my chart.
>
> I wonder: **Why** do you use grams? I'll write that on my chart.

The "What I Wonder" section of this chart is important because I'll be thinking of my questions while I read the information. Notice I used the words "who, when, what, and why" in my questions. When you're thinking of questions, try to use those words to help you make up questions.

Why is it important to ask questions before I read? (Idea: *Asking questions gets you interested in what you're going to learn—it makes you think about what you're going to read.*)

Lesson 32

Save the KWL Chart for Lesson 33.

The text I read may or may not have the answers to my questions. That is okay. Just asking the questions helps me be smarter. If I don't find the answers to my questions, I might need to read more in another book to find the answers.

Activity 2 Comprehension Monitoring: Reread Expository Text—A During-Reading Strategy

 Direct students to Lesson 31, pages 184–184 in Reading *Textbook A*.

Elicit responses to questions. **Guide** as needed.
Comprehension means "understanding what you read." Sometimes when you read, you get confused and you don't understand the meaning of what you are reading. While you read, you should always ask yourself, "Does this make sense?" A great strategy to use when reading doesn't make sense is to reread the part that didn't make sense.

What's the strategy called? *Rereading.*

Rereading works for both **narrative text** like "Nancy Gets Some Water" and **expository text** like "More About the Skin That Water Has." I'll show you how I reread a part of expository text.
Model think-aloud for rereading strategy for expository text.

> **Sample Wording for Think-Aloud**
>
> I'm reading "More about the Skin That Water Has," and so far I think I understand what I'm reading. When I get to the part that says "the hair won't even get wet," I don't understand how something that is in water does not get wet. That doesn't make sense. So I stop and go back to **reread** the part that is confusing. I'll also look at the pictures to see if they will help me understand. After I go back and reread the sentence, finish the paragraph, and look at the picture, I can see how the skin of the water works. That's amazing. When you put hair on top of water, it doesn't get wet. Now it makes sense. I can keep reading.

Rereading is a great strategy to use for both narrative and expository text any time you have a problem understanding what you read.

What's this strategy called? *Rereading.*

What question should you be asking yourself all the time when you read? (Idea: *Does this make sense?*)

When should you use rereading as a strategy? (Idea: *Whenever I don't understand what I'm reading.*)

5 minutes

Student Materials:
Reading *Textbook A*

Part C: Fluency Building

 Conduct after the lesson, using the story of the day.

Activity 1 Partner Reading

It's time for partner reading.

Direct students to the story of the day. **Assign** student partners as Partner 1 and Partner 2. **Monitor** partner reading. **Guide** as needed.

Lesson 33

Materials
Teacher: 7-KWL Chart (partially completed in Lessons 31–32); Reading *Textbook A*
Student: Vocabulary notebook; Reading *Textbook A*

8 minutes

Teacher Materials:
Reading *Textbook A*

Student Materials:
Vocabulary notebook

Reading *Textbook A*

Part A: Vocabulary Development

Activity 1 Learn New Vocabulary Word

Elicit responses to questions. **Guide** as needed.
Today you'll learn a new vocabulary word. **Search. Search** means "to try to find something." What does **Search** mean? *To try to find something.*

Another way to say "to try to find something" is **search.** What's another way to say "to try to find something"? *Search.*

Nancy had made her way to the kitchen and was **trying to find something** to eat. She even crawled up on the counter to **search** for food.

Discuss things that a person may search for.

What's another way to say "to try to find something"? *Search.*

Direct students to write search and its definition in their vocabulary notebook. **Guide** as needed.
Write **search** and what it means in your vocabulary notebook.

Activity 2 Review Vocabulary Word

Elicit responses to questions. **Guide** as needed.
What's another way to say "wanted to know something"? *Wondered.*

Tell me a sentence using the word **wondered.** (Student responses.)
Discuss sentence.

 Review vocabulary words in appropriate context in Reading *Textbook A*.

Lesson 33 **99**

12 minutes

Teacher Materials:
KWL Chart (partially completed in Lessons 31–32)

Reading *Textbook A*

Student Materials:
Reading *Textbook A*

Part B: Comprehension Strategies

Activity 1 KWL Chart: What I Learned—An After-Reading Strategy

 Direct students to Lesson 32, pages 191–192 in Reading *Textbook A*.

Show the KWL Chart (partially completed in Lessons 31–32).
Today you'll learn how to fill out the last section of your KWL chart. This section is called "What I Learned." This section is actually an important one because this is where you write all the things you learned after reading the text. Writing what you learned on your chart will help you organize the information and remember it for later.

When you write what you learned, you should write it in your own words rather than copy it right from the book. When you write what you learned in your own words, it will help you remember the information later.

 Read "Grams" again on pages 191–192 of Reading *Textbook A*.

I'll show you how I fill out the "What I Learned" section of the chart.
Model think-aloud to write information for "What I Learned" section of KWL Chart.

Read first paragraph from Lesson 32 of Reading *Textbook A*. **Write** information learned on the chart.

Read the next sentence from Lesson 32 of Reading *Textbook A*. **Write** information learned on the chart.

Read the next paragraph from Lesson 32 of Reading *Textbook A*. **Write** information learned on the chart.

Read the next paragraph from Lesson 32 of Reading *Textbook A*. **Write** information learned on the chart.

Sample Wording for Think-Aloud
I'll say in my own words, "We use grams to weigh things that are very small." I'll write that on my chart.
I'll say in my own words, "One gram is the same weight as another gram." I'll write that on my chart.
I'll say in my own words, "Water the size of a one centimeter cube weighs one gram." I'll write that on my chart.
I'll say in my own words, "Long pencil = 5 grams; short pencil = 2 grams." I'll write that on my chart.

I've now written new things I've learned from the expository text I read. I wrote the information in my own words. That's a very tough thing to do, but you'll get really good at doing it as you practice. **Writing things in your own words** helps you remember the information later.

Activity 2 Comprehension Monitoring: Reread Expository or Narrative Texts—A During-Reading Strategy

 Direct students to Lesson 32, pages 191–193 in Reading *Textbook A*.

Elicit responses to questions. **Guide** as needed.

Comprehension means "understanding what you read." Sometimes when you read, you get confused and you don't understand the meaning of what you're reading. While you read, you should always ask yourself, "Does this make sense?" A great strategy to use when reading doesn't make sense is to **reread** the part that didn't make sense. You can also **read ahead** a little bit to see whether that helps you understand.

What's the strategy called? *Rereading.*

Does this strategy work for both expository and narrative text? *Yes.*

Read the sentence on page 192 that is bold. What does that sentence mean? (Student responses.)

Guide students to reread or read ahead if they do not understand the sentence.

Today when you read Lesson 33, be sure to think about using the rereading strategy if you don't understand what you're reading for both the expository and narrative sections.

5 minutes

Student Materials:
Reading *Textbook A*

Part C: Fluency Building

 Conduct after the lesson, using the story of the day.

Activity 1 Partner Reading

It's time for partner reading.
Direct students to the story of the day. **Assign** student partners as Partner 1 and Partner 2. **Monitor** partner reading. **Guide** as needed.

Lesson 33 **101**

Lesson 34

Materials
Teacher: 7-KWL Chart (partially completed in Lessons 31–33); Reading *Textbook A*
Student: Vocabulary notebook; Reading *Textbook A*

8 minutes

Teacher Materials:
Reading *Textbook A*

Student Materials:
Vocabulary notebook
Reading *Textbook A*

Part A: Vocabulary Development

Activity 1 Learn New Vocabulary Word

Elicit responses to questions. **Guide** as needed.
Today you'll learn a new vocabulary word. **Moment. Moment** means "very short period of time." What does **moment** mean? *Very short period of time.*

Another way to say "very short period of time" is **moment.** What's another way to say "very short period of time"? *Moment.*

Nancy did not think it would only take her **a short period of time** to get to sleep because she was not very tired. However, a **moment** later she went to sleep.

Discuss examples of things that take a moment.

What's another way to say "very short period of time"? *Moment.*

Direct students to write moment and its definition in their vocabulary notebook.
Guide as needed.
Write **moment** and what it means in your vocabulary notebook.

Activity 2 Review Vocabulary Word

Elicit responses to questions. **Guide** as needed.
What's another way to say "to try to find something"? *Search.*

Tell me a sentence using the word **search.** (Student responses).
Discuss sentence.

 Review vocabulary words in appropriate context in Reading *Textbook A*.

102   Lesson 34

12 minutes

Teacher Materials:
KWL Chart (partially completed in Lessons 31–33)

Reading *Textbook A*

Student Materials:
Reading *Textbook A*

Part B: Comprehension Strategies

Activity 1 KWL Chart: What I Learned—An After-Reading Strategy

 Direct students to Lesson 33, pages 196–198 in Reading *Textbook A*.

Show the KWL Chart (partially completed in Lessons 31–33).
Today you'll continue to fill out the last section of your KWL chart to add more information from another passage about grams. This passage is called "More about Grams."

When you write sentences for what you learned, you should write them in your own words rather than copy them right from the book. Writing the sentences in your own words, it will help you remember the information later.

 Read "More About Grams" again on pages 196–198 of Reading *Textbook A*.

I'll show you how I add more information to the "What I Learned" section of the chart.
Model think-aloud to write information for the "What I Learned" section of the KWL Chart.

 Read the first two paragraphs of Lesson 33 in Reading *Textbook A*.

Read the next paragraph of Lesson 33 in Reading *Textbook A*.
Skim rest of the passage from Lesson 33 in Reading *Textbook A*.
Read the paragraphs and record the weight of items from sentences in the passage on the chart.

Lesson 34

> **Sample Wording for Think-Aloud**
>
> The first part tells information that I already wrote on my chart so I don't need to write anything for this part.
>
> This paragraph tells about how many grams an apple and a cherry weigh. I could maybe put the information in a chart to help me remember. I'll look ahead and skim the rest of the passage.
>
> When I skim the passage, I see that it tells more information about what different things weigh. I think I can make a chart to record the information.
>
> | Item | How Many Grams? |
> |---|---|
> | cherry | 10 grams |
> | apple | 200 grams |
> | 100 ants | 1 gram |
> | 30 flies | 1 gram |
> | 200 fleas | 1 gram |
> | beetle | 2 grams |

I've now written more new things I learned from the expository text I read. I organized the information in a chart to help me remember it. Writing things in your own words helps you remember the information later.

Activity 2 Comprehension Monitoring: Reread Expository or Narrative Texts—A During-Reading Strategy

 Direct students to Lesson 33, pages 196–201 in Reading *Textbook A*.

Elicit responses to questions. **Guide** as needed.
Comprehension means "understanding what you read." Sometimes when you read, you get confused and you don't understand the meaning of what you're reading. While you read, you should always ask yourself, "Does this make sense?" A great strategy to use when reading doesn't make sense is to reread the part that didn't make sense. You can also read ahead a little bit to see if that helps you understand.

What's the strategy called? *Rereading.*

Does this strategy work for both expository and narrative text? *Yes.*

When you read this story, did the whole story make sense?
(Student responses.)

What do you do if something does not make sense? (Idea: *Reread the sentence that did not make sense or read ahead a little to see whether that helps you understand.*)

Today when you read Lesson 34, be sure to think about using the rereading strategy if you don't understand what you're reading for the narrative sections.

Part C: Fluency Building

  5 minutes

Student Materials:
Reading *Textbook A*

 Conduct after the lesson, using the story of the day.

Activity 1 Partner Reading

It's time for partner reading.

Direct students to the story of the day. **Assign** student partners as Partner 1 and Partner 2. **Monitor** partner reading. **Guide** as needed.

Lesson 34 **105**

Lesson 35

Materials

Teacher: Reading *Textbook A*, 2-Vocabulary Acquisition and Use

Student: Vocabulary notebook; Reading *Textbook A*, Copy of 2-Vocabulary Acquisition and Use; Lined paper; balance scale for weighing items; gram weights; assorted small items to weigh

8 minutes

Teacher Materials:
Reading *Textbook A*

Vocabulary Acquisition and Use

Student Materials:
Vocabulary notebook

Reading *Textbook A*

Vocabulary Acquisition and Use

Part A: Vocabulary Development

Activity 1 Vocabulary Notebook Review

Guide students through all words.
Today you'll study from your vocabulary notebook. Studying your words and what they mean will help you know your words even better. You'll look at the four words we studied this week.

Activity 2 Cumulative Vocabulary Review

Elicit responses to questions. **Guide** as needed.
Directions: Listen and tell me whether I use our vocabulary words the right way or the wrong way. If I use the word the right way, say **"yes."** If I use the word the wrong way, say **"no."** Then we'll talk about each word.

1. Jacob pounded on the table with a hammer leaving many **dents.**

   Did I use the word **dents** the right way? *Yes.*

   How do you know? (Student responses.)

2. The 2-hour volleyball game lasted only a **moment.**

   Did I use the word **moment** the right way? *No.*

   How do you know? (Student responses.)

3. Frances put on a blue dress and **wondered** what she should wear that day.

   Did I use the word **wondered** the right way? *No.*

   How do you know? (Student responses.)

4. The neighbors helped Frank **search** for his lost dog.

   Did I use the word **search** the right way? *Yes.*

   How do you know? (Student responses.)

Review vocabulary words as needed.

 Review vocabulary words in appropriate context in Reading *Textbook A*.

Activity 3 Vocabulary Acquisition and Use

Display Vocabulary Acquisition and Use. **Have** students work with a neighbor to complete Vocabulary Acquisition and Use.
Today's vocabulary words are ____ and ____ [and ____ and ____].
Vocabulary words: **search** and **look; round** and **circular**
Write the words on the lines provided. Then write the words in the boxes based on whether you think each word is less/smaller or more/larger than the other word. Below the boxes, write why you think word 1 is less/smaller and word 2 is more/larger than word 1.

Repeat for words 3 and 4. **Have** students share what they wrote. **Discuss** examples of how these words might be used.

Part B: Comprehension Strategies

12 minutes

Teacher Materials:
Reading *Textbook A*

Student Materials:
Balance scale for weighing items; gram weights; assorted small items to weigh

Lined Paper

Reading *Textbook A*

Display directions for activity.
Directions: Discuss what grams are and why you use them. Choose items to weigh. Draw a chart and complete it as you weigh items to find the weight.

Item	Grams

Activity 1 Pair-Share Activity—Apply Knowledge (Level 3 of Bloom's Taxonomy)

 Direct students to Lesson 32, pages 191–192 and Lesson 33, pages 196–198 in Reading *Textbook A*.

Discuss the steps in Pair-Share.
You'll do an activity called **Pair-Share** to show some things you have learned about grams in previous lessons. The directions are on the board. I'll read them to you.

Assign partners. **Provide** lined paper, balance scale, gram weights, and assorted small items to weigh.
Step 1 is the **Pair** part of the activity. Discuss what grams are and why you use them with your partner. Then work with your partner to see how many grams each item weighs. Draw a chart and record your information. Decide who'll weigh the items and who'll record the information before you start. Work quickly. You have 7 minutes.
Guide students as they discuss grams and then complete the chart as they weigh items.

Call on as many students to share as time allows.
Step 2 is to **Share.** I'll call on pairs of students to share their work with the rest of the class.

Lesson 35

5 minutes

Student Materials:
Reading *Textbook A*

Part C: Fluency Building

 Conduct after the lesson, using the story of the day.

Activity 1 Partner Reading

It's time for partner reading.

Direct students to the story of the day. **Assign** student partners as Partner 1 and Partner 2. **Monitor** partner reading. **Guide** as needed.

Lesson 36

> **Materials**
> **Teacher:** 7-KWL Chart; Reading *Textbook A*
> **Student:** Vocabulary notebook; Reading *Textbook A*

Part A: Vocabulary Development

8 minutes

Teacher Materials:
Reading *Textbook A*

Student Materials:
Vocabulary notebook
Reading *Textbook A*

Activity 1 Learn New Vocabulary Word

Elicit responses to questions. **Guide** as needed.
Today you'll learn a new vocabulary word. **Forward. Forward** means "in front." What does **forward** mean? *In front.*

Another way to say "in front" is **forward.** What's another way to say "in front"? *Forward.*

The boy stood on a block of ice. Then he **moved in front.** He jumped **forward** to the ground.

Discuss examples of when people or things move forward.

What's another way to say "in front"? *Forward.*

Direct students to write forward and its definition in their vocabulary notebook. **Guide** as needed.
Write **forward** and what it means in your vocabulary notebook.

Activity 2 Review Vocabulary Word

Elicit responses to questions. **Guide** as needed.
What's another way to say "very short period of time"? *Moment.*

Tell me a sentence using the word **moment.** (Student responses.)
Discuss sentence.

 Review vocabulary words in their appropriate context in Reading *Textbook A*.

Lesson 36 **109**

Part B: Comprehension Strategies

12 minutes

Teacher Materials:
KWL Chart

Reading *Textbook A*

Student Materials:
Reading *Textbook A*

Activity 1 KWL Chart: Topic and What I Know— A Before-Reading Strategy

Elicit responses to questions. **Guide** as needed.
You're going to activate your background knowledge for a new topic.

What do you do when you activate your background knowledge? (Idea: *Think about what you already know.*)

You'll be reading text about "A Push in the Opposite Direction" in today's lesson. Before you read, it's a great idea to think about **what you know already** about this topic. Then you'll be able to **connect** what you know to what you learned. That'll make it easier for you to understand or remember the new information you learn.

Show KWL Chart.
You'll use a KWL chart to help you organize your thinking about expository text.

Why do you use a KWL chart? (Idea: *To organize thinking about expository text.*)

The first box we write in is the "Topic" box. A topic is what the text is mostly about. What's a topic? *What the text is mostly about.*

Write topic on KWL Chart.
We'll read about "A Push in the Opposite Direction," so I'll write that in the section for "Topic."

Now I'll show you how I activate my background knowledge about pushes in the opposite direction for the "What I Know" section of the KWL chart.

Model how to activate background knowledge for the "What I Know" section of KWL Chart. Suggested ideas: 1. **A push** makes me think of kids pushing a swing. If someone pushes a swing up, it goes back or the opposite direction. 2. **Opposite** makes me think of going in a different direction. 3. I remember the Goad story where air came out and Goad went the other way. I'll write that. **Write** three sentences on the chart.

When you connect what you already know with the text, you'll be building more background knowledge in your brain and you'll be smarter.

Activity 2 KWL Chart: What I Wonder—A Before-Reading Strategy

Elicit responses to questions. **Guide** as needed. **Show** KWL Chart (partially completed in Activity 1).
Next you'll write the questions you have about the topic in the "What I Wonder" section of the chart.

What will you write in this section of the chart? (Ideas: *Questions you have, what you wonder about.*)

I know that questions start with words like **who, when, where, why, what,** and **how.**

What words can you use to help you think of questions? (Ideas: *Who, when, where, why, what, and how.*)

I'll show you how I think of questions for the "What I Wonder" section of the KWL chart.

Model how to generate questions for the "What I Wonder" section of KWL Chart. Suggested questions: 1.What is pushing? 2. How do pushes work? 3. Why is there a push in an opposite direction? 4. What happens when there is a push in one direction? **Write** questions on chart.

Why is it important to ask questions before I read? (Idea: *Asking questions gets you interested in what you're going to learn—it makes you think about what you're going to read.*)

Save the KWL Chart for Lesson 37.

The text I read may or may not have the answers to my questions. That is okay. Just asking the questions helps me be smarter. If I don't find the answers to my questions, I might need to read more in another book to find the answers.

Activity 3 Comprehension Monitoring: Reread Expository or Narrative Texts—A During-Reading Strategy

 Direct students to Lesson 35, pages 211–215 in Reading *Textbook A*.

Elicit responses to questions. **Guide** as needed.
Comprehension means "understanding what you read." Sometimes when you read, you get confused and you don't understand the meaning of what you're reading. While you read, you should always ask yourself, "Does this make sense?" A great strategy to use when reading doesn't make sense is to **reread** the part that didn't make sense. You can also read ahead a little bit to see whether that helps you understand.

What's the strategy called? *Rereading.*

Does this strategy work for both expository and narrative text? *Yes.*

When you read this story, did the whole story make sense?
(Student responses.)

Discuss what did not make sense and the strategy students used to fix the problem.

What do you do if something does not make sense? (Idea: *Reread the sentence that did not make sense or read ahead a little to see whether that helps you understand.*)

Today when you read Lesson 36, be sure to think about using the rereading strategy if you don't understand what you're reading for the expository section.

Lesson 36 **111**

5 minutes

Student Materials:
Reading *Textbook A*

Part C: Fluency Building

 Conduct after the lesson, using the story of the day.

Activity 1 Partner Reading

It's time for partner reading.
Direct students to the story of the day. **Assign** student partners as Partner 1 and Partner 2. **Monitor** partner reading. **Guide** as needed.

112   *Lesson 36*

Lesson 37

Materials
Teacher: 7-KWL Chart (partially completed in Lesson 36); Reading *Textbook A*
Student: Vocabulary notebook; Reading *Textbook A*

8 minutes

Teacher Materials:
Reading *Textbook A*

Student Materials:
Vocabulary notebook

Reading *Textbook A*

Part A: Vocabulary Development

Activity 1 Learn New Vocabulary Word

Elicit responses to questions. **Guide** as needed.
Today you'll learn a new vocabulary word. **Rotten. Rotten** means "something that's bad." What does **rotten** mean? *Something that's bad.*

Another way to say "something that's bad" is **rotten.** What's another way to say "something that's bad"? *Rotten.*

Herman had many brothers and sisters. They were all familiar with **things that were bad** because they were all born on **rotten** cabbage leaves.

Discuss things that are rotten.

What's another way to say "something that is bad"? *Rotten.*

Direct students to write rotten and its definition in their vocabulary notebook. **Guide** as needed.
Write **rotten** and what it means in your vocabulary notebook.

Activity 2 Review Vocabulary Word

Elicit responses to questions. **Guide** as needed.
What's another way to say "in front"? *Forward.*

Tell me a sentence using the word **forward.** (Student responses.)
Discuss sentence.

 Review vocabulary words in their appropriate context in Reading *Textbook A*.

Lesson 37 113

12 minutes

Teacher Materials:
KWL Chart (partially completed in Lesson 36)

Reading *Textbook A*

Student Materials:
Reading *Textbook A*

Part B: Comprehension Strategies

Activity 1 KWL Chart: What I Learned—An After-Reading Strategy

 Direct students to Lesson 36, pages 221–224 in Reading *Textbook A*.

Elicit responses to questions. **Guide** as needed. **Show** the KWL Chart (partially completed in Lesson 36).
In the last lesson you read about "A Push in the Opposite Direction." It's time to write what you learned from the passage in the "What I Learned" section of the KWL chart.

When you write what you learned, you should write it in your own words rather than copy it right from the book. When you write what you learned in your own words, it will help you remember the information later. I'll show you how I fill out the "What I Learned" section of the chart.

Model how to write the information learned for the "What I Learned" section of KWL Chart.

 Read paragraphs from Lesson 36 in Reading *Textbook A*.

Write sentences on the chart as you summarize information. Suggested ideas: 1. When air comes out of a balloon, the balloon moves the opposite way. 2. When air comes out of Goad, Goad moves the opposite way. 3. When a boy jumps off a block of ice, the ice moves the opposite way. 4. When a girl jumps from a boat, the boat moves the opposite way. 5. The rule is any time something moves one way, there is a push the opposite way.

I've now written new things I have learned from the expository text I read. I wrote the information in my own words. That's a very tough thing to do but you'll get really good at doing it as you practice. Writing things in your own words helps you remember the information later.

Activity 2 Comprehension Monitoring: Reread Expository or Narrative Texts—A During-Reading Strategy

 Direct students to Lesson 36, pages 220–224 in Reading *Textbook A*.

Elicit responses to questions. **Guide** as needed.
Comprehension means "understanding what you read." What should you ask yourself while you are reading? (Idea: *Does this make sense?*)

A great strategy to use when reading doesn't make sense is to **reread** the part that didn't make sense. You can also read ahead a little bit to see if that helps you understand.

What's the strategy called? *Rereading.*

Does this strategy work for both expository and narrative text? *Yes.*

When you read this story, did the whole story make sense? (Student responses.)

Discuss what did not make sense and the strategy students used fix the problem.

What do you do if something does not make sense? (Idea: *Reread the sentence that did not make sense or read ahead a little to see if that helps you understand.*)

Today when you read Lesson 37, be sure to think about using the rereading strategy if you don't understand what you're reading for both the expository section and the narrative section.

Part C: Fluency Building

5 minutes

Student Materials:
Reading *Textbook A*

 Conduct after the lesson, using the story of the day.

Activity 1 Partner Reading

It's time for partner reading.
Direct students to the story of the day. **Assign** student partners as Partner 1 and Partner 2. **Monitor** partner reading. **Guide** as needed.

Lesson 37 **115**

Lesson 38

Materials

Teacher: Reading *Textbook A;* sample expository trade book with labels, captions, maps, photographs, cutaways, diagrams; sample narrative trade book with characters, setting, problem, and events (beginning, middle, end); 8-T-Chart

Student: Vocabulary notebook; Reading *Textbook A*

8 minutes

Teacher Materials:
Reading *Textbook A*

Student Materials:
Vocabulary notebook

Reading *Textbook A*

Part A: Vocabulary Development

Activity 1 Learn New Vocabulary Word

Elicit responses to questions. **Guide** as needed.
Today you'll learn a new vocabulary word. **Travel. Travel** means "move from place to place." What does **travel** mean? *Move from place to place.*

Another way to say "move from place to place" is **travel.** What's another way to say "move from place to place"? *Travel.*

Herman would **go from place to place.** He would look for food while he would **travel** around.

Discuss examples of how people or things travel.

What's another way to say "move from place to place"? *Travel.*

Direct students to write travel and its definition in their vocabulary notebook. **Guide** as needed.
Write **travel** and what it means in your vocabulary notebook.

Activity 2 Review Vocabulary Word

Elicit responses to questions. **Guide** as needed.
What's another way to say "something that's bad"? *Rotten.*

Tell me a sentence using the word **rotten.** (Student responses.)
Discuss sentence.

 Review vocabulary words in their appropriate context in Reading *Textbook A*.

116   Lesson 38

12 minutes

Teacher Materials:
Reading *Textbook A*

T-Chart

sample expository trade book with labels, captions, maps, photographs, cutaways, diagrams

sample narrative trade book with characters, setting, problem, and events (beginning, middle, end)

Student Materials:
Reading *Textbook A*

Part B: Comprehension Strategies

Activity 1 Determine Text Type: Features of Expository Text—A Before-Reading Strategy

Elicit responses to questions. **Guide** as needed.
Today you'll read two types of text. The first type of text is called expository text. You'll read "Speedometers" which is expository text. **Expository text** is written to teach you new information or facts about something.

Why do you read expository text? *To learn new information or facts about something.*

Expository text is different from narrative text in lots of ways. It's good to know some of the ways that the two types of text are different. That'll help you decide whether text is expository or narrative.
Discuss differences between expository and narrative text.

Display T-Chart. **List** features on the T-Chart as you discuss them.

 Note some examples of features in Reading *Textbook A* (maps, labels, captions, diagrams, table of contents, headings).
Let's list some items you often find in expository text.
Labels—help identify parts
Photographs—help you understand what something looks like
Captions—tell what's in a picture
Cutaways—show what something looks like inside
Diagrams—show parts of things
Maps—help you know where something is in the world
Bold print—shows you important words
Headings—show what a section of text is about
Tables of contents—helps you find information in a book
Index—tells you an alphabetized list with page numbers of what's in the book
Glossary—defines words in the book

Another important thing to remember about expository text is that it does not have to be read in order. You can hop around and read different parts in any order and you'll still learn new information.

Do you have to read expository text in order? *No.*

What kinds of text are you reading when you're reading to learn new facts or information? *Expository text.*

What are some of the items you find in expository text? (Student responses.)

Activity 2 Determine Text Type: Features of Narrative Text—A Before-Reading Strategy

Elicit responses to questions. **Guide** as needed.
A second type of text is called **narrative text.** You'll read "Herman Goes to Kennedy Airport," which is narrative text. Narrative text tells you a story. What does narrative text tell you? *A story.*

Lesson 38   **117**

You'll often read narrative texts for fun. Narrative texts might include new facts or information that you did not know before. You'll often notice information in your narrative stories in your reading book. But the main purpose of narrative text is to tell you a story.

What kind of text are you reading when you read a story? *Narrative text.*

List features of narrative text on the T-Chart as you discuss them.

Note some examples of features in Reading *Textbook A* (characters, setting, problem, events).

Let's list some items you find in stories or narrative text.
Characters—people, animals, or objects that do things in the story
Setting—where and when the story happens
Problem—thing that goes wrong in the story that makes you want to read more
Events—beginning, middle, and end of story

Another important thing to remember is that narratives have to be read in order, from the beginning to the end. Otherwise, they do not make sense.

Do you have to read narrative text in order? *Yes.*

What kind of text are you reading when you read a story? *Narrative text.*

What are some items you find in narrative text? (Student responses.)

Activity 3 Comprehension Monitoring: Reread Expository or Narrative Texts—A During-Reading Strategy

Direct students to Lesson 37, pages 228–231 in Reading *Textbook A*.

Elicit responses to questions. **Guide** as needed.
Comprehension means "understanding what you read." What should you ask yourself while you are reading? (Idea: *Does this make sense?*)

What do you do if something does not make sense? (Idea: *Reread the sentence that did not make sense or read ahead a little to see if that helps you understand.*)

What's the strategy called? *Rereading.*

Does this strategy work for both expository and narrative text? *Yes.*

When you read this story, did the whole story make sense? (Student responses.)

Discuss what did not make sense and the strategy students used fix the problem.

Today when you read Lesson 38, be sure to think about using the rereading strategy if you don't understand what you're reading for both the expository section and the narrative section.

5 minutes

Student Materials:
Reading *Textbook A*

Part C: Fluency Building

 Conduct after the lesson, using the story of the day.

Activity 1 Partner Reading

It's time for partner reading.

Direct students to the story of the day. **Assign** student partners as Partner 1 and Partner 2. **Monitor** partner reading. **Guide** as needed.

Lesson 38

Lesson 39

Materials
Teacher: 6-Narrative Story Map; Reading *Textbook A*
Student: Vocabulary notebook; copy of 6-Narrative Story Map; Reading *Textbook A*

8 minutes

Teacher Materials:
Reading *Textbook A*

Student Materials:
Vocabulary notebook
Reading *Textbook A*

Part A: Vocabulary Development

Activity 1 Learn New Vocabulary Word

Elicit responses to questions. **Guide** as needed.
Today you'll learn a new vocabulary word. **Jumbo. Jumbo** means "very large." What does **jumbo** mean? *Very large.*

Another way to say "very large" is **jumbo.** What's another way to say **very large?** *Jumbo.*

There are some **very large** jets that fly in the sky. A **jumbo** jet can carry many people.

Discuss things that are jumbo.

What's another way to say "very large"? *Jumbo.*

Direct students to write jumbo and its definition in their vocabulary notebook. **Guide** as needed.
Write **jumbo** and what it means in your vocabulary notebook.

Activity 2 Review Vocabulary Word

Elicit responses to questions. **Guide** as needed.
What's another way to say "move from place to place"? *Travel.*

Tell me a sentence using the word **travel.** (Student responses.)
Discuss sentence.

 Review vocabulary words in their appropriate context in Reading *Textbook A*.

120   Lesson 39

12 minutes

Teacher Materials:
Narrative Story Map

Reading *Textbook A*

Student Materials:
Narrative Story Map

Reading *Textbook A*

Part B: Comprehension Strategies

Activity 1 — Narrative Story Map: Identify Title, Characters, Setting, Events, and Problem—An After-Reading Strategy

 Direct students to Lesson 38, pages 236–239 in Reading *Textbook A*.

Elicit responses to questions. **Guide** as needed.
Narratives have a title, characters, settings, a problem, and events. Skim "Herman Goes to Kennedy Airport," and then work by yourself to fill in the title, important characters, setting, problem, and events on your Narrative Story Map.

Monitor students as they write the title, characters, setting, problem, and events. **Discuss** answers for the title, characters, setting, problem, and events. **Write** answers on Narrative Story Map.
What did you write on your Narrative Story Map? (Ideas: *Title—"Herman Goes to Kennedy Airport;" Main Character—Herman; Setting—Where: New York City, Kennedy Airport, When: Chapter does not say, so leave blank; Problem—Herman will fly farther than any other fly; Beginning—Herman was buzzing around looking for food when he landed on a taxi; Middle—Herman hung on to the taxi while it went to Kennedy Airport; End—Herman flew into a purse to get some candy when the purse shut with him inside.*)

Activity 2 — Use Narrative Story Map: Retell the Story—An After-Reading Strategy

Show Narrative Story Map completed in Activity 1.
You have completed the Narrative Story Map and now you can use it to help you retell the story. When you retell the story, you want to be sure to tell about the title, the characters, the setting, the problem, and the events that happened in the right order. Use your Narrative Story Map to help you retell the story.

Assign student partners. **Monitor** student partners as they retell the narrative story to a partner by using the Narrative Story Map they completed in Activity 1.
Retell the story to your partner from your Narrative Story Map. Then your partner can take a turn retelling the story to you.

Who wants to retell the story to the whole class? (Student responses.)
Retelling the story helps you remember all the parts of the story.

Lesson 39

5 minutes

Student Materials:
Reading *Textbook A*

Part C: Fluency Building

 Conduct after the lesson, using the story of the day.

Activity 1 Partner Reading

It's time for partner reading.

Direct students to the story of the day. **Assign** student partners as Partner 1 and Partner 2. **Monitor** partner reading. **Guide** as needed.

Lesson 40

> **Materials**
> **Teacher:** Reading *Textbook A,* 2-Vocabulary Acquisition and Use, Writing Prompts, 3-My Writing Checklist
> **Student:** Reading *Textbook A,* Vocabulary notebook; Copy of 2-Vocabulary Acquisition and Use, Copy of 6-Narrative Story Map, Copy of 3-My Writing Checklist, Lined paper

8 minutes

Teacher Materials:
Reading *Textbook A*

Vocabulary Acquisition and Use

Student Materials:
Vocabulary Notebook

Reading *Textbook A*

Vocabulary Acquisition and Use

Part A: Vocabulary Development

Activity 1 Vocabulary Notebook Review

Guide students as they study all words.
Today you'll study from your vocabulary notebook. Studying your words and what they mean will help you know your words even better. You'll study the eight words we studied over the past two weeks.

Activity 2 Cumulative Vocabulary Review

Elicit responses to questions. **Guide** as needed.
Directions: Listen and tell me whether I use our vocabulary words the right way or the wrong way. If I use the word the right way, say **"yes."** If I use the word the wrong way, say **"no."** Then we'll talk about each word.

1. Tony **wondered** what it would be like to walk on the moon.

   Did I use the word **wondered** the right way? *Yes.*

   How do you know? (Student responses.)

2. Sam bought an old car that had several **dents** on it.

   Did I use the word **dents** the right way? *Yes.*

   How do you know? (Student responses.)

3. David was not very hungry so he ordered a **jumbo** pizza for dinner.

   Did I use the word **jumbo** the right way? *No.*

   How do you know? (Student responses.)

4. Maria wanted to make a salad but all she had was **rotten** lettuce in her refrigerator. She didn't make the salad and threw the lettuce away.

   Did I use the word **rotten** the right way? *Yes.*

   How do you know? (Student responses.)

Lesson 40   123

5. Carlos remembered he left his book on his nightstand. So he had to **search** the entire house to find it.

   Did I use the word **search** the right way? *No.*

   How do you know? (Student responses.)

6. Mr. Rahn would **travel** to many cities to do his job. He often traveled by bus.

   Did I use the word **travel** the right way. *Yes.*

   How do you know? (Student responses.)

7. The teacher asked Molly to come **forward** and write her answer on the board.

   Did I use the word **forward** the right way? *Yes.*

   How do you know? (Student responses.)

8. It took Martha only a **moment** to prepare the three-layered cake. She worked many hours on it.

   Did I use the word **moment** correctly? *No.*

   How do you know? (Student responses.)

Review vocabulary words as needed.

 Review vocabulary words in their appropriate context in Reading *Textbook A*.

Activity 3 Vocabulary Acquisition and Use

Display Vocabulary Acquisition and Use. **Have** students work with a neighbor to complete Vocabulary Acquisition and Use.
Today's vocabulary words are _____ and _____ [and _____ and _____].
Vocabulary words: **rotten** and **bad; travel** and **move**
Write the words on the lines provided. Then write the words in the boxes based on whether you think each word is less/smaller or more/larger than the other word. Below the boxes, write why you think word 1 is less/smaller and word 2 is more/larger than word 1.
Repeat for words 3 and 4. **Have** students share what they wrote. **Discuss** examples of how these words might be used.

8 minutes

Teacher Materials:
Reading *Textbook A*

Student Materials:
Narrative Story Map

Reading *Textbook A*

Part B: Comprehension Strategies

Display directions for the activity.
Directions: Discuss what parts are found in all narrative stories. Show your understanding of these parts by choosing any narrative story from your reading book and completing a Narrative Story Map for that story.

Activity 1 Pair-Share Activity—Apply Knowledge (Level 3 of Bloom's Taxonomy)

Discuss the steps in Pair-Share.
You'll do an activity called **Pair-Share** to show some things you have learned in previous lessons. The directions are on the board. I'll read them to you.

Assign partners. **Provide** the copy of the Narrative Story Map to each pair of students.

 Guide students to choose a narrative story from the Reading Textbook A and to complete the Narrative Story Map.

Step 1 is the **Pair** part of the activity. Discuss what parts you find in all narrative stories. Then work with your partner to choose a narrative story from your reading book. Complete a Narrative Story Map for that story. You have 10 minutes to complete this job.

Call on as many students to share as time allows.
Step 2 is to **Share.** I'll call on pairs of students to share their work with the rest of the class.

5 minutes

Student Materials:
Reading *Textbook A*

Part C: Fluency Building

 Conduct after the lesson, using the story of the day.

Activity 1 Partner Reading

It's time for partner reading.
Direct students to the story of the day. **Assign** student partners as Partner 1 and Partner 2. **Monitor** partner reading. **Guide** as needed.

Lesson 40   **125**

Part D: Writing/Language Arts

10 minutes

Teacher Materials:
Writing Prompts

My Writing Checklist

Student Materials:
Lined Paper

My Writing Checklist

Activity 1 Write and Use Parts of Speech and Conventions

Time to write using a writing prompt based on the stories we've been reading.

Assign student partners. **Distribute** lined paper to students. **Display** writing prompts and have students choose one to write about or assign a writing prompt of your choice. **Review** parts of speech and punctuation as well as the writing checklist with students. **Tell** students to write one to two paragraphs (minimum of four sentences per paragraph) on their own to answer the writing prompt. **Tell** them to use their writing checklist (first column labeled "Did I use them?") to ensure they include important parts of speech or punctuation in their writing. **Tell** students which parts of speech or punctuation to focus on, if you wish. **Model** what it means to answer a writing prompt and to use the writing checklist during and after the writing process, as needed. **Monitor** and guide students as needed. **Model** what it means to have a neighbor look over his or her neighbor's writing and to complete the writing checklist (second column labeled "Did my neighbor use them?"), as needed. **Have** students share what they wrote as time permits.

Writing Prompt 1	Writing Prompt 2	Writing Prompt 3
If you were as small as Nancy, describe one thing you would be able to do better than if you were regular size.	If you were as small as Nancy, describe one thing you would not be able to do as well as if you were regular size.	What would it be like to have 80 brothers and 90 sisters, like Herman had?

Lesson 41

Materials
Teacher: 7-KWL Chart; Reading *Textbook A*
Student: Vocabulary notebook; copy of 7-KWL Chart; Reading *Textbook A*

 8 minutes

Teacher Materials:
Reading *Textbook A*

Student Materials:
Vocabulary notebook
Reading *Textbook A*

Part A: Vocabulary Development

Activity 1 Learn New Vocabulary Word

Elicit responses to questions. **Guide** as needed.
Today you'll learn a new vocabulary word. **Peaceful. Peaceful means** "quiet."
What does **peaceful** mean? *Quiet.*

Another word for "quiet" is **peaceful.** What's another word for **quiet?**
Peaceful.

Herman was flying all around looking for a **quiet** place in the airplane. He just wanted to go somewhere where it was **peaceful.**

Discuss examples of things that are peaceful.

What's another word for "quiet"? *Peaceful.*

Direct students to write peaceful and its definition in their vocabulary notebooks.
Guide as needed.
Write **peaceful** and what it means in your vocabulary notebook.

Activity 2 Review Vocabulary Word

Elicit responses to questions. **Guide** as needed.
What's another way to say "very large"? *Jumbo.*

Tell me a sentence using the word **jumbo.** (Student responses.)
Discuss sentences.

 Review vocabulary words in appropriate context in Reading *Textbook A*.

Lesson 41   **127**

Part B: Comprehension Strategies

12 minutes

Teacher Materials:
KWL Chart

Reading *Textbook A*

Student Materials:
KWL Chart

Reading *Textbook A*

Activity 1 KWL Chart: Topic and What I Know— A Before-Reading Strategy

Elicit responses to questions. **Guide** as needed.
You're going to activate your background knowledge for a new topic. What do you do when you activate your background knowledge? (Idea: *Think about what you already know.*)

You'll be reading a passage called "Insects" in today's lesson. Before you read, it's a great idea to think about what you know already about insects. Then you'll be able to connect what you know to what you learn.

Show KWL Chart.
You'll use your KWL chart to help you organize your thinking about expository text. Why do you use a KWL chart? (Idea: *To organize thinking about expository text.*)

Write topic on KWL Chart. **Guide** students as they copy the topic on their charts.
The first box we write in is the "Topic" box. What's our topic? *Insects.*

Write *insects* in the "Topic" box.

Discuss students' background knowledge. **Record** three items in "What I Know" section of KWL Chart. **Guide** students as they copy items on their charts.
Now let's work together to activate your background knowledge about insects for the "What I Know" section of the KWL chart.

When you connect what you already know with the text, you'll be building more background knowledge in your mind and you'll be smarter.

Activity 2 KWL Chart: What I Wonder— A Before-Reading Strategy

Elicit responses to questions. **Guide** as needed. **Show** KWL Chart (partially completed in Activity 1).
Next you'll write the questions you have about the topic in the "What I Wonder" section of the chart.

What will you write in this section of the chart? (Ideas: *Questions you have, what you wonder about.*)

What words can you use to help you think of questions? (Ideas: *Who, when, where, why, what, and how.*)

Let's work together to think of questions for the "What I Wonder" section of the KWL chart.

Discuss possible questions. **Record** three questions in the "What I Wonder" section of the KWL Chart. Possible questions: 1. How many kinds of insects are there? 2. What do insects eat? 3. Where do insects live? 4. Why do insects bite? 5. How long do insects live? **Guide** students as they copy the questions on their charts.

128 Lesson 41

Why is it important to ask questions before you read? (Idea: *Asking questions gets you interested in what you're going to learn—it makes you think about what you're going to read.*)

The text you read may or may not have the answers to your questions. That is okay. Just asking the questions helps you be smarter. If you don't find the answers to your questions, you might need to read more in another book to find out the answers.

Save teacher and student copies of KWL Chart for Lesson 42.

5 minutes

Student Materials:
Reading *Textbook A*

Part C: Fluency Building

 Conduct after the lesson, using the story of the day.

Activity 1 Partner Reading

It's time for partner reading.

Direct students to the story of the day. **Assign** student partners as Partner 1 and Partner 2. **Monitor** partner reading. **Guide** as needed.

Lesson 41 **129**

Lesson 42

Materials

Teacher: 7-KWL Chart (partially completed in Lesson 41); Reading *Textbook A*

Student: Vocabulary notebook; copy of 7-KWL Chart (partially completed in Lesson 41); Reading *Textbook A*

8 minutes

Teacher Materials:
Reading *Textbook A*

Student Materials:
Vocabulary notebook

Reading *Textbook A*

Part A: Vocabulary Development

Activity 1 Learn New Vocabulary Word

Elicit responses to questions. **Guide** as needed.
Today you'll learn a new vocabulary word. **Rush. Rush** means "go very quickly." What does **rush** mean? *Go very quickly.*

Another way to say "go very quickly" is **rush.** What's another way to say "go very quickly"? *Rush.*

Goad knew many things. She knew she needed to **go very quickly.**
Goad knew if she let her air **rush** out she would get away.

Discuss examples of how people or things rush.

What's another way to say "go very quickly"? *Rush.*

Direct students to write rush and its definition in their vocabulary notebooks.
Guide as needed.
Write **rush** and what it means in your vocabulary notebook.

Activity 2 Review Vocabulary Word

Elicit responses to questions. **Guide** as needed.
What's another word for "quiet"? *Peaceful.*

Tell me a sentence using the word **peaceful.** (Student responses.)
Discuss sentences.

  Review vocabulary words in appropriate context in Reading *Textbook A*.

130   *Lesson 42*

12 minutes

Teacher Materials:
KWL Chart (partially completed in Lesson 41)

Reading *Textbook A*

Student Materials:
KWL Chart (partially completed in Lesson 41)

Reading *Textbook A*

Part B: Comprehension Strategies

Activity 1 KWL Chart: What I Learned—An After-Reading Strategy

  Direct students to Lesson 41, pages 258–259 in Reading *Textbook A*.

Elicit responses to questions. **Guide** as needed. **Show** KWL Chart (partially completed in Lesson 41).

In the last lesson you read "Insects." It's time to write what you learned from the passage on the KWL chart.

When you write what you learned, you should write it in your own words rather than copy it right from the book. That will help you remember the information later.

Let's work together to fill out the "What I Learned" section of the chart.

Call on students to read the passage in parts. **Record** the best sentences on the "What I Learned" section of KWL Chart. **Guide** students as they copy sentences on their charts.
Read the first part of the passage on insects. How can we put that part in our own words to record on our chart? (Student responses.)

We can write "Not all bugs are insects."

Read the next part. How can we put that part in our own words? (Student responses.)

We can write "Ants, flies, butterflies, beetles, bees, and grasshoppers are insects, but spiders are not."

Read the next part. How can we put that part in our own words? (Student responses.)

We can write "All insects have six legs and three body parts."

Read the next part. How can we put that part in our own words? (Student responses.)

We can write "A spider is not an insect because it has eight legs and two body parts."

You have now written the new things you learned from the expository text you read. You wrote the information in your own words.

Lesson 42   **131**

Activity 2 Generate Questions—A During-Reading Strategy

 Direct students to Lesson 39, page 248 in Reading *Textbook A*.

Elicit response to question. **Guide** as needed.
Another strategy you can use to help you have better comprehension in both expository and narrative text is to ask questions. You have asked questions before reading for your KWL chart. You can also use the strategy while you're reading.

Model think-aloud for generating questions.
Watch me as I show you what I mean.

Sample Wording for Think-Aloud

I'm reading the last page of the story. It says that Herman found a nice warm red. I wonder: What could that be? As I keep reading, I find out that it's the back of the seat on the airplane.

Asking questions while you read keeps you interested in what you are reading.

Why should you ask questions while you read? (Idea: *It keeps you interested in what you read.*)

5 minutes

Student Materials:
Reading *Textbook A*

Part C: Fluency Building

 Conduct after the lesson, using the story of the day.

Activity 1 Partner Reading

It's time for partner reading.
Direct students to the story of the day. Assign student partners as Partner 1 and Partner 2. **Monitor** partner reading. **Guide** as needed.

Lesson 43

Materials
Teacher: 7-KWL Chart; Reading *Textbook A*
Student: Vocabulary notebook; Copy of 7-KWL Chart; Reading *Textbook A*

Part A: Vocabulary Development

8 minutes

Teacher Materials:
Reading *Textbook A*

Student Materials:
Vocabulary notebook
Reading *Textbook A*

Activity 1 Learn New Vocabulary Word

Elicit responses to questions. **Guide** as needed.
Today you'll learn a new vocabulary word. **Trays. Trays** means "something you use to carry things." What does **trays** mean? *Something you use to carry things.*

Another way to say "something you use to carry things" is **trays.** What's another way to say "something you use to carry things"? *Trays.*

The people who work on the jets need to use **something to carry things.** The **trays** made it easy for them to serve food to the passengers.

Discuss examples of when trays are used.

What's another way to say "something you use to carry things"? *Trays.*

Direct students to write trays and its definition in their vocabulary notebooks. **Guide** as needed.
Write **trays** and what it means in your vocabulary notebook.

Activity 2 Review Vocabulary Word

Elicit responses to questions. **Guide** as needed.
What's another way to say "go very quickly"? *Rush.*

Tell me a sentence using the word **rush.** (Student responses.)
Discuss sentences.

 Review vocabulary words in appropriate context in Reading *Textbook A.*

Lesson 43 133

Part B: Comprehension Strategies

12 minutes

Teacher Materials:
KWL Chart

Reading *Textbook A*

Student Materials:
KWL Chart

Reading *Textbook A*

Activity 1 KWL Chart: Topic and What I Know— A Before-Reading Strategy

Elicit responses to questions. **Guide** as needed.
You're going to activate your background knowledge for a new topic.
What do you do when you activate your background knowledge? (Idea: *Think about what you already know.*)

You'll be reading a passage called "Degrees" in today's lesson. Before you read, it's a great idea to think about what you already know about this topic. Then you'll be able to connect what you know to what you learn.

Show KWL Chart.

You'll use a KWL chart to help you organize your thinking about expository text. Why do you use a KWL chart? (Idea: *To organize thinking about expository text.*)

Write topic on KWL Chart. **Guide** students as they copy the topic on their charts.
The first box you write in is the "Topic" box. What should we write for the topic? *Degrees.*

Write *degrees* in the "Topic" box.

Discuss students' background knowledge. **Record** three items in "What I Know" section of KWL Chart. **Guide** students as they copy items on their charts.
Now let's work together to activate your background knowledge about degrees for the "What I Know" section of the KWL chart.

When you connect what you already know with the text, you'll be building more background knowledge in your brain and you'll be smarter.

Activity 2 KWL Chart: What I Wonder—A Before-Reading Strategy

Elicit responses to questions. **Guide** as needed. **Show** KWL Chart (partially completed in Activity 1).
Next you'll write questions you have about the topic in the "What I Wonder" section of the chart.

What will you write in this section of the chart? (Ideas: *Questions you have; what you wonder about.*)

What words can you use to help you think of questions? (Ideas: *Who, when, where, why, what, and how.*)

Let's work together to think of questions for the "What I Wonder" section of the KWL chart.

134 *Lesson 43*

Discuss possible questions. **Record** three questions in the "What I Wonder" section of KWL Chart. Possible questions: 1. What are degrees? 2. Why do you use degrees? 3. Who found out about degrees? 4. How do you use degrees? 5. Why do we learn about degrees? **Guide** students as they copy the questions on their charts.

Why is it important to ask questions before you read? (Idea: *Asking questions gets you interested in what you're going to learn—it makes you think about what you're going to read.*)

The text you read may or may not have the answers to your questions. That's okay. Just asking the questions helps you be smarter. If you don't find the answers to your questions, you might need to read more in another book to find out the answers.

Save teacher and student copies of KWL Chart for Lesson 44.

Activity 3 Generate Questions—A During-Reading Strategy

 Direct students to Lesson 42, page 267 in Reading *Textbook A*.

Elicit response to question. **Guide** as needed.
Another strategy you can use to help you have better comprehension in both expository and narrative text is to ask questions. You've asked questions before reading for your KWL chart. You can also use the strategy while you're reading.

Model generating questions.
Watch me as I show you what I mean.

Asking questions while you read keeps you interested in what you're reading.

Why should you ask questions while you read? (Idea: *It keeps you interested in what you read.*)

Part C: Fluency Building

5 minutes

Student Materials:
Reading *Textbook A*

 Conduct after the lesson, using the story of the day.

Activity 1 Partner Reading

It's time for partner reading.
Direct students to the story of the day. **Assign** student partners as Partner 1 and Partner 2. **Monitor** partner reading. **Guide** as needed.

Lesson 43 **135**

Lesson 44

Materials
Teacher: 7-KWL Chart (partially completed in Lesson 43); Reading *Textbook A*
Student: Vocabulary notebook; 7-KWL Chart (partially completed in Lesson 43); Reading *Textbook A*

8 minutes

Teacher Materials:
Reading *Textbook A*

Student Materials:
Vocabulary notebook
Reading *Textbook A*

Part A: Vocabulary Development

Activity 1 Learn New Vocabulary Word

Elicit responses to questions. **Guide** as needed.
Today you'll learn a new vocabulary word. **Stacked. Stacked** means "put things on top of each other." What does **stacked** mean? *Put things on top of each other.*

Another way to say "put things on top of each other" is **stacked.** What's another way to say "put things on top of each other"? *Stacked.*

The workers cleaned up the plane and **put things on top of each other. They stacked** the dinners while the dinners were still frozen to save room.

Discuss things that are stacked.

What's another way to say "put things on top of each other"? *Stacked.*

Direct students to write stacked and its definition in their vocabulary notebooks. **Guide** as needed.

Write **stacked** and what it means in your vocabulary notebook.

Activity 2 Review Vocabulary Word

Elicit responses to questions. **Guide** as needed.
What's another way to say "something you use to carry things"? *Trays.*

Tell me a sentence using the word **trays.** (Student responses.)
Discuss sentences.

 Review vocabulary words in appropriate context in Reading *Textbook A*.

136   Lesson 44

12 minutes

Teacher Materials:
KWL Chart (partially completed in Lesson 43)

Reading *Textbook A*

Student Materials:
KWL Chart (partially completed in Lesson 43)

Reading *Textbook A*

Part B: Comprehension Strategies

Activity 1 KWL Chart: What I Learned—An After-Reading Strategy

 Direct students to Lesson 43, pages 272–273 in Reading *Textbook A*.

Elicit responses to questions. **Guide** as needed. **Show** KWL Chart (partially completed in Lesson 43).

In the last lesson, you read "Degrees." It's time to write what you learned from the passage in the "What I Learned" section of the KWL chart.

When you write what you learned, you should write it in your own words rather than copy it right from the book. That will help you remember the information later.

Let's work together to fill out the "What I Learned" section of the chart.

Call on students to read the passage in parts. **Guide** students as they copy the sentences on their charts. **Record** the best sentences on the "What I Learned" section of KWL Chart.

Read the first part of the passage on degrees. How can we put that part in our own words to record on our chart? (Student responses.)

We can write "Degrees measure temperature."

Read the next part. How can we put that part in our own words? (Student responses.)

We can write "If temperature goes up, degrees go up."

Read the next part. How can we put that part in our own words? (Student responses.)

We can write "The hotter an object is, the higher the degrees."

Read the next part. How can we put that part in our own words? (Student responses.)

We can write "Hot days can be 100°, cold days can be 0°, and the temperature at school is 70°."

You have now written the new things you learned from the expository text you read. You wrote the information in your own words.

Lesson 44 **137**

Activity 2 Generate Questions—A During-Reading Strategy

 Direct students to Lesson 43, page 273 in Reading *Textbook A*.

Elicit responses to questions. **Guide** as needed.
Another strategy you can use to help you have better comprehension in both expository and narrative text is to ask questions. You've asked questions before reading for your KWL chart. You can also use the strategy while you're reading.

Sometimes it is hard to think of questions. Let's look at the story and see whether we can think of a question while we are reading. On page 273 it says that Herman "went from a city on the east coast to a city on the west coast."

Guide students to generate questions from the text.
Who can think of a good question after reading that sentence? (Student responses.)

Yes. "What city did Herman come from and what city did he go to?" is a great question. Read on to find the answer. Oops. The story doesn't tell me the answer to my question. I have to think and figure it out.

In what city on the east coast did Herman start his trip? (Idea: *New York City*)

What city did Herman go to on the west coast? (Idea: *San Francisco*)

Remember, asking questions while you read keeps you interested in what you are reading.

Why should you ask questions while you read? (Idea: *It keeps you interested in what you read.*)

Part C: Fluency Building

5 minutes

Student Materials:
Reading *Textbook A*

 Conduct after the lesson, using the story of the day.

Activity 1 Partner Reading

It's time for partner reading.
Direct students to the story of the day. **Assign** student partners as Partner 1 and Partner 2. **Monitor** partner reading. **Guide** as needed.

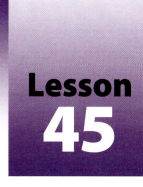

Lesson 45

Materials

Teacher: Reading *Textbook A*, 2-Vocabulary Acquisition and Use

Student: Vocabulary notebook; Reading *Textbook A*, Copy of 2-Vocabulary Acquisition and Use; Lined paper

8 minutes

Teacher Materials:
Reading *Textbook A*

Vocabulary Acquisition and Use

Student Materials:
Vocabulary notebook

Reading *Textbook A*

Vocabulary Acquisition and Use

Part A: Vocabulary Development

Activity 1 — Vocabulary Notebook Review

Guide students through all the words.
Today you'll study from your vocabulary notebook. Studying your words and what they mean will help you know your words even better. You'll look at the four words we studied this week.

Activity 2 — Cumulative Vocabulary Review

Elicit responses to questions. **Guide** as needed.
Directions: Listen and tell me whether I use our vocabulary words the right way or the wrong way. If I use the word the right way, say **"yes."** If I use the word the wrong way, say **"no."** Then we'll talk about each word.

1. Riley **stacked** the cars in the driveway.

   Did I use the word **stacked** the right way? *No.*

   How do you know? (Student responses.)

2. Dion was playing his radio loudly while the television was on. It was very **peaceful** in the house.

   Did I use the word **peaceful** the right way? *No.*

   How do you know? (Student responses.)

3. The waitress needed two **trays** to get all the food to our table. Our entire family, including our aunts and uncles, went with us.

   Did I use the word **trays** the right way? *Yes.*

   How do you know? (Student responses.)

4. Tricia had to **rush** so she wouldn't miss the bus.

   Did I use the word **rush** the right way? *Yes.*

   How do you know? (Student responses.)

Review vocabulary words as needed.

 Review vocabulary words in appropriate context in Reading *Textbook A*.

Activity 3 Vocabulary Acquisition and Use

Display Vocabulary Acquisition and Use. **Have** students work with a neighbor to complete Vocabulary Acquisition and Use.
Today's vocabulary words are ____ and ____ [and ____ and ____].
Vocabulary words: **peaceful** and **quiet; place** and **spot**
Write the words on the lines provided. Then write the words in the boxes based on whether you think each word is less/smaller or more/larger than the other word. Below the boxes, write why you think word 1 is less/smaller and word 2 is more/larger than word 1.
Repeat for words 3 and 4. **Have** students share what they wrote. **Discuss** examples of how these words might be used.

Part B: Comprehension Strategies

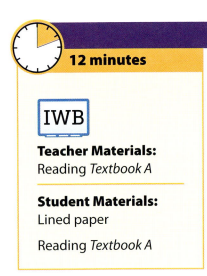

12 minutes

Teacher Materials:
Reading *Textbook A*

Student Materials:
Lined paper

Reading *Textbook A*

Display directions for activity.
Directions: Discuss how you know that Herman is an insect. Complete the writing frame with words that tell how you know Herman is an insect.

Writing Frame
Herman is an _____ because he has _____, and _____. He does not have _____ or _____.

Activity 1 Pair-Share Activity—Apply Knowledge (Level 3 of Bloom's Taxonomy)

 Direct students to Lessons 37–44, pages 228–284 in Reading *Textbook A*.

Discuss the steps in Pair-Share.
You'll do an activity called **Pair-Share** to describe some things you have learned about Herman. The directions are on the board. I'll read them to you.

Assign partners. **Provide** lined paper.
Step 1 is the **Pair** part of the activity. Discuss with your partner what you know about insects. Then complete the writing frame to show how you know that Herman is an insect. Work quickly. You have 7 minutes.

Guide students as they complete writing frame with "Herman is an insect because he has <u>six legs</u> and <u>three body parts</u>. He does not have <u>two body parts</u> or <u>eight legs</u>."

Call on as many students to share as time allows.
Step 2 is to **Share.** I'll call on pairs of students to share their work with the rest of the class.

5 minutes

Student Materials:
Reading Textbook A

Part C: Fluency Building

 Conduct after the lesson, using the story of the day.

Activity 1 Partner Reading

It's time for partner reading.
Direct students to the story of the day. **Assign** student partners as Partner 1 and Partner 2. **Monitor** partner reading. **Guide** as needed.

Lesson 45 **141**

Lesson 46

Materials
Teacher: 9-Compare and Contrast Chart; Reading *Textbook A*
Student: Vocabulary notebook; Reading *Textbook A*

8 minutes

Teacher Materials:
Reading Textbook A

Student Materials:
Vocabulary notebook

Reading Textbook A

Part A: Vocabulary Development

Activity 1 Learn New Vocabulary Word

Elicit responses to questions. **Guide** as needed.
Today you'll learn a new vocabulary word. **Cleared. Cleared** means "get rid of something you don't want." What does **cleared** mean? *Get rid of something you don't want.*

Another way to say "get rid of something you don't want" is **cleared.** What's another way to say "get rid of something you don't want"? *Cleared.*

The crew let the cleaning people know there were insects on the plane that they **did not want** and asked them **to get rid of** them. They sprayed and then told the crew the plane had been **cleared** of insects.

Discuss things examples of things that are cleared.

What's another way to say "get rid of something you don't want"? *Cleared.*

Direct students to write cleared and its definition in their vocabulary notebooks. **Guide** as needed.
Write **cleared** and what it means in your vocabulary notebook.

Activity 2 Review Vocabulary Word

Elicit responses to questions. **Guide** as needed.
What's another way to say "put things on top of each other"? *Stacked.*

Tell me a sentence using the word **stacked.** (Student responses.)
Discuss sentences.

 Review vocabulary words in appropriate context in Reading *Textbook A*.

142   Lesson 46

12 minutes

Teacher Materials:
Compare and Contrast Chart

Reading *Textbook A*

Student Materials:
Reading *Textbook A*

Part B: Comprehension Strategies

Activity 1 Identify Characters: Compare and Contrast—An After-Reading Strategy

Refer to the Nancy stories, Lessons 25–35, pages 152–215 and the Herman stories, Lessons 37–45, pages 229–293 in Reading *Textbook A*.
Elicit responses to questions. **Guide** as needed.
You've learned how to tell how things are the same and how they're different. You have practiced doing that skill with shapes, cups, animals, and dice. This strategy is called compare and contrast.

What's this strategy called? *Compare and contrast.*

You're going to use this strategy to tell how characters are the same and how they're different. When you tell how characters are the same, you compare the characters.

What do you do when you compare characters? *Tell how characters are the same.*

When you tell how characters are different, you contrast characters.

What do you do when you contrast characters? *Tell how characters are different.*

Today I want you to think about two characters—Nancy and Herman. We'll compare and contrast these two characters.

Show Compare and Contrast Chart. **Model** think-aloud to compare and contrast the characters.
I'll show you how I compare and contrast characters. I will use my Compare and Contrast chart.

Write sentences in the "How Same?" section of the chart. **Write** sentences in "How Different?" section of chart.

Lesson 46   **143**

Sample Wording for Think-Aloud

I'll think back to the stories about Nancy and Herman and try to think about how they're the same. When I write about how characters are the same, my sentences should begin, "They both…"

Sample Sentences for "How Same?" Box

They both are characters.
They both are small.
They both have names.
They both do things in the stories.
They both are in danger.
They both eat.
They both take naps.

When you write about how characters are different it is a little harder. Your sentence needs to tell about each character and tell how they are different. You say the name of the character, tell about that character, and then use the word "but" before you tell about the next character.

The Compare and Contrast chart makes this easier for you because it shows you the place to put in the word "but."

One more thing to think about when you contrast. You have to tell about the same quality. That means if you tell about size for the first character, you tell about size for the second character. If you tell about shape for the first character, you tell about shape for the second character. You can't tell about size for the first character and shape for the second character. This is tricky. Let me show you how I do it on the chart.

Sample Sentences for "How Different?" Box

Nancy		Herman
Nancy is human,	but	Herman is an insect.
Nancy thinks,	but	Herman does not think.
Nancy solves problems,	but	Herman does not solve problems.
Nancy stays home,	but	Herman travels on an airplane.
Nancy's mother tries to find her,	but	Herman's mother does not try to find him.
Nancy gets small,	but	Herman stays the same size.
Nancy has two legs,	but	Herman has six legs.

When you can tell how characters are the same and different, you're smart.

144　*Lesson 46*

Activity 2 Generate Questions—A During-Reading Strategy

 Direct students to Lesson 45, page 291 in Reading *Textbook A*.

Elicit responses to questions. **Guide** as needed.
Another strategy you can use to help you have better comprehension in both expository and narrative text is to ask questions. You've asked questions before reading for your KWL chart. You can also use the strategy while you are reading.

Sometimes it is hard to think of questions. Let's look at the story and see whether we can think of a question while we are reading. On page 291, it says that the passengers "were in for some rough air."

Guide students to generate questions from the text.
Who can think of a good question after reading that sentence? (Student responses.)

Yes, "I wonder what rough air is?" is a great question. Read on to find out the answer.

What is rough air? (Idea: *Windy air that makes an airplane bounce.*)

Remember, asking questions while you read keeps you interested in what you are reading.

Why should you ask questions while you read? (Idea: *It keeps you interested in what you read.*)

Part C: Fluency Building

5 minutes

Student Materials:
Reading *Textbook A*

 Conduct after the lesson, using the story of the day.

Activity 1 Partner Reading

It's time for partner reading.
Direct students to the story of the day. **Assign** student partners as Partner 1 and Partner 2. **Monitor** partner reading. **Guide** as needed.

Lesson 46

Lesson 47

Materials
Teacher: 7-KWL Chart; Reading *Textbook A*
Student: Vocabulary notebook; copy of 7-KWL Chart; Reading *Textbook A*

Part A: Vocabulary Development

8 minutes

Teacher Materials:
Reading *Textbook A*

Student Materials:
Vocabulary notebook
Reading *Textbook A*

Activity 1 Learn New Vocabulary Word

Elicit responses to questions. **Guide** as needed.
Today you'll learn a new vocabulary word. **Tugged. Tugged** means "pulled suddenly." What does **tugged** mean? *Pulled suddenly.*

Another way to say "pulled suddenly" is **tugged.** What's another way to say "pulled suddenly"? *Tugged.*

Herman was stuck in the spider web so he **pulled suddenly** to try and get out. Herman **tugged** as hard as he could but he seemed to be stuck.

Discuss things that are tugged.

What's another way to say "pulled suddenly"? *Tugged.*

Direct students to write tugged and its definition in their vocabulary notebooks. **Guide** as needed.
Write **tugged** and what it means in your vocabulary notebook.

Activity 2 Review Vocabulary Word

Elicit responses to questions. **Guide** as needed.
What's another way to say "get rid of something you don't want"? *Cleared.*

Tell me a sentence using the word **cleared.** (Student responses.)
Discuss sentences.

 Review vocabulary words in appropriate context in Reading *Textbook A*.

146 *Lesson 47*

Part B: Comprehension Strategies

12 minutes

Teacher Materials:
KWL Chart

Reading *Textbook A*

Student Materials:
KWL Chart

Reading *Textbook A*

Activity 1 KWL Chart: Topic and What I Know— A Before-Reading Strategy

Elicit responses to questions. **Guide** as needed.
You're going to activate your background knowledge for a new topic.

What do you do when you activate your background knowledge? (Idea: *Think about what you already know.*)

You'll be reading a passage called "The Eye of a Fly" in today's lesson. Before you read, it's a great idea to think about what you already know about this topic. Then you'll be able to connect what you know to what you learn.

Show KWL Chart.
You'll use a KWL chart to help you organize your thinking about expository text. Why do you use a KWL chart? (Idea: *To organize thinking about expository text.*)

Write the topic on KWL Chart. **Guide** students as they copy the topic on their charts.
The first box you write in is "Topic" box.

What should we write for the topic? *Fly eyes.*

Discuss students' background knowledge. **Record** three items in the "What I Know" section of KWL Chart. **Guide** students as they copy items on their charts.
Now let's work together to activate your background knowledge about fly eyes for the "What I Know" section of the KWL chart.

When you connect what you already know with the text, you'll be building more background knowledge in your mind and you'll be smarter.

Activity 2 KWL Chart: What I Wonder—A Before-Reading Strategy

Elicit responses to questions. **Guide** as needed. Show KWL Chart.

Next you'll write the questions you have about the topic in the "What I Wonder" section of the chart.

What will you write in this section of the chart? (Ideas: *Questions you have, what you wonder about.*)

What words can you use to help you think of questions? (Ideas: *Who, when, where, why, what, and how.*)

Let's work together to think of questions for the "What I Wonder" section of the KWL chart.

Lesson 47

Discuss possible questions. **Record** three questions in the "What I Wonder" section of KWL Chart. Possible questions: 1. How many eyes do flies have? 2. Do flies see color? 3. What do flies see? 4. What shape are flies' eyes? 5. Are flies' eyes the same as human eyes? **Guide** students as they copy questions on their charts.

Why is it important to ask questions before you read? (Idea: *Asking questions gets you interested in what you're going to learn—it makes you think about what you're going to read.*)

The text you read may or may not have the answers to your questions. That's okay. Just asking the questions helps you be smarter. If you don't find the answers to your questions, you might need to read more in another book to find out the answers.

Save teacher and student copies of KWL Chart for Lesson 48.

Activity 3 Generate Questions—A During-Reading Strategy

 Direct students to Lesson 46, page 301 in Reading *Textbook A*.

Elicit responses to questions. **Guide** as needed.
Another strategy you can use to help you have better comprehension in both expository and narrative text is to ask questions. You've asked questions before reading for your KWL chart. You can also use the strategy while you're reading.
What strategy can you use while you are reading to help keep you interested in what you are reading? (Idea: *Asking questions.*)

Assign student partners.
Sometimes it is hard to think of questions. Look at the story with a partner and see whether you can think of a question while you are reading.

Monitor students as they generate questions from the text. **Elicit** answers to student-generated questions.
Find a sentence that makes you think of a question. Write the sentence and the question and then we'll see who can answer your question.

Remember, asking questions while you read keeps you interested in what you are reading.

Why should you ask questions while you read? (Idea: *It keeps you interested in what you read.*)

Lesson 47

5 minutes

Student Materials:
Reading *Textbook A*

Part C: Fluency Building

 Conduct after the lesson, using the story of the day.

Activity 1 Partner Reading

It's time for partner reading.
Direct students to the story of the day. **Assign** student partners as Partner 1 and Partner 2. **Monitor** partner reading. **Guide** as needed.

Lesson 47

Lesson 48

Materials

Teacher: 7-KWL Chart (partially completed in Lesson 47); Reading *Textbook A*

Student: Vocabulary notebook; 7-KWL Chart (partially completed in Lesson 47); Reading *Textbook A*

Part A: Vocabulary Development

10 minutes

Teacher Materials:
Reading *Textbook A*

Student Materials:
Vocabulary notebook

Reading *Textbook A*

Activity 1 Learn New Vocabulary Word

Elicit responses to questions. **Guide** as needed.
Today you'll learn a new vocabulary word. **Eager. Eager** means "want very much." What does **eager** mean? *Want very much.*

Another way to say "want very much" is **eager.** What's another way to say "want very much"? *Eager.*

It was a long flight to Japan so the passengers **wanted very much** to get there. They all felt very **eager** to get to Japan.

Discuss examples of when someone seems eager.

What's another way to say "want very much"? *Eager.*

Direct students to write eager and its definition in their vocabulary notebooks. **Guide** as needed.

Write **eager** and what it means in your vocabulary notebook.

Activity 2 Review Vocabulary Word

Elicit responses to questions. **Guide** as needed.
What's another way to say "pulled suddenly"? *Tugged.*

Tell me a sentence using the word **tugged.** (Student responses.)
Discuss sentences.

 Review vocabulary words in appropriate context in Reading *Textbook A*.

150 Lesson 48

Part B: Comprehension Strategies

12 minutes

Teacher Materials:
KWL Chart (partially completed in Lesson 47)

Reading *Textbook A*

Student Materials:
KWL Chart (partially completed in Lesson 47)

Reading *Textbook A*

Activity 1 KWL Chart: What I Learned—An After-Reading Strategy

 Direct students to Lesson 47, pages 306–307 in Reading *Textbook A*.

Elicit responses to questions. **Guide** as needed. **Show** KWL Chart (partially completed in Lesson 47).

In the last lesson you read "The Eye of a Fly." It's time to write what you learned from the passage in the "What I Learned" section of the KWL chart.

When you write what you learned, you should write it in your own words rather than copy it right from the book.

Why should you write the ideas in your own words? (Idea: *That will help you remember the information later.*)

Call on students to read passage in parts. **Guide** students as they copy the sentences on their charts. **Record** the best sentences on the "What I Learned" section of KWL Chart.

Let's work together to fill out the "What I Learned" section of the chart.

Read the first part of the passage on the eyes of a fly. How can we put that part in our own words to record on our chart? (Student responses.)

We can write "Eyes catch pictures like water drops."

Read the next section. How can we put that part in our own words? (Student responses.)

We can write "Fly eyes are different than human eyes."

Read the next section. How can we put that part in our own words? (Student responses.)

We can write "Fly eyes have many drops."

Read the next section and study the diagram. How can we put that part in our own words? (Student responses.)

We can write "The two sides of a fly's eye catch different pictures at the same time."

You have now written the new things you learned from the expository text you read. You wrote the information in your own words.

Lesson 48

Activity 2 Generate Questions—A During-Reading Strategy

 Direct students to Lesson 47, pages 308–309 in Reading *Textbook A*.

Elicit responses to questions. **Guide** as needed. **Assign** student partners.
What strategy can you use while you're reading to help keep you interested in what you are reading? (Idea: *Asking questions.*)

Look at the story with a partner and see whether you can think of a question while you're reading. Find a sentence that makes you think of a question. Write the sentence and the question and then we will see who can answer your question.

Monitor students as they generate questions from the text. **Elicit** answers to student-generated questions.

Remember, asking questions while you read keeps you interested in what you are reading.

Why should you ask questions while you read? (Idea: *It keeps you interested in what you read.*)

Part C: Fluency Building

5 minutes

Student Materials:
Reading *Textbook A*

 Conduct after the lesson, using the story of the day.

Activity 1 Partner Reading

It's time for partner reading.
Direct students to the story of the day. **Assign** student partners as Partner 1 and Partner 2. **Monitor** partner reading. **Guide** as needed.

152 Lesson 48

Lesson 49

Materials
Teacher: 9-Compare and Contrast Chart; Reading *Textbook A*
Student: Vocabulary notebook; Reading *Textbook A*

8 minutes

Teacher Materials:
Reading *Textbook A*

Student Materials:
Vocabulary notebook

Reading *Textbook A*

Part A: Vocabulary Development

Activity 1 Learn New Vocabulary Word

Elicit responses to questions. **Guide** as needed.
Today you'll learn a new vocabulary word. **Temperature. Temperature** means "how hot or cold something is." What does **temperature** mean? *How hot or cold something is.*

Another way to say "how hot or cold something is" is **temperature.** What's another way to say "how hot or cold something is"? *Temperature.*

How hot or how cold an animal is depends on whether the animal is warm-blooded or cold-blooded. If an animal is warm-blooded, its **temperature** always stays the same.

Discuss examples of different temperatures.

What's another way to say "how hot or cold something is"? *Temperature.*

Direct students to write temperature and its definition in their vocabulary notebooks. **Guide** as needed.
Write **temperature** and what it means in your vocabulary notebook.

Activity 2 Review Vocabulary Word

Elicit responses to questions. **Guide** as needed.
What's another way to say "want very much"? *Eager.*

Tell me a sentence using the word **eager.** (Student responses.)
Discuss sentences.

 Review vocabulary words in appropriate context in Reading *Textbook A*.

12 minutes

Teacher Materials:
Compare and Contrast Chart

Reading *Textbook A*

Student Materials:
Reading *Textbook A*

Part B: Comprehension Strategies

Activity 1 Identify Characters: Compare and Contrast— An After-Reading Strategy

Refer to the Goad stories, Lessons 15–23, pages 85–138 and the Herman, stories, Lessons 37–48, pages 229–319 in Reading *Textbook A*.

Elicit responses to questions. **Guide** as needed.
You have learned how to tell how things are the same and how they are different. This strategy is called compare and contrast.

What's this strategy called? *Compare and contrast.*

You're going to use this strategy to tell how characters are the same and how they're different. When you tell how characters are the same, you compare the characters.

What do you do when you compare characters? *Tell how they are the same.*

When you tell how characters are different, you contrast characters.

What do you do when you contrast characters? *Tell how they are different.*

Today I want you think about two characters—Goad and Herman. You'll compare and contrast these two characters.

Show Compare and Contrast Chart.

Help me think about how to compare and contrast characters. We'll use the Compare and Contrast chart.

Let's think back to the stories about Goad and Herman and try to think about how they are the same. When I write about how characters are the same, my sentences should begin, "They both . . ."

Elicit sentences for "How Same?" section of chart. **Write** the best sentences on Compare and Contrast Chart.

Sample Sentences for "How Same?" Box
They both are characters.
They both are small.
They both have names.
They both do things in the stories.
They both are in danger.
They both eat.
They both escape from humans.

154 *Lesson 49*

When you write about how characters are different, it's a little harder. Your sentences need to tell about each character and tell how they are different. You say the name of the character, tell about that character and then use the word "but" before you tell about the next character.

Remember, when you tell how characters are different, you have to tell about the same quality. That means if you tell about what kind of animal for the first character, you tell about what kind of animal for the second character. If you tell about color for the first character, you tell about color for the second character. You can't tell about what kind of animal for the first character and what color for the second character. This is tricky. Let's think together about ways that Herman and Goad are different.

Elicit sentences for "How Different?" section of chart. **Write** best sentences on Compare and Contrast Chart.

Sample Sentences for "How Different?" Box		
Herman		**Goad**
Herman is a fly,	but	Goad is a toad.
Herman is not smart,	but	Goad is smart.
Herman has six legs,	but	Goad has four legs.
Herman travels in an airplane,	but	Goad stays at Four Mile Lake.
Herman eats garbage,	but	Goad eats flies.
Herman is not tricky,	but	Goad is tricky.
Herman gets caught in a spider web,	but	Goad does not get caught in traps.
Herman develops from a maggot,	but	Goad develops from a tadpole.

When you can tell how characters are the same and different, you're smart.

Activity 2 Generate Questions—A During-Reading Strategy

 Direct students to Lesson 48, pages 318–319 in Reading *Textbook A*.

Elicit responses to questions. **Guide** as needed.
What strategy can you use while you're reading to help keep you interested in what you are reading? (Idea: *Asking questions.*)

Sometimes it is hard to think of questions. Look at the story and see whether you can think of a question by yourself while you're reading. Find a sentence that makes you think of a question. Write the sentence and the question and then we will see who can answer your question.
Monitor students as they generate questions from the text. **Elicit** answers to student-generated questions.

Lesson 49

Remember, asking questions while you read keeps you interested in what you're reading.

Why should you ask questions while you read? (Idea: *It keeps you interested in what you read.*)

5 minutes

Student Materials:
Reading *Textbook A*

Part C: Fluency Building

 Conduct after the lesson, using the story of the day.

Activity 1 Partner Reading

It's time for partner reading.
Direct students to the story of the day. **Assign** student partners as Partner 1 and Partner 2. **Monitor** partner reading. **Guide** as needed.

Lesson 50

Materials
Teacher: Reading *Textbook A*, 2-Vocabulary Acquisition and Use, Writing Prompts, 3-My Writing Checklist
Student: Reading *Textbook A*, Vocabulary notebook; Copy of 2-Vocabulary Acquisition and Use, Copy of 3-My Writing Checklist, Lined paper

8 minutes

Teacher Materials:
Reading *Textbook A*
Vocabulary Acquisition and Use

Student Materials:
Vocabulary Notebook
Reading *Textbook A*
Vocabulary Acquisition and Use

Part A: Vocabulary Development

Activity 1 Vocabulary Notebook Review

Guide students as they study all words.
Today you'll study from your vocabulary notebook. Studying your words and what they mean will help you know your words even better. You'll study the eight words we studied over the past two weeks.

Activity 2 Cumulative Vocabulary Review

Elicit responses to questions. **Guide** as needed.
Directions: Listen and tell me whether I use our vocabulary words the right way or the wrong way. If I use the word the right way, say **"yes."** If I use the word the wrong way, say **"no."** Then we'll talk about each word.

1. Watching the sun come up in the early hours of the morning is very peaceful. No one is awake and it is very quiet in the house.

   Did I use the word **peaceful** the right way? *Yes.*

   How do you know? (Student responses.)

2. Miguel had to **rush** to get his letter in the mailbox before the mail was picked up. He didn't want his letter to be late.

   Did I use the word **rush** the right way? *Yes.*

   How do you know? (Student responses.)

3. Terri was sunburned, so she was **eager** to get back out into the sun for a few more hours.

   Did I use the word **eager** the right way? *No.*

   How do you know? (Student responses.)

4. Peter **tugged** at his mother's purse to get her attention. She was busy talking to someone else.

   Did I use the word **tugged** the right way? *Yes.*

   How do you know? (Student responses.)

Lesson 50

5. Stacey **cleared** the table after dinner. She liked to help her parents.

   Did I use the word **cleared** the right way? *Yes.*

   How do you know? (Student responses.)

6. As he went around the table, Paul **stacked** the milk on top of the glasses.

   Did I use the word **stacked** the right way? *No.*

   How do you know? (Student responses.)

7. Zack's mother put out **trays** of cookies for a snack at the birthday party.

   Did I use the word **trays** the right way? *Yes.*

   How do you know? (Student responses.)

8. Della wanted to know what the **temperature** was going to be outside so she could decide what indoor movie to see.

   Did I use the word **temperature** the right way? *No.*

   How do you know? (Student responses.)

Review vocabulary words as needed.

 Review vocabulary words in appropriate context in Reading *Textbook A*.

Activity 3 Vocabulary Acquisition and Use

Display Vocabulary Acquisition and Use. **Have** students work with a neighbor to complete Vocabulary Acquisition and Use.
Today's vocabulary words are ____ and ____ [and ____ and ____].
Vocabulary words: **cleared** and **removed; tugged** and **pulled**
Write the words on the lines provided. Then write the words in the boxes based on whether you think each word is less/smaller or more/larger than the other word. Below the boxes, write why you think word 1 is less/smaller and word 2 is more/larger than word 1.
Repeat for words 3 and 4. **Have** students share what they wrote. **Discuss** examples of how these words might be used.

12 minutes

Student Materials:
Lined paper

Part B: Comprehension Strategies

Display directions for the activity. **Assign** partners.
Directions: Discuss how you and your partner are the same. Write three sentences on how you're the same that begin with "We both…" Examine these sentences, and choose your favorite one.

Activity 1 Pair-Share Activity—Apply Knowledge (Level 3 of Bloom's Taxonomy)

Discuss the steps in Pair-Share. **Provide** writing paper.
You'll do an activity called **Pair-Share** to show some things you have learned in previous lessons. The directions are on the board. I'll read them to you.

Step 1 is the **Pair** part of the activity. Discuss how you and your partner are the same. Write 3 sentences that tell how you both are the same. Remember to use the word "both" in those sentences. Think about how you look, what you like to do, what you like to eat, and what you are good at. Then choose your favorite sentence. You have 8 minutes to complete this job. Work quickly so you'll finish on time.
Guide students as they write sentences.

Call on as many students to share as time allows.
Step 2 is to **Share.** I'll call on pairs of students to share their work with the rest of the class.

5 minutes

Student Materials:
Reading *Textbook A*

Part C: Fluency Building

 Conduct after the lesson, using the story of the day.

Activity 1 Partner Reading

It's time for partner reading.
Direct students to the story of the day. **Assign** student partners as Partner 1 and Partner 2. **Monitor** partner reading. Guide as needed.

Lesson 50 **159**

Part D: Writing/Language Arts

10 minutes

Teacher Materials:
Writing Prompts

My Writing Checklist

Student Materials:
Lined Paper

My Writing Checklist

Activity 1 Write and Use Parts of Speech and Conventions

Time to write using a writing prompt based on the stories we've been reading.

Assign student partners. **Distribute** lined paper to students. **Display** writing prompts and have students choose one to write about or assign a writing prompt of your choice. **Review** parts of speech and punctuation as well as the writing checklist with students. **Tell** students to write one to two paragraphs (minimum of four sentences per paragraph) on their own to answer the writing prompt. **Tell** them to use their writing checklist (first column labeled "Did I use them?") to ensure they include important parts of speech or punctuation in their writing. **Tell** students which parts of speech or punctuation to focus on, if you wish. **Model** what it means to answer a writing prompt and to use the writing checklist during and after the writing process, as needed. **Monitor** and guide students as needed. **Model** what it means to have a neighbor look over his or her neighbor's writing and to complete the writing checklist (second column labeled "Did my neighbor use them?"), as needed. **Have** students share what they wrote as time permits.

Writing Prompt 1	Writing Prompt 2	Writing Prompt 3
Describe what Herman could do on a plane that you couldn't do on a plane.	Would you rather live in San Francisco, California, or New York City? Why?	Would you rather live near an ocean or in the mountains? Why?

160 Lesson 50

Lesson 51

Materials
Teacher: Reading *Textbooks A and B*
Student: Vocabulary notebook; Reading *Textbooks A and B*

8 minutes

Teacher Materials:
Reading *Textbooks A and B*

Student Materials:
Vocabulary notebook

Reading *Textbooks A and B*

Part A: Vocabulary Development

Activity 1 Learn New Vocabulary Word

Elicit responses to questions. **Guide** as needed.
Today you'll learn a new vocabulary word. **Aisle. Aisle** means "pathway between things." What does **aisle** mean? *Pathway between things.*

Another way to say "pathway between things" is **aisle.** What's another way to say "pathway between things"? *Aisle.*

There is not a lot of room on an airplane. There is only a **pathway between things** on both sides to walk up and down. The **aisle** is used by both the passengers and the flight attendants.

Discuss places where students have used an aisle.

What's another way to say "pathway between things"? *Aisle.*

Direct students to write aisle and its definition in their vocabulary notebooks. **Guide** as needed.
Write **aisle** and what it means in your vocabulary notebook.

Activity 2 Review Vocabulary Word

What's another way to say "how hot or how cold something is"? *Temperature.*

Tell me a sentence using the word **temperature.** (Student responses.)
Discuss sentences.

  Review vocabulary words in their appropriate context in Reading *Textbook B*.

Lesson 51   **161**

12 minutes

Teacher Materials:
Reading *Textbook A*

Student Materials:
Reading *Textbook A*

Part B: Comprehension Strategies

Activity 1 Comprehension Monitoring: Mental Imaging—A During-Reading Strategy

Elicit responses to questions. **Guide** as needed.
Today you're going to learn a new strategy to use when you're reading. It'll help you understand what you read while you're reading. The strategy is called mental imaging. What's the strategy called? *Mental imaging.*

Mental imaging helps you understand and enjoy a story more. What does mental imaging help you do? *Understand and enjoy a story more.*

Mental imaging is making pictures in your mind about what you're reading. What's mental imaging? *Making pictures in your mind about what you're reading.*

You can use this strategy with expository or narrative text. When you use mental imaging with narrative text, you can make pictures in your mind of the characters, setting, and events to help you understand the story better.

 Direct students to Lesson 47 on pages 308–309 of Reading *Textbook A*.

Model think-aloud for mental imaging.
In an earlier lesson you read, "Herman Tries to Escape." I'm going to show you how I use mental imaging to help me understand the passage.

Sample Wording for Think-Aloud

The first paragraph of the story tells about Herman trying to escape from the spider. As I read it, I make pictures in my mind. I imagine Herman stuck in the web and buzzing his wings very hard. Then I imagine the spider moving toward him, kind of like a scary movie. I picture Herman trying and trying to get free.

The next paragraph tells that the spider is three times bigger than Herman. Now I imagine a huge spider, as big as the palm of my hand trying to bite poor little Herman. The more Herman tries to get away, the harder he gets stuck in the web. I'm feeling scared inside while I read that part. I'm afraid that Herman will not get away.

The sixth paragraph tells about the spider trying to wrap Herman in silk. I see a picture in my mind of the huge spider grabbing Herman with two of its eight legs and turning Herman over. Then as the spider turns Herman, he gets free and flies away. I imagine him flying away as fast as he can. I feel happy that he escaped from the spider and the web. I think that Herman must feel happy too.

162 *Lesson 51*

Mental imaging is making pictures in your mind about what you're reading. What's mental imaging? *Making pictures in your mind about what you're reading.*

We'll practice using mental imaging in future lessons.

Part C: Fluency Building

5 minutes

Student Materials:
Reading *Textbook B*

 Conduct after the lesson, using the story of the day.

Activity 1 Partner Reading

It's time for partner reading.
Direct students to the story of the day. **Assign** student partners as Partner 1 and Partner 2. **Monitor** partner reading. **Guide** as needed.

Lesson 51   163

Lesson 52

Materials
Teacher: Reading *Textbook B*
Student: Vocabulary notebook; Reading *Textbook B*

8 minutes

Teacher Materials:
Reading *Textbook B*

Student Materials:
Vocabulary notebook
Reading *Textbook B*

Part A: Vocabulary Development

Activity 1 Learn New Vocabulary Word

Elicit responses to questions. **Guide** as needed.
Today you'll learn a new vocabulary word. **Fuel. Fuel** means "gas." What does **fuel** mean? *Gas.*

Another word for "gas" is **fuel.** What's another word for "gas"? *Fuel.*

When a plane gets where it's going, it needs **gas.** Once the plane has gotten **fuel,** it can take off again.

Discuss things that need fuel.

What's another word for "gas"? *Fuel.*

Direct students to write fuel and its definition in their vocabulary notebooks. **Guide** as needed.
Write **fuel** and what it means in your vocabulary notebook.

Activity 2 Review Vocabulary Word

Elicit responses to questions. **Guide** as needed.
What's another way to say "pathway between seats"? *Aisle.*

Tell me a sentence using the word **aisle.** (Student responses.)
Discuss sentences.

 Review vocabulary words in their appropriate context in Reading *Textbook B*.

164 Lesson 52

12 minutes

Teacher Materials:
Reading *Textbook B*

Student Materials:
Reading *Textbook B*

Part B: Comprehension Strategies

Activity 1 Comprehension Monitoring: Mental Imaging—A During-Reading Strategy

Elicit responses to questions. **Guide** as needed.
In the last lesson, you learned about a strategy to help you understand what you read while you're reading. Mental imaging helps you understand and enjoy a story more. What does mental imaging help you do? *Understand and enjoy a story more.*

Mental imaging is making pictures in your mind about what you're reading. What's mental imaging? *Making pictures in your mind about what you're reading.*

When you use mental imaging with narrative text, you can make pictures in your mind of the characters, setting, and events to help you understand the story better.

 Direct students to Lesson 51 on pages 2–4 of Reading *Textbook B*.

Model mental imaging by looking at the title and pictures and reading the text.
In the last lesson, you read "Herman Flies to Italy." I'm going to show you how I use mental imaging to make pictures in my mind as I read.

You'll practice using mental imaging in upcoming lessons.

5 minutes

Student Materials:
Reading *Textbook B*

Part C: Fluency Building

 Conduct after the lesson, using the story of the day.

Activity 1 Partner Reading

It's time for partner reading.
Direct students to the story of the day. **Assign** student partners as Partner 1 and Partner 2. **Monitor** partner reading. **Guide** as needed.

Lesson 52 **165**

Lesson 53

Materials
Teacher: 7-KWL Chart; Reading *Textbook B*
Student: Vocabulary notebook; copy of 7-KWL Chart; Reading *Textbook B*

8 minutes

Teacher Materials:
Reading *Textbook B*

Student Materials:
Vocabulary notebook

Reading *Textbook B*

Part A: Vocabulary Development

Activity 1 Learn New Vocabulary Word

Elicit responses to questions. **Guide** as needed.
Today you'll learn a new vocabulary word. **Objects. Objects** means "things you can see, hold, or touch." What does **objects** mean? *Things you can see, hold, or touch.*

Another word for "things you can see, hold, or touch" is **objects.** What's another word for "things you can see, hold, or touch"? *Objects.*

Whirlpools catch **things you can see, hold, or touch** and spin them around and around. **Objects** could get stuck going around and around in a whirlpool.

Discuss examples of objects.

What's another word for "things you can see, hold, or touch"? *Objects*

Direct students to write objects and its definition in their vocabulary notebooks. **Guide** as needed.
Write **objects** and what it means in your vocabulary notebook.

Activity 2 Review Vocabulary Word

Elicit responses to questions. **Guide** as needed.
What's another word for "gas"? *Fuel.*

Tell me a sentence using the word **fuel.** (Student responses.)
Discuss sentences.

  Review vocabulary words in their appropriate context in Reading *Textbook B*.

166   Lesson 53

Part B: Comprehension Strategies

Teacher Materials:
KWL Chart

Reading *Textbook B*

Student Materials:
KWL Chart

Reading *Textbook B*

Activity 1 KWL Chart: Topic and What I Know— A Before-Reading Strategy

Elicit responses to questions. **Guide** as needed.
You're going to activate your background knowledge for a new topic. What do you do when you activate your background knowledge? (Idea: *Think about what you already know.*)

You'll be reading a passage called "Facts about an Ocean Liner" in today's lesson.

Why is it a good idea to think about your background knowledge before you read? (Idea: *Then you'll be able to connect what you know to what you learn.*)

Show KWL Chart.
You'll use a KWL Chart to help you organize your thinking about expository text. Why do you use a KWL Chart? (Idea: *To organize thinking about expository text.*)

Write topic on KWL Chart. **Guide** students as they copy the topic on their charts.
The first box you write in is the "Topic" box.

What should we write for the topic? *Ocean liners.*

Discuss students' background knowledge. **Record** three items in "What I Know" section of KWL Chart. **Guide** students as they write items on their charts.
Now let's work together to activate your background knowledge about ocean liners for the "What I Know" section of the KWL Chart.

When you connect what you already know with the text, you'll be building more background knowledge in your brain and you'll be smarter.

Activity 2 KWL Chart: What I Wonder— A Before-Reading Strategy

Elicit responses to questions. **Guide** as needed. **Show** KWL Chart.
Next you'll write the questions you have about the topic in the "What I Wonder" section of the chart.

What will you write in this section of the chart? (Ideas: *Questions you have; what you wonder about.*)

What words can you use to help you think of questions? (Ideas: *Who, when, where, why, what, and how.*)

Let's work together to think of questions about ocean liners for the "What I Wonder" section of the KWL Chart.

Discuss possible questions. **Record** three questions in the "What I Wonder" section of KWL Chart. **Guide** students as they write questions on their charts.

Lesson 53   **167**

Why is it important to ask questions before you read? (Idea: *Asking questions gets you interested in what you're going to learn—it makes you think about what you're going to read.*)

The text you read may or may not have the answers to your questions. That's okay. Just asking the questions helps you be smarter. If you don't find the answers to your questions, you might need to read more in another book to find out the answers.

Save teacher and student copies of KWL Chart for Lesson 54.

Activity 3 Comprehension Monitoring: Mental Imaging— A During-Reading Strategy

Elicit responses to questions. **Guide** as needed.
You are learning about a strategy to help you understand what you read while you're reading. Mental imaging helps you understand and enjoy a story more. What does mental imaging help you do? *Understand and enjoy a story more.*

Mental imaging is making pictures in your mind about what you're reading. What's mental imaging? *Making pictures in your mind about what you're reading.*

When you use mental imaging with narrative text, you can make pictures in your mind of the characters, setting, and events to help you understand the story better.

 Direct students to Lesson 52 on page 10 of Reading *Textbook B*.

Elicit student responses for mental images.
In the last lesson, you read, "Herman's Last Trip." Look at the first sentence in the fifth paragraph and see whether you can make a mental image for " . . . Herman caught a good smell and followed it."

You'll practice using mental imaging in upcoming lessons.

Part C: Fluency Building

5 minutes

Student Materials:
Reading Textbook B

 Conduct after the lesson, using the story of the day.

Activity 1 Partner Reading

It's time for partner reading.
Direct students to the story of the day. **Assign** student partners as Partner 1 and Partner 2. **Monitor** partner reading. **Guide** as needed.

Lesson 54

Materials
Teacher: 7-KWL Chart (partially completed in Lesson 53); Reading *Textbook B*
Student: Vocabulary notebook; 7-KWL Chart (partially completed in Lesson 53); Reading *Textbook B*

Part A: Vocabulary Development

8 minutes

Teacher Materials:
Reading *Textbook B*

Student Materials:
Vocabulary notebook
Reading *Textbook B*

Activity 1 Learn New Vocabulary Word

Elicit responses to questions. **Guide** as needed.
Today you'll learn a new vocabulary word. **Disappeared. Disappeared** means "left your sight." What does **disappeared** mean? *Left your sight.*

Another way to say "left your sight" is **disappeared.** What's another way to say "left your sight"? *Disappeared.*

The girls could no longer see the lifeboats; the lifeboats had **left their sight.** They looked and looked but the lifeboats had **disappeared.**

Discuss things that have disappeared.

What's another way to say "left your sight"? *Disappeared.*

Direct students to write disappeared and its definition in their vocabulary notebooks. **Guide** as needed.
Write **disappeared** and what it means in your vocabulary notebook.

Activity 2 Review Vocabulary Word

Elicit responses to questions. **Guide** as needed.
What's another word for "things you can see, hold, or touch"? *Objects.*

Tell me a sentence using the word **objects.** (Student responses.)
Discuss sentences.

 Review vocabulary words in appropriate context in Reading *Textbook B*.

Lesson 54 **169**

12 minutes

Teacher Materials:
KWL Chart (partially completed in Lesson 53)

Reading *Textbook B*

Student Materials:
KWL Chart (partially completed in Lesson 53)

Reading *Textbook B*

Part B: Comprehension Strategies

Activity 1 KWL Chart: What I Learned— An After-Reading Strategy

 Direct students to Lesson 53 on pages 20–21 of Reading *Textbook B*.

Elicit responses to questions. **Guide** as needed. **Show** KWL Chart (partially completed in Lesson 53).
In the last lesson you read "Facts about an Ocean Liner." It's time to write what you learned from the passage in the "What I Learned" section of the KWL Chart.

When you write what you learned, you should write it in your own words rather than copy it right from the book.

Why should you write the ideas in your own words? (Idea: *That will help you remember the information later.*)

Let's work together to fill out the "What I Learned" section of the chart.

Call on students to read passage in parts. **Guide** students as they copy the sentences on their charts. **Record** the best sentences on the "What I Learned" section of KWL Chart.
Read the first part of the passage on ocean liners. How can we put that part in our own words to record on our chart? (Student responses.)

We can write: "Very large ships are ocean liners."

Read the next section. How can we put that part in our own words? (Student responses.)

We can write: "Ocean liners are ships that carry passengers."

Read the next section. How can we put that part in our own words? (Student responses.)

We can write: "Parts of the ocean liner have special names."

Read the next section and study the diagram. How can we put that part in our own words? (Student responses.)

We can write: "Names on ocean liners: bow is the front, stern is the back, decks are floors, and bulkheads are walls."

You've now written the new things you learned from the expository text you read. You wrote the information in your own words.

170 Lesson 54

Activity 2 Comprehension Monitoring: Mental Imaging— A During-Reading Strategy

Elicit responses to questions. **Guide** as needed.
You are learning about a strategy to help you understand what you read while you're reading. Mental imaging helps you understand and enjoy a story more. What does mental imaging help you do? *Understand and enjoy a story more.*

Mental imaging is making pictures in your mind about what you're reading. What's mental imaging? *Making pictures in your mind about what you're reading.*

When you use mental imaging with narrative text, you can make pictures in your mind of the characters, setting, and events to help you understand the story better. You can also use it to help you remember facts in expository texts.

 Direct students to Lesson 53 on page 18 of Reading *Textbook B*.

Elicit student responses for mental images.
In the last lesson, you read "Facts about Whirlpools." Look at the first sentence in the second paragraph and see whether you can make a mental image for "You have seen whirlpools in sinks."

Making a mental image when you read expository text can help you remember facts in the passage. You'll practice using mental imaging in upcoming lessons.

Part C: Fluency Building

5 minutes

Student Materials:
Reading Textbook B

 Conduct after the lesson, using the story of the day.

Activity 1 Partner Reading

It's time for partner reading.
Direct students to the story of the day. **Assign** student partners as Partner 1 and Partner 2. **Monitor** partner reading. **Guide** as needed.

Lesson 54 **171**

Lesson 55

Materials

Teacher: Reading *Textbook B,* 2-Vocabulary Acquisition and Use

Student: Vocabulary notebook; Reading *Textbook B,* Copy of 2-Vocabulary Acquisition and Use; Drawing paper

8 minutes

Teacher Materials:
Reading *Textbook B*

Vocabulary Acquisition and Use

Student Materials:
Vocabulary notebook

Reading *Textbook B*

Vocabulary Acquisition and Use

Part A: Vocabulary Development

Activity 1 Vocabulary Notebook Review

Today you'll study from your vocabulary notebook. Studying your words and what they mean will help you know your words even better. You'll look at the four words we studied this week.

Activity 2 Cumulative Vocabulary Review

Elicit responses to questions. **Guide** as needed.
Directions: Listen and tell me whether I use our vocabulary words the right way or the wrong way. If I use the word the right way, say **"yes."** If I use the word the wrong way, say **"no."** Then we'll talk about each word.

1. Leeza asked in what **aisle** in the store she could find the ketchup.

    Did I use the word **aisle** the right way? *Yes.*

    How do you know? (Student responses.)

2. Thomas asked his mother if they could stop and get **fuel** for his bicycle.

    Did I use the word **fuel** the right way? *No.*

    How do you know? (Student responses.)

3. Troy watched the balloon he had let go until it **disappeared** in the sky.

    Did I use the word **disappeared** the right way? *Yes.*

    How do you know? (Student responses.)

4. Air and wind are **objects.**

    Did I use the word **objects** the right way? *No.*

    How do you know? Student responses.

Review vocabulary words as needed.

 Review vocabulary words in appropriate context in Reading *Textbook B.*

172   Lesson 55

Activity 3 Vocabulary Acquisition and Use

Display Vocabulary Acquisition and Use. **Have** students work with a neighbor to complete Vocabulary Acquisition and Use.
Today's vocabulary words are ____ and ____ [and ____ and ____].
Vocabulary words: **peaceful** and **quiet**; **place** and **spot**
Write the words on the lines provided. Then write the words in the boxes based on whether you think each word is less/smaller or more/larger than the other word. Below the boxes, write why you think word 1 is less/smaller and word 2 is more/larger than word 1.

Repeat for words 3 and 4. **Have** students share what they wrote. **Discuss** examples of how these words might be used.

Part B: Comprehension Strategies

12 minutes

Teacher Materials:
Reading *Textbook B*

Student Materials:
Drawing paper

Reading *Textbook B*

Display directions for activity.
Directions: Discuss the parts of an ocean liner. Illustrate an ocean liner by making a sketch and labeling the parts of the ocean liner. Write a sentence that explains how ocean liners are used.

Activity 1 Pair-Share Activity—Apply Knowledge (Level 3 of Bloom's Taxonomy)

 Direct students to Lesson 53 on pages 20–21 of Reading *Textbook B*.

Discuss the steps in the Pair-Share activity.
You'll do an activity called **Pair-Share** to describe some things you have learned in recent lessons. The directions are on the board. I'll read them to you.

Assign partners. **Provide** drawing paper.
Step 1 is the **Pair** part of the activity. Discuss the parts of an ocean liner with your partner to make a drawing of an ocean liner. Label the parts of the ocean liner with the special names used for the parts of an ocean liner. Then write a sentence in your own words to explain how ocean liners are used. Decide who will do what part of the job. Work quickly. You have 7 minutes.
Guide students to draw and label an ocean liner and then write a sentence to explain that ocean liners are used to carry passengers.

Call on as many students to share as time allows.
Step 2 is to **Share.** I'll call on pairs of students to share their work with the rest of the class.

Lesson 55

5 minutes

Student Materials:
Reading *Textbook B*

Part C: Fluency Building

 Conduct after the lesson, using the story of the day.

Activity 1 Partner Reading

It's time for partner reading.
Direct students to the story of the day. **Assign** student partners as Partner 1 and Partner 2. **Monitor** partner reading. **Guide** as needed.

Lesson 56

Materials

Teacher: Reading *Textbook B*

Student: Vocabulary notebook; photocopy of Story 54 for each student group; 4 highlighters of varying colors for each student group

8 minutes

Teacher Materials:
Reading *Textbook B*

Student Materials:
Vocabulary notebook

Reading *Textbook B*

Part A: Vocabulary Development

Activity 1 — Learn New Vocabulary Word

Elicit responses to questions. **Guide** as needed.
Today you'll learn a new vocabulary word. **Bunches. Bunches** means "groups of things." What does **bunches** mean? *Groups of things.*

Another way to say "groups of things" is **bunches.** What's another way to say "groups of things"? *Bunches.*

Kathy and her sister were hungry, so they looked around for something to eat. They found **groups of** bananas. The girls ate most of the **bunches** of bananas they found.

Discuss examples of things that are in <u>bunches</u>.

What's another way to say "groups of things"? *Bunches.*

Direct students to write <u>bunches</u> and its definition in their vocabulary notebooks. **Guide** as needed.
Write **bunches** and what it means in your vocabulary notebook.

Activity 2 — Review Vocabulary Word

What's another way to say "left your sight"? *Disappeared.*

Tell me a sentence using the word **disappeared.** (Student responses.) **Discuss** sentences.

 Review vocabulary words in appropriate context in Reading *Textbook B*.

Lesson 56 **175**

Part B: Comprehension Strategies

12 minutes

Teacher Materials:
Reading *Textbook B*

Student Materials:
Photocopy of Story 54 for each student group

4 highlighters of varying colors for each student group

Activity 1 Comprehension Monitoring: Reading Dialogue with Prosody—A During-Reading Strategy

Show what quotation marks look like on the board.
In order to read with high comprehension, it is important to pay attention to the punctuation marks in a story. Quotation marks are punctuation marks that show that a character is talking in a story. The words characters say in narratives are called dialogue. Often, narratives have lots of dialogue. Sometimes the dialogue can get confusing. We will practice paying attention to the quotation marks and reading the story in a way that will help us understand which character is saying the words.

Dialogue is marked with quotation marks. How's dialogue marked in stories? (Idea: *With quotation marks or talking marks.*)

What's dialogue? (Idea: *The words characters say in the story.*)

Group students in groups of 4. **Provide** copies of story for students to mark the dialogue. **Have** students mark dialogue with highlighters—4 colors needed.
Monitor groups as they mark the story.

This is the story "Linda and Kathy Escape from a Sinking Ship." I want you to mark the dialogue for the characters. One color will be for the words that Linda says. Mark what Kathy says with another color. Mark the words from the loudspeaker, the shouting voice, and the man's voice in a third color. You also need a narrator to read all the parts not in quotation marks, so those words should be in a fourth color.

Monitor groups as they practice dialogue.
Your turn to read the story with four people. Try to read with expression. Decide who'll read which part. The colors will help you know when it's your turn. Take turns, and try to make the dialogue interesting.

When you read dialogue and pay attention to the quotation marks, you will better understand what you read.
Encourage students to perform parts of the dialogue in front of the class, after practice.

176 Lesson 56

Activity 2 | Comprehension Monitoring: Mental Imaging— A During-Reading Strategy

Elicit responses to questions. **Guide** as needed.
You are learning about a strategy to help you understand what you read while you're reading. Mental imaging helps you understand and enjoy a story more. What does mental imaging help you do? *Understand and enjoy a story more.*

Mental imaging is making pictures in your mind about what you're reading. What's mental imaging? *Making pictures in your mind about what you're reading.* Why do you use mental imaging with narrative text? (Idea: *You can make pictures in your mind of the characters, setting, and events to help you understand the story better.*)

 Direct students to Lesson 54 on page 29 of Reading *Textbook B*.

Assign student partners. **Elicit** student responses for mental images.
In Lesson 54, you read "Linda and Kathy Escape from a Sinking Ship." Look at page 29 with a partner and see whether you can find a sentence where you can make a mental image. Then we'll talk about the sentence you found and the mental image you made.

You'll practice using mental imaging in upcoming lessons.

5 minutes

Student Materials:
Reading *Textbook B*

Part C: Fluency Building

 Conduct after the lesson, using the story of the day.

Activity 1 | Partner Reading

It's time for partner reading.
Direct students to the story of the day. **Assign** student partners as Partner 1 and Partner 2. **Monitor** partner reading. **Guide** as needed.

Lesson 56 **177**

Lesson 57

Materials
Teacher: Reading *Textbook B*
Student: Vocabulary notebook; Reading *Textbook B*

8 minutes

Teacher Materials:
Reading *Textbook B*

Student Materials:
Vocabulary notebook

Reading *Textbook B*

Part A: Vocabulary Development

Activity 1 Prefix Introduction

Elicit response to question. **Guide** as needed.
Today you'll learn about a **prefix.** A **prefix** is a "word part added to the beginning of a word that changes its meaning." What do we call a "word part added to the beginning of a word that changes its meaning"? *Prefix.*

Activity 2 Learn New Prefix

Elicit responses to questions. **Guide** as needed.
Today you'll learn a new prefix. **Re-. Re-** means "again." What does **re-** mean? *Again.*

The prefix that means "again" is **re-.** What's the prefix that means "again"? *Re-.*

Redo. **Re**do means do **again. Re**try. **Re**try means try **again. Re**play. What does **re**play mean? *Play again.*

So when we add the prefix **re-** to the beginning of words we change what they mean. **Write.** Adding **re-** to **write** makes it **re**write. What does **re**write mean? *Write again.*

Tell me a **re-** word. (Student responses.)
Discuss responses.

What prefix means "again"? *Re-.*

Activity 3 Review Vocabulary Word

Elicit responses to questions. **Guide** as needed.
What's another way to say "groups of things"? *Bunches.*

Tell me a sentence using the word **bunches.** (Student responses.)
Discuss sentences.

 Review vocabulary words in appropriate context in Reading *Textbook B*.

178 Lesson 57

12 minutes

Teacher Materials:
Reading *Textbook B*

Student Materials:
Reading *Textbook B*

Part B: Comprehension Strategies

Activity 1 — Comprehension Monitoring: Mental Imaging—A During-Reading Strategy

Elicit responses to questions. **Guide** as needed.
You are learning about a strategy to help you understand what you read while you're reading. What does mental imaging help you do? *Understand and enjoy a story more.*

What's mental imaging? *Making pictures in your mind about what you're reading.*

Why do you use mental imaging with narrative text? (Idea: *You can make pictures in your mind of the characters, setting, and events to help you understand the story better.*)

 Direct students to Lesson 56 on page 51 of Reading *Textbook B*.

Assign student partners. **Elicit** student responses for mental images.
In Lesson 56, you read "Alone on an Island." Look at page 51 with a partner and see if you can find a sentence in which you can make a mental image. Then we'll talk about the sentence you found and the mental image you made.

Remember to use mental imaging when you read to help you understand and enjoy the story.

Activity 2 — Determine Text Type and Establish Purpose for Reading—A Before-Reading Strategy

 Direct students to Lesson 57, pages 55–56 in Reading *Textbook B*.

Elicit responses to questions. **Guide** as needed.
Today you'll read both narrative and expository text in your reading lesson.

What's the title of the first section you'll read? *"Facts about Coconuts."*

Do you think this section is expository or narrative? *Expository.*

Why do you think it's expository? (Idea: *It looks like it teaches information about coconuts.*)

Why do you read expository text? *To learn new facts or information.*

Why will you read "Facts about Coconuts"? (Idea: *To learn new information about coconuts.*)

Lesson 57

The author wrote "Facts about Coconuts" to build your background knowledge. If you don't know about coconuts, it'll be hard to understand the narrative story about Linda and Kathy. So you're reading this expository passage in order to understand the narrative passage you'll read. You're adding information to your background knowledge about coconuts.

Why will you read "Facts about Coconuts?" (Idea: *To build background knowledge about coconuts so you can understand the narrative story you will read.*)

Part C: Fluency Building

5 minutes

Student Materials:
Reading *Textbook B*

 Conduct after the lesson, using the story of the day.

Activity 1 Partner Reading

It's time for partner reading.

Direct students to the story of the day. **Assign** student partners as Partner 1 and Partner 2. **Monitor** partner reading. **Guide** as needed.

180 *Lesson 57*

Lesson 58

Materials
Teacher: 6-Narrative Story Map; Reading *Textbook B*
Student: Vocabulary notebook; copy of 6-Narrative Story Map; Reading *Textbook B*

8 minutes

Teacher Materials:
Reading *Textbook B*

Student Materials:
Vocabulary notebook
Reading *Textbook B*

Part A: Vocabulary Development

Activity 1 Learn New Vocabulary Word

Elicit responses to questions. **Guide** as needed.
Today you'll learn a new vocabulary word. **Vines. Vines** means "climbing plants." What does **vines** mean? *Climbing plants.*

Another way to say "climbing plants" is **vines.** What's another way to say "climbing plants"? *Vines.*

Linda and Kathy noticed there were **climbing plants.** They decided they could use the **vines** for fishing lines.

Discuss examples of vines.

What's another way to say **climbing plants?** *Vines.*

Direct students to write vines. and its definition in their vocabulary notebooks. **Guide** as needed.
Write **vines** and what it means in your vocabulary notebook.

Activity 2 Review Vocabulary Word

Elicit responses to questions. **Guide** as needed.
What prefix means "again"? *Re-.*

Tell me a sentence using a word with the prefix **re-.** (Student responses.)
Discuss sentences.

 Review vocabulary words in their appropriate context in Reading *Textbook B*.

Lesson 58 **181**

12 minutes

Teacher Materials:
Narrative Story Map

Reading *Textbook B*

Student Materials:
Narrative Story Map

Reading *Textbook B*

Part B: Comprehension Strategies

Activity 1 Narrative Story Map: Identify Title, Characters, Setting, Problem, and Events— An After-Reading Strategy

 Direct students to Lesson 57, page 56–59 in Reading *Textbook A*.

Elicit responses to questions. **Guide** as needed.
Narratives have a title, characters, settings, a problem, and events.
Skim "Linda and Kathy Find More Food" and then work by yourself to fill in the title, important characters, setting, problem, and events on your Narrative Story Map.
Monitor students as they write the title, characters, setting, problem, and events.

Discuss answers for the title, characters, setting, problem, and events. **Write** answers on Narrative Story Map.
What did you write on your Narrative Story Map? (Ideas: *Title—"Linda and Kathy Find More Food;" Main Characters—Linda and Kathy; Setting: Where—island, on the beach; When—chapter does not say: leave blank; Problem—Linda and Kathy are tired of eating bananas; Beginning—Linda and Kathy find a coconut to eat; Middle—Linda and Kathy figure out how to open the coconut to eat it; End—Linda and Kathy figure out how to get monkeys to throw coconuts down from the trees so Linda and Kathy can eat more coconuts.*)

Save teacher and student copy of Narrative Story Map for Lesson 59.

You'll use your Narrative Story Map to retell the story in the next lesson.

Activity 2 Comprehension Monitoring: Mental Imaging— A During-Reading Strategy

Elicit responses to questions. **Guide** as needed.
You are learning about a strategy to help you understand what you read while you're reading. What does mental imaging help you do? *Understand and enjoy a story more.*

What's mental imaging? *Making pictures in your mind about what you're reading.*

Why do you use mental imaging with narrative text? (Idea: *You can make pictures in your mind of the characters, setting, and events to help you understand the story better.*)

 Direct students to Lesson 57, page 58 in Reading *Textbook B*.

Elicit student responses for mental images.

In Lesson 57, you read "Linda and Kathy Find More Food." Look at page 58 by yourself and see whether you can find a sentence where you can make a mental image. Then we'll talk about the sentence you found and the mental image you made.

Remember to use mental imaging when you read to help you understand and enjoy the story.

5 minutes

Student Materials:
Reading *Textbook B*

Part C: Fluency Building

 Conduct after the lesson, using the story of the day.

Activity 1 Partner Reading

It's time for partner reading.

Direct students to the story of the day. **Assign** student partners as Partner 1 and Partner 2. **Monitor** partner reading. **Guide** as needed.

Lesson 58 **183**

Lesson 59

Materials
Teacher: 6-Narrative Story Map (completed in Lesson 58); Reading *Textbook B*
Student: Vocabulary notebook; 6-Narrative Story Map (completed in Lesson 58); Reading *Textbook B*

8 minutes

Teacher Materials:
Reading *Textbook B*

Student Materials:
Vocabulary notebook
Reading *Textbook B*

Part A: Vocabulary Development

Activity 1 Learn New Vocabulary Word

Elicit responses to questions. **Guide** as needed.
Today you'll learn a new vocabulary word. **Attached. Attached** means "hooked together." What does **attached** mean? *Hooked together.*

Another way to say "hooked together" is **attached.** What's another way to say "hooked together"? *Attached.*

Kathy and Linda needed to get some things **hooked together.** They needed to get the handle **attached** to one of the logs so they could pull the net in.

Discuss examples of things that are <u>attached</u>.

What's another way to say "hooked together"? *Attached.*

Direct students to write <u>attached</u> and its definition in their vocabulary notebooks. **Guide** as needed.
Write **attached** and what it means in your vocabulary notebook.

Activity 2 Review Vocabulary Word

Elicit responses to questions. **Guide** as needed.
What's another way to say "climbing plants"? *Vines.*

Tell me a sentence using the word **vines.** (Student responses.)
Discuss sentences.

 Review vocabulary words in appropriate context in Reading *Textbook B*.

184   Lesson 59

12 minutes

Teacher Materials:
Narrative Story Map (completed in Lesson 58)

Reading *Textbook B*

Student Materials:
Narrative Story Map (completed in Lesson 58)

Reading *Textbook B*

Part B: Comprehension Strategies

Activity 1 — Use Narrative Story Map: Retell the Story—An After-Reading Strategy

 Direct students to Lesson 57, pages 56–59 in Reading *Textbook B*.

Show Narrative Story Map (completed in Lesson 58). **Assign** student partners for retelling the story.
You did a great job of completing your Narrative Story Maps in the last lesson.

Now it's your turn to use your Narrative Story Maps to retell the story to your partner. Remember to start by telling the title and something about the characters and setting. Tell something about the problem and then tell the events that happened. Use your own words to retell the story. Then let your partner use his or her own words to retell the story.

Retelling the story helps you remember all the parts of the story.

Activity 2 — Comprehension Monitoring: Mental Imaging— A During-Reading Strategy

Elicit responses to questions. **Guide** as needed.
You are learning about a strategy to help you understand what you read while you're reading. What does mental imaging help you do? *Understand and enjoy a story more.*

What's mental imaging? *Making pictures in your mind about what you're reading.*

Why do you use mental imaging with narrative text? (Idea: *You can make pictures in your mind of the characters, setting, and events to help you understand the story better.*)

 Direct students to Lesson 58, page 68 in Reading *Textbook B*.

Elicit student responses for mental images.
In Lesson 58, you read "Making Tools." Look at page 68 by yourself and see whether you can find a sentence where you can make a mental image. Then we'll talk about the sentence you found and the mental image you made.

Remember to use mental imaging when you read to help you understand and enjoy the story.

Lesson 59

Activity 3 Comprehension Monitoring: Reading Dialogue with Prosody—A During-Reading Strategy

 Direct students to Lesson 58, page 68 in Reading *Textbook B*.

In order to read with better comprehension, it is important to pay attention to the punctuation marks in a story. Quotation marks are punctuation marks that show that a character is talking in a story. The words characters say in narratives are called dialogue.

Dialogue is marked with quotation marks. How's dialogue marked in stories? (Idea: *With quotation marks or talking marks.*)

What's dialogue? (Idea: *The words characters say in the story.*)

Assign student groups of 3. **Monitor** groups as they practice dialogue.
Decide who'll read Linda's words, who'll read Kathy's words, and who'll be the narrator and read the rest of the words. Read just page 68, practicing dialogue.

Part C: Fluency Building

5 minutes

Student Materials:
Reading *Textbook B*

 Conduct after the lesson, using the story of the day.

Activity 1 Partner Reading

It's time for partner reading.
Direct students to the story of the day. **Assign** student partners as Partner 1 and Partner 2. **Monitor** partner reading. **Guide** as needed.

Lesson 60

> **Materials**
> **Teacher:** Reading *Textbook B,* 2-Vocabulary Acquisition and Use, Writing Prompts, 3-My Writing Checklist
> **Student:** Reading *Textbook B,* Vocabulary notebook; Copy of 2-Vocabulary Acquisition and Use, Copy of 3-My Writing Checklist, Drawing paper, Lined paper

8 minutes

Teacher Materials:
Reading *Textbook B*
Vocabulary Acquisition and Use

Student Materials:
Vocabulary Notebook
Reading *Textbook B*
Vocabulary Acquisition and Use

Part A: Vocabulary Development

Activity 1 Vocabulary Notebook Review

Guide students as they study all words.
Today you'll study from your vocabulary notebook. Studying your words and what they mean will help you know your words even better. You'll study the eight words we studied over the past two weeks.

Activity 2 Cumulative Vocabulary Review

Elicit responses to questions. **Guide** as needed.
Directions: Listen and tell me whether I use our vocabulary words the right way or the wrong way. If I use the word the right way, say **"yes."** If I use the word the wrong way, say **"no."** Then we'll talk about each word.

1. Louise **hooked** her pillow on her bed.

   Did I use the word **hooked** the right way? *No.*

   How do you know? (Student responses.)

2. Patrick had to go all the way down the **aisle** to find a good seat in the movie theater.

   Did I use the word **aisle** the right way? *Yes.*

   How do you know? (Student responses.)

3. Timothy ate one banana after dinner. He ate **bunches** of bananas.

   Did I use the word **bunches** the right way? *No.*

   How do you know? (Student responses.)

4. Pamela's mother was a very good gardener. She grew beautiful **vines** that wrapped themselves around tall posts in her yard.

   Did I use the word **vines** the right way? *Yes.*

   How do you know? (Student responses.)

Lesson 60   187

5. The car was parked on the side of the road because it had run out of **fuel.**
   Did I use the word **fuel** the right way? *Yes.*

   How do you know? (Student responses.)

6. Mr. Olson could not read John's paper because it was sloppy. He asked John to **rewrite** it.

   Did I use the word **rewrite** the right way? *Yes.*

   How do you know? (Student responses.)

7. The smell of grilled food is an **object.**

   Did I use the word **object** the right way? *No.*

   How do you know? (Student responses.)

8. Sarita watched the sun until it **disappeared** behind a mountain.

   Did I use the word **disappeared** the right way? *Yes.*

   How do you know? (Student responses.)

Review vocabulary words as needed.

 Review vocabulary words in appropriate context in Reading *Textbook B.*

Activity 3 Vocabulary Acquisition and Use

Display Vocabulary Acquisition and Use. **Have** students work with a neighbor to complete Vocabulary Acquisition and Use.
Today's vocabulary words are _____ and _____ [and _____ and _____].
Vocabulary words: **attached** and **hooked; foul** and **bad**
Write the words on the lines provided. Then write the words in the boxes based on whether you think each word is less/smaller or more/larger than the other word. Below the boxes, write why you think word 1 is less/smaller and word 2 is more/larger than word 1.
Repeat for words 3 and 4. **Have** students share what they wrote. **Discuss** examples of how these words might be used.

12 minutes

Teacher Materials:
Reading *Textbook B*

Student Materials:
drawing paper

Reading *Textbook B*

Part B: Comprehension Strategies

Display directions for the activity.
Directions: Discuss what you learned about how tools or machines help you do work. Draw a tool or machine that you could construct to help Linda and Kathy get coconuts out of the tall trees (in case the monkeys won't throw them down). Write instructions to explain how to use the tool or machine.

Activity 1 Pair-Share Activity—Apply Knowledge (Level 3 of Bloom's Taxonomy)

 Direct students to Lessons 58–59, pages 65–79 in Reading *Textbook B*.

Discuss the steps in Pair-Share.
You'll do an activity called **Pair-Share** to show some things you have learned in previous lessons. The directions are on the board. I'll read them to you.

Assign partners. **Provide** drawing paper.
Step 1 is the **Pair** part of the activity. Think about the problem of picking coconuts from a tall tree. Think about the supplies that Kathy and Linda have on the island. Then talk with your partner to think of a tool or a machine you could construct to help them get coconuts out of the trees. Draw the tool or the machine, and write instructions for using it. You have 8 minutes to complete this job, so work quickly.
Guide students as they draw a tool or machine and write instructions for it.

Call on as many students to share as time allows.
Step 2 is to **Share.** I'll call on pairs of students to share their work with the rest of the class.

5 minutes

Student Materials:
Reading *Textbook B*

Part C: Fluency Building

 Conduct after the lesson, using the story of the day.

Activity 1 Partner Reading

It's time for partner reading.
Direct students to the story of the day. **Assign** student partners as Partner 1 and Partner 2. **Monitor** partner reading. **Guide** as needed.

Lesson 60

Part D: Writing/Language Arts

10 minutes

Teacher Materials:
Writing Prompts

My Writing Checklist

Student Materials:
Lined Paper

My Writing Checklist

Activity 1 Write and Use Parts of Speech and Conventions

Time to write using a writing prompt based on the stories we've been reading.

Assign student partners. **Distribute** lined paper to students. **Display** writing prompts and have students choose one to write about or assign a writing prompt of your choice. **Review** parts of speech and punctuation as well as the writing checklist with students. **Tell** students to write one to two paragraphs (minimum of four sentences per paragraph) on their own to answer the writing prompt. **Tell** them to use their writing checklist (first column labeled "Did I use them?") to ensure they include important parts of speech or punctuation in their writing. **Tell** students which parts of speech or punctuation to focus on, if you wish. **Model** what it means to answer a writing prompt and to use the writing checklist during and after the writing process, as needed. **Monitor** and guide students as needed. **Model** what it means to have a neighbor look over his or her neighbor's writing and to complete the writing checklist (second column labeled "Did my neighbor use them?"), as needed. **Have** students share what they wrote as time permits.

Writing Prompt 1	Writing Prompt 2	Writing Prompt 3
What foreign country would you like to visit? Why?	Would you like to take a cruise on an ocean liner? Where might you go?	If you were stranded on a faraway island, what might you miss about your home?

190   Lesson 60

Lesson 61

> **Materials**
> **Teacher:** Reading *Textbook B*
> **Student:** Vocabulary notebook; Reading *Textbook B*

8 minutes

Teacher Materials:
Reading *Textbook B*

Student Materials:
Vocabulary notebook

Reading *Textbook B*

Part A: Vocabulary Development

Activity 1 Learn New Vocabulary Word

Elicit responses to questions. **Guide** as needed.
Today you'll learn a new vocabulary word. **Unpleasant. Unpleasant** means "not nice." What does **unpleasant** mean? *Not nice.*

Another way to say "not nice" is **unpleasant.** What's another way to say **not nice?** *Unpleasant.*

The girls were able to catch some fish but now they had the job that was **not nice** of cleaning the fish. The girls did not know that cleaning fish would be so **unpleasant.**

Discuss things that are unpleasant.

What's another way to say "not nice"? *Unpleasant.*

Direct students to write unpleasant and its definition in their vocabulary notebooks. **Guide** as needed.
Write **unpleasant** and what it means in your vocabulary notebook.

Activity 2 Review Vocabulary Word

Elicit responses to questions. **Guide** as needed.
What's another way to say "hooked together"? *Attached.*

Tell me a sentence using the word **attached.** (Student responses.)
Discuss sentences.

 Review vocabulary words in appropriate context in Reading *Textbook B*.

12 minutes

Teacher Materials:
Reading *Textbook B*

Student Materials:
Reading *Textbook B*

Part B: Comprehension Strategies

Activity 1 Retell Narrative Text Through Readers' Theater—An After-Reading Strategy

 Direct students to Lesson 59, pages 74–79 in Reading *Textbook B*.

Elicit responses to questions. **Guide** as needed.

Lesson 61   191

Another way to retell a narrative story is to put on a play. When you put on a play, you tell the story by acting it out. We're going to act out "Linda and Kathy Construct a Machine." We call putting on a play **Readers' Theater.**

First we have to make some decisions. What's the setting of the Linda and Kathy story? (Idea: *The beach of the island.*)

Where will that be in our classroom? (Student responses.)

Who are the main characters in the story? (Idea: *Kathy and Linda.*)

Who'll play the part of Kathy? (Student responses.)

Who'll play the part of Linda? (Student responses.)

Who are the other characters in the story? (Idea: *Fish in the net.*)

Who'll play those parts? (Student responses.)

Assign roles.

I'll tell the story. Sometimes I'll tell you to say a part. You can move around to act out the story as I tell the story. Here we go.

Guide actors to perform the play for the class as you side coach the dialogue and actions.

Sample Wording for Think-Aloud

Kathy and Linda could not pull the net from the water because it was too heavy. (Prompt Kathy and Linda to be unsuccessful in pulling imaginary net.) Linda sat on the rocks to try to think of a solution to the problem. (Prompt Linda to tell her solution.) The girls looked for supplies for their machine. (Prompt Kathy to see first-aid kit in water.) Linda pulled the kit to shore. (Prompt Linda to discover matches in the kit.) Kathy wanted to try the matches right away. (Prompt Linda to tell Kathy to save matches for later.) Kathy and Linda worked hard to make supports for the machine. (Prompt girls to pantomime building supports.) Then they put a log on the supports. (Prompt girls to lift heavy log onto supports.) Next the girls added a handle and tied the net to the machine with vines. (Prompt girls to pantomime actions.) The girls put the net in the water and waited. When a lot of fish swam in the net the girls ran to the machine and turned the handle. (Prompt "fish" to be "pulled" to shore as girls turn the handle.) When the net was on the shore, the girls ran to the net. (Prompt girls to sort fish and put some back in the water.) The girls collected twigs and dry grass. (Prompt girls to prepare to make a fire.) Linda lit the first two matches but the wind blew them out. (Prompt Linda to show discouragement.) The next match worked. (Prompt the girls to celebrate because they will have a fish dinner.)

Prompt actors to bow and audience to applaud.

5 minutes

Student Materials:
Reading *Textbook B*

Part C: Fluency Building

 Conduct after the lesson, using the story of the day.

Activity 1 Partner Reading

It's time for partner reading.
Direct students to the story of the day. **Assign** student partners as Partner 1 and Partner 2. **Monitor** partner reading. **Guide** as needed.

Lesson 61 **193**

Lesson 62

Materials
Teacher: Reading *Textbook B*
Student: Vocabulary notebook; Reading *Textbook B*

8 minutes

Teacher Materials:
Reading *Textbook B*

Student Materials:
Vocabulary notebook

Reading *Textbook B*

Part A: Vocabulary Development

Activity 1 Learn New Vocabulary Word

Elicit responses to questions. **Guide** as needed.
Today you'll learn a new vocabulary word. **Sliver. Sliver** means "a small piece of something." What does **sliver** mean? *A small piece of something.*

Another way to say "a small piece of something" is **sliver.** What's another way to say "a small piece of something"? *Sliver.*

Linda could not believe what she saw. She saw **a small piece of something** in the distance. She saw a **sliver** of a ship.

Discuss examples of a sliver.

What's another way to say "a small piece of something"? *Sliver.*

Direct students to write sliver and its definition in their vocabulary notebooks. **Guide** as needed.
Write **sliver** and what it means in your vocabulary notebook.

Activity 2 Review Vocabulary Word

Elicit responses to questions. **Guide** as needed.
What's another word for "groups of things"? *Bunches.*

Tell me a sentence using the word **bunches.** (Student responses.)
Discuss sentence.

 Review vocabulary words in appropriate context in Reading *Textbook B*.

Part B: Comprehension Strategies

12 minutes

Teacher Materials:
Reading *Textbook B*

Student Materials:
Reading *Textbook B*

Activity 1 Activate Background Knowledge— A Before-Reading Strategy

Elicit responses to questions. **Guide** as needed.
Remember that information is organized in your mind so that you can remember it. Everything you know in your mind is called background knowledge. What do you call everything you know in your mind? *Background knowledge.*

When you think about what you know, you activate your background knowledge.

What do you do when you activate your background knowledge? (Idea: *Think about what you already know.*)

You used this skill when you filled out the "What I Know" part of a KWL chart for expository text. This skill is also useful when you read narrative text. Connecting what you know to the story you are reading helps you understand the story better.

You'll read about fevers in the next story. I'll show you how I think about my background knowledge about fevers.

Model think-aloud for activating background knowledge.

> **Sample Wording for Think-Aloud**
>
> When I think about a fever, I remember being really sick. I was hot and sweaty and I felt really weak and uncomfortable. I took some medicine to help my fever go down. After my fever went down, I felt cold. It was not fun to have a fever.

Connecting what you know about fevers may help you understand what you read in the next story.

Lesson 62

Activity 2 Determine Text Type and Establish Purpose for Reading—A Before-Reading Strategy

 Direct students to Lesson 62, pages 100–101 in Reading *Textbook B*.

Elicit responses to questions. **Guide** as needed.
Today you'll read both narrative and expository text in your reading lesson.

What's the title of the first section you'll read? *"Facts about Fevers."*

Do you think this section is expository or narrative? *Expository.*

Why do you think it's expository? (Idea: *It looks like it teaches information about fevers.*)

Why do you read expository text? *To learn new facts or information.*

Why will you read "Facts about Fevers"? (Idea: To *learn new information about fevers.*)

The author wrote "Facts about Fevers" to build your background knowledge. If you don't know about fevers, it'll be hard to understand the narrative story about Linda and Kathy. So you're reading this expository passage to understand the narrative passage you'll read. You're adding information to your background knowledge about fevers.

Why will you read "Facts about Fevers?" (Idea: *To build background knowledge about fevers so you can understand the narrative story you will read.*)

Part C: Fluency Building

5 minutes

Student Materials:
Reading *Textbook B*

 Conduct after the lesson, using the story of the day.

Activity 1 Partner Reading

It's time for partner reading.
Direct students to the story of the day. **Assign** student partners as Partner 1 and Partner 2. **Monitor** partner reading. **Guide** as needed.

Lesson 63

Materials

Teacher: 9-Compare and Contrast Chart; Reading *Textbook A*; Reading *Textbook B*

Student: Vocabulary notebook; copy of 9-Compare and Contrast Chart; Reading *Textbook A*; Reading *Textbook B*

Part A: Vocabulary Development

8 minutes

Teacher Materials:
Reading *Textbook B*

Student Materials:
Vocabulary notebook

Reading *Textbook B*

Activity 1 Learn New Vocabulary Word

Elicit responses to questions. **Guide** as needed.
Today you'll learn a new vocabulary word. **Occasionally. Occasionally** means "sometimes." What does **occasionally** mean? *Sometimes.*

Another word for "sometimes" is **occasionally.** What's another word for **sometimes?** *Occasionally.*

Kathy was not feeling well so she was sleeping a lot. **Sometimes** she would wake up and say things. **Occasionally** she would think she saw a ship.

Discuss examples of things people do <u>occasionally</u>.

What's another word for "sometimes"? *Occasionally.*

Direct students to write <u>occasionally</u> and its definition in their vocabulary notebooks. **Guide** as needed.
Write **occasionally** and what it means in your vocabulary notebook.

Activity 2 Review Vocabulary Word

Elicit responses to questions. **Guide** as needed.
What's another way to say "not nice"? *Unpleasant.*

Tell me a sentence using the word "unpleasant." (Student responses.)
Discuss sentences.

 Review vocabulary words in appropriate context in Reading *Textbook B*.

Lesson 63   197

12 minutes

Teacher Materials:
Compare and Contrast Chart

Reading *Textbook A*

Reading *Textbook B*

Student Materials:
Compare and Contrast Chart

Reading *Textbook A*

Reading *Textbook B*

Part B: Comprehension Strategies

Activity 1 Identify Characters: Compare and Contrast— An After-Reading Strategy

Direct students to Nancy stories, Lessons 25–35, pages 152–215 in Reading *Textbook A* and Linda stories, Lessons 54–61, pages 28–96 in Reading *Textbook B*.
Elicit responses to questions. **Guide** as needed.
You've learned how to tell how things are the same and how they're different.

What's this strategy called? *Compare and contrast.*

What do you do when you compare characters? *Tell how characters are the same.*

What do you do when you contrast characters? *Tell how characters are different.*

Show Compare and Contrast Chart.
Today I want you to think about two characters—Nancy and Linda.
You'll compare and contrast these two characters.

First think back to the stories about Nancy and Linda and try to think about how they're the same. When you write about how characters are the same, your sentences should begin, "They both…"
Guide students to compare and contrast characters. **Elicit** answers from students and complete the chart with the best suggestions. **Write** sentences in "How Same?" section of chart.

Sample Sentences for "How Same?" Box
They both are girls.
They both solve problems.
They both have an adventure.
They both are in danger.
They both eat.

Guide students to copy three sentences on their charts.

Now think back to the stories about Nancy and Linda and try to think about how they're different. When you write about how characters are different, it's a little harder. Your sentence needs to tell about the characters and tell how they are different. You say the name of the character, tell about that character, and then use the word "but" before you tell about the next character. Remember, when you tell about how the characters are different, you have to tell about the same quality.
Elicit answers from students and complete the chart with the best suggestions.
Write sentences in "How Different?" section of chart.

198 Lesson 63

Sample Sentences for "How Different?" Box

Nancy		Linda
Nancy is a little girl,	but	Linda is a big girl.
Nancy thinks only of herself,	but	Linda helps her sister.
Nancy stays home,	but	Linda travels on an ocean liner.
Nancy gets small,	but	Linda does not change size.

Guide students to copy three sentences on their charts.

Activity 2 Activate Background Knowledge— A Before-Reading Strategy

Elicit responses to questions. **Guide** as needed.

Remember that information is organized in your mind so that you can remember it. Everything you know in your mind is called background knowledge. What do you call everything you know in your mind? *Background knowledge.*

When you think about what you know, you activate your background knowledge.

What do you do when you activate your background knowledge? (Idea: *Think about what you already know.*)

You used this skill when you filled out the "What I Know" part of a KWL chart for expository text. This skill is also useful when you read narrative text. Connecting what you know to the story you are reading helps you understand the story better.

You'll read about "being a star" in the next story. I'll show you how I think about my background knowledge about "being a star."

Model activating background knowledge. Suggested ideas: Stars are people who are famous. Movie stars and sports heroes are famous. So being a star means being someone that everyone wants to talk to and know.

Connecting what you know about "being a star" may help you understand what you read in the next story.

Lesson 63   **199**

5 minutes

Student Materials:
Reading *Textbook B*

Part C: Fluency Building

 Conduct after the lesson, using the story of the day.

Activity 1 Partner Reading

It's time for partner reading.
Direct students to the story of the day. **Assign** student partners as Partner 1 and Partner 2. **Monitor** partner reading. Guide as needed.

Lesson 64

Materials
Teacher: 9-Compare and Contrast Chart; Reading *Textbook B*
Student: Vocabulary notebook; Copy of 9-Compare and Contrast Chart; Reading *Textbook B*

Part A: Vocabulary Development

8 minutes

Teacher Materials:
Reading *Textbook B*

Student Materials:
Vocabulary notebook
Reading *Textbook B*

Activity 1 Learn New Vocabulary Word

Elicit responses to questions. **Guide** as needed.
Today you'll learn a new vocabulary word. **Tugboat. Tugboat** means "a small boat for pulling ships." What does **tugboat** mean? *A small boat for pulling ships.*

Another way to say "a small boat for pulling ships" is **tugboat.** What's another way to say "a small boat for pulling ships"? *Tugboat.*

The **small boat** was used to **pull** the big **ships** to the docks. A **tugboat** is very small but it is able to pull big ships.

Discuss examples of where students have seen a tugboat.

What's another way to say "a small boat for pulling ships"? *Tugboat.*

Direct students to write tugboat and its definition in their vocabulary notebooks. **Guide** as needed.
Write **tugboat** and what it means in your vocabulary notebook.

Activity 2 Review Vocabulary Word

Elicit responses to questions. **Guide** as needed.
What word means "a small piece of something"? *Sliver.*

Tell me a sentence using the word **sliver.** *Student response.*
Discuss sentences.

 Review vocabulary words in appropriate context in Reading *Textbook B*.

Lesson 64   **201**

Part B: Comprehension Strategies

12 minutes

Teacher Materials:
Compare and Contrast Chart

Reading *Textbook B*

Student Materials:
Compare and Contrast Chart

Reading *Textbook B*

Activity 1 Compare and Contrast—An After-Reading Strategy

 Direct students to Lesson 63, pages 108–109 in Reading *Textbook B*.

Elicit responses to questions. **Guide** as needed.
You've learned how to tell how characters are the same and how they're different. The Compare and Contrast strategy also works with expository text. You read "Landing a Ship" in the last lesson. That passage contrasts a ship and an airplane.

Show Compare and Contrast Chart.
Today you'll compare and contrast a ship and an airplane. What will you do when you compare a ship and an airplane? (Idea: *Tell how a ship and an airplane are the same.*)

What will you do when you contrast a ship and an airplane? (Idea: *Tell how a ship and an airplane are different.*)

Write "ship" for one name and "airplane" for the other name. They are both vehicles.
Guide students to compare and contrast vehicles.

First think about how they're the same. When you write about how the vehicles are the same your sentences should begin, "They both…"

Elicit answers from students and complete the chart with the best suggestions.
Write sentences in "How Same?" section of chart.

Sample Sentences for "How Same?" Box
They both carry passengers.
They both are large.
They both can travel long distances.
They both land.
They both load and unload passengers.
They both have pilots to steer them.

Guide students to copy three sentences on their charts.

Now think about how the vehicles are different. When you write about how vehicles are different, it's a little harder. Your sentence needs to tell about each vehicle and tell how each is different. You say the name of the vehicle, tell about that vehicle, and then use the word "but" before you tell about the next vehicle. Remember, when you tell about how the vehicles are different, you have to tell about the same quality.

202 Lesson 64

Elicit answers from students and complete the chart with the best suggestions. **Write** sentences in "How Different?" section of chart.

Sample Sentences for "How Different?" Box		
Ship		**Airplane**
A ship lands at a harbor,	but	an airplane lands at an airport.
A ship unloads at docks,	but	an airplane unloads at gates.
A ship is pulled by a tugboat,	but	an airplane is pulled by a truck.
A ship does not have wings,	but	an airplane has wings.

Guide students to copy three sentences on their charts.

Activity 2 Activate Background Knowledge— A Before-Reading Strategy

Elicit responses to questions. **Guide** as needed.
Remember, everything you know in your mind is called background knowledge. What do you call everything you know in your mind? *Background knowledge.*

When you think about what you know, you activate your background knowledge.

What do you do when you activate your background knowledge? (Idea: *Think about what you already know.*)

Connecting what you know to the story you are reading helps you understand the story better.

You'll read about a time line in the next story. Let's talk about your background knowledge about time lines.
Discuss students' background knowledge about time lines. **Guide** as needed.

Connecting what you know about time lines may help you understand what you read in the next story.

Part C: Fluency Building

5 minutes

Student Materials:
Reading *Textbook B*

 Conduct after the lesson, using the story of the day.

Activity 1 Partner Reading

It's time for partner reading.
Direct students to the story of the day. **Assign** student partners as Partner 1 and Partner 2. **Monitor** partner reading. **Guide** as needed.

Lesson 64   **203**

Lesson 65

> **Materials**
> **Teacher:** Reading *Textbook B*, 2-Vocabulary Acquisition and Use
> **Student:** Vocabulary notebook; Lined paper; Reading *Textbook B*, Copy of 2-Vocabulary Acquisition and Use

8 minutes

Teacher Materials:
Reading *Textbook B*

Vocabulary Acquisition and Use

Student Materials:
Vocabulary notebook

Reading *Textbook B*

Vocabulary Acquisition and Use

Part A: Vocabulary Development

Activity 1 Vocabulary Notebook Review

Guide students through all words.
Today you'll study from your vocabulary notebook. Studying your words and what they mean will help you know your words even better. You'll look at the four words we studied this week.

Activity 2 Cumulative Vocabulary Review

Elicit responses to questions. **Guide** as needed.
Directions: Listen and tell me whether I use our vocabulary words the right way or the wrong way. If I use the word the right way, say **"yes."** If I use the word the wrong way, say **"no."** Then we'll talk about each word.

1. We had so much fun on our vacation to Disneyland. It was really **unpleasant.**

   Did I use the word **unpleasant** the right way? *No.*

   How do you know? (Student responses.)

2. Matt got a **sliver** in his foot from walking on the old, rickety dock.

   Did I use the word **sliver** the right way? *Yes.*

   How do you know? (Student responses.)

3. **Occasionally,** Elijah would go with his friends to the lake.

   Did I use the word **occasionally** the right way? *Yes.*

   How do you know? (Student responses.)

4. Ships use a **tugboat** in case they sink and passengers need a place to go for safety.

   Did I use the word **tugboat** the right way? *No.*

   How do you know? (Student responses.)

Review vocabulary words as needed.

 Review vocabulary words in appropriate context in Reading *Textbook B*.

204 Lesson 65

Activity 3 Vocabulary Acquisition and Use

Display Vocabulary Acquisition and Use. **Have** students work with a neighbor to complete Vocabulary Acquisition and Use.
Today's vocabulary words are ____ and ____ [and ____ and ____].
Vocabulary words: **unpleasant** and **uncomfortable**; **shows** and **illustrates**
Write the words on the lines provided. Then write the words in the boxes based on whether you think each word is less/smaller or more/larger than the other word. Below the boxes, write why you think word 1 is less/smaller and word 2 is more/larger than word 1.
Repeat for words 3 and 4. **Have** students share what they wrote. **Discuss** examples of how these words might be used.

Part B: Comprehension Strategies

12 minutes

Teacher Materials:
Reading *Textbook B*

Student Materials:
Lined paper
Reading *Textbook B*

Display directions for the activity.
Directions: Discuss Linda's and Kathy's experiences on the island. Apply your knowledge of the stories to help you write three questions you'd like to ask Linda and Kathy about their experiences.

Activity 1 Pair-Share Activity—Apply Knowledge (Level 3 of Bloom's Taxonomy)

 Direct students to Linda and Kathy stories, Lessons 54–63, pages 28–112 in Reading *Textbook B*.
Discuss the steps in Pair-Share.
You'll do an activity called **Pair-Share** to show some things you have learned in previous lessons. The directions are on the board. I'll read them to you.

Assign partners. **Provide** lined paper.
Step 1 is the **Pair** part of the activity. Discuss some of the experiences that Linda and Kathy had while they were on the island. Work with your partner to write three questions you would like to ask Linda and Kathy about what it was like to live on the island. Remember that questions can begin with "who, where, what, when, why, and how." Decide who'll write the questions. You have 8 minutes to complete this job. Work quickly so you'll finish on time.
Guide the students as they write questions.

Call on as many students to share as time allows.
Step 2 is to **Share.** I'll call on pairs of students to share their work with the rest of the class.

Part C: Fluency Building

5 minutes

Student Materials:
Reading *Textbook B*

 Conduct after the lesson, using the story of the day.

Activity 1 Partner Reading

It's time for partner reading.
Direct students to the story of the day. **Assign** student partners as Partner 1 and Partner 2. **Monitor** partner reading. **Guide** as needed.

Lesson 65   205

Lesson 66

Materials
Teacher: 9-Compare and Contrast Chart; Reading *Textbook B*
Student: Vocabulary notebook; Copy of 9-Compare and Contrast Chart; Reading *Textbook B*

Part A: Vocabulary Development

8 minutes

Teacher Materials:
Reading *Textbook B*

Student Materials:
Vocabulary notebook
Reading *Textbook B*

Activity 1 Learn New Vocabulary Word

Elicit responses to questions. **Guide** as needed.
Today you'll learn a new vocabulary word. **Battle. Battle** means "a short fight." What does **battle** mean? *A short fight.*

Another way to say "a short fight" is **battle.** What's another way to say "a short fight"? *Battle.*

There was **a short fight** between the soldiers from Greece and the soldiers of Troy. The soldiers from Greece did not win the **battle.**

Discuss examples of a battle.

What's another word for "a short fight"? *Battle.*

Direct students to write battle and its definition in their vocabulary notebooks. **Guide** as needed.
Write **battle** and what it means in your vocabulary notebook.

Activity 2 Review Vocabulary Word

Elicit responses to questions. **Guide** as needed.
What's another way to say "a small boat for pulling ships"? *Tugboat.*

Tell me a sentence using the word **tugboat.** (Student responses.)
Discuss sentences.

 Review vocabulary words in appropriate context in Reading *Textbook B.*

206 *Lesson 66*

Part B: Comprehension Strategies

12 minutes

Teacher Materials:
Compare and Contrast Chart

Reading *Textbook B*

Student Materials:
Compare and Contrast Chart

Reading *Textbook B*

Activity 1 Compare and Contrast—An After-Reading Strategy

 Direct students to Lesson 65, pages 129–134 in Reading *Textbook B*.

Elicit responses to questions. **Guide** as needed.
You've learned how to tell how characters are the same and how they're different. The compare and contrast strategy also works with expository text. You read "The City of Troy" in the last lesson. That passage contrasts Troy with a city today.

Show Compare and Contrast Chart.
Today you'll compare and contrast Troy and the city where you live. What will you do when you compare Troy and your city? (Idea: *Tell how Troy and my city are the same.*)

What will you do when you contrast Troy and your city? (Idea: *Tell how Troy and my city are different.*)

Write "Troy" for one name and the name of your city for the other name. They are both cities.
Guide students to compare and contrast cities.

First think about how they're the same. When you write about how the cities are the same your sentences should begin, "They both…"
Elicit answers from students and complete the chart with the best suggestions. **Write** sentences in "How Same?" section of chart. **Guide** students to copy three sentences on their charts.

Now think about how the cities are different. When you write about how the cities are different, it's a little harder. Your sentence needs to tell about each city and tell how each is different. You say the name of the city, tell about that city, and then use the word "but" before you tell about the next city. Remember, when you tell about how the cities are different, you have to tell about the same quality.
Elicit answers from students and complete the chart with the best suggestions. **Write** sentences in "How Different?" section of chart. **Guide** students to copy three sentences on their charts.

Lesson 66

Activity 2 Activate Background Knowledge—A Before-Reading Strategy

 Direct students to Lesson 65, pages 129–134 in Reading *Textbook B*.

Elicit responses to questions. **Guide** as needed.
Remember that information is organized in your mind so that you can remember it. Everything you know in your mind is called background knowledge. What do you call everything you know in your mind? *Background knowledge.*

What do you do when you think about what you already know? (Idea: *Activate your background knowledge.*)

Can you use this skill in both narrative and expository text? *Yes.*

Connecting what you know to the story you're reading helps you understand the story better.

In the last lesson, you read "The City of Troy." That passage was written to give you background knowledge about what the city of Troy was like and what kind of things the people of Troy used when they had a war. Let's activate your background knowledge about what you learned in the last lessons before you read the narrative story "A Great War at Troy."
Elicit information from students about background knowledge learned in last lesson. **List** information on a chart.

Connecting what you have learned about Troy to the narrative story you read today may help you understand what you read better.

Part C: Fluency Building

5 minutes

Teacher Materials:
Reading *Textbook B*

 Conduct after the lesson, using the story of the day.

Activity 1 Partner Reading

It's time for partner reading.
Direct students to the story of the day. **Assign** student partners as Partner 1 and Partner 2. **Monitor** partner reading. **Guide** as needed.

Lesson 67

Materials
Teacher: Reading *Textbook B*
Student: Vocabulary notebook; Reading *Textbook B*

8 minutes

Teacher Materials:
Reading *Textbook B*

Student Materials:
Vocabulary notebook

Reading *Textbook B*

Part A: Vocabulary Development

Activity 1 Learn New Vocabulary Word

Elicit responses to questions. **Guide** as needed.
Today you'll learn a new vocabulary word. **Trick. Trick** means "something done to make someone else look bad." What does **trick** mean? *Something done to make someone else look bad.*

Another way to say "something done to make someone else look bad" is **trick.** What's another way to say "something done to make someone else look bad"? *Trick.*

The soldiers from Greece **did something to make someone else look bad.** They used a horse to **trick** the soldiers of Troy into thinking they had given up.

Discuss examples of a <u>trick</u>.

What's another way to say "something done to make someone else look bad"? *Trick.*

Direct students to write <u>trick</u> and its definition in their vocabulary notebooks.
Guide as needed.
Write **trick** and what it means in your vocabulary notebook.

Activity 2 Review Vocabulary Word

Elicit responses to questions. **Guide** as needed.
What's another way to say "a short fight"? *Battle.*

Tell me a sentence using the word **battle.** (Student responses.)
Discuss sentences.

 Review vocabulary words in appropriate context in Reading *Textbook B*.

Lesson 67 **209**

12 minutes

Teacher Materials:
Reading *Textbook B*

Student Materials:
Reading *Textbook B*

Part B: Comprehension Strategies

Activity 1 Comprehension Monitoring: Mental Imaging—A During-Reading Strategy

Elicit responses to questions. **Guide** as needed.
You learned about a strategy to help you understand what you read while you're reading. Mental imaging helps you understand and enjoy a story more. What does mental imaging help you do? *Understand and enjoy a story more.*

What's mental imaging? *Making pictures in your mind about what you're reading.*

When you use mental imaging with narrative text, you can make pictures in your mind of the characters, setting, and events to help you understand the story better.

 Direct students to Lesson 66, pages 141–143 in Reading *Textbook B*.

In the last lesson, you read "A Great War at Troy." We're going to skim the story to find places where you can make a mental image. Then we'll discuss the mental image you have.

Elicit mental images from students as they read passage. **Guide** as needed.
The second paragraph says, "The woman from Greece was named Helen. She was supposed to be the most beautiful woman in the world."

What mental images do you have when you read those sentences? **(Student responses.)**

The next paragraph tells about how many ships came from Greece to Troy.

What mental images do you have when you read those sentences? **(Student responses.)**

Skim more of the story and see whether you can find a place in the passage where you can make a mental image. Tell both the part you read and the mental images you made. **(Student responses.)**

You can practice using mental imaging whenever you read to help you understand and enjoy what you read. Try it today when you read "The Great Wooden Horse."

Lesson 67

Activity 2 — Activate Background Knowledge— A Before-Reading Strategy

Elicit responses to questions. **Guide** as needed.
Remember, everything you know in your mind is called background knowledge. What do you call everything you know in your mind? *Background knowledge.*

When you think about what you know, you activate your background knowledge.

What do you do when you activate your background knowledge? (Idea: *Think about what you already know.*)

Why do you activate your background knowledge? (Idea: *Connecting what you know to the story you are reading helps you better understand the story.*)

You'll read about a trick in the next story. Let's talk about your background knowledge about tricks.

Discuss students' background knowledge about tricks. **Guide** as needed.
Connecting what you know about tricks may help you understand what you read in the next story.

5 minutes

Student Materials:
Reading *Textbook B*

Part C: Fluency Building

 Conduct after the lesson, using the story of the day.

Activity 1 Partner Reading

It's time for partner reading.
Direct students to the story of the day. **Assign** student partners as Partner 1 and Partner 2. **Monitor** partner reading. **Guide** as needed.

Lesson 68

Materials

Teacher: 9-Compare and Contrast Chart; Reading *Textbook B*

Student: Vocabulary notebook; Copy of 9-Compare and Contrast Chart for each student pair; Reading *Textbook B*

Part A: Vocabulary Development

8 minutes

Teacher Materials:
Reading *Textbook B*

Student Materials:
Vocabulary notebook

Reading *Textbook B*

Activity 1 Learn New Vocabulary Word

Elicit responses to questions. **Guide** as needed.
Today you'll learn a new vocabulary word. **Blindfold. Blindfold** means "a piece of cloth covering your eyes so you can't see." What does **blindfold** mean? *A piece of cloth covering your eyes so you can't see.*

Another way to say "a piece of cloth covering your eyes so you can't see" is **blindfold.** What's another way to say "a piece of cloth covering your eyes so you can't see"? *Blindfold.*

At the party, they played a game where they had to put **a piece of cloth covering your eyes so you can't see.** Wearing a **blindfold** makes the game more fun.

Discuss examples when someone might wear a blindfold.

What's another way to say "a piece of cloth covering your eyes so you can't see"? *Blindfold.*

Direct students to write blindfold and its definition in their vocabulary notebooks. **Guide** as needed.
Write **blindfold** and what it means in your vocabulary notebook.

Activity 2 Review Vocabulary Word

Elicit responses to questions. **Guide** as needed.
What's another way to say "something done to make someone else look bad"? *Trick.*

Tell me a sentence using the word **trick.** (Student responses.)
Discuss sentences.

 Review vocabulary words in appropriate context in Reading *Textbook B*.

212 Lesson 68

Part B: Comprehension Strategies

12 minutes

Teacher Materials:
Compare and Contrast Chart

Reading *Textbook B*

Student Materials:
Compare and Contrast Chart for each student pair

Reading *Textbook B*

Activity 1 Compare and Contrast—An After-Reading Strategy

 Direct students to Lesson 65, pages 129–134 in Reading *Textbook B*.

Elicit responses to questions. **Guide** as needed. **Assign** student partners.
Show Compare and Contrast Chart.
You've learned how to tell how characters are the same and how they're different. Today you'll compare and contrast you and your partner.

What will you do when you compare you and your partner? (Idea: *Tell how my partner and I are the same.*)

What will you do when you contrast you and your partner? (Idea: *Tell how my partner and I are different.*)

Write your name for one name and the name of your partner for the other name. You are both kids.

Guide students to compare and contrast student partners.

First think about how you're the same. When you write about how you're the same, your sentences should begin, "They both…"
Monitor student partners as they write three sentences for "How Same?" box on Compare and Contrast Chart.

Now think about how you are different. When you write about how you are different, it's a little harder. Your sentence needs to tell about each person and tell how each is different. You say the name of the person, tell about that person, and then use the word "but" before you tell about the next person. Remember, when you tell about how you're different, you have to tell about the same quality. **Hint:** Think about how you look, what you like or dislike, food you eat, and sports you play.
Monitor student partners as they write three sentences for "How Different?" box on Compare and Contrast Chart.

Lesson 68 **213**

Activity 2   Activate Background Knowledge— A Before-Reading Strategy

Elicit responses to questions. **Guide** as needed.

Remember, everything you know in your mind is called background knowledge. What do you call everything you know in your mind? *Background knowledge.*

What do you do when you activate your background knowledge? (Idea: *Think about what you already know.*)

Why do you activate your background knowledge? (Idea: *Connecting what you know to the story you are reading helps you better understand the story.*)

You'll read about the sense of smell in the next story. Let's talk about your background knowledge about sense of smell.

Discuss students' background knowledge about sense of smell. **Guide** as needed.

Connecting what you know about the sense of smell may help you understand what you read in the next story.

Part C: Fluency Building

5 minutes

Student Materials:
Reading *Textbook B*

 Conduct after the lesson, using the story of the day.

Activity 1   Partner Reading

It's time for partner reading.

Direct students to the story of the day. **Assign** student partners as Partner 1 and Partner 2. **Monitor** partner reading. **Guide** as needed.

214   Lesson 68

Lesson 69

Materials
Teacher: 6-Narrative Story Map; Reading *Textbook B*
Student: Vocabulary notebook; Copy of 6-Narrative Story Map; Reading *Textbook B*

8 minutes

Teacher Materials:
Reading *Textbook B*

Student Materials:
Vocabulary notebook
Reading *Textbook B*

Part A: Vocabulary Development

Activity 1 Learn New Vocabulary Word

Elicit responses to questions. **Guide** as needed.
Today you'll learn a new vocabulary word. **Shrugged. Shrugged** means "to move your shoulders up and down." What does **shrugged** mean? *To move your shoulders up and down.*

Another way to say "to move your shoulders up and down" is **shrugged.** What's another way to say "to move your shoulders up and down"? *Shrugged.*

Bertha did not understand what Maria said so she **moved** her **shoulders up and down** to let her know she did not understand. Bertha often **shrugged** when she was not sure about something.

Discuss examples of when someone has shrugged.

What's another way to say "to move your shoulders up and down"? *Shrugged.*

Direct students to write shrugged and its definition in their vocabulary notebooks. **Guide** as needed.
Write **shrugged** and what it means in your vocabulary notebook.

Activity 2 Review Vocabulary Word

Elicit responses to questions. **Guide** as needed.
What's another way to say "a piece of cloth covering your eyes so you can't see"? *Blindfold.*

Tell me a sentence using the word **blindfold.** (Student responses.)
Discuss sentences.

 Review vocabulary words in appropriate context in Reading *Textbook B*.

Lesson 69   215

Part B: Comprehension Strategies

12 minutes

Teacher Materials:
Narrative Story Map

Reading *Textbook B*

Student Materials:
Narrative Story Map

Reading *Textbook B*

Activity 1 Narrative Story Map: Identify Title, Characters, Setting, Problem, and Events—An After-Reading Strategy

 Direct students to Lesson 68, pages 156–159 in Reading *Textbook B*.

Show Narrative Story Map. **Elicit** responses to questions. **Guide** as needed.
Narrative text has a title, characters, settings, a problem, and events.
Skim "Bertha Has a Great Sense of Smell," and then work by yourself to fill in the title, important characters, setting, problem, and events on your Narrative Story Map.

Monitor students as they write the title, characters, setting, problem, and events on: Narrative Story Map.

Discuss answers for the title, characters, setting, problem, and events. **Write** answers on Narrative Story Map.
What did you write on your Narrative Story Map? (Ideas: *Title—"Bertha Has a Great Sense of Smell;" Main Character— Bertha; Setting: Where—At a party and at school; When— last summer; Problem—Bertha has a strange ability to smell things better than a hound; Beginning— With her sense of smell, Bertha tells everyone at a party what they are doing while she faces the other way; Middle— Bertha's sense of smell is tested at school; End—Bertha feels bad because everyone thinks she is strange.*)

Save student copies of Narrative Story Map for Lessons 70.

You'll use your Narrative Story Map to help you think about how to illustrate an event in the next lesson.

Activity 2 Use Narrative Story Map: Retell the Story—An After-Reading Strategy

Show Narrative Story Map (completed in Activity 1). **Assign** student partners for retelling the story.
You did a great job of completing your Narrative Story Maps. Now it's your turn to use your Narrative Story Maps to retell the story to your partner. Remember to start by telling the title and something about the characters and setting. Tell something about the problem and then tell the events that happened. Use your own words to retell the story. Then let your partner use his or her own words to retell the story.

Retelling the story helps you remember all the parts of the story.

5 minutes

Student Materials:
Reading *Textbook B*

Part C: Fluency Building

 Conduct after the lesson, using the story of the day.

Activity 1 Partner Reading

It's time for partner reading.
Direct students to the story of the day. **Assign** student partners as Partner 1 and Partner 2. **Monitor** partner reading. **Guide** as needed.

Lesson 69 **217**

Lesson 70

> **Materials**
>
> **Teacher:** Reading *Textbook B,* 2-Vocabulary Acquisition and Use, Writing Prompts, 3-My Writing Checklist
>
> **Student:** Vocabulary notebook; drawing paper; 6-Narrative Story Map (completed in Lesson 69); Reading *Textbook B,* Copy of 2-Vocabulary Acquisition and Use, Copy of 3-My Writing Checklist, Lined paper

8 minutes

Teacher Materials:
Reading *Textbook B*

Vocabulary Acquisition and Use

Student Materials:
Vocabulary Notebook

Reading *Textbook B*

Vocabulary Acquisition and Use

Part A: Vocabulary Development

Activity 1 Vocabulary Notebook Review

Guide students as they study all words.
Today you'll study from your vocabulary notebook. Studying your words and what they mean will help you know your words even better. You'll study the eight words we studied over the past two weeks.

Activity 2 Cumulative Vocabulary Review

Elicit responses to questions. **Guide** as needed.
Directions: Listen and tell me whether I use our vocabulary words the right way or the wrong way. If I use the word the right way, say **"yes."** If I use the word the wrong way, say **"no."** Then we'll talk about each word.

1. Joe was not very hungry so for dessert he ate only a **sliver** of pie.

    Did I use the word **sliver** the right way? *Yes.*

    How do you know? (Student responses.)

2. Ann played a **trick** on her sister when she popped out of the closet and scared her sister in front of her friends.

    Did I use the word **trick** the right way? *Yes.*

    How do you know? (Student responses.)

3. Alex's mother did not like the music he listened to. She thought the music he liked was **unpleasant.**

    Did I use the word **unpleasant** the right way? *Yes.*

    How do you know? (Student responses.)

4. **Occasionally,** Victoria liked to see a movie at the mall.

    Did I use the word **occasionally** the right way? *Yes.*

    How do you know? (Student responses.)

5. The **tugboat** took the children water skiing.

218   Lesson 70

Did I use the word **tugboat** the right way? *No.*

How do you know? (Student responses.)

6. Anna wanted to surprise her daughter with a new puppy. She put a **blindfold** on her daughter and led her into the house.

   Did I use the word **blindfold** the right way? *Yes.*

   How do you know? (Student responses.)

7. Frank **shrugged** his leg before he kicked the ball.

   Did I use the word **shrugged** the right way? *No.*

   How do you know? (Student responses.)

8. When there is a **battle,** many people can be hurt or even killed.

   Did I use the word **battle** the right way? *Yes.*

   How do you know? (Student responses.)

Review vocabulary words as needed.

 Review vocabulary words in appropriate context in Reading *Textbook B*.

Activity 3 Vocabulary Acquisition and Use

Display Vocabulary Acquisition and Use. **Have** students work with a neighbor to complete Vocabulary Acquisition and Use.
Today's vocabulary words are ____ and ____ [and ____ and ____].
Vocabulary words: **shrugged** and **moved; bunch** and **group**
Write the words on the lines provided. Then write the words in the boxes based on whether you think each word is less/smaller or more/larger than the other word. Below the boxes, write why you think word 1 is less/smaller and word 2 is more/larger than word 1.
Repeat for words 3 and 4. **Have** students share what they wrote. **Discuss** examples of how these words might be used.

Part B: Comprehension Strategies

8 minutes

Teacher Materials:
Reading *Textbook B*

Student Materials:
Drawing paper

Narrative Story Map (completed in Lesson 69)

Reading *Textbook B*

Display directions for the activity.
Directions: Discuss the Narrative Story Map you made for "Bertha Has a Great Sense of Smell." Illustrate one of the events from the story that you put on your Narrative Story Map.

Activity 1 Pair-Share Activity—Apply Knowledge (Level 3 of Bloom's Taxonomy)

 Direct students to Lesson 68, pages 156–159 in Reading *Textbook B*.

Discuss the steps in Pair-Share.

Lesson 70   219

You'll do an activity called **Pair-Share** to show some things you have learned in previous lessons. The directions are on the board. I'll read them to you.

Assign partners. **Provide** drawing paper.
Step 1 is the **Pair** part of the activity. Discuss some of the events that happened to Bertha that are written on your Narrative Story Map from the last lesson. Work with your partner to pick one event on your map and illustrate it. You have 8 minutes to complete this job. Work quickly so you'll finish on time.
Guide students as they draw illustration.

Call on as many students to share as time allows.
Step 2 is to **Share.** I'll call on pairs of students to share their work with the rest of the class.

5 minutes

Student Materials:
Reading Textbook B

Part C: Fluency Building

 Conduct after the lesson, using the story of the day.

Activity 1 Partner Reading

It's time for partner reading.
Direct students to the story of the day. **Assign** student partners as Partner 1 and Partner 2. **Monitor** partner reading. **Guide** as needed.

10 minutes

Teacher Materials:
Writing Prompts
My Writing Checklist

Student Materials:
Lined Paper
My Writing Checklist

Part D: Writing/Language Arts

Activity 1 Write and Use Parts of Speech and Conventions

Time to write using a writing prompt based on the stories we've been reading.
Assign student partners. **Distribute** lined paper to students. **Display** writing prompts and have students choose one to write about or assign a writing prompt of your choice. **Review** parts of speech and punctuation as well as the writing checklist with students. **Tell** students to write one to two paragraphs (minimum of four sentences per paragraph) on their own to answer the writing prompt. **Tell** them to use their writing checklist (first column labeled "Did I use them?") to ensure they include important parts of speech or punctuation in their writing. **Tell** students which parts of speech or punctuation to focus on, if you wish. **Model** what it means to answer a writing prompt and to use the writing checklist during and after the writing process, as needed. **Monitor** and guide students as needed. **Model** what it means to have a neighbor look over his or her neighbor's writing and to complete the writing checklist (second column labeled "Did my neighbor use them?"), as needed. **Have** students share what they wrote as time permits.

Writing Prompt 1	Writing Prompt 2	Writing Prompt 3
How might you signal for help if you were stranded on an island?	Would you rather take an airplane or a ship to a faraway place? Why?	How do you think you could have sneaked into the city of Troy if you were there?

Lesson 71

Materials
Teacher: Reading *Textbook B,* 10-Prediction Chart
Student: Vocabulary notebook; Reading *Textbook B*

8 minutes

Teacher Materials:
Reading *Textbook B*

Student Materials:
Vocabulary notebook
Reading *Textbook B*

Part A: Vocabulary Development

Activity 1 Learn New Vocabulary Word

Elicit responses to questions. **Guide** as needed.
Today you'll learn a new vocabulary word. **Honest. Honest** means "tells the truth." What does **honest** mean? *Tells the truth.*

Another way to say "tells the truth" is **honest.** What's another way to say "tells the truth"? *Honest.*

Bertha always **tells the truth.** She was **honest** about how she could smell things.

Discuss examples of being honest.

What's another way to say "tells the truth"? *Honest.*

Direct students to write honest and its definition in their vocabulary notebooks. **Guide** as needed.
Write **honest** and what it means in your vocabulary notebook.

Activity 2 Review Vocabulary Word

Elicit responses to questions. **Guide** as needed.
What's another way to say "to move your shoulders up and down"? *Shrugged.*

Tell me a sentence using the word **shrugged.** (Student response.)
Discuss sentences.

 Review vocabulary words in appropriate context in Reading *Textbook B.*

Lesson 71 **221**

12 minutes

Teacher Materials:
Reading *Textbook B*

Prediction Chart

Student Materials:
Reading *Textbook B*

Part B: Comprehension Strategies

Activity 1 Activate Background Knowledge—A Before-Reading Strategy

Elicit responses to questions. **Guide** as needed.
Remember, everything you know in your mind is called background knowledge. What do you call everything you know in your mind? *Background knowledge.*

What do you do when you activate your background knowledge? (Idea: *Think about what you already know.*)

Why do you activate your background knowledge? (Idea: *Connecting what you know to the story you are reading helps you better understand the story.*)

Assign partners.
You'll read about amazing things in the next story. Talk with your partner about your background knowledge for amazing things.

Monitor student discussion. **Elicit** student background knowledge about amazing things. **Guide** as needed.
Share what you and your partner talked about when you think of amazing things.

Connecting what you know about the amazing things may help you understand what you read in the next story.

Activity 2 Make Predictions—A Before-Reading Strategy

 Direct students to Lesson 71, pages 176–177 in Reading *Textbook B*.

Show Prediction Chart. **Elicit** responses to questions. **Guide** as needed.
When you read narrative stories, it's a good strategy to make predictions about what you're going to read to help you understand the story better. Predictions are good guesses about what's in the story based on clues.

What are predictions? (Idea: *Good guesses about what's in the story based on clues.*)

You'll use clues from the title, pictures, and skimming the text so you can make a good prediction.

What will you use to get clues? (Idea: *The title, pictures, and skimming the text.*)

I'm going to show you what I mean. I'll predict what'll happen in the next story by looking at the title "Maria Tests Bertha's Talent." I'll also skim the story and remember what I know about the story so far to predict what'll happen to Bertha and Maria.
Model think-aloud for prediction from the title, skimming the text, and remembering the last story.

222   *Lesson 71*

Sample Wording for Think-Aloud

The title gives me a big hint about what will happen next. I know that Bertha can smell really well, and I know from the last story that Bertha has a plan for Maria's problem. I bet Maria does not think that Bertha can help her with a sense of smell. So I bet Maria tests Bertha's sense of smell by making her smell water that comes from different places. That's my prediction.

I make a prediction about what I'm going to read and as I read I'll try to see whether my prediction is correct. It doesn't matter whether my prediction is exactly right. What's important is that I'm checking as I read to see whether my prediction is correct.

Record prediction for further discussion in Lesson 72.

5 minutes

Student Materials:
Reading *Textbook B*

Part C: Fluency Building

 Conduct after the lesson, using the story of the day.

Activity 1 Partner Reading

It's time for partner reading.

Direct students to the story of the day. **Assign** student partners as Partner 1 and Partner 2. **Monitor** partner reading. **Guide** as needed.

Lesson 72

Materials
Teacher: Prediction recorded in Lesson 71; Reading *Textbook B,* 10-Prediction Chart
Student: Vocabulary notebook; Reading *Textbook B*

Part A: Vocabulary Development

8 minutes

Teacher Materials:
Reading *Textbook B*

Student Materials:
Vocabulary notebook

Reading *Textbook B*

Activity 1 Learn New Vocabulary Word

Elicit responses to questions. **Guide** as needed.
Today you'll learn a new vocabulary word. **Narrow. Narrow** means "small from one side to another." What does **narrow** mean? *Small from one side to another.*

Another way to say "small from one side to another" is **narrow.** What's another way to say "small from one side to another"? *Narrow.*

Bertha and Maria had been driving a long time down a road that was **small from one side to another.** There was no one else on the **narrow** road.

Discuss things that are narrow.

What's another way to say "small from one side to another"? *Narrow.*

Direct students to write narrow and its definition in their vocabulary notebooks. **Guide** as needed.
Write **narrow** and what it means in your vocabulary notebook.

Activity 2 Review Vocabulary Word

Elicit responses to questions. **Guide** as needed.
What's another way to say "tells the truth"? *Honest.*

Tell me a sentence using the word **honest.** (Student response.)
Discuss sentences.

 Review vocabulary words in appropriate context in Reading *Textbook B.*

224 Lesson 72

12 minutes

Teacher Materials:
Prediction recorded in Lesson 71

Prediction Chart

Reading *Textbook B*

Student Materials:
Reading *Textbook B*

Part B: Comprehension Strategies

Activity 1 Confirm Predictions—An After-Reading Strategy

 Direct students to Lesson 71, pages 176–177 in Reading *Textbook B*.

Show Prediction Chart. **Elicit** responses to questions. **Guide** as needed.
In the last lesson, I made a prediction about what happens to Bertha and Maria in the story. I made the prediction before I read the story. Making predictions helps you understand the story better.

You confirm predictions when you check to see whether your predictions were correct. What do you do when you check to see whether your predictions were right? *Confirm predictions.*

Now that you've read the story, let's check to see whether my prediction was correct or incorrect.

Guide discussion based on prediction recorded in Lesson 71.
I predicted that Maria would test Bertha's sense of smell. Was my prediction correct? *Yes.*

Sometimes, we don't predict correctly. That's okay. Just trying to make predictions and then confirming them will help you better understand what you read.

Activity 2 Activate Background Knowledge— A Before-Reading Strategy

Elicit responses to questions. **Guide** as needed.
Remember, everything you know in your mind is called background knowledge. What do you call everything you know in your mind? *Background knowledge.*

What do you do when you activate your background knowledge? (Idea: *Think about what you already know.*)

Why do you activate your background knowledge? (Idea: *Connecting what you know to the story you are Reading helps you better understand the story.*)

Assign partners. **Monitor** student discussion. **Guide** as needed.
You read about a refinery in the passage "Oil Wells" in Lesson 71 to build your background knowledge. Talk with your partner about your background knowledge about refineries.

Connecting what you know about the refineries may help you understand what you read in the next story.

Lesson 72

Activity 3 | Make Predictions—A Before-Reading Strategy

 Direct students to Lesson 72, pages 181–184 in Reading *Textbook B*.

Elicit responses to questions. **Guide** as needed.
When you read narrative stories, it's a good strategy to make predictions about what you're going to read to help you understand the story better. Predictions are good guesses about what's in the story based on clues.

What are predictions? (Idea: *Good guesses about what's in the story based on clues.*)

You'll use clues from the title, pictures, remembering the story so far, and skimming the text so you can make a good prediction.

What will you use to get clues? (Idea: *The title, pictures, remembering the story so far, and skimming the text.*)

I'm going to show you what I mean.

Model making a prediction from the title, skimming the text, looking at the picture, and remembering the last story. Suggested idea: I predict that Bertha will figure out where the water comes from.
I'll predict what'll happen in the next story by looking at the title "Maria and Bertha Go to the Oil Refinery." I'll also skim the story, look at the picture, and remember what I know about the story so far to predict what'll happen to Bertha and Maria.

Record prediction for further discussion in Lesson 73.

I make a prediction about what I'm going to read and as I read, I'll try to see whether my prediction is correct or not. It doesn't matter whether my prediction is exactly right. What's important is that I'm checking as I read to see whether my prediction is correct.

Part C: Fluency Building

5 minutes

Student Materials:
Reading *Textbook B*

 Conduct after the lesson, using the story of the day.

Activity 1 | Partner Reading

It's time for partner reading.
Direct students to the story of the day. **Assign** student partners as Partner 1 and Partner 2. **Monitor** partner reading. **Guide** as needed.

226 Lesson 72

Lesson 73

Materials
Teacher: Prediction recorded in Lesson 72; Reading *Textbook B,* 10-Prediction Chart
Student: Vocabulary notebook; Reading *Textbook B,* Copy of 10-Prediction Chart

8 minutes

Teacher Materials:
Reading *Textbook B*

Student Materials:
Vocabulary notebook
Reading *Textbook B*

Part A: Vocabulary Development

Activity 1 Learn New Vocabulary Word

Elicit responses to questions. **Guide** as needed.
Today you'll learn a new vocabulary word. **Doubt. Doubt** means "not sure about something." What does **doubt** mean? *Not sure about something.*

Another way to say "not sure about something" is **doubt.** What's another way to say "not sure about something"? *Doubt.*

Maria was **not sure about something** so she brought Bertha with her to figure things out. Bertha had no **doubt** where the water came from.

Discuss examples of when people have doubt.

What's another way to say "not sure about something"? *Doubt.*

Direct students to write doubt and its definition in their vocabulary notebooks.
Guide as needed.
Write **doubt** and what it means in your vocabulary notebook.

Activity 2 Review Vocabulary Word

Elicit responses to questions. **Guide** as needed.
What's another way to say "small from one side to another"? *Narrow.*

Tell me a sentence using the word **narrow.** (Student responses.)
Discuss sentences.

 Review vocabulary words in appropriate context in Reading *Textbook B.*

Lesson 73   **227**

Part B: Comprehension Strategies

12 minutes

Teacher Materials:
Prediction recorded in Lesson 72

Prediction Chart

Reading *Textbook B*

Student Materials:
Prediction Chart

Reading *Textbook B*

Activity 1 Confirm Predictions—An After-Reading Strategy

 Direct students to Lesson 72, pages 181–184 in Reading *Textbook B*.

Elicit responses to questions. **Guide** as needed.
In the last lesson, I made a prediction about what happens to Bertha and Maria in the story. I made the prediction before I read the story. Making predictions helps you understand the story better.

You confirm predictions when you check to see whether your predictions were correct. What do you do when you check to see whether your predictions were right? *Confirm predictions.*

Guide discussion based on prediction recorded in Lesson 72.
Now that you've read the story, let's check to see whether my predictions were correct or incorrect. I predicted that Bertha would figure out where the water was coming from. Was my prediction correct? *No.*

Sometimes, we don't predict correctly. That's okay. Just trying to make predictions and then trying to confirm them when you read will help you understand better what you read.

Activity 2 Activate Background Knowledge— A Before-Reading Strategy

Elicit responses to questions. **Guide** as needed.
What do you call everything you know in your mind? *Background knowledge.*

What do you do when you activate your background knowledge? (Idea: *Think about what you already know.*)

Why do you activate your background knowledge? (Idea: *Connecting what you know to the story you are reading helps you better understand the story.*)

Elicit student background knowledge about "pretending to be polite." **Guide** as needed.
You'll read about "pretending to be polite." Think about what your background knowledge is about "pretending to be polite."

Connecting what you know about "pretending to be polite" may help you understand what you read in the next story.

Activity 3 Make Predictions—A Before-Reading Strategy

 Direct students to Lesson 73, pages 188–191 in Reading *Textbook B*.

Elicit responses to questions. **Guide** as needed.
When you read narrative stories, it's a good strategy to make predictions about what you're going to read to help you understand the story better. Predictions are good guesses about what's in the story based on clues.

What are predictions? (Idea: *Good guesses about what's in the story based on clues.*)

You'll use clues from the title, pictures, remembering the story so far, and skimming the text so you can make a good prediction.

What will you use to get clues? (Idea: *The title, picture, remembering the story so far, and skimming the text.*)

Discuss the title, picture, remembering the story so far, and skimming the text.
Let's predict what'll happen in the next story by looking at the title "Maria and Bertha Meet Mr. Daniels." Let's also skim the story, look at the picture, and remember what I know about the story so far to predict what'll happen to Bertha and Maria.

Elicit predictions from students about what will happen next. **Record** predictions on prediction chart for further discussion in Lesson 74.

You make predictions about what you're going to read, and as you read, try to see whether your predictions are correct. It doesn't matter whether your predictions are exactly right. What's important is that you're checking as you read to see whether your predictions are correct.

Part C: Fluency Building

 5 minutes

Student Materials:
Reading *Textbook B*

 Conduct after the lesson, using the story of the day.

Activity 1 Partner Reading

It's time for partner reading.
Direct students to the story of the day. **Assign** student partners as Partner 1 and Partner 2. **Monitor** partner reading. **Guide** as needed.

Lesson 73   **229**

Lesson 74

Materials

Teacher: Predictions recorded in Lesson 73; Reading *Textbook B,* 11-Before, During, After Reading Strategies

Student: Vocabulary notebook; Reading *Textbook B*

8 minutes

Teacher Materials:
Reading *Textbook B*

Student Materials:
Vocabulary notebook

Reading *Textbook B*

Part A: Vocabulary Development

Activity 1 Learn New Vocabulary Word

Elicit responses to questions. **Guide** as needed.
Today you'll learn a new vocabulary word. **Expression. Expression** means "look on someone's face." What does **expression** mean? *Look on someone's face.*

Another way to say "look on someone's face" is **expression.** What's another way to say "look on someone's face"? *Expression.*

Bertha could tell Mr. Daniels was not happy **by the look on his face.** His **expression** told her he was very mad.

Discuss examples of an <u>expression</u>.

What's another way to say "look on someone's face"? *Expression.*

Direct students to write <u>expression</u> and its definition in their vocabulary notebooks. **Guide** as needed.
Write **expression** and what it means in your vocabulary notebook.

Activity 2 Review Vocabulary Word

Elicit responses to questions. **Guide** as needed.
What's another way to say "not sure about something"? *Doubt.*

Tell me a sentence using the word **doubt.** (Student responses.)
Discuss sentences.

 Review vocabulary words in appropriate context in Reading *Textbook B.*

230 Lesson 74

Part B: Comprehension Strategies

12 minutes

Teacher Materials:
Prediction recorded in Lesson 73

Before, During, After Reading Strategies

Reading *Textbook B*

Student Materials:
Reading *Textbook B*

Activity 1 Confirm Predictions—An After-Reading Strategy

 Direct students to Lesson 73, pages 188–191 in Reading *Textbook B*.

Elicit responses to questions. **Guide** as needed.
In the last lesson, you made some predictions about what happens to Bertha and Maria in the story. You made the predictions before you read the story. Making predictions helps you understand the story better.

You confirm predictions when you check to see whether your predictions were correct. What do you do when you check to see whether your predictions were right? *Confirm predictions.*

Now that you've read the story, let's check to see whether your predictions were correct or incorrect.
Guide discussion based on predictions recorded in Lesson 73.

Sometimes, we don't predict correctly. That's okay. Just trying to make predictions and then trying to confirm them when you read will help you understand better what you read.

Activity 2 Review Before-, During- and After-Reading Strategies

Elicit responses to questions. **Guide** as needed. **List** before-reading, during-reading, and after-reading strategies on the strategy chart as you review them to post in the classroom.
You've learned some strategies to use before you read. What are they called? (Ideas: *Activate background knowledge; set a purpose for reading; ask questions about what you want to learn (KWL chart).*)

When you activate background knowledge, what do you do? (Ideas: *Think about what you already know.*)

Why do you activate your background knowledge? (Ideas: *To connect what you know to what you will learn.*)

How do you set a purpose for reading? (Ideas: *Decide whether you are reading a narrative story for fun or an expository text to learn.*)

What do you do in the first two sections of a KWL chart before you read? (Ideas: *Activate background knowledge (What You Know) and ask questions (What You Wonder).*)

Why do you use the first two sections of the KWL chart before you read expository text? (Ideas: *To connect to what you already know and to get interested in what you will read.*)

You've learned two strategies to use during reading to help you understand what you're reading. What are they called? (Ideas: *Rereading and mental imaging.*)

Lesson 74 **231**

When you use the rereading strategy, what question do you ask yourself? (Ideas: *Do I understand this?*)

Then what do you do? (Ideas: *Reread to find the answer to your question.*)

When you use mental imaging what do you do? (Ideas: *Make pictures in your mind about what you're reading.*)

Remember, mental imaging with narrative text helps you understand the details of a story better. What does using mental imaging with narrative text do? (Ideas: *Helps you understand the details of a story better.*)

When you use mental imaging with expository text, you can make pictures in your mind of facts or true information to help you remember better. What does using mental imaging with expository text do? (Ideas: *Helps you remember facts or true information better.*)

You've learned some strategies to use after reading to help you understand what you read. What are some of those strategies? (Ideas: *Complete a Narrative Story Map, complete the What I Learned part of the KWL chart, complete a Compare and Contrast Chart, and retell the story.*)

Why do you use a Narrative Story Map? (Ideas: *To organize thinking about a story.*)

What parts do you fill in for a Narrative Story Map? (Ideas: *Title, characters, setting, problem, and events.*)

Why do you complete a KWL Chart? (Ideas: *To organize thinking about an expository text.*)

What are the parts of the KWL Chart? (Ideas: *What I Know, What I Wonder, and What I Learned.*)

Why do you complete a Compare and Contrast Chart? (Ideas: *To show how things are the same and different from each other.*)

What are the parts of the Compare and Contrast Chart? (Ideas: *A part for "How Same?" and a part for "How Different?"*)

What do you do when you retell a narrative story? (Ideas: *Tell a narrative story in your own words.*)

Why do you retell a narrative story? (Ideas: *To help you remember it.*)

These strategies will help you have better comprehension.

232   *Lesson 74*

5 minutes

Student Materials:
Reading *Textbook B*

Part C: Fluency Building

 Conduct after the lesson, using the story of the day.

Activity 1 Partner Reading

It's time for partner reading.

Direct students to the story of the day. **Assign** student partners as Partner 1 and Partner 2. **Monitor** partner reading. **Guide** as needed.

Lesson 74 **233**

Lesson 75

Materials

Teacher: Reading *Textbook B*, 2-Vocabulary Acquisition and Use

Student: Vocabulary notebook; Copy of 2-Vocabulary Acquisition and Use, Reading *Textbook B*; Lined paper

8 minutes

Teacher Materials:
Reading *Textbook B*

Vocabulary Acquisition and Use

Student Materials:
Vocabulary notebook

Reading *Textbook B*

Vocabulary Acquisition and Use

Part A: Vocabulary Development

Activity 1 Vocabulary Notebook Review

Guide students through all words.
Today you'll study from your vocabulary notebook. Studying your words and what they mean will help you know your words even better. You'll look at the four words we studied this week.

Activity 2 Cumulative Vocabulary Review

Elicit responses to questions. **Guide** as needed.
Directions: Listen and tell me whether I use our vocabulary words the right way or the wrong way. If I use the word the right way, say **"yes."** If I use the word the wrong way, say **"no."** Then we'll talk about each word.

1. Ray's **expression** told Mark that he was not happy with him.

   Did I use the word **expression** the right way? *Yes.*

   How do you know? (Student responses.)

2. The bridge was so **narrow** that only one car could cross at a time.

   Did I use the word **narrow** the right way? *Yes.*

   How do you know? (Student responses.)

3. Paco had some **doubt** that he could run the ten-mile race. He had never raced before.

   Did I use the word **doubt** the right way? *Yes.*

   How do you know? (Student responses.)

4. Lori always made up things and her friends knew it. They said she was very **honest.**

   Did I use the word **honest** the right way? *No.*

   How do you know? (Student responses.)

Review vocabulary words as needed.

 Review vocabulary words in appropriate context in Reading *Textbook B*.

Activity 3 | Vocabulary Acquisition and Use

Display Vocabulary Acquisition and Use. **Have** students work with a neighbor to complete Vocabulary Acquisition and Use.
Today's vocabulary words are ____ and ____ [and ____ and ____].
Vocabulary words: **pounding** and **beating**; **pointed** and **gestured**
Write the words on the lines provided. Then write the words in the boxes based on whether you think each word is less/smaller or more/larger than the other word. Below the boxes, write why you think word 1 is less/smaller and word 2 is more/larger than word 1.
Repeat for words 3 and 4. **Have** students share what they wrote. **Discuss** examples of how these words might be used.

Part B: Comprehension Strategies

12 minutes

Teacher Materials:
Reading *Textbook B*

Student Materials:
Reading *Textbook B*
Lined paper

Display directions for activity.
Directions: Skim "Bertha Tests Some Water" to find a clue that something is not quite right at the Oil Refinery. Discuss the clues you find and then select and write the best clue as an example of what's wrong at the refinery.

Activity 1 | Pair-Share Activity—Apply Knowledge (Level 3 of Bloom's Taxonomy)

 Direct students to Lesson 74, pages 195–199 in Reading *Textbook B*.

Discuss the steps in the Pair-Share activity.
You'll do an activity called **Pair-Share** to show some things you have learned in recent lessons. The directions are on the board. I'll read them to you.

Assign partners. **Provide** writing paper.
Step 1 is the **Pair** part of the activity. Skim "Bertha Tests Some Water" to find clues that something is wrong at the Refinery. Discuss the clues with your partner. Decide what the best example is to show that things aren't right. Then write your example on your paper. Decide who'll do the writing. Work quickly. You have 8 minutes.

Guide students to skim the text and find clues in the text for what is wrong at the Refinery. Ideas: 1. Donna felt uneasy with Bertha and Maria. 2. Big Ted was unfriendly. 3. Ted turned and winked at another man. 4. Big Ted yells, "Are you calling me a liar?" 5. No one looked at or talked to Bertha or Maria. 6. Mr. Daniels won't let Bertha and Maria go to the refinery. 7. Mr. Daniels' expression was filled with hate.

Call on as many students to share as time allows.
Step 2 is to **Share.** I'll call on pairs of students to share their work with the rest of the class.

Lesson 75   235

5 minutes

Student Materials:
Reading *Textbook B*

Part C: Fluency Building

 Conduct after the lesson, using the story of the day.

Activity 1 Partner Reading

It's time for partner reading.

Direct students to the story of the day. **Assign** student partners as Partner 1 and Partner 2. **Monitor** partner reading. **Guide** as needed.

Lesson 76

Materials
Teacher: Reading *Textbook B,* 10-My Prediction Chart
Student: Vocabulary notebook; Reading *Textbook B,* Copy of 10-Prediction Chart

Part A: Vocabulary Development

8 minutes

Teacher Materials:
Reading *Textbook B*

Student Materials:
Vocabulary notebook
Reading *Textbook B*

Activity 1 Learn New Vocabulary Word

Elicit responses to questions. **Guide** as needed.
Today you'll learn a new vocabulary word. **Faded. Faded** means "disappeared slowly." What does **faded** mean? *Disappeared slowly.*

Another way to say "disappeared slowly" is **faded.** What's another way to say "disappeared slowly"? *Faded.*

The voices Maria heard **disappeared slowly.** The voices **faded** as Maria went inside.

Discuss examples of things that have faded.

What's another way to say "disappeared slowly"? *Faded.*

Direct students to write faded and its definition in their vocabulary notebooks. **Guide** as needed.
Write **faded** and what it means in your vocabulary notebook.

Activity 2 Review Vocabulary Word

Elicit responses to questions. **Guide** as needed.
What's another way to say "look on someone's face"? *Expression.*

Tell me a sentence using the word **expression.** (Student responses.)
Discuss sentences.

 Review vocabulary words in appropriate context in Reading *Textbook B.*

Lesson 76 **237**

12 minutes

Teacher Materials:
Reading *Textbook B*

Prediction Chart

Student Materials:
Prediction Chart

Reading *Textbook B*

Part B: Comprehension Strategies

Activity 1 Summarize Narrative Text— An After-Reading Strategy

 Direct students to Lesson 75, pages 202–205 in Reading *Textbook B*.

Elicit response to question. **Guide** as needed.
You're going to learn about a strategy called summarizing. Summarizing is telling part of a story or the whole story in your own words. You tell only the important parts of the story when you summarize and you leave out the details.

What do you do when you summarize? (Idea: *Tell the story in your own words and tell only the most important parts.*)

You've been practicing retelling the story in your own words from a Narrative Story Map. You've also told what you learned in your own words on a KWL chart. So you already have an idea how to do this.

Model think-aloud for summarizing a story. **Tell** the title, characters, setting, and problem. **Tell** the important events in the story.

You read the story in the last lesson. Now, I'll show you how I summarize the story "Maria and Bertha Make Up a New Plan."

Sample Wording for Think-Aloud

I'll think of the parts of a narrative from a Narrative Story Map. That'll help me think of the important parts so I can summarize the story.

The title is "Maria and Bertha Make Up a New Plan." Maria, the state investigator, and Bertha, the 15-year-old girl with the great sense of smell, were trying to figure out how to show that the Oil Refinery was breaking the law by using the wrong water. Maria and Bertha had made Mr. Daniels, the boss of the Refinery, very mad. Mr. Daniels was trying to get Maria in trouble with her boss by saying that she had said and done things that she didn't do. So Bertha and Maria were trying to figure out how to get Maria's boss to go to the Refinery with Maria. They decided that Bertha would go hidden under a blanket so she could tell Maria where the water really came from. Maria and her boss went to the Refinery. Bertha was hidden under a blanket in the back of the van. Maria's boss did not know Bertha was in the car. But as they waited in the van, Bertha began to get so hot, she began to feel sick.

Putting part of the story in my own words helps me remember it and helps me understand it. You'll be learning to summarize stories too.

Activity 2 | Make Predictions—A Before-Reading Strategy

 Direct students to Lesson 76, pages 209–212 in Reading *Textbook B*.

Show Prediction Chart. **Elicit** answer to question. **Guide** as needed.
When you read narrative stories, it's a good strategy to make predictions about what you're going to read to help you understand the story better. Predictions are good guesses about what's in the story based on clues.

What are predictions? (Idea: *Good guesses about what's in the story based on clues.*)

You'll use clues from the title, pictures, remembering the story so far, and skimming the text so you can make a good prediction.

What will you use to get clues? (Idea: *The title, picture, remembering the story so far, and skimming the text.*)

Assign partners.
Work with a partner to predict what'll happen in the next story by looking at the title "Inside a Hot Van." Skim the story, look at the picture, and remember what you know about the story so far to predict what'll happen to Bertha and Maria.

Monitor students as they discuss the title, picture, remember the story so far, and skim the text to make a prediction. **Elicit** predictions from students about what will happen next. **Record** predictions for further discussion in Lesson 77.

You make predictions about what you're going to read, and as you read, try to see whether your predictions are correct or not. It doesn't matter whether your predictions are exactly right. What's important is that you're checking as you read to see whether your predictions are correct.

Part C: Fluency Building

5 minutes

Student Materials:
Reading *Textbook B*

 Conduct after the lesson, using the story of the day.

Activity 1 | Partner Reading

It's time for partner reading.
Direct students to the story of the day. **Assign** student partners as Partner 1 and Partner 2. **Monitor** partner reading. **Guide** as needed.

Lesson 76   **239**

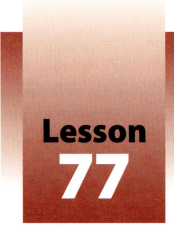

Lesson 77

Materials

Teacher: Reading *Textbook B*; predictions recorded in Lesson 76

Student: Vocabulary notebook; Reading *Textbook B*, predictions recorded in Lesson 76, Copy of 10-Prediction Chart

8 minutes

Teacher Materials:
Reading *Textbook B*

Student Materials:
Vocabulary notebook

Reading *Textbook B*

Part A: Vocabulary Development

Activity 1 Learn New Vocabulary Word

Elicit responses to questions. **Guide** as needed.
Today you'll learn a new vocabulary word. **Silence. Silence** means "no sound." What does **silence** mean? *No sound.*

Another way to say "no sound" is **silence.** What's another way to say "no sound"? *Silence.*

When Maria said that Bertha smelled, there was **no sound** from anyone. The **silence** told Maria that she had said something wrong.

Discuss examples of silence.

What's another way to say "no sound"? *Silence.*

Direct students to write silence and its definition in their vocabulary notebooks. **Guide** as needed.
Write **silence** and what it means in your vocabulary notebook.

Activity 2 Review Vocabulary Word

Elicit responses to questions. **Guide** as needed.
What's another way to say "disappeared slowly"? *Faded.*

Tell me a sentence using the word **faded.** (Student responses.)
Discuss sentences.

 Review vocabulary words in appropriate context in Reading *Textbook B*.

240   *Lesson 77*

12 minutes

Teacher Materials:
Reading *Textbook B*

Student Materials:
Predictions recorded in Lesson 76

Prediction Chart

Reading *Textbook B*

Part B: Comprehension Strategies

Activity 1 Confirm Predictions—An After-Reading Strategy

 Direct students to Lesson 76, pages 209–212 in Reading *Textbook B*.

Elicit responses to questions. **Guide** as needed.
In the last lesson, you made some predictions about what happens to Bertha and Maria in the story. You made the predictions before you read the story. Making predictions helps you understand the story better.

What do you do when you check to see whether your predictions were right? *Confirm predictions.*

Guide discussion based on predictions recorded in Lesson 76.
Now that you've read the story, let's check to see whether your predictions were correct or incorrect.

Sometimes, you don't predict correctly. That's okay. Just trying to make predictions and then confirming them will help you better understand what you read.

Activity 2 Summarize Narrative Text—An After-Reading Strategy

 Direct students to Lesson 76, pages 209–212 in Reading *Textbook B*.

Elicit responses to questions. **Guide** as needed.
You are learning about a strategy called summarizing. Summarizing is telling a part of a story or the whole story in your own words. You tell the important parts of the story when you summarize and you leave out the details.

What do you do when you summarize? (Idea: *Tell the story in your own words and tell only the most important parts.*)

You've been practicing retelling the story from a Narrative Story Map. You've also told what you learned in your own words on a KWL chart. So you already have an idea how to do this.

You read the story in the last lesson. Now I'll show you how I summarize the story "Inside a Hot Van."

Model summarizing a story. **Tell** the title, characters, setting, and problem. **Tell** the important events in the story.

Putting the story in my own words helps me remember and understand it. You'll summarize stories in future lessons too.

Lesson 77

Activity 3 — Make Predictions—A Before-Reading Strategy

 Direct students to Lesson 77, pages 216–219 in Reading *Textbook B*.

Elicit responses to questions. **Guide** as needed.
When you read narrative stories, it's a good strategy to make predictions about what you're going to read to help you understand the story better. Predictions are good guesses about what's in the story based on clues.

What are predictions? (Idea: *Good guesses about what's in the story based on clues.*)

You'll use clues from the title, pictures, remembering the story so far, and skimming the text so you can make a good prediction.

What will you use to get clues? (Idea: *The title, picture, remembering the story so far, and skimming the text.*)

Assign partners.
Work with a partner to predict what'll happen in the next story by looking at the title "The Chief Listens to Bertha." Skim the story, look at the picture, and remember what you know about the story so far to predict what'll happen to Bertha and Maria.

Monitor students as they discuss the title, picture, remember the story so far, and skim the text to make a prediction. **Elicit** predictions from students. **Record** predictions for further discussion in Lesson 78.

You make predictions about what you're going to read, and as you read, try to see whether your predictions are correct or not. It doesn't matter whether your predictions are exactly right. What's important is that you're checking as you read to see whether your predictions are correct.

Part C: Fluency Building

5 minutes

Student Materials:
Reading *Textbook B*

 Conduct after the lesson, using the story of the day.

Activity 1 — Partner Reading

It's time for partner reading.
Direct students to the story of the day. **Assign** student partners as Partner 1 and Partner 2. **Monitor** partner reading. **Guide** as needed.

242 Lesson 77

Lesson 78

Materials
Teacher: Reading *Textbook B;* 10-My Prediction Chart
Student: Vocabulary notebook; Reading *Textbook B;* predictions recorded in Lesson 77, Copy of 10-My Prediction Chart

8 minutes

Teacher Materials:
Reading *Textbook B*

Student Materials:
Vocabulary notebook

Reading *Textbook B*

Part A: Vocabulary Development

Activity 1 Learn New Vocabulary Word

Elicit responses to questions. **Guide** as needed.
Today you'll learn a new vocabulary word. **Hood. Hood** means "a covering for the head and neck." What does **hood** mean? *A covering for the head and neck.*

Another way to say "a covering for the head and neck" is **hood.** What's another way to say "a covering for the head and neck"? *Hood.*

Bertha was wearing **a covering for** her **head and neck.** The chief put her **hood** up and covered her eyes with a cloth.

Discuss things with a hood.

What's another way to say "a covering for the head and neck"? *Hood.*

Direct students to write hood and its definition in their vocabulary notebooks.
Guide as needed.
Write **hood** and what it means in your vocabulary notebook.

Activity 2 Review Vocabulary Word

Elicit responses to questions. **Guide** as needed.
What's another way to say "no sound"? *Silence.*

Tell me a sentence using the word **silence.** (Student responses.)
Discuss sentences.

 Review vocabulary words in appropriate context in Reading *Textbook B*.

Lesson 78 243

12 minutes

Teacher Materials:
Reading *Textbook B*

Student Materials:
predictions recorded in Lesson 77

Prediction Chart

Reading *Textbook B*

Part B: Comprehension Strategies

Activity 1 Confirm Predictions—An After-Reading Strategy

 Direct students to Lesson 77, pages 216–219 in Reading *Textbook B*.

Show Prediction Chart. **Elicit** responses to questions. **Guide** as needed.
In the last lesson, you made some predictions about what happens to Bertha and Maria in the story. You made the predictions before you read the story. Making predictions helps you understand the story better.

You confirm predictions when you check to see whether your predictions were correct. What do you do when you check to see whether your predictions were right? *Confirm predictions.*

Guide discussion based on predictions recorded in Lesson 77.
Now that you've read the story, let's check to see whether your predictions were correct or incorrect.

Sometimes, we don't predict correctly. That's okay. Just trying to make predictions and then confirming them will help you understand better what you read.

Activity 2 Summarize Narrative Text—An After-Reading Strategy

 Direct students to Lesson 77, pages 216–219 in Reading *Textbook B*.

Elicit responses to questions. **Guide** as needed.
You're learning about a strategy called summarizing. Summarizing is telling a part of a story or the whole story in your own words. You tell only the important parts of the story when you summarize and you leave out the details.

What do you do when you summarize? (Idea: *Tell the story in your own words and tell only the most important parts.*)

You've been practicing retelling the story from a Narrative Story Map. You have also told what you learned in your own words on a KWL Chart. So you already have an idea how to do this.

Elicit summary, characters, setting, problem, and events from students.
You read the story in the last lesson. Now we'll work together to summarize the story "The Chief Listens to Bertha."

What are the main characters and the setting of the story? (Student responses.)

Yes, Bertha and Maria are at the Oil Refinery.

What's the problem in the story? (Student responses.)

244 Lesson 78

Yes, Bertha fainted from the heat in the back of the van. Also, Bertha and Maria are trying to show the chief that the people at the Oil Refinery are breaking the law by using the wrong water.

What are some events in the story? Try to tell just the important events, not all the details. (**Student responses.**)

Yes, first Bertha started to feel better. Then Maria told the chief that Bertha could tell about things with her sense of smell. Mr. Daniels was really mad because he didn't want to be caught breaking the law. But Bertha proved to the chief that she could really smell things and tell where they came from. So the chief told Mr. Daniels to be quiet and asked Maria to get six jars of water, three from the creek and three from the well, in order to test Bertha.

Putting part of the story in your own words helps you remember it and helps you understand it. You're learning to summarize stories.

Activity 3 Make Predictions—A Before-Reading Strategy

 Direct students to Lesson 78, pages 224–227 in Reading *Textbook B*.

Elicit responses to questions. **Guide** as needed.
When you read narrative stories, it's a good strategy to make predictions about what you're going to read to help you understand the story better. Predictions are good guesses about what's in the story based on clues.

What are predictions? (Idea: *Good guesses about what's in the story based on clues.*)

You'll use clues from the title, pictures, remembering the story so far, and skimming the text so you can make a good prediction.

What'll you use to get clues? (Idea: *The title, picture, remembering the story so far, and skimming the text.*)

Work by yourself to predict what'll happen in the next story by looking at the title "Bertha Tests the Water." Skim the story, look at the picture, and remember what you know about the story so far to predict what'll happen to Bertha and Maria.

Monitor students as they review the title, picture, remember the story so far, and skim the text to make a prediction. **Elicit** predictions from students. **Record** predictions for further discussion in Lesson 79.

You made a prediction about what you're going to read. What do you do with that prediction as you read? (Idea: *Try to see whether your predictions are correct.*)

Does it matter if the prediction is exactly correct? *No.*

That's right. What's important is that you're checking as you read to see whether your predictions are correct.

Lesson 78

5 minutes

Student Materials:
Reading *Textbook B*

Part C: Fluency Building

 Conduct after the lesson, using the story of the day.

Activity 1 Partner Reading

It's time for partner reading.

Direct students to the story of the day. **Assign** student partners as Partner 1 and Partner 2. **Monitor** partner reading. **Guide** as needed.

Lesson 79

> **Materials**
> **Teacher:** Reading *Textbook B*; 9-Compare and Contrast Chart
> **Student:** Vocabulary notebook; predictions recorded in Lesson 78, Copy of 9-Compare and Contrast Chart for student pairs; Reading *Textbook B*

Part A: Vocabulary Development

 8 minutes

Teacher Materials:
Reading *Textbook B*

Student Materials:
Vocabulary notebook
Reading *Textbook B*

Activity 1 Learn New Vocabulary Word

Elicit responses to questions. **Guide** as needed.
Today you'll learn a new vocabulary word. **Special. Special** means "something really great." What does **special** mean? *Something really great.*

Another way to say "something really great" is **special.** What's another way to say "something really great"? *Special.*

There was a river that was magical. People who came to the river were **really great.** People who were **special** were brought to the river.

Discuss things that are special.

What's another way to say "something really great"? *Special.*

Direct students to write special and its definition in their vocabulary notebooks. **Guide** as needed.

Write **special** and what it means in your vocabulary notebook.

Activity 2 Review Vocabulary Word

Elicit responses to questions. **Guide** as needed.
What word means "a covering for the head and neck"? *Hood.*

Tell me a sentence using the word **hood.** (Student responses.)
Discuss sentences.

 Review vocabulary words in appropriate context in Reading *Textbook B*.

12 minutes

Teacher Materials:
Reading *Textbook B*

Compare and Contrast Chart

Student Materials:
predictions recorded in Lesson 78

Compare and Contrast Chart

Reading *Textbook B*

Part B: Comprehension Strategies

Activity 1 Confirm Predictions—An After-Reading Strategy

 Direct students to Lesson 78, pages 224–227 in Reading *Textbook B*.

Elicit response to question. **Guide** as needed.
In the last lesson, you made some predictions about what happens to Bertha and Maria in the story. You made the predictions before you read the story. Making predictions helps you understand the story better.

You confirm predictions when you check to see whether your predictions were correct. What do you do when you check to see whether your predictions were right? *Confirm predictions.*

Guide discussion based on predictions recorded in Lesson 78.
Now that you've read the story, let's check to see whether your predictions were correct or incorrect.

Sometimes, we don't predict correctly. That's okay. Just trying to make predictions and then confirming them will help you understand better what you read.

Activity 2 Compare and Contrast—An After-Reading Strategy

 Direct students to Lessons 68–78, pages 156–227 in Reading *Textbook B*.

Elicit response to question. **Guide** as needed.
You've learned how to tell how characters are the same and how they're different. Today you'll compare and contrast Bertha and Maria.

What will you do when you compare Bertha and Maria? (Idea: *Tell how Bertha and Maria are the same.*)

What will you do when you contrast Bertha and Maria? (Idea: *Tell how Bertha and Maria are different.*)

Show Compare and Contrast Chart.
Write Bertha for one name and Maria for the other name. They are both characters.

First think about how they're the same. When you write about how they're the same your sentences should begin, "They both…"
Monitor students as they write two sentences for "How Same?" box on Compare and Contrast Chart.

248 *Lesson 79*

Now think about how they are different. When you write about how they are different, it's a little harder. Your sentence needs to tell about each person and tell how each is different. You say the name of the person, tell about that person, and then use the word "but" before you tell about the next person. Remember, when you tell about how they're different, you have to tell about the same quality.

Monitor students as they write two sentences for "How Different?" box on Compare and Contrast Chart.

Activity 3 Summarize Narrative Text—An After-Reading Strategy

 Direct students to Lesson 78, pages 224–227 in Reading *Textbook B*.

Elicit response to question. **Guide** as needed.
You're learning about a strategy called summarizing. Summarizing is telling a part of a story or the whole story in your own words. You tell the important parts of the story when you summarize and you leave out the details. Summarizing helps you remember and understand the story better.

What do you do when you summarize? (Idea: *Tell the story in your own words and tell only the most important parts.*)

Guide students to summarize a story. **Elicit** characters, setting, problem, and events from students.
You read the story in the last lesson. Now we'll work together to summarize the story "Bertha Tests the Water."

Who can tell the main characters and the setting of the story? (Student responses.)

Yes, Bertha, Maria, the chief, and Mr. Daniels are at the Oil Refinery.

Who can tell the problem of this story? (Student responses.)

Yes, Bertha needed to prove to the chief that she could tell the difference between creek water and well water.

Who can tell some events in the story? Try to tell just the important events, not all the details. (Student responses.)

Yes, Bertha tested six jars of water by smelling them and got all the answers right. That made Mr. Daniels furious. But the chief believed Bertha and ordered that the Oil Refinery be closed immediately because it was breaking the law. The chief told Bertha that she should fill out the papers to be a special consultant to the state and so she would be paid $500 per day. Bertha was very happy.

Putting the story in your own words helps you remember it and helps you understand it. You're learning to summarize stories.

Lesson 79 **249**

5 minutes

Student Materials:
Reading *Textbook B*

Part C: Fluency Building

 Conduct after the lesson, using the story of the day.

Activity 1 Partner Reading

It's time for partner reading.

Direct students to the story of the day. **Assign** student partners as Partner 1 and Partner 2. **Monitor** partner reading. **Guide** as needed.

Lesson 80

Materials

Teacher: Reading *Textbook B,* 2-Vocabulary Acquisition and Use, Writing Prompts, 3-My Writing Checklist

Student: Vocabulary notebook; drawing paper; Reading *Textbook B,* Copy of 2-Vocabulary Acquisition and Use, Copy of 3-My Writing Checklist, Lined paper

Part A: Vocabulary Development

8 minutes

Teacher Materials:
Reading Textbook B

Vocabulary Acquisition and Use

Student Materials:
Vocabulary Notebook

Reading Textbook B

Vocabulary Acquisition and Use

Activity 1 Vocabulary Notebook Review

Guide students as they study all the words.
Today you'll study from your vocabulary notebook. Studying your words and what they mean will help you know your words even better. You'll study the eight words we studied over the past two weeks.

Activity 2 Cumulative Vocabulary Review

Elicit responses to questions. **Guide** as needed.
Directions: Listen and tell me whether I use our vocabulary words the right way or the wrong way. If I use the word the right way, say **"yes."** If I use the word the wrong way, say **"no."** Then we'll talk about each word.

1. Shannon had a ring that was **special** to her because her grandmother gave it to her.

   Did I use the word **special** the right way? *Yes.*

   How do you know? (Student responses.)

2. It was getting colder outside so Trina put her **hood** up.

   Did I use the word **hood** the right way? *Yes.*

   How do you know? (Student responses.)

3. The kids made a jump, but it was too **narrow** to ride their bikes over. They decided to redesign their jump.

   Did I use the word **narrow** the right way? *Yes.*

   How do you know? (Student responses.)

4. You could tell Noah was happy by the **expression** on his face.

   Did I use the word **expression** the right way? *Yes.*

   How do you know? (Student responses.)

Lesson 80

5. After the ball shattered the window, there was **silence.** Everyone was shocked at what had just happened.

   Did I use the word **silence** the right way? *Yes.*

   How do you know? (Student responses.)

6. James found a wallet on the floor in the gym. He knew the **honest** thing to do was to turn it into the office.

   Did I use the word **honest** the right way? *Yes.*

   How do you know? (Student responses.)

7. The sound of the siren **faded** as it got farther away.

   Did I use the word **faded** the right way? *Yes.*

   How do you know? (Student responses.)

8. Brandon had **doubt** that his answer was right. He asked the teacher for help.

   Did I use the word **doubt** the right way? *Yes.*

   How do you know? (Student responses.)

Review vocabulary words as needed.

 Review vocabulary words in appropriate context in Reading *Textbook B*.

Activity 3 Vocabulary Acquisition and Use

Display Vocabulary Acquisition and Use. **Have** students work with a neighbor to complete Vocabulary Acquisition and Use.
Today's vocabulary words are ____ and ____ [and ____ and ____].
Vocabulary words: **faded** and **disappeared; special** and **great**
Write the words on the lines provided. Then write the words in the boxes based on whether you think each word is less/smaller or more/larger than the other word. Below the boxes, write why you think word 1 is less/smaller and word 2 is more/larger than word 1.
Repeat for words 3 and 4. **Have** students share what they wrote. **Discuss** examples of how these words might be used.

Part B: Comprehension Strategies

12 minutes

Teacher Materials:
Reading *Textbook B*

Student Materials:
Drawing paper

Reading *Textbook B*

Display directions for the activity.
Directions: Bertha was happy at the end of the story. Discuss an experience you had that made you very happy. Then illustrate the time you were so happy. Explain why you were happy and how that experience helps you understand how Bertha felt.

Activity 1 Pair-Share Activity—Apply Knowledge (Level 3 of Bloom's Taxonomy)

 Direct students to Lesson 78, pages 224–227 in Reading *Textbook B*.

Discuss the steps in the Pair-Share activity.
You'll do an activity called **Pair-Share** to show some things you have learned in recent lessons. The directions are on the board. I'll read them to you.

Assign partners. **Provide** drawing paper.
Step 1 is the **Pair** part of the activity. Think of an experience you've had that made you happy. Illustrate that experience. Then tell how that experience helps you understand Bertha's feelings. Decide what to draw and who will draw. Work quickly. You have 8 minutes.

Guide students to think of an experience that made them happy and have them draw that experience. They should then explain how that experience helps them understand Bertha's feelings.

Call on as many students to share as time allows.
Step 2 is to **Share.** I'll call on pairs of students to share their work with the rest of the class.

Part C: Fluency Building

5 minutes

Student Materials:
Reading Textbook B

 Conduct after the lesson, using the story of the day.

Activity 1 Partner Reading

It's time for partner reading.
Direct students to the story of the day. **Assign** student partners as Partner 1 and Partner 2. **Monitor** partner reading. **Guide** as needed.

Lesson 80 **253**

Part D: Writing/Language Arts

10 minutes

Teacher Materials:
Writing Prompts

My Writing Checklist

Student Materials:
Lined Paper

My Writing Checklist

Activity 1 Write and Use Parts of Speech and Conventions

Time to write using a writing prompt based on the stories we've been reading.

Assign student partners. **Distribute** lined paper to students. **Display** writing prompts and have students choose one to write about or assign a writing prompt of your choice. **Review** parts of speech and punctuation as well as the writing checklist with students. **Tell** students to write one to two paragraphs (minimum of four sentences per paragraph) on their own to answer the writing prompt. **Tell** them to use their writing checklist (first column labeled "Did I use them?") to ensure they include important parts of speech or punctuation in their writing. **Tell** students which parts of speech or punctuation to focus on, if you wish. **Model** what it means to answer a writing prompt and to use the writing checklist during and after the writing process, as needed. **Monitor** and guide students as needed. **Model** what it means to have a neighbor look over his or her neighbor's writing and to complete the writing checklist (second column labeled "Did my neighbor use them?"), as needed. **Have** students share what they wrote as time permits.

Writing Prompt 1	*Writing Prompt 2*	*Writing Prompt 3*
If you were an investigator for the state, what would you like to investigate? Why?	Would you like to have the sense of smell that Bertha had? Why or why not?	If you could dip your body in a magic river like Achilles' mother did to him, would you? Why or why not?

254 *Lesson 80*

Lesson 81

Materials

Teacher: Alternate version of a story about Achilles; Reading *Textbook B*, 10-Prediction Chart

Student: Vocabulary notebook; Reading *Textbook B*

8 minutes

Teacher Materials:
Reading *Textbook B*

Student Materials:
Vocabulary notebook

Reading *Textbook B*

Part A: Vocabulary Development

Activity 1 Learn New Vocabulary Word

Elicit responses to questions. **Guide** as needed.
Today you'll learn a new vocabulary word. **Prove. Prove** means "show that something is true." What does **prove** mean? *Show that something is true.*

Another way to say "show that something is true" is **prove.** What's another way to say "show that something is true"? *Prove.*

Achilles wanted Hector to know that he was the greatest soldier of all and this was **something that was true.** He wanted him to know that he could **prove** this.

Discuss examples of things someone can prove.

What's another way to say "show that something is true"? *Prove.*

Direct students to write prove and its definition in their vocabulary notebooks.
Guide as needed.
Write **prove** and what it means in your vocabulary notebook.

Activity 2 Review Vocabulary Word

Elicit responses to questions. **Guide** as needed.
What's another way to say "something really great"? *Special.*

Tell me a sentence using the word **special.** (Student responses.)
Discuss sentences.

 Review vocabulary words in appropriate context in Reading *Textbook B*.

Lesson 81   **255**

12 minutes

Teacher Materials:
Alternate version of a story about Achilles

Prediction Chart

Reading *Textbook B*

Student Materials:
Reading *Textbook B*

Part B: Comprehension Strategies

Activity 1 Prepare for Text-to-Text Connections— A Before-Reading Strategy

When you make text-to-text connections, you think about stories you've read that remind you of the story you're reading. Making a connection to another story may help you understand the story you are reading better.

You read the beginning of the story of Achilles in Lesson 79. This story is a Greek myth that was written thousands of years ago. Since then, many people have written their own versions of the myth. The story in your reading book is just one version of the story. I'll read another version of the story, written by a different author, so that we can make a text-to-text connection in the next lesson.

Read an alternate version of the story of Achilles with prosody. **Elicit** the title, characters, setting, problem, and main events after reading story.

In the next lesson, we'll make a text-to-text connection. We'll compare and contrast the stories to see how they're the same and how they're different. Making text-to-text connections helps you understand stories better.

Activity 2 Make Predictions—A Before-Reading Strategy

 Direct students to Lesson 81, pages 241–244 in Reading *Textbook B*.

Show Prediction Chart. **Elicit** answers to questions. **Guide** as needed.
When you read narrative stories, it's a good strategy to make predictions about what you're going to read to help you understand the story better.

What are predictions? (Idea: *Good guesses based on clues about what's in the story.*)

Where do you get the clues for your prediction? (Idea: *The title, the picture, skimming the text, and remembering what you know about the story so far.*)

Work by yourself to predict what'll happen in the next story by looking at the title "The Greatest Soldier." You'll also skim the story, look at the picture, and remember what you know about the story so far to predict what will happen to Achilles.
Monitor students as they review the title, picture, remember the story so far, and skim the text to make a prediction. **Elicit** predictions from the students. **Record** predictions for further discussion in Lesson 82.

You made a prediction about what you're going to read.

What do you do with that prediction as you read? (Idea: *Try to see whether your predictions are correct or not.*)

Does it matter whether the prediction is exactly correct? *No.*

That's right. What's important is that you're checking as you read to see whether your predictions are correct.

256 Lesson 81

5 minutes

Student Materials:
Reading *Textbook B*

Part C: Fluency Building

 Conduct after the lesson, using the story of the day.

Activity 1 Partner Reading

It's time for partner reading.
Direct students to the story of the day. **Assign** student partners as Partner 1 and Partner 2. **Monitor** partner reading. **Guide** as needed.

Lesson 81 **257**

Lesson 82

Materials

Teacher: Alternate version of a story about Achilles (from Lesson 81); 10-Prediction Chart (from Lesson 81); Reading *Textbook B*
Student: Vocabulary notebook; Reading *Textbook B*

Part A: Vocabulary Development

8 minutes

Teacher Materials:
Reading *Textbook B*

Student Materials:
Vocabulary notebook
Reading *Textbook B*

Activity 1 Learn New Vocabulary Word

Elicit responses to questions. **Guide** as needed.
Today you'll learn a new vocabulary word. **Clues. Clues** mean "things that help you find an answer." What does **clues** mean? *Things that help you find an answer.*

Another way to say "things that help you find an answer" is **clues.** What's another way to say "things that help you find an answer"? *Clues.*

People who lived eighty thousand years ago left **things that help us find answers** about how they lived. They left **clues** that show us how they lived.

Discuss examples of clues.

What's another way to say "things that help you find an answer"? *Clues.*

Direct students to write clues and its definition in their vocabulary notebooks. **Guide** as needed.
Write **clues** and what it means in your vocabulary notebook.

Activity 2 Review Vocabulary Word

Elicit responses to questions. **Guide** as needed.
What's another way to say "show that something is true"? *Prove.*

Tell me a sentence using the word **prove.** (Student responses.)
Discuss sentences.

 Review vocabulary words in appropriate context in Reading *Textbook B*.

258   Lesson 82

Part B: Comprehension Strategies

12 minutes

Teacher Materials:
Alternate version of a story about Achilles (from Lesson 81)

Prediction Chart

Reading *Textbook B*

Student Materials:
Reading *Textbook B*

Activity 1 Confirm Predictions—An After-Reading Strategy

 Direct students to Lesson 81, pages 241–244 in Reading *Textbook B*.

Elicit response to question. **Guide** as needed.
In the last lesson, you made some predictions about what happens to Achilles in the story. You made the predictions before you read the story. Making predictions helps you better understand the story.

What do you do when you check to see whether your predictions were right? *Confirm predictions.*

Now that you've read the story, let's check to see whether your predictions were correct or incorrect.
Guide discussion based on predictions recorded in Lesson 81.

Sometimes, we don't predict correctly.

Why is that okay? (Idea: *Just trying to make a prediction and then confirming it will help you better understand what you read.*)

Activity 2 Make Text-to-Text Connections— An After-Reading Strategy

Direct students to Lesson 79 pages 232–233 and Lesson 81, pages 241–244.
Direct students to alternate version of story about Achilles from Lesson 81.
You're learning about making text-to-text connections. When you make text-to-text connections, you think about stories you've read that remind you of the story you're reading. Making a connection to another story may help you understand the story you are reading better.

The story of Achilles is a Greek myth. A myth is a story that is not true. This story was written thousands of years ago, and it has been written many times by many authors. Different authors write the same story many different ways. So we'll make a text-to-text connection today to tell how these two stories are the same and how they're different.

Elicit suggestions for how the stories are the same. **Elicit** suggestions for how the stories are different. **Guide** as needed.

When you compare and contrast the stories to see how they're the same and how they're different, you're making text-to-text connections that helps you better understand stories.

Lesson 82 **259**

5 minutes

Student Materials:
Reading *Textbook B*

Part C: Fluency Building

 Conduct after the lesson, using the story of the day.

Activity 1 Partner Reading

It's time for partner reading.
Direct students to the story of the day. **Assign** student partners as Partner 1 and Partner 2. **Monitor** partner reading. **Guide** as needed.

Lesson 83

Materials

Teacher: Reading *Textbook B*, 10-Prediction Chart
Student: Vocabulary notebook; Reading *Textbook B*, Copy of 10-Prediction Chart

Part A: Vocabulary Development

8 minutes

Teacher Materials:
Reading *Textbook B*

Student Materials:
Vocabulary notebook

Reading *Textbook B*

Activity 1 Learn New Vocabulary Word

Elicit responses to questions. **Guide** as needed.
Today you'll learn a new vocabulary word. **Bits. Bits** mean "small pieces."
What does **bits** mean? *Small pieces.*

Another way to say "small pieces" is **bits.** What's another way to say "small pieces"? *Bits.*

We look at piles left from the past and find **small pieces** of things. These **bits** help us to determine things like whether the people who lived before us cooked with fire.

Discuss examples of things that are <u>bits</u>.

What's another way to say "small pieces"? *Bits.*

Direct students to write <u>bits</u> and its definition in their vocabulary notebooks. **Guide** as needed.
Write **bits** and what it means in your vocabulary notebook.

Activity 2 Review Vocabulary Word

Elicit responses to questions. **Guide** as needed.
What's another way to say "things that help you find an answer"? *Clues.*

Tell me a sentence using the word **clues.** (Student responses.)
Discuss sentences.

 Review vocabulary words in appropriate context in Reading *Textbook B*.

12 minutes

Teacher Materials:
Reading *Textbook B*

Prediction Chart

Student Materials:
Reading *Textbook B*

Prediction Chart

Part B: Comprehension Strategies

Activity 1 Summarize Expository Text—An After-Reading Strategy

 Direct students to Lesson 82, pages 248–253 in Reading *Textbook B*.

Elicit response to question. **Guide** as needed.
You're learning a strategy called **summarizing.** When you summarize narrative text, you **tell part of a story or the whole story in your own words.** You tell only the important parts of the story when you summarize and leave out the details.

What do you do when you summarize narrative text? (Idea: *Tell the story in your own words and tell only the most important parts.*)

Today you'll learn to summarize expository text. You summarized expository text when you filled out the "What I Learned" section of your KWL chart. You wrote the facts you learned in your own words.

Now I'll show you how I summarize the passage "Clues from Thousands of Years Ago."
Model think-aloud for summarizing expository text. **Tell** the topic of passage. **Tell** the important facts from the passage and try to leave out the details.

Sample Wording for Think-Aloud

I'll think of why I read expository text. I read to learn new information and facts. So when I **summarize** expository text, I want to **tell the topic of the passage and the most important facts from the passage**. I want to try to leave out the details.

The title is "Clues from Thousands of Years Ago." The topic is "how to learn about people long ago from garbage piles."

The first part of the passage tells about a time line. I think it is a detail, so I will not include that part in my summary. The next part tells that things were very different 80,000 years ago. That part is important, so it's part of my summary. The things that were different are details, so I will not include them in my summary. The next part tells about clues. I think this part tells details. But then there's a part about how garbage gives clues to how people lived. That's important, so I'll include it in my summary. Things at the bottom of the garbage pile are older than the things at the top of the garbage pile. So the things at the bottom of the garbage pile were used longer ago than things at the top of the pile. That's important, so I'll include it in my summary. The way things change in a garbage pile from the bottom to the top, gives us clues for how people changed from long ago until now. That's important. We can tell from the garbage pile that people ate things raw a very long time ago, but then people changed and started cooking their food. That's important and I'll include that in my summary.

Putting the facts in the passage in my own words helps me remember and understand them. You'll be learning to summarize expository text, too.

262 Lesson 83

Activity 2 Make Predictions—A Before-Reading Strategy

Direct students to Lesson 83, pages 257–261 in Reading *Textbook B*.

Show Prediction Chart. **Elicit** responses to questions. **Guide** as needed.
When you read narrative stories, it's a good strategy to make predictions about what you're going to read to help you understand the story better. You can also make predictions when you read expository text. It works exactly the same way.

What are predictions? (Idea: *Good guesses based on clues about what's in the story.*)

Where do you get the clues for your prediction? (Idea: *The title, the picture, skimming the text, and remembering what you know about the story so far.*)

Work by yourself to predict what will happen in the next story by looking at the title "Digging into Piles." You'll also skim the passage and look at the picture. You haven't read about this topic before so you can't remember the story so far this time. Try to make a prediction, based on the clues you have.

Elicit predictions from students. **Have** students record predictions for further discussion in Lesson 84.

You made a prediction about what you're going to read.

What do you do with that prediction as you read? (Idea: *Try to see whether your prediction is correct.*)

Does it matter whether the prediction is exactly correct? *No.*

That's right. What's important is that you're checking as you read to see if your predictions are correct.

5 minutes

Student Materials:
Reading *Textbook B*

Part C: Fluency Building

Conduct after the lesson, using the story of the day.

Activity 1 Partner Reading

It's time for partner reading.
Direct students to the story of the day. **Assign** student partners as Partner 1 and Partner 2. **Monitor** partner reading. **Guide** as needed.

Lesson 83 **263**

Lesson 84

Materials
Teacher: Reading *Textbook B*; 10-Prediction Chart
Student: Vocabulary notebook; Reading *Textbook B*, predictions recorded in Lesson 83

8 minutes

Teacher Materials:
Reading *Textbook B*

Student Materials:
Vocabulary notebook
Reading *Textbook B*

Part A: Vocabulary Development

Activity 1 Learn New Vocabulary Word

Elicit responses to questions. **Guide** as needed.
Today you'll learn a new vocabulary word. **Gather. Gather** means "come together." What does **gather** mean? *Come together.*

Another way to say "come together" is **gather.** What's another way to say "come together"? *Gather.*

The people all **come together** to see the tree that is burning because it has been struck by lightning. They **gather** to watch the fire burn.

Discuss examples of when people gather.

What's another way to say "come together"? *Gather.*

Direct students to write gather and its definition in their vocabulary notebooks. **Guide** as needed.
Write **gather** and what it means in your vocabulary notebook.

Activity 2 Review Vocabulary Word

Elicit responses to questions. **Guide** as needed.
What's another way to say "small pieces"? *Bits.*

Tell me a sentence using the word **bits.** (Student responses).
Discuss sentences.

 Review vocabulary words in appropriate context in Reading *Textbook B*.

264 *Lesson 84*

12 minutes

Teacher Materials:
Reading *Textbook B*
Prediction Chart

Student Materials:
Reading *Textbook B*
Prediction Chart

Part B: Comprehension Strategies

Activity 1 Confirm Predictions—An After-Reading Strategy

 Direct students to Lesson 83, pages 257–265 in Reading *Textbook B*.

Show Prediction Chart. **Elicit** response to questions. **Guide** as needed.
In the last lesson, you made some predictions about what you would read in the expository passage "Digging into Piles." You made the predictions before you read the story. Making predictions helps you better understand the story.

What do you do when you check to see whether your predictions were right? *Confirm predictions.*

Now that you've read the story, let's check to see whether your predictions were correct or incorrect.
Guide discussion based on predictions recorded in Lesson 83.

Sometimes, we don't predict correctly. Why is that okay? (Idea: *Just trying to make a prediction and then confirming it will help you better understand what you read.*)

Activity 2 Summarize Expository Text—An After-Reading Strategy

 Direct students to Lesson 83, pages 257–262 in Reading *Textbook B*.

Elicit response to question. **Guide** as needed.
You're learning a strategy called summarizing. When you summarize narrative text you tell part of a story or the whole story in your own words. You tell only the important parts of the story when you summarize and leave out the details.

Today you'll learn more about how to summarize expository text. You summarized expository text when you filled out the "What I Learned" section of your KWL chart. You wrote the facts you learned in your own words. When you summarize expository text, you tell the topic and the important facts you learn from the passage.

What do you do when you summarize expository text? (Idea: *Tell the topic and the important facts you learn from the passage.*)

Now I'll show you how I summarize the passage "Digging into Piles."
Hint: Words in bold print are usually important ideas.

Lesson 84

Model summarizing expository text. **Tell** the topic of passage. Idea: The topic is garbage piles. **Tell** the important facts from the passage and try to leave out the details. Possible important facts: Things at the bottom of garbage piles went in earlier than things at the top so they are older. We learn what people used by looking in garbage piles. The order in which things are thrown in a garbage pile is like a time line. The things at the bottom are oldest and tell about the earliest people. Things at the top tell about later people.

Putting the facts in the passage in my own words helps me remember and understand them. You'll be learning to summarize expository text too.

Part C: Fluency Building

5 minutes

Student Materials:
Reading *Textbook B*

Conduct after the lesson, using the story of the day.

Activity 1 Partner Reading

It's time for partner reading.

Direct students to the story of the day. **Assign** student partners as Partner 1 and Partner 2. **Monitor** partner reading. **Guide** as needed.

Lesson 85

> **Materials**
> **Teacher:** Reading *Textbook B*, 2-Vocabulary Acquisition and Use
> **Student:** Vocabulary notebook; Copy of 2-Vocabulary Acquisition and Use, Reading *Textbook B*; Drawing paper

8 minutes

Teacher Materials:
Reading *Textbook B*

Vocabulary Acquisition and Use

Student Materials:
Reading *Textbook B*

Vocabulary Acquisition and Use

Part A: Vocabulary Development

Activity 1 Vocabulary Notebook Review

Guide students through all vocabulary words.
Today you'll study from your vocabulary notebook. Studying your words and what they mean will help you know your words even better. You'll look at the four words we studied this week.

Activity 2 Cumulative Vocabulary Review

Elicit responses to questions. **Guide** as needed.
Directions: Listen and tell me whether I use our vocabulary words the right way or the wrong way. If I use the word the right way, say **"yes."** If I use the word the wrong way, say **"no."** Then we'll talk about each word.

1. Geoff had a picture to **prove** he had red hair as a baby.

   Did I use the word **prove** the right way? *Yes.*

   How do you know? (Student responses.)

2. The children were asked to **gather** around for story time.

   Did I use the word **gather** the right way? *Yes.*

   How do you know? (Student responses.)

3. Alana knew exactly where Terry lived. She needed **clues** to help her get to Terry's house.

   Did I use the word **clues** the right way? *No.*

   How do you know? (Student responses.)

4. The dog chewed my shoe to **bits.**

   Did I use the word bits the right way? *Yes.*

   How do you know? (Student responses.)

Review vocabulary words as needed.

 Review vocabulary words in appropriate context in Reading *Textbook B*.

Activity 3 — Vocabulary Acquisition and Use

Display Vocabulary Acquisition and Use. **Have** students work with a neighbor to complete Vocabulary Acquisition and Use.
Today's vocabulary words are ____ and ____ [and ____ and ____].
Vocabulary words: **prove** and **show**; **gather** and **assemble**
Write the words on the lines provided. Then write the words in the boxes based on whether you think each word is less/smaller or more/larger than the other word. Below the boxes, write why you think word 1 is less/smaller and word 2 is more/larger than word 1.
Repeat for words 3 and 4. **Have** students share what they wrote. **Discuss** examples of how these words might be used.

Part B: Comprehension Strategies

12 minutes

Teacher Materials:
Reading *Textbook B*

Student Materials:
Drawing paper

Reading *Textbook B*

Display directions for activity.
Directions: Draw a garbage pile to show a time line of your life. Show the things you threw away when you were a baby at the bottom of the pile. Show things you threw away when you were three in the middle and things you would throw away now at the top. Explain how your garbage pile shows parts of your life from the beginning until now.

Activity 1 — Pair-Share Activity—Apply Knowledge (Level 3 of Bloom's Taxonomy)

 Direct students to Lesson 83, pages 257–262 in Reading *Textbook B*.

Discuss the steps in the Pair-Share activity.
You'll do an activity called **Pair-Share** to show some things you've learned in recent lessons. The directions are on the board. I'll read them to you.

Assign partners. **Provide** drawing paper.
Step 1 is the **Pair** part of the activity. Work with your partner to draw a garbage pile to show things you would throw away when you were a baby at the bottom, things you would throw away when you were three in the middle, and things you would throw away now at the top. Explain how that shows a time line of your life. Decide what to draw and who will draw. Work quickly. You have 8 minutes.
Guide students to draw garbage pile to show a time line of their lives.

Call on as many students to share as time allows.
Step 2 is to **Share.** I'll call on pairs of students to share their work with the rest of the class.

268 Lesson 85

5 minutes

Student Materials:
Reading *Textbook B*

Part C: Fluency Building

 Conduct after the lesson, using the story of the day.

Activity 1 Partner Reading

It's time for partner reading.
Direct students to the story of the day. **Assign** student partners as Partner 1 and Partner 2. **Monitor** partner reading. **Guide** as needed.

Lesson 85 **269**

Lesson 86

Materials
Teacher: 7-KWL Chart, Reading *Textbook B*
Student: Vocabulary notebook; 7-KWL Chart; Reading *Textbook B*

8 minutes

Teacher Materials:
Reading *Textbook B*

Student Materials:
Vocabulary notebook
Reading *Textbook B*

Part A: Vocabulary Development

Activity 1 Learn New Vocabulary Word

Elicit responses to questions. **Guide** as needed.
Today you'll learn a new vocabulary word. **Slim. Slim** means "thin." What does **slim** mean? *Thin.*

Another word for "thin" is **slim.** What's another word for "thin"? *Slim.*

There are many varieties of horses. Some are **thin** and some are big. Some horses have muscular legs and some have **slim** legs.

Discuss things that are slim.

What's another word for "thin"? *Slim.*

Direct students to write slim and its definition in their vocabulary notebooks. **Guide** as needed.
Write **slim** and what it means in your vocabulary notebook.

Activity 2 Review Vocabulary Word

Elicit responses to questions. **Guide** as needed.
What's another way to say "come together"? *Gather.*

Tell me a sentence using the word **gather.** (Student responses.)
Discuss sentences.

 Review vocabulary words in appropriate context in Reading *Textbook B*.

270 Lesson 86

Part B: Comprehension Strategies

12 minutes

Teacher Materials:
KWL Chart

Student Materials:
KWL Chart

Activity 1 KWL Chart: Topic and What I Know— A Before-Reading Strategy

Elicit responses to questions. **Guide** as needed.
You're going to activate your background knowledge for a new topic. What do you do when you activate your background knowledge? (Idea: *Think about what you already know.*)

You'll be reading passages about different kinds of horses in the next few lessons.

Why is it a good idea to think about your background knowledge before you read? (Idea: *Then you'll be able to connect what you know to what you learn.*)

Show KWL Chart.
You'll use a KWL chart to help you organize your thinking about expository text. Why do you use a KWL chart? (Idea: *To organize thinking about expository text.*)

The first box you write in is the "Topic" box.

What should we write for the topic? *Horses.*

Write the topic on KWL Chart. **Guide** students as they write topic on their charts.

Now let's work together to activate your background knowledge about horses for the "What I Know" section of the KWL chart.

Discuss student background knowledge. **Record** three items in "What I Know" section of KWL Chart. **Guide** students as they write items on their charts.

When you connect what you already know with the text, you'll be building more background knowledge in your mind.

Activity 2 KWL Chart: What I Wonder—A Before-Reading Strategy

Elicit responses to questions. **Guide** as needed. **Show** KWL Chart.
Next you'll write the questions you have about the topic in the "What I Wonder" section of the chart.

What'll you write in this section of the chart? (Ideas: *Questions you have; what you wonder about.*)

What words can you use to help you think of questions? (Idea: *Who, what, when, where, how, and why.*)

Let's work together to think of questions about horses for the "What I Wonder" section of the KWL chart.

Lesson 86 **271**

Discuss possible questions. **Record** three questions in "What I Wonder" section of KWL Chart. **Guide** students as they copy questions on their charts.

Why is it important to ask questions before you read? (Idea: *Asking questions gets you interested in what you're going to learn—it makes you think about what you're going to read.*)

The text you read may or may not have the answers to your questions. That's okay. Just asking the questions helps you be smarter. If you don't find the answers to your questions, you might need to read more in another book to find out the answers.

Save teacher and student copies of KWL Chart for Lesson 87.

5 minutes

Student Materials:
Reading *Textbook B*

Part C: Fluency Building

 Conduct after the lesson, using the story of the day.

Activity 1 Partner Reading

It's time for partner reading.
Direct students to the story of the day. **Assign** student partners as Partner 1 and Partner 2. **Monitor** partner reading. **Guide** as needed.

Lesson 87

Materials
Teacher: 7-KWL Chart (from Lesson 86); Reading *Textbook B*
Student: Vocabulary notebook; 7-KWL Chart (from Lesson 86); Reading *Textbook B*

Part A: Vocabulary Development

8 minutes

Teacher Materials:
Reading *Textbook B*

Student Materials:
Vocabulary notebook
Reading *Textbook B*

Activity 1 Learn New Vocabulary Word

Elicit responses to questions. **Guide** as needed.
Today you'll learn a new vocabulary word. **Earliest. Earliest** means "could not happen any sooner." What does **earliest** mean? *Could not happen any sooner.*

Another way to say "could not happen any sooner" is **earliest.** What's another way to say "could not happen any sooner"? *Earliest.*

We look at layers of rock to determine what things **could not have happened any sooner.** The things that were here the earliest are found in the deepest layer of rock.

Discuss examples of things that are the earliest.

What's another way to say "could not happen any sooner"? *Earliest.*

Direct students to write earliest and its definition in their vocabulary notebook. **Guide** as needed.
Write **earliest** and what it means in your vocabulary notebook.

Activity 2 Review Vocabulary Word

Elicit responses to questions. **Guide** as needed.
What's another word that means "thin"? *Slim.*

Tell me a sentence using the word **slim.** (Student responses.)
Discuss sentences.

 Review vocabulary words in appropriate context in Reading *Textbook B*.

Lesson 87   273

12 minutes

Teacher Materials:
KWL Chart

Reading *Textbook B*

Student Materials:
KWL Chart

Reading *Textbook B*

Part B: Comprehension Strategies

Activity 1 KWL Chart: What I Learned—An After-Reading Strategy

 Direct students to Lesson 86, pages 285–288 in Reading *Textbook B*.

Show KWL Chart (partially completed in Lesson 86). **Elicit** responses to questions. **Guide** as needed.

In the last lesson you read "Different Kinds of Horses." It's time to write what you learned from the passage in the "What I Learned" section of the KWL chart.

When you write what you learned, you should write it in your own words rather than copy it right from the book.

Why should you write the ideas in your own words? (Idea: *That will help you remember the information later.*)

Let's work together to fill out the "What I Learned" section of the chart.

Call on students to read passage in parts. **Guide** students to summarize parts of the passage. **Record** best sentences on the "What I Learned" section of KWL Chart. **Guide** students as they write the sentences on their charts.

Read the first part of the passage on horses. How can we put that part in our own words to record on our chart? (**Student responses.**)

We can write: "Not all horses are the same."

Read the next part. How can we put that part in our own words? (**Student responses.**)

We can write: "Draft horses are very large, pull heavy things, and weigh as much as 30 children."

Read the next part. How can we put that part in our own words? (**Student responses.**)

We can write: "Racehorses are smaller than draft horses, run fast, have thin legs, and weigh as much as 15 children."

Read the next part. How can we put that part in our own words? (**Student responses.**)

We can write: "Quarter horses are smaller than racehorses, have a shorter back, can stop and turn fast, and weigh as much as 15 children."

Read the next part. How can we put that part in our own words? (**Student responses.**)

We can write: "Mongolian horses are small horses, lived 30,000 years ago, look like pictures of horses in caves, and weigh as much as 8 children."

274 Lesson 87

Read the next part. How can we put that part in our own words? (Student responses.)

We can write: "A full-grown pony is no bigger than a large dog and weighs as much as 4 children."
Save teacher and student copies of KWL Chart for Lesson 88.

You've now written the new things you learned from the expository text you read. You wrote the information in your own words.

Activity 2 Summarize Expository Text—An After-Reading Strategy

 Direct students to Lesson 86, pages 285–288 in Reading *Textbook B*.

Elicit responses to questions. **Guide** as needed.
You're learning a strategy called summarizing. When you summarize text, you tell about what you read in your own words. You tell only the important parts of the passage when you summarize and you leave out the details. When you summarize expository text, you tell the topic and the important facts.

What do you tell when you summarize expository text? (Idea: *The topic and the important facts.*)

You have summarized as you write the topic and important facts on your KWL chart. You can further summarize by telling about the whole passage in a few sentences that tell the most important thing you learned from the passage. Watch me as I think about summarizing "Different Kinds of Horses" in a few sentences.
Model think-aloud for summarizing expository text in a few sentences.

Sample Wording for Think-Aloud

I'm thinking of the text I just read and of all the sentences I wrote on my KWL chart. I want to put all that information together in a few sentences. My sentences are all about different kinds of horses and how they are different from each other. So I will say, "This passage tells about how there are many kinds of horses that are different from each other. They are different sizes and they are good at different skills."

I told the main thing I learned from the passage, and I left out all the details.

Lesson 87 **275**

5 minutes

Student Materials:
Reading *Textbook B*

Part C: Fluency Building

 Conduct after the lesson, using the story of the day.

Activity 1 Partner Reading

It's time for partner reading.

Direct students to the story of the day. **Assign** student partners as Partner 1 and Partner 2. **Monitor** partner reading. **Guide** as needed.

Lesson 88

Materials
Teacher: 7-KWL Chart (from Lesson 87); Reading *Textbook B*
Student: Vocabulary notebook; 7-KWL Chart (from Lesson 87); Reading *Textbook B*

8 minutes

Teacher Materials:
Reading *Textbook B*

Student Materials:
Vocabulary notebook
Reading *Textbook B*

Part A: Vocabulary Development

Activity 1 Learn New Vocabulary Word

Elicit responses to questions. **Guide** as needed.
Today you'll learn a new vocabulary word. **Row. Row** means "a neat line of people or things." What does **row** mean? *A neat line of people or things.*

Another way to say "a neat line of people or things" is **row.** What's another way to say "a neat line of people or things"? *Row.*

When we compare things, we make **a neat line of people or things.** By putting things in a **row**, we can easily see the differences.

Discuss things that are in a row.

What's another way to say "a neat line of people or things"? *Row.*

Direct students to write row and its definition in their vocabulary notebooks. **Guide** as needed.
Write **row** and what it means in your vocabulary notebook.

Activity 2 Review Vocabulary Word

Elicit responses to questions. **Guide** as needed.
What's another way to say "could not happen any sooner"? *Earliest.*

Tell me a sentence using the word **earliest.** (Student responses.)
Discuss sentences.

 Review vocabulary words in appropriate context in Reading *Textbook B*.

Lesson 88   **277**

12 minutes

Teacher Materials:
KWL Chart

Reading *Textbook B*

Student Materials:
KWL Chart

Reading *Textbook B*

Part B: Comprehension Strategies

Activity 1 KWL Chart: What I Learned—An After-Reading Strategy

 Direct students to Lesson 87, pages 291–295 in Reading *Textbook B*.

Show KWL Chart (partially completed in Lesson 87). **Elicit** responses to questions. **Guide** as needed.

In the last lesson, you read "Horses from Millions of Years Ago." It's time to add what you learned from the passage in the "What I Learned" section of the KWL chart that you started in Lesson 86.

Should you copy the words from the book? *No.*

What should you do instead? (Idea: *Write the ideas in your own words.*)

Why should you write the ideas in your own words? (Idea: *That will help you remember the information later.*)

Today you'll work with a partner to fill out the "What I Learned" section of the chart.

Guide students to work with a partner to summarize parts of the passage and to write two sentences to add to the "What I Learned" section of the KWL chart started in Lesson 86. **Elicit** sentences from students to add to "What I Learned" section. **Record** the best sentences on the "What I Learned" section of the KWL Chart for students to copy as necessary.

Save teacher and student copies of the KWL Chart for Lesson 89.

You've now written the new things you learned from the expository text you read. You wrote the information in your own words.

Activity 2 Summarize Expository Text—An After-Reading Strategy

 Direct students to Lesson 87, pages 291–295 in Reading *Textbook B*.

Elicit responses to questions. **Guide** as needed.
You're learning a strategy called summarizing. When you summarize text, you tell about what you read in your own words. You tell only the important parts of the passage when you summarize and you leave out the details. When you summarize expository text, you tell the topic and the important facts.

What do you tell when you summarize expository text? (Idea: *The topic and the important facts.*)

You have summarized as you wrote the topic and important facts on your KWL chart. You can further summarize by telling about the whole passage in a few sentences that tell the most important thing you learned from the passage.

278 Lesson 88

Watch me as I think about summarizing "Horses from Millions of Years Ago" in a few sentences.

Model summarizing expository text in a few sentences. Suggested sentence: We have learned from digging up horse skeletons from deep in the ground that horses looked different millions of years ago from horses today.

I told the main thing I learned from the passage, and I left out all the details.

Part C: Fluency Building

5 minutes

Student Materials:
Reading *Textbook B*

  Conduct after the lesson, using the story of the day.

Activity 1 Partner Reading

It's time for partner reading.

Direct students to the story of the day. **Assign** student partners as Partner 1 and Partner 2. **Monitor** partner reading. **Guide** as needed.

Lesson 88

Lesson 89

Materials
Teacher: 7-KWL Chart (from Lesson 88); Reading *Textbook B*
Student: Vocabulary notebook; 7-KWL Chart (from Lesson 88); Reading *Textbook B*

Part A: Vocabulary Development

8 minutes

Teacher Materials:
Reading *Textbook B*

Student Materials:
Vocabulary notebook

Reading *Textbook B*

Activity 1 Learn New Vocabulary Word

Elicit responses to questions. **Guide** as needed.
Today you'll learn a new vocabulary word. **Daydreaming. Daydreaming** means "thinking about happy things during the day." What does **daydreaming** mean? *Thinking about happy things during the day.*

Another way to say "thinking about happy things during the day" is **daydreaming.** What's another way to say "thinking about happy things during the day"? *Daydreaming.*

Andrew was not good enough to play most sports. So Andrew would spend a lot of time **thinking about happy things during the day.** When he was **daydreaming,** he would be the star of the team.

Discuss examples of daydreaming.

What's another way to say **thinking about happy things during the day?** *Daydreaming.*

Direct students to write daydreaming and its definition in their vocabulary notebooks.
Guide as needed.
Write **daydreaming** and what it means in your vocabulary notebook.

Activity 2 Review Vocabulary Word

Elicit responses to questions. **Guide** as needed.
What's another way to say "a neat line of people or things"? *Row.*

Tell me a sentence using the word **row.** (Student responses.)
Discuss sentences.

 Review vocabulary words in appropriate context in Reading *Textbook B*.

280 Lesson 89

12 minutes

Teacher Materials:
KWL Chart

Reading *Textbook B*

Student Materials:
KWL Chart

Reading *Textbook B*

Part B: Comprehension Strategies

Activity 1 KWL Chart: What I Learned—An After-Reading Strategy

 Direct students to Lesson 88, pages 300–303 in Reading *Textbook B*.

Show KWL Chart (partially completed in Lesson 88). **Elicit** responses to questions. **Guide** as needed.
In the last lesson, you read "How Horses Changed." It's time to add what you learned from the passage in the "What I Learned" section of the KWL chart that you started in Lesson 86.

Should you copy the words from the book? *No.*

What should you do instead? (Idea: *Write the ideas in your own words.*)

Why should you write the ideas in your own words? (Idea: *That will help you remember the information later.*)

Today you'll work with a partner to fill out the "What I Learned" section of the chart. **Hint:** Important information is often printed in bold print.

Guide students to work with a partner to summarize parts of the passage and to write 2 sentences to add to the "What I Learned" section of the KWL Chart started in Lesson 86. **Elicit** sentences from students to add to the "What I Learned" section. **Record** the best sentences on the "What I Learned" section of the KWL Chart for students to copy as necessary.

You've now written the new things you learned from the expository text you read. You wrote the information in your own words.

Activity 2 Summarize Expository Text—An After-Reading Strategy

 Direct students to Lesson 87, pages 291–295 in Reading *Textbook B*.

Elicit responses to questions. **Guide** as needed.
You're learning a strategy called summarizing. When you summarize text, you tell about what you read in your own words. You tell only the important parts of the passage when you summarize, and you leave out the details. When you summarize expository text, you tell the topic and the important facts.

What do you tell when you summarize expository text? (Idea: *The topic and the important facts.*)

You have summarized as you wrote the topic and important facts on your KWL chart. You can further summarize by telling about the whole passage in a few sentences that tell the most important thing you learned from the passage.

Lesson 89   **281**

Let's work together to summarize "How Horses Changed" in a few sentences. Look at the topic and look at the new sentences you wrote for your KWL chart.

How can we put those ideas into a few sentences? (Student responses.)
Elicit student ideas for summary sentences. Guide students to the idea that the eohippus was a horse millions of years ago that was very different from horses today. It changed over many years from a small, hiding animal to a large, fast, running animal.

We told the main things we learned from the passage in a few sentences, and we left out all the details.

Part C: Fluency Building

5 minutes

Student Materials:
Reading *Textbook B*

 Conduct after the lesson, using the story of the day.

Activity 1 Partner Reading

It's time for partner reading.
Direct students to the story of the day. **Assign** student partners as Partner 1 and Partner 2. **Monitor** partner reading. **Guide** as needed.

Lesson 90

Materials

Teacher: Reading *Textbook B*, 2-Vocabulary Acquisition and Use, Writing Prompts, 3-My Writing Checklist

Student: Vocabulary notebook; drawing paper; Reading *Textbook B*, Copy of 2-Vocabulary Acquisition and Use, Copy of 3-My Writing Checklist, Lined paper

8 minutes

Teacher Materials:
Reading *Textbook B*

Vocabulary Acquisition and Use

Student Materials:
Vocabulary Notebook

Reading Textbook B

Vocabulary Acquisition and Use

Part A: Vocabulary Development

Activity 1 Vocabulary Notebook Review

Guide students as they study all vocabulary words.
Today you'll study from your vocabulary notebook. Studying your words and what they mean will help you know your words even better. You'll study the eight words we studied over the past two weeks.

Activity 2 Cumulative Vocabulary Review

Elicit responses to questions. **Guide** as needed.
Directions: Listen and tell me whether I use our vocabulary words the right way or the wrong way. If I use the word the right way, say **"yes."** If I use the word the wrong way, say **"no."** Then we'll talk about each word.

1. Sam would **row** his wagon around the neighborhood.

   Did I use the word **row** the right way? *No.*

   How do you know? (Student responses.)

2. Jacob said the **earliest** he could be to the party was noon.

   Did I use the word **earliest** the right way? *Yes.*

   How do you know? (Student responses.)

3. Andrea showed her test to Ben to **prove** she passed it.

   Did I use the word **prove** the right way? *Yes.*

   How do you know? (Student responses.)

4. When the teacher called on Steve, he didn't know the answer because he'd been **daydreaming.**

   Did I use the word **daydreaming** the right way? *Yes.*

   How do you know? (Student responses.)

Lesson 90 283

5. Carol was tall and **slim.**

   Did I use the word **slim** the right way? *Yes.*

   How do you know? (Student responses.)

6. Everyone at the party was asked to **gather** so Marcy could take a picture.

   Did I use the word **gather** the right way? *Yes.*

   How do you know? (Student responses.)

7. Shelly was so hungry that she ate in big bites. Shelly ate **bits** of things.

   Did I use the word **bits** the right way? *No.*

   How do you know? (Student responses.)

8. The police had no **clues** to help them find the robber.

   Did I use the word **clues** the right way? *Yes.*

   How do you know? (Student responses.)

Review vocabulary words as needed.

 Review vocabulary words in appropriate context in Reading *Textbook B.*

Activity 3 Vocabulary Acquisition and Use

Display Vocabulary Acquisition and Use. **Have** students work with a neighbor to complete Vocabulary Acquisition and Use.
Today's vocabulary words are ____ and ____ [and ____ and ____].
Vocabulary words: **slim** and **thin; daydreaming** and **thinking**
Write the words on the lines provided. Then write the words in the boxes based on whether you think each word is less/smaller or more/larger than the other word. Below the boxes, write why you think word 1 is less/smaller and word 2 is more/larger than word 1.
Repeat for words 3 and 4. **Have** students share what they wrote. **Discuss** examples of how these words might be used.

12 minutes

Teacher Materials:
Reading *Textbook B*

Student Materials:
Drawing paper

Reading *Textbook B*

Part B: Comprehension Strategies

Display directions for the activity.
Directions: Discuss how horses have changed over time. Draw a time line to show how horses have changed from 38 million years ago to today. Draw the earliest horse at the bottom and what horses look like today at the top. Add how horses changed in the middle. Explain your drawing.

Activity 1 Pair-Share Activity—Apply Knowledge (Level 3 of Bloom's Taxonomy)

 Direct students to Lesson 87, pages 291–295 and Lesson 88, pages 300–303 in Reading *Textbook B*.

Discuss the steps in the Pair-Share activity.
You'll do an activity called **Pair-Share** to show some things you've learned in recent lessons. The directions are on the board. I'll read them to you.

Assign partners. **Provide** drawing paper.
Step 1 is the **Pair** part of the activity. Discuss how horses have changed over time with your partner. Then draw horses on a time line to show the changes. Draw the horse from 38 million years ago at the bottom, what horses look like today at the top, and how horses changed in the middle. Decide what to draw and who will draw. Be ready to explain your drawing. Work quickly. You have 8 minutes.
Guide students to draw a time line showing the changes in horses over time.

Call on as many students to share as time allows.
Step 2 is to **Share**. I'll call on pairs of students to share their work with the rest of the class.

5 minutes

Student Materials:
Reading *Textbook B*

Part C: Fluency Building

 Conduct after the lesson, using the story of the day.

Activity 1 Partner Reading

It's time for partner reading.
Direct students to the story of the day. **Assign** student partners as Partner 1 and Partner 2. **Monitor** partner reading. **Guide** as needed.

Lesson 90 **285**

Part D: Writing/Language Arts

10 minutes

Teacher Materials:
Writing Prompts
My Writing Checklist

Student Materials:
Lined Paper
My Writing Checklist

Activity 1 — Write and Use Parts of Speech and Conventions

Time to write using a writing prompt based on the stories we've been reading. **Assign** student partners. **Distribute** lined paper to students. **Display** writing prompts and have students choose one to write about or assign a writing prompt of your choice. **Review** parts of speech and punctuation as well as the writing checklist with students. **Tell** students to write one to two paragraphs (minimum of four sentences per paragraph) on their own to answer the writing prompt. **Tell** them to use their writing checklist (first column labeled "Did I use them?") to ensure they include important parts of speech or punctuation in their writing. **Tell** students which parts of speech or punctuation to focus on, if you wish. **Model** what it means to answer a writing prompt and to use the writing checklist during and after the writing process, as needed. **Monitor** and guide students as needed. **Model** what it means to have a neighbor look over his or her neighbor's writing and to complete the writing checklist (second column labeled "Did my neighbor use them?"), as needed. **Have** students share what they wrote as time permits.

Writing Prompt 1	Writing Prompt 2	Writing Prompt 3
Would you be noticed if you took a chariot to your school? Why?	Would you rather have a modern day horse or a horse from long ago? Why?	If you were a caveperson and got to decorate the wall of your cave, what would you draw? What would you use to draw your picture?

Lesson 91

Materials
Teacher: 12-Cause and Effect Map; Reading *Textbook B*
Student: Vocabulary notebook; Reading *Textbook B*

8 minutes

Teacher Materials:
Reading *Textbook B*

Student Materials:
Vocabulary notebook
Reading *Textbook B*

Part A: Vocabulary Development

Activity 1 Learn New Vocabulary Word

Elicit responses to questions. **Guide** as needed.
Today you'll learn a new vocabulary word. **Shoved. Shoved** means "pushed." What does **shoved** mean? *Pushed.*

Another word for "pushed" is **shoved.** What's another word for "pushed"? *Shoved.*

Andrew had customers who would come into the bank with lots of money that they would **push** over the counter at him. Every day people would **shove** their money at him.

Discuss things that are shoved.

What's another word for "pushed"? *Shoved.*

Direct students to write shoved and its definition in their vocabulary notebooks. **Guide** as needed.
Write **shoved** and what it means in your vocabulary notebook.

Activity 2 Review Vocabulary Word

Elicit responses to questions. **Guide** as needed.
What's another way to say "thinking about happy things during the day"? *Daydreaming.*

Tell me a sentence using the word **daydreaming.** (Student responses.)
Discuss sentences.

 Review vocabulary words in appropriate context in Reading *Textbook B*.

Lesson 91 287

12 minutes

Teacher Materials:
Cause and Effect Map

Reading *Textbook B*

Student Materials:
Reading *Textbook B*

Part B: Comprehension Strategies

Activity 1 Identify Cause-and-Effect Relationships—A During-Reading Strategy

 Direct students to Lesson 89, pages 307–310 in Reading *Textbook B*.

Elicit responses to questions. **Guide** as needed.
Today you're going to learn how to identify cause and effect in a passage. Identifying cause and effect will help you understand what you read.

Cause means to "make something happen." What does **cause** mean? *To make something happen.*

An **effect** is "what happens." What's an **effect?** *What happens.*

Show Cause and Effect Map.
In Lesson 89 you read "Andrew Dexter Has Daydreams." Today I'm going to show you how I fill out my Cause and Effect Map for that story.
Model think-aloud for identifying cause and effect. **Write** cause-and-effect relationships on map.

Sample Wording for Think-Aloud

I'm thinking about the story "Andrew Dexter Has Daydreams." I'm thinking about Andrew and how he was not big or strong. I look at the Cause and Effect Map. I see the first box says Cause: To Make Something Happen. Andrew wanted to make the team in baseball, football, and basketball. But he never did. So I write in the Cause box, "Andrew was not big or strong when he tried out for the teams." Because Andrew was not big or strong, something happened. He did not make the team. So I write in the Effect box, "Andrew did not make the team."

Because Andrew did not make the team, he daydreamed about being a star on a team. So I can fill in the next set of boxes. In the Cause box, I can write, "Andrew did not make the team." Because Andrew did not make the team, something happened. He daydreamed. So I write in the Effect box, "Andrew daydreamed about being a star."

We'll practice identifying cause and effect in the next lesson.

Activity 2 Summarize Narrative Text—An After-Reading Strategy

  Direct students to Lesson 87, pages 291–295 in Reading *Textbook B*.

Elicit responses to questions. **Guide** as needed.

You're learning a strategy called summarizing. When you summarize text, you tell about what you read in your own words. You tell only the important parts of the passage when you summarize and you leave out the details. When you summarize narrative text, you tell the characters, the setting, and a few important events.

What do you tell when you summarize narrative text? (Idea: *The characters, the setting, and a few important events.*)

You can summarize by telling about the whole passage in a few sentences that tell the most important things you learned about the passage.

Let's work together to summarize "Andrew Dexter Has Daydreams" in a few sentences. Think about the characters, setting, and the most important events.

How can we put those ideas into a few sentences? (**Student responses.**)

Elicit student ideas for summary sentences. **Guide** students to the idea that Andrew Dexter worked in a bank but he daydreamed about being a super sports star.

We told the main things we learned from the passage in a few sentences, and we left out all the details.

5 minutes

Student Materials:
Reading *Textbook B*

Part C: Fluency Building

  Conduct after the lesson, using the story of the day.

Activity 1 Partner Reading

It's time for partner reading.
Direct students to the story of the day. **Assign** student partners as Partner 1 and Partner 2. **Monitor** partner reading. **Guide** as needed.

Lesson 91   **289**

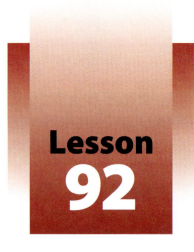

Lesson 92

Materials
Teacher: 12-Cause and Effect Map; Reading *Textbook B,* 10-Prediction Chart
Student: Vocabulary notebook; Reading *Textbook B,* Copy of 10-Prediction Chart

8 minutes

Teacher Materials:
Reading *Textbook B*

Student Materials:
Vocabulary notebook
Reading *Textbook B*

Part A: Vocabulary Development

Activity 1 Learn New Vocabulary Word

Elicit responses to questions. **Guide** as needed.
Today you'll learn a new vocabulary word. **Paused. Paused** means "took a short break between activities." What does **paused** mean? *Took a short break between activities.*

Another way to say "took a short break between activities" is **paused.** What's another way to say "took a short break between activities"? *Paused.*

Andrew **took a short break** to think about what he should do since he could not see in the building to see if anyone was there. He **paused** before deciding to open the door and enter.

Discuss examples of when someone has paused.

What's another way to say "took a short break between activities"? *Paused.*

Direct students to write paused and its definition in their vocabulary notebooks. **Guide** as needed.
Write **paused** and what it means in your vocabulary notebook.

Activity 2 Review Vocabulary Word

Elicit responses to questions. **Guide** as needed.
What's another way to say "pushed"? *Shoved.*

Tell me a sentence using the word **shoved.** (Student responses.)
Discuss sentences.

 Review vocabulary words in their appropriate context in Reading *Textbook B.*

290 Lesson 92

12 minutes

Teacher Materials:
Cause and Effect Map

Prediction Chart

Reading *Textbook B*

Student Materials:
Reading *Textbook B*

My Prediction Chart

Part B: Comprehension Strategies

Activity 1 Identify Cause-and-Effect Relationships—A During-Reading Strategy

 Direct students to Lesson 91, pages 319–322 in Reading *Textbook B*.

Elicit responses to questions. **Guide** as needed.
Learning to identify cause and effect in a passage will help you understand what you read.

Cause means "to make something happen." What does **cause** mean? *To make something happen.*

An **effect** is "what happens." What's an **effect?** *What happens.*

Discuss examples of cause-and-effect relationships. Suggested ideas: 1. tease your sister—go to time-out; 2. go to school—learn to read; 3. help someone—make a friend.

Show Cause and Effect Map.
In Lesson 91 you read, "Andrew Visits Magnetic Research Company." Today I'm going to show you how I fill out my Cause and Effect Map for that story.

Model identifying cause and effect. Suggested ideas: 1. Cause—Andrew is daydreaming. Effect—Andrew's boss tells him to get back to work; 2. Cause—Andrew's boss asks him to take a package to Magnetic Research Company. Effect—Andrew gets in his car; 3. Cause—Andrew drives out of his lane because he is daydreaming. Effect—A woman tells him to stay in his lane. **Record** cause-and-effect relationships on the map.

We'll practice identifying cause and effect in the next lesson.

Activity 2 Summarize Narrative Text—An After-Reading Strategy

 Direct students to Lesson 91, pages 319–322 in Reading *Textbook B*.

Elicit responses to questions. **Guide** as needed.
You're learning a strategy called summarizing. When you summarize text, you tell about what you read in your own words. You tell only the important parts of the passage when you summarize and you leave out the details. When you summarize narrative text, you tell the characters, the setting, and a few important events.

What do you tell when you summarize narrative text? (Idea: *The characters, the setting, and a few important events.*)

You can summarize by telling about the whole passage in a few sentences that tell the most important things you learned about the passage.

Lesson 92

Let's work together to summarize "Andrew Visits Magnetic Research Company" in a few sentences. Think about the characters, setting, and the most important events.

How can we put those ideas into a few sentences? (Student responses.)

Elicit student ideas for summary sentences. **Guide** students to the idea that Andrew found a small package on his counter at the bank that his boss wants him to take to Magnetic Research Company. He daydreams about being a sports star while driving to the company.

We told the main things we learned from the passage in a few sentences, and we left out all the details.

Activity 3 Make Predictions—A Before-Reading Strategy

 Direct students to Lesson 92, pages 328–331 in Reading *Textbook B*.

Show Prediction Chart. **Elicit** responses to questions. **Guide** as needed.
When you read narrative stories, it's a good strategy to make predictions about what you're going to read to help you understand the story better.

What are predictions? (Idea: *Good guesses based on clues about what is in the story.*)

Where do you get the clues for your prediction? (Idea: *The title, the picture, skimming the text, and remembering what you know about the story so far.*)

Let's work together to predict what'll happen in the next story by looking at the title "Andrew Is a Changed Person." You'll also skim the story, look at the picture, and remember what you know about the story so far to predict what'll happen to Andrew.

Elicit predictions. **Record** predictions for further discussion in Lesson 93.

You make predictions about what you're going to read and, as you read, you'll check to see whether your prediction is correct or not. It doesn't matter whether your prediction is exactly right. What's important is that you're checking as you read to see whether your prediction is correct.

Part C: Fluency Building

5 minutes

Student Materials:
Reading *Textbook B*

 Conduct after the lesson, using the story of the day.

Activity 1 Partner Reading

It's time for partner reading.
Direct students to the story of the day. **Assign** student partners as Partner 1 and Partner 2. **Monitor** partner reading. **Guide** as needed.

292 Lesson 92

Lesson 93

> **Materials**
>
> **Teacher:** 12-Cause and Effect Map; 10-Prediction Chart (from Lesson 92); Reading *Textbook B*
>
> **Student:** Vocabulary notebook; Copy of 12-Cause and Effect Map; Copy of 10-Prediction Chart (from Lesson 92); Reading *Textbook B*

Part A: Vocabulary Development

8 minutes

Teacher Materials:
Reading *Textbook B*

Student Materials:
Vocabulary notebook

Reading *Textbook B*

Activity 1 Learn New Vocabulary Word

Elicit responses to questions. **Guide** as needed.
Today you'll learn a new vocabulary word. **Scolded. Scolded** means "talked to someone in an angry voice." What does **scolded** mean? *Talked to someone in an angry voice.*

Another way to say "talked to someone in an angry voice" is **scolded.** What's another way to say "talked to someone in an angry voice"? *Scolded.*

Mr. Franks **talked** to Andrew **in an angry voice.** He **scolded** him by telling him that the Magnetic Research Company was not happy with what he had done.

Discuss examples of when someone might be scolded.

What's another way to say "talked to someone in an angry voice"? *Scolded.*

Direct students to write scolded and its definition in their vocabulary notebooks.
Guide as needed.
Write **scolded** and what it means in your vocabulary notebook.

Activity 2 Review Vocabulary Word

Elicit responses to questions. **Guide** as needed.
What's another way to say "took a short break between activities"? *Paused.*

Tell me a sentence using the word **paused.** (Student responses.)
Discuss sentences.

 Review vocabulary words in their appropriate context in Reading *Textbook B*.

12 minutes

Teacher Materials:
Cause and Effect Map

Prediction Chart

Reading *Textbook B*

Student Materials:
Prediction Chart

Cause and Effect Map

Reading *Textbook B*

Part B: Comprehension Strategies

Activity 1 Confirm Predictions—An After-Reading Strategy

 Direct students to Lesson 92, pages 328–331 in Reading *Textbook B*.

Show Prediction Chart. **Elicit** responses to questions. **Guide** as needed.
In the last lesson, you made some predictions about what happens to Andrew in the story. You made the predictions before you read the story. Making predictions helps you better understand the story.

You confirm predictions when you check to see whether your predictions were correct. What do you do when you check to see whether your predictions were right? *Confirm predictions.*

Now that you've read the story, let's check to see whether your predictions were correct or incorrect.

Guide discussion based on predictions recorded in Lesson 92.

Sometimes, we don't predict correctly. That's okay. Just trying to make a prediction and then confirming it will help you better understand what you read.

Activity 2 Identify Cause-and-Effect Relationships—A During-Reading Strategy

 Direct students to Lesson 92, pages 328–331 in Reading *Textbook B*.

Elicit responses to questions. **Guide** as needed.
Learning to identify cause and effect in a passage will help you understand what you read.

Cause means "to make something happen." What does **cause** mean? *To make something happen.*

An **effect** is "what happens." What's an **effect?** *What happens.*
Discuss examples of cause-and-effect relationships. Suggested ideas: 1. kick a soccer ball—the ball goes across the field; 2. fall off a horse—get hurt; 3. do something nice for a friend—get a smile.

Show Cause and Effect Map.
In Lesson 92, you read "Andrew Is a Changed Person." Today we'll work together to fill out your Cause and Effect Map for that story.

Record cause-and-effect relationships. **Monitor** students as they write sentences to fill out their Cause and Effect Maps.
Read the first paragraph and see whether you can find a cause and effect relationship.

294 *Lesson 93*

Name a cause-and-effect relationship. (Idea: *Cause: Andrew tugs a door. Effect: The door opens.*)

Read the third paragraph and see whether you can find a cause-and-effect relationship.

Name a cause-and-effect relationship. (Idea: *Cause: Turn off the switch. Effect: The car drops.*)

Read some more paragraphs and see if you can find a cause-and-effect relationship.

What are some more cause-and-effect relationships? (Idea: *1. Cause: Andrew got electrocuted. Effect: Andrew feels funny; 2. Cause: Man touches package. Effect: Man gets shocked; 3 Cause: Andrew tugs car door. Effect: Door came off car.*)

Discuss further cause-and-effect relationships in the story but do not record on Cause and Effect Map.
We'll practice identifying cause and effect in the next lesson.

Activity 3 Summarize Narrative Text—An After-Reading Strategy

Direct students to Lesson 92, pages 328–331 in Reading *Textbook B*.

Elicit responses to questions. **Guide** as needed.
You're learning a strategy called summarizing. When you summarize text, you tell about what you read in your own words. You tell only the important parts of the passage when you summarize and you leave out the details. When you summarize narrative text, you tell the characters, the setting, and a few important events.

What do you tell when you summarize narrative text? (Idea: *The characters, the setting, and a few important events.*)

You can summarize by telling about the whole passage in a few sentences that tell the most important things you learned about the passage.

Let's work together to summarize, "Andrew's a Changed Person" in a few sentences. Think about the characters, setting, and the most important events.

Lesson 94 **295**

How can we put those ideas into a few sentences? (Student responses.)

Elicit student ideas for summary sentences. **Guide** students to the idea that Andrew drove to the Magnetic Research Company to deliver the package, and when he walked into a dark room he got an enormous electric shock. He tingled all over and discovered later that he could pull the door off his car.

We told the main things we learned from the passage in a few sentences, and we left out all the details.

Part C: Fluency Building

5 minutes

Student Materials:
Reading *Textbook B*

 Conduct after the lesson, using the story of the day.

Activity 1 Partner Reading

It's time for partner reading.
Direct students to the story of the day. **Assign** student partners as Partner 1 and Partner 2. **Monitor** partner reading. **Guide** as needed.

Lesson 94

Materials
Teacher: 12-Cause and Effect Map; Reading *Textbook B*
Student: Vocabulary notebook; Copy of 12-Cause and Effect Map; sticky notes; Reading *Textbook B*

8 minutes

Teacher Materials:
Reading *Textbook B*

Student Materials:
Vocabulary notebook
Reading *Textbook B*

Part A: Vocabulary Development

Activity 1 Learn New Vocabulary Word

Elicit responses to questions. **Guide** as needed.
Today you'll learn a new vocabulary word. **Impossible. Impossible** means "can't be done." What does **impossible** mean? *Can't be done.*

Another way to say "can't be done" is **impossible.** What's another way to say "can't be done"? *Impossible.*

There were a lot of things that just **can't be done** by Andrew. But all of a sudden, he was doing things that were **impossible.**

Discuss things that are impossible.

What's another way to say **can't be done?** *Impossible.*

Direct students to write impossible and its definition in their vocabulary notebooks. **Guide** as needed.
Write **impossible** and what it means in your vocabulary notebook.

Activity 2 Review Vocabulary Word

Elicit responses to questions. **Guide** as needed.
What's another way to say "talked to someone in an angry voice"? *Scolded.*

Tell me a sentence using the word **scolded.** (Student responses.)
Discuss sentences.

 Review vocabulary words in their appropriate context in Reading *Textbook B*.

Lesson 94   **297**

12 minutes

Teacher Materials:
Cause and Effect Map

Reading *Textbook B*

Student Materials:
Cause and Effect Map

Sticky notes

Reading *Textbook B*

Part B: Comprehension Strategies

Activity 1 Identify Cause-and-Effect Relationships—A During-Reading Strategy

 Direct students to Lesson 93, pages 338–340 in Reading *Textbook B*.

Elicit responses to questions. **Guide** as needed.
Learning to identify cause and effect in a passage will help you understand what you read.

Cause means "to make something happen." What does **cause** mean? *To make something happen.*

An **effect** is "what happens." What's an **effect?** *What happens.*

Show Cause and Effect Map.
In Lesson 93 you read "Andrew Gets Fired." Today we'll work together to fill out your Cause and Effect Map for that story.

Record cause-and-effect relationships. **Monitor** students as they write sentences to fill out their Cause and Effect Maps.
Read the first paragraph and see whether you can find a cause-and-effect relationship.

Name a cause-and-effect relationship. (Idea: *Cause: Andrew drove a car with no door. Effect: Andrew felt silly.*)

Read the fifth paragraph and see whether you can find a cause-and-effect relationship.

Name a cause-and-effect relationship. (Idea: *Cause: Andrew does not pay attention. Effect: Andrew got fired.*)

Read some more paragraphs and see whether you can find a cause and effect relationship.

What are some cause and effect relationships? (Idea: *1. Cause: Andrew jumped three yards high. Effect: Andrew was high enough to catch a baseball; 2. Cause: Andrew threw the ball 100 miles per hour. Effect: The ball hit the mitt with a loud "Whap"; 3. Cause: The ball hit the mitt hard. Effect: The catcher fell over backward.*)

Discuss further cause-and-effect relationships in the story but do not record on Cause and Effect Map as time permits.

Activity 2 Summarize Narrative Text—An After-Reading Strategy

 Direct students to Lesson 93, pages 338–340 in Reading *Textbook B*.

Elicit responses to questions. **Guide** as needed.
You're learning a strategy called summarizing. When you summarize text, you tell about what you read in your own words. You tell only the important parts of the passage when you summarize and you leave out the details. When you summarize narrative text, you tell the characters, the setting, and a few important events.

What do you tell when you summarize narrative text? (Idea: *The characters, the setting, and a few important events.*)

You can summarize by telling about the whole passage in a few sentences that tell the most important things you learned about the passage.

Assign partners. **Monitor** students as they think of summary sentences. **Elicit** student ideas for summary sentences. **Discuss** best ideas and why they are good summaries.
Now work with a partner to summarize "Andrew Gets Fired" in a few sentences. Think about the characters, setting, and the most important events. Then put together a few sentences to summarize the story.

What summary sentences did you and your partner think of? (**Student responses.**)

We told the main things we learned from the passage in a few sentences, and we left out all the details.

Activity 3 Comprehension Monitoring: Mental Imaging—A During-Reading Strategy

 Direct students to Lesson 93, pages 335–340 in Reading *Textbook B*.

Elicit responses to questions. **Guide** as needed.
Mental imaging helps you understand and enjoy a story more. What does mental imaging help you do? *Understand and enjoy a story more.*

Mental imaging is making pictures in your mind about what you're reading. What's mental imaging? *Making pictures in your mind about what you're reading.*

Remember, mental imaging with narrative text helps you understand the details of a story better. What does using mental imaging with narrative text do? (Idea: *Helps you better understand the details of a story.*)

When you use mental imaging with expository text, you can make pictures in your mind of facts or true information to help you remember better. What does using mental imaging with expository text do? (Idea: *Helps you better remember facts or true information.*)

Lesson 94   **299**

Discuss how remembering the pictures can help you remember the text.

In the last lesson, you read "The Strength of Animals." Was that expository text or narrative text? *Expository text.*

Guide students to make mental images by looking at the text and drawing mental images on sticky notes.

Remember, you can use mental imaging of the expository text to help you remember the information better. Look at the text and at the pictures. The illustrator is trying to help you make a mental picture of the text with the illustrations.

You also read "Andrew Gets Fired." Let's work together to see whether we can make some mental images. Look at the text and see whether you can find a place to make a mental image. Mark the place in your text with a yellow sticky note and draw your mental image on the sticky note. Then we'll talk about your mental images.

Discuss mental images students make for as long as time permits.

Remember to make mental images when you read to help you understand and remember what you read.

Part C: Fluency Building

5 minutes

Student Materials:
Reading *Textbook B*

 Conduct after the lesson, using the story of the day.

Activity 1 Partner Reading

It's time for partner reading.

Direct students to the story of the day. **Assign** student partners as Partner 1 and Partner 2. **Monitor** partner reading. **Guide** as needed.

300 Lesson 94

Lesson 95

Materials
Teacher: 2-Vocabulary Acquisition and Use; Reading *Textbook B*
Student: Vocabulary notebook; Copy of 2-Vocabulary Acquisition and Use, Copy of 12-Cause and Effect Map for each student pair, Reading *Textbook B*

Part A: Vocabulary Development

8 minutes

Teacher Materials:
Reading *Textbook B*
Vocabulary Acquisition and Use

Student Materials:
Vocabulary notebook
Reading *Textbook B*
Vocabulary Acquisition and Use

Activity 1 Vocabulary Notebook Review

Guide students through all vocabulary words.
Today you'll study from your vocabulary notebook. Studying your words and what they mean will help you know your words even better. You'll look at the four words we studied this week.

Activity 2 Cumulative Vocabulary Review

Elicit responses to questions. **Guide** as needed.
Directions: Listen and tell me whether I use our vocabulary words the right way or the wrong way. If I use the word the right way, say **"yes."** If I use the word the wrong way, say **"no."** Then we'll talk about each word.

1. After mowing the lawn, Seth **paused** before watering the plants.

   Did I use the word **paused** the right way? *Yes.*

   How do you know? (Student responses.)

2. Jim told his mother that it was **impossible** to brush his own teeth.

   Did I use the word **impossible** the right way? *No.*

   How do you know? (Student responses.)

3. Ms. Levi **scolded** the children for sharing their toys so nicely.

   Did I use the word **scolded** the right way? *No.*

   How do you know? (Student responses.)

4. Jerry **shoved** his little sister to school.

   Did I use the word **shoved** the right way? *No.*

   How do you know? (Student responses.)

Review vocabulary words as needed.

 Review vocabulary words in their appropriate context in Reading *Textbook B*.

Lesson 95

Activity 3 Vocabulary Acquisition and Use

Display Vocabulary Acquisition and Use. **Have** students work with a neighbor to complete Vocabulary Acquisition and Use.

Today's vocabulary words are ____ and ____ [and ____ and ____].
Vocabulary words: **shoved** and **pushed**; **scolded** and **reprimanded**
Write the words on the lines provided. Then write the words in the boxes based on whether you think each word is less/smaller or more/larger than the other word. Below the boxes, write why you think word 1 is less/smaller and word 2 is more/larger than word 1.

Repeat for words 3 and 4. **Have** students share what they wrote. **Discuss** examples of how these words might be used.

Part B: Comprehension Strategies

12 minutes

Student Materials:
Cause and Effect Map for each student pair

Display directions for activity.
Directions: Discuss something that happened in your life that caused something else to happen (the effect). Apply your understanding of cause and effect by drawing pictures in your Cause and Effect Map showing the cause and the effect. (**Hint:** I dropped a plate equals cause; the plate broke equals effect.) Your partner will do the same thing by filling in the second set of pictures. Explain your cause-and-effect relationship.

Activity 1 Pair-Share Activity—Apply Knowledge (Level 3 of Bloom's Taxonomy)

Discuss the steps in the Pair-Share activity.
You'll do an activity called Pair-Share to show some things you have learned in recent lessons. The directions are on the board. I'll read them to you.

Assign partners. **Provide** Cause and Effect Map to each student pair.
Step 1 is the Pair part of the activity. Discuss with your partner something that happened in your life that caused something else to happen. Draw the cause and the effect. Your partner will do the same thing by filling in the next set of pictures. Be ready to explain your cause-and-effect relationship. Work quickly. You have 8 minutes.

Guide students to fill in the map with their cause-and-effect relationships.

Call on as many students to share as time allows.
Step 2 is to Share. I'll call on pairs of students to share their work with the rest of the class.

5 minutes

Student Materials:
Reading *Textbook B*

Part C: Fluency Building

 Conduct after the lesson, using the story of the day.

Activity 1 Partner Reading

It's time for partner reading.

Direct students to the story of the day. **Assign** student partners as Partner 1 and Partner 2. **Monitor** partner reading. **Guide** as needed.

Lesson 95

Lesson 96

Materials

Teacher: 6-Narrative Story Map; 12-Cause and Effect Map; Reading *Textbook B*

Student: Vocabulary notebook; Copy of 6-Narrative Story Map; Copy of 12-Cause and Effect Map for student pairs; Reading *Textbook B*

Part A: Vocabulary Development

8 minutes

Teacher Materials:
Reading *Textbook B*

Student Materials:
Vocabulary notebook

Reading *Textbook B*

Activity 1 Learn New Vocabulary Word

Elicit responses to questions. **Guide** as needed.
Today you'll learn a new vocabulary word. **Trotted. Trotted** means "ran slowly." What does **trotted** mean? *Ran slowly.*

Another way to say "ran slowly" is trotted. What's another way to say "ran slowly"? *Trotted.*

The players **ran slowly** away from Andrew. They all **trotted** back onto the field.
Discuss examples of things that students have seen that trotted.

What's another way to say "ran slowly"? *Trotted.*

Direct students to write trotted and its definition in their vocabulary notebooks. **Guide** as needed.
Write **trotted** and what it means in your vocabulary notebook.

Activity 2 Review Vocabulary Word

Elicit responses to questions. **Guide** as needed.
What's another way to say "can't be done"? *Impossible.*

Tell me a sentence using the word **impossible.** (Student responses.)
Discuss sentences.

 Review vocabulary words in their appropriate context in Reading *Textbook B*.

304   Lesson 96

12 minutes

Teacher Materials:
Narrative Story Map

Cause and Effect Map

Reading *Textbook B*

Student Materials:
Narrative Story Map

Cause and Effect Map for student pairs

Reading *Textbook B*

Part B: Comprehension Strategies

Activity 1 Identify Cause-and-Effect Relationships—A During-Reading Strategy

 Direct students to Lesson 95, pages 355–358 in Reading *Textbook B*.

Elicit responses to questions. **Guide** as needed.

Learning to identify cause and effect in a passage will help you understand what you read.

Cause means "to make something happen." What does **cause** mean? *To make something happen.*

An **effect** is "what happens." What's an **effect?** *What happens.*

Show Cause and Effect Map. **Assign** student partners.

In Lesson 95 you read "The Titans Make Fun of Andrew." Today you'll work with a partner to fill out your Cause and Effect Map for that story. Skim page 356 and see whether you and your partner can find one cause-and-effect relationship to write on your Cause and Effect Map.

Monitor students as they write sentences to fill out one cause-and-effect relationship on their Cause and Effect Maps. Suggested relationships: 1. Denny tries to get rid of Andrew—Andrew gets angry. 2. Andrew says he can kick—He goes on the field to prove it. 3. A player makes fun of Andrew—All the players laugh.

Discuss cause-and-effect relationships in the story and record on Cause and Effect Map as time permits.
Share the cause-and-effect relationships you found. (Student responses.)

Activity 2 Narrative Story Map: Identify Title, Characters, Setting, Problem, and Events—An After-Reading Strategy

 Direct students to Lesson 95, pages 355–358 in Reading *Textbook B*.

Show Narrative Story Map. **Elicit** responses to questions. **Guide** as needed.
Narratives have a title, characters, settings, a problem, and events.
Skim "The Titans Make Fun of Andrew," and then work by yourself to fill in the Narrative Story Map with the title, important characters, setting, problem, and events.

Monitor students as they write the title, characters, setting, problem, and events.

Discuss answers for title, characters, setting, problem, and events. **Write** answers on Narrative Story Map.

What did you write on your Narrative Story Map? (Ideas: *Title—"The Titans Make Fun of Andrew;" Main Characters—Andrew, Denny Brock; Setting: Where— the ball park; When—Chapter does not say: leave blank; Problem—The best kicker on the football team hurt his leg; Beginning—Andrew offers to kick for the football team; Middle—The football players make fun of Andrew; End—Andrew gets ready to kick the ball.*)

Save teacher and student copies of Narrative Story Map for Lesson 97.

You'll use your Narrative Story Map to retell the story in the next lesson.

5 minutes

Student Materials:
Reading *Textbook B*

Part C: Fluency Building

Conduct after the lesson, using the story of the day.

Activity 1 Partner Reading

It's time for partner reading.
Direct students to the story of the day. **Assign** student partners as Partner 1 and Partner 2. **Monitor** partner reading. **Guide** as needed.

Lesson 97

> **Materials**
> **Teacher:** 6-Narrative Story Map (from Lesson 96); Reading *Textbook B*, 12-Cause-and-Effect Map
> **Student:** Vocabulary notebook; Copy of 6-Narrative Story Map (from Lesson 96); Reading *Textbook B*, Copy of 12-Cause-and-Effect Map

8 minutes

Teacher Materials:
Reading *Textbook B*

Student Materials:
Vocabulary notebook
Reading *Textbook B*

Part A: Vocabulary Development

Activity 1 Suffix Introduction

Elicit responses to questions. **Guide** as needed.
Today you'll learn about a **suffix**. A **suffix** is a "word part added to the end of a word that changes its meaning." What do we call a "word part added to the end of a word that changes its meaning"? *Suffix.*

Activity 2 Learn New Suffix

Elicit responses to questions. **Guide** as needed.
Today you'll learn a new suffix. **S** and **e-s. S** and **e-s** means "more than one." What does **s** and **e-s** mean? *More than one.*

The suffix that means "more than one" is **s** and **e-s**. What's the suffix that means "more than one"? *S and e-s.*

Boxes. Box**es** means **more than one** box. Flower**s**. Flower**s** means **more than one** flower. Question**s**. What does **questions** mean? *More than one question.*

So when we add the suffix **s** and **e-s** to the end of words, we change what the words mean. Game**s**. Adding **s** to **game** makes it **games.** What does **games** mean? *More than one game.*

Tell me an **s** and **e-s** word. (Student responses.)
Discuss responses.

What suffix means "more than one"? *S and e-s.*

Activity 3 Review Vocabulary Word

Elicit responses to questions. **Guide** as needed.
What's another way to say "ran slowly"? *Trotted.*

Tell me a sentence using the word **trotted.** (Student responses.)
Discuss sentences.

 Review vocabulary words in their appropriate context in Reading *Textbook B*.

12 minutes

Teacher Materials:
Narrative Story Map

Cause and Effect Map

Reading *Textbook B*

Student Materials:
Narrative Story Map

Cause and Effect Map

Reading *Textbook B*

Part B: Comprehension Strategies

Activity 1 Use Narrative Story Map: Retell the Story—An After-Reading Strategy

 Direct students to Lesson 95, pages 355–358 in Reading *Textbook B*.

Show Narrative Story Map (completed in Lesson 96).
You did a great job of completing your Narrative Story Maps in the last lesson. Now it's time to use the Narrative Story Maps to retell the story. Watch me as I use my map to retell the story of "The Titans Make Fun of Andrew." First I'll tell the title and something about the characters and the setting. Then I'll tell about the problem. Finally I'll tell the events that happened.

Model retelling a narrative text from the Narrative Story Map filled out in Lesson 96.
Assign student partners for retelling the story.
Now it's your turn to use your Narrative Story Map to retell the story to your partner. Remember to start by telling the title and something about the characters and setting. Tell something about the problem and then tell the events that happened. Use your own words to retell the story. Then let your partner use his or her own words to retell the story.

Retelling the story helps you remember all the parts of the story.

Activity 2 Identify Cause-and-Effect Relationships—A During-Reading Strategy

 Direct students to Lesson 96, pages 360–363 in Reading *Textbook B*.

Show Cause and Effect Map. **Elicit** responses to questions. **Guide** as needed.
Learning to identify cause and effect in a passage will help you understand what you read.

Cause means "to make something happen." What does **cause** mean? *To make something happen.*

An **effect** is "what happens." What's an **effect?** *What happens.*

Assign student partners.
In Lesson 96 you read "Andrew Kicks." Today you'll work with a partner to fill out your Cause and Effect Map for that story. Skim page 363 and see whether you and your partner can find two cause-and-effect relationships to write on your Cause and Effect Map.

Monitor students as they write sentences to fill out two cause-and-effect relationship on their Cause and Effect Maps. Suggested relationships: 1. Andrew kicked the ball—The sound was so loud, players put their hands over their ears. 2. The ball came down—Everyone checked the hang time of the ball. 3. Denny tells players to get back to work—Players put on helmets. 4. Players tell Andrew that he did a good job—Andrew says thanks.

308 *Lesson 97*

Discuss cause-and-effect relationships in story and record on Cause and Effect Map as time permits.

Share the cause-and-effect relationships you found. (Student responses.)

Activity 3 Activate Background Knowledge and Set Purpose for Reading—A Before-Reading Strategy

 Direct students to Lesson 97, pages 367–371 in Reading *Textbook B*.

Elicit responses to questions. **Guide** as needed.
Remember everything you know in your mind is called background knowledge. What do you call everything you know in your mind? *Background knowledge.*

What do you do when you think about what you already know? (Idea: *Activate your background knowledge.*)

Can you use this skill in both narrative and expository text? *Yes.*

In the next lesson, you will read "Professional Football Players." That passage was written to give you background knowledge about professional football players. What do you know about football players? (Student responses.)

When you read "Professional Football Players," you'll learn more about football players. Connecting what you learn about football players to the narrative story you will read today will help you better understand what you read.

Why will you read "Professional Football Players?" (Idea: *To increase background knowledge about football players.*)

What strategy will you use when you read the narrative passage "Denny Gives Andrew a Job"? (Idea: *Connect what you know—background knowledge—to the story to understand the story better.*)

Part C: Fluency Building

5 minutes

Student Materials:
Reading *Textbook B*

 Conduct after the lesson, using the story of the day.

Activity 1 Partner Reading

It's time for partner reading.
Direct students to the story of the day. **Assign** student partners as Partner 1 and Partner 2. **Monitor** partner reading. **Guide** as needed.

Lesson 97   **309**

Lesson 98

Materials

Teacher: Simple biography of a football player; 12-Cause and Effect Map; Reading *Textbook B*

Student: Vocabulary notebook; Copy of 12-Cause and Effect Map; Reading *Textbook B*, Lined paper

Part A: Vocabulary Development

8 minutes

Teacher Materials:
Reading *Textbook B*

Student Materials:
Vocabulary notebook
Reading *Textbook B*

Activity 1 Learn New Vocabulary Word

Elicit responses to questions. **Guide** as needed.
Today you'll learn a new vocabulary word. **Hollered. Hollered** means "shouted." What does **hollered** mean? *Shouted.*

Another word for "shouted" is **hollered.** What's another word for "shouted"? *Hollered.*

The fans **shouted** when the team came on the field. They **hollered** even louder when Andrew came on the field.

Discuss examples of when people have hollered.

What's another word for "shouted"? *Hollered.*

Direct students to write hollered and its definition in their vocabulary notebooks. **Guide** as needed.
Write **hollered** and what it means in your vocabulary notebook.

Activity 2 Review Vocabulary Word

Elicit responses to questions. **Guide** as needed.
What suffix means "more than one"? *S and e-s.*

Tell me a sentence using a word with the suffix **s** and **e-s.**
(Student responses.)
Discuss sentences.

 Review vocabulary words in their appropriate context in Reading *Textbook B*.

310 Lesson 98

12 minutes

Teacher Materials:
Simple biography of a football player

Cause and Effect Map

Reading *Textbook B*

Student Materials:
Cause and Effect Map

Reading *Textbook B*

Lined paper

Part B: Comprehension Strategies

Activity 1 Summarize Narrative Text—An After-Reading Strategy

 Direct students to Lesson 97, pages 368–371 in Reading *Textbook B*.

Elicit responses to questions. **Guide** as needed.
You're learning a strategy called summarizing. What do you do when you summarize text? (Idea: *Tell the important parts of the text and you leave out the details.*)

When you summarize narrative text, you tell the characters, the setting, and a few important events.

What do you tell when you summarize narrative text? (Idea: *The characters, the setting, and a few important events.*)

You can summarize by telling about the whole passage in a few sentences that tell the most important things you learned about the passage.

Now work by yourself to summarize "Denny Gives Andrew a Job" in a few sentences. Think about the characters, setting, and the most important events. Then write a few sentences to summarize the story.
Monitor students as they write summary sentences.

What summary sentences did you think of? (Student responses.)
Elicit student ideas for summary sentences. **Discuss** best ideas and why they are good summaries.

We told the main things we learned from the passage in a few sentences, and we left out all the details.

Activity 2 Identify Cause-and-Effect Relationships—A During-Reading Strategy

 Direct students to Lesson 97, pages 368–371 in Reading *Textbook B*.

Show Cause and Effect Map. **Elicit** responses to questions. **Guide** as needed.
Learning to identify cause-and-effect in a passage will help you understand what you read.

What does **cause** mean? *To make something happen.*

What's an **effect?** *What happens.*

In Lesson 97 you read "Denny Gives Andrew a Job." Today you'll work by yourself to fill out your Cause and Effect Map for that story. Skim page 370 and see if you can find one cause-and-effect relationship to write on your Cause and Effect Map.

Lesson 98 **311**

Monitor students as they write sentences to fill out one cause-and-effect relationship on their Cause and Effect Maps. Suggested relationships: 1. Denny asks Andrew what his name is—Andrew tells him. 2. Denny asks how much money Andrew wants—Andrew tells him $2,000/month. 3. Andrew tells Denny he wants $2,000/month—Denny smiles and shakes his head.

Share the cause-and-effect relationships you found. (Student responses.)
Discuss cause-and-effect relationships in story and record on Cause and Effect Map as time permits.

Activity 3 Prepare for Text-to-Text Connections—A Before-Reading Strategy

When you make text-to-text connections, you think about stories you've read that remind you of the story you're reading. Making a connection to another story may help you understand the story you're reading better.

Read simple biography of a football player with prosody. **Elicit** the title, characters, setting, problem, and events after reading story.
You're reading the story of Andrew. I'll read a story about a real football player today. When you read a story about a real person, it's called a biography. Then we'll make a text-to-text connection between the story of Andrew and the biography of _____.

In the next lesson, we'll make a text-to-text connection. We'll compare and contrast the stories to see how they're the same and how they're different. Making text-to-text connections helps you better understand stories.

Part C: Fluency Building

5 minutes

Student Materials:
Reading *Textbook B*

 Conduct after the lesson, using the story of the day.

Activity 1 Partner Reading

It's time for partner reading.
Direct students to the story of the day. **Assign** student partners as Partner 1 and Partner 2. **Monitor** partner reading. **Guide** as needed.

312 *Lesson 98*

Lesson 99

> **Materials**
> **Teacher:** Teacher choice of a simple biography of a football player; Reading *Textbook B*, 12-Cause-and-Effect Map
> **Student:** Vocabulary notebook; Reading *Textbook B*, Copy of 12-Cause-and-Effect Map, Lined paper

8 minutes

Teacher Materials:
Reading *Textbook B*

Student Materials:
Vocabulary notebook
Reading *Textbook B*

Part A: Vocabulary Development

Activity 1 Learn New Vocabulary Word

Elicit responses to questions. **Guide** as needed.
Today you'll learn a new vocabulary word. **Whooped. Whooped** means "made a loud shout of joy." What does **whooped** mean? *Made a loud shout of joy.*

Another way to say "made a loud shout of joy" is **whooped.** What's another way to say "made a loud shout of joy"? *Whooped.*

The fans made **a loud shout of joy** when Andrew kicked the ball. They **whooped** very loudly.

Discuss examples of when students have heard someone who whooped.

What's another way to say "made a loud shout of joy"? *Whooped.*

Direct students to write whooped and its definition in their vocabulary notebooks. **Guide** as needed.
Write **whooped** and what it means in your vocabulary notebook.

Activity 2 Review Vocabulary Word

Elicit responses to questions. **Guide** as needed.
What's another word for "shouted"? *Hollered.*

Tell me a sentence using the word **hollered.** (Student responses.)
Discuss sentences.

 Review vocabulary words in their appropriate context in Reading *Textbook B*.

Lesson 99   313

12 minutes

Teacher Materials:
Teacher choice of a simple biography of a football player

Cause and Effect Map

Reading *Textbook B*

Student Materials:
Cause and Effect Map

Reading *Textbook B*

Lined paper

Part B: Comprehension Strategies

Activity 1 Summarize Narrative Text—An After-Reading Strategy

 Direct students to Lesson 97, pages 368–371 in Reading *Textbook B*.

Elicit response to question. **Guide** as needed.
You're learning a strategy called summarizing. When you summarize text, you tell about what you read in your own words. You tell only the important parts of the passage when you summarize and you leave out the details. When you summarize narrative text, you tell the characters, the setting, and a few important events.

What do you tell when you summarize narrative text? (Idea: *The characters, the setting, and a few important events.*)

You can summarize by telling about the whole passage in a few sentences that tell the most important things you learned about the passage.

Monitor students as they write summary sentences.
Now work by yourself to summarize "Denny Gives Andrew a Job" in a few sentences. Think about the characters, setting, and the most important events. Then write a few sentences to summarize the story.

What summary sentences did you think of? (Student responses.)

Elicit student ideas for summary sentences. **Discuss** the best ideas and why they are good summaries.

We told the main things we learned from the passage in a few sentences, and we left out all the details.

314 Lesson 99

Activity 2   Identify Cause-and-Effect Relationships—A During-Reading Strategy

 Direct students to Lesson 98, pages 374–378 in Reading *Textbook B*.

Show Cause and Effect Map. **Elicit** response to question. **Guide** as needed.
Learning to identify cause and effect in a passage will help you understand what you read.

What does **cause** mean? *To make something happen.*

What's an **effect**? *What happens.*

In Lesson 98 you read "Andrew Plays in His First Game." Today you'll work by yourself to fill out your Cause and Effect Map for that story.
Skim page 378 and see whether you can find two cause-and-effect relationships to write on your Cause and Effect Map.

Monitor the students as they write sentences to fill out two cause-and-effect relationships on their Cause and Effect Maps.

Share the cause-and-effect relationships you found. (**Student responses.**)

Discuss cause-and-effect relationships in the story and record them on the Cause and Effect Map as time permits.

Activity 3   Make Text-to-Text Connections—An After-Reading Strategy

 Direct students to Lessons 89–98, pages 307–378 in Reading *Textbook B*.

Direct students to remember biography of football player read in last lesson.
When you make text-to-text connections, you think about stories you've read that remind you of the story you're reading. Making a connection to another story may help you understand the story you're reading better.

The story of Andrew is a narrative story. It is not true. The biography of _____ is true. So we'll make a text-to-text connection today to tell how these two stories are the same and how they're different.

Elicit suggestions for how stories are the same and how they're different. **Guide** as needed.

When you compare and contrast the stories to see how they're the same and how they're different, you're making text-to-text connections that help you better understand stories.

Lesson 99   **315**

5 minutes

Student Materials:
Reading *Textbook B*

Part C: Fluency Building

 Conduct after the lesson, using the story of the day.

Activity 1 Partner Reading

It's time for partner reading.

Direct students to the story of the day. **Assign** student partners as Partner 1 and Partner 2. **Monitor** partner reading. **Guide** as needed.

Lesson 100

Materials

Teacher: Reading *Textbook B,* 2-Vocabulary Acquisition and Use, 12-Cause-and-Effect Map, Writing Prompts, 3-My Writing Checklist

Student: Vocabulary notebook; Reading *Textbook B,* Copy of 2-Vocabulary Acquisition and Use, 12-Cause-and-Effect Map, and 3-My Writing Checklist, Lined paper

Part A: Vocabulary Development

8 minutes

Teacher Materials:
Reading *Textbook B*

Vocabulary Acquisition and Use

Student Materials:
Vocabulary Notebook

Reading *Textbook B*

Vocabulary Acquisition and Use

Activity 1 Vocabulary Notebook Review

Guide students as they study all vocabulary words.
Today you'll study from your vocabulary notebook. Studying your words and what they mean will help you know your words even better. You'll study the eight words we studied over the past two weeks.

Activity 2 Cumulative Vocabulary Review

Elicit responses to questions. **Guide** as needed.
Directions: Listen and tell me whether I use our vocabulary words the right way or the wrong way. If I use the word the right way, say **"yes."** If I use the word the wrong way, say **"no."** Then we'll talk about each word.

1. Because the stadium was so noisy, the coach **hollered** at his players to make the tackles.

   Did I use the word **hollered** the right way? *Yes.*

   How do you know? (Student responses.)

2. Alice **scolded** the puppy for wetting in the house.

   Did I use the word **scolded** the right way? *Yes.*

   How do you know? (Student responses.)

3. Allen accidentally **shoved** the bowl of cherries and they landed in his father's lap.

   Did I use the word **shoved** the right way? *Yes.*

   How do you know? (Student responses.)

4. When the horse race started, the fastest horse **trotted** to the finish line.

   Did I use the word **trotted** the right way? *No.*

   How do you know? (Student responses.)

Lesson 100   317

5. It would be **impossible** to get a sun tan in your dark basement.

   Did I use the word **impossible** the right way? *Yes.*

   How do you know? (Student responses.)

6. When the other team lost the game, they were very quiet. They **whooped** loudly to show how happy they were.

   Did I use the word **whooped** the right way? *No.*

   How do you know? (Student responses.)

7. The teacher finished teaching math then **paused** before going on to teach spelling.

   Did I use the word **paused** the right way? *Yes.*

   How do you know? (Student responses.)

8. The family looked at many **houses** before buying one.

   Did I use the word **houses** the right way? *Yes.*

   How do you know? (Student responses.)

Review vocabulary words as needed.

 Review vocabulary words in their appropriate context in Reading *Textbook B.*

Activity 3 Vocabulary Acquisition and Use

Display Vocabulary Acquisition and Use. **Have** students work with a neighbor to complete Vocabulary Acquisition and Use.
Today's vocabulary words are _____ and _____ [and _____ and _____].
Vocabulary words: **whooped** and **yelled; hollered** and **shouted**
Write the words on the lines provided. Then write the words in the boxes based on whether you think each word is less/smaller or more/larger than the other word. Below the boxes, write why you think word 1 is less/smaller and word 2 is more/larger than word 1.
Repeat for words 3 and 4. **Have** students share what they wrote. **Discuss** examples of how these words might be used.

12 minutes

Teacher Materials:
Reading *Textbook B*

Cause and Effect Map

Student Materials:
Reading *Textbook B*

Cause and Effect Map

Part B: Comprehension Strategies

Display directions for the activity.
Directions: Discuss the last story you read about Andrew. Apply what you know about cause and effect to find two cause-and-effect relationships in the story. Fill out your Cause and Effect Map to show those two causes and their effects. Explain these cause-and-effect relationships.

Activity 1 Pair-Share Activity—Apply Knowledge (Level 3 of Bloom's Taxonomy)

 Direct students to Lesson 99, pages 382–386 in Reading *Textbook B*.

Discuss the steps in the Pair-Share activity.
You'll do an activity called Pair-Share to show some things you've learned in recent lessons. The directions are on the board. I'll read them to you.

Assign partners. **Provide** Cause and Effect Map.
Step 1 is the Pair part of the activity. Discuss two cause-and-effect relationships in the story "Andrew Meets Smiling Sam." Draw pictures of these cause-and-effect relationships. Decide what to draw and who will draw. Be ready to explain the causes and the effects. Work quickly. You have 8 minutes.
Guide students to fill out Cause and Effect Map to show two cause-and-effect relationships.

Call on as many students to share as time allows.
Step 2 is to Share. I'll call on pairs of students to share their work with the rest of the class.

5 minutes

Student Materials:
Reading *Textbook B*

Part C: Fluency Building

 Conduct after the lesson, using the story of the day.

Activity 1 Partner Reading

It's time for partner reading.
Direct students to the story of the day. **Assign** student partners as Partner 1 and Partner 2. **Monitor** partner reading. **Guide** as needed.

Lesson 100   **319**

10 minutes

Part D: Writing/Language Arts

Activity 1 Write and Use Parts of Speech and Conventions

Teacher Materials:
Writing Prompts

My Writing Checklist

Student Materials:
Lined Paper

My Writing Checklist

Time to write using a writing prompt based on the stories we've been reading.

Assign student partners. **Distribute** lined paper to students. **Display** writing prompts and have students choose one to write about or assign a writing prompt of your choice. **Review** parts of speech and punctuation as well as the writing checklist with students. **Tell** students to write one to two paragraphs (minimum of four sentences per paragraph) on their own to answer the writing prompt. **Tell** them to use their writing checklist (first column labeled "Did I use them?") to ensure they include important parts of speech or punctuation in their writing. **Tell** students which parts of speech or punctuation to focus on, if you wish. **Model** what it means to answer a writing prompt and to use the writing checklist during and after the writing process, as needed. **Monitor** and guide students as needed. **Model** what it means to have a neighbor look over his or her neighbor's writing and to complete the writing checklist (second column labeled "Did my neighbor use them?"), as needed. **Have** students share what they wrote as time permits.

Writing Prompt 1	Writing Prompt 2	Writing Prompt 3
Would you rather be a fan, a football coach, or a football player? Why?	What is your favorite sport? Why?	If you could play a sport professionally and be paid for it, would you? Why or why not?

Lesson 101

Materials

Teacher: Reading *Textbook C*
Student: Vocabulary notebook; Reading *Textbook C*

8 minutes

Teacher Materials:
Reading *Textbook C*

Student Materials:
Vocabulary notebook

Reading *Textbook C*

Part A: Vocabulary Development

Activity 1 Learn New Vocabulary Word

Elicit responses to questions. **Guide** as needed.
Today you'll learn a new vocabulary word. **Awful. Awful** means "very bad."
What does **awful** mean? *Very bad.*

Another way to say "very bad" is **awful.** What's another way to say
"very bad"? *Awful.*

The Titans were a **very bad** team. But after they got Andrew on their team,
people no longer said they were **awful.**

Discuss things that are <u>awful</u>.

What's another way to say "very bad"? *Awful.*

Direct students to write <u>awful</u> and its definition in their vocabulary notebooks.
Guide as needed.
Write **awful** and what it means in your vocabulary notebook.

Activity 2 Review Vocabulary Word

Elicit responses to questions. **Guide** as needed.
What's another way to say "made a loud shout of joy"? *Whooped.*

Tell me a sentence using the word **whooped.** (Student responses.)
Discuss sentences.

 Review vocabulary words in their appropriate context in Reading *Textbook C*.

Lesson 101 **321**

12 minutes

Teacher Materials:
Reading *Textbook C*

Student Materials:
Reading *Textbook C*

Part B: Comprehension Strategies

Activity 1 Choose a Comprehension Strategy—A Before-Reading Strategy

 Direct students to Lesson 101, pages 1–5 in Reading *Textbook C*.

Elicit responses to questions. **Guide** as needed.
You've learned strategies to use before you read a passage. What are those strategies? (Ideas: *Activate background knowledge, predict what is in the story, determine text type and set a purpose for reading, and fill out the first two parts of a KWL chart.*)

Take a look at the story you'll read today. How would you use these strategies while you read the story? (Student responses.)

Activity 2 Choose a Comprehension Strategy—A During-Reading Strategy

Elicit responses to questions. **Guide** as needed.
You've learned strategies to use while you read a passage. What are those strategies? (Ideas: *Mental imaging,* rereading, *reading with prosody, and generating questions.*)

Take a look at the story you'll read today. How would you use these strategies while you read the story? (Student responses.)

Activity 3 Choose a Comprehension Strategy—An After-Reading Strategy

Elicit responses to questions. **Guide** as needed.
You've learned strategies to use after you read a passage. What are those strategies? (Ideas: *Narrative Story Map, retell the story, fill in the last section of KWL chart, summarize the story, make a text-to-text connection, confirm a prediction, compare and contrast, and identify cause and effect.*)

Assign student partners. **Monitor** students as they discuss after-reading strategies.
Choose what after-reading strategy you'll use in the next lesson. Discuss this strategy with a partner.

5 minutes

Student Materials:
Reading *Textbook C*

Part C: Fluency Building

 Conduct after the lesson, using the story of the day.

Activity 1 Partner Reading

It's time for partner reading.

Direct students to the story of the day. **Assign** student partners as Partner 1 and Partner 2. **Monitor** partner reading. **Guide** as needed.

Lesson 101 **323**

Lesson 102

Materials
Teacher: Reading *Textbook C*; 6-Narrative Story Map
Student: Vocabulary notebook; Copy of 6-Narrative Story Map if chosen by student for after-reading strategy; Reading *Textbook C*

8 minutes

Teacher Materials:
Reading *Textbook C*

Student Materials:
Vocabulary notebook
Reading *Textbook C*

Part A: Vocabulary Development

Activity 1 Learn New Vocabulary Word

Elicit responses to questions. **Guide** as needed.
Today you'll learn a new vocabulary word. **Announcer. Announcer** means "someone who tells the news." What does **announcer** mean? *Someone who tells the news.*

Another way to say "someone who tells the news" is **announcer.** What's another way to say "someone who tells the news"? *Announcer.*

The **person who told the news** to the crowd about Andrew's kick said it was an okay kick. The **announcer** could tell that Andrew was not kicking as well as normal.

Discuss examples of an announcer.

What's another way to say "someone who tells the news"? *Announcer.*

Direct students to write announcer and its definition in their vocabulary notebooks. **Guide** as needed.
Write **announcer** and what it means in your vocabulary notebook.

Activity 2 Review Vocabulary Word

Elicit responses to questions. **Guide** as needed.
What's another way to say "very bad"? *Awful.*

Tell me a sentence using the word **awful.** (Student responses.)
Discuss sentences.

 Review vocabulary words in their appropriate context in Reading *Textbook C*.

324   Lesson 102

12 minutes

Teacher Materials:
Reading *Textbook C*

Narrative Story Map

Student Materials:
Narrative Story Map

Reading *Textbook C*

Part B: Comprehension Strategies

Activity 1 Choose a Comprehension Strategy—An After-Reading Strategy

 Direct students to Lesson 101, pages 1–5 in Reading *Textbook C*.

Monitor students as they complete Narrative Story Map as needed.

In the last lesson, you chose a strategy to use after reading the passage, "Andrew Begins to Change" from Lesson 101. Follow the steps you need to complete the strategy. If you need a Narrative Story Map, I can provide you one.

Activity 2 Text-to-Self Connection—An After-Reading Strategy

 Direct students to Lesson 101, pages 1–5 in Reading *Textbook C*.

When you read narrative text, it helps you understand the passage you're reading if you connect what you're reading to an experience you've had. That's called making a text-to-self connection. I'll read, "Andrew Begins to Change" and show you how I connect that story to my own experience.
Model think-aloud for making text-to-self connections.

> **Sample Wording for Think-Aloud**
>
> The beginning of the story says that the "newspapers were filled with stories about Andrew." That reminds me about a time that I was in the newspaper. I didn't do anything famous, like Andrew did, but the newspaper was doing an article about big families, and I have a big family. They took a picture of us and put it in the newspaper. I understand a little of what it's like to be in the newspaper, so I understand a little how Andrew feels.

I made a text-to-self connection by making a connection between something in the story and an experience I've had. It's a good strategy to help you understand what you read.

Activity 3 Comprehension Monitoring: Read with Prosody—A During-Reading Strategy

 Direct students to Lesson 101, pages 1–5 in Reading *Textbook C*.

You've learned a lot about reading stories with expression. You know how to read and pay attention to the punctuation. You even know about dialogue. You know that your voice should go up a little when you read a question.

Assign student partners. **Monitor** student reading to ensure that they take turns and read with prosody.

Today you'll practice reading the story with expression with your partner. Take turns reading paragraphs with your partner. You each will be listening for reading with expression. Make your voice really interesting. Read the dialogue with different voices. Make sure your voice goes up at the end of the questions. Take a small breath between sentences. Reread a sentence if you make a little mistake. It should be fun to listen to you and your partner read the whole story.

Remember that reading with expression helps you have good comprehension.

Student Materials:
Reading *Textbook C*

Part C: Fluency Building

 Conduct after the lesson, using the story of the day.

Activity 1 Partner Reading

It's time for partner reading.
Direct students to the story of the day. **Assign** student partners as Partner 1 and Partner 2. **Monitor** partner reading. **Guide** as needed.

Lesson 103

Materials
Teacher: Reading *Textbook C*
Student: Vocabulary notebook; Reading *Textbook C*

8 minutes

Teacher Materials:
Reading *Textbook C*

Student Materials:
Vocabulary notebook

Reading *Textbook C*

Part A: Vocabulary Development

Activity 1 Learn New Vocabulary Word

Elicit responses to questions. **Guide** as needed.
Today you'll learn a new vocabulary word. **Experts. Experts** means "people who know a lot about something." What does **experts** mean? *People who know a lot about something.*

Another way to say "people who know a lot about something" is **experts.**
What's another way to say "people who know a lot about something"? *Experts.*

People who know a lot about football said the Wildcats would be tough to beat. The **experts** were not sure who would win.

Discuss examples of experts.

What's another way to say "someone who knows a lot about something"? *Experts.*

Direct students to write experts and its definition in their vocabulary notebooks. **Guide** as needed.
Write **experts** and what it means in your vocabulary notebook.

Activity 2 Review Vocabulary Word

Elicit responses to questions. **Guide** as needed.
What's another way to say "someone who tells the news"? *Announcer.*

Tell me a sentence using the word **announcer.** (Student responses.)

Discuss sentences.

 Review vocabulary words in their appropriate context in Reading *Textbook C*.

12 minutes

Teacher Materials:
Reading *Textbook C*

Student Materials:
Reading *Textbook C*

Part B: Comprehension Strategies

Activity 1 Text-to-Self Connection—An After-Reading Strategy

 Direct students to Lesson 102, pages 8–12 in Reading *Textbook C*.

When you read narrative text, it helps you understand the passage you're reading if you connect what you're reading to an experience you've had. That's called making a text-to-self connection. I'll read "Andrew Plays Harder" and show you how I connect that story to my own experience.

Skim text to show places to make connections. **Model** making text-to-self connections. Suggested ideas: Andrew shouted because he was frightened; Andrew said he would do his best; Andrew tried harder.

I made a text-to-self connection by making a connection between something in the story and an experience I've had. It's a good strategy to help you understand what you read.

Activity 2 Comprehension Monitoring: Reread Narrative or Expository Text—A During-Reading Strategy

 Direct students to Lesson 102, pages 8–12 in Reading *Textbook C*.

Elicit response to question. **Guide** as needed.
Rereading is a strategy to use while you read to help you have high comprehension.

What should you ask yourself while you're reading? (Idea: *Does this make sense?*)

What do you do if something doesn't make sense? (Idea: *Reread the sentence that didn't make sense or read ahead a little to see if that helps you understand.*)

What's the strategy called? *Rereading.*

Does this strategy work for both expository and narrative text? *Yes.*

Discuss what did not make sense and the strategy students used to fix the problem. When you read this story, did the whole story make sense? (Student responses.)

Today when you read Lesson 103, be sure to think about using the rereading strategy if you don't understand what you're reading for both the expository section and the narrative section.

Lesson 103

Activity 3 Activate Background Knowledge—A Before-Reading Strategy

Elicit responses to questions. **Guide** as needed.
Remember, everything you know in your brain is called background knowledge. What do you call everything you know in your brain? *Background knowledge.*

What do you do when you activate your background knowledge? (Idea: *Think about what you already know.*)

Why do you activate your background knowledge? (Idea: *Connecting what you know to the story you're reading helps you better understand the story.*)

You'll read about a field goal in the next story. Let's talk about your background knowledge about a field goal.
Discuss the students' background knowledge about a field goal. **Guide** as needed.

Connecting what you know about a field goal to the next story may help you understand what you read.

Part C: Fluency Building

5 minutes

Student Materials:
Reading *Textbook C*

 Conduct after the lesson, using the story of the day.

Activity 1 Partner Reading

It's time for partner reading.
Direct students to the story of the day. **Assign** student partners as Partner 1 and Partner 2. **Monitor** partner reading. **Guide** as needed.

Lesson 103 **329**

Lesson 104

Materials
Teacher: 6-Narrative Story Map; Reading *Textbook C*
Student: Vocabulary notebook; Copy of 6-Narrative Story Map; Reading *Textbook C*

Part A: Vocabulary Development

8 minutes

Teacher Materials:
Reading *Textbook C*

Student Materials:
Vocabulary notebook
Reading *Textbook C*

Activity 1 Learn New Vocabulary Word

Elicit responses to questions. **Guide** as needed.
Today you'll learn a new vocabulary word. **Bare. Bare** means "not covered."
What does **bare** mean? *Not covered.*

Another way to say "not covered." is **bare.** What's another way to say "not covered."? *Bare.*

The electric cord was **not covered,** and Andrew touched it. Because it was **bare,** Andrew got shocked.

Discuss things that are bare.

What's another way to say "not covered"? *Bare.*

Direct students to write bare and its definition in their vocabulary notebooks.
Guide as needed.
Write **bare** and what it means in your vocabulary notebook.

Activity 2 Review Vocabulary Word

Elicit responses to questions. **Guide** as needed.
What's another way to say "people who know a lot about something"? *Experts.*

Tell me a sentence using the word **experts.** (Student responses.)
Discuss sentences.

 Review vocabulary words in their appropriate context in Reading *Textbook C.*

330   Lesson 104

12 minutes

Teacher Materials:
Narrative Story Map

Reading *Textbook C*

Student Materials:
Narrative Story Map

Reading *Textbook C*

Part B: Comprehension Strategies

Activity 1 Text-to-Self Connection—An After-Reading Strategy

 Direct students to Lesson 103, pages 16–19 in Reading *Textbook C*.

Elicit responses to questions. **Guide** as needed.
When you read narratives, it helps you understand the passage you're reading if you connect what you're reading to an experience you've had. That's called making a text-to-self connection.

What's the strategy called? *Making a text-to-self connection.*

Skim the text to find places to make connections. **Guide** students to make text-to-self connections.
Let's skim "The Titans Play Harder" and see whether we can connect that story to our own experience.

Have you ever practiced something hard? (Student responses.)

How can you make a connection from your experience of practicing hard to the Titans practicing hard all week? (Student responses.)

We made a text-to-self connection by making a connection between something in the story and an experience you've had. It's a good strategy to help you understand what you read.

Activity 2 Narrative Story Map: Identify Title, Characters, Setting, Problem, and Events—An After-Reading Strategy

 Direct students to Lesson 103, pages 16–19 in Reading *Textbook C*.

Show Narrative Story Map. **Elicit** responses to questions. **Guide** as needed.
Narratives have a title, characters, settings, a problem, and events.
Skim "The Titans Play Harder," and then work by yourself to fill in the Narrative Story Map with the title, important characters, setting, problem, and events.

Discuss answers for the title, characters, setting, problem, and events. **Write** answers on Narrative Story Map. **Monitor** students as they write the title, characters, setting, problem, and events.

What did you write on your Narrative Story Map? (Ideas: *Title—"The Titans Play Harder;" Main Characters—Andrew; Setting: Where—the ball park; When—Sunday; Problem—Andrew is losing his strength; Beginning—The Titans were one point behind with a minute left in the game; Middle—Andrew kicked a field goal from 50 yards; End—The Titans won a chance to play in the championship game, but Andrew is losing his strength fast.*)

Now you'll use your Narrative Story Map to retell the story.

Lesson 104 **331**

Activity 3 | Use Narrative Story Map: Retell the Story—An After-Reading Strategy

Show Narrative Story Map (completed in Activity 2).
You did a great job of completing your Narrative Story Maps.

Assign student partners.
Now it's your turn to use your Narrative Story Maps to retell the story to your partner. Remember to start by telling the title and something about the characters and setting. Tell something about the problem, and then tell the events that happened. Use your own words to retell the story. Then let your partner use his or her own words to retell the story.

Retelling the story helps you remember all the parts of the story.

Part C: Fluency Building

5 minutes

Student Materials:
Reading *Textbook C*

Conduct after the lesson, using the story of the day.

Activity 1 | Partner Reading

It's time for partner reading.
Direct students to the story of the day. **Assign** student partners as Partner 1 and Partner 2. **Monitor** partner reading. **Guide** as needed.

Lesson 105

> **Materials**
> **Teacher:** Reading *Textbooks B and C,* 2-Vocabulary Acquisition and Use
> **Student:** Vocabulary notebook; drawing paper; Reading *Textbooks B and C,* Copy of 2-Vocabulary Acquisition and Use

8 minutes

Teacher Materials:
Reading *Textbook C*
Vocabulary Acquisition and Use

Student Materials:
Vocabulary notebook
Reading *Textbook C*
Vocabulary Acquisition and Use

Part A: Vocabulary Development

Activity 1 — Vocabulary Notebook Review

Guide students through all vocabulary words.
Today you'll study from your vocabulary notebook. Studying your words and what they mean will help you know your words even better. You'll look at the four words we studied this week.

Activity 2 — Cumulative Vocabulary Review

Elicit responses to questions. **Guide** as needed.
Directions: Listen and tell me whether I use our vocabulary words the right way or the wrong way. If I use the word the right way, say **"yes."** If I use the word the wrong way, say **"no."** Then we'll talk about each word.

1. The **announcer's** job was to write happy stories.

   Did I use the word **announcer** the right way? *No.*

   How do you know? (Student responses.)

2. Vera did not know the names of the flowers growing in her yard because she was not a flower **expert.**

   Did I use the word **expert** the right way? *Yes.*

   How do you know? (Student responses.)

3. Maria felt **awful** that she had forgotten her friend's birthday.

   Did I use the word **awful** the right way? *Yes.*

   How do you know? (Student responses.)

4. Katie was wearing shoes so her feet were **bare.**

   Did I use the word **bare** the right way? *No.*

   How do you know? (Student responses.)

Review vocabulary words as needed.

 Review vocabulary words in their appropriate context in Reading *Textbook C.*

Activity 3 Vocabulary Acquisition and Use

Display Vocabulary Acquisition and Use. **Have** students work with a neighbor to complete Vocabulary Acquisition and Use.
Today's vocabulary words are ____ and ____ [and ____ and ____].
Vocabulary words: **awful** and **bad; bare** and **uncovered**
Write the words on the lines provided. Then write the words in the boxes based on whether you think each word is less/smaller or more/larger than the other word. Below the boxes, write why you think word 1 is less/smaller and word 2 is more/larger than word 1.
Repeat for words 3 and 4. **Have** students share what they wrote. **Discuss** examples of how these words might be used.

Part B: Comprehension Strategies

12 minutes

Teacher Materials:
Reading *Textbook B*

Reading *Textbook C*

Student Materials:
Drawing paper

Reading *Textbook B*

Reading *Textbook C*

Display directions for activity.
Directions: You know from the story about Andrew that he changed because he got an electric shock. Discuss the changes in Andrew that occurred because of the shock. Illustrate one of the changes by drawing pictures to show Andrew before the shock and after the shock. For example, before the shock, Andrew daydreamed about being a star; after the shock, he was a star. Under each picture, write an explanation of your picture to help us understand the change in Andrew that you are illustrating.

Activity 1 Pair-Share Activity—Apply Knowledge (Level 3 of Bloom's Taxonomy)

Direct students to Andrew stories, Lessons 89–104, pages 306–386 in *Textbook B* and pages 1–26 in Reading *Textbook C*.

Discuss the steps in the Pair-Share activity.
You'll do an activity called **Pair-Share** to show some things you've learned in recent lessons. The directions are on the board. I'll read them to you.

Assign partners. **Provide** drawing paper to students.
Step 1 is the **Pair** part of the activity. Discuss with your partner the changes in Andrew from before to after his electric shock. Decide what change in Andrew you'll illustrate. Draw before and after pictures and then write under each picture an explanation of the change you're illustrating. Decide with your partner who'll do what part. Work quickly. You have 8 minutes.
Guide students to illustrate Andrew before and after his electric shock and explain the change in Andrew.

Call on as many students to share as time allows.
Step 2 is to **Share.** I'll call on pairs of students to share their work with the rest of the class.

5 minutes

Student Materials:
Reading *Textbook C*

Part C: Fluency Building

 Conduct after the lesson, using the story of the day.

Activity 1 Partner Reading

It's time for partner reading.
Direct students to the story of the day. **Assign** student partners as Partner 1 and Partner 2. **Monitor** partner reading. **Guide** as needed.

Lesson 106

Materials
Teacher: 12-Cause and Effect Map; Reading *Textbook C*, 10-Prediction Chart
Student: Vocabulary notebook; Copy of 12-Cause and Effect Map; Reading *Textbook C*

8 minutes

Teacher Materials:
Reading *Textbook C*

Student Materials:
Vocabulary notebook
Reading *Textbook C*

Part A: Vocabulary Development

Activity 1 Learn New Vocabulary Word

Elicit responses to questions. **Guide** as needed.
Today you'll learn a new vocabulary word. **Dodged. Dodged** means "not being hit by something because you moved out of the way." What does **dodged** mean? *Not being hit by something because you moved out of the way.*

Another way to say "not being hit by something because you moved out of the way" is **dodged.** What's another way to say "not being hit by something because you moved out of the way"? *Dodged.*

Football players try to **not get hit** by the other players **by moving out of the way.** By the end of the game, they have **dodged** many of the other team's players.

Discuss things that are dodged.

What's another way to say "not being hit by something because you moved out of the way"? *Dodged.*

Direct students to write dodged and its definition in their vocabulary notebooks. **Guide** as needed.
Write **dodged** and what it means in your vocabulary notebook.

Activity 2 Review Vocabulary Word

Elicit responses to questions. **Guide** as needed.
What's another way to say "not covered"? *Bare.*

Tell me a sentence using the word **bare.** (Student responses.)

Discuss sentences.

 Review vocabulary words in their appropriate context in Reading *Textbook C.*

336 Lesson 106

12 minutes

Teacher Materials:
Cause and Effect

Prediction Chart

Reading *Textbook C*

Student Materials:
Cause and Effect Map

Reading *Textbook C*

Part B: Comprehension Strategies

Activity 1 Text-to-Self Connection—An After-Reading Strategy

 Direct students to Lesson 105, pages 30–33 in Reading *Textbook C*.

When you read narrative text, it helps you understand the passage you're reading if you connect what you're reading to an experience you've had. That's called making a text-to-self connection.

What's the strategy called? *Making a text-to-self connection.*

Skim the text to find places to make connections. **Guide** students to make text-to-self connections.
Let's skim "The Championship Game" and see if we can connect that story to our own experience.

Have you ever heard a crowd cheer? (Student responses.)

How can you make a connection from your experience of hearing a crowd cheer to this story? (Student responses.)

We made a text-to-self connection by making a connection between something in the story and an experience you had. It's a good strategy to help you understand what you read.

Activity 2 Identify Cause-and-Effect Relationships—A During-Reading Strategy

 Direct students to Lesson 105, pages 30–33 in Reading *Textbook C*.

Show Cause and Effect Map. **Elicit** responses to questions. **Guide** as needed.
Learning to identify cause and effect in a passage will help you understand what you read.

Cause means "to make something happen." What does **cause** mean? *To make something happen.*

An **effect** is "what happens." What's an **effect?** *What happens.*

In Lesson 105 you read "The Championship Game." Today you'll work to fill out your Cause and Effect Map for that story. Skim page 30 and see whether you can find one or two cause-and-effect relationships to write on your Cause and Effect Map.
Monitor students as they write sentences to fill out one cause-and-effect relationship on the Cause and Effect Map.

Discuss cause-and-effect relationships and record on the Cause and Effect Map as time permits.
Share the cause-and-effect relationships you found. (Student responses.)

Lesson 106 **337**

Activity 3 Make Predictions—A Before-Reading Strategy

 Direct students to Lesson 106, pages 37–41 in Reading *Textbook C*.

Show Prediction Chart. **Elicit** responses to questions. **Guide** as needed.
When you read narrative text, it's a good strategy to make predictions about what you're going to read to help you understand the story better.

What are predictions? (*Idea: Good guesses based on clues about what's in the story.*)

Where do you get the clues for your prediction? (*Idea: The title, the picture, skimming the text, and remembering what you know about the story so far.*)

Let's work together to predict what will happen in the next story by looking at the title "The End of the Game." You'll also skim the story, look at the picture, and remember what you know about the story so far to predict what will happen next.
Elicit predictions. **Record** predictions for further discussion in Lesson 107.

You made a prediction about what you're going to read.

What do you do with that prediction as you read? (*Idea: Try to see whether your predictions are correct or not.*)

Does it matter if the prediction is exactly correct? *No.*

That's right. What's important is that you're checking as you read to see whether your predictions are correct.

Part C: Fluency Building

5 minutes

Student Materials:
Reading *Textbook C*

 Conduct after the lesson, using the story of the day.

Activity 1 Partner Reading

It's time for partner reading.
Direct students to the story of the day. **Assign** student partners as Partner 1 and Partner 2. **Monitor** partner reading. **Guide** as needed.

338   Lesson 106

Lesson 107

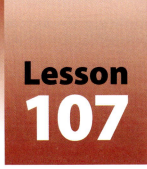

Materials

Teacher: 9-Compare and Contrast Chart; Prediction Chart (from Lesson 106); Reading *Textbooks B and C*

Student: Vocabulary notebook; Copy of 9-Compare and Contrast Chart; Reading *Textbooks B and C*

8 minutes

Teacher Materials:
Reading *Textbook C*

Student Materials:
Vocabulary notebook

Reading *Textbook C*

Part A: Vocabulary Development

Activity 1 Learn New Vocabulary Word

Elicit responses to questions. **Guide** as needed.
Today you'll learn a new vocabulary word. **Dive. Dive** means "jump headfirst." What does **dive** mean? *Jump headfirst.*

Another way to say "jump headfirst" is **dive.** What's another way to say "jump headfirst"? *Dive.*

People **jump headfirst** into the water to go deeper into the water. Some people **dive** into the water to look for ships and treasures.

Discuss examples of when and where students dive.

What's another way to say "jump headfirst"? *Dive.*

Direct students to write dive and its definition in their vocabulary notebooks. **Guide** as needed.
Write **dive** and what it means in your vocabulary notebook.

Activity 2 Review Vocabulary Word

Elicit responses to questions. **Guide** as needed.
What's another way to say "not being hit by something because you moved out of the way"? *Dodged.*

Tell me a sentence using the word **dodged.** (Student responses.)
Discuss sentences.

 Review vocabulary words in their appropriate context in Reading *Textbook C.*

Lesson 107   **339**

12 minutes

Teacher Materials:
Prediction Chart

Compare and Contrast Chart

Reading *Textbook B*

Reading *Textbook C*

Student Materials:
Compare and Contrast Chart

Reading *Textbook B*

Reading *Textbook C*

Part B: Comprehension Strategies

Activity 1 Confirm Predictions—An After-Reading Strategy

 Direct students to Lesson 106, pages 37–41 in Reading *Textbook C*.

Show Prediction Chart from Lesson 106. **Elicit** responses to questions. **Guide** as needed.
In the last lesson, you made some predictions about what happens to Andrew in the story. You made the predictions before you read the story. Making predictions helps you better understand the story.

You confirm predictions when you check to see whether your predictions were correct. What do you do when you check to see whether your predictions were right? *Confirm predictions.*

Now that you've read the story, let's check to see if your predictions were correct or incorrect.
Guide the discussion based on the predictions recorded in Lesson 106.

Sometimes, we don't predict correctly. That's okay. Just trying to make a prediction and then confirming it will help you better understand what you read.

Activity 2 Text-to-Self Connection—An After-Reading Strategy

 Direct students to Lesson 106, pages 37–41 in Reading *Textbook C*.

When you read narrative text, it helps you understand the passage you're reading if you connect what you're reading to an experience you've had. That's called making a text-to-self connection.

What's the strategy called? *Making a text-to-self connection.*

Assign student partners. **Skim** the text to find places to make connections. **Monitor** students as they make text-to-self connections.
Skim "The End of the Game" with your partner and see whether you can connect something in the story to your own experience. Put a sticky note in your book to mark the spot where you find a connection so you can find it again when we talk about text-to-self connections.

What text-to-self connections were you and your partner able to make in this story? (Student responses.)
Elicit as many text-to-self connections as time permits.

340   Lesson 107

You made text-to-self connections by making a connection between events in the story and experiences you had. It's a good strategy to help you understand what you read.

Activity 3 Compare and Contrast—An After-Reading Strategy

Direct students to Andrew stories, Lessons 89–106, pages 306–386 in *Textbook B* and pages 1–41 in Reading *Textbook C.*

Show the Compare and Contrast Chart. **Elicit** responses to questions. **Guide** as needed. You've learned how to tell how characters are the same and how they're different. Today you'll compare and contrast Andrew and you.

What will you do when you compare Andrew and you? (Idea: *Tell how Andrew and you are the same.*)

What will you do when you contrast Andrew and you? (Idea: *Tell how Andrew and you are different.*)

Write your name for one name and Andrew for the other name.
You are both people.

First, think about how you're the same as Andrew. Write two sentences. When you write about how you're the same, your sentences should begin, "We both…"
Monitor students as they write two sentences for "How Same?" box on Compare and Contrast Chart.

Now think about how you're different. Write two sentences. When you write about how you're different, it's a little harder. Your sentence needs to tell about each person and tell how each is different. You say the name of the person, tell about that person, and then use the word "but" before you tell about the next person. Remember, when you tell about how you're different, you have to tell about the same quality.
Monitor students as they write two sentences for "How Different?" box on Compare and Contrast Chart.

Lesson 107   **341**

5 minutes

Student Materials:
Reading *Textbook C*

Part C: Fluency Building

 Conduct after the lesson, using the story of the day.

Activity 1 Partner Reading

It's time for partner reading.

Direct students to the story of the day. **Assign** student partners as Partner 1 and Partner 2. **Monitor** partner reading. **Guide** as needed.

Lesson 108

> **Materials**
> **Teacher:** 9-Compare and Contrast Chart; Reading *Textbook C*
> **Student:** Vocabulary notebook; Copy of 9-Compare and Contrast Chart; Reading *Textbook C*

8 minutes

Teacher Materials:
Reading *Textbook C*

Student Materials:
Vocabulary notebook

Reading *Textbook C*

Part A: Vocabulary Development

Activity 1 Learn New Vocabulary Word

Elicit responses to questions. **Guide** as needed.
Today you'll learn a new vocabulary word. **Guess. Guess** means "think of something without having the facts." What does **guess** mean? *Think of something without having the facts.*

Another way to say "think of something without having the facts" is **guess.** What's another way to say "think of something without having the facts"? *Guess.*

In the word bank, you could never **think** you knew who would be sitting where **without having the facts.** It was anyone's **guess** who would be sitting in the front and who would be sitting in the back.

Discuss examples of when you guess.

What's another way to say "think of something without having the facts"? *Guess.*

Direct students to write guess and its definition in their vocabulary notebooks. **Guide** as needed.
Write **guess** and what it means in your vocabulary notebook.

Activity 2 Review Vocabulary Word

Elicit responses to questions. **Guide** as needed.
What's another way to say "jump headfirst"? *Dive.*

Tell me a sentence using the word **dive.** (Student responses.)
Discuss sentences.

  Review vocabulary words in their appropriate context in Reading *Textbook C*.

Lesson 108   343

8 minutes

Teacher Materials:
Compare and Contrast Chart

Reading *Textbook C*

Student Materials:
Compare and Contrast Chart

Reading *Textbook C*

Part B: Comprehension Strategies

Activity 1 Text-to-Self Connection—An After-Reading Strategy

 Direct students to Lesson 107, pages 48–52 in Reading *Textbook C*.

When you read narrative text, it helps you understand the passage you're reading if you connect what you're reading to an experience you've had. That's called making a text-to-self connection.

What's the strategy called? *Making a text-to-self connection.*

You can also make text-to-self connections with expository text. Today you'll skim the expository passage "Looking for Treasure." It might be hard to connect this passage with an experience, but you may be able to connect it to something you know about because you've seen a TV show or a movie.

Assign student partners. **Skim** the text to find places to make connections. **Monitor** students as they make text-to-self connections.
Skim "Looking for Treasure" with your partner and see whether you can connect something in the story to your own experience or something you know about. Put a sticky note in your book to mark the spot where you find a connection so you can find it again when we talk about text-to-self connections.

What text-to-self connections were you and your partner able to make in this story? (Student responses.)

You made text-to-self connections by making a connection between events in the story and experiences you had. It's a good strategy to help you understand what you read.

Activity 2 Compare and Contrast—An After-Reading Strategy

 Direct students to Lesson 107, pages 48–52 in Reading *Textbook C*.

Show the Compare and Contrast Chart. **Elicit** responses to questions. **Guide** as needed. You've learned how to tell how characters are the same and how they're different. Today you'll compare and contrast vehicles: ships from 200 years ago and ships of today.

What will you do when you compare ships from 200 years ago and ships of today? (Idea: *Tell how they're the same.*)

What will you do when you contrast ships from 200 years ago and ships of today? (Idea: *Tell how they're different.*)

Write "Ships from 200 years ago" for one name and "Ships of today" for the other name. They're both vehicles.

First think about how they're the same. Write two sentences. When you write about how they're the same your sentences should begin, "They both…"
Monitor students as they write two sentences for "How Same?" box on the Compare and Contrast Chart.

Now think about how they're different. Write two sentences. When you write about how they're different, it's a little harder. Your sentence needs to tell about each ship and tell how each is different. You say the name of the ship, tell about that ship, and then use the word "but" before you tell about the next ship. Remember, when you tell about how they're different, you have to tell about the same quality.
Monitor students as they write two sentences for "How Different?" box on the Compare and Contrast Chart.

Part C: Fluency Building

5 minutes

Student Materials:
Reading *Textbook C*

Conduct after the lesson, using the story of the day.

Activity 1 Partner Reading

It's time for partner reading.
Direct students to the story of the day. **Assign** student partners as Partner 1 and Partner 2. **Monitor** partner reading. **Guide** as needed.

Lesson 108   **345**

Lesson 109

Materials
Teacher: Reading *Textbook C*
Student: Vocabulary notebook; narrative story selected by student; sticky notes; Reading *Textbook C*; lined paper

8 minutes

Teacher Materials:
Reading *Textbook C*

Student Materials:
Vocabulary notebook
Reading *Textbook C*

Part A: Vocabulary Development

Activity 1 Learn New Vocabulary Word

Elicit responses to questions. **Guide** as needed.
Today you'll learn a new vocabulary word. **Cool. Cool** means "a little bit cold." What does **cool** mean? *A little bit cold.*

Another way to say "a little bit cold" is **cool.** What's another way to say "a little bit cold"? *Cool.*

Liz liked weather that was **a little bit cold.** She wanted to go to a city where it was **cool** rather than hot all the time.

Discuss things that are cool.

What's another way to say "a little bit cold"? *Cool.*

Direct students to write cool and its definition in their vocabulary notebooks. **Guide** as needed.
Write **cool** and what it means in your vocabulary notebook.

Activity 2 Review Vocabulary Word

Elicit responses to questions. **Guide** as needed.
What's another way to say "think of something without having the facts"? *Guess.*

Tell me a sentence using the word **guess.** (Student responses.)
Discuss sentences.

 Review vocabulary words in their appropriate context in Reading *Textbook C*.

346 Lesson 109

12 minutes

Teacher Materials:
Reading *Textbook C*

Student Materials:
Narrative story

Sticky notes

Reading *Textbook C*

Lined paper

Part B: Comprehension Strategies

Activity 1 Text-to-Self Connection—An After-Reading Strategy

 Direct students to choose a narrative story for making a text-to-self connection.

When you read narrative text, it helps you understand the passage you're reading if you connect what you're reading to an experience you've had. That's called making a text-to-self connection.

What's the strategy called? *Making a text-to-self connection.*

Skim stories to find places to make connections. **Monitor** students as they make text-to-self connections.
Read your story and find a place to make a text-to-self connection. Put a sticky note in your book to mark the spot where you find a connection so you can find it again when we talk about text-to-self connections.

Elicit as many text-to-self connections as time permits.
What text-to-self connections were you able to make in your story? (Student responses.)

You made text-to-self connections by making a connection between events in the story and experiences you had. It's a good strategy to help you understand what you read.

Activity 2 Generate Questions—A During-Reading Strategy

 Direct students to Lesson 108, pages 57–59 in Reading *Textbook C*.

Elicit responses to questions. **Guide** as needed.
Remember that asking questions while you read is one way to help you have better comprehension while you read because it keeps you interested in what you read.

What strategy can you use while you're reading to help keep you interested in what you're reading? (Idea: *Asking questions.*)

Provide lined paper to students. **Monitor** students as they generate questions from the text.
Sometimes it's hard to think of questions. Look at the story and see whether you can think of a question by yourself while you're reading. Find a sentence that makes you think of a question. Write the sentence and the question and then we'll see who can answer your questions.
Elicit answers to student-generated questions.

Remember, asking questions while you read keeps you interested in what you're reading. Why should you ask questions while you read? (Idea: *It keeps you interested in what you read.*)

Lesson 109

Activity 3 Choose a Comprehension Strategy—A During-Reading Strategy

Elicit responses to questions. **Guide** as needed.
You've learned strategies to use while you read a passage. What are those strategies? (Ideas: *Mental imaging, rereading, reading with prosody, and generating questions.*)

What strategies would you like to use on the passage in Lesson 109 that you'll read today? (Student responses.)

How would you use these strategies while you read the story? (Student responses).

Part C: Fluency Building

5 minutes

Student Materials:
Reading *Textbook C*

 Conduct after the lesson, using the story of the day.

Activity 1 Partner Reading

It's time for partner reading.
Direct students to the story of the day. **Assign** student partners as Partner 1 and Partner 2. **Monitor** partner reading. **Guide** as needed.

Lesson 110

Materials

Teacher: Reading *Textbook B and C,* 2-Vocabulary Acquisition and Use, Writing Prompts, 3-My Writing Checklist

Student: Vocabulary notebook; Reading *Textbook B and C,* Copy of 2-Vocabulary Acquisition and Use and 3-My Writing Checklist, Lined paper, Drawing paper

Part A: Vocabulary Development

8 minutes

Teacher Materials:
Reading *Textbook C*

Vocabulary Acquisition and Use

Student Materials:
Vocabulary Notebook

Reading *Textbook C*

Vocabulary Acquisition and Use

Activity 1 Vocabulary Notebook Review

Guide students as they study all vocabulary words.
Today you'll study from your vocabulary notebook. Studying your words and what they mean will help you know your words even better. You'll study the eight words we studied over the past two weeks.

Activity 2 Cumulative Vocabulary Review

Elicit responses to questions. **Guide** as needed.
Directions: Listen and tell me whether I use our vocabulary words the right way or the wrong way. If I use the word the right way, say **"yes."** If I use the word the wrong way, say **"no."** Then we'll talk about each word.

1. Sue asked Carla to **guess** how much money she made babysitting.

   Did I use the word **guess** the right way? *Yes.*

   How do you know? (Student responses.)

2. The walls in Emily's room had pictures all over them. They were **bare.**

   Did I use the word **bare** the right way? *No.*

   How do you know? (Student responses.)

3. Tino had a second helping of spaghetti because he thought it tasted **awful.**

   Did I use the word **awful** the right way? *No.*

   How do you know? (Student responses.)

4. Jasmine left her sweater at home because it was getting **cool** outside.

   Did I use the word **cool** the right way? *No.*

   How do you know? (Student responses.)

Lesson 110   349

5. The **announcer** said that there was a fire in a building downtown.

    Did I use the word **announcer** the right way? *Yes.*

    How do you know? (Student responses.)

6. Kelly **dodged** the kickball when it was thrown at him.

    Did I use the word **dodged** the right way? *Yes.*

    How do you know? (Student responses.)

7. The **experts** on TV said that the weather this summer would be hotter than normal. They always reported on sports and did not know about the weather.

    Did I use the word **experts** the right way? *No.*

    How do you know? (Student responses.)

8. The sign says that you are not to **dive** in the shallow end of the pool.

    Did I use the word **dive** the right way? *Yes.*

    How do you know? (Student responses.)

Review vocabulary words as needed.

Review vocabulary words in their appropriate context in Reading *Textbook C*.

Activity 3 Vocabulary Acquisition and Use

Display Vocabulary Acquisition and Use. **Have** students work with a neighbor to complete Vocabulary Acquisition and Use.
Today's vocabulary words are ____ and ____ [and ____ and ____].
Vocabulary words: **dive** and **jump**; **dodged** and **avoided**
Write the words on the lines provided. Then write the words in the boxes based on whether you think each word is less/smaller or more/larger than the other word. Below the boxes, write why you think word 1 is less/smaller and word 2 is more/larger than word 1.
Repeat for words 3 and 4. **Have** students share what they wrote. **Discuss** examples of how these words might be used.

12 minutes

Teacher Materials:
Reading *Textbook B*

Reading *Textbook C*

Student Materials:
Drawing paper

Reading *Textbook B*

Reading *Textbook C*

Part B: Comprehension Strategies

Display directions for the activity. **Note:** Discuss with students the dangers of electricity and that they shouldn't try to get an electric shock. The Andrew story is make-believe and couldn't really happen.

Directions: Discuss a pretend change that might happen to you if you got a pretend electric shock like Andrew. Apply your understanding of the Andrew story by drawing a pretend illustration of you before your electric shock and after your electric shock. Write under the pictures a quality you had before the shock and what changed after the shock.

Activity 1 Pair-Share Activity—Apply Knowledge (Level 3 of Bloom's Taxonomy)

 Direct students to Andrew stories, Lessons 89–106, pages 306–386 in *Textbook B* and pages 1–41 in Reading *Textbook C*.

Discuss the steps in the Pair-Share activity.
You'll do an activity called **Pair-Share** to show some things you have learned in recent lessons. The directions are on the board. I'll read them to you.

Assign student partners. **Provide** drawing paper to students.
Step 1 is the **Pair** part of the activity. Discuss with your partner what this make-believe experience of an electric shock would do to you and how it would change you. Both of you should illustrate yourselves before and after the pretend electric shock. Then write what quality changed in you by writing what you were like before the shock under the "before" picture. Write about the change in you under the picture of you after the shock. Each of you should draw and write about yourselves after discussing what to do. Work quickly. You have 8 minutes.

Guide students to illustrate themselves before and after a pretend electric shock, then write a quality and how it changes due to the electric shock.

Call on as many students to share as time allows.
Step 2 is to **Share.** I'll call on pairs of students to share their work with the rest of the class.

5 minutes

Student Materials:
Reading *Textbook C*

Part C: Fluency Building

Conduct after the lesson, using the story of the day.

Activity 1 Partner Reading

It's time for partner reading.
Direct students to the story of the day. **Assign** student partners as Partner 1 and Partner 2. **Monitor** partner reading. **Guide** as needed.

Lesson 110 **351**

Part D: Writing/Language Arts

10 minutes

Teacher Materials:
Writing Prompts

My Writing Checklist

Student Materials:
Lined Paper

My Writing Checklist

Activity 1 Write and Use Parts of Speech and Conventions

Time to write using a writing prompt based on the stories we've been reading.

Assign student partners. **Distribute** lined paper to students. **Display** writing prompts and have students choose one to write about or assign a writing prompt of your choice. **Review** parts of speech and punctuation as well as the writing checklist with students. **Tell** students to write one to two paragraphs (minimum of four sentences per paragraph) on their own to answer the writing prompt. **Tell** them to use their writing checklist (first column labeled "Did I use them?") to ensure they include important parts of speech or punctuation in their writing. **Tell** students which parts of speech or punctuation to focus on, if you wish. **Model** what it means to answer a writing prompt and to use the writing checklist during and after the writing process, as needed. **Monitor** and guide students as needed. **Model** what it means to have a neighbor look over his or her neighbor's writing and to complete the writing checklist (second column labeled "Did my neighbor use them?"), as needed. **Have** students share what they wrote as time permits.

Writing Prompt 1	Writing Prompt 2	Writing Prompt 3
Would you be nervous before a big game or event? Why or why not?	If you found treasure, what would you do with the money you'd get from it?	Would you like to dive deep in the ocean to find treasure? Why or why not?

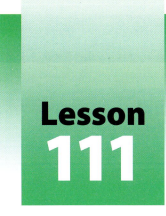

Lesson 111

Materials
Teacher: 13-KWL Chart; Reading *Textbook C*
Student: Vocabulary notebook; Copy of 13-KWL Chart; Reading *Textbook C*

Part A: Vocabulary Development

8 minutes

Teacher Materials:
Reading *Textbook C*

Student Materials:
Vocabulary notebook
Reading *Textbook C*

Activity 1 Learn New Vocabulary Word

Elicit responses to questions. **Guide** as needed.
Today you'll learn a new vocabulary word. **Opposite. Opposite** means "as different as possible." What does **opposite** mean? *As different as possible.*

Another way to say "as different as possible" is **opposite.** What's another way to say "as different as possible"? *Opposite.*

In Hohoboho, if a word was said a lot, it got moved to the front. But this was **as different as possible** when a word was not said very often. The **opposite** would happen, and the word would be moved to the back.

Discuss things that are opposite.

What's another way to say "as different as possible"? *Opposite.*

Direct students to write opposite and its definition in their vocabulary notebooks. **Guide** as needed.
Write **opposite** and what it means in your vocabulary notebook.

Activity 2 Review Vocabulary Word

Elicit responses to questions. **Guide** as needed.
What's another way to say "a little bit cold"? *Cool.*

Tell me a sentence using the word **cool.** (Student responses.)
Discuss sentences.

 Review vocabulary words in their appropriate context in Reading *Textbook C*.

Lesson 111   353

12 minutes

Teacher Materials:
KWL Chart

Reading *Textbook C*

Student Materials:
KWL Chart

Reading *Textbook C*

Part B: Comprehension Strategies

Activity 1 Determine Text Type and Establish Purpose for Reading—A Before-Reading Strategy

 Direct students to Lesson 111, pages 73–74 in Reading *Textbook C*.

Elicit responses to questions. **Guide** as needed.
Today you'll read an expository passage in your reading lesson.

What's the title of the first section you'll read? *Facts about Canada.*

Do you think this section is expository or narrative? *Expository.*

Why do you think it's expository? (Idea: *It looks like it teaches information about Canada.*)

Why do you read expository text? *To learn new facts or information.*

Why will you read "Facts about Canada"? (Idea: *To learn new information about Canada.*)

Activity 2 Choose a Comprehension Strategy—A Before-Reading Strategy

 Direct students to Lesson 111, pages 73–74 in Reading *Textbook C*.

Elicit responses to questions. **Guide** as needed.
You've learned strategies to use before you read a passage. What are those strategies? (Ideas: *Activate background knowledge, predict what is in the story, determine text type and set a purpose for reading, and fill out the first two parts of a KWL chart.*)

Take a look at the story you'll read today. Tell what strategy you should use before you read this story. (Idea: *Fill out the first two parts of a KWL chart because it's expository text.*)

Activity 3 KWL Chart: Topic and What I Know—A Before-Reading Strategy

Show the KWL Chart. **Elicit** responses to questions. **Guide** as needed.
You're going to activate your background knowledge for a new topic. What do you do when you activate your background knowledge? (Idea: *Think about what you already know.*)

You'll be reading a passage about Canada in the next lesson.

Why is it a good idea to think about your background knowledge before you read? (Idea: *Then you'll be able to connect what you know to what you learn.*)

354 Lesson 111

You'll use a KWL chart to help you organize your thinking about expository text. Why do you use a KWL chart? (Idea: *To organize thinking about expository text.*)

What should we write for the topic? *Canada.*
Write the topic on the KWL Chart. **Monitor** students as they write the topic on their charts.

Now work by yourself to think about your background knowledge about Canada for the "What I Know" section of the KWL chart.
Monitor students as they write what they know on their charts.

Tell me what you wrote in the "What I Know" section of your chart. (Student responses.)
Discuss background knowledge recorded by students on their KWL charts.

When you connect what you already know with the text, you'll be building more background knowledge in your mind.

Activity 4 KWL Chart: What I Wonder—A Before-Reading Strategy

Show the KWL Chart. **Elicit** responses to questions. **Guide** as needed.
Next you'll write the questions you have about the topic in the "What I Wonder" section of the chart.

What will you write in this section of the chart? (Ideas: *Questions you have; what you wonder about.*)

Think of questions you have about Canada for the "What I Wonder" section of the KWL chart and write them on the chart.
Monitor students as they write questions on their charts.

What questions did you think of? (Student responses.)

Discuss questions recorded by students on their KWL charts. **Record** three questions in "What I Wonder" section of the KWL Chart.

Why is it important to ask questions before you read? (Idea: *Asking questions gets you interested in what you're going to learn—it makes you think about what you're going to read.*)

Save teacher and student copies of the KWL Chart for Lesson 112.

The text you read may or may not have the answers to your questions. That's okay. Just asking the questions helps you be smarter. If you don't find the answers to your questions, you might need to read more in another book to find out the answers.

Lesson 111   **355**

5 minutes

Student Materials:
Reading *Textbook C*

Part C: Fluency Building

 Conduct after the lesson, using the story of the day.

Activity 1 Partner Reading

It's time for partner reading.

Direct students to the story of the day. **Assign** student partners as Partner 1 and Partner 2. **Monitor** partner reading. **Guide** as needed.

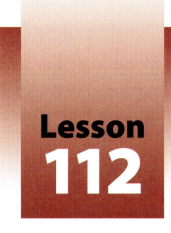

Lesson 112

Materials
Teacher: 13-KWL Chart (from Lesson 111); Reading *Textbook C;* additional book or Web site on Canada
Student: Vocabulary notebook; 13-KWL Chart (from Lesson 111); Reading *Textbook C*

Part A: Vocabulary Development

8 minutes

Teacher Materials:
Reading *Textbook C*

Student Materials:
Vocabulary notebook
Reading *Textbook C*

Activity 1 Learn New Vocabulary Word

Elicit responses to questions. **Guide** as needed.
Today you'll learn a new vocabulary word. **Forever. Forever** means "a very long time." What does **forever** mean? *A very long time.*

Another way to say "a very long time" is **forever.** What's another way to say "a very long time"? *Forever.*

Some things we remember for **a very long time.** For instance, Run had a chance to be up front. Although he was going to be moved, he didn't care because he knew he would remember the time up front **forever.**

Discuss things that are <u>forever</u>.

What's another way to say "a very long time"? *Forever.*

Direct students to write <u>forever</u> and its definition in their vocabulary notebooks. **Guide** as needed.
Write **forever** and what it means in your vocabulary notebook.

Activity 2 Review Vocabulary Word

Elicit responses to questions. **Guide** as needed.
What's another way to say "as different as possible"? *Opposite.*

Tell me a sentence using the word **opposite.** (Student responses.)
Discuss sentences.

 Review vocabulary words in their appropriate context in Reading *Textbook C.*

Lesson 112   357

12 minutes

Teacher Materials:
KWL Chart

Reading *Textbook C*

Additional book or Web site on Canada

Student Materials:
KWL Chart

Reading *Textbook C*

Part B: Comprehension Strategies

Activity 1 Choose a Comprehension Strategy—An After-Reading Strategy

 Direct students to Lesson 111, pages 73–74 in Reading *Textbook C*.

Elicit response to question. **Guide** as needed.
In the last lesson, you filled out the first two sections of your KWL chart. Then you read the passage "Facts about Canada."

What after-reading strategy should you use today? (Idea: *Fill in the "What I Learned" section of the KWL chart.*)

Activity 2 KWL Chart: What I Learned—An After-Reading Strategy

 Direct students to Lesson 111, pages 73–74 in Reading *Textbook C*.

Show the KWL Chart (partially completed in Lesson 111). **Elicit** responses to questions. **Guide** as needed.
In the last lesson, you read "Facts about Canada." It's time to add what you learned from the passage in the "What I Learned" section of the KWL chart that you started in Lesson 111.

Should you copy the words from the book? *No.*

What should you do instead? (Idea: *Write the ideas in your own words.*)

Why should you write the ideas in your own words? (Idea: *That will help you remember the information later.*)

Today you'll work to fill out the "What I Learned" section of the chart.

Monitor students as they write two sentences to add to the "What I Learned" section of the KWL Chart started in Lesson 111. **Record** the best sentences on the "What I Learned" section of the KWL Chart for students to copy as necessary.

You've now written the new things you learned from the expository text you read. You wrote the information in your own words.

There's a new part on your KWL chart that says, "Questions I Still Have."

Did you have all your questions about Canada answered? (Idea: *No.*)

Model writing questions in "Questions I Still Have" box. **Guide** students to copy one or two questions in the box.
I'm going to write a couple of questions I still have in this box.

Show additional resources for information about Canada. **Model** writing resources in the "Where to Look for More Information" box.

358 Lesson 112

Let's think about how we could find the answers to your questions. (Ideas: *Another book, a magazine, a video, the Internet, or an encyclopedia.*)

Model writing resources in the "Where to Look for More Information" box.
Write where you could look for more information in the last box.

Activity 3 Summarize Expository Text—An After-Reading Strategy

Direct students to Lesson 111, pages 73–74 in Reading *Textbook C*.

Elicit responses to questions. **Guide** as needed.
When you summarize text, you tell about what you read in your own words. You tell only the important parts of the passage when you summarize, and you leave out the details. When you summarize expository text, you tell the topic and the important facts.

What do you tell when you summarize expository text? (Idea: *The topic and the important facts.*)

You've summarized as you wrote the topic and important facts on your KWL chart. You can further summarize by telling about the whole passage in a few sentences that tell the most important thing you learned from the passage.

Let's work together to summarize "Facts about Canada" in a few sentences. Look at the topic and look at the new sentences you wrote for your KWL chart.

How can we put those ideas into a few sentences? (Student responses.)

Elicit student ideas for summary sentences. Idea: Canada is north of the U.S. and much larger than the U.S.

We told the main things we learned from the passage in a few sentences, and we left out all the details.

Part C: Fluency Building

5 minutes

Student Materials:
Reading *Textbook C*

Conduct after the lesson, using the story of the day.

Activity 1 Partner Reading

It's time for partner reading.
Direct students to the story of the day. **Assign** student partners as Partner 1 and Partner 2. **Monitor** partner reading. **Guide** as needed.

Lesson 112   **359**

Lesson 113

Materials
Teacher: 13-KWL Chart; Reading *Textbook C*
Student: Vocabulary notebook; Copy of 13-KWL Chart; Reading *Textbook C*

8 minutes

Teacher Materials:
Reading *Textbook C*

Student Materials:
Vocabulary notebook
Reading *Textbook C*

Part A: Vocabulary Development

Activity 1 Learn New Vocabulary Word

Elicit responses to questions. **Guide** as needed.
Today you'll learn a new vocabulary word. **Finest. Finest** means "nicest." What does **finest** mean? *The nicest.*

Another way to say "nicest" is **finest.** What's another way to say "nicest"? *Finest.*

Sometimes we say some of the **nicest** things. Toby was the last kangaroo, but he had the **finest** tail there was.

Discuss examples of things that are the finest.

What's another way to say "nicest?" *Finest.*

Direct students to write finest and its definition in their vocabulary notebooks.
Guide as needed.
Write **finest** and what it means in your vocabulary notebook.

Activity 2 Review Vocabulary Word

Elicit responses to questions. **Guide** as needed.
What's another way to say "a very long time"? *Forever.*

Tell me a sentence using the word **forever.** (Student responses.)
Discuss sentences.

 Review vocabulary words in their appropriate context in Reading *Textbook C*.

360 Lesson 113

12 minutes

Teacher Materials:
KWL Chart

Reading *Textbook C*

Student Materials:
KWL Chart

Reading *Textbook C*

Part B: Comprehension Strategies

Activity 1 Determine Text Type and Establish Purpose for Reading—A Before-Reading Strategy

 Direct students to Lesson 113, pages 88–89 in Reading *Textbook C*.

Elicit responses to questions. **Guide** as needed.
Today you'll read an expository passage in your reading lesson.

What's the title of the first section you'll read? *Facts about Australia.*

Do you think this section is expository or narrative? *Expository.*

Why do you think it's expository? (Idea: *It looks like it teaches information about Australia.*)

Why do you read expository text? *To learn new facts or information.*

Why will you read "Facts about Australia"? (Idea: *To learn new information about Australia.*)

Activity 2 Choose a Comprehension Strategy—A Before-Reading Strategy

 Direct students to Lesson 113, pages 88–89 in Reading *Textbook C*.

Elicit responses to questions. **Guide** as needed.
You've learned strategies to use before you read a passage. What are those strategies? (Ideas: *Activate background knowledge, predict what is in the story, determine text type and set a purpose for reading, and fill out the first two parts of a KWL chart.*)

Take a look at the story you'll read today. Tell what strategy you should use before you read this story. (Idea: *Fill out the first two parts of a KWL chart because it is expository text.*)

Activity 3 KWL Chart: Topic and What I Know—A Before-Reading Strategy

Show the KWL Chart. **Elicit** responses to questions. **Guide** as needed.
What do you do when you activate your background knowledge? (Idea: *Think about what you already know.*)

You'll be reading a passage about Australia in the next lesson. Why is it a good idea to think about your background knowledge before you read? (Idea: *Then you'll be able to connect what you know to what you learn.*)

You'll use a KWL chart to help you organize your thinking about expository text. Why do you use a KWL chart? (Idea: *To organize thinking about expository text.*)

Lesson 113 **361**

What should we write for the topic? *Australia.*
Write the topic on the KWL Chart. **Monitor** students as they write the topic on their charts.

Now work by yourself to think about your background knowledge about Australia for the "What I Know" section of the KWL chart.
Monitor students as they write what they know on their charts.

Tell me what you wrote in the "What I Know" section of your chart? (Student responses).
Discuss background knowledge recorded by students on their KWL charts.

When you connect what you already know with the text, you'll be building more background knowledge in your mind.

Activity 4 KWL Chart: What I Wonder—A Before-Reading Strategy

Show the KWL Chart. **Elicit** responses to questions. **Guide** as needed.
Next you'll write the questions you have about the topic in the "What I Wonder" section of the chart.

What will you write in this section of the chart? (Ideas: *Questions you have; what you wonder about.*)

Think of questions you have about Australia for the "What I Wonder" section of the KWL chart and write them on the chart.
Monitor students as they write questions on their charts.

What questions did you think of? (Student responses).
Discuss questions recorded by students on their KWL charts. **Record** three questions in "What I Wonder" section of the KWL Chart.

Why is it important to ask questions before you read? (Idea: *Asking questions gets you interested in what you're going to learn—it makes you think about what you're going to read.*)

Save teacher and student copies of the KWL Chart for Lesson 114.

The text you read may or may not have the answers to your questions. That's okay. Just asking the questions helps you be smarter. If you don't find the answers to your questions, you might need to read more in another book to find out the answers.

Part C: Fluency Building

5 minutes

Student Materials:
Reading *Textbook C*

 Conduct after the lesson, using the story of the day.

Activity 1 Partner Reading

It's time for partner reading.
Direct students to the story of the day. **Assign** student partners as Partner 1 and Partner 2. **Monitor** partner reading. **Guide** as needed.

Lesson 114

Materials

Teacher: KWL Chart (from Lesson 113); Reading *Textbook C*; additional book or Web site on Australia

Student: Vocabulary notebook; Copy of 13-KWL Chart (from Lesson 113); Reading *Textbook C*

Part A: Vocabulary Development

8 minutes

Teacher Materials:
Reading *Textbook C*

Student Materials:
Vocabulary notebook
Reading *Textbook C*

Activity 1 Learn New Vocabulary Word

Elicit responses to questions. **Guide** as needed.
Today you'll learn a new vocabulary word. **Smack. Smack** means "hit." What does **smack** mean? *Hit.*

Another word for "hit" is **smack.** What's another word for "hit"? *Smack.*

Toby was put on lookout duty for the rest of the kangaroos. His job was to let the others know if there was any trouble. He was supposed to **hit** the ground with his foot if there was trouble. He hoped he wouldn't need to **smack** his foot.

Discuss things that you smack.

What's another word for "hit"? *Smack.*

Direct students to write smack and its definition in their vocabulary notebooks. **Guide** as needed.
Write **smack** and what it means in your vocabulary notebook.

Activity 2 Review Vocabulary Word

Elicit responses to questions. **Guide** as needed.
What's another way to say "nicest"? *Finest.*

Tell me a sentence using the word **finest.** (Student responses.)
Discuss sentences.

  Review vocabulary words in their appropriate context in Reading *Textbook C*.

Lesson 114   **363**

12 minutes

Teacher Materials:
KWL Chart

Reading *Textbook C*

Additional book or Web site on Australia

Student Materials:
KWL Chart

Reading *Textbook C*

Part B: Comprehension Strategies

Activity 1 Choose a Comprehension Strategy—An After-Reading Strategy

 Direct students to Lesson 113, pages 88–89 in Reading *Textbook C*.

Elicit responses to questions. **Guide** as needed.
In the last lesson, you filled out the first two sections of your KWL chart. Then you read the passage "Facts about Australia."

What after-reading strategy should you use today? (Idea: *Fill in the What I Learned section of the KWL chart.*)

Activity 2 KWL Chart: What I Learned—An After-Reading Strategy

 Direct students to Lesson 113, pages 88–89 in Reading *Textbook C*.

Show the KWL Chart (partially completed in Lesson 113). **Elicit** responses to questions. **Guide** as needed.
In the last lesson, you read "Facts about Australia." It's time to add what you learned from the passage in the "What I Learned" section of the KWL chart that you started in Lesson 113.

Should you copy the words from the book? *No.*

What should you do instead? (Idea: *Write the ideas in your own words.*)

Why should you write the ideas in your own words? (Idea: *That will help you remember the information later.*)

Today you'll work to fill out the "What I Learned" section of the chart.
Monitor students as they write two sentences to add to the "What I Learned" section of the KWL Chart started in Lesson 113. **Record** the best sentences on the "What I Learned" section of the KWL Chart for students to copy as necessary.

You've now written the new things you learned from the expository text you read. You wrote the information in your own words.

There's a new part on your KWL chart that says "Questions I Still Have."

Did you have all your questions about Australia answered? (Idea: *No.*)

Write one or two questions you still have in this box.
Guide students as they write questions in the "Questions I Still Have" box.

Show additional resources for information about Australia.
Let's think about how we could find the answers to your questions. (Ideas: *Read another book, look on the Internet, and look in an encyclopedia.*)

Guide students as they write resources in the "Where to Look for More Information" box.
Write where you could look for more information in the last box.

364 Lesson 114

Activity 3 Summarize Expository Text—An After-Reading Strategy

 Direct students to Lesson 113, pages 88–89 in Reading *Textbook C*.

Show KWL Chart. **Elicit** response to question. **Guide** as needed.
When you summarize text, you tell about what you read in your own words. You tell only the important parts of the passage when you summarize, and you leave out the details. When you summarize expository text, you tell the topic and the important facts.

What do you tell when you summarize expository text? (Idea: *The topic and the important facts.*)

You have summarized as you wrote the topic and important facts on your KWL chart. You can further summarize by telling about the whole passage in a few sentences that tell the most important thing you learned from the passage.

Let's work together to summarize "Facts about Australia" in a few sentences. Look at the topic and look at the new sentences you wrote for your KWL chart.

How can we put those ideas into a few sentences? (Student responses.)
Elicit student ideas for summary sentences. Idea: Australia a continent west of the U.S. that has some unusual animals.

We told the main things we learned from the passage in a few sentences, and we left out all the details.

5 minutes

Student Materials:
Reading *Textbook C*

Part C: Fluency Building

 Conduct after the lesson, using the story of the day.

Activity 1 Partner Reading

It's time for partner reading.
Direct students to the story of the day. **Assign** student partners as Partner 1 and Partner 2. **Monitor** partner reading. **Guide** as needed.

Lesson 114 **365**

Lesson 115

Materials

Teacher: Reading *Textbook C*, 2-Vocabulary Acquisition and Use

Student: Vocabulary notebook; Reading *Textbook C*, Copy of 2-Vocabulary Acquisition and Use, Drawing paper

Part A: Vocabulary Development

8 minutes

Teacher Materials:
Reading *Textbook C*

Vocabulary Acquisition and Use

Student Materials:
Vocabulary notebook

Reading *Textbook C*

Vocabulary Acquisition and Use

Activity 1 Vocabulary Notebook Review

Guide students through all vocabulary words.
Today you'll study from your vocabulary notebook. Studying your words and what they mean will help you know your words even better. You'll look at the four words we studied this week.

Activity 2 Cumulative Vocabulary Review

Elicit responses to questions. **Guide** as needed.
Directions: Listen and tell me whether I use our vocabulary words the right way or the wrong way. If I use the word the right way, say **"yes."** If I use the word the wrong way, say **"no."** Then we'll talk about each word.

1. Joni told Sara they would be friends **forever.**

    Did I use the word **forever** the right way? *Yes.*

    How do you know? (Student responses.)

2. Diane and Tami wore the same outfit to school. They dressed the **opposite** of one another.

    Did I use the word **opposite** the right way? *No.*

    How do you know? (Student responses.)

3. A queen wears only the **finest** jewels.

    Did I use the word **finest** the right way? *Yes.*

    How do you know? (Student responses.)

4. Paco laid his hand gently on the glass tabletop. His mother said not to **smack** the tabletop.

Did I use the word **smack** the right way? *Yes.*

How do you know? (Student responses.)

Review vocabulary words as needed.

 Review vocabulary words in their appropriate context in Reading *Textbook C.*

Activity 3 Vocabulary Acquisition and Use

Display Vocabulary Acquisition and Use. **Have** students work with a neighbor to complete Vocabulary Acquisition and Use.
Today's vocabulary words are ____ and ____ [and ____ and ____].
Vocabulary words: **finest** and **nicest**; **smack** and **hit**
Write the words on the lines provided. Then write the words in the boxes based on whether you think each word is less/smaller or more/larger than the other word. Below the boxes, write why you think word 1 is less/smaller and word 2 is more/larger than word 1.
Repeat for words 3 and 4. **Have** students share what they wrote. **Discuss** examples of how these words might be used.

Part B: Comprehension Strategies

12 minutes

Teacher Materials:
Reading *Textbook C*

Student Materials:
Drawing paper

Reading *Textbook C*

Display directions for activity.
Directions: Discuss the events that happened at the end of the story entitled "A Job for Toby." Apply your knowledge of the story by making a map to show the characters and the setting for Toby, the mob, and the hunters. Label all the parts of the map. Explain where and why you put each item on your map.

Activity 1 Pair-Share Activity—Apply Knowledge
            (Level 3 of Bloom's Taxonomy)

Discuss the steps in the Pair-Share activity.
You'll do an activity called **Pair-Share** to show some things you have learned in recent lessons. The directions are on the board. I'll read them to you.

Assign partners. **Provide** drawing paper.
Step 1 is the **Pair** part of the activity. Discuss with your partner the events at the end of the story "A Job for Toby." Then draw a map to show the setting and the characters in the story. Label each part of the map. Be ready to explain what is on your map and why you put it there. Work quickly. You have 8 minutes.
Guide students to draw and label a map.

Call on as many students to share as time allows.
Step 2 is to **Share.** I'll call on pairs of students to share their work with the rest of the class.

Lesson 115   **367**

5 minutes

Student Materials:
Reading Textbook C

Part C: Fluency Building

 Conduct after the lesson, using the story of the day.

Activity 1 Partner Reading

It's time for partner reading.
Direct students to the story of the day. **Assign** student partners as Partner 1 and Partner 2. **Monitor** partner reading. **Guide** as needed.

Lesson 116

Materials

Teacher: Locate an expository trade book of teacher choice about kangaroos; Reading *Textbook C*

Student: Vocabulary notebook; Reading *Textbook C*

Part A: Vocabulary Development

8 minutes

Teacher Materials:
Reading *Textbook C*

Student Materials:
Vocabulary notebook

Reading *Textbook C*

Activity 1 Learn New Vocabulary Word

Elicit responses to questions. **Guide** as needed.
Today you'll learn a new vocabulary word. **Lovely. Lovely** means "beautiful." What does **lovely** mean? *Beautiful.*

Another word for "beautiful" is **lovely.** What's another word for "beautiful"? *Lovely.*

As Toby's eyes adjusted to the dark, he could see something in the distance that was **beautiful.** It was a **lovely** peacock.

Discuss things that are lovely.

What's another word for "beautiful"? *Lovely.*

Direct students to write lovely and its definition in their vocabulary notebooks. **Guide** as needed.
Write **lovely** and what it means in your vocabulary notebook.

Activity 2 Review Vocabulary Word

Elicit responses to questions. **Guide** as needed.

What's another word for "hit"? *Smack.*

Tell me a sentence using the word **smack.** (Student responses.)
Discuss sentences.

 Review vocabulary words in their appropriate context in Reading *Textbook C.*

Lesson 116   **369**

Part B: Comprehension Strategies

12 minutes

Teacher Materials:
Locate an expository trade book of teacher choice about kangaroos

Reading *Textbook C*

Student Materials:
Reading *Textbook C*

Activity 1 Determine Text Type and Establish Purpose for Reading—A Before-Reading Strategy

Direct students to look at an expository book of the teacher's choice about kangaroos. **Elicit** responses to questions. **Guide** as needed.

Today we'll read an expository book about kangaroos. The title is "_____."

Why do you read expository text? *To learn new facts or information.*

Why will you read, "_____"? (Idea: *To learn new information about kangaroos.*)

Activity 2 Identify Features of Expository Text—A Before-Reading Strategy

Direct students to look through the book with you to find features of expository text. **Elicit** responses to questions. **Guide** as needed.

Expository text is different from narrative text in lots of ways. Before we read this book, it's a good idea to look at some of the features that you find in expository text. Let's look through the book and see what features we can find. Remember, when you read expository text, you need to read all the features you find to help you learn the facts that the book is teaching you.

Identify following features if found in your text.
Labels—help identify parts
Photographs—help you understand what something looks like
Captions—tell what's in a picture
Cutaways—show what something looks like inside
Diagrams—show parts of things
Maps—help you know where something is in the world
Bold print—shows you important words
Headings—show what a section of text is about
Table of contents—helps you find information in a book
Index—tells you an alphabetized list with page numbers of what's in the book
Glossary—defines words in the book

Another important thing to remember about expository text is that it does not have to be read in order. You can hop around and read different parts in any order and you'll still learn new information.

Do you have to read expository text in order? *No.*

Why will we read this book? *To learn about kangaroos.*

370 Lesson 116

Activity 3 Prepare for Text-to-Text Connections—A Before-Reading Strategy

Read expository text about kangaroos with prosody noting text features as you read. When you make text-to-text connections, you think about stories you've read that remind you of the story you're reading. Making a connection to another story may help you understand the story you're reading better.

You're reading the story of Toby the kangaroo. That story is a narrative story. I'll read an expository book about kangaroos. Then we'll make a text-to-text connection between the story of Toby and the book about kangaroos.

Elicit from students the topic, important facts, and features of text after reading book.

In the next lesson, we'll make a text-to-text connection. We'll compare and contrast the stories to see how they're the same and how they're different. Making text-to-text connections helps you better understand stories.

Part C: Fluency Building

5 minutes

Student Materials:
Reading *Textbook C*

  Conduct after the lesson, using the story of the day.

Activity 1 Partner Reading

It's time for partner reading.
Direct students to the story of the day. **Assign** student partners as Partner 1 and Partner 2. **Monitor** partner reading. **Guide** as needed.

Lesson 116

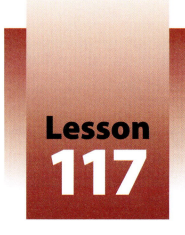

Lesson 117

Materials

Teacher: Expository book of teacher choice about kangaroos (from Lesson 116); Reading *Textbook C;* 13-KWL Chart

Student: Vocabulary notebook; Reading *Textbook C;* copy of 13-KWL Chart

Part A: Vocabulary Development

8 minutes

Teacher Materials:
Reading *Textbook C*

Student Materials:
Vocabulary notebook
Reading *Textbook C*

Activity 1 Learn New Vocabulary Word

Elicit responses to questions. **Guide** as needed.
Today you'll learn a new vocabulary word. **Entertain. Entertain** means "make people laugh." What does **entertain** mean? *Make people laugh.*

Another way to say "make people laugh" is **entertain.** What's another way to say "make people laugh"? *Entertain.*

The ship was headed for Canada. It would take many days to get there. The peacock told everyone not to worry about the time, because she would keep them busy by **making them laugh.** She planned to **entertain** them.

Discuss examples of ways people entertain.

What's another way to say "make people laugh"? *Entertain.*

Direct students to write entertain and its definition in their vocabulary notebooks. **Guide** as needed.
Write **entertain** and what it means in your vocabulary notebook.

Activity 2 Review Vocabulary Word

Elicit responses to questions. **Guide** as needed.
What's another word for "beautiful"? *Lovely.*

Tell me a sentence using the word **lovely.** (Student responses.)
Discuss sentences.

 Review vocabulary words in their appropriate context in Reading *Textbook C*.

12 minutes

Teacher Materials:
Expository book of teacher choice about kangaroos (from Lesson 116)

KWL Chart

Reading *Textbook C*

Student Materials:
KWL Chart

Reading *Textbook C*

Part B: Comprehension Strategies

Activity 1 Make Text-to-Text Connections—An After-Reading Strategy

 Direct students to Lessons 113–116, pages 90–116 in Reading *Textbook C*.

Direct students to remember expository text about kangaroos read in last lesson.
When you make text-to-text connections, you think about stories you've read that remind you of the story you're reading. Making a connection to another story may help you understand the story you're reading better.

The story of Toby the kangaroo is a narrative story. It's not true. The expository text about kangaroos has true information about kangaroos. So we'll make a text-to-text connection today to tell how the book and the story are the same and how they're different.

Elicit ideas from students for how stories are the same and how they're different. Note differences in features of texts; topics and information in expository texts; characters, settings, and events in narratives. **Guide** as needed.

When you compare and contrast the stories to see how they're the same and how they're different, you're making text-to-text connections that help you better understand stories.

Activity 2 Generate Questions—An After-Reading Strategy

Direct students to Lessons 113–116, pages 90–116 in Reading *Textbook C* and the expository text about kangaroos read in the last lesson.

Show KWL Chart. **Elicit** responses to questions. **Guide** as needed.
You've learned to ask questions before you read so you can record them on your KWL chart. You've learned to ask questions while you read.

Why do you ask questions while you read? (Idea: *It keeps you interested in what you read.*)

You can also ask questions after you read. When you ask questions after you read, you ask because you want to know more information. You have read about Toby, and we read a book about kangaroos.

Guide students to generate questions for information they want to know.
Tell me a question you still have about kangaroos. (Student responses.)

Where do you think we could look to find more information about kangaroos? (Idea: *Other resources such as books, magazines, videos, and the internet.*)

Allow students with further questions to seek answers in additional resources.

Asking questions after you read and looking for more answers is a great way to keep learning new information.

Lesson 117 **373**

5 minutes

Student Materials:
Reading *Textbook C*

Part C: Fluency Building

 Conduct after the lesson, using the story of the day.

Activity 1 Partner Reading

It's time for partner reading.

Direct students to the story of the day. **Assign** student partners as Partner 1 and Partner 2. **Monitor** partner reading. **Guide** as needed.

Lesson 118

Materials
Teacher: Reading *Textbook C*
Student: Vocabulary notebook; sticky notes; Reading *Textbook C*

8 minutes

Teacher Materials:
Reading *Textbook C*

Student Materials:
Vocabulary notebook
Reading *Textbook C*

Part A: Vocabulary Development

Activity 1 Learn New Vocabulary Word

Elicit responses to questions. **Guide** as needed.
Today you'll learn a new vocabulary word. **Hauled. Hauled** means "carried away." What does **hauled** mean? *Carried away.*

Another way to say "carried away" is **hauled.** What's another way to say "carried away"? *Hauled.*

Toby tried to sneak up the stairs and get away, but he got caught and was **carried away.** He was **hauled** onto a cart and sent down a ramp.

Discuss things that are hauled.

What's another way to say "carried away"? *Hauled.*

Direct students to write hauled and its definition in their vocabulary notebooks. **Guide** as needed.
Write **hauled** and what it means in your vocabulary notebook.

Activity 2 Review Vocabulary Word

Elicit responses to questions. **Guide** as needed.
What's another way to say "make people laugh"? *Entertain.*

Tell me a sentence using the word **entertain.** (Student responses.)
Discuss sentences.

 Review vocabulary words in their appropriate context in Reading *Textbook C.*

Lesson 118 375

12 minutes

Teacher Materials:
Reading Textbook C

Student Materials:
Sticky notes

Reading Textbook C

Part B: Comprehension Strategies

Activity 1 Comprehension Monitoring: Mental Imaging—A During-Reading Strategy

 Direct students to Lesson 117, page 123 in Reading *Textbook C*.

Elicit responses to questions. **Guide** as needed.
You've learned a strategy called mental imaging to help you understand what you read while you're reading. What does mental imaging help you do? *Understand and enjoy a story more.*

What's mental imaging? *Making pictures in your mind about what you're reading.*

Why do you use mental imaging with narrative text? (Idea: *You can make pictures in your mind of the characters, setting, and events to help you understand the story better.*)

In Lesson 117, you read "The End of the Trip." Look at page 123 by yourself and see if you can find a sentence or two where you can make a mental image. Mark the sentences with a sticky note and make a quick sketch to remind you of your mental image. Then we'll talk about the sentences you found and the mental image you made.
Elicit student responses for mental images.

Remember to use mental imaging when you read to help you understand and enjoy the story.

Activity 2 Text-to-Self Connection—An After-Reading Strategy

 Direct students to Lesson 117, page 120 in Reading *Textbook C*.

Elicit responses to questions. **Guide** as needed.
When you read narratives, it helps you understand the passage you're reading if you connect what you're reading to an experience you've had. That's called making a text-to-self connection.

What's the strategy called? *Making a text-to-self connection.*

Skim page 120 to find places to make connections.
Read your story and find a place to make a text-to-self connection.
Put a sticky note in your book to mark the spot where you find a connection so you can find it again when we talk about text-to-self connections.
Monitor students as they make text-to-self connections.

Elicit as many text-to-self connections as time permits.
What text-to-self connections were you able to make in your story?
(Student responses.)

376   Lesson 118

You made text-to-self connections by making a connection between events in the story and experiences you had. It's a good strategy to help you understand what you read.

Activity 3 Text-to-World Connection—An After-Reading Strategy

 Direct students to Lesson 117, pages 120–121 in Reading *Textbook C*.

You have made text-to-self and text-to-text connections. There is a third kind of connection to make and that is a text-to-world connection. When you make a text-to-world connection, you're making a connection to something that happens in the world.

Model think-aloud for text-to-world connection.
Listen as I make a text-to-world connection.

> **Sample Wording for Think-Aloud**
>
> I read that Pip told Toby that he had lived on a game preserve. A game preserve is a place where animals live so that they are safe. It is illegal to hunt, kill, or take animals from a game preserve.
>
> That's a problem in this story, but it's also a real problem in the world. There are game preserves for all kinds of animals. I'm thinking of game preserves for elephants. Often, elephants are hunted on game preserves and killed for their tusks. After the elephant is killed, the hunter cuts off the tusks and sells them for a lot of money. It's a huge problem.
>
> So Toby's problem is like a problem in the real world.

I made a text-to-world connection by connecting a problem in the story to a problem that really happens in the world. It helps me better understand the story.

Part C: Fluency Building

5 minutes

Student Materials:
Reading *Textbook C*

 Conduct after the lesson, using the story of the day.

Activity 1 Partner Reading

It's time for partner reading.
Direct students to the story of the day. **Assign** student partners as Partner 1 and Partner 2. **Monitor** partner reading. **Guide** as needed.

Lesson 118   **377**

Lesson 119

Materials

Teacher: 12-Cause and Effect Map; Reading *Textbook C*
Student: Vocabulary notebook; Copy of 12-Cause and Effect Map; Reading *Textbook C*

Part A: Vocabulary Development

8 minutes

Teacher Materials:
Reading *Textbook C*

Student Materials:
Vocabulary notebook

Reading *Textbook C*

Activity 1 Learn New Vocabulary Word

Elicit responses to questions. **Guide** as needed.
Today you'll learn a new vocabulary word. **Shabby. Shabby** means "old or worn out." What does **shabby** mean? *Old or worn out.*

Another way to say "old or worn out" is **shabby.** What's another way to say "old or worn out"? *Shabby.*

Toby was told he was going to be doing tricks for people who came to watch the circus. They took him into a place that looked **old and worn out.** It was a **shabby** tent where he was to perform his tricks.

Discuss things that are shabby.

What's another way to say "old or worn out"? *Shabby.*

Direct students to write shabby and its definition in their vocabulary notebooks.
Guide as needed.
Write **shabby** and what it means in your vocabulary notebook.

Activity 2 Review Vocabulary Word

Elicit responses to questions. **Guide** as needed.
What's another way to say "carried away"? *Hauled.*

Tell me a sentence using the word **hauled**. (Student responses.)
Discuss sentences.

 Review vocabulary words in their appropriate context in Reading *Textbook C*.

378   Lesson 119

12 minutes

Teacher Materials:
Cause and Effect Map

Reading *Textbook C*

Student Materials:
Cause and Effect Map

Reading *Textbook C*

Part B: Comprehension Strategies

Activity 1 Identify Cause-and-Effect Relationships— A During-Reading Strategy

 Direct students to Lesson 118, pages 128–129 in Reading *Textbook C*.

Elicit responses to questions. **Guide** as needed.
Today you'll identify cause and effect in a passage to help you understand what you read.

Cause means "to make something happen." What does **cause** mean? *To make something happen.*

An **effect** is "what happens." What's an **effect?** *What happens.*

Show the Cause and Effect Map.
In Lesson 118 you read "The Ship Arrives in Canada." Today you'll work to fill out your Cause and Effect Map for that story. Skim pages 128–129 and see if you can find one or two cause-and-effect relationships to write on your Cause and Effect Map.

Monitor students as they write sentences to fill out one or two cause-and-effect relationships on the Cause and Effect Map.

Discuss cause-and-effect relationships and record on the Cause and Effect Map as time permits.
Share the cause-and-effect relationships you found. (Student responses.)

Activity 2 Activate Background Knowledge— A Before-Reading Strategy

Elicit responses to questions. **Guide** as needed.

Remember, everything you know in your mind is called background knowledge. What do you call everything you know in your mind? *Background knowledge.*

What do you do when you activate your background knowledge? (Idea: *Think about what you already know.*)

Why do you activate your background knowledge? (Idea: *Connecting what you know to the story you're reading helps you better understand the story.*)

You'll read about a circus in the next story. Let's talk about your background knowledge about a circus.
Discuss student background knowledge about a circus. **Guide** as needed.

Connecting what you know about a circus to the next story may help you understand what you read.

Lesson 119 **379**

5 minutes

Student Materials:
Reading *Textbook C*

Part C: Fluency Building

 Conduct after the lesson, using the story of the day.

Activity 1 Partner Reading

It's time for partner reading.

Direct students to the story of the day. **Assign** student partners as Partner 1 and Partner 2. **Monitor** partner reading. **Guide** as needed.

Lesson 120

> **Materials**
> **Teacher:** Reading *Textbook C*, 2-Vocabulary Acquisition and Use, Writing Prompts, 3-My Writing Checklist
> **Student:** Vocabulary notebook; Reading *Textbook C*, Copy of 2-Vocabulary Acquisition and Use and 3-My Writing Checklist, Lined paper, Drawing paper

8 minutes

Teacher Materials:
Reading *Textbook C*

Vocabulary Acquisition and Use

Student Materials:
Vocabulary Notebook

Reading *Textbook C*

Vocabulary Acquisition and Use

Part A: Vocabulary Development

Activity 1 Vocabulary Notebook Review

Guide students as they study all vocabulary words.
Today you'll study from your vocabulary notebook. Studying your words and what they mean will help you know your words even better. You'll study the eight words we studied over the past two weeks.

Activity 2 Cumulative Vocabulary Review

Elicit responses to questions. **Guide** as needed.
Directions: Listen and tell me whether I use our vocabulary words the right way or the wrong way. If I use the word the right way, say **"yes."** If I use the word the wrong way, say **"no."** Then we'll talk about each word.

1. Ming did not want to wear the old dress her mother picked out for her from her closet. She thought it looked **shabby.**

   Did I use the word **shabby** the right way? *Yes.*

   How do you know? (Student responses.)

2. Tomás told the bride how **lovely** she looked. Her gown was long and white with lots of beads and flowers.

   Did I use the word **lovely** the right way? *Yes.*

   How do you know? (Student responses.)

3. A doctor's job is to **entertain** her patients.

   Did I use the word **entertain** the right way? *No.*

   How do you know? (Student responses.)

4. David had lots of new clothes to wear. He put on an old sweatshirt to wear outside. It was the **finest** thing he owned.

   Did I use the word **finest** the right way? *No.*

   How do you know? (Student responses.)

5. A big tree fell on the Olson's yard. The tree removal company came and **hauled** it away.

   Did I use the word **hauled** the right way? *Yes.*

   How do you know? (Student responses.)

6. Adam did not mean to **smack** his knee on the table when he was getting up.

   Did I use the word **smack** the right way? *Yes.*

   How do you know? (Student responses.)

7. Chris always agreed with what his friends said. He always said the **opposite** of what they would say.

   Did I use the word **opposite** the right way? *No.*

   How do you know? (Student responses.)

8. Cole moved away from New York twenty years ago. He said it felt like **forever** since he had lived there.

   Did I use the word **forever** the right way? *Yes.*

   How do you know? (Student responses.)

Review vocabulary words as needed.

 Review vocabulary words in their appropriate context in Reading *Textbook C*.

Activity 3 Vocabulary Acquisition and Use

Display Vocabulary Acquisition and Use. **Have** students work with a neighbor to complete Vocabulary Acquisition and Use.
Today's vocabulary words are _____ and _____ [and _____ and _____].
Vocabulary words: **lovely** and **beautiful; hauled** and **carried**
Write the words on the lines provided. Then write the words in the boxes based on whether you think each word is less/smaller or more/larger than the other word. Below the boxes, write why you think word 1 is less/smaller and word 2 is more/larger than word 1.
Repeat for words 3 and 4. **Have** students share what they wrote. **Discuss** examples of how these words might be used.

Part B: Comprehension Strategies

12 minutes

Student Materials:
Drawing paper

Display directions for the activity.
Directions: Toby the kangaroo has been sold to a circus. Discuss the acts that Toby is supposed to perform. Apply your understanding of the story by drawing a sign to advertise the acts he is supposed to do for the circus. Your sign should have pictures and words to try to get people to come to the circus and see the acts.

Activity 1 Pair-Share Activity—Apply Knowledge (Level 3 of Bloom's Taxonomy)

Direct students to Lesson 119, pages 135–138 in Reading *Textbook C*.

Discusss the steps in the Pair-Share activity.
You'll do an activity called **Pair-Share** to show some things you have learned in recent lessons. The directions are on the board. I'll read them to you.

Assign partners. **Provide** drawing paper.
Step 1 is the **Pair** part of the activity. Discuss with your partner the acts that Toby is supposed to do in the circus. Draw a sign to advertise the acts that Toby is supposed to do. Remember that good signs have pictures and words to get people interested in coming to the circus and paying for the show. Decide who will do what part. Work quickly. You have 8 minutes.
Guide students to draw a sign advertising the acts that Toby will do in the circus.

Call on as many students to share as time allows.
Step 2 is to **Share.** I'll call on pairs of students to share their work with the rest of the class.

Part C: Fluency Building

5 minutes

Student Materials:
Reading *Textbook C*

Conduct after the lesson, using the story of the day.

Activity 1 Partner Reading

It's time for partner reading.
Direct students to the story of the day. **Assign** student partners as Partner 1 and Partner 2. **Monitor** partner reading. **Guide** as needed.

Lesson 120 **383**

10 minutes

Teacher Materials:
Writing Prompts

My Writing Checklist

Student Materials:
Lined Paper

My Writing Checklist

Part D: Writing/Language Arts

Activity 1 Write and Use Parts of Speech and Conventions

Time to write using a writing prompt based on the stories we've been reading.

Assign student partners. **Distribute** lined paper to students. **Display** writing prompts and have students choose one to write about or assign a writing prompt of your choice. **Review** parts of speech and punctuation as well as the writing checklist with students. **Tell** students to write one to two paragraphs (minimum of four sentences per paragraph) on their own to answer the writing prompt. **Tell** them to use their writing checklist (first column labeled "Did I use them?") to ensure they include important parts of speech or punctuation in their writing. **Tell** students which parts of speech or punctuation to focus on, if you wish. **Model** what it means to answer a writing prompt and to use the writing checklist during and after the writing process, as needed. **Monitor** and guide students as needed. **Model** what it means to have a neighbor look over his or her neighbor's writing and to complete the writing checklist (second column labeled "Did my neighbor use them?"), as needed. **Have** students share what they wrote as time permits.

Writing Prompt 1	Writing Prompt 2	Writing Prompt 3
Would you want to live in Hohoboho? Why or why not?	Tell me what word you would like to be in Hohoboho and why you'd like to be this word.	What would it be like to have a kangaroo as a pet?

Lesson 121

Materials

Teacher: Reading *Textbook C;* 10-My Prediction Chart
Student: Vocabulary notebook; Reading *Textbook C;* Copy of 10-My Prediction Chart

Part A: Vocabulary Development

8 minutes

Teacher Materials:
Reading *Textbook C*

Student Materials:
Vocabulary notebook
Reading *Textbook C*

Activity 1 Learn New Vocabulary Word

Elicit responses to questions. **Guide** as needed.
Today you'll learn a new vocabulary word. **Crowded. Crowded** means "full of people or things." What does **crowded** mean? *Full of people or things.*

Another way to say "full of people or things" is **crowded.** What's another way to say "full of people or things"? *Crowded.*

Toby was put in a cage that was very small. It was a small place that got **full** when they added a second kangaroo. The little cage was very **crowded** with both kangaroos in it.

Discuss examples of places that are crowded.

What's another way to say "full of people or things"? *Crowded.*

Direct students to write crowded and its definition in their vocabulary notebook.
Guide as needed.
Write **crowded** and what it means in your vocabulary notebook.

Activity 2 Review Vocabulary Word

Elicit responses to questions. **Guide** as needed.
What's another way to say "old or worn out"? *Shabby.*

Tell me a sentence using the word **shabby.** (Student responses.)
Discuss sentence.

 Review vocabulary words in appropriate context in Reading *Textbook C.*

Lesson 121 **385**

8 minutes

Teacher Materials:
Reading *Textbook C*

Prediction Chart

Student Materials:
Reading *Textbook C*

Prediction Chart

Part B: Comprehension Strategies

Activity 1 Summarize Narrative Text—An After-Reading Strategy

 Direct students to Lesson 119, pages 135–138 in Reading *Textbook C*.

Elicit responses to questions. **Guide** as needed.
You've learned a strategy called **summarizing.** When you summarize text, you tell about what you read in your own words. You tell only the important parts of the passage when you summarize and you leave out the details. When you summarize narrative text, you tell the characters, the setting, and a few important events.

What do you tell when you summarize narrative text? (Idea: *The characters, the setting, and a few important events.*)

You can summarize by telling about the whole passage in a few sentences that tell the most important things you learned about the passage.

Now work by yourself to summarize "Toby's New Job" in a few sentences. Think about the characters, setting, and the most important events. Then write down a few sentences to summarize the story.
Monitor students as they write summary sentences.

Elicit student ideas for summary sentences. **Discuss** the best ideas and why they are good summaries.
What summary sentences did you think of? (Student responses.)

You told the main things you learned from the passage in a few sentences, and you left out all the details.

Activity 2 Comprehension Monitoring: Read with Prosody—A During-Reading Strategy

 Direct students to Lesson 119, pages 135–138 in Reading *Textbook C*.

You've learned a lot about reading stories with expression. You know how to read and pay attention to the punctuation. You even know about dialogue. You know that your voice should go up a little when you read a question.

Assign student partners.
Today you'll practice reading the story with expression with your partner. Take turns reading paragraphs with your partner. You each will be listening for reading with expression. Make your voice really interesting. Read the dialogue with different voices. Make sure your voice goes up at the end of the questions. Take a small breath between sentences. Reread a sentence if you make a little mistake. It should be fun to listen to you and your partner read the first two pages of the story.
Monitor student reading to ensure that they take turns and read with prosody.

Remember that reading with expression helps you have good comprehension.

386 Lesson 121

Activity 3 Make Predictions—A Before-Reading Strategy

 Direct students to Lesson 121, pages 146–149 in Reading *Textbook C*.

Show Prediction Chart. **Elicit** responses to questions. **Guide** as needed.
When you read narrative text, it's a good strategy to make predictions about what you're going to read to help you understand the story better.

What are predictions? (Idea: *Good guesses based on clues about what's in the story.*)

Where do you get the clues for your prediction? (Idea: *The title, the picture, skimming the text, and remembering what you know about the story so far.*)

Work by yourself to make a prediction about what'll happen in the next story by looking at the title "Toby Leaves the Circus." You'll also skim the story, look at the picture, and remember what you know about the story so far to predict what'll happen next.

Monitor students as they make predictions. **Elicit** predictions. **Record** predictions made by students for further discussion in Lesson 122.

You made a prediction about what you're going to read.

What do you do with that prediction as you read? (Idea: *Try to see if your predictions are correct or not.*)

Does it matter if the prediction is exactly correct? *No.*

That's right. What's important is that you're checking as you read to see if your predictions are correct.

Part C: Fluency Building

5 minutes

Student Materials:
Reading *Textbook C*

 Conduct after the lesson, using the story of the day.

Activity 1 Partner Reading

It's time for partner reading.
Direct students to the story of the day. **Assign** student partners as Partner 1 and Partner 2. **Monitor** partner reading. **Guide** as needed.

Lesson 121 **387**

Lesson 122

Materials

Teacher: Prediction Chart (from Lesson 121); Reading *Textbook C*

Student: Vocabulary notebook; lined paper; Reading *Textbook C*, Copy of Prediction Chart (from Lesson 121)

Part A: Vocabulary Development

8 minutes

Teacher Materials:
Reading *Textbook C*

Student Materials:
Vocabulary notebook

Reading *Textbook C*

Activity 1 Learn New Vocabulary Word

Elicit responses to questions. **Guide** as needed.
Today, you'll learn a new vocabulary word. **Important. Important** means "matters a lot." What does **important** mean? *Matters a lot.*

Another way to say "matters a lot" is **important.** What's another way to say "matters a lot"? *Important.*

When Toby and his father returned to Australia, the others were thrilled to have them back. They knew that the two kangaroos **mattered a lot** to their mob. It was good to have two **important** kangaroos return.

Discuss things that are important.

What's another way to say "matters a lot"? *Important.*

Direct students to write important and its definition in their vocabulary notebook. **Guide** as needed.
Write **important** and what it means in your vocabulary notebook.

Activity 2 Review Vocabulary Word

Elicit responses to questions. **Guide** as needed.
What's another way to say "full of people or things"? *Crowded.*

Tell me a sentence using the word **crowded.** (Student responses.)
Discuss sentence.

 Review vocabulary words in appropriate context in Reading *Textbook C*.

388 Lesson 122

12 minutes

Teacher Materials:
Prediction Chart

Reading *Textbook C*

Student Materials:
Lined paper

Reading *Textbook C*

My Prediction Chart

Part B: Comprehension Strategies

Activity 1 Confirm Predictions—An After-Reading Strategy

 Direct students to Lesson 121, pages 146–149 in Reading *Textbook C*.

Show Prediction Chart. **Elicit** response to question. **Guide** as needed.
In the last lesson, you made some predictions about what happens to Toby in the story. You made the predictions before you read the story.

You confirm predictions when you check to see if your predictions were correct. What do you do when you check to see if your predictions were right? *Confirm predictions.*

Now that you've read the story, let's check to see if your predictions were correct or incorrect.
Guide discussion based on predictions recorded in Lesson 121.

Sometimes, we don't predict correctly. That's okay. Just trying to make a prediction and then confirming it will help you better understand what you read.

Activity 2 Generate Questions—A During-Reading Strategy

 Direct students to Lesson 121, page 146 in Reading *Textbook C*.

Elicit responses to questions. **Guide** as needed.
Remember that asking questions while you read is one way to help you have better comprehension because it keeps you interested in what you read.

What strategy can you use while you're reading to help keep you interested in what you're reading? (Idea: *Asking questions*.)

Provide lined paper to students. **Monitor** students as they generate questions from the text.
Sometimes it's hard to think of questions. Look at the first page of the story and see if you can think of a question by yourself while you're reading. Find a sentence that makes you think of a question. Write the sentence and the question and then we'll see who can answer your questions.
Elicit answers to student-generated questions.

Remember, asking questions while you read keeps you interested in what you're reading. Why should you ask questions while you read? (Idea: *It keeps you interested in what you read*.)

Lesson 122

Activity 3 Make Predictions—A Before-Reading Strategy

 Direct students to Lesson 122, pages 152–159 in Reading *Textbook C*.

Elicit responses to questions. **Guide** as needed.
When you read narrative text, it's a good strategy to make predictions about what you're going to read to help you understand the story better.

What are predictions? (Idea: *Good guesses based on clues about what's in the story.*)

Where do you get the clues for your prediction? (Idea: *The title, the picture, skimming the text, and remembering what you know about the story so far.*)

Work by yourself to make a prediction about what'll happen in the next story by looking at the title "The Big Fight." You'll also skim the story, look at the picture, and remember what you know about the story so far to predict what will happen next.
Monitor students as they make predictions. **Elicit** predictions. **Record** predictions made by students for further discussion in Lesson 123.

You made a prediction about what you're going to read.

What do you do with that prediction as you read? (Idea: *Try to see if your predictions are correct or not.*)

Does it matter if the prediction is exactly correct? *No.*

That's right. What's important is that you're checking as you read to see if your predictions are correct.

5 minutes

Student Materials:
Reading *Textbook C*

Part C: Fluency Building

 Conduct after the lesson, using the story of the day.

Activity 1 Partner Reading

It's time for partner reading.
Direct students to the story of the day. **Assign** student partners as Partner 1 and Partner 2. **Monitor** partner reading. **Guide** as needed.

390 Lesson 122

Lesson 123

Materials

Teacher: Prediction Chart (from Lesson 122); Reading *Textbook C*

Student: Vocabulary notebook; sticky notes; Reading *Textbook C*, Copy of Prediction Chart (from Lesson 122)

Part A: Vocabulary Development

8 minutes

Teacher Materials:
Reading *Textbook C*

Student Materials:
Vocabulary notebook

Reading *Textbook C*

Activity 1 Learn New Vocabulary Word

Elicit responses to questions. **Guide** as needed.
Today, you'll learn a new vocabulary word. **Single. Single** means "one." What does **single** mean? *One.*

Another word for "one" is **single.** What's another word for "one"? *Single.*

There have been many bad fights in the word bank. A word would attack and sometimes leave **one** scar on a word. Other times, instead of a **single** scar, a word would leave many scars on another word.

Discuss examples of things that are single.

What's another word for "one"? *Single.*

Direct student to write single and its definition in their vocabulary notebook. **Guide** as needed.
Write **single** and what it means in your vocabulary notebook.

Activity 2 Review Vocabulary Word

Elicit responses to questions. **Guide** as needed.
What's another way to say "matters a lot"? *Important.*

Tell me a sentence using the word **important.** (Student responses.)
Discuss sentence.

 Review vocabulary words in appropriate context in Reading *Textbook C*.

Lesson 123   391

12 minutes

Teacher Materials:
Prediction Chart

Reading *Textbook C*

Student Materials:
Prediction Chart

Sticky notes

Reading *Textbook C*

Part B: Comprehension Strategies

Activity 1 Confirm Predictions—An After-Reading Strategy

 Direct students to Lesson 122, pages 152–155 in Reading *Textbook C*.

Show Prediction Chart. **Elicit** response to question. **Guide** as needed.
In the last lesson, you made some predictions about what happens to Toby in the story. You made the predictions before you read the story.

Now you'll confirm your predictions.

What do you do when you confirm your predictions? (Idea: *Check to see if your predictions were correct.*)

Now that you've read the story, let's check to see if your predictions were correct or incorrect.
Guide discussion based on predictions recorded in Lesson 122.

Sometimes, we don't predict correctly. That's okay. Just trying to make a prediction and then confirming it will help you better understand what you read.

Activity 2 Comprehension Monitoring: Mental Imaging—A During-Reading Strategy

 Direct students to Lesson 122, page 155 in Reading *Textbook C*.

Elicit responses to questions. **Guide** as needed. **Provide** stick notes.
You've learned a strategy called mental imaging to help you understand what you read while you're reading. What does mental imaging help you do? *Understand and enjoy a story more.*

What's mental imaging? *Making pictures in your mind about what you're reading.*

Why do you use mental imaging with narrative text? (Idea: *You can make pictures in your mind of the characters, setting, and events to help you understand and enjoy the story better.*)

In Lesson 122, you read "The Big Fight." Look at page 155 by yourself and see if you can find a sentence or two where you can make a mental image. Mark the sentences with a sticky note and make a quick sketch to remind you of your mental image. Then we'll talk about the sentences you found and the mental image you made.
Elicit student responses for mental images.

Remember to use mental imaging when you read to help you understand and enjoy the story.

Activity 3 Comprehension Monitoring: Reread Narrative or Expository Text—A During-Reading Strategy

 Direct students to Lesson 122, pages 152–155 in Reading *Textbook C*.

Elicit responses to questions. **Guide** as needed.
Rereading is a strategy to use while you read to help you have high comprehension.

What should you ask yourself while you're reading? (Idea: *Does this make sense?*)

What do you do if something doesn't make sense? (Idea: *Reread the sentence that didn't make sense or read ahead a little to see if that helps you understand.*)

What's the strategy called? *Rereading.*

Does this strategy work for both expository and narrative text? *Yes.*

When you read this story, did the whole story make sense? (Idea: *No.*)
Discuss what did not make sense and the strategy students used to fix the problem.

Today when you read Lesson 123, be sure to think about using the rereading strategy if you don't understand what you're reading for both the expository section and the narrative section.

5 minutes

Student Materials:
Reading *Textbook C*

Part C: Fluency Building

 Conduct after the lesson, using the story of the day.

Activity 1 Partner Reading

It's time for partner reading.
Direct students to the story of the day. **Assign** student partners as Partner 1 and Partner 2. **Monitor** partner reading. **Guide** as needed.

Lesson 123 **393**

Lesson 124

Materials

Teacher: Selection of narrative trade books; 6-Narrative Story Map

Student: Vocabulary notebook; narrative trade book of student choice; Copy of 6-Narrative Story Map

8 minutes

Teacher Materials:
Reading *Textbook C*

Student Materials:
Vocabulary notebook
Reading *Textbook C*

Part A: Vocabulary Development

Activity 1 Learn New Vocabulary Word

Elicit responses to questions. **Guide** as needed.
Today, you'll learn a new vocabulary word. **Reason. Reason** means "why something happened." What does **reason** mean? *Why something happened.*

Another way to say "why something happened" is **reason.** What's another way to say "why something happened"? *Reason.*

The word two has many scars. **Why this would happen** is that the word two could be spelled different ways, yet it always sounds the same. The **reason** two was so beaten up is that you can spell the word three different ways.

Discuss examples of a reason.

What's another way to say "why something happened"? *Reason.*

Direct students to write reason and its definition in their vocabulary notebook.
Guide as needed.
Write **reason** and what it means in your vocabulary notebook.

Activity 2 Review Vocabulary Word

Elicit responses to questions. **Guide** as needed.
What's another word for "one"? *Single.*

Tell me a sentence using the word **single.** (Student responses.)
Discuss sentence.

 Review vocabulary words in appropriate context in Reading *Textbook C.*

394 Lesson 124

Part B: Comprehension Strategies

12 minutes

Teacher Materials:
Selection of narrative trade books

Narrative Story Map

Student Materials:
Narrative trade book

Narrative Story Map

Activity 1 — Choose a Comprehension Strategy—An After-Reading Strategy

Elicit response to question. **Guide** as needed. **Discuss** after-reading strategies.
You've learned strategies to use after you read a passage. What are those strategies? (Ideas: *Narrative Story Map, retell the story, fill in the last section of KWL chart, summarize the story, make a text-to-text connection, make a text-to self connection, make a text-to-world connection; confirm a prediction, compare and contrast, and identify cause and effect.*)

You will read a narrative story in the next activity. What after-reading strategies would be appropriate after you read the story? (Student responses.)

Activity 2 — Narrative Story Map: Identify Title, Characters, Setting, Problem, and Events—An After-Reading Strategy

Direct students to choose a narrative trade book. **Show** Narrative Story Map. **Monitor** students as they write the title, characters, setting, problem, and events.
Narratives have a title, characters, settings, a problem, and events.
Read your narrative story and then work by yourself to fill in the Narrative Story Map with the title, important characters, setting, problem, and events.

Now you'll use your Narrative Story Map to retell the story.

Activity 3 — Use Narrative Story Map: Retell the Story—An After-Reading Strategy

You did a great job completing your Narrative Story Maps.

Assign student partners. **Monitor** students as they retell the story from Narrative Story Maps.
Now it's your turn to use your Narrative Story Maps to retell the story to your partner. Remember to start by telling the title and something about the characters and setting. Tell something about the problem and then tell the events that happened. Use your own words to retell the story. Then let your partner use his/her own words to retell the story.

Retelling the story helps you remember all the parts of the story.

Part C: Fluency Building

5 minutes

Student Materials:
Reading *Textbook C*

 Conduct after the lesson, using the story of the day.

Activity 1 — Partner Reading

It's time for partner reading.
Direct students to the story of the day. **Assign** student partners as Partner 1 and Partner 2. **Monitor** partner reading. **Guide** as needed.

Lesson 124   **395**

Lesson 125

> **Materials**
> **Teacher:** Reading *Textbook C*, 2-Vocabulary Acquisition and Use
> **Student:** Vocabulary notebook; Reading *Textbook C*, Copy of 2-Vocabulary Acquisition and Use, Drawing paper

8 minutes

Teacher Materials:
Reading *Textbook C*

Vocabulary Acquisition and Use

Student Materials:
Vocabulary notebook

Reading *Textbook C*

Vocabulary Acquisition and Use

Part A: Vocabulary Development

Activity 1 Vocabulary Notebook Review

Guide students through all words.
Today you'll study from your vocabulary notebook. Studying your words and what they mean will help you know your words even better. You'll look at the four words we studied this week.

Activity 2 Cumulative Vocabulary Review

Elicit responses to questions. **Guide** as needed.
Directions: Listen and tell me if I use our vocabulary words the right way or the wrong way. If I use the word the right way, say **"yes."** If I use the word the wrong way, say **"no."** Then we'll talk about each word.

1. Blake and his entire family went up to the counter and asked for a **single** movie ticket.

   Did I use the word **single** the right way? *No.*

   How do you know? (Student responses.)

2. James told Carmen the **reason** he could not come over was because he had the chicken pox.

   Did I use the word **reason** the right way? *Yes.*

   How do you know? (Student responses.)

3. Jamal was late for an **important** meeting.

   Did I use the word **important** the right way? *Yes.*

   How do you know? (Student responses.)

4. The restaurant was **crowded.** Linda was the only customer.

   Did I use the word **crowded** the right way? *No.*

   How do you know? (Student responses.)

Review vocabulary words as needed.

 Review vocabulary words in their appropriate context in Reading *Textbook C*.

Activity 3 | Vocabulary Acquisition and Use

Display Vocabulary Acquisition and Use. **Have** students work with a neighbor to complete Vocabulary Acquisition and Use.
Today's vocabulary words are ____ and ____ [and ____ and ____].
Vocabulary words: **stupid** and **unintelligent; glad** and **happy**
Write the words on the lines provided. Then write the words in the boxes based on whether you think each word is less/smaller or more/larger than the other word. Below the boxes, write why you think word 1 is less/smaller and word 2 is more/larger than word 1.
Repeat for words 3 and 4. **Have** students share what they wrote. **Discuss** examples of how these words might be used.

Part B: Comprehension Strategies

12 minutes

Teacher Materials:
Reading *Textbook C*

Student Materials:
Drawing paper

Reading *Textbook C*

Display directions for activity.
Directions: Discuss how Toby and his father may have traveled back to Australia. Apply what you know about the world to draw a map illustrating where they traveled from, how they traveled, and where they ended up. Label all the parts of your map. Explain what each part is and why you put it on the map.

Activity 1 | Pair-Share Activity—Apply Knowledge (Level 3 of Bloom's Taxonomy)

 Direct students to Lesson 122, pages 152–155 in Reading *Textbook C*.

Discuss the steps in the Pair-Share activity.
You'll do an activity called **Pair-Share** to show some things you've learned in recent lessons. The directions are on the board. I'll read them to you.

Assign partners. **Provide** drawing paper.
Step 1 is the **Pair** part of the activity. Discuss with your partner how Toby and his father might have traveled back to Australia. Draw a map showing the country they leave, the ocean they have to cross, and the country to which they travel. Show what kind of vehicle they travel in. Label all the parts of your map. Be ready to explain what each part is and why you put it on the map. Decide who'll do what part. Work quickly. You have 8 minutes.
Guide students to draw a map showing how Toby and his father travel back to Australia from Canada.

Call on as many students to share as time allows.
Step 2 is to **Share.** I'll call on pairs of students to share their work with the rest of the class.

Lesson 125

Part C: Fluency Building

Student Materials:
Reading *Textbook C*

  Conduct after the lesson, using the story of the day.

Activity 1 Partner Reading

It's time for partner reading.
Direct students to the story of the day. **Assign** student partners as Partner 1 and Partner 2. **Monitor** partner reading. **Guide** as needed.

Lesson 126

Materials
Teacher: Selection of expository trade books; 13-KWL Chart
Student: Vocabulary notebook; expository trade book of student choice; Copy of 13-KWL Chart

8 minutes

Teacher Materials:
Reading *Textbook C*

Student Materials:
Vocabulary notebook
Reading *Textbook C*

Part A: Vocabulary Development

Activity 1 Learn New Vocabulary Word

Elicit responses to questions. **Guide** as needed.
Today you'll learn a new vocabulary word. **Pair. Pair** means "two of the same kind." What does **pair** mean? *Two of the same kind.*

Another way to say "two of the same kind" is **pair.** What's another way to say "two of the same kind"? *Pair.*

There were many **two of the same** words in Hohoboho. Each **pair** would have terrible fights, because each of them would always think that it was the one being talked to.

Discuss examples of a pair.

What's another way to say "two of the same kind"? *Pair.*

Direct students to write pair and its definition in their vocabulary notebook.
Guide as needed.
Write **pair** and what it means in your vocabulary notebook.

Activity 2 Review Vocabulary Word

Elicit responses to questions. **Guide** as needed.
What's another way to say "why something happened"? *Reason.*

Tell me a sentence using the word **reason.** (Student responses.)
Discuss sentence.

 Review vocabulary words in appropriate context in Reading *Textbook C.*

Lesson 126   **399**

Part B: Comprehension Strategies

12 minutes

Teacher Materials:
Selection of expository trade books

KWL Chart

Student Materials:
Expository trade book

KWL Chart

Activity 1 Choose a Comprehension Strategy—A Before-Reading Strategy

Direct students to choose an expository trade book. **Show** KWL Chart. **Elicit** responses to questions. **Guide** as needed.

You've learned strategies to use before you read a passage. What are those strategies? (Ideas: *Activate background knowledge, predict what is in the story, determine text type and set a purpose for reading, and fill out the first two parts of a KWL chart.*)

Take a look at the story you'll read today. Tell what strategy you should use before you read this story. (Idea: *Fill out the first two parts of a KWL chart because it's expository text.*)

Activity 2 KWL Chart: Topic and What I Know—A Before-Reading Strategy

Elicit responses to questions. **Guide** as needed.
You're going to activate your background knowledge for a new topic. What do you do when you activate your background knowledge? (Idea: *Think about what you already know.*)

You'll be reading an expository book of your choice.

Why is it a good idea to think about your background knowledge before you read? (Idea: *Then you'll be able to connect what you know to what you learn.*)

Show KWL Chart.
You'll use a KWL chart to help you organize your thinking about expository text. Why do you use a KWL chart? (Idea: *To organize thinking about expository text.*)

Monitor students as they write the topic on their charts.
What should you write for the topic? (Student responses.)

Monitor students as they write what they know on their charts.
Now work by yourself to think about your background knowledge about your topic for the "What I Know" section of the KWL chart.

Remember, you're doing this to connect what you already know with the text that you'll be reading.

Activity 3 KWL Chart: What I Wonder—A Before-Reading Strategy

Elicit responses to questions. **Guide** as needed. **Show** KWL Chart.
Next you'll write the questions you have about the topic in the "What I Wonder" section of the chart.

What will you write in this section of the chart? (Ideas: *Questions you have; what you wonder about.*)

Monitor students as they write questions on their charts.
Think of questions you have about your topic for the "What I Wonder" section of the KWL chart and write them on the chart.

Why is it important to ask questions before you read? (Idea: *Asking questions gets you interested in what you're going to learn—it makes you think about what you're going to read.*)

The text you read may or may not have the answers to your questions. That's okay. Just asking the questions helps you be smarter. If you don't find the answers to your questions, you might need to read more in another book to find out the answers.
Save student copies of KWL Chart for Lesson 127.

5 minutes

Student Materials:
Reading *Textbook C*

Part C: Fluency Building

 Conduct after the lesson, using the story of the day.

Activity 1 Partner Reading

It's time for partner reading.
Direct students to the story of the day. **Assign** student partners as Partner 1 and Partner 2. **Monitor** partner reading. **Guide** as needed.

Lesson 126 **401**

Lesson 127

Materials

Teacher: 13-KWL Chart; Reading *Textbook C*

Student: Vocabulary notebook; expository trade book (from Lesson 126), Copy of 13-KWL Chart (from Lesson 126); Reading *Textbook C*

Part A: Vocabulary Development

8 minutes

Teacher Materials:
Reading *Textbook C*

Student Materials:
Vocabulary notebook

Reading *Textbook C*

Activity 1 Learn New Vocabulary Word

Elicit responses to questions. **Guide** as needed.
Today you'll learn a new vocabulary word. **Solved. Solved** means "found an answer." What does **solved** mean? *Found an answer.*

Another way to say "found an answer" is **solved.** What's another way to say "found an answer"? *Solved.*

It seemed that the word bank had **found an answer** to its fighting problem. But just when they thought their problems were **solved,** the contractions started fighting.

Discuss examples of things that are solved.

What's another way to say "found an answer"? *Solved.*

Direct students to write solved and its definition in their vocabulary notebook. **Guide** as needed.
Write **solved** and what it means in your vocabulary notebook.

Activity 2 Review Vocabulary Word

Elicit responses to questions. **Guide** as needed.
What's another way to say "two of the same kind"? *Pair*

Tell me a sentence using the word **pair.** (Student responses.)
Discuss sentence.

 Review vocabulary words in appropriate context in Reading *Textbook C*.

402 *Lesson 127*

Part B: Comprehension Strategies

12 minutes

Teacher Materials:
KWL Chart

Student Materials:
KWL Chart

Expository trade book

Activity 1 Choose a Comprehension Strategy—An After-Reading Strategy

Direct students to expository trade book chosen in Lesson 126. **Elicit** response to question. **Guide** as needed.
In the last lesson, you filled out the first two sections of your KWL chart. Then you read your book.

What after-reading strategy should you use today? (Idea: *Fill in the "What I Learned" section of the KWL chart.*)

Activity 2 KWL Chart: What I Learned—An After-Reading Strategy

Direct students to expository trade book chosen in Lesson 126. **Show** KWL Chart. **Elicit** responses to questions. **Guide** as needed.
In the last lesson, you read your book. It's time to add what you learned from the book to the "What I Learned" section of the KWL chart that you started in Lesson 126.

Should you copy the words from the book? *No.*

What should you do instead? (Idea: *Write the ideas in your own words.*)

Why should you write the ideas in your own words? (Idea: *That will help you remember the information later.*)

Today you'll work to fill out the "What I Learned" section of the chart.
Monitor students as they write 3 sentences to add to the "What I Learned" section of KWL Chart started in Lesson 126.

You've now written the new things you learned from the expository text you read. You wrote the information in your own words.

There's a part on your KWL chart that says, "Questions I still have."

Did you have all your questions about your topic answered? (**Student responses.**)

If not, copy the questions that were not answered in the "Questions I still have" box.
Guide students to write one or two questions from "What I Wonder" section to the "Questions I Still Have" box.

Lesson 127 **403**

Let's think about how we could find the answers to your questions?
(Ideas: *Another book, a magazine, a video, look on the internet, or look in an encyclopedia.*)
Discuss additional resources for information about topics.

Write where you could look for more information in the last box.
Model writing resources in the "Where to Look for More Information" box. **Guide** students to write a list of resources in the "Where to Look for More Information" box.

5 minutes

Student Materials:
Reading *Textbook C*

Part C: Fluency Building

 Conduct after the lesson, using the story of the day.

Activity 1 Partner Reading

It's time for partner reading.
Direct students to the story of the day. **Assign** student partners as Partner 1 and Partner 2. **Monitor** partner reading. **Guide** as needed.

404 Lesson 127

Lesson 128

Materials
Teacher: Examples of narrative and expository trade books
Student: Vocabulary notebook; Reading *Textbook C*.

8 minutes

Teacher Materials:
Reading *Textbook C*

Student Materials:
Vocabulary notebook
Reading *Textbook C*

Part A: Vocabulary Development

Activity 1 Learn New Vocabulary Word

Elicit responses to questions. **Guide** as needed.
Today you'll learn a new vocabulary word. **Nearby. Nearby** means "close." What does **nearby** mean? *Close.*

Another way to say "close" is **nearby.** What's another way to say "close?" *Nearby.*

The problem with building wood buildings **close** to each other is that if there were a fire, the **nearby** buildings might also catch fire.

Discuss things that are nearby.

What's another way to say "close"? *Nearby.*

Direct students to write nearby and its definition in their vocabulary notebook. **Guide** as needed.
Write **nearby** and what it means in your vocabulary notebook.

Activity 2 Review Vocabulary Word

Elicit responses to questions. **Guide** as needed.
What's another way to say "found an answer"? *Solved.*

Tell me a sentence using the word **solved.** (Student responses.)
Discuss sentence.

 Review vocabulary words in appropriate context in Reading *Textbook C*.

12 minutes

Teacher Materials:
Examples of narrative and expository trade books

Part B: Comprehension Strategies

Activity 1 Determine Text Type: Review Features of Expository Text—A Before-Reading Strategy

Show example of expository trade book. **Elicit** responses to questions. **Guide** as needed.
Expository and narrative texts have different features. If you know what those features are, it'll help you decide before you read what kind of text you're reading.

Lesson 128   **405**

Why is it a good idea to think about what you're going to read before you read? (Idea: *It helps you decide what you'll do during reading—learn new information or read a story.*)

What are some of the features that you might find in expository text? (Student responses.)

Discuss features and look in trade book to see if it contains the feature under discussion.

Labels—help identify parts

Photographs—help you understand what something looks like

Captions—tell what's in a picture

Cutaways—show what something looks like inside

Diagrams—show parts of things

Maps—help you know where something is in the world

Bold print—shows you important words

Headings—show what a section of text is about

Tables of contents—help you find information in a book

Index—tells you an alphabetized list with page numbers of what's in the book

Glossary—defines words in the book

Do you have to read expository text in order? *No.*

What kinds of text are you reading when you're reading to learn new facts or information? *Expository text.*

Activity 2 Determine Text Type: Review Features of Narrative Text—A Before-Reading Strategy

Show example of narrative trade book. **Elicit** responses to questions. **Guide** as needed.

A second type of text is called narrative text. What does narrative text tell you? *A story.*

You'll often read narrative texts for fun. Narrative texts might include new facts or information that you didn't know before. But the main purpose of narrative text is to tell you a story.

What are some of the features that you might find in narrative texts? (Student responses.)

Discuss features and look in trade book to see if it contains the feature under discussion.

Characters—people, animals, or objects that do things in the story

Setting—where and when the story happens

Problem—thing that goes wrong in the story that makes you want to read more

Events—beginning, middle, and end of story

Do you have to read narrative text in order? *Yes.*

What kind of text are you reading when you read a story? *Narrative text.*

406 *Lesson 128*

Activity 3 | Activate Background Knowledge—A Before-Reading Strategy

Elicit responses to questions. **Guide** as needed.
Remember, everything you know in your brain is called background knowledge. What do you call everything you know in your brain? *Background knowledge.*

What do you do when you activate your background knowledge? (Idea: *Think about what you already know.*)

Why do you activate your background knowledge? (Idea: *Connecting what you know to the story you're reading helps you better understand the story.*)

You'll read about a time machine in the next story. Let's talk about your background knowledge about a time machine.
Discuss student background knowledge about a time machine. **Guide** as needed.

Connecting what you know about a time machine to the next story may help you understand what you read.

Part C: Fluency Building

5 minutes

Student Materials:
Reading *Textbook C*

 Conduct after the lesson, using the story of the day.

Activity 1 | Partner Reading

It's time for partner reading.
Direct students to the story of the day. **Assign** student partners as Partner 1 and Partner 2. **Monitor** partner reading. **Guide** as needed.

Lesson 128   **407**

Lesson 129

Materials

Teacher: 9-Compare and Contrast Chart; Reading *Textbook C*

Student: Vocabulary notebook; Copy of 9-Compare and Contrast Chart; Reading *Textbook C*, Lined paper

8 minutes

Teacher Materials:
Reading *Textbook C*

Student Materials:
Vocabulary notebook
Reading *Textbook C*

Part A: Vocabulary Development

Activity 1 Learn New Vocabulary Word

Elicit responses to questions. **Guide** as needed.
Today you'll learn a new vocabulary word. **Distance. Distance** means "close enough to be seen." What does **distance** mean? *Close enough to be seen.*

Another way to say "close enough to be seen" is **distance.** What's another way to say "close enough to be seen"? *Distance.*

The boys had just finished a picnic. As they started walking down the mountain, they noticed that the town was **close enough to be seen.** They were glad to see the town in the **distance.**

Discuss things that are in the distance.

What's another way to say "close enough to be seen"? *Distance.*

Direct students to write distance and its definition in their vocabulary notebook. **Guide** as needed.
Write **distance** and what it means in your vocabulary notebook.

Activity 2 Review Vocabulary Word

Elicit responses to questions. **Guide** as needed.
What's another way to say "close by"? *Nearby.*

Tell me a sentence using the word **nearby.** (Student responses.)
Discuss sentence.

 Review vocabulary words in appropriate context in Reading *Textbook C*.

408 Lesson 129

12 minutes

Teacher Materials:
Compare and Contrast Chart

Reading *Textbook C*

Student Materials:
Compare and Contrast Chart

Reading *Textbook C*

Lined paper

Part B: Comprehension Strategies

Activity 1 Compare and Contrast—An After-Reading Strategy

 Direct students to Lesson 128, pages 190–191 in Reading *Textbook C*.

Show Compare and Contrast Chart. **Elicit** responses to questions. **Guide** as needed.
You've learned how to tell how characters are the same and how they're different. Today you'll compare and contrast buildings: wooden buildings and steel, concrete, and brick buildings.

What will you do when you compare wooden buildings to steel, concrete, and brick buildings? (Idea: *Tell how they're the same.*)

What will you do when you contrast wooden buildings to steel, concrete, and brick buildings? (Idea: *Tell how they're different.*)

Write "wooden buildings" for one name and "steel, concrete, and brick buildings" for the other name. They're both buildings.

First, think about how they're the same. Write two sentences. When you write about how they're the same your sentences should begin, "They both…"
Monitor students as they write two sentences for "How Same?" box on Compare and Contrast Chart.

Now, think about how they're different. Write two sentences. When you write about how they're different, it's a little harder. Your sentence needs to tell about each kind of building and tell how each is different. You say the name of the building, tell about that building, and then use the word "but" before you tell about the next building. Remember, when you tell about how they're different, you have to tell about the same quality.
Monitor students as they write two sentences for "How Different?" box on Compare and Contrast Chart.

Lesson 129 **409**

Activity 2 Generate Questions—A During-Reading Strategy

 Direct students to Lesson 128, pages 190–191 in Reading *Textbook C*.

Elicit responses to questions. **Guide** as needed.
Remember that asking questions while you read is one way to help you have better comprehension while you read because it keeps you interested in what you read.

What strategy can you use while you're reading to help keep you interested in what you're reading? (Idea: *Asking questions.*)

Provide lined paper to students.
Sometimes it's hard to think of questions. Look at the first page of the story and see if you can think of a question by yourself while you're reading. Find a sentence that makes you think of a question. Write the sentence and the question and then we'll see who can answer your questions.

Monitor students as they generate questions from the text. **Elicit** answers to student-generated questions.

Remember, asking questions while you read keeps you interested in what you're reading. Why should you ask questions while you read? (Idea: *It keeps you interested in what you read.*)

Part C: Fluency Building

5 minutes

Student Materials:
Reading *Textbook C*

 Conduct after the lesson, using the story of the day.

Activity 1 Partner Reading

It's time for partner reading.
Direct students to the story of the day. **Assign** student partners as Partner 1 and Partner 2. **Monitor** partner reading. **Guide** as needed.

Lesson 130

> **Materials**
> **Teacher:** Reading *Textbook C*, 2-Vocabulary Acquisition and Use, Writing Prompts, 3-My Writing Checklist
> **Student:** Vocabulary notebook; Reading *Textbook C*, Copy of 2-Vocabulary Acquisition and Use and 3-My Writing Checklist, Lined paper, Drawing paper

8 minutes

Teacher Materials:
Reading *Textbook C*
Vocabulary Acquisition and Use

Student Materials:
Vocabulary Notebook
Reading *Textbook C*
Vocabulary Acquisition and Use

Part A: Vocabulary Development

Activity 1 Vocabulary Notebook Review

Guide students as they study all words.
Today you'll study from your vocabulary notebook. Studying your words and what they mean will help you know your words even better. You'll study the eight words we studied over the past two weeks.

Activity 2 Cumulative Vocabulary Review

Elicit responses to questions. **Guide** as needed.
Directions: Listen and tell me if I use our vocabulary words the right way or the wrong way. If I use the word the right way, say **"yes."** If I use the word the wrong way, say **"no."** Then we'll talk about each word.

1. Larry ordered a **single** sandwich. He normally ordered two, but he was not very hungry today.

   Did I use the word **single** the right way? *Yes*.

   How do you know? (Student responses.)

2. Looking at the sky, Leila could see the Big Dipper in the **distance.**

   Did I use the word **distance** the right way? *Yes*.

   How do you know? (Student responses.)

3. It's **important** to drink lots of water when the weather is very hot.

   Did I use the word **important** the right way? *Yes*.

   How do you know? (Student responses.)

4. Beth's friend Cheng lives 2,000 miles away. Beth likes that Cheng lives **nearby.**

   Did I use the word **nearby** the right way? *No*.

   How do you know? (Student responses.)

Lesson 130   411

5. Beta wanted to buy a **pair** of sandals to wear on the beach. She went to the store and bought one sandal.

   Did I use the word **pair** the right way? *No.*

   How do you know? (Student responses.)

6. Crystal did not have a good **reason** for being late to practice.

   Did I use the word **reason** the right way? *Yes.*

   How do you know? (Student responses.)

7. Brian **solved** the crossword puzzle in the paper.

   Did I use the word **solved** the right way. *Yes.*

   How do you know? (Student responses.)

8. Elizabeth could sit anywhere she wanted at the basketball game because it was so **crowded.**

   Did I use the word **crowded** the right way? *No.*

   How do you know? (Student responses.)

Review vocabulary words as needed.

 Review vocabulary words in appropriate context in Reading *Textbook C*.

Activity 3 Vocabulary Acquisition and Use

Display Vocabulary Acquisition and Use. **Have** students work with a neighbor to complete Vocabulary Acquisition and Use.

Today's vocabulary words are ____ and ____ [and ____ and ____].
Vocabulary words: **fight** and **brawl**; **raw** and **uncooked**
Write the words on the lines provided. Then write the words in the boxes based on whether you think each word is less/smaller or more/larger than the other word. Below the boxes, write why you think word 1 is less/smaller and word 2 is more/larger than word 1.

Repeat for words 3 and 4. **Have** students share what they wrote. **Discuss** examples of how these words might be used.

12 minutes

Student Materials:
Drawing paper

Part B: Comprehension Strategies

Display directions for the activity.
Directions: Tom and Eric found a time machine that travels through time. Discuss what it would be like to time travel. Illustrate a time machine and write where and when you would like to travel in a time machine. Explain why you would like to travel to that place and/or time.

Activity 1 Pair-Share Activity—Apply Knowledge (Level 3 of Bloom's Taxonomy)

 Direct students to Lesson 129, pages 199–203 in Reading *Textbook C*.

Discuss the steps in the Pair-Share activity.
You'll do an activity called **Pair-Share** to show some things you have learned in recent lessons. The directions are on the board. I'll read them to you.

Assign partners. **Provide** drawing paper.
Step 1 is the **Pair** part of the activity. Discuss with your partner what it would be like to time travel. Draw your own time travel machine and write where and when you would like to go in your time travel machine. Explain why you would like to go to that particular place and time. Decide who'll do what part. Work quickly. You have 8 minutes.
Guide students to draw a time travel machine and write where and when they would like to travel.

Call on as many students to share as time allows.
Step 2 is to **Share.** I'll call on pairs of students to share their work with the rest of the class.

5 minutes

Student Materials:
Reading *Textbook C*

Part C: Fluency Building

 Conduct after the lesson, using the story of the day.

Activity 1 Partner Reading

It's time for partner reading.
Direct students to the story of the day. **Assign** student partners as Partner 1 and Partner 2. **Monitor** partner reading. **Guide** as needed.

Lesson 130 **413**

Part D: Writing/Language Arts

10 minutes

Teacher Materials:
Writing Prompts

My Writing Checklist

Student Materials:
Lined Paper

My Writing Checklist

Activity 1 Write and Use Parts of Speech and Conventions

Time to write using a writing prompt based on the stories we've been reading.

Assign student partners. **Distribute** lined paper to students. **Display** writing prompts and have students choose one to write about or assign a writing prompt of your choice. **Review** parts of speech and punctuation as well as the writing checklist with students. **Tell** students to write one to two paragraphs (minimum of four sentences per paragraph) on their own to answer the writing prompt. **Tell** them to use their writing checklist (first column labeled "Did I use them?") to ensure they include important parts of speech or punctuation in their writing. **Tell** students which parts of speech or punctuation to focus on, if you wish. **Model** what it means to answer a writing prompt and to use the writing checklist during and after the writing process, as needed. **Monitor** and guide students as needed. **Model** what it means to have a neighbor look over his or her neighbor's writing and to complete the writing checklist (second column labeled "Did my neighbor use them?"), as needed. **Have** students share what they wrote as time permits.

Writing Prompt 1	Writing Prompt 2	Writing Prompt 3
If you were to take a vacation, where would you go and why?	If you could go back in time in a time machine, what time would you visit? Why?	If you could go to the future in a time machine, what time would you visit? Why?

Lesson 131

Materials
Teacher: Student dictionary; Reading *Textbook C*
Student: Vocabulary notebook; Reading *Textbook C*

8 minutes

Teacher Materials:
Student dictionary

Reading *Textbook C*

Student Materials:
Vocabulary notebook

Reading *Textbook C*

Part A: Vocabulary Development

Activity 1 Learn New Vocabulary Word

Elicit responses to questions. **Guide** as needed.
Today you'll learn a new vocabulary word. **Dizzy. Dizzy** means "feeling like you are about to fall." What does **dizzy** mean? *Feeling like you are about to fall.*

Another way to say "feeling like you are about to fall" is **dizzy.** What's another way to say "feeling like you are about to fall"? *Dizzy.*

Tom and Eric did not know where the time machine had taken them. When Tom saw a newspaper and read the date, he **felt** like he **was about to fall.** The fact that the paper's date showed they had gone back one hundred years in time made Tom **dizzy.**

Discuss examples of when someone might be <u>dizzy</u>.

What's another way to say "feeling like you are about to fall"? *Dizzy.*

Direct students to write <u>dizzy</u> and its definition in their vocabulary notebooks.
Guide as needed.
Write **dizzy** and what it means in your vocabulary notebook.

Activity 2 Dictionary Use

Today you'll learn how to use the dictionary. Looking up words in a dictionary will help you learn their meanings. I often look up words in the dictionary to find out what they mean. It helps me understand what I'm reading when I know what all of the words mean. I'll show you how to look up the word **dizzy.**

Model think-aloud for looking up words in dictionary.

Lesson 131   415

Sample Wording for Think-Aloud

I'm not sure I understand the meaning of **dizzy.** I need to look it up in the dictionary. I thumb through the dictionary like this until I come to the section labeled **D.** Then I check the spelling of **dizzy.** I look up at the tops of the pages in the dictionary and try to get as close to the spelling of **dizzy** as I can. Watch as I check the tops of the pages. Now I know the word **dizzy** will be found on one of these two pages, between these two words. I skim the pages of the dictionary like this and find the word **dizzy.** I see that the word **dizzy** is defined as _____. This will help me understand the word **dizzy.**

Activity 3 Review Vocabulary Word

Elicit responses to questions. **Guide** as needed.
What's another way to say "close enough to be seen"? *Distance.*

Tell me a sentence using the word **distance.** (Student responses.)
Discuss sentence.

 Review vocabulary words in appropriate context in Reading *Textbook C.*

Part B: Comprehension Strategies

12 minutes

Teacher Materials:
Reading *Textbook C*

Student Materials:
Reading *Textbook C*

Activity 1 Retell Narrative Text through Readers' Theater—An After-Reading Strategy

 Direct students to Lesson 129, pages 199–203 in Reading *Textbook C.*

Elicit responses to questions. **Guide** as needed.
Another way to retell a narrative story is to put on a play. When you put on a play, you tell the story by acting it out. We're going to perform "Eric and Tom Find a Time Machine." We call putting on a play Readers' Theater.

First we have to make some decisions. What's the setting of the Eric and Tom story? (Idea: *Halfway up a mountain and in the time machine.*)

Where will those places be in our classroom? (Student responses.)

Who are the main characters in the story? (Idea: *Eric and Tom.*)

Assign roles.
Who will play the part of Eric? (Student responses.)

Who will play the part of Tom? (Student responses.)

Who's the other character in the story? (Idea: *Thrig.*)

Who will play that part? (Student responses.)

416 Lesson 131

We'll need some sounds in the play. We need a loud sound when the time machine lands. How could we make that loud sound? (Student responses.)

We need the sound of buzzing and clicking for the dials in the time machine. How could we make that sound? (Student responses.)

We need the sound of the time machine door closing. How could we make that sound? (Student responses.)

I'll tell the story. Sometimes I'll tell you to say a part. You can move around to perform the story as I tell the story. Here we go.

Guide the actors to perform the play for the class as you side coach the dialogue and actions. When the play is completed, **prompt** the actors to bow and the audience to applaud.

Sample Wording for Think-Aloud

Eric and Tom were walking down the mountain with their friends after a picnic. They got tired so they talked about resting. (Prompt Eric and Tom to discuss whether to rest and whether they will get lost trying to get home.) Suddenly, they heard a loud sound. (Prompt loud sound to happen. Prompt Eric and Tom to react by saying and doing the appropriate actions.) A big pill-shaped object that was as big as a tree had landed on the mountain side. (Prompt Thrig to step out, wave, and say "hello.") Tom said, "_____." (Prompt Tom to say the appropriate words.) Eric started running toward Thrig and said "_____." (Prompt Eric to run to Thrig and say "hello.") Tom was really scared and wanted to get out of there. (Prompt Tom to show fear and try to get Eric to come back.) But Eric and Thrig talked. (Prompt Eric and Thrig to say appropriate dialogue about who Thrig is and where he came from.) When Thrig said he lived in a different time than the boys, they were amazed. (Prompt boys to pantomime action.) They asked, "_____?" (Prompt Thrig to tell them what year he came from, what machine he had made, and why he can't return to the year 2400.) Thrig was so tired he decided to rest and went to sleep. Tom wanted to get out of there. (Prompt Tom to try to persuade Eric to leave.) But Eric had a different idea. He said, "_____." (Prompt Eric to go to time machine.) Inside the time machine were all kinds of lights and dials. (Prompt appropriate sounds.) Tom still wanted to get out of there. He said,"_____." (Prompt Tom to try to get Eric to get out of the time machine.) But Eric sat in the time machine. The door of the time machine closed. (Prompt the sound of the door closing.) He touched a handle and said, "_____." (Prompt Tom to try to persuade Eric not to touch it.) Suddenly the dials clicked and buzzed (prompt appropriate sounds) and the boys felt a great push. (Prompt Eric's and Tom's reaction and dialogue as they time travel.) When everything got quiet, the boys looked outside. They were amazed at what they saw.

Lesson 131   **417**

5 minutes

Student Materials:
Reading *Textbook C*

Part C: Fluency Building

 Conduct after the lesson, using the story of the day.

Activity 1 Partner Reading

It's time for partner reading.

Direct students to the story of the day. **Assign** student partners as Partner 1 and Partner 2. **Monitor** partner reading. **Guide** as needed.

Lesson 132

Materials
Teacher: Student dictionary; 12-Cause and Effect Map; Reading *Textbook C*
Student: Vocabulary notebook; Copy of 12-Cause and Effect Map; sticky notes; Reading *Textbook C*

Part A: Vocabulary Development

5 minutes

Teacher Materials:
Student dictionary
Reading *Textbook C*

Student Materials:
Vocabulary notebook
Reading *Textbook C*

Activity 1 Learn New Vocabulary Word

Elicit responses to questions. **Guide** as needed.
Today you'll learn a new vocabulary word. **Dragging. Dragging** means "pulling something heavy." What does **dragging** mean? *Pulling something heavy.*

Another way to say "pulling something heavy" is **dragging.** What's another way to say "pulling something heavy"? *Dragging.*

The boys landed by a river that had boats and rafts. It did not look like anything they had ever seen. They saw men **pulling heavy things.** The men were **dragging** big pieces of stone toward a pyramid.

Discuss examples of things someone would be dragging.

What's another way to say "pulling something heavy"? *Dragging.*

Direct students to write dragging and its definition in their vocabulary notebooks. **Guide** as needed.
Write **dragging** and what it means in your vocabulary notebook.

Activity 2 Dictionary Use

In the last lesson, you learned how to look up the word **dizzy.** Watch again as I look up the word **dragging.**

Activity 3 Review Vocabulary Word

Elicit responses to questions. **Guide** as needed.
What's another way to say "feeling like you are about to fall"? *Dizzy.*

Tell me a sentence using the word **dizzy.** (Student responses.)
Discuss sentence.

 Review vocabulary words in appropriate context in Reading *Textbook C*.

Lesson 132 **419**

12 minutes

Teacher Materials:
Cause and Effect Map

Reading *Textbook C*

Student Materials:
Cause and Effect Map

Sticky notes

Reading *Textbook C*

Part B: Comprehension Strategies

Activity 1 Identify Cause-and-Effect Relationships—A During- Reading Strategy

 Direct students to Lesson 131, page 215 in Reading *Textbook C*.

Elicit responses to questions. **Guide** as needed.
Today you'll identify cause and effect in a passage to help you understand what you read.

What does cause mean? *To make something happen.*

What's an effect? *What happens.*

Show Cause and Effect Map.
In Lesson 131 you read "The San Francisco Earthquake." Today you'll work to fill out your Cause and Effect Map for that story. Skim page 215 and see whether you can find one or two cause-and-effect relationships to write on your Cause and Effect Map.
Monitor students as they write sentences to fill out one or two cause-and-effect relationships on Cause and Effect Map.

Share the cause and effect relationships you found. (Student responses.)
Discuss cause-and-effect relationships and record on Cause and Effect Map as time permits.

Activity 2 Comprehension Monitoring: Mental Imaging—A During-Reading Strategy

 Direct students to Lesson 131, page 215 in Reading *Textbook C*.

Elicit responses to questions. **Guide** as needed.
You've learned a strategy called mental imaging to help you understand what you read while you're reading. What does mental imaging help you do? *Understand and enjoy a story more.*

What's mental imaging? *Making pictures in your mind about what you're reading.*

Why do you use mental imaging with narrative text? (Idea: *You can make pictures in your mind of the characters, setting, and events to help you understand and enjoy the story better.*)

In Lesson 131 you read, "The San Francisco Earthquake." Look at page 215 by yourself and see whether you can find a sentence or two where you can make a mental image. Mark the sentences with a sticky note and make a quick sketch to remind you of your mental image. Then we'll talk about the sentences you found and the mental image you made.
Elicit student responses for mental images.

Remember to use mental imaging when you read to help you understand and enjoy the story.

420 *Lesson 132*

Activity 3 Activate Background Knowledge—A Before-Reading Strategy

Elicit responses to questions. **Guide** as needed.

Remember, everything you know in your mind is called background knowledge. What do you call everything you know in your mind? *Background knowledge.*

What do you do when you activate your background knowledge? (Idea: *Think about what you already know.*)

Why do you activate your background knowledge? (Idea: *Connecting what you know to the story you're reading helps you better understand the story.*)

You'll read about Egypt in the next story. Let's talk about your background knowledge about Egypt.
Discuss students' background knowledge about Egypt. **Guide** as needed.

Connecting what you know about Egypt to the next story may help you understand what you read.

Part C: Fluency Building

5 minutes

Student Materials:
Reading *Textbook C*

 Conduct after the lesson, using the story of the day.

Activity 1 Partner Reading

It's time for partner reading.
Direct students to the story of the day. **Assign** student partners as Partner 1 and Partner 2. **Monitor** partner reading. **Guide** as needed.

Lesson 132   **421**

Lesson 133

Materials
Teacher: Student dictionary; Reading *Textbook C*
Student: Vocabulary notebook; student dictionary; lined paper; Reading *Textbook C*

Part A: Vocabulary Development

5 minutes

Teacher Materials:
Student dictionary
Reading *Textbook C*

Student Materials:
Vocabulary notebook
Student dictionary
Reading *Textbook C*

Activity 1 Learn New Vocabulary Word

Elicit responses to questions. **Guide** as needed.
Today you'll learn a new vocabulary word. **Softly. Softly** means "quietly."
What does **softly** mean? *Quietly.*

Another word for "quietly" is **softly.** What's another word for "quietly"? *Softly.*

Tom had a flashlight in his hand. When Tom turned it on, the soldier said something **quietly.** The soldier **softly** said, "On kon urub."

Discuss examples of softly.

What's another word for "quietly"? *Softly.*

Direct students to write softly and its definition in their vocabulary notebooks.
Guide as needed.
Write **softly** and what it means in your vocabulary notebook.

Activity 2 Dictionary Use

Guide as needed.
In the last lesson you learned how to look up the word **dragging.** Now let's use our dictionaries to look up the word **softly** together.

Activity 3 Review Vocabulary Word

Elicit responses to questions. **Guide** as needed.
What's another way to say "pulling something heavy"? *Dragging.*

Tell me a sentence using the word **dragging.** (Student responses.)
Discuss sentence.

 Review vocabulary words in appropriate context in Reading *Textbook C.*

Part B: Comprehension Strategies

12 minutes

Teacher Materials:
Reading *Textbook C*

Student Materials:
Lined paper

Reading *Textbook C*

Activity 1 Generate Questions—A During-Reading Strategy

 Direct students to Lesson 132, page 223 in Reading *Textbook C*.

Elicit responses to questions. **Guide** as needed.
Remember that asking questions while you read is one way to help you have better comprehension because it keeps you interested in what you read.

What strategy can you use while you're reading to help keep you interested in what you're reading? (Idea: *Asking questions.*)

Provide lined paper to students. **Monitor** students as they generate questions from the text.
Sometimes it's hard to think of questions. Look at the first page of the story and see whether you can think of a question by yourself while you're reading. Find a sentence that makes you think of a question. Write the sentence and the question and then we'll see who can answer your questions.
Elicit answers to student-generated questions.

Remember, asking questions while you read keeps you interested in what you're reading. Why should you ask questions while you read? (Idea: *It keeps you interested in what you read.*)

Activity 2 Summarize Narrative Text—An After-Reading Strategy

 Direct students to Lesson 132, pages 222–223 in Reading *Textbook C*.

Elicit responses to questions. **Guide** as needed.
You've learned a strategy called summarizing. What do you do when you summarize? (Idea: *You tell the important parts and leave out the details.*)

What do you tell when you summarize narrative text? (Idea: *The characters, the setting, and a few important events.*)

You can summarize by telling about the whole passage in a few sentences that tell the most important things you learned about the passage.

Provide lined paper to students. **Monitor** students as they write summary sentences.
Now skim the first two pages of the story as you work by yourself to summarize "Eric and Tom in Egypt" in a few sentences. Think about the characters, setting, and the most important events. Then write a few sentences to summarize part of the story.

Lesson 133 **423**

What summary sentences did you think of? (Student responses.)
Elicit student ideas for summary sentences. **Discuss** best ideas and why they are good summaries.

You told the main things you learned from the passage in a few sentences, and you left out all the details.

5 minutes

Student Materials:
Reading *Textbook C*

Part C: Fluency Building

 Conduct after the lesson, using the story of the day.

Activity 1 Partner Reading

It's time for partner reading.
Direct students to the story of the day. **Assign** student partners as Partner 1 and Partner 2. **Monitor** partner reading. **Guide** as needed.

Lesson 134

Materials
Teacher: Student dictionary; Reading *Textbook C*
Student: Vocabulary notebook; student dictionary; Reading *Textbook C*

5 minutes

Teacher Materials:
Student dictionary
Reading *Textbook C*

Student Materials:
Vocabulary notebook
Student dictionary
Reading *Textbook C*

Part A: Vocabulary Development

Activity 1 Learn New Vocabulary Word

Elicit responses to questions. **Guide** as needed.
Today you'll learn a new vocabulary word. **Throne. Throne** means "a seat for a queen or king." What does **throne** mean? *A seat for a queen or king.*

Another way to say a "seat for a queen or king" is **throne.** What's another way to say a "seat for a queen or king"? *Throne.*

When the boys woke up in the morning, they were taken to a room at the end of the hall. In the room was a **seat for a queen or king.** A young man sat on the **throne** made of silver and gold.

Discuss examples of where students have seen or heard of a throne.

What's another way to say "a seat for a queen or king"? *Throne.*

Direct students to write throne and its definition in their vocabulary notebooks.
Guide as needed.
Write **throne** and what it means in your vocabulary notebook.

Activity 2 Dictionary Use

Guide as needed.
Let's use our dictionaries to look up the word **throne** together.

Activity 3 Review Vocabulary Word

Elicit responses to questions. **Guide** as needed.
What's another word that means "quietly"? *Softly.*

Tell me a sentence using the word **softly.** (Student responses.)
Discuss sentence.

 Review vocabulary words in appropriate context in Reading *Textbook C*.

Lesson 134   **425**

12 minutes

Teacher Materials:
Reading *Textbook C*

Student Materials:
Student dictionary

Reading *Textbook C*

Part B: Comprehension Strategies

Activity 1 — Comprehension Monitoring: Reading Dialogue with Prosody—A During-Reading Strategy

 Direct students to Lesson 133, pages 229–232 in Reading *Textbook C*.

Elicit responses to questions. **Guide** as needed.
In order to read with better comprehension, it is important to pay attention to the punctuation marks in a story. Quotation marks are punctuation marks that show that a character is talking in a story. The words characters say in narratives are called dialogue.

Dialogue is marked with quotation marks. How is dialogue marked in stories? (Idea: *With quotation marks or talking marks.*)

What's dialogue? (Idea: *The words characters say in the story.*)

Who are the characters in this story? (Idea: *Tom, Eric, soldier, and the old man.*)

Assign student groups of 5.
Decide which person in each group will read what part. Assign someone to read Tom's words, someone to read Eric's words, someone to read the soldier's words, someone to read the old man's words, and someone to be the narrator and read all the rest of the words. Read the story, practicing dialogue.
Monitor groups as they practice dialogue.

Activity 2 — Choose a Comprehension Strategy—A Before-Reading Strategy

 Direct students to Lesson 134, pages 238–241 in Reading *Textbook C*.

Elicit responses to questions. **Guide** as needed.
You've learned strategies to use before you read a passage. What are those strategies? (Ideas: *Activate background knowledge, predict what is in the story, determine text type and set a purpose for reading, and fill out the first two parts of a KWL chart.*)

Take a look at the story you'll read today. How would you use these strategies while you read the story? (Student responses.)

5 minutes

Student Materials:
Reading *Textbook C*

Part C: Fluency Building

 Conduct after the lesson, using the story of the day.

Activity 1 — Partner Reading

It's time for partner reading.
Direct students to the story of the day. **Assign** student partners as Partner 1 and Partner 2. **Monitor** partner reading. **Guide** as needed.

426 Lesson 134

Lesson 135

Materials

Teacher: Reading *Textbook C*, 2-Vocabulary Acquisition and Use

Student: Vocabulary notebook; Reading *Textbook C*, Copy of 2-Vocabulary Acquisition and Use, Drawing paper

Part A: Vocabulary Development

5 minutes

Teacher Materials:
Reading *Textbook C*

Vocabulary Acquisition and Use

Student Materials:
Vocabulary notebook

Reading *Textbook C*

Vocabulary Acquisition and Use

Activity 1 Vocabulary Notebook Review

Guide students through all words.
Today you'll study from your vocabulary notebook. Studying your words and what they mean will help you know your words even better. You'll look at the four words we studied this week.

Activity 2 Cumulative Vocabulary Review

Elicit responses to questions. **Guide** as needed.
Directions: Listen and tell me whether I use our vocabulary words the right way or the wrong way. If I use the word the right way, say **"yes."** If I use the word the wrong way, say **"no."** Then we'll talk about each word.

1. Maria was named the queen for the homecoming dance. She got to sit on the **throne** and have her picture taken.

    Did I use the word **throne** the right way? *Yes.*

    How do you know? (Student responses.)

2. As soon as my father woke up from his nap, everyone started speaking **softly.**

    Did I use the word **softly** the right way? *No.*

    How do you know? (Student responses.)

3. Lauren went on five roller coasters. Afterward, every time she tried to get up, she had to sit down because she felt **dizzy.**

    Did I use the word **dizzy** the right way? *Yes.*

    How do you know? (Student responses.)

4. The children were **dragging** their sleds up the snowy hill.

   Did I use the word **dragging** the right way? *Yes.*

   How do you know? (Student responses.)

Review vocabulary words as needed.

 Review vocabulary words in appropriate context in Reading *Textbook C.*

Activity 3 Vocabulary Acquisition and Use

Display Vocabulary Acquisition and Use. **Have** students work with a neighbor to complete Vocabulary Acquisition and Use.
Today's vocabulary words are ____ and ____ [and _____ and ____].
Vocabulary words: **dragging** and pulling; **shook** and **moved**
Write the words on the lines provided. Then write the words in the boxes based on whether you think each word is less/smaller or more/larger than the other word. Below the boxes, write why you think word 1 is less/smaller and word 2 is more/larger than word 1.
Repeat for words 3 and 4. **Have** students share what they wrote. **Discuss** examples of how these words might be used.

Part B: Comprehension Strategies

12 minutes

Teacher Materials:
Reading *Textbook C*

Student Materials:
Drawing paper

Reading *Textbook C*

Display directions for activity.
Directions: Tom and Eric were in danger when their flashlight, a modern invention, broke. Discuss what modern invention you would use to help you trick the Egyptians into letting you go if you were Tom or Eric. Draw an illustration of an item you use all the time that the Egyptians would never have seen before, and explain how that item would trick the Egyptians into letting you go.

Activity 1 Pair-Share Activity—Apply Knowledge (Level 3 of Bloom's Taxonomy)

 Direct students to Lesson 134, pages 238–241 in Reading *Textbook C.*

Discuss the steps in the Pair-Share activity.
You'll do an activity called **Pair-Share** to show some things you have learned in recent lessons. The directions are on the board. I'll read them to you.

Assign partners. Provide drawing paper.
Step 1 is the **Pair** part of the activity. Discuss with your partner what item invented in the last 200 years could be used to trick the Egyptians into letting you escape from their soldiers. Illustrate that item, and explain why that item would trick the Egyptians into letting you go. Decide who'll do what part. Work quickly. You have 8 minutes.

Guide students to draw an item that has been invented in the last 200 years to trick the Egyptians into letting them escape.

Call on as many students to share as time allows.
Step 2 is to **Share.** I'll call on pairs of students to share their work with the rest of the class.

5 minutes

Student Materials:
Reading *Textbook C*

Part C: Fluency Building

 Conduct after the lesson, using the story of the day.

Activity 1 Partner Reading

It's time for partner reading.
Direct students to the story of the day. **Assign** student partners as Partner 1 and Partner 2. **Monitor** partner reading. **Guide** as needed.

Lesson 135 **429**

Lesson 136

Materials
Teacher: 6-Narrative Story Map; Reading *Textbook C*
Student: Vocabulary notebook; student dictionary; Copy of 6-Narrative Story Map; Reading *Textbook C*

5 minutes

Teacher Materials:
Reading *Textbook C*

Student Materials:
Vocabulary notebook

Student dictionary

Reading *Textbook C*

Part A: Vocabulary Development

Activity 1 Learn New Vocabulary Word

Elicit responses to questions. **Guide** as needed.
Today you'll learn a new vocabulary word. **Tame. Tame** means "gentle." What does **tame** mean? *Gentle.*
Another word for "gentle" is **tame.** What's another word for "gentle"? *Tame.*

Eric and Tom were sitting in their time machine when a lion came to the door. When a man appeared next to it, the boys knew the lion was **gentle.** Eric and Tom went walking with the **tame** lion and the man.

Discuss examples of animals that are tame.

What's another word for "gentle"? *Tame.*

Direct students to write tame and its definition in their vocabulary notebooks.
Guide as needed.
Write **tame** and what it means in your vocabulary notebook.

Activity 2 Dictionary Use

Guide as needed.
Now you'll look up the word **tame** in the dictionary on your own.

Activity 3 Review Vocabulary Word

Elicit responses to questions. **Guide** as needed.
What's another way to say "a seat for a queen or king"? *Throne.*

Tell me a sentence using the word **throne.** (Student responses.)
Discuss sentence.

 Review vocabulary words in appropriate context in Reading *Textbook C*.

430 Lesson 136

12 minutes

Teacher Materials:
Narrative Story Map

Reading *Textbook C*

Student Materials:
Narrative Story Map

Reading *Textbook C*

Part B: Comprehension Strategies

Activity 1 Choose a Comprehension Strategy—An After-Reading Strategy

Elicit response to question. **Guide** as needed.
You've learned strategies to use after you read a passage. What are those strategies? (Ideas: *Narrative Story Map, retell the story, fill in the last section of the KWL chart, summarize the story, make a text-to-text connection, make a text-to-self connection, make a text-to-world connection, confirm a prediction, compare and contrast, and identify cause and effect.*)

Discuss after-reading strategies.
You read a narrative story in the last lesson. What after-reading strategies would be appropriate to use now that you have read the story? (Student responses.)

Activity 2 Narrative Story Map: Identify Title, Characters, Setting, Problem, and Events—An After-Reading Strategy

Direct students to Lesson 135, pages 244–246 in Reading *Textbook C*.
Show Narrative Story Map.
Narrative stories have a title, characters, settings, a problem, and events. Read your narrative story and then work by yourself to fill in the Narrative Story Map with the title, important characters, setting, problem, and events.
Monitor students as they write the title, characters, setting, problem, and events.

Now you'll use your Narrative Story Map to retell the story.

Activity 3 Use Narrative Story Map: Retell the Story— An After-Reading Strategy

You did a great job completing your Narrative Story Maps.

Assign student partners.
Now it's your turn to use your Narrative Story Maps to retell the story to your partner. Remember to start by telling the title and something about the characters and setting. Tell something about the problem and then tell the events that happened. Use your own words to retell the story. Then let your partner use his or her own words to retell the story.
Monitor students as they retell the story from the Narrative Story Maps.

Retelling the story helps you remember all the parts of the story.

5 minutes

Student Materials:
Reading *Textbook C*

Part C: Fluency Building

 Conduct after the lesson, using the story of the day.

Activity 1 Partner Reading

It's time for partner reading.
Direct students to the story of the day. **Assign** student partners as Partner 1 and Partner 2. **Monitor** partner reading. **Guide** as needed.

Lesson 136   **431**

Lesson 137

Materials
Teacher: Reading *Textbook C*, 10-Prediction Chart
Student: Vocabulary notebook; Reading *Textbook C*, Copy of 10-Prediction Chart

5 minutes

Teacher Materials:
Reading *Textbook C*

Student Materials:
Vocabulary notebook

Reading *Textbook C*

Part A: Vocabulary Development

Activity 1 Suffix Introduction

Elicit response to question. **Guide** as needed.
Today you'll learn about a **suffix.** A **suffix** is "a word part added to the end of a word that changes its meaning." What do we call "a word part added to the end of a word that changes its meaning"? *Suffix.*

Activity 2 Learn New Suffix

Elicit responses to questions. **Guide** as needed.
Today you'll learn a new suffix: **e-d. E-d** means "in the past." What does **e-d** mean? *In the past.*

The suffix that means "in the past" is **e-d.** What's the suffix that means "in the past"? *E-d.*

Jump**ed.** Jump**ed** means **jump** "in the past." Deliver**ed.** Deliver**ed** means **deliver** "in the past." Pack**ed.** What does pack**ed** mean? *Pack in the past.*

So when we add the suffix **e-d** to the end of words, we change what they mean. Brush**ed.** Adding **e-d** to **brush** makes it brush**ed.** What does brush**ed** mean? *Brush in the past.*

Tell me an **e-d** word. (Student responses.)
Discuss responses.

What suffix means **in the past?** *E-d.*

Activity 3 Review Vocabulary Word

Elicit responses to questions. **Guide** as needed.
What's another word for "gentle"? *Tame.*

Tell me a sentence using the word **tame.** (Student responses.)
Discuss sentence.

 Review vocabulary words in appropriate context in Reading *Textbook C.*

432 Lesson 137

12 minutes

Teacher Materials:
Reading *Textbook C*

Prediction Chart

Student Materials:
Reading *Textbook C*

Prediction Chart

Part B: Comprehension Strategies

Activity 1 Comprehension Monitoring: Read with Prosody—A During-Reading Strategy

 Direct students to Lesson 136, page 252 in Reading *Textbook C*.

You've learned a lot about reading stories with expression. You know how to read and pay attention to the punctuation. You even know about dialogue. You know that your voice should go up a little when you read a question.

Assign student partners.
Today you'll practice reading the first page of the story with expression with your partner. Take turns reading paragraphs with your partner. You each will be listening for reading with expression. Make your voice really interesting. Read the dialogue with different voices. Make sure your voice goes up at the end of the questions. Take a small breath between sentences. Reread a sentence if you make a little mistake. It should be fun to listen to you and your partner read the first two pages of the story.
Monitor student reading to ensure that they take turns and read with prosody.

Remember that reading with expression helps you have good comprehension.

Activity 2 Make Predictions—A Before-Reading Strategy

 Direct students to Lesson 137, pages 259–262 in Reading *Textbook C*.

Show Prediction Chart. **Elicit** responses to questions. **Guide** as needed.
When you read narrative text, it's a good strategy to make predictions about what you're going to read to help you understand the story better.

What are predictions? (Idea: *Good guesses based on clues about what's in the story.*)

Where do you get the clues for your prediction? (Idea: *The title, the picture, skimming the text, and remembering what you know about the story so far.*)

Work by yourself to make a prediction about what'll happen in the next story by looking at the title "Eric and Tom See Cave People." You'll also skim the story, look at the picture, and remember what you know about the story so far to predict what'll happen next.
Monitor students as they make predictions. **Elicit** predictions. **Record** predictions made by students for further discussion in Lesson 138.

Lesson 137

You made a prediction about what you're going to read.

What do you do with that prediction as you read? (Idea: *Try to see whether your predictions are correct or not.*)

Does it matter whether the prediction is exactly correct? *No.*

That's right. What's important is that you're checking as you read to see whether your predictions are correct.

Activity 3 Choose a Comprehension Strategy—A Before-Reading Strategy

 Direct students to Lesson 137, pages 259–262 in Reading *Textbook C*.

Elicit responses to questions. **Guide** as needed.
You've learned strategies to use before you read a passage. What are those strategies? (Ideas: *Activate background knowledge, predict what is in the story, determine text type and set a purpose for reading, and fill out the first two parts of a KWL chart.*)

Take a look at the story you'll read today. How would you use these strategies while you read the story? (Student responses.)

Part C: Fluency Building

5 minutes

Student Materials:
Reading *Textbook C*

 Conduct after the lesson, using the story of the day.

Activity 1 Partner Reading

It's time for partner reading.
Direct students to the story of the day. **Assign** student partners as Partner 1 and Partner 2. **Monitor** partner reading. **Guide** as needed.

434 Lesson 137

Lesson 138

Materials

Teacher: Predictions Chart (from Lesson 137); 9-Compare and Contrast Chart; Reading *Textbook C*

Student: Vocabulary notebook; student dictionary; Predictions Chart (from Lesson 137); Copy of 9-Compare and Contrast Chart; Reading *Textbook C*

5 minutes

Teacher Materials:
Reading *Textbook C*

Student Materials:
Vocabulary notebook
Student dictionary
Reading *Textbook C*

Part A: Vocabulary Development

Activity 1 Learn New Vocabulary Word

Elicit responses to questions. **Guide** as needed.
Today you'll learn a new vocabulary word. **Study. Study** means "spend time learning." What does **study** mean? *Spend time learning.*

Another way to say "spend time learning" is **study.** What's another way to say "spend time learning"? *Study.*

Tom and Eric found an old man and asked him to help them fix their time machine. The old man had **spent time learning** old languages so he understood the boys. He knew the language the boys were speaking because he would **study** often.

Discuss examples of things people can study.

What's another way to say "spend time learning"? *Study.*

Direct students to write study and its definition in their vocabulary notebooks. **Guide** as needed.
Write **study** and what it means in your vocabulary notebook.

Activity 2 Dictionary Use

Guide as needed.
Now you'll look up the word **study** in the dictionary on your own.

Activity 3 Review Vocabulary Word

Elicit responses to questions. **Guide** as needed.
What suffix means "in the past"? *E-d.*

Tell me a sentence using a word with the suffix **e-d.** (Student responses.)
Discuss sentence.

 Review vocabulary words in appropriate context in Reading *Textbook C*.

Lesson 138 **435**

12 minutes

Teacher Materials:
Prediction Chart

Compare and Contrast Chart

Reading *Textbook C*

Student Materials:
Compare and Contrast Chart

Prediction Chart

Reading *Textbook C*

Part B: Comprehension Strategies

Activity 1 Confirm Predictions—An After-Reading Strategy

  Direct students to Lesson 137, pages 259–262 in Reading *Textbook C*.

Show Prediction Chart. **Elicit** response to question. **Guide** as needed.
In the last lesson you made some predictions about what happens to Eric and Tom in the story. You made the predictions before you read the story.

You confirm predictions when you check to see whether your predictions were correct. What do you do when you check to see whether your predictions were right? *Confirm predictions.*

Now that you've read the story, let's check to see whether your predictions were correct or incorrect.
Guide discussion based on predictions recorded in Lesson 137.

Sometimes, we don't predict correctly. That's okay. Just trying to make a prediction and then confirming it will help you better understand what you read.

Activity 2 Compare and Contrast—An After-Reading Strategy

  Direct students to Lesson 137, pages 258–259 in Reading *Textbook C*.

Show Compare and Contrast Chart. **Elicit** responses to questions. **Guide** as needed.
You've learned how to tell how characters are the same and how they're different. Today you'll compare and contrast how things look: how things looked 40 thousand years ago and how things look now. Read pages 258–259 to get ideas for your chart.

What will you do when you compare how things looked long ago to how things look now? (Idea: *Tell how they're the same.*)

What will you do when you contrast how things looked long ago to how things look now? (Idea: *Tell how they're different.*)

Write "how things looked long ago" for one name and "how things look now" for the other name.

First think about how they're the same. Write two sentences. When you write about how they're the same your sentences should begin, "They both…"
Monitor students as they write two sentences for "How Same?" box on Compare and Contrast Chart.

Now think about how they're different. Write two sentences. When you write about how they're different, it's a little harder. Your sentence needs to tell about each period of time and tell how each is different. You say the name of the time, tell about that time, and then use the word "but" before you tell about the next period of time. Remember, when you tell about how they're different, you have to tell about the same quality.
Monitor students as they write two sentences for "How Different?" box on Compare and Contrast Chart.

5 minutes

Student Materials:
Reading *Textbook C*

Part C: Fluency Building

 Conduct after the lesson, using the story of the day.

Activity 1 Partner Reading

It's time for partner reading.
Direct students to the story of the day. **Assign** student partners as Partner 1 and Partner 2. **Monitor** partner reading. **Guide** as needed.

Lesson 138 **437**

Lesson 139

Materials
Teacher: Reading *Textbook C*
Student: Vocabulary notebook; student dictionary; Reading *Textbook C*; sticky notes

5 minutes

Teacher Materials:
Reading *Textbook C*

Student Materials:
Vocabulary notebook
student dictionary
Reading *Textbook C*

Part A: Vocabulary Development

Activity 1 Learn New Vocabulary Word

Elicit responses to questions. **Guide** as needed.
Today you'll learn a new vocabulary word. **Obese. Obese** means "fat." What does **obese** mean? *Fat.*

Another word for "fat" is **obese.** What's another word for "fat"? *Obese.*

This time the boys landed near an ocean. They could see a **fat** man wearing funny pants standing near a shack. The **obese** man told the boys he spoke English.

Discuss the term obese.

What's another word for "fat"? *Obese.*

Direct students to write obese and its definition in their vocabulary notebooks. **Guide** as needed.
Write **obese** and what it means in your vocabulary notebook.

Activity 2 Dictionary Use

Guide as needed.
Now you'll look up the word **obese** in the dictionary on your own.

Activity 3 Review Vocabulary Word

Elicit responses to questions. **Guide** as needed.
What's another way to say "spend time learning"? *Study.*

Tell me a sentence using the word **study.** (Student responses.)
Discuss sentence.

 Review vocabulary words in appropriate context in Reading *Textbook C.*

438 Lesson 139

12 minutes

Teacher Materials:
Reading *Textbook C*

Student Materials:
Sticky notes

Reading *Textbook C*

Part B: Comprehension Strategies

Activity 1 Text-to-Self Connection—An After-Reading Strategy

 Direct students to Lesson 138, page 269 in Reading *Textbook C*.

When you read narrative text, it helps you understand the passage you're reading if you connect what you're reading to an experience you've had. That's called making a text-to-self connection.

What's the strategy called? *Making a text-to-self connection.*

 Skim page 269 of the story to find places to make connections.

Monitor students as they make text-to-self connections.
Read page 269 of your story, and find a place to make a text-to-self connection. Put a sticky note in your book to mark the spot where you find a connection so you can find it again when we talk about text-to-self connections.

Elicit as many text-to-self connections as time permits.
What text-to-self connections were you able to make in your story? (Student responses.)

You made text-to-self connections by making a connection between events in the story and experiences you had. It's a good strategy to help you understand what you read.

Activity 2 Comprehension Monitoring: Reread Narrative or Expository Text—A During-Reading Strategy

Elicit responses to questions. **Guide** as needed.
Rereading is a strategy to use while you read to help you have high comprehension.

What should you ask yourself while you're reading? (Idea: *Does this make sense?*)

What do you do if something doesn't make sense? (Idea: *Reread the sentence that didn't make sense or read ahead a little to see whether that helps you understand.*)

What's the strategy called? *Rereading.*

Does this strategy work for both expository and narrative text? *Yes.*

Today when you read Lesson 139, be sure to think about using the rereading strategy if you don't understand what you're reading for both the expository section and the narrative section.

Lesson 139 **439**

Activity 3 Choose a Comprehension Strategy—A During-Reading Strategy

Elicit responses to questions. **Guide** as needed.
You've learned strategies to use while you read a passage besides rereading. What are those other strategies? (Ideas: *Mental imaging, reading with prosody, and generating questions.*)

Take a look at the story you'll read today. How would you use these strategies while you read the story? (Student responses.)

Part C: Fluency Building

5 minutes

Student Materials:
Reading *Textbook C*

 Conduct after the lesson, using the story of the day.

Activity 1 Partner Reading

It's time for partner reading.
Direct students to the story of the day. **Assign** student partners as Partner 1 and Partner 2. **Monitor** partner reading. **Guide** as needed.

Lesson 140

Materials

Teacher: Reading *Textbook C*, 2-Vocabulary Acquisition and Use, Writing Prompts, 3-My Writing Checklist

Student: Vocabulary notebook; Reading *Textbook C*, Copy of 2-Vocabulary Acquisition and Use and 3-My Writing Checklist, Lined paper, Drawing paper

Part A: Vocabulary Development

5 minutes

Teacher Materials:
Reading *Textbook C*
Vocabulary Acquisition and Use

Student Materials:
Vocabulary Notebook
Reading *Textbook C*
Vocabulary Acquisition and Use

Activity 1 Vocabulary Notebook Review

Guide students as they study all words.
Today you'll study from your vocabulary notebook. Studying your words and what they mean will help you know your words even better. You'll study the eight words we studied over the past two weeks.

Activity 2 Cumulative Vocabulary Review

Elicit responses to questions. **Guide** as needed.
Directions: Listen and tell me whether I use our vocabulary words the right way or the wrong way. If I use the word the right way, say **"yes."** If I use the word the wrong way, say **"no."** Then we'll talk about each word.

1. After Charlie wrote his answer on the board, his teacher told him to go back to his **throne.**

   Did I use the word **throne** the right way? *No.*

   How do you know? (Student responses.)

2. John needed to **study.** His mother agreed and said he should go to a movie with his friends.

   Did I use the word **study** the right way? *No.*

   How do you know? (Student responses.)

3. Sitting quietly in his chair always made Lewis **dizzy.**

   Did I use the word **dizzy** the right way? *No.*

   How do you know? (Student responses.)

4. Armando could not understand what Phillip said because he spoke so **softly.**

   Did I use the word **softly** the right way? *Yes.*

   How do you know? (Student responses.)

Lesson 140   441

5. The children went on a field trip to a petting zoo where they could pet the **tame** animals.

   Did I use the word **tame** the right way? *Yes.*

   How do you know? (Student responses.)

6. The Wilson's dog was twenty pounds overweight. The veterinarian told them that their dog was **obese** and needed to lose some weight.

   Did I use the word **obese** the right way? *Yes.*

   How do you know? (Student responses.)

7. Mary's father cook**ed** ham and potatoes for dinner last night.

   Did I use the word cook**ed** the right way? *Yes.*

   How do you know? (Student responses.)

8. Russ was **dragging** the cake for the party over to the table.

   Did I use the word **dragging** the right way? *No.*

   How do you know? (Student responses.)

Review vocabulary words as needed.

 Review vocabulary words in appropriate context in Reading *Textbook C*.

Activity 3 Vocabulary Acquisition and Use

Display Vocabulary Acquisition and Use. **Have** students work with a neighbor to complete Vocabulary Acquisition and Use.
Today's vocabulary words are ____ and ____ [and ____ and ____].
Vocabulary words: **fat** and **obese**; **bend** and **twist**
Write the words on the lines provided. Then write the words in the boxes based on whether you think each word is less/smaller or more/larger than the other word. Below the boxes, write why you think word 1 is less/smaller and word 2 is more/larger than word 1.
Repeat for words 3 and 4. **Have** students share what they wrote. **Discuss** examples of how these words might be used.

12 minutes

Teacher Materials:
Reading *Textbook C*

Student Materials:
Drawing paper

Reading *Textbook C*

Part B: Comprehension Strategies

Display directions for the activity.
Directions: Discuss what Tom and Eric would see if they went to Australia in their time machine. Draw an illustration of the kinds of things they would see there. Label all the parts of the illustration and explain what and why you put each item on your picture.

Activity 1 Pair-Share Activity—Apply Knowledge (Level 3 of Bloom's Taxonomy)

 Direct students to Lesson 113, pages 88–96 in Reading *Textbook C*.

Discuss the steps in the Pair-Share activity.
You'll do an activity called **Pair-Share** to show some things you have learned in recent lessons. The directions are on the board. I'll read them to you.

Assign partners. **Provide** drawing paper.
Step 1 is the **Pair** part of the activity. Discuss with your partner what Tom and Eric would see if their time machine took them to Australia. Draw a picture of the kinds of things they'd see and label the picture. Be ready to explain what's in your picture and why you put it there. Decide who'll do what part. Work quickly. You have 8 minutes.
Guide students to draw and label what Tom and Eric would see if they traveled to Australia in their time machine.

Call on as many students to share as time allows.
Step 2 is to **Share.** I'll call on pairs of students to share their work with the rest of the class.

5 minutes

Student Materials:
Reading *Textbook C*

Part C: Fluency Building

 Conduct after the lesson, using the story of the day.

Activity 1 Partner Reading

It's time for partner reading.
Direct students to the story of the day. **Assign** student partners as Partner 1 and Partner 2. **Monitor** partner reading. **Guide** as needed.

Lesson 140   443

Part D: Writing/Language Arts

10 minutes

Teacher Materials:
Writing Prompts

My Writing Checklist

Student Materials:
Lined Paper

My Writing Checklist

Activity 1 Write and Use Parts of Speech and Conventions

Time to write using a writing prompt based on the stories we've been reading.

Assign student partners. **Distribute** lined paper to students. **Display** writing prompts and have students choose one to write about or assign a writing prompt of your choice. **Review** parts of speech and punctuation as well as the writing checklist with students. **Tell** students to write one to two paragraphs (minimum of four sentences per paragraph) on their own to answer the writing prompt. **Tell** them to use their writing checklist (first column labeled "Did I use them?") to ensure they include important parts of speech or punctuation in their writing. **Tell** students which parts of speech or punctuation to focus on, if you wish. **Model** what it means to answer a writing prompt and to use the writing checklist during and after the writing process, as needed. **Monitor** and guide students as needed. **Model** what it means to have a neighbor look over his or her neighbor's writing and to complete the writing checklist (second column labeled "Did my neighbor use them?"), as needed. **Have** students share what they wrote as time permits.

Writing Prompt 1	Writing Prompt 2	Writing Prompt 3
What things would you miss if you went back in time and why would you miss them?	Would you rather visit ancient Greece or ancient Egypt? Why?	Describe what a city in the future might be like.

Lesson 141

Materials
Teacher: 6-Narrative Story Map; Reading *Textbook C*
Student: Vocabulary notebook; student dictionary; Copy of 6-Narrative Story Map; Reading *Textbook C*

5 minutes

Teacher Materials:
Reading *Textbook C*

Student Materials:
Vocabulary notebook
Student dictionary
Reading *Textbook C*

Part A: Vocabulary Development

Activity 1 Learn New Vocabulary Word

Elicit responses to questions. **Guide** as needed.
Today you'll learn a new vocabulary word. **Crouched. Crouched** means "lowered your body by bending your knees." What does **crouched** mean?
Lowered your body by bending your knees.

Another way to say "lowered your body by bending your knees" is **crouched.** What's another way to say "lowered your body by bending your knees"?
Crouched.

The boys ran back to the time machine only to find a dog with **its body lowered at the knees** standing by the handle. They did not think the dog **crouched** there looked friendly.

Discuss examples of when someone might be crouched.

What's another way to say "lowered your body by bending your knees"?
Crouched.

Direct students to write crouched and its definition in their vocabulary notebooks. **Guide** as needed.
Write **crouched** and what it means in your vocabulary notebook.

Monitor students as they use the dictionary to double-check the meaning of crouched, as time permits.

Activity 2 Review Vocabulary Word

Elicit responses to questions. **Guide** as needed.
What's another way to say "fat"? *Obese.*

Tell me a sentence using the word **obese.** (Student responses.)
Discuss sentence.

 Review vocabulary words in appropriate context in Reading *Textbook C*.

Lesson 141   **445**

12 minutes

Teacher Materials:
Narrative Story Map

Reading *Textbook C*

Student Materials:
Narrative Story Map

Reading *Textbook C*

Part B: Comprehension Strategies

Activity 1 Narrative Story Map: Identify Title, Characters, Setting, Problem, and Events—An After-Reading Strategy

 Direct students to choose a narrative story from Reading *Textbook C*.

Show Narrative Story Map.
Narrative stories have a title, characters, settings, a problem, and events. Read your narrative story and then work by yourself to fill in the Narrative Story Map with the title, important characters, setting, problem, and events.

Pick a narrative story of your choice from *Textbook C* and fill out a Narrative Story Map for the story you choose.
Monitor students as they write the title, characters, setting, problem, and events.

Now you'll use your Narrative Story Map to retell the story.

Activity 2 Use Narrative Story Map: Retell the Story—An After-Reading Strategy

You did a great job completing your Narrative Story Maps.

Assign student partners. **Monitor** students as they retell the story from Narrative Story Maps.
Now it's your turn to use your Narrative Story Maps to retell the story to your partner. Remember to start by telling the title and something about the characters and setting. Tell something about the problem and then tell the events that happened. Use your own words to retell the story. Then let your partner use his or her own words to retell the story.

Retelling the story helps you remember all the parts of the story.

5 minutes

Student Materials:
Reading *Textbook C*

Part C: Fluency Building

 Conduct after the lesson, using the story of the day.

Activity 1 Partner Reading

It's time for partner reading.
Direct students to the story of the day. **Assign** student partners as Partner 1 and Partner 2. **Monitor** partner reading. **Guide** as needed.

Lesson 141

Lesson 142

Materials

Teacher: 13-KWL Chart; Reading *Textbook C*

Student: Vocabulary notebook; student dictionary; Copy of 13-KWL Chart; Reading *Textbook C*

Part A: Vocabulary Development

5 minutes

Teacher Materials:
Reading *Textbook C*

Student Materials:
Vocabulary notebook

Student dictionary

Reading *Textbook C*

Activity 1 Learn New Vocabulary Word

Elicit responses to questions. **Guide** as needed.
Today you'll learn a new vocabulary word. **Huts. Huts** means "small, simple buildings." What does **huts** mean? *Small, simple buildings.*

Another way to say "small, simple buildings" is **huts.** What's another way to say "small, simple buildings"? *Huts.*

Tom and Eric followed a Viking to a village with several **small, simple buildings.** The boys noticed that the village had many **huts** and many dogs.

Discuss examples of huts.

What's another way to say "small, simple buildings"? *Huts.*

Direct students to write huts and its definition in their vocabulary notebooks. **Guide** as needed.
Write **huts** and what it means in your vocabulary notebook.

Monitor students as they use the dictionary to double-check the meaning of huts, as time permits.

Activity 2 Review Vocabulary Word

Elicit responses to questions. **Guide** as needed.
What's another way to say "lowered your body by bending your knees"? *Crouched.*

Tell me a sentence using the word **crouched.** (Student responses.)
Discuss sentence.

 Review vocabulary words in appropriate context in Reading *Textbook C*.

Lesson 142 **447**

Part B: Comprehension Strategies

12 minutes

Teacher Materials:
KWL Chart

Reading *Textbook C*

Student Materials:
KWL Chart

Reading *Textbook C*

Activity 1 Choose a Comprehension Strategy—A Before-Reading Strategy

 Direct students to Lesson 142, pages 296–297 in Reading *Textbook C*.

Elicit responses to questions. **Guide** as needed.
You've learned strategies to use before you read a passage. What are those strategies? (Ideas: *Activate background knowledge, predict what is in the story, determine text type and set a purpose for reading, and fill out the first two parts of a KWL chart.*)

Take a look at the passage you'll read today about Vikings. Tell what strategy you should use before you read this passage. (Idea: *Fill out the first two parts of a KWL chart because it's expository text.*)

Activity 2 KWL Chart: Topic and What I Know—A Before-Reading Strategy

Show KWL Chart. **Elicit** responses to questions. **Guide** as needed.
You're going to activate your background knowledge for a new topic. What do you do when you activate your background knowledge? (Idea: *Think about what you already know.*)

Why is it a good idea to think about your background knowledge before you read? (Idea: *Then you'll be able to connect what you know to what you learn.*)

Why do you use a KWL chart? (Idea: *To organize thinking about expository text.*)

Monitor students as they write the topic on their charts.
What should you write for the topic? *Vikings.*

Monitor students as they write what they know on their charts.
Now work by yourself to think about your background knowledge about Vikings for the "What I Know" section of the KWL chart.

Remember, you're doing this to connect what you already know with the text that you'll be reading.

448 Lesson 142

Activity 3 KWL Chart: What I Wonder—A Before-Reading Strategy

Show KWL Chart. **Elicit** responses to questions. **Guide** as needed.
Next you'll write the questions you have about the Vikings in the "What I Wonder" section of the chart.

What'll you write in this section of the chart? (Ideas: *Questions you have; what you wonder about.*)

Think of questions you have about the Vikings for the "What I Wonder" section of the KWL chart, and write them on the chart.
Monitor students as they write questions on their charts.

Why is it important to ask questions before you read? (Idea: *Asking questions gets you interested in what you're going to learn—it makes you think about what you're going to read.*)

The text you read may or may not have the answers to your questions. That's okay. Just asking the questions helps you be smarter. If you don't find the answers to your questions, you might need to read more in another book to find out the answers.
Save student copies of KWL Chart for Lesson 143.

5 minutes

Student Materials:
Reading *Textbook C*

Part C: Fluency Building

 Conduct after the lesson, using the story of the day.

Activity 1 Partner Reading

It's time for partner reading.
Direct students to the story of the day. **Assign** student partners as Partner 1 and Partner 2. **Monitor** partner reading. **Guide** as needed.

Lesson 142   **449**

Lesson 143

Materials

Teacher: 13-KWL Chart; Reading *Textbook C*

Student: Vocabulary notebook; student dictionary; Copy of 13-KWL Chart (from Lesson 142); Reading *Textbook C*

5 minutes

Teacher Materials:
Reading *Textbook C*

Student Materials:
Vocabulary notebook

Student dictionary

Reading *Textbook C*

Part A: Vocabulary Development

Activity 1 Learn New Vocabulary Word

Elicit responses to questions. **Guide** as needed.
Today you'll learn a new vocabulary word. **Blast. Blast** means "strong movement of air." What does **blast** mean? *Strong movement of air.*

Another way to say "strong movement of air" is **blast.** What's another way to say "strong movement of air"? *Blast.*

Tom pushed the handle and they were off again. When they landed, Tom opened the door and a **strong movement of air** came in. The cold **blast** of air made Eric want to leave because it was so cold outside.

Discuss examples of a blast.

What's another way to say "strong movement of air"? *Blast.*

Direct students to write blast and its definition in their vocabulary notebooks. **Guide** as needed.
Write **blast** and what it means in your vocabulary notebook.

Monitor students as they use the dictionary to double-check the meaning of blast, as time permits.

Activity 2 Review Vocabulary Word

Elicit responses to questions. **Guide** as needed.
What's another way to say "small, simple buildings"? *Huts.*

Tell me a sentence using the word huts. (Student responses.)
Discuss sentence.

 Review vocabulary words in appropriate context in Reading *Textbook C.*

450   Lesson 143

12 minutes

Teacher Materials:
KWL Chart

Reading *Textbook C*

Student Materials:
KWL Chart

Reading *Textbook C*

Part B: Comprehension Strategies

Activity 1 Choose a Comprehension Strategy—An After-Reading Strategy

Elicit response to question. **Guide** as needed.
In the last lesson you filled out the first two sections of your KWL chart. Then you read your book.

What after-reading strategy should you use today? (Idea: *Fill in the What I Learned section of the KWL chart.*)

Activity 2 KWL Chart: What I Learned—An After-Reading Strategy

 Direct students to Lesson 142, pages 296–297 in Reading *Textbook C*.

Show KWL Chart. **Elicit** responses to questions. **Guide** as needed.
In the last lesson you read your book. It's time to add what you learned from the book to the "What I Learned" section of the KWL chart that you started in Lesson 142.

Should you copy the words from the book? *No.*

What should you do instead? (Idea: *Write the ideas in your own words.*)

Why should you write the ideas in your own words? (Idea: *That will help you remember the information later.*)

Today you'll work to fill out the "What I Learned" section of the chart.
Monitor students as they write 2–3 sentences to add to the "What I Learned" section of KWL Chart started in Lesson 142.

You've now written the new things you learned from the expository text you read. You wrote the information in your own words.

There's a part on your KWL chart that says, "Questions I Still Have."

Did you have all your questions about your topic answered? (Idea: *No.*)

If not, copy the questions that were not answered in the "Questions I Still Have" box.
Guide students to write one or two questions from the "What I Wonder" section in the "Questions I Still Have" box.

Lesson 143   **451**

Discuss additional resources for information about topics. **Model** writing resources in the "Where to Look for More Information" box.

Let's think about how we could find the answers to your questions?
(Ideas: *Another book, a magazine, a video, look on the Internet, or look in an encyclopedia.*)

Guide students to write list of resources in the box for "Where to Look for More Information."

Write where you could look for more information in the last box.

Part C: Fluency Building

Student Materials:
Reading *Textbook C*

  Conduct after the lesson, using the story of the day.

Activity 1 Partner Reading

It's time for partner reading.
Direct students to the story of the day. **Assign** student partners as Partner 1 and Partner 2. **Monitor** partner reading. **Guide** as needed.

452   Lesson 143

Lesson 144

Materials
Teacher: Reading *Textbook C*
Student: Vocabulary notebook; student dictionary; Reading *Textbook C*

5 minutes

Teacher Materials:
Reading *Textbook C*

Student Materials:
Vocabulary notebook
Student dictionary
Reading *Textbook C*

Part A: Vocabulary Development

Activity 1 Learn New Vocabulary Word

Elicit responses to questions. **Guide** as needed.
Today you'll learn a new vocabulary word. **Lad. Lad** means "boy." What does **lad** mean? *Boy.*

Another word for "boy" is **lad.** What's another word for "boy"? *Lad.*

Tom was running in front of the church when the door opened and someone told the **boy** to come inside. Some men took Tom into the church and told the **lad** to sit by the fire.

Discuss examples of a lad.

What's another word for "boy"? *Lad.*

Direct students to write lad and its definition in their vocabulary notebooks.
Guide as needed.
Write **lad** and what it means in your vocabulary notebook.

Monitor students as they use the dictionary to double-check the meaning of lad as time permits.

Activity 2 Review Vocabulary Word

Elicit responses to questions. **Guide** as needed.
What's another way to say "strong movement of air"? *Blast.*

Tell me a sentence using the word **blast.** (Student responses.)
Discuss sentence.

 Review vocabulary words in appropriate context in Reading *Textbook C.*

Lesson 144   453

12 minutes

Teacher Materials:
Reading *Textbook C*

Student Materials:
Reading *Textbook C*

Part B: Comprehension Strategies

Activity 1 Determine Text Type: Review Features of Expository Text—A Before-Reading Strategy

 Direct students to *Textbook C*.

Elicit responses to questions. **Guide** as needed.
Expository and narrative texts have different features. If you know what those features are, this will help you decide before you read what kind of text you're reading.

Why is it a good idea to think about what you're going to read before you read? (Idea: *It helps you decide what you'll do during reading—learn new information or read a story.*)

What are some of the features that you might find in expository text? (Student responses.)

See whether you can find any features of expository text in *Textbook C* and show them to me. (Student responses.)

 Discuss features and look in *Textbook C* to see whether it contains the feature under discussion.

Labels—help identify parts
Photographs—help you understand what something looks like
Captions—tell what's in a picture
Cutaways—show what something looks like inside
Diagrams—show parts of things
Maps—help you know where something is in the world
Bold print—shows you important words
Headings—show what a section of text is about
Tables of contents—help you find information in a book
Index—tells you an alphabetized list with page numbers of what's in the book
Glossary—defines words in the book

Do you have to read expository text in order? *No.*

What kind of text are you reading when you're reading to learn new facts or information? *Expository text.*

Activity 2 Determine Text Type: Review Features of Narrative Text—A Before-Reading Strategy

 Direct students to *Textbook C*.

Elicit responses to questions. **Guide** as needed.
A second type of text is called narrative text. What does narrative text tell you? *A story.*

454 Lesson 144

You'll often read narrative texts for fun. Narrative texts might include new facts or information that you didn't know before. But the main purpose of narrative text is to tell you a story.

What are some of the features that you might find in narrative texts? (Student responses.)

See whether you can find any features of narrative text in Reading *Textbook C* and show them to me. (Student responses.)

 Discuss features and look in *Textbook C* to see whether it contains the feature under discussion.
Characters—people, animals, or objects that do things in the story
Setting—where and when the story happens
Problem—thing that goes wrong in the story that makes you want to read more
Events—beginning, middle, and end of story

Do you have to read narrative text in order? *Yes.*

What kind of text are you reading when you read a story? *Narrative text.*

Activity 3 Determine Text Type and Establish Purpose for Reading—A Before-Reading Strategy

 Direct students to Lesson 144, pages 313–318 in Reading *Textbook C.*

Elicit responses to questions. **Guide** as needed.
What's the title of the first section you'll read? *Facts About the United States.*

What kind of text is it? *Expository.*

Why will you read "Facts about the United States"? (Idea: *To learn new information about the United States.*)

What's the title of the next section you'll read? *Concord.*

What kind of text is it? *Narrative.*

Why will you read "Concord"? (Idea: *To read a story.*)

Part C: Fluency Building

5 minutes

Student Materials:
Reading *Textbook C*

 Conduct after the lesson, using the story of the day.

Activity 1 Partner Reading

It's time for partner reading.
Direct students to the story of the day. **Assign** student partners as Partner 1 and Partner 2. **Monitor** partner reading. **Guide** as needed.

Lesson 144   **455**

Lesson 145

Materials

Teacher: Reading *Textbook C*, 2-Vocabulary Acquisition and Use

Student: Vocabulary notebook; Reading *Textbook C*, Copy of 2-Vocabulary Acquisition and Use, Drawing paper

Part A: Vocabulary Development

5 minutes

Teacher Materials:
Reading *Textbook C*
Vocabulary Acquisition and Use

Student Materials:
Vocabulary notebook
Reading *Textbook C*
Vocabulary Acquisition and Use

Activity 1 Vocabulary Notebook Review

Guide students through all words.
Today you'll study from your vocabulary notebook. Studying your words and what they mean will help you know your words even better. You'll look at the four words we studied this week.

Activity 2 Cumulative Vocabulary Review

Elicit responses to questions. **Guide** as needed.
Directions: Listen and tell me whether I use our vocabulary words the right way or the wrong way. If I use the word the right way, say **"yes."** If I use the word the wrong way, say **"no."** Then we'll talk about each word.

1. Scott **crouched** to get a better look during the game. He stood straight and tall as he watched others play.

   Did I use the word **crouched** the right way? *No.*

   How do you know? (Student responses.)

2. The **lad** helped others in town. Everyone said she was the nicest girl in town.

   Did I use the word **lad** the right way? *No.*

   How do you know? (Student responses.)

3. The **blast** of cold air sent a shiver down Sharon's spine.

   Did I use the word **blast** the right way? *Yes.*

   How do you know? (Student responses.)

4. There are many **huts** in Chicago. They are the biggest buildings in town.

   Did I use the word **huts** the right way? *No.*

   How do you know? (Student responses.)

Review vocabulary words as needed.

 Review vocabulary words in appropriate context in Reading *Textbook C*.

Activity 3 Vocabulary Acquisition and Use

Display Vocabulary Acquisition and Use. **Have** students work with a neighbor to complete Vocabulary Acquisition and Use.
Today's vocabulary words are ____ and ____ [and ____ and ____].
Vocabulary words: **crouched** and **lowered**; **hurt** and **injured**
Write the words on the lines provided. Then write the words in the boxes based on whether you think each word is less/smaller or more/larger than the other word. Below the boxes, write why you think word 1 is less/smaller and word 2 is more/larger than word 1.

Repeat for words 3 and 4. **Have** students share what they wrote. **Discuss** examples of how these words might be used.

Part B: Comprehension Strategies

Student Materials:
Drawing paper

Display directions for activity.
Directions: Discuss what a time line is and why it is useful. Draw a time line for your life. Show when you were born, when you learned to walk, when you started school, and any other important events in your life up until now, in the order in which they happened. Explain the important events in your life in the order in which they happened.

Activity 1 Pair-Share Activity—Apply Knowledge
             (Level 3 of Bloom's Taxonomy)

Discuss the steps in the Pair-Share activity.
You'll do an activity called Pair-Share to show some things you have learned in recent lessons. The directions are on the board. I'll read them to you.

Assign partners. **Provide** drawing paper.
Step 1 is the Pair part of the activity. Discuss with your partner what a time line is and why it's useful. Draw your time line and include important events in your life, in the order in which they happened. Each partner can do one for his or her life. Be ready to explain your time line. Work quickly. You have 8 minutes.
Guide students to draw and label a time line of their lives.

Call on as many students to share as time allows.
Step 2 is to Share. I'll call on pairs of students to share their work with the rest of the class.

Lesson 145   **457**

5 minutes

Student Materials:
Reading *Textbook C*

Part C: Fluency Building

 Conduct after the lesson, using the story of the day.

Activity 1 Partner Reading

It's time for partner reading.
Direct students to the story of the day. **Assign** student partners as Partner 1 and Partner 2. **Monitor** partner reading. **Guide** as needed.

Appendix A

Name _____   Date _____

1: Narrative Story Map

Title: _____

Characters

Setting

Where:

When:

Problem

Events

Beginning:

Middle:

End:

Copyright © The McGraw-Hill Companies, Inc. Permission is granted to reproduce for classroom use.

Name _____   Date _____

2: Vocabulary Acquisition and Use

Words: _____   _____

Less/Smaller   More/Larger

⟵——————————————————————————————————⟶

| Word 1: | Word 2: |

Why do you think Word 1 is less/smaller and Word 2 is more/larger?

_____

_____

_____

_____

Words: _____   _____

Less/Smaller   More/Larger

⟵——————————————————————————————————⟶

| Word 3: | Word 4: |

Why do you think Word 3 is less/smaller and Word 4 is more/larger?

_____

_____

_____

_____

Name _____   Date _____

3: My Writing Checklist
Level 2

My Neighbor's Name _____

Parts to include:	Did I use them? (circle one)		Did my neighbor use them? (circle one)	
1. Nouns (person, place, thing, names, ownership)	Yes	No	Yes	No
2. Pronouns (he, she, him, her, I, me, my, they, them, their, anyone, everything)	Yes	No	Yes	No
3. Conjunctions (and, but, or, so, because)	Yes	No	Yes	No
4. Determiners (a, an, the)	Yes	No	Yes	No
5. Prepositions (in, on, over, under, during, beyond, toward)	Yes	No	Yes	No
6. Commas (dates, separate words in a series)	Yes	No	Yes	No
7. Collective nouns (group, herd, flock, litter)	Yes	No	Yes	No
8. Reflexive pronouns (myself, ourselves, yourself, himself, herself)	Yes	No	Yes	No

Name _____ Date _____

4: Vocabulary Notebook

	Word	Definition

Name _____   Date _____

5: Narrative Story Map

Title: _____

Characters	Setting
	Where:
	When:

Problem

Events

Beginning:

Middle:

End:

Copyright © The McGraw-Hill Companies, Inc. Permission is granted to reproduce for classroom use.

Name _____   Date _____

6: Narrative Story Map

Title: _____

Characters

Setting

Where:

When:

Problem

Events

Beginning:

Middle:

End:

Copyright © The McGraw-Hill Companies, Inc. Permission is granted to reproduce for classroom use.

Name _____   Date _____

7: KWL Chart

Topic:

What I **K**now	What I **W**onder	What I **L**earned

Questions I still have:

Where to look to find answers:

Copyright © The McGraw-Hill Companies, Inc. Permission is granted to reproduce for classroom use.

Name _____   **Date** _____

8: T-Chart

Name _____   Date _____

9: Compare and Contrast Chart

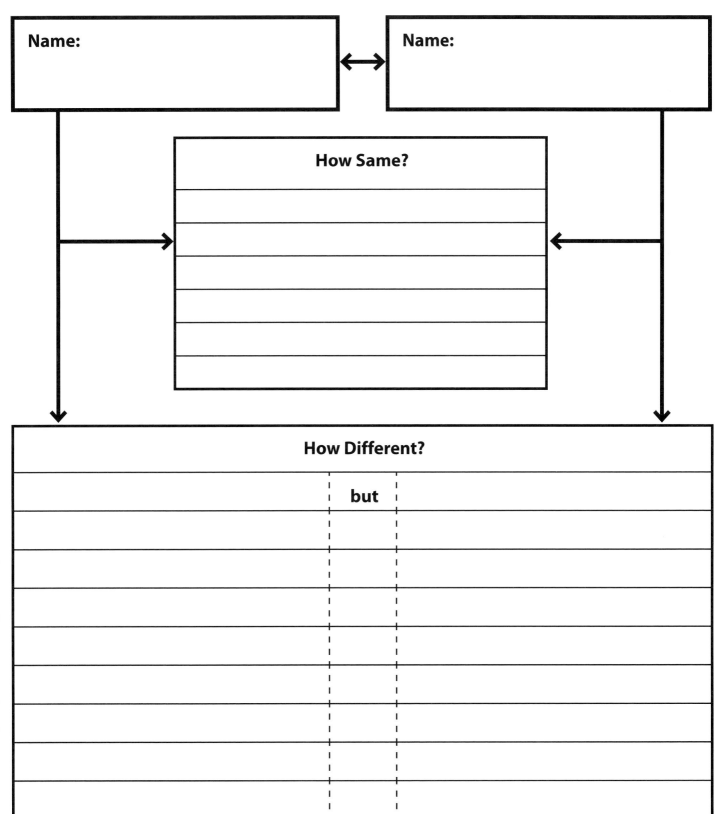

Name _____ Date _____

10: My Prediction Chart

Book Title:

I Predict That:

Was My Prediction Correct?

Yes   No

Copyright © The McGraw-Hill Companies, Inc. Permission is granted to reproduce for classroom use.

Name _____   Date _____

11: Before-During-After

Before	During	After

Copyright © The McGraw-Hill Companies, Inc. Permission is granted to reproduce for classroom use.

Name _____ **Date** _____

12: Cause and Effect Map

Cause:
To Make Something Happen

Effect:
What Happens

Cause:
To Make Something Happen

Effect:
What Happens

Copyright © The McGraw-Hill Companies, Inc. Permission is granted to reproduce for classroom use.

Name _____   Date _____

13: KWL Chart

Topic:

What I **K**now	What I **W**onder	What I **L**earned

Questions I still have:

Where to look to find answers:

Copyright © The McGraw-Hill Companies, Inc. Permission is granted to reproduce for classroom use.

Appendix B

Test	Tips for Teachers	Home Connections
Fluency Checkout (Lesson 10) **Approaching Mastery**	• See guidelines for students who do not read within error or time limit for Lesson 10 on page 58 in *Presentation Book A*. • Partner with "at mastery" student and have him or her model reading story; have student read story. • Re-teach difficult words using "good-bye" list: Write difficult words on board; place check mark for each day completed correctly; after 3 consecutive days completed correctly, say "good-bye" to word. • Review finger placement and tracking for sentence reading. • Have adult model reading story; have student read story until firm. • Use paired reading: Good reader reads until student signals for his or her turn to read. • Use "cold timing" and "hot timing" to improve fluency: First timing is colored on graph in blue (words correct per minute); student reads story 3 times and then is timed by the teacher; this final timing is graphed in red. • Develop tape of story read by good reader (e.g., at mastery student, adult); have student listen to tape and whisper read.	• Provide word flash cards for students to take home for additional practice. • Have an adult model reading story; have students listen and track during story reading; have students read story; have an adult review difficult words following story reading. • Have students read story to a pet, stuffed animal, or sibling for extra practice.
At Mastery	• See guidelines for students who read within error and time limit for Lesson 10 on page 58 in *Presentation Book A*. • Partner with "approaching mastery" or ELL student and model reading story; have student read story. • Have student assist "approaching mastery" or ELL student with "cold and hot timings" and repeated readings. • Have student tape him or herself reading story as model for "approaching mastery" or ELL student. • Direct student to reading and writing center in classroom to reinforce literacy and writing skills.	

Test	Tips for Teachers	Home Connections
ELL **Test**	• See "Tips for Teachers" for "approaching mastery" and "at mastery" students. • Describe and model mouth formations for difficult sounds and words, then guide students while practicing with mirror. • Use sentence strips to practice reading sentences in story. • Show realia or other visuals of objects (e.g., picture of construction worker) and concepts (e.g., next to). • Use role-play to act out monologue or dialogue (e.g., act out Joe talking to himself about how he feels). • Use primary language equivalents when available and then ask students to say words and sentences in English.	• See "Home Connections" for "approaching mastery" and "at mastery" students. • Provide audiotape to use with sentence strips and word flash cards for additional practice; encourage students to practice with mirror at home, as needed. • Provide audiotape of story; have students listen and track during story reading; then students read aloud with tape while tracking; then students read aloud and track independently; have an adult review difficult words following independent story reading. • Encourage an adult to help students tell a similar story using primary language equivalents. • Encourage an adult to help students identify realia and other visuals illustrating meaning of sentences in story. • Encourage an adult to help students practice using primary language equivalents and English words when possible.
Test 1 (Lesson 10) **Approaching Mastery**	• See guidelines noted on Group Summary Chart (see Appendix H of *Teacher's Guide*) and Test Summary Sheet (see Appendix I of *Teacher's Guide*) for students who do not meet passing criterion. • See test remedies noted on pages 69–72 of *Teacher's Guide* as well as Test 1 Firming Table noted on page 59 of *Presentation Book A*. • Partner with "at mastery" student and review previous lessons in Reading *Textbook A*. • Implement note-taking study strategy using 2-column note-taking method: left column lists questions, right column lists answers; review notes before test. • Write lesson summaries on index cards as study strategy and review before test. • Review key vocabulary words/terms until firm; write vocabulary words and their definitions on index cards.	• Encourage students to reread previous lessons at home, particularly before the test; provide another text to be kept at home for this purpose. • Have an adult "quiz" students from notes or index cards before test. • Provide vocabulary flash cards for students to take home for additional practice.
At Mastery	• See guidelines noted on Group Summary Chart (see Appendix H of *Teacher's Guide*) and Test Summary Sheet (see Appendix I of *Teacher's Guide*) for students who meet passing criterion. • Have student "be the teacher": Partner with "approaching mastery" or ELL student and review previous lessons in Reading *Textbook A*. • Have student assist "approaching mastery" or ELL student with note-taking and index card study strategies. • Direct student to reading and writing center in classroom to reinforce literacy and writing skills (e.g., books on tape, worksheets, books, writing paper, computer).	

B3

Test	Tips for Teachers	Home Connections
ELL	• See "Tips for Teachers" for "approaching mastery" and "at mastery" students. • Explain key terms in rules and vocabulary sentences by using realia or other visuals to illustrate examples and non-examples (e.g., explain "living things," by using realia or other visuals of living and non-living things). • Explain key terms in vocabulary sentences by using realia, other visuals, or pantomime (e.g., pantomime wading into a stream and scooping up tadpoles). • Implement web diagram to group facts about key concept (e.g., write "living things" in a circle in the center of the board, write facts about all living things in separate circles surrounding "living things" and connect each fact circle with a line to "living things"). • When writing vocabulary words and definitions on index cards, include primary language equivalents when available. • Show related videos with captioning to help students associate printed text to spoken word.	• See "Home Connections" for "approaching mastery" and "at mastery" students. • Encourage an adult to help students review vocabulary flash cards including primary language equivalents. • Encourage students to study web about key concept. • Encourage an adult to turn on television captioning at home.
Test **Fluency Checkout** (Lesson 15) **Approaching Mastery**	• See guidelines for students who do not read within error or time limit for Lesson 15 on page 85 in *Presentation Book A*. • Partner with "at mastery" student and have him or her model reading story; have student read story. • Re-teach difficult words using "good-bye" list. • Review finger placement and tracking for sentence reading. • Have adult model reading story; have student read story until firm. • Use paired reading. • Use "cold timing" and "hot timing" to improve fluency. • Develop tape of story read by good reader; have student listen to tape and whisper read.	• Provide word flash cards for students to take home for additional practice. • Have an adult model reading story; have students listen and track during story reading; have students read story; have an adult review difficult words following story reading. • Have students read story to a pet, stuffed animal, or sibling for extra practice.
At Mastery	• See guidelines for students who read within error and time limit for Lesson 15 on page 85 in *Presentation Book A*. • Partner with "approaching mastery" or ELL student and model reading story; have student read story. • Have student assist "approaching mastery" or ELL student with "cold and hot timings" and repeated readings. • Have student tape him or herself reading story as model for "approaching mastery" or ELL student. • Direct student to reading and writing center in classroom to reinforce literacy and writing skills.	

B4

Test	Tips for Teachers	Home Connections
ELL	• See "Tips for Teachers" for "approaching mastery" and "at mastery" students. • Describe and model mouth formations for difficult sounds and words, then guide students while practicing with mirror. • Use sentence strips to practice reading sentences in story. • Show realia or other visuals of objects and concepts. • Use role-play to act out how characters must have felt. • Use primary language equivalents when available and then ask students to say words and sentences in English.	• See "Home Connections" for "approaching mastery" and "at mastery" students. • Provide audiotape to use with sentence strips and word flash cards for additional practice; encourage students to practice with mirror at home, as needed. • Provide audiotape of story; have students listen and track during story reading; then students read aloud with tape while tracking; then students read aloud and track independently; have an adult review difficult words following independent story reading. • Encourage an adult to help students identify realia and other visuals illustrating meaning of sentences in story. • Encourage an adult to help students practice using primary language equivalents and English words when possible.
Fluency Checkout (Lesson 20) **Approaching Mastery**	• See guidelines for students who do not read within error or time limit for Lesson 20 on page 110 in *Presentation Book A*. • Partner with "at mastery" student and have him or her model reading story; have student read story. • Re-teach difficult words using "good-bye" list. • Review finger placement and tracking for sentence reading. • Have adult model reading story; have student read story until firm. • Use paired reading. • Use "cold timing" and "hot timing" to improve fluency. • Develop tape of story read by good reader; have student listen to tape and whisper read.	• Provide word flash cards for students to take home for additional practice. • Have an adult model reading story; have students listen and track during story reading; have students read story; have an adult review difficult words following story reading. • Have students read story to a pet, stuffed animal, or sibling for extra practice.
At Mastery	• See guidelines for students who read within error and time limit for Lesson 20 on page 110 in *Presentation Book A*. • Partner with "approaching mastery" or ELL student and model reading story; have student read story. • Have student assist "approaching mastery" or ELL student with "cold and hot timings" and repeated readings. • Have student tape him or herself reading story as model for "approaching mastery" or ELL student. • Direct student to reading and writing center in classroom to reinforce literacy and writing skills.	

B5

Test	Tips for Teachers	Home Connections
ELL	• See "Tips for Teachers" for "approaching mastery" and "at mastery" students. • Describe and model mouth formations for difficult sounds and words, then guide students while practicing with mirror. • Use sentence strips to practice reading sentences in story. • Show realia or other visuals of objects and concepts. • Use primary language equivalents when available and then ask students to say words and sentences in English.	• See "Home Connections" for "approaching mastery" and "at mastery" students. • Provide audiotape to use with sentence strips and word flash cards for additional practice; encourage students to practice with mirror at home, as needed. • Provide audiotape of story; have students listen and track during story reading; then students read aloud with tape while tracking; then students read aloud and track independently; have an adult review difficult words following independent story reading. • Encourage an adult to help students identify realia and other visuals illustrating meaning of sentences in story. • Encourage an adult to help students practice using primary language equivalents and English words when possible.
Test 2 (Lesson 20) **Lesson 20 Assessment** **Approaching Mastery**	• See guidelines noted on Group Summary Chart (see Appendix H of *Teacher's Guide*) and Test Summary Sheet (see Appendix I of *Reading Teacher's Guide*) for students who do not meet passing criterion. • See test remedies noted on pages 69-72 of *Teacher's Guide* as well as Test 2 Firming Table noted on page 111 of *Presentation Book A*. • Partner with "at mastery" student and review previous lessons in Reading *Textbook A*. • Implement note-taking study strategy using 2-column note-taking method; review notes before test. • Write lesson summaries on index cards as study strategy and review before test. • Review key vocabulary words/terms until firm; write vocabulary words and their definitions on index cards. • For **Lesson 20 Assessment,** review assessment story and comprehension questions.	• Encourage students to reread previous lessons at home, particularly before the test; provide another text to be kept at home for this purpose. • Have an adult "quiz" students from notes or index cards before test. • Provide vocabulary flash cards for students to take home for additional practice.
At Mastery	• See guidelines noted on Group Summary Chart (see Appendix H of *Teacher's Guide*) and Test Summary Sheet (see Appendix I of *Teacher's Guide*) for students who meet passing criterion. • Have student "be the teacher": Partner with "approaching mastery" or ELL student and review previous lessons in Reading *Textbook A*. • Have student assist "approaching mastery" or ELL student with note-taking and index card study strategies. • Direct student to reading and writing center in classroom to reinforce literacy and writing skills.	

Test	Tips for Teachers	Home Connections
ELL	• See "Tips for Teachers" for "approaching mastery" and "at mastery" students. • Explain key terms in rules by using realia or other visuals to illustrate examples and non-examples. • Explain key terms in vocabulary sentences by using realia, other visuals, pantomime, or a quick sketch (e.g., draw a quick sketch on the board of a rectangle with two hunters, one at each end of the rectangle, to show "opposite ends"). • Use web diagram to group facts about key concept. • When writing vocabulary words and definitions on index cards include primary language equivalents when available. • Show related videos with captioning to help students associate printed text to spoken word.	• See "Home Connections" for "approaching mastery" and "at mastery" students. • Have an adult help students review vocabulary flash cards including primary language equivalents. • Encourage students to study web about key concept. • Encourage an adult to turn on television captioning at home.
Test **Fluency Checkout** (Lesson 25) **Approaching Mastery**	• See guidelines for students who do not read within error or time limit for Lesson 25 on page 140 in *Presentation Book A*. • Partner with "at mastery" student and have him or her model reading story; have student read story. • Re-teach difficult words using "good-bye" list. • Review finger placement and tracking for sentence reading. • Have adult model reading story; have student read story until firm. • Use paired reading. • Use "cold timing" and "hot timing" to improve fluency. • Develop tape of story read by good reader; have student listen to tape and whisper read.	• Provide word flash cards for students to take home for additional practice. • Have an adult model reading story; have students listen and track during story reading; have students read story; have an adult review difficult words following story reading. • Have students read story to a pet, stuffed animal, or sibling for extra practice.
At Mastery	• See guidelines for students who read within error and time limit for Lesson 25 on page 140 in *Presentation Book A*. • Partner with "approaching mastery" or ELL student and model reading story; have student read story. • Have student assist "approaching mastery" or ELL student with "cold and hot timings" and repeated readings. • Have student tape him or herself reading story as model for "approaching mastery" or ELL student. • Direct student to reading and writing center in classroom to reinforce literacy and writing skills.	

B7

Test	Tips for Teachers	Home Connections
ELL **Test**	• See "Tips for Teachers" for "approaching mastery" and "at mastery" students. • Describe and model mouth formations for difficult sounds and words, then guide students while practicing with mirror. • Use sentence strips to practice reading sentences in story. • Show realia or other visuals of objects and concepts. • Use primary language equivalents when available and then ask students to say words and sentences in English.	• See "Home Connections" for "approaching mastery" and "at mastery" students. • Provide audiotape to use with sentence strips and word flash cards for additional practice; encourage students to practice with mirror at home, as needed. • Provide audiotape of story; have students listen and track during story reading; then students read aloud with tape while tracking; then students read aloud and track independently; have an adult review difficult words following independent story reading. • Encourage an adult to help students identify realia and other visuals illustrating meaning of sentences in story. • Encourage an adult to help students practice using primary language equivalents and English words when possible.
Fluency Checkout (Lesson 30) **Approaching Mastery**	• See guidelines for students who do not read within error or time limit for Lesson 30 on page 164 in *Presentation Book A*. • Partner with "at mastery" student and have him or her model reading story; have student read story. • Re-teach difficult words using "good-bye" list. • Review finger placement and tracking for sentence reading. • Have adult model reading story; have student read story until firm. • Use paired reading. • Use "cold timing" and "hot timing" to improve fluency. • Develop tape of story read by good reader; have student listen to tape and whisper read.	• Provide word flash cards for students to take home for additional practice. • Have an adult model reading story; have students listen and track during story reading; have students read story; have an adult review difficult words following story reading. • Have students read story to a pet, stuffed animal, or sibling for extra practice.
At Mastery	• See guidelines for students who read within error and time limit for Lesson 30 on page 164 in *Presentation Book A*. • Partner with "approaching mastery" or ELL student and model reading story; have student read story. • Have student assist "approaching mastery" or ELL student with "cold and hot timings" and repeated readings. • Have student tape him or herself reading story as model for "approaching mastery" or ELL student. • Direct student to reading and writing center in classroom to reinforce literacy and writing skills.	

Test	Tips for Teachers	Home Connections
ELL	• See "Tips for Teachers" for "approaching mastery" and "at mastery" students. • Describe and model mouth formations for difficult sounds and words, then guide students while practicing with mirror. • Use sentence strips to practice reading sentences in story. • Show realia or other visuals of objects and concepts. • Use primary language equivalents when available and then ask students to say words and sentences in English.	• See "Home Connections" for "approaching mastery" and "at mastery" students. • Provide audiotape to use with sentence strips and word flash cards for additional practice; encourage students to practice with mirror at home, as needed. • Provide audiotape of story; have students listen and track during story reading; then students read aloud with tape while tracking; then students read aloud and track independently; have an adult review difficult words following independent story reading. • Encourage an adult to help students identify realia and other visuals illustrating meaning of sentences in story. • Encourage an adult to help students practice using primary language equivalents and English words when possible.
Test 3 (Lesson 30) **Approaching Mastery**	• See guidelines noted on Group Summary Chart (see Appendix H of *Teacher's Guide*) and Test Summary Sheet (see Appendix I of *Teacher's Guide*) for students who do not meet passing criterion. • See test remedies noted on pages 69–72 of *Teacher's Guide* as well as Test 3 Firming Table noted on page 164 of *Presentation Book A*. • Partner with "at mastery" student and review previous lessons in Reading *Textbook A*. • Implement note-taking study strategy using 2-column note-taking method; review notes before test. • Write lesson summaries on index cards as study strategy and review before test. • Review key vocabulary words/terms until firm; write vocabulary words and their definitions on index cards.	• Encourage students to reread previous lessons at home, particularly before the test; provide another text to be kept at home for this purpose. • Have an adult "quiz" students from notes or index cards before test. • Provide vocabulary flash cards for students to take home for additional practice.
At Mastery	• See guidelines noted on Group Summary Chart (see Appendix H of *Teacher's Guide*) and Test Summary Sheet (see Appendix I of *Teacher's Guide*) for students who meet passing criterion. • Have student "be the teacher": Partner with "approaching mastery" or ELL student and review previous lessons in Reading *Textbook A*. • Have student assist "approaching mastery" or ELL student with note-taking and index card study strategies. • Direct student to reading and writing center in classroom to reinforce literacy and writing skills.	

Test	Tips for Teachers	Home Connections
ELL	• See "Tips for Teachers" for "approaching mastery" and "at mastery" students. • Explain key terms in rules by using realia or other visuals to illustrate examples and non-examples. • Explain key terms in vocabulary sentences by using realia, other visuals, pantomime, or a quick sketch. • When writing vocabulary words and definitions on index cards, include primary language equivalents when available. • Use web diagram to group facts about key concept. • Model rereading strategy to improve comprehension by using think-aloud (e.g., "I'm looking back at the passage called, "Facts About Miles." I'm seeing that a mile is a little more than five thousand feet. That will help me the next time I read a map."). • Show related videos with captioning to help students associate printed text to spoken word.	• See "Home Connections" for "approaching mastery" and "at mastery" students. • Have an adult help students review vocabulary flash cards including primary language equivalents. • Encourage students to study web about key concept. • Encourage an adult to turn on television captioning at home.

Test

Test	Tips for Teachers	Home Connections
Fluency Checkout (Lesson 35) **Approaching Mastery**	• See guidelines for students who do not read within error or time limit for Lesson 35 on pages 190 and 191 in *Presentation Book A*. • Partner with "at mastery" student and have him or her model reading story; have student read story. • Re-teach difficult words using "good-bye" list. • Review finger placement and tracking for sentence reading. • Have adult model reading story; have student read story until firm. • Use paired reading. • Use "cold timing" and "hot timing" to improve fluency. • Develop tape of story read by good reader; have student listen to tape and whisper read.	• Provide word flash cards for students to take home for additional practice. • Have an adult model reading story; have students listen and track during story reading; have students read story; have an adult review difficult words following story reading. • Have students read story to a pet, stuffed animal, or sibling for extra practice.
At Mastery	• See guidelines for students who read within error and time limit for Lesson 35 on pages 190 and 191 in *Presentation Book A*. • Partner with "approaching mastery" or ELL student and model reading story; have student read story. • Have student assist "approaching mastery" or ELL student with "cold and hot timings" and repeated readings. • Have student tape him or herself reading story as model for "approaching mastery" or ELL student. • Direct student to reading and writing center in classroom to reinforce literacy and writing skills.	

Test	Tips for Teachers	Home Connections
ELL / **Test**	• See "Tips for Teachers" for "approaching mastery" and "at mastery" students. • Describe and model mouth formations for difficult sounds and words, then guide students while practicing with mirror. • Use sentence strips to practice reading sentences in story. • Show realia or other visuals of objects and concepts. • Use primary language equivalents when available and then ask students to say words and sentences in English.	• See "Home Connections" for "approaching mastery" and "at mastery" students. • Provide audiotape to use with sentence strips and word flash cards for additional practice; encourage students to practice with mirror at home, as needed. • Provide audiotape of story; have students listen and track during story reading; then students read aloud with tape while tracking; then students read aloud and track independently; have an adult review difficult words following independent story reading. • Encourage an adult to help students identify realia and other visuals illustrating meaning of sentences in story. • Encourage an adult to help students practice using primary language equivalents and English words when possible.
Fluency Checkout (Lesson 40) **Approaching Mastery**	• See guidelines for students who do not read within error or time limit for Lesson 40 on pages 213 and 214 in *Presentation Book A*. • Partner with "at mastery" student and have him or her model reading story; have student read story. • Re-teach difficult words using "good-bye" list. • Review finger placement and tracking for sentence reading. • Have adult model reading story; have student read story until firm. • Use paired reading. • Use "cold timing" and "hot timing" to improve fluency. • Develop tape of story read by good reader; have student listen to tape and whisper read.	• Provide word flash cards for students to take home for additional practice. • Have an adult model reading story; have students listen and track during story reading; have students read story; have an adult review difficult words following story reading. • Have students read story to a pet, stuffed animal, or sibling for extra practice.
At Mastery	• See guidelines for students who read within error and time limit for Lesson 40 on pages 213 and 214 in *Presentation Book A*. • Partner with "approaching mastery" or ELL student and model reading story; have student read story. • Have student assist "approaching mastery" or ELL student with "cold and hot timings" and repeated readings. • Have student tape him or herself reading story as model for "approaching mastery" or ELL student. • Direct student to reading and writing center in classroom to reinforce literacy and writing skills.	

B11

Test	Tips for Teachers	Home Connections
ELL **Test**	• See "Tips for Teachers" for "approaching mastery" and "at mastery" students. • Describe and model mouth formations for difficult sounds and words, then guide students while practicing with mirror. • Use sentence strips to practice reading sentences in story. • Show students how to recognize punctuation (e.g., commas) when reading with prosody using a model think-aloud (e.g., I see the first sentence has a comma in it; I know that I need to pause after the comma, so I can understand the sentence better). • Show realia or other visuals of objects and concepts. • Use primary language equivalents when available and then ask students to say words and sentences in English.	• See "Home Connections" for "approaching mastery" and "at mastery" students. • Provide audiotape to use with sentence strips and word flash cards for additional practice; encourage students to practice with mirror at home, as needed. • Provide audiotape of story; have students listen and track during story reading; then students read aloud with tape while tracking; then students read aloud and track independently; have an adult review difficult words following independent story reading. • Encourage an adult to help students identify realia and other visuals illustrating meaning of sentences in story. • Encourage an adult to help students practice using primary language equivalents and English words when possible.
Test 4 (Lesson 40) **Lesson 40 Assessment** **Approaching Mastery**	• See guidelines noted on Group Summary Chart (see Appendix H of *Teacher's Guide*) and Test Summary Sheet (see Appendix I of *Teacher's Guide*) for students who do not meet passing criterion. • See test remedies noted on pages 69–72 of *Teacher's Guide* as well as Test 4 Firming Table noted on page 214 of *Presentation Book A*. • Partner with "at mastery" student and review previous lessons in Reading *Textbook A*. • Implement note-taking study strategy using 2-column note-taking method; review notes before test. • Write lesson summaries on index cards as study strategy and review before test. • Review key vocabulary words/terms until firm; write vocabulary words and their definitions on index cards. • For **Lesson 40 Assessment,** review assessment story and comprehension questions.	• Encourage students to reread previous lessons at home, particularly before the test; provide another text to be kept at home for this purpose. • Have an adult "quiz" students from notes or index cards before test. • Provide vocabulary flash cards for students to take home for additional practice.
At Mastery	• See guidelines noted on Group Summary Chart (see Appendix H of *Teacher's Guide*) and Test Summary Sheet (see Appendix I of *Teacher's Guide*) for students who meet passing criterion. • Have student "be the teacher": Partner with "approaching mastery" or ELL student and review previous lessons in Reading *Textbook A*. • Have student assist "approaching mastery" or ELL student with note-taking and index card study strategies. • Direct student to reading and writing center in classroom to reinforce literacy and writing skills.	

Test	Tips for Teachers	Home Connections
ELL	• See "Tips for Teachers" for "approaching mastery" and "at mastery" students. • Explain key terms in rules by using realia or other visuals to illustrate examples and non-examples. • Explain key terms in vocabulary sentences by using realia, other visuals, pantomime, or a quick sketch. • When writing vocabulary words and definitions on index cards, include primary language equivalents when available. • Use web diagram to group facts about key concept. • Use rereading strategy to improve comprehension. • Show related videos with captioning to help students associate printed text to spoken word.	• See "Home Connections" for "approaching mastery" and "at mastery" students. • Have an adult help students review vocabulary flash cards including primary language equivalents. • Encourage students to study web about key concept. • Encourage an adult to turn on television captioning at home.
Test **Fluency Checkout** (Lesson 45) **Approaching Mastery**	• See guidelines for students who do not read within error or time limit for Lesson 45 on pages 241 and 242 in *Presentation Book A*. • Partner with "at mastery" student and have him or her model reading story; have student read story. • Re-teach difficult words using "good-bye" list. • Review finger placement and tracking for sentence reading. • Have adult model reading story; have student read story until firm. • Use paired reading. • Use "cold timing" and "hot timing" to improve fluency. • Develop tape of story read by good reader; have student listen to tape and whisper read.	• Provide word flash cards for students to take home for additional practice. • Have an adult model reading story; have students listen and track during story reading; have students read story; have an adult review difficult words following story reading. • Have students read story to a pet, stuffed animal, or sibling for extra practice.
At Mastery	• See guidelines for students who read within error and time limit for Lesson 45 on pages 241 and 242 in *Presentation Book A*. • Partner with "approaching mastery" or ELL student and model reading story; have student read story. • Have student assist "approaching mastery" or ELL student with "cold and hot timings" and repeated readings. • Have student tape him or herself reading story as model for "approaching mastery" or ELL student. • Direct student to reading and writing center in classroom to reinforce literacy and writing skills.	

B13

Test	Tips for Teachers	Home Connections
ELL	• See "Tips for Teachers" for "approaching mastery" and "at mastery" students. • Describe and model mouth formations for difficult sounds and words, then guide students while practicing with mirror. • Use sentence strips to practice reading sentences in story. • Show students how to recognize punctuation when reading with prosody. • Show realia or other visuals of objects and concepts. • Use primary language equivalents when available and then ask students to say words and sentences in English.	• See "Home Connections" for "approaching mastery" and "at mastery" students. • Provide audiotape to use with sentence strips and word flash cards for additional practice; encourage students to practice with mirror at home, as needed. • Provide audiotape of story; have students listen and track during story reading; then students read aloud with tape while tracking; then students read aloud and track independently; have an adult review difficult words following independent story reading. • Encourage an adult to help students identify realia and other visuals illustrating meaning of sentences in story. • Encourage an adult to help students practice using primary language equivalents and English words when possible.
Fluency Checkout (Lesson 50) **Approaching Mastery**	• See guidelines for students who do not read within error or time limit for Lesson 50 on pages 264 and 265 in *Presentation Book A.* • Partner with "at mastery" student and have him or her model reading story; have student read story. • Re-teach difficult words using "good-bye" list. • Review finger placement and tracking for sentence reading. • Have adult model reading story; have student read story until firm. • Use paired reading. • Use "cold timing" and "hot timing" to improve fluency. • Develop tape of story read by good reader; have student listen to tape and whisper read.	• Provide word flash cards for students to take home for additional practice. • Have an adult model reading story; have students listen and track during story reading; have students read story; have an adult review difficult words following story reading. • Have students read story to a pet, stuffed animal, or sibling for extra practice.
At Mastery	• See guidelines for students who read within error and time limit for Lesson 50 on pages 264 and 265 in *Presentation Book A.* • Partner with "approaching mastery" or ELL student and model reading story; have student read story. • Have student assist "approaching mastery" or ELL student with "cold and hot timings" and repeated readings. • Have student tape him or herself reading story as model for "approaching mastery" or ELL student. • Direct student to reading and writing center in classroom to reinforce literacy and writing skills.	

Test	Tips for Teachers	Home Connections
ELL	• See "Tips for Teachers" for "approaching mastery" and "at mastery" students. • Describe and model mouth formations for difficult sounds and words, then guide students while practicing with mirror. • Use sentence strips to practice reading sentences in story. • Show students how to recognize punctuation when reading with prosody. • Show realia or other visuals of objects and concepts. • Use primary language equivalents when available and then ask students to say words and sentences in English.	• See "Home Connections" for "approaching mastery" and "at mastery" students. • Provide audiotape to use with sentence strips and word flash cards for additional practice; encourage students to practice with mirror at home, as needed. • Provide audiotape of story; have students listen and track during story reading; then students read aloud with tape while tracking; then students read aloud and track independently; have an adult review difficult words following independent story reading. • Encourage an adult to help students identify realia and other visuals illustrating meaning of sentences in story. • Encourage an adult to help students practice using primary language equivalents and English words when possible.
Test 5 (Lesson 50) **Approaching Mastery**	• See guidelines noted on Group Summary Chart (see Appendix H of *Teacher's Guide*) and Test Summary Sheet (see Appendix I of *Teacher's Guide*) for students who do not meet passing criterion. • See test remedies noted on pages 69-72 of *Teacher's Guide* as well as Test 5 Firming Table noted on page 265 of *Presentation Book A*. • Partner with "at mastery" student and review previous lessons in Reading *Textbook A*. • Implement note-taking study strategy using 2-column note-taking method; review notes before test. • Write lesson summaries on index cards as study strategy and review before test. • Review key vocabulary words/terms until firm; write vocabulary words and their definitions on index cards.	• Encourage students to reread previous lessons at home, particularly before the test; provide another text to be kept at home for this purpose. • Have an adult "quiz" students from notes or index cards before test. • Provide vocabulary flash cards for students to take home for additional practice.
At Mastery	• See guidelines noted on Group Summary Chart (see Appendix H of *Teacher's Guide*) and Test Summary Sheet (see Appendix I of *Teacher's Guide*) for students who meet passing criterion. • Have student "be the teacher": Partner with "approaching mastery" or ELL student and review previous lessons in Reading *Textbook A*. • Have student assist "approaching mastery" or ELL student with note-taking and index card study strategies. • Direct student to reading and writing center in classroom to reinforce literacy and writing skills.	

B15

Test	Tips for Teachers	Home Connections
ELL	• See "Tips for Teachers" for "approaching mastery" and "at mastery" students. • Explain key terms in rules by using realia or other visuals to illustrate examples and non-examples. • Explain key terms in vocabulary sentences by using realia, other visuals, pantomime, or a quick sketch. • When writing vocabulary words and definitions on index cards, include primary language equivalents when available. • Use web diagram to group facts about key concept. • Implement compare-contrast diagram to illustrate similarities and differences (e.g., cold-blooded animals compared to warm-blooded animals; examples of similarities-all are living things, all grow, all need water, all make babies; examples of differences-body temperature of a cold-blooded animal changes, body temperature of a warm-blooded animal stays the same). • Use rereading strategy to improve comprehension. • Show related videos with captioning to help students associate printed text to spoken word.	• See "Home Connections" for "approaching mastery" and "at mastery" students. • Have an adult help students review vocabulary flash cards including primary language equivalents. • Encourage students to study web about key concept. • Encourage an adult to turn on captioning at home.

Test

Test	Tips for Teachers	Home Connections
Fluency Checkout (Lesson 55) **Approaching Mastery**	• See guidelines for students who do not read within error or time limit for Lesson 55 on page 30 in *Presentation Book B*. • Partner with "at mastery" student and have him or her model reading story; have student read story. • Re-teach difficult words using "good-bye" list. • Review finger placement and tracking for sentence reading. • Have adult model reading story; have student read story until firm. • Use paired reading. • Use "cold timing" and "hot timing" to improve fluency. • Develop tape of story read by good reader; have student listen to tape and whisper read.	• Provide word flash cards for students to take home for additional practice. • Have an adult model reading story; have students listen and track during story reading; have students read story; have an adult review difficult words following story reading. • Have students read story to a pet, stuffed animal, or sibling for extra practice.
At Mastery	• See guidelines for students who read within error and time limit for Lesson 55 on page 30 in *Presentation Book B*. • Partner with "approaching mastery" or ELL student and model reading story; have student read story. • Have student assist "approaching mastery" or ELL student with "cold and hot timings" and repeated readings. • Have student tape him or herself reading story as model for "approaching mastery" or ELL student. • Direct student to reading and writing center in classroom to reinforce literacy and writing skills.	

Test	Tips for Teachers	Home Connections
ELL	• See "Tips for Teachers" for "approaching mastery" and "at mastery" students. • Describe and model mouth formations for difficult sounds and words, then guide students while practicing with mirror. • Use sentence strips to practice reading sentences in story. • Show students how to recognize punctuation when reading with prosody. • Show realia or other visuals of objects and concepts. • Use primary language equivalents when available and then ask students to say words and sentences in English.	• See "Home Connections" for "approaching mastery" and "at mastery" students. • Provide audiotape to use with sentence strips and word flash cards for additional practice; encourage students to practice with mirror at home, as needed. • Provide audiotape of story; have students listen and track during story reading; then students read aloud with tape while tracking; then students read aloud and track independently; have an adult review difficult words following independent story reading. • Encourage an adult to help students identify realia and other visuals illustrating meaning of sentences in story. • Encourage an adult to help students practice using primary language equivalents and English words when possible.
Fluency Checkout (Lesson 60) **Approaching Mastery**	• See guidelines for students who do not read within error or time limit for Lesson 60 on page 55 in *Presentation Book B*. • Partner with "at mastery" student and have him or her model reading story; have student read story. • Re-teach difficult words using "good-bye" list. • Review finger placement and tracking for sentence reading. • Have adult model reading story; have student read story until firm. • Use paired reading. • Use "cold timing" and "hot timing" to improve fluency. • Develop tape of story read by good reader; have student listen to tape and whisper read.	• Provide word flash cards for students to take home for additional practice. • Have an adult model reading story; have students listen and track during story reading; have students read story; have an adult review difficult words following story reading. • Have students read story to a pet, stuffed animal, or sibling for extra practice.
At Mastery	• See guidelines for students who read within error and time limit for Lesson 60 on page 55 in *Presentation Book B*. • Partner with "approaching mastery" or ELL student and model reading story; have student read story. • Have student assist "approaching mastery" or ELL student with "cold and hot timings" and repeated readings. • Have student tape him or herself reading story as model for "approaching mastery" or ELL student. • Direct student to reading and writing center in classroom to reinforce literacy and writing skills.	

B17

Test	Tips for Teachers	Home Connections
ELL	• See "Tips for Teachers" for "approaching mastery" and "at mastery" students. • Describe and model mouth formations for difficult sounds and words, then guide students while practicing with mirror. • Use sentence strips to practice reading sentences in story. • Show students how to recognize punctuation when reading with prosody. • Show realia or other visuals of objects and concepts. • Use primary language equivalents when available and then ask students to say words and sentences in English.	• See "Home Connections" for "approaching mastery" and "at mastery" students. • Provide audiotape to use with sentence strips and word flash cards for additional practice; encourage students to practice with mirror at home, as needed. • Provide audiotape of story; have students listen and track during story reading; then students read aloud with tape while tracking; then students read aloud and track independently; have an adult review difficult words following independent story reading. • Encourage an adult to help students identify realia and other visuals illustrating meaning of sentences in story. • Encourage an adult to help students practice using primary language equivalents and English words when possible.

Test

Test	Tips for Teachers	Home Connections
Test 6 (Lesson 60) **Lesson 60 Assessment** **Approaching Mastery**	• See guidelines noted on Group Summary Chart (see Appendix H of *Teacher's Guide*) and Test Summary Sheet (see Appendix I of *Teacher's Guide*) for students who do not meet passing criterion. • See test remedies noted on pages 69-72 of *Teacher's Guide* as well as Test 6 Firming Table noted on page 56 of *Presentation Book B*. • Partner with "at mastery" student and review previous lessons in Reading *Textbook B*. • Implement note-taking study strategy using 2-column note-taking method; review notes before test. • Write lesson summaries on index cards as study strategy and review before test. • Review key vocabulary words/terms until firm; write vocabulary words and their definitions on index cards. • For **Lesson 60 Assessment,** review assessment story and comprehension questions. • Review country locations and directions until firm.	• Encourage students to reread previous lessons at home, particularly before the test; provide another text to be kept at home for this purpose. • Have an adult "quiz" students from notes or index cards before test. • Provide vocabulary flash cards for students to take home for additional practice.
At Mastery	• See guidelines noted on Group Summary Chart (see Appendix H of *Teacher's Guide*) and Test Summary Sheet (see Appendix I of *Teacher's Guide*) for students who meet passing criterion. • Have student "be the teacher": Partner with "approaching mastery" or ELL student and review previous lessons in Reading *Textbook B*. • Have student assist "approaching mastery" or ELL student with note-taking and index card study strategies. • Direct student to reading and writing center in classroom to reinforce literacy and writing skills.	

B18

Test	Tips for Teachers	Home Connections
ELL	• See "Tips for Teachers" for "approaching mastery" and "at mastery" students. • Explain key terms in rules by using realia or other visuals to illustrate examples and non-examples. • Explain key terms in vocabulary sentences by using realia, other visuals, pantomime, or a quick sketch. • When writing vocabulary words and definitions on index cards, include primary language equivalents when available. • Use web diagram to group facts about key concept. • Use compare-contrast diagram to illustrate similarities and differences. • Use rereading strategy to improve comprehension. • Show related videos with captioning to help students associate printed text to spoken word.	• See "Home Connections" for "approaching mastery" and "at mastery" students. • Have an adult help students review vocabulary flash cards including primary language equivalents. • Encourage students to study web about key concept. • Encourage an adult to turn on television captioning at home.

Test

Test	Tips for Teachers	Home Connections
Fluency Checkout (Lesson 65) **Approaching Mastery**	• See guidelines for students who do not read within error or time limit for Lesson 65 on page 88 in *Presentation Book B*. • Partner with "at mastery" student and have him or her model reading story; have student read story. • Re-teach difficult words using "good-bye" list. • Review finger placement and tracking for sentence reading. • Have adult model reading story; have student read story until firm. • Use paired reading. • Use "cold timing" and "hot timing" to improve fluency. • Develop tape of story read by good reader; have student listen to tape and whisper read.	• Provide word flash cards for students to take home for additional practice. • Have an adult model reading story; have students listen and track during story reading; have students read story; have an adult review difficult words following story reading. • Have students read story to a pet, stuffed animal, or sibling for extra practice.
At Mastery	• See guidelines for students who read within error and time limit for Lesson 65 on page 88 in *Presentation Book B*. • Partner with "approaching mastery" or ELL student and model reading story; have student read story. • Have student assist "approaching mastery" or ELL student with "cold and hot timings" and repeated readings. • Have student tape him or herself reading story as model for "approaching mastery" or ELL student. • Direct student to reading and writing center in classroom to reinforce literacy and writing skills.	

B19

Test	Tips for Teachers	Home Connections
ELL **Test**	• See "Tips for Teachers" for "approaching mastery" and "at mastery" students. • Describe and model mouth formations for difficult sounds and words, then guide students while practicing with mirror. • Use sentence strips to practice reading sentences in story. • Show students how to recognize punctuation when reading with prosody. • Show realia or other visuals of objects and concepts. • Use primary language equivalents when available and then ask students to say words and sentences in English.	• See "Home Connections" for "approaching mastery" and "at mastery" students. • Provide audiotape to use with sentence strips and word flash cards for additional practice; encourage students to practice with mirror at home, as needed. • Provide audiotape of story; have students listen and track during story reading; then students read aloud with tape while tracking; then students read aloud and track independently; have an adult review difficult words following independent story reading. • Encourage an adult to help students identify realia and other visuals illustrating meaning of sentences in story. • Encourage an adult to help students practice using primary language equivalents and English words when possible.
Fluency Checkout (Lesson 70) **Approaching Mastery**	• See guidelines for students who do not read within error or time limit for Lesson 70 on pages 113 and 114 in *Presentation Book B*. • Partner with "at mastery" student and have him or her model reading story; have student read story. • Re-teach difficult words using "good-bye" list. • Review finger placement and tracking for sentence reading. • Have adult model reading story; have student read story until firm. • Use paired reading. • Use "cold timing" and "hot timing" to improve fluency. • Develop tape of story read by good reader; have student listen to tape and whisper read.	• Provide word flash cards for students to take home for additional practice. • Have an adult model reading story; have students listen and track during story reading; have students read story; have an adult review difficult words following story reading. • Have students read story to a pet, stuffed animal, or sibling for extra practice.
At Mastery	• See guidelines for students who read within error and time limit for Lesson 70 on pages 113 and 114 in *Presentation Book B*. • Partner with "approaching mastery" or ELL student and model reading story; have student read story. • Have student assist "approaching mastery" or ELL student with "cold and hot timings" and repeated readings. • Have student tape him or herself reading story as model for "approaching mastery" or ELL student. • Direct student to reading and writing center in classroom to reinforce literacy and writing skills.	

Test	Tips for Teachers	Home Connections
ELL **Test**	• See "Tips for Teachers" for "approaching mastery" and "at mastery" students. • Describe and model mouth formations for difficult sounds and words, then guide students while practicing with mirror. • Use sentence strips to practice reading sentences in story. • Show students how to recognize punctuation when reading with prosody. • Show realia or other visuals of objects and concepts. • Use primary language equivalents when available and then ask students to say words and sentences in English.	• See "Home Connections" for "approaching mastery" and "at mastery" students. • Provide audiotape to use with sentence strips and word flash cards for additional practice; encourage students to practice with mirror at home, as needed. • Provide audiotape of story; have students listen and track during story reading; then students read aloud with tape while tracking; then students read aloud and track independently; have an adult review difficult words following independent story reading. • Encourage an adult to help students identify realia and other visuals illustrating meaning of sentences in story. • Encourage an adult to help students practice using primary language equivalents and English words when possible.
Test 7 (Lesson 70) **Approaching Mastery**	• See guidelines noted on Group Summary Chart (see Appendix H of *Teacher's Guide*) and Test Summary Sheet (see Appendix I of *Teacher's Guide*) for students who do not meet passing criterion. • See test remedies noted on pages 69–72 of *Teacher's Guide* as well as Test 7 Firming Table noted on page 114 of *Presentation Book B*. • Partner with "at mastery" student and review previous lessons in Reading *Textbook B*. • Implement note-taking study strategy using 2-column note-taking method; review notes before test. • Write lesson summaries on index cards as study strategy and review before test. • Review key vocabulary words/terms until firm; write vocabulary words and their definitions on index cards. • Play "Jeopardy-like" game before taking test; student provides answers to questions posed by adult or "at mastery" student.	• Encourage students to reread previous lessons at home, particularly before the test; provide another text to be kept at home for this purpose. • Have an adult "quiz" students from notes or index cards before test. • Provide vocabulary flash cards for students to take home for additional practice.
At Mastery	• See guidelines noted on Group Summary Chart (see Appendix H of *Teacher's Guide*) and Test Summary Sheet (see Appendix I of *Teacher's Guide*) for students who meet passing criterion. • Have student "be the teacher": Partner with "approaching mastery" or ELL student and review previous lessons in Reading *Textbook B*. • Have student assist "approaching mastery" or ELL student with note-taking and index card study strategies. • Have student assist with conducting "Jeopardy-like" game. • Direct student to reading and writing center in classroom to reinforce literacy and writing skills.	

B21

Test	Tips for Teachers	Home Connections
ELL	• See "Tips for Teachers" for "approaching mastery" and "at mastery" students. • Explain key terms in rules by using realia or other visuals to illustrate examples and non-examples. • Explain key terms in vocabulary sentences by using realia, other visuals, pantomime, or a quick sketch. • Implement cognate word wall and cognate journal by introducing the term "cognates" as "words in two languages that share a similar meaning, spelling, and pronunciation." • When writing vocabulary words and definitions on index cards, include primary language equivalents when available. • Use web diagram to group facts about key concept. • Use compare-contrast diagram to illustrate similarities and differences. • Use rereading strategy to improve comprehension. • Show related videos with captioning to help students associate printed text to spoken word.	• See "Home Connections" for "approaching mastery" and "at mastery" students. • Encourage students to take home cognate journal for review and encourage an adult to add to list when possible. • Have an adult help students review vocabulary flash cards including primary language equivalents. • Encourage students to study web about key concept. • Encourage an adult to turn on television captioning at home.
Fluency Checkout (Lesson 75) **Approaching Mastery**	• See guidelines for students who do not read within error or time limit for Lesson 75 on pages 142 and 143 in *Presentation Book B*. • Partner with "at mastery" student and have him or her model reading story; have student read story. • Re-teach difficult words using "good-bye" list. • Review finger placement and tracking for sentence reading. • Have adult model reading story; have student read story until firm. • Use paired reading. • Use "cold timing" and "hot timing" to improve fluency. • Develop tape of story read by good reader; have student listen to tape and whisper read.	• Provide word flash cards for students to take home for additional practice. • Have an adult model reading story; have students listen and track during story reading; have students read story; have an adult review difficult words following story reading. • Have students read story to a pet, stuffed animal, or sibling for extra practice.
At Mastery	• See guidelines for students who read within error and time limit for Lesson 75 on pages 142 and 143 in *Presentation Book B*. • Partner with "approaching mastery" or ELL student and model reading story; have student read story. • Have student assist "approaching mastery" or ELL student with "cold and hot timings" and repeated readings. • Have student tape him or herself reading story as model for "approaching mastery" or ELL student. • Direct student to reading and writing center in classroom to reinforce literacy and writing skills.	

Test	Tips for Teachers	Home Connections
ELL	• See "Tips for Teachers" for "approaching mastery" and "at mastery" students. • Describe and model mouth formations for difficult sounds and words, then guide students while practicing with mirror. • Use sentence strips to practice reading sentences in story. • Show students how to recognize punctuation when reading with prosody. • Show realia or other visuals of objects and concepts. • Use primary language equivalents when available and then ask students to say words and sentences in English.	• See "Home Connections" for "approaching mastery" and "at mastery" students. • Provide audiotape to use with sentence strips and word flash cards for additional practice; encourage students to practice with mirror at home, as needed. • Provide audiotape of story; have students listen and track during story reading; then students read aloud with tape while tracking; then students read aloud and track independently; have an adult review difficult words following independent story reading. • Encourage an adult to help students identify realia and other visuals illustrating meaning of sentences in story. • Encourage an adult to help students practice using primary language equivalents and English words when possible.
Fluency Checkout (Lesson 80) **Approaching Mastery**	• See guidelines for students who do not read within error or time limit for Lesson 80 on pages 165 and 166 in *Presentation Book B*. • Partner with "at mastery" student and have him or her model reading story; have student read story. • Re-teach difficult words using "good-bye" list. • Review finger placement and tracking for sentence reading. • Have adult model reading story; have student read story until firm. • Use paired reading. • Use "cold timing" and "hot timing" to improve fluency. • Develop tape of story read by good reader; have student listen to tape and whisper read.	• Provide word flash cards for students to take home for additional practice. • Have an adult model reading story; have students listen and track during story reading; have students read story; have an adult review difficult words following story reading. • Have students read story to a pet, stuffed animal, or sibling for extra practice.
At Mastery	• See guidelines for students who read within error and time limit for Lesson 80 on pages 165 and 166 in *Presentation Book B*. • Partner with "approaching mastery" or ELL student and model reading story; have student read story. • Have student assist "approaching mastery" or ELL student with "cold and hot timings" and repeated readings. • Have student tape him or herself reading story as model for "approaching mastery" or ELL student. • Direct student to reading and writing center in classroom to reinforce literacy and writing skills.	

B23

Test	Tips for Teachers	Home Connections
ELL **Test**	• See "Tips for Teachers" for "approaching mastery" and "at mastery" students. • Describe and model mouth formations for difficult sounds and words, then guide students while practicing with mirror. • Use sentence strips to practice reading sentences in story. • Show students how to recognize punctuation when reading with prosody. • Show realia or other visuals of objects and concepts. • Use primary language equivalents when available and then ask students to say words and sentences in English.	• See "Home Connections" for "approaching mastery" and "at mastery" students. • Provide audiotape to use with sentence strips and word flash cards for additional practice; encourage students to practice with mirror at home, as needed. • Provide audiotape of story; have students listen and track during story reading; then students read aloud with tape while tracking; then students read aloud and track independently; have an adult review difficult words following independent story reading. • Encourage an adult to help students identify realia and other visuals illustrating meaning of sentences in story. • Encourage an adult to help students practice using primary language equivalents and English words when possible.
Test 8 (Lesson 80) **Lesson 80 Assessment** **Approaching Mastery**	• See guidelines noted on Group Summary Chart (see Appendix H of *Teacher's Guide*) and Test Summary Sheet (see Appendix I of *Teacher's Guide*) for students who do not meet passing criterion. • See test remedies noted on pages 69–72 of *Teacher's Guide* as well as Test 8 Firming Table noted on page 166 of *Presentation Book B*. • Partner with "at mastery" student and review previous lessons in Reading *Textbook B*. • Implement note-taking study strategy. • Write lesson summaries on index cards as study strategy and review before test. • Review key vocabulary words/terms until firm; write vocabulary words and their definitions on index cards. • Play "Jeopardy-like" game before taking test. • For **Lesson 80 Assessment,** review assessment story and comprehension questions. • Review timelines and sun placement in sky until firm.	• Encourage students to reread previous lessons at home, particularly before the test; provide another text to be kept at home for this purpose. • Have an adult "quiz" students from notes or index cards before test. • Provide vocabulary flash cards for students to take home for additional practice.
At Mastery	• See guidelines noted on Group Summary Chart (see Appendix H of *Teacher's Guide*) and Test Summary Sheet (see Appendix I of *Teacher's Guide*) for students who meet passing criterion. • Have student "be the teacher": Partner with "approaching mastery" or ELL student and review previous lessons in Reading *Textbook B*. • Have student assist "approaching mastery" or ELL student with note-taking and index card study strategies. • Have student assist with conducting "Jeopardy-like" game. • Direct student to reading and writing center in classroom to reinforce literacy and writing skills.	

Test	Tips for Teachers	Home Connections
ELL	• See "Tips for Teachers" for "approaching mastery" and "at mastery" students. • Explain key terms in rules by using realia or other visuals to illustrate examples and non-examples. • Explain key terms in vocabulary sentences by using realia, other visuals, pantomime, or a quick sketch. • Add to cognate word wall and cognate journal. • When writing vocabulary words and definitions on index cards, include primary language equivalents when available. • Use web diagram to group facts about key concept. • Use compare-contrast diagram to illustrate similarities and differences. • Use rereading strategy to improve comprehension. • Show related videos with captioning to help students associate printed text to spoken word.	• See "Home Connections" for "approaching mastery" and "at mastery" students. • Encourage students to take home cognate journal for review and encourage an adult to add to list when possible. • Have an adult help students review vocabulary flash cards including primary language equivalents. • Encourage students to study web about key concept. • Encourage an adult to turn on television captioning at home.

Test

Test	Tips for Teachers	Home Connections
Fluency Checkout (Lesson 85) **Approaching Mastery**	• See guidelines for students who do not read within error or time limit for Lesson 85 on page 194 in *Presentation Book B*. • Partner with "at mastery" student and have him or her model reading story; have student read story. • Re-teach difficult words using "good-bye" list. • Review finger placement and tracking for sentence reading. • Have adult model reading story; have student read story until firm. • Use paired reading. • Use "cold timing" and "hot timing" to improve fluency. • Develop tape of story read by good reader; have student listen to tape and whisper read.	• Provide word flash cards for students to take home for additional practice. • Have an adult model reading story; have students listen and track during story reading; have students read story; have an adult review difficult words following story reading. • Have students read story to a pet, stuffed animal, or sibling for extra practice.
At Mastery	• See guidelines for students who read within error and time limit for Lesson 85 on page 194 in *Presentation Book B*. • Partner with "approaching mastery" or ELL student and model reading story; have student read story. • Have student assist "approaching mastery" or ELL student with "cold and hot timings" and repeated readings. • Have student tape him or herself reading story as model for "approaching mastery" or ELL student. • Direct student to reading and writing center in classroom to reinforce literacy and writing skills.	

B25

Test	Tips for Teachers	Home Connections
ELL	• See "Tips for Teachers" for "approaching mastery" and "at mastery" students. • Describe and model mouth formations for difficult sounds and words, then guide students while practicing with mirror. • Use sentence strips to practice reading sentences in story. • Show students how to recognize punctuation when reading with prosody. • Show realia or other visuals of objects and concepts. • Use primary language equivalents when available and then ask students to say words and sentences in English.	• See "Home Connections" for "approaching mastery" and "at mastery" students. • Provide audiotape to use with sentence strips and word flash cards for additional practice; encourage students to practice with mirror at home, as needed. • Provide audiotape of story; have students listen and track during story reading; then students read aloud with tape while tracking; then students read aloud and track independently; have an adult review difficult words following independent story reading. • Encourage an adult to help students identify realia and other visuals illustrating meaning of sentences in story. • Encourage an adult to help students practice using primary language equivalents and English words when possible.

Test

Test	Tips for Teachers	Home Connections
Fluency Checkout (Lesson 90) **Approaching Mastery**	• See guidelines for students who do not read within error or time limit for Lesson 90 on pages 216 and 217 in *Presentation Book B*. • Partner with "at mastery" student and have him or her model reading story; have student read story. • Re-teach difficult words using "good-bye" list. • Review finger placement and tracking for sentence reading. • Have adult model reading story; have student read story until firm. • Use paired reading. • Use "cold timing" and "hot timing" to improve fluency. • Develop tape of story read by good reader; have student listen to tape and whisper read.	• Provide word flash cards for students to take home for additional practice. • Have an adult model reading story; have students listen and track during story reading; have students read story; have an adult review difficult words following story reading. • Have students read story to a pet, stuffed animal, or sibling for extra practice.
At Mastery	• See guidelines for students who read within error and time limit for Lesson 90 on pages 216 and 217 in *Presentation Book B*. • Partner with "approaching mastery" or ELL student and model reading story; have student read story. • Have student assist "approaching mastery" or ELL student with "cold and hot timings" and repeated readings. • Have student tape him or herself reading story as model for "approaching mastery" or ELL student. • Direct student to reading and writing center in classroom to reinforce literacy and writing skills.	

B26

Test	Tips for Teachers	Home Connections
ELL / **Test**	• See "Tips for Teachers" for "approaching mastery" and "at mastery" students. • Describe and model mouth formations for difficult sounds and words, then guide students while practicing with mirror. • Use sentence strips to practice reading sentences in story. • Show students how to recognize punctuation when reading with prosody. • Show realia or other visuals of objects and concepts. • Use primary language equivalents when available and then ask students to say words and sentences in English.	• See "Home Connections" for "approaching mastery" and "at mastery" students. • Provide audiotape to use with sentence strips and word flash cards for additional practice; encourage students to practice with mirror at home, as needed. • Provide audiotape of story; have students listen and track during story reading; then students read aloud with tape while tracking; then students read aloud and track independently; have an adult review difficult words following independent story reading. • Encourage an adult to help students identify realia and other visuals illustrating meaning of sentences in story. • Encourage an adult to help students practice using primary language equivalents and English words when possible.
Test 9 (Lesson 90) **Approaching Mastery**	• See guidelines noted on Group Summary Chart (see Appendix H of *Teacher's Guide*) and Test Summary Sheet (see Appendix I of *Teacher's Guide*) for students who do not meet passing criterion. • See test remedies noted on pages 69–72 of *Teacher's Guide* as well as Test 9 Firming Table noted on page 217 of *Presentation Book B.* • Partner with "at mastery" student and review previous lessons in Reading *Textbook B.* • Implement note-taking study strategy using 2-column note-taking method; review notes before test. • Write lesson summaries on index cards as study strategy and review before test. • Review key vocabulary words/terms until firm; write vocabulary words and their definitions on index cards. • Play "Jeopardy-like" game before taking test; student provides answers to questions posed by adult or "at mastery" student.	• Encourage students to reread previous lessons at home, particularly before the test; provide another text to be kept at home for this purpose. • Have an adult "quiz" students from notes or index cards before test. • Provide vocabulary flash cards for students to take home for additional practice.
At Mastery	• See guidelines noted on Group Summary Chart (see Appendix H of *Teacher's Guide*) and Test Summary Sheet (see Appendix I of *Teacher's Guide*) for students who meet passing criterion. • Have student "be the teacher": Partner with "approaching mastery" or ELL student and review previous lessons in Reading *Textbook B.* • Have student assist "approaching mastery" or ELL student with note-taking and index card study strategies. • Have student assist with conducting "Jeopardy-like" game. • Direct student to reading and writing center in classroom to reinforce literacy and writing skills.	

B27

Test	Tips for Teachers	Home Connections
ELL	• See "Tips for Teachers" for "approaching mastery" and "at mastery" students. • Explain key terms in rules by using realia or other visuals to illustrate examples and non-examples. • Explain key terms in vocabulary sentences by using realia, other visuals, pantomime, or a quick sketch. • Add to cognate word wall and cognate journal. • When writing vocabulary words and definitions on index cards, include primary language equivalents when available. • Use web diagram to group facts about key concept. • Use compare-contrast diagram to illustrate similarities and differences. • Use rereading strategy to improve comprehension. • Show related videos with captioning to help students associate printed text to spoken word.	• See "Home Connections" for "approaching mastery" and "at mastery" students. • Encourage students to take home cognate journal for review and encourage an adult to add to list when possible. • Have an adult help students review vocabulary flash cards including primary language equivalents. • Encourage students to study web about key concept. • Encourage an adult to turn on television captioning at home.

Test

Test	Tips for Teachers	Home Connections
Fluency Checkout (Lesson 95) **Approaching Mastery**	• See guidelines for students who do not read within error or time limit for Lesson 95 on pages 247 and 248 in *Presentation Book B*. • Partner with "at mastery" student and have him or her model reading story; have student read story. • Re-teach difficult words using "good-bye" list. • Review finger placement and tracking for sentence reading. • Have adult model reading story; have student read story until firm. • Use paired reading. • Use "cold timing" and "hot timing" to improve fluency. • Develop tape of story read by good reader; have student listen to tape and whisper read.	• Provide word flash cards for students to take home for additional practice. • Have an adult model reading story; have students listen and track during story reading; have students read story; have an adult review difficult words following story reading. • Have students read story to a pet, stuffed animal, or sibling for extra practice.
At Mastery	• See guidelines for students who read within error and time limit for Lesson 95 on pages 247 and 248 in *Presentation Book B*. • Partner with "approaching mastery" or ELL student and model reading story; have student read story. • Have student assist "approaching mastery" or ELL student with "cold and hot timings" and repeated readings. • Have student tape him or herself reading story as model for "approaching mastery" or ELL student. • Direct student to reading and writing center in classroom to reinforce literacy and writing skills.	

Test	Tips for Teachers	Home Connections
ELL	• See "Tips for Teachers" for "approaching mastery" and "at mastery" students. • Describe and model mouth formations for difficult sounds and words, then guide students while practicing with mirror. • Use sentence strips to practice reading sentences in story. • Show students how to recognize punctuation when reading with prosody. • Show realia or other visuals of objects and concepts. • Use primary language equivalents when available and then ask students to say words and sentences in English.	• See "Home Connections" for "approaching mastery" and "at mastery" students. • Provide audiotape to use with sentence strips and word flash cards for additional practice; encourage students to practice with mirror at home, as needed. • Provide audiotape of story; have students listen and track during story reading; then students read aloud with tape while tracking; then students read aloud and track independently; have an adult review difficult words following independent story reading. • Encourage an adult to help students identify realia and other visuals illustrating meaning of sentences in story. • Encourage an adult to help students practice using primary language equivalents and English words when possible.

Test

Test	Tips for Teachers	Home Connections
Fluency Checkout (Lesson 100) **Approaching Mastery**	• See guidelines for students who do not read within error or time limit for Lesson 100 on page 271 in *Presentation Book B*. • Partner with "at mastery" student and have him or her model reading story; have student read story. • Re-teach difficult words using "good-bye" list. • Review finger placement and tracking for sentence reading. • Have adult model reading story; have student read story until firm. • Use paired reading. • Use "cold timing" and "hot timing" to improve fluency. • Develop tape of story read by good reader; have student listen to tape and whisper read.	• Provide word flash cards for students to take home for additional practice. • Have an adult model reading story; have students listen and track during story reading; have students read story; have an adult review difficult words following story reading. • Have students read story to a pet, stuffed animal, or sibling for extra practice.
At Mastery	• See guidelines for students who read within error and time limit for Lesson 100 on page 271 in *Presentation Book B*. • Partner with "approaching mastery" or ELL student and model reading story; have student read story. • Have student assist "approaching mastery" or ELL student with "cold and hot timings" and repeated readings. • Have student tape him or herself reading story as model for "approaching mastery" or ELL student. • Direct student to reading and writing center in classroom to reinforce literacy and writing skills.	

B29

Test	Tips for Teachers	Home Connections
ELL **Test**	• See "Tips for Teachers" for "approaching mastery" and "at mastery" students. • Describe and model mouth formations for difficult sounds and words, then guide students while practicing with mirror. • Use sentence strips to practice reading sentences in story. • Show students how to recognize punctuation when reading with prosody. • Show realia or other visuals of objects and concepts. • Use primary language equivalents when available and then ask students to say words and sentences in English.	• See "Home Connections" for "approaching mastery" and "at mastery" students. • Provide audiotape to use with sentence strips and word flash cards for additional practice; encourage students to practice with mirror at home, as needed. • Provide audiotape of story; have students listen and track during story reading; then students read aloud with tape while tracking; then students read aloud and track independently; have an adult review difficult words following independent story reading. • Encourage an adult to help students identify realia and other visuals illustrating meaning of sentences in story. • Encourage an adult to help students practice using primary language equivalents and English words when possible.
Test 10 **(Lesson 100)** **Lesson 100** **Assessment** **Approaching** **Mastery**	• See guidelines noted on Group Summary Chart (see Appendix H of *Teacher's Guide*) and Test Summary Sheet (see Appendix I of *Teacher's Guide*) for students who do not meet passing criterion. • See test remedies noted on pages 69–72 of *Teacher's Guide* as well as Test 10 Firming Table noted on page 272 of *Presentation Book B*. • Partner with "at mastery" student and review previous lessons in Reading *Textbook B*. • Implement note-taking study strategy. • Write lesson summaries on index cards as study strategy and review before test. • Review key vocabulary words/terms until firm; write vocabulary words and their definitions on index cards. • Play "Jeopardy-like" game before taking test. • For **Lesson 100 Assessment,** review assessment story and comprehension questions. • Review "What things went into the pile first?" until firm.	• Encourage students to reread previous lessons at home, particularly before the test; provide another text to be kept at home for this purpose. • Have an adult "quiz" students from notes or index cards before test. • Provide vocabulary flash cards for students to take home for additional practice.
At Mastery	• See guidelines noted on Group Summary Chart (see Appendix H of *Teacher's Guide*) and Test Summary Sheet (see Appendix I of *Teacher's Guide*) for students who meet passing criterion. • Have student "be the teacher": Partner with "approaching mastery" or ELL student and review previous lessons in Reading *Textbook B*. • Have student assist "approaching mastery" or ELL student with note-taking and index card study strategies. • Have student assist with conducting "Jeopardy-like" game. • Direct student to reading and writing center in classroom to reinforce literacy and writing skills.	

Test	Tips for Teachers	Home Connections
ELL	• See "Tips for Teachers" for "approaching mastery" and "at mastery" students. • Explain key terms in rules by using realia or other visuals to illustrate examples and non-examples. • Explain key terms in vocabulary sentences by using realia, other visuals, pantomime, or a quick sketch. • Add to cognate word wall and cognate journal. • When writing vocabulary words and definitions on index cards, include primary language equivalents when available. • Use web diagram to group facts about key concept. • Use compare-contrast diagram to illustrate similarities and differences. • Use rereading strategy to improve comprehension. • Show related videos with captioning to help students associate printed text to spoken word.	• See "Home Connections" for "approaching mastery" and "at mastery" students. • Encourage students to take home cognate journal for review and encourage an adult to add to list when possible. • Have an adult help students review vocabulary flash cards including primary language equivalents. • Encourage students to study web about key concept. • Encourage an adult to turn on television captioning at home.
Test **Fluency Checkout** (Lesson 105) **Approaching Mastery**	• See guidelines for students who do not read within error or time limit for Lesson 105 on page 25 in *Presentation Book C*. • Partner with "at mastery" student and have him or her model reading story; have student read story. • Re-teach difficult words using "good-bye" list. • Review finger placement and tracking for sentence reading. • Have adult model reading story; have student read story until firm. • Use paired reading. • Use "cold timing" and "hot timing" to improve fluency. • Develop tape of story read by good reader; have student listen to tape and whisper read.	• Provide word flash cards for students to take home for additional practice. • Have an adult model reading story; have students listen and track during story reading; have students read story; have an adult review difficult words following story reading. • Have students read story to a pet, stuffed animal, or sibling for extra practice.
At Mastery	• See guidelines for students who read within error and time limit for Lesson 105 on page 25 in *Presentation Book C*. • Partner with "approaching mastery" or ELL student and model reading story; have student read story. • Have student assist "approaching mastery" or ELL student with "cold and hot timings" and repeated readings. • Have student tape him or herself reading story as model for "approaching mastery" or ELL student. • Direct student to reading and writing center in classroom to reinforce literacy and writing skills.	

B31

Test	Tips for Teachers	Home Connections
ELL **Test**	• See "Tips for Teachers" for "approaching mastery" and "at mastery" students. • Describe and model mouth formations for difficult sounds and words, then guide students while practicing with mirror. • Use sentence strips to practice reading sentences in story. • Show students how to recognize punctuation when reading with prosody. • Show realia or other visuals of objects and concepts. • Use primary language equivalents when available and then ask students to say words and sentences in English.	• See "Home Connections" for "approaching mastery" and "at mastery" students. • Provide audiotape to use with sentence strips and word flash cards for additional practice; encourage students to practice with mirror at home, as needed. • Provide audiotape of story; have students listen and track during story reading; then students read aloud with tape while tracking; then students read aloud and track independently; have an adult review difficult words following independent story reading. • Encourage an adult to help students identify realia and other visuals illustrating meaning of sentences in story. • Encourage an adult to help students practice using primary language equivalents and English words when possible.
Fluency Checkout (Lesson 110) **Approaching Mastery**	• See guidelines for students who do not read within error or time limit for Lesson 110 on pages 52 and 53 in *Presentation Book C*. • Partner with "at mastery" student and have him or her model reading story; have student read story. • Re-teach difficult words using "good-bye" list. • Review finger placement and tracking for sentence reading. • Have adult model reading story; have student read story until firm. • Use paired reading. • Use "cold timing" and "hot timing" to improve fluency. • Develop tape of story read by good reader; have student listen to tape and whisper read.	• Provide word flash cards for students to take home for additional practice. • Have an adult model reading story; have students listen and track during story reading; have students read story; have an adult review difficult words following story reading. • Have students read story to a pet, stuffed animal, or sibling for extra practice.
At Mastery	• See guidelines for students who read within error and time limit for Lesson 110 on pages 52 and 53 in *Presentation Book C*. • Partner with "approaching mastery" or ELL student and model reading story; have student read story. • Have student assist "approaching mastery" or ELL student with "cold and hot timings" and repeated readings. • Have student tape him or herself reading story as model for "approaching mastery" or ELL student. • Direct student to reading and writing center in classroom to reinforce literacy and writing skills.	

Test	Tips for Teachers	Home Connections
ELL **Test**	• See "Tips for Teachers" for "approaching mastery" and "at mastery" students. • Describe and model mouth formations for difficult sounds and words, then guide students while practicing with mirror. • Use sentence strips to practice reading sentences in story. • Show students how to recognize punctuation when reading with prosody. • Show realia or other visuals of objects and concepts. • Use primary language equivalents when available and then ask students to say words and sentences in English.	• See "Home Connections" for "approaching mastery" and "at mastery" students. • Provide audiotape to use with sentence strips and word flash cards for additional practice; encourage students to practice with mirror at home, as needed. • Provide audiotape of story; have students listen and track during story reading; then students read aloud with tape while tracking; then students read aloud and track independently; have an adult review difficult words following independent story reading. • Encourage an adult to help students identify realia and other visuals illustrating meaning of sentences in story. • Encourage an adult to help students practice using primary language equivalents and English words when possible.
Test 11 (Lesson 110) **Approaching Mastery**	• See guidelines noted on Group Summary Chart (see Appendix H of *Teacher's Guide*) and Test Summary Sheet (see Appendix I of *Teacher's Guide*) for students who do not meet passing criterion. • See test remedies noted on pages 69–72 of *Teacher's Guide* as well as Test 11 Firming Table noted on page 53 of *Presentation Book C.* • Partner with "at mastery" student and review previous lessons in Reading *Textbook C.* • Implement note-taking study strategy using 2-column note-taking method; review notes before test. • Write lesson summaries on index cards as study strategy and review before test. • Review key vocabulary words/terms until firm; write vocabulary words and their definitions on index cards. • Play "Jeopardy-like" game before taking test; student provides answers to questions posed by adult or "at mastery" student.	• Encourage students to reread previous lessons at home, particularly before the test; provide another text to be kept at home for this purpose. • Have an adult "quiz" students from notes or index cards before test. • Provide vocabulary flash cards for students to take home for additional practice.
At Mastery	• See guidelines noted on Group Summary Chart (see Appendix H of *Teacher's Guide*) and Test Summary Sheet (see Appendix I of *Teacher's Guide*) for students who meet passing criterion. • Have student "be the teacher": Partner with "approaching mastery" or ELL student and review previous lessons in Reading *Textbook C.* • Have student assist "approaching mastery" or ELL student with note-taking and index card study strategies. • Have student assist with conducting "Jeopardy-like" game. • Direct student to reading and writing center in classroom to reinforce literacy and writing skills.	

B33

Test	Tips for Teachers	Home Connections
ELL **Test**	• See "Tips for Teachers" for "approaching mastery" and "at mastery" students. • Explain key terms in rules by using realia or other visuals to illustrate examples and non-examples. • Explain key terms in vocabulary sentences by using realia, other visuals, pantomime, or a quick sketch. • Add to cognate word wall and cognate journal. • When writing vocabulary words and definitions on index cards, include primary language equivalents when available. • Use web diagram to group facts about key concept. • Use compare-contrast diagram to illustrate similarities and differences. • Use rereading strategy to improve comprehension. • Show related videos with captioning to help students associate printed text to spoken word.	• See "Home Connections" for "approaching mastery" and "at mastery" students. • Encourage students to take home cognate journal for review and encourage an adult to add to list when possible. • Have an adult help students review vocabulary flash cards including primary language equivalents. • Encourage students to study web about key concept. • Encourage an adult to turn on television captioning at home.
Fluency Checkout (Lesson 115) **Approaching Mastery**	• See guidelines for students who do not read within error or time limit for Lesson 115 on page 79 in *Presentation Book C*. • Partner with "at mastery" student and have him or her model reading story; have student read story. • Re-teach difficult words using "good-bye" list. • Review finger placement and tracking for sentence reading. • Have adult model reading story; have student read story until firm. • Use paired reading. • Use "cold timing" and "hot timing" to improve fluency. • Develop tape of story read by good reader; have student listen to tape and whisper read.	• Provide word flash cards for students to take home for additional practice. • Have an adult model reading story; have students listen and track during story reading; have students read story; have an adult review difficult words following story reading. • Have students read story to a pet, stuffed animal, or sibling for extra practice.
At Mastery	• See guidelines for students who read within error and time limit for Lesson 115 on page 79 in *Presentation Book C*. • Partner with "approaching mastery" or ELL student and model reading story; have student read story. • Have student assist "approaching mastery" or ELL student with "cold and hot timings" and repeated readings. • Have student tape him or herself reading story as model for "approaching mastery" or ELL student. • Direct student to reading and writing center in classroom to reinforce literacy and writing skills.	

B34

Test	Tips for Teachers	Home Connections
ELL	• See "Tips for Teachers" for "approaching mastery" and "at mastery" students. • Describe and model mouth formations for difficult sounds and words, then guide students while practicing with mirror. • Use sentence strips to practice reading sentences in story. • Show students how to recognize punctuation when reading with prosody. • Show realia or other visuals of objects and concepts. • Use primary language equivalents when available and then ask students to say words and sentences in English.	• See "Home Connections" for "approaching mastery" and "at mastery" students. • Provide audiotape to use with sentence strips and word flash cards for additional practice; encourage students to practice with mirror at home, as needed. • Provide audiotape of story; have students listen and track during story reading; then students read aloud with tape while tracking; then students read aloud and track independently; have an adult review difficult words following independent story reading. • Encourage an adult to help students identify realia and other visuals illustrating meaning of sentences in story. • Encourage an adult to help students practice using primary language equivalents and English words when possible.
Test		
Fluency Checkout (Lesson 120) **Approaching Mastery**	• See guidelines for students who do not read within error or time limit for Lesson 120 on page 103 in *Presentation Book C*. • Partner with "at mastery" student and have him or her model reading story; have student read story. • Re-teach difficult words using "good-bye" list. • Review finger placement and tracking for sentence reading. • Have adult model reading story; have student read story until firm. • Use paired reading. • Use "cold timing" and "hot timing" to improve fluency. • Develop tape of story read by good reader; have student listen to tape and whisper read.	• Provide word flash cards for students to take home for additional practice. • Have an adult model reading story; have students listen and track during story reading; have students read story; have an adult review difficult words following story reading. • Have students read story to a pet, stuffed animal, or sibling for extra practice.
At Mastery	• See guidelines for students who read within error and time limit for Lesson 120 on page 103 in *Presentation Book C*. • Partner with "approaching mastery" or ELL student and model reading story; have student read story. • Have student assist "approaching mastery" or ELL student with "cold and hot timings" and repeated readings. • Have student tape him or herself reading story as model for "approaching mastery" or ELL student. • Direct student to reading and writing center in classroom to reinforce literacy and writing skills.	

B35

Test	Tips for Teachers	Home Connections
ELL **Test**	• See "Tips for Teachers" for "approaching mastery" and "at mastery" students. • Describe and model mouth formations for difficult sounds and words, then guide students while practicing with mirror. • Use sentence strips to practice reading sentences in story. • Show students how to recognize punctuation when reading with prosody. • Show realia or other visuals of objects and concepts. • Use primary language equivalents when available and then ask students to say words and sentences in English.	• See "Home Connections" for "approaching mastery" and "at mastery" students. • Provide audiotape to use with sentence strips and word flash cards for additional practice; encourage students to practice with mirror at home, as needed. • Provide audiotape of story; have students listen and track during story reading; then students read aloud with tape while tracking; then students read aloud and track independently; have an adult review difficult words following independent story reading. • Encourage an adult to help students identify realia and other visuals illustrating meaning of sentences in story. • Encourage an adult to help students practice using primary language equivalents and English words when possible.
Test 12 (Lesson 120) **Lesson 120 Assessment** **Approaching Mastery**	• See guidelines noted on Group Summary Chart (see Appendix H of *Teacher's Guide*) and Test Summary Sheet (see Appendix I of *Teacher's Guide*) for students who do not meet passing criterion. • See test remedies noted on pages 69–72 of *Teacher's Guide* as well as Test 12 Firming Table noted on page 104 of *Presentation Book C*. • Partner with "at mastery" student and review previous lessons in Reading *Textbook C*. • Implement note-taking study strategy. • Write lesson summaries on index cards as study strategy and review before test. • Review key vocabulary words/terms until firm; write vocabulary words and their definitions on index cards. • Play "Jeopardy-like" game before taking test. • For **Lesson 120 Assessment,** review assessment story and comprehension questions. • Review parts of a ship until firm.	• Encourage students to reread previous lessons at home, particularly before the test; provide another text to be kept at home for this purpose. • Have an adult "quiz" students from notes or index cards before test. • Provide vocabulary flash cards for students to take home for additional practice.
At Mastery	• See guidelines noted on Group Summary Chart (see Appendix H of *Teacher's Guide*) and Test Summary Sheet (see Appendix I of *Teacher's Guide*) for students who meet passing criterion. • Have student "be the teacher": Partner with "approaching mastery" or ELL student and review previous lessons in Reading *Textbook C*. • Have student assist "approaching mastery" or ELL student with note-taking and index card study strategies. • Have student assist with conducting "Jeopardy-like" game. • Direct student to reading and writing center in classroom to reinforce literacy and writing skills.	

Test	Tips for Teachers	Home Connections
ELL	• See "Tips for Teachers" for "approaching mastery" and "at mastery" students. • Explain key terms in rules by using realia or other visuals to illustrate examples and non-examples. • Explain key terms in vocabulary sentences by using realia, other visuals, pantomime, or a quick sketch. • Add to cognate word wall and cognate journal. • When writing vocabulary words and definitions on index cards, include primary language equivalents when available. • Use web diagram to group facts about key concept. • Use compare-contrast diagram to illustrate similarities and differences. • Use rereading strategy to improve comprehension. • Show related videos with captioning to help students associate printed text to spoken word	• See "Home Connections" for "approaching mastery" and "at mastery" students. • Encourage students to take home cognate journal for review and encourage an adult to add to list when possible. • Have an adult help students review vocabulary flash cards including primary language equivalents. • Encourage students to study web about key concept. • Encourage an adult to turn on television captioning at home.

Test

Test	Tips for Teachers	Home Connections
Fluency Checkout (Lesson 125) **Approaching Mastery**	• See guidelines for students who do not read within error or time limit for Lesson 125 on pages 130 and 131 in *Presentation Book C.* • Partner with "at mastery" student and have him or her model reading story; have student read story. • Re-teach difficult words using "good-bye" list. • Review finger placement and tracking for sentence reading. • Have adult model reading story; have student read story until firm. • Use paired reading. • Use "cold timing" and "hot timing" to improve fluency. • Develop tape of story read by good reader; have student listen to tape and whisper read.	• Provide word flash cards for students to take home for additional practice. • Have an adult model reading story; have students listen and track during story reading; have students read story; have an adult review difficult words following story reading. • Have students read story to a pet, stuffed animal, or sibling for extra practice.
At Mastery	• See guidelines for students who read within error and time limit for Lesson 125 on pages 130 and 131 in *Presentation Book C.* • Partner with "approaching mastery" or ELL student and model reading story; have student read story. • Have student assist "approaching mastery" or ELL student with "cold and hot timings" and repeated readings. • Have student tape him or herself reading story as model for "approaching mastery" or ELL student. • Direct student to reading and writing center in classroom to reinforce literacy and writing skills.	

B37

Test	Tips for Teachers	Home Connections
ELL **Test**	• See "Tips for Teachers" for "approaching mastery" and "at mastery" students. • Describe and model mouth formations for difficult sounds and words, then guide students while practicing with mirror. • Use sentence strips to practice reading sentences in story. • Show students how to recognize punctuation when reading with prosody. • Show realia or other visuals of objects and concepts. • Use primary language equivalents when available and then ask students to say words and sentences in English.	• See "Home Connections" for "approaching mastery" and "at mastery" students. • Provide audiotape to use with sentence strips and word flash cards for additional practice; encourage students to practice with mirror at home, as needed. • Provide audiotape of story; have students listen and track during story reading; then students read aloud with tape while tracking; then students read aloud and track independently; have an adult review difficult words following independent story reading. • Encourage an adult to help students identify realia and other visuals illustrating meaning of sentences in story. • Encourage an adult to help students practice using primary language equivalents and English words when possible.
Fluency Checkout (Lesson 130) **Approaching Mastery**	• See guidelines for students who do not read within error or time limit for Lesson 130 on page 153 in *Presentation Book C*. • Partner with "at mastery" student and have him or her model reading story; have student read story. • Re-teach difficult words using "good-bye" list. • Review finger placement and tracking for sentence reading. • Have adult model reading story; have student read story until firm. • Use paired reading. • Use "cold timing" and "hot timing" to improve fluency. • Develop tape of story read by good reader; have student listen to tape and whisper read.	• Provide word flash cards for students to take home for additional practice. • Have an adult model reading story; have students listen and track during story reading; have students read story; have an adult review difficult words following story reading. • Have students read story to a pet, stuffed animal, or sibling for extra practice.
At Mastery	• See guidelines for students who read within error and time limit for Lesson 130 on page 153 in *Presentation Book C*. • Partner with "approaching mastery" or ELL student and model reading story; have student read story. • Have student assist "approaching mastery" or ELL student with "cold and hot timings" and repeated readings. • Have student tape him or herself reading story as model for "approaching mastery" or ELL student. • Direct student to reading and writing center in classroom to reinforce literacy and writing skills.	

Test	Tips for Teachers	Home Connections
ELL **Test**	• See "Tips for Teachers" for "approaching mastery" and "at mastery" students. • Describe and model mouth formations for difficult sounds and words, then guide students while practicing with mirror. • Use sentence strips to practice reading sentences in story. • Show students how to recognize punctuation when reading with prosody. • Show realia or other visuals of objects and concepts. • Use primary language equivalents when available and then ask students to say words and sentences in English.	• See "Home Connections" for "approaching mastery" and "at mastery" students. • Provide audiotape to use with sentence strips and word flash cards for additional practice; encourage students to practice with mirror at home, as needed. • Provide audiotape of story; have students listen and track during story reading; then students read aloud with tape while tracking; then students read aloud and track independently; have an adult review difficult words following independent story reading. • Encourage an adult to help students identify realia and other visuals illustrating meaning of sentences in story. • Encourage an adult to help students practice using primary language equivalents and English words when possible.
Test 130 (Lesson 130) **Approaching Mastery**	• See guidelines noted on Group Summary Chart (see Appendix H of *Teacher's Guide*) and Test Summary Sheet (see Appendix I of *Teacher's Guide*) for students who do not meet passing criterion. • See test remedies noted on pages 69–72 of *Teacher's Guide* as well as Test 13 Firming Table noted on page 154 of *Presentation Book C*. • Partner with "at mastery" student and review previous lessons in Reading *Textbook C*. • Implement note-taking study strategy using 2-column note-taking method; review notes before test. • Write lesson summaries on index cards as study strategy and review before test. • Review key vocabulary words/terms until firm; write vocabulary words and their definitions on index cards.	• Encourage students to reread previous lessons at home, particularly before the test; provide another text to be kept at home for this purpose. • Have an adult "quiz" students from notes or index cards before test. • Provide vocabulary flash cards for students to take home for additional practice.
At Mastery	• See guidelines noted on Group Summary Chart (see Appendix H of *Teacher's Guide*) and Test Summary Sheet (see Appendix I of *Teacher's Guide*) for students who meet passing criterion. • Have student "be the teacher": Partner with "approaching mastery" or ELL student and review previous lessons in Reading *Textbook C*. • Have student assist "approaching mastery" or ELL student with note-taking and index card study strategies. • Have student assist with conducting "Jeopardy-like" game. • Direct student to reading and writing center in classroom to reinforce literacy and writing skills.	

B39

Test	Tips for Teachers	Home Connections
ELL	• See "Tips for Teachers" for "approaching mastery" and "at mastery" students. • Explain key terms in rules by using realia or other visuals to illustrate examples and non-examples. • Explain key terms in vocabulary sentences by using realia, other visuals, pantomime, or a quick sketch. • Add to cognate word wall and cognate journal. • When writing vocabulary words and definitions on index cards, include primary language equivalents when available. • Use web diagram to group facts about key concept. • Use compare-contrast diagram to illustrate similarities and differences. • Use rereading strategy to improve comprehension. • Show related videos with captioning to help students associate printed text to spoken word.	• See "Home Connections" for "approaching mastery" and "at mastery" students. • Encourage students to take home cognate journal for review and encourage an adult to add to list when possible. • Have an adult help students review vocabulary flash cards including primary language equivalents. • Encourage students to study web about key concept. • Encourage an adult to turn on television captioning at home.
Test		
Fluency Checkout (Lesson 135) **Approaching Mastery**	• See guidelines for students who do not read within error or time limit for Lesson 135 on page 182 in *Presentation Book C*. • Partner with "at mastery" student and have him or her model reading story; have student read story. • Re-teach difficult words using "good-bye" list. • Review finger placement and tracking for sentence reading. • Have adult model reading story; have student read story until firm. • Use paired reading. • Use "cold timing" and "hot timing" to improve fluency. • Develop tape of story read by good reader; have student listen to tape and whisper read.	• Provide word flash cards for students to take home for additional practice. • Have an adult model reading story; have students listen and track during story reading; have students read story; have an adult review difficult words following story reading. • Have students read story to a pet, stuffed animal, or sibling for extra practice.
At Mastery	• See guidelines for students who read within error and time limit for Lesson 135 on page 182 in *Presentation Book C*. • Partner with "approaching mastery" or ELL student and model reading story; have student read story. • Have student assist "approaching mastery" or ELL student with "cold and hot timings" and repeated readings. • Have student tape him or herself reading story as model for "approaching mastery" or ELL student. • Direct student to reading and writing center in classroom to reinforce literacy and writing skills.	

Test	Tips for Teachers	Home Connections
ELL	• See "Tips for Teachers" for "approaching mastery" and "at mastery" students. • Describe and model mouth formations for difficult sounds and words, then guide students while practicing with mirror. • Use sentence strips to practice reading sentences in story. • Show students how to recognize punctuation when reading with prosody. • Show realia or other visuals of objects and concepts. • Use primary language equivalents when available and then ask students to say words and sentences in English.	• See "Home Connections" for "approaching mastery" and "at mastery" students. • Provide audiotape to use with sentence strips and word flash cards for additional practice; encourage students to practice with mirror at home, as needed. • Provide audiotape of story; have students listen and track during story reading; then students read aloud with tape while tracking; then students read aloud and track independently; have an adult review difficult words following independent story reading. • Encourage an adult to help students identify realia and other visuals illustrating meaning of sentences in story. • Encourage an adult to help students practice using primary language equivalents and English words when possible.
Fluency Checkout (Lesson 140) **Approaching Mastery**	• See guidelines for students who do not read within error or time limit for Lesson 140 on page 205 in *Presentation Book C*. • Partner with "at mastery" student and have him or her model reading story; have student read story. • Re-teach difficult words using "good-bye" list. • Review finger placement and tracking for sentence reading. • Have adult model reading story; have student read story until firm. • Use paired reading. • Use "cold timing" and "hot timing" to improve fluency. • Develop tape of story read by good reader; have student listen to tape and whisper read.	• Provide word flash cards for students to take home for additional practice. • Have an adult model reading story; have students listen and track during story reading; have students read story; have an adult review difficult words following story reading. • Have students read story to a pet, stuffed animal, or sibling for extra practice.
At Mastery	• See guidelines for students who read within error and time limit for Lesson 140 on page 205 in *Presentation Book C*. • Partner with "approaching mastery" or ELL student and model reading story; have student read story. • Have student assist "approaching mastery" or ELL student with "cold and hot timings" and repeated readings. • Have student tape him or herself reading story as model for "approaching mastery" or ELL student. • Direct student to reading and writing center in classroom to reinforce literacy and writing skills.	

Test	Tips for Teachers	Home Connections
ELL	• See "Tips for Teachers" for "approaching mastery" and "at mastery" students. • Describe and model mouth formations for difficult sounds and words, then guide students while practicing with mirror. • Use sentence strips to practice reading sentences in story. • Show students how to recognize punctuation when reading with prosody. • Show realia or other visuals of objects and concepts. • Use primary language equivalents when available and then ask students to say words and sentences in English.	• See "Home Connections" for "approaching mastery" and "at mastery" students. • Provide audiotape to use with sentence strips and word flash cards for additional practice; encourage students to practice with mirror at home, as needed. • Provide audiotape of story; have students listen and track during story reading; then students read aloud with tape while tracking; then students read aloud and track independently; have an adult review difficult words following independent story reading. • Encourage an adult to help students identify realia and other visuals illustrating meaning of sentences in story. • Encourage an adult to help students practice using primary language equivalents and English words when possible.
Test 14 (Lesson 140) **Lesson 140 Assessment** **Approaching Mastery**	• See guidelines noted on Group Summary Chart (see Appendix H of *Teacher's Guide*) and Test Summary Sheet (see Appendix I of *Teacher's Guide*) for students who do not meet passing criterion. • See test remedies noted on pages 69–72 of *Teacher's Guide* as well as Test 14 Firming Table noted on page 206 of *Presentation Book C*. • Partner with "at mastery" student and review previous lessons in Reading *Textbook C*. • Implement note-taking study strategy. • Write lesson summaries on index cards as study strategy and review before test. • Review key vocabulary words/terms until firm; write vocabulary words and their definitions on index cards. • Play "Jeopardy-like" game before taking test. • For **Lesson 140 Assessment,** review assessment story and comprehension questions. • Review contractions and homonyms until firm.	• Encourage students to reread previous lessons at home, particularly before the test; provide another text to be kept at home for this purpose. • Have an adult "quiz" students from notes or index cards before test. • Provide vocabulary flash cards for students to take home for additional practice.
At Mastery	• See guidelines noted on Group Summary Chart (see Appendix H of *Teacher's Guide*) and Test Summary Sheet (see Appendix I of *Teacher's Guide*) for students who meet passing criterion. • Have student "be the teacher": Partner with "approaching mastery" or ELL student and review previous lessons in Reading *Textbook C*. • Have student assist "approaching mastery" or ELL student with note-taking and index card study strategies. • Have student assist with conducting "Jeopardy-like" game. • Direct student to reading and writing center in classroom to reinforce literacy and writing skills.	

B42

Test	Tips for Teachers	Home Connections
ELL	• See "Tips for Teachers" for "approaching mastery" and "at mastery" students. • Explain key terms in rules by using realia or other visuals to illustrate examples and non-examples. • Explain key terms in vocabulary sentences by using realia, other visuals, pantomime, or a quick sketch. • Add to cognate word wall and cognate journal. • When writing vocabulary words and definitions on index cards, include primary language equivalents when available. • Use web diagram to group facts about key concept. • Use compare-contrast diagram to illustrate similarities and differences. • Use rereading strategy to improve comprehension. • Show related videos with captioning to help students associate printed text to spoken word.	• See "Home Connections" for "approaching mastery" and "at mastery" students. • Encourage students to take home cognate journal for review and encourage an adult to add to list when possible. • Have an adult help students review vocabulary flash cards including primary language equivalents. • Encourage students to study web about key concept. • Encourage an adult to turn on television captioning at home.

Test

Test	Tips for Teachers	Home Connections
Fluency Checkout (Lesson 145) **Approaching Mastery**	• See guidelines for students who do not read within error or time limit for Lesson 145 on page 235 in *Presentation Book C.* • Partner with "at mastery" student and have him or her model reading story; have student read story. • Re-teach difficult words using "good-bye" list. • Review finger placement and tracking for sentence reading. • Have adult model reading story; have student read story until firm. • Use paired reading. • Use "cold timing" and "hot timing" to improve fluency. • Develop tape of story read by good reader; have student listen to tape and whisper read.	• Provide word flash cards for students to take home for additional practice. • Have an adult model reading story; have students listen and track during story reading; have students read story; have an adult review difficult words following story reading. • Have students read story to a pet, stuffed animal, or sibling for extra practice.
At Mastery	• See guidelines for students who read within error and time limit for Lesson 145 on page 235 in *Presentation Book C.* • Partner with "approaching mastery" or ELL student and model reading story; have student read story. • Have student assist "approaching mastery" or ELL student with "cold and hot timings" and repeated readings. • Have student tape him or herself reading story as model for "approaching mastery" or ELL student. • Direct student to reading and writing center in classroom to reinforce literacy and writing skills.	

Test	Tips for Teachers	Home Connections
ELL	• See "Tips for Teachers" for "approaching mastery" and "at mastery" students. • Describe and model mouth formations for difficult sounds and words, then guide students while practicing with mirror. • Use sentence strips to practice reading sentences in story. • Show students how to recognize punctuation when reading with prosody. • Show realia or other visuals of objects and concepts. • Use primary language equivalents when available and then ask students to say words and sentences in English.	• See "Home Connections" for "approaching mastery" and "at mastery" students. • Provide audiotape to use with sentence strips and word flash cards for additional practice; encourage students to practice with mirror at home, as needed. • Provide audiotape of story; have students listen and track during story reading; then students read aloud with tape while tracking; then students read aloud and track independently; have an adult review difficult words following independent story reading. • Encourage an adult to help students identify realia and other visuals illustrating meaning of sentences in story. • Encourage an adult to help students practice using primary language equivalents and English words when possible.

Test	Tips for Teachers	Home Connections
ELL	• See "Tips for Teachers" for "approaching mastery" and "at mastery" students.	• See "Home Connections" for "approaching mastery" and "at mastery" students.

B44

Appendix C

Levels of Support for Students with Intellectual Disabilities

The following table presents helpful tips to help ensure maximum access for students with intellectual disabilities. These suggestions use foundational skills that are clearly linked to the *Reading Mastery* content to aid such students in achieving academic success. These suggestions are provided at three levels of support (from least to most) to allow all learners the opportunity to access learning at the highest possible in program materials.

Levels of Support for Students with Intellectual Disabilities *Reading Mastery Signature Edition* **Grade 2**
***Level 1 (less support needed):* The student will**
<ul><li>identify initial and final phonemes in CVC words.</li><li>blend individual phonemes in one-syllable words.</li><li>produce the most common sounds associated with all letters of the alphabet.</li><li>use self-correction strategies.</li><li>recognize and read high frequency sight words.</li><li>decode phonetically regular CVC words.</li><li>use new vocabulary that is taught directly.</li><li>identify and sort pictures of common words into categories.</li><li>identify meaning of words that show spatial and temporal relationships.</li><li>use picture dictionary to identify word meaning.</li><li>determine if verbal statements about pictures are true or false.</li><li>use strategies to repair comprehension.</li><li>select fiction and nonfiction materials to listen to.</li><li>identify text features and answer literal comprehension questions.</li></ul>
***Level 2 (more support needed):* The student will**
<ul><li>orally blend and segment compound words with picture prompts.</li><li>name five or more letters and produce their sounds.</li><li>identify the first letter and sound in CVC words.</li><li>use new vocabulary that is taught directly.</li><li>identify and name words paired with pictures.</li><li>identify details of familiar read-aloud stories.</li><li>identify literary forms in read-aloud stories.</li><li>determine if pictures represent real or make believe.</li><li>identify pictures that evoke feelings in familiar read-aloud stories.</li><li>identify key information in fiction and nonfiction materials.</li><li>respond to literal yes/no questions.</li><li>select and listen to a variety of fiction and nonfiction materials.</li></ul>

C3

Level 3 (most support needed): The student will

- respond to a familiar person reading a book aloud.
- respond to spoken words/objects/gestures/signs/pictures/symbols used as prompts in familiar stories or activities.
- attend to print by touching/looking/listening.
- respond to the book cover or illustrations of a familiar story.
- respond to spoken words in familiar stories.
- request continuation of a familiar story when it is interrupted.
- respond to new vocabulary that is taught directly.
- match familiar objects to tasks in routines.
- respond to events in familiar read-aloud stories.
- respond accurately and consistently to referent objects or pictures used in routines.
- seek assistance to clarify meaning of pictures and activities with prompting.
- respond to emotions expressed by familiar persons.
- express a preference for read-aloud stories.
- attend to read-aloud fiction and nonfiction materials.

Appendix D

Professional Development
Fluency Building and Reading Level Determination

What is Fluency Building?

Fluency is the ability to read text quickly, accurately, and with expression (Armbruster et al., 2003; Hasbrouck, 2006; NICHD, 2000). It goes beyond automaticity and fast, effortless reading to include prosody or reading with expression as a critical aspect. Students who know how to read fluently read text smoothly with few, if any, decoding errors; they also read with proper expression, placing vocal emphasis and inflection where needed in the text (e.g., dialogue, punctuation, key words).

Why Fluency Building?

Fluency building is critical because "it provides a bridge between word recognition and comprehension. Because fluent readers do not have to concentrate on decoding the words, they can focus their attention on what the text means. They can make connections among the ideas in the text and between the text and their background knowledge" (Armbruster et al., 2003, p. 22).

However, Hasbrouck (2006) notes "fluency is necessary, but not sufficient, for understanding the meaning of text. When children read too slowly or haltingly, the text devolves into a broken string of words and/or phrases; it's a struggle just to remember what's been read, much less extract its meaning" (p. 24). Thus, reading programs should focus not only on building fluency but also on building vocabulary and text comprehension strategies to ensure that students read with understanding. *Core Lesson Connections* includes fluency practice as well as vocabulary and comprehension strategies as key aspects of the reading program.

Is Fluency Building Included in Core Lesson Connections?

Yes. Each lesson of *Core Lesson Connections* (starting at Lesson 1) includes **Part C: Fluency Building**. After each *Reading Mastery Signature Edition* program lesson, you will have students reread the story of the day with a partner. This rereading is done orally; repeated oral reading has been shown to substantially improve reading fluency and overall reading achievement (Armbruster et al., 2003; Hasbrouck, 2006; NICHD, 2000). Oral reading with a partner is a key part of *Core Lesson Connections* and takes no more than 5 minutes of instructional time, with long-lasting results. The fluency-building activities in *Core Lesson Connections* are further extensions of the individual fluency checkouts already found in the *Reading Mastery Signature Edition* program.

Conduct after the lesson, using the story of the day.	**Part C: Fluency Building**
Direct students to story of day.	**Activity 1** **Partner Reading**
Assign student partners as Partner 1 and Partner 2.	It's time for partner reading.
Read or **explain** Activity 1.	
Monitor partner reading.	
Guide as needed.	

D3

What are Accurate Descriptions of Independent, Instructional, and Frustrational Reading Levels for Individual Students?

"Fluency develops as a result of many opportunities to practice reading with a high degree of success. Therefore, your students should practice orally rereading text that is reasonably easy for them" (Armbruster et al., 2003, p. 27). Students can encounter three types of text (Katz, Polkoff, & Gurvitz, 2005; Osborn, Lehr, & Hiebert, 2003):

- Independent level text (relatively easy for the reader, with no more than approximately 1 in 20 words difficult for the reader; 95% success or higher; with 90% comprehension).
- Instructional level text (challenging but manageable text for the reader, with no more than approximately 1 in 10 words difficult for the reader; 90% to 94% success; with 75% comprehension).
- Frustrational level text (problematic text for the reader, with more than 1 in 10 words difficult for the reader; less than 90% success; with 50% comprehension).

Most researchers advocate the use of text containing words students know or can decode easily (e.g., Allington, 2002; Armbruster et al., 2003; Hasbrouck, 2006). You can determine if a story or text is appropriate for students to read independently using the following steps:

1. Select a 50–100 word passage from a book that the student has not read previously.

2. Have the student read the passage aloud. Make sure you start at the beginning of a paragraph and avoid paragraphs with lots of dialogue. Count substitutions, mispronunciations, omissions, reversals, and hesitations (of more than 3 seconds) as errors; insertions, self corrects, and repetitions do not count as errors.

3. Subtract the number of errors the student made from the total number of words—this will yield the number of correct words read by the student; divide the number of correct words read by the student by the total number of words in the passage and multiply by 100.

Example: passage length = 50 words; student makes 3 errors yielding 47 correct words read; divide 47 correct words by 50 total words equaling .94; multiply .94 by 100 to get 94%.

4. Compare the student's calculated accuracy level to the reading level percentages (i.e., 95% or higher = independent level; 90%–94% = instructional; below 90% = frustrational); in the above example, the student would be at an instructional reading level (94% falls in the 90% to 94% range).

5. Develop 5-8 comprehension questions (at least one "who, what, where, why, and inference-type" question). Ask these comprehension questions after the student reads the passage.

6. Subtract the number of questions answered incorrectly from the total number of questions; divide the number of correctly answered questions by the total number of questions and multiply by 100.

Example: number of questions = 6; student answers 1 incorrectly yielding 5 correctly answered questions; divide 5 correctly answered questions by 6 total questions yielding .83; multiply .83 by 100 to get 83%.

7. Compare the student's calculated percentage correct to the comprehension levels (i.e., 90% = independent; 75% = instructional; 50% = frustrational); in the above example, the student would be at an instructional level (83% is above 75% and less than 90%).

How Can You Tell If Students Are Working At The Appropriate Instructional Level in Reading Mastery Signature Edition?

The *Reading Mastery Signature Edition* program is designed with student success in mind.

- Only a small amount of new learning (10%–15% of the total lesson) occurs in each lesson.
- New concepts and skills are presented in two or three consecutive lessons to provide students with enough exposure to new material to use it in other applications.
- The majority of each lesson firms and reviews material and skills presented earlier in the program.

The small-step design of the program promises successful learning for students who are placed appropriately. Four criteria help you determine if students are working at the appropriate instructional level during lessons (Engelmann,1999).

1. Each time a task is presented, the group either responds correctly (all students respond correctly and in unison) or incorrectly (some students give the wrong response, no response, or do not respond in unison). Students should be at least 70% correct on information that is being introduced for the first time. If students are much below 70%, they will find it difficult to learn the skills being presented. If they are only at 50%, they are at chance levels and are probably guessing.

2. Students should be at least 90% correct on parts of the lesson that deal with skills and information taught earlier in the program (assuming previous skill mastery). For example, when students read a passage, they should read at least 90% of the words correctly on the first reading because virtually all of the words should be familiar. If students are consistently below the 90% correct level, the amount of new learning is too great.

3. At the end of a lesson, all students should be "virtually 100% firm on all tasks and activities" (p. 6). For example, on the second reading of the passage, students should read with close to 100% accuracy.

4. Students should be at least 85% correct on independent work.

To determine student-reading level, you should complete the reading checkout and words correct per minute (WCPM) calculation as scripted.

You can compare your student's WCPM to the 2005 Hasbrouck and Tindal Oral Reading Fluency Data Chart (see *How do You Help Readers who Struggle with Fluency?* below) to establish who is in need of additional fluency practice.

D5

How Can You Help Students Select Appropriate Material to Read for Personal Pleasure?

Independent reading is the key to success as a life-long reader (Katz et al., 2005). Scaffolded independent reading should be done daily in the classroom; up to 30 minutes of independent reading time is advocated. Scaffolded independent reading involves opportunities for pleasurable, student-selected reading.

To accomplish this scaffolded independent reading, students should be taught a good way to self-select books that are "just right" for their independent reading level. The "Five Finger Rule" or "Goldilocks Method" helps students determine if books are "too easy."

Goldilocks Method

Level	Ask Yourself:
Too Easy	• Have you read it many times? • Do you understand the story very well? • Do you know almost every word? • Can you read it smoothly?
Too Hard	• Are there more than 5 words on the page you don't know? • Are you confused about what is happening in most of this book? • When you read, does it sound choppy?
Just Right	• Is the book new to you? • Do you understand a lot of the book? • Are there just a few words on a page that you don't know? • When you read, are some places smooth and some places choppy?

Routman (2003).

Students may ask themselves these questions or use the steps below to choose an independent-level book:

1. Choose a book

2. Open it anywhere

3. Make a fist

4. Read the page and hold up one finger for every unknown word or mistake you come across

5. Determine book level: 0–1 mistakes = too easy; 2–3 mistakes = just right; 4 or more mistakes = too hard.

How Should a Fluency Building Lesson Be Conducted?

You should assign student partners for the fluency building activity. To ensure success, students should be matched as closely as possible both in terms of their reading levels and their fluency rates. Given the emphasis on placement testing and flexible skill grouping in the *Reading Mastery Signature Edition* program, this matching should be relatively easy to accomplish.

Next, you should introduce and teach students how to conduct fluency practice properly in the classroom; this training should be conducted over 1 week. Even after training, you should carefully monitor student pairs during fluency practice activities. The following table presents an overview of what should be taught and how to teach it. If students struggle with fluency goals even after partner reading, they can be encouraged to repeat fluency practice two or more times with their partners (Note: Armbruster et al., 2003 report up to four repeated reads of the same passage may be needed to build fluency). However, if students continue to struggle, fluency intervention may be needed (see "How do you Help Readers Who Struggle with Fluency" below).

What to Teach	How to Teach It
Importance of fluency	• Discuss why fluent reading is important.
Fluency partnership behavior	• Discuss how to treat others (e.g., no arguing, be positive). • Set rules/expectations.
Fluency practice procedure	• Model and practice how/where to sit (across from one another in desks or at table; side by side in desks or at table). • Model and practice set up (one student gets own textbook, one student has copy of textbook story on which to record errors/last word read). • Model and practice what errors are (unknown/incorrect words). • Model and practice partner reading procedure (teacher times all students for 1 minute; recording partners underline unknown/incorrect words and draw slash after last word read when timer sounds; following timing, recording partners go over errors and follow standard error correct procedure [i.e., "That word is brother. What word?"]; recording partners record last word read, number of errors, calculate CWPM [correct words per minute], and graph partners' data; student roles are reversed and same procedure is followed).

D7

How do You Help Readers who Struggle with Fluency?

Hasbrouck and Tindal (2006) completed an extensive study of oral reading fluency. They recommended using the 2005 Hasbrouck and Tindal Oral Reading Fluency Data Chart (at end of section) to establish who is in need of additional fluency practice beyond that accomplished by partner reading in the classroom. Students scoring below the 50th percentile using an average of two unpracticed readings from grade-level materials need a regimented fluency-building intervention. Additionally, teachers can use the chart to establish long-range goals for students or "aim lines" that can appear on graphs as a visual aid for students.

Students scoring at the frustrational reading level may be an indication of the following:

- A failure to achieve 70% correct on new information, 90% on skills taught earlier in the program, and virtually 100% on all tasks/activities by the end of a lesson—further training on the program may be warranted.
- Program placement that is too high—re-administer placement test to ensure appropriate program placement.
- Double-dosing or completing a lesson a second time to ensure skill mastery—once students are above the 90% accuracy level, they can participate more successfully in fluency building activities; fluency building should occur on independent level text although some researchers advocate the use of independent or instructional level text—see Osborn et al., 2003 for details).

Several research-validated strategies can be used to improve fluency.

Problem	Fluency Strategy	How to Do It
Reading without prosody	Teacher modeling of prosody (echo reading)	Teacher reads story with prosody; approaching-mastery student tracks as teacher models prosody; teacher provides guided practice on reading with prosody; sentences or paragraphs can be alternated between teacher and student.
	Tape-assisted modeling of prosody	Approaching-mastery student listens to tape of story read with prosody; student whisper reads and tracks as tape is played a second time.
	Tutoring	At-mastery student paired with approaching-mastery student; at-mastery student reads, modeling prosody; at-mastery student provides guided practice on reading with prosody.

Problem	Fluency Strategy	How to Do It
Failure to meet individual rate and accuracy checkout goals or score below 50% percentile on Hasbrouck and Tindal (2006) fluency data chart	Choral reading	Teacher models reading at appropriate pace; approaching-mastery students then read along with teacher at appropriate pace.
	Student-adult reading	Adult reads story first, modeling appropriate pace (and prosody); approaching-mastery student reads same story with adult providing assistance as needed.
	Tape-assisted reading	Approaching-mastery student listens to tape of story read at appropriate pace; student whisper reads and tracks as tape is played a second time.
	Paired or tandem reading	At-mastery student is paired with an approaching-mastery student; at-mastery student reads along with approaching-mastery student at appropriate pace noting, "whenever you want to read alone, just tap the back of my hand"); at-mastery student fades him/herself from reading as approaching-mastery student reads more and more of story.

Problem	Fluency Strategy	How to Do It
Errors occur on particular words.	Error word drill.	At end of fluency building session, teacher records all "error" words on whiteboard or index cards; approaching-mastery student reviews cards 3-4 times with teacher.
	Reading racetrack.	Teacher records troublesome words on "track segments" forming a racetrack; approaching-mastery student points to words on racetrack and reads them for 1 minute, circling the track as many times as possible (Falk, Band, & McLaughlin, 2003).
	Good-bye list.	Teacher writes troublesome words on board; teacher practices words on daily basis; teacher has approaching-mastery students say "good-bye" to words that are stated correctly 3 sessions in a row.
	Cloze reading.	Teacher models reading at appropriate pace; once or twice every few sentences, teacher omits important words and approaching-mastery students read words aloud in choral fashion.

Hasbrouck & Tindal Oral Reading Fluency Data

Jan Hasbrouck and Gerald Tindal completed an extensive study of oral reading fluency in 2004. The results of their study are published in a technical report entitled "Oral Reading Fluency: 90 Years of Measurement," which is available on the University of Oregon's Web site and in THE READING TEACHER volume 59, 2006.

This table shows the oral reading fluency rates of students in grades 1 through 8 as determined by Hasbrouck and Tindal's data.

You can use the information in this table to draw conclusions and make decisions about the oral reading fluency of your students. **Students scoring below the 50th percentile using the average score of two unpracticed readings from grade-level materials need a fluency-building program.** In addition, teachers can use the table to set the long-term fluency goals for their struggling readers.

Average weekly improvement is the average words per week growth you can expect from a student. It was calculated by subtracting the fall score from the spring score and dividing the difference by 32, the typical number of weeks between the fall and spring assessments. For grade 1, since there is no fall assessment, the average weekly improvement was calculated by subtracting the winter score from the spring score and dividing the difference by 16, the typical number of weeks between the winter and spring assessments.

Grade	Percentile	Fall WCPM*	Winter WCPM*	Spring WCPM*	Avg. Weekly Improvement**
1	90		81	111	1.9
	75		47	82	2.2
	50		23	53	1.9
	25		12	28	1.0
	10		6	15	0.6
2	90	106	125	142	1.1
	75	79	100	117	1.2
	50	51	72	89	1.2
	25	25	42	61	1.1
	10	11	18	31	0.6
3	90	128	146	162	1.1
	75	99	120	137	1.2
	50	71	92	107	1.1
	25	44	62	78	1.1
	10	21	36	48	0.8
4	90	145	166	180	1.1
	75	119	139	152	1.0
	50	94	112	123	0.9
	25	68	87	98	0.9
	10	45	61	72	0.8
5	90	166	182	194	0.9
	75	139	156	168	0.9
	50	110	127	139	0.9
	25	85	99	109	0.8
	10	61	74	83	0.7
6	90	177	195	204	0.8
	75	153	167	177	0.8
	50	127	140	150	0.7
	25	98	111	122	0.8
	10	68	82	93	0.8
7	90	180	192	202	0.7
	75	156	165	177	0.7
	50	128	136	150	0.7
	25	102	109	123	0.7
	10	79	88	98	0.6
8	90	185	199	199	0.4
	75	161	173	177	0.5
	50	133	146	151	0.6
	25	106	115	124	0.6
	10	77	84	97	0.6

*WCPM = Words Correct per Minute

**Average Words per Week Growth

Oral Reading Fluency Data Chart from Oral Reading Fluency: 90 Years of Measurement

NAEP Oral Reading Fluency Scale

Fluent		
	Level 4	Reads primarily in larger, meaningful phrase groups. Although some regressions, repetitions, and deviations from text may be present, these do not appear to detract from the overall structure of the story. Preservation of the author's syntax is consistent. Some or most of the story is read with expressive interpretation.
	Level 3	Reads primarily in three- or four-word phrase groups. Some small groupings may be present. However, the majority of phrasing seems appropriate and preserves the syntax of the author. Little or no expressive interpretation is present.
Nonfluent		
	Level 2	Reads primarily in two-word phrases with some three- or four-word groupings. Some word-by-word reading may be present. Word groupings may seem awkward and unrelated to larger context of sentence or passage.
	Level 1	Reads primarily word-by-word. Occasional two-word or three-word phrases may occur— but these are infrequent and/or they do not preserve meaningful syntax.

National Center for Education Statistics, U.S. Department of Education

References

Allington, R. L. (2002). What I've learned about effective reading instruction from a decade of studying exemplary elementary classroom teachers. *Phi Delta Kappan*, 83, 740-747.

Armbruster, B., Lehr, F., & Osborn, J. (2003). *Put reading first: The research building blocks of reading instruction: Grades K-3* (2nd ed.). Washington, DC: Center for the Improvement of Early Reading Achievement, National Institute for Literacy, U.S. Department of Education.

Carnine, D. W., Silbert, J., Kame'enui, E. J., & Tarver, S. G. (2004). *Direct Instruction reading* (4th ed.). Upper Saddle River, NJ: Pearson Education.

Engelmann, S. (1999, July). *Student-program alignment and teaching to mastery*. Paper presented at the 25th National Direct Instruction Conference, Eugene, OR.

Falk, M., Band, M., & McLaughlin, T. F. (2003). The effects of reading racetracks and flashcards on sight word vocabulary of three third grade students with a specific learning disability: A further replication and analysis. *International Journal of Special Education*, 18(2), 57-61.

Hasbrouck, J. (2006). Drop everything and read—but how?: For students who are not yet fluent, silent reading is not the best use of classroom time. *American Educator*, 30(2), 22-27, 30-31, 46-47.

Hasbrouck, J., & Tindal, G. A. (2006). ORF norms: A valuable assessment tool for reading teachers. *The Reading Teacher*, 59, 636-644.

Katz, C. A., Polkoff, L., & Gurvitz, D. (2005, January). "Shhh…I'm reading:" Scaffolded independent-level reading. *School Talk*. Urbana, IL: National Council of Teachers of English.

National Institute of Child Health and Human Development [NICHD]. (2000). *Report of the National Reading Panel. Teaching children to read: An evidence-based assessment of the scientific research literature on reading and its implications for reading instruction: Reports of the subgroups* (NIH Publication NO. 00-4754). Washington, DC: U.S. Government Printing Office.

Osborn, J., Lehr, F., & Hiebert, E. (2003). *A focus on fluency*. Honolulu, HI: Pacific Resources for Education and Learning.

Routman, R. (2003). *Reading essentials: The specifics you need to teach reading well*. Portsmouth, NH: Heineman.

Vaughn, S., & Linan-Thompson, S. (2004). *Research-based methods of reading instruction: Grades K-3*. Alexandria, VA: ASCD.

Appendix E

Fluency/Paired Reading Guidelines

Lesson 1

Part C: Fluency Building

Conduct after lesson, using story of day.

Activity 1 Partner Reading

Direct students to story of day.

The more time you spend reading, the better your reading skills will be. You're going to learn to read with a partner to help improve your reading skills. When you partner read, you'll take turns reading with your partner. You'll do this every day using the story we just read during reading group.

Before you learn how to do partner reading, it's important to learn how to **act** as a partner. While you're **listening** to your partner read, you should sit quietly and listen very carefully for errors. You should follow along with your finger so you don't lose your place. You should also be very positive, saying things like "good job" or "nice reading." You should treat your partner the way you'd like to be treated.

Discuss partner behavior, adding points not mentioned by students.

What kinds of things should you be doing as your partner is reading? (Ideas: *Follow along in story by tracking with finger; listen for errors; listen carefully; sit quietly; be positive.*)

Why is it important to do these things? (Student responses.)

When you're **reading** to your partner, you should read with expression so you're interesting to listen to. You should also read loud enough so your partner can hear you. Finally, when your partner helps you with troublesome words, make the correction and go on. You shouldn't argue. You should be positive—your partner is trying to help you become an even better reader.

What kinds of things should you do as you're reading the story to your partner? (Ideas: *Read with expression; read loudly enough; accept corrections without arguing; be positive.*)

Being a good partner is an important responsibility. I know you can do it!

As your partner is reading, you also need to know how to correct errors. First, let's talk about what errors are.

Discuss errors one could make during reading: mispronunciations, substitutions, omissions, reversals, skipping line(s); give examples.

E3

Write error correction steps on the board.

Second, let's review the steps to correcting an error. Here they are:

Discuss each step.

Step 1: Stop your partner and tell your partner what he/she did.

Step 2: Tell partner what it should be.

Step 3: Have your partner say it correctly.

Step 4: Have your partner start over at the beginning of the sentence.

Model think-aloud for partner reading. **Call** on student to serve as sample "partner." **Model** error correction steps for each error. **Model** praise. **Guide** student volunteer as necessary as he/she serves as partner.

Now, watch as I show you how to partner read.

Sample Wording for Think-Aloud

(Student's name) and I are going to show you how to do partner reading. (Student's name) will read today's story and make three or four different kinds of errors. I'll listen to him/her read and correct the errors I hear. Follow along in your story as (Student's name) reads. Here we go.

1. Stop. You said _____.
2. The word is _____.
3. What word?
4. Start over at the beginning of the sentence.

Super job reading this story.

Now (Student's name) and I are going to switch roles. I'll read the story and (Student's name) will listen to me read. I'll make a few errors so we can practice our error correction steps. Here we go.

We'll practice this more later.

Lesson 2

Part C: Fluency Building

Conduct after lesson, using story of day.

Activity 1 Partner Reading

Direct students to story of day.

In the last lesson, you learned that when you partner read, you take turns reading with your partner. You'll do this every day using the story we just read during reading group.

Discuss with students.

You learned how to act during partner reading. How should the person who is **listening** act? (Student responses.)

How should the person who is **reading** act? (Student responses.)

Write error correction steps on the board.

As your partner is reading, you also need to know how to correct errors. Give me some examples of what errors are. (Student responses.)

Discuss each step. **Point** to each step on board as you read them together.

What are the steps to correcting an error?

Step 1: Stop your partner, and tell your partner what he/she did.

Step 2: Tell partner what it should be.

Step 3: Have your partner say it correctly.

Step 4: Have your partner start over at the beginning of the sentence.

Now, watch as I show you how to partner read once again.

Model partner reading. **Call** on student to serve as sample "partner." **Model** error correction steps for each error. **Model** praise. **Guide** student volunteer as necessary as he/she serves as partner.

We'll practice this more later.

E5

Part C: Fluency Building

Conduct after lesson, using story of day.

Activity 1 Partner Reading

Direct students to story of day. **Elicit** responses to questions. **Guide** as needed.

What is partner reading? (Idea: *Taking turns reading with a partner.*)

What story do you read? (Idea: *The story from today's lesson.*)

You learned how to act during partner reading. How should the person who is **listening** act? (Student responses.)

How should the person who is **reading** act? (Student responses.)

As your partner is reading, you also need to correct errors. Give me some examples of errors. (Student responses.)

Write error correction steps on the board. **Point** to each step on board as you read them together. **Discuss** each step.

What are the steps to correcting an error?

Step 1: Stop your partner, and tell your partner what he/she did.

Step 2: Tell partner what it should be.

Step 3: Have your partner say it correctly.

Step 4: Have your partner start over at the beginning of the sentence.

Assign student partners as Partner 1 and Partner 2. **Monitor** partner reading. **Guide** as needed.

Now, you'll practice partner reading with another student. Partner 1 will read and Partner 2 will listen. Partner 1, remember to make a couple of errors to allow your partner a chance to practice using the error correction steps.

Reverse roles. Now Partner 2 will read and Partner 1 will listen. Partner 2, remember to make a couple of errors to allow your partner a chance to practice using the error correction steps.

Discuss with students.

Let's talk about how this went. What questions do you have?

We'll practice this more later.

Lessons 7–9

Part C: Fluency Building

Conduct after lesson, using story of day.

Activity 1 Partner Reading

Direct students to story of day. **Assign** student partners as Partner 1 and Partner 2. **Monitor** partner reading. **Guide** as needed.

Partner 1 will read to Partner 2. When you're done, reverse roles. Partner 2 will then read to Partner 1. Remember to be positive and treat your partner as you would like to be treated.

Discuss with students.

Let's talk about how this went. What questions do you have?

Lessons 10 to end of program

Part C: Fluency Building

Conduct after lesson, using story of day.

Activity 1 Partner Reading

Direct students to story of day. **Assign** student partners as Partner 1 and Partner 2. **Monitor** partner reading. **Guide** as needed.

It's time for partner reading.

E7

Appendix F

Strand Component	Lessons 1-5	Lessons 6-10	Lessons 11-15	Lessons 16-20
Core Lesson Connections	**A. Vocabulary** *New Vocabulary* – 1.A2, 2.A1, 3.A1, 4.A1 **B. Comprehension Strategies** *Determine Text Type* – 1.B2, 2.B2, 3.B2, 4.B2 **C. Fluency** – 1.C, 2.C, 3.C, 4.C, 5.C	**A. Vocabulary** *New Vocabulary* – 6.A1, 7.A1, 8.A1, 9.A1 **B. Comprehension Strategies** *Determine Text Type* – 6.B2 *Comprehension Monitoring* – 7.B2, 8.B2, 9.B2 **C. Fluency** – 6.C, 7.C, 8.C, 9.C, 10.C **D. Writing/Language Arts** – 10 D 1	**A. Vocabulary** *New Vocabulary* – 11.A1, 12.A1, 13.A1, 14.A1 **B. Comprehension Strategies** *Comprehension Monitoring* – 11.B2, 12.B3, 13.B3, 14.B3 **C. Fluency** – 11.C, 12.C, 13.C, 14.C, 15.C	**A. Vocabulary** *New Vocabulary* – 16.A1, 17.A2, 18.A1, 19.A1 **B. Comprehension Strategies** *Determine Text Type* – 18.B1 *Comprehension Monitoring* – 16.B2, 17.B2, 18.B2, 19.B2 **C. Fluency** – 16.C, 17.C, 18.C, 19.C, 20.C **D. Writing/Language Arts** – 20 D 1
Reading Strand *Reading Mastery*	**Presentation Book A** **Vocabulary** – 1.1, 2.1, 3.1, 4.1–4.3, 5.1, 5.2 **Decoding/Word Analysis** – 1.1, 2.1, 3.1, 4.1–4.3, 5.1, 5.2 **Story Reading/ Comprehension** – 1.2–1.5, 2.2–2.5, 3.2–3.5, 4.4–4.7, 5.3–5.6 **Fluency** **Paired Practice** **Study Skills** – 1.4, 1.5, 2.5, 3.5, 4.7, 5.6 **Informal Assessment Workcheck** – 1, 2, 3, 4, 5 **Formal Assessment** **Spelling** – 1, 2, 3, 4, 5	**Presentation Book A** **Vocabulary** – 6.1, 6.2, 7.1–7.3, 8.1, 8.2, 9.1, 9.2 **Decoding/Word Analysis** – 6.1, 6.2, 7.1–7.3, 8.1, 8.2, 9.1, 9.2 **Story Reading/ Comprehension** – 6.3, 6.4, 6.6, 7.4, 7.5, 7.7, 8.3, 8.4, 8.6, 9.3, 9.4, 9.6 **Fluency** **Paired Practice** – 6.5, 7.6, 8.5, 9.5 **Study Skills** – 6.6, 7.7, 8.6, 9.6 **Informal Assessment Workcheck** – 6, 7, 8, 9 **Formal Assessment** – 10.1, 10.2 **Spelling** – 6, 7, 8, 9	**Presentation Book A** **Vocabulary** – 11.1–11.3, 12.1, 12.2, 13.1, 13.2, 14.1–14.3, 15.1, 15.2 **Decoding/Word Analysis** – 11.1–11.3, 12.1, 12.2, 13.1, 13.2, 14.1–14.3, 15.1, 15.2 **Story Reading/ Comprehension** – 11.4, 11.5, 11.7, 12.3, 12.4, 12.6, 13.3, 13.4, 13.6, 14.4, 14.5, 14.7, 15.3–15.6 **Fluency** **Paired Practice** – 11.6, 12.5, 13.5, 14.6 **Study Skills** – 11.7, 13.6, 14.7, 15.5 **Informal Assessment Workcheck** – 11, 12, 13, 14, 15 **Formal Assessment** **Spelling** – 11, 12, 13, 14, 15	**Presentation Book A** **Vocabulary** – 16.1, 16.2, 17.1–17.3, 18.1, 18.2, 19.1, 19.2 **Decoding/Word Analysis** – 16.1, 16.2, 17.1–17.3, 18.1, 18.2, 19.1, 19.2 **Story Reading/ Comprehension** – 16.3, 16.4, 16.6, 17.4, 17.5, 17.7, 18.3, 18.4, 18.6, 19.3, 19.4, 19.6 **Fluency** **Paired Practice** – 17.6, 18.5, 19.5 **Study Skills** – 16.5, 17.5, 18.6, 19.6 **Informal Assessment Workcheck** – 16, 17, 18, 19 **Formal Assessment** – 20.1, 20.1 **Spelling** – 16, 17, 18, 19
Language Arts Strand *Reading Mastery*	**Vocabulary** *Left, right* – 1.2, 2.2, 3.1, 5.5 **Comprehension** *Classification* – 1.3, 1.4, 2.5, 3.3, 4.3, 5.4 *Sequence* – 1.5, 2.4 *Listening Comprehension* – 1.7, 2.6, 3.5, 4.4, 5.6 *Recalling Details* – 1.8, 2.8, 3.6, 4.5, 5.7 *True, False* – 2.3, 2.7, 3.2, 4.2, 5.3 **Grammar/Usage/ Mechanics**	**Vocabulary** *Left, right* – 9.4, 10.2 **Comprehension** *Classification* – 6.3, 7.2 *Listening Comprehension* – 6.4, 7.4, 8.6, 9.6, 10.3 *If-then Reasoning* – 8.3, 9.3 *Deduction* – 8.5, 9.5 *Recalling Details* – 8.7, 9.7 **Grammar/Usage/ Mechanics** *Correcting Word Usage Errors* – 6.5, 6.6, 7.5, 8.4	**Vocabulary** *Seasons* – 11.4, 12.1, 13.1 *Initial Letter Substitution* – 15.5 **Comprehension** *Deduction* – 11.2, 12.3, 13.3, 14.4, 15.2 *Listening Comprehension* – 11.5, 12.5, 13.5, 14.5, 15.4 *Recalling Details* – 11.6, 14.6	**Vocabulary** **Comprehension** *Listening Comprehension* – 16.4, 17.3, 18.3, 19.3 *True, false* – 16.5 *Deduction* – 17.2 *Comparisons* – 17.4, 18.4, 19.4 *Listening to Directions* – 20.3 **Grammar/Usage/ Mechanics** **Writing/Composition/ Speaking** *Sentences* 17.1, 18.1, 19.1, 20.1

F2

Strand Component	Lessons 1-5	Lessons 6-10	Lessons 11-15	Lessons 16-20
Language Arts Strand *(continued)*	**Writing/Composition/Speaking** *Sentences* – 1.6, 2.1, 3.4, 4.1, 5.1 **Study Skills** *Cardinal Directions* – 5.2	**Writing/Composition/Speaking** *Sentences* – 6.2, 7.3, 8.2, 9.2, 10.1 **Study Skills** *Cardinal Directions* – 6.1, 7.1, 8.1, 9.1	**Grammar/Usage/Mechanics** *Correcting Word Usage Errors* – 12.6, 13.6 **Writing/Composition/Speaking** *Sentences* – 11.3, 12.4, 13.4, 14.1, 15.3 **Study Skills** *Cardinal Directions* – 11.1, 14.2 *Maps* – 12.2, 13.2, 14.3, 15.1	**Study Skills** *Cardinal Directions* 16.1, 16.2 *Maps* 16.3, 20.2 *Maze Directions* 18.2, 19.2
Literature Strand *Reading Mastery*		**Literature Lesson 1** (presented with RM Lesson 6) setting, characters, plot **Literature Lesson 2** (presented with RM Lesson 10) *Stephanie's Ponytail;* theme individual tastes vary; setting, characters, plot		**Literature Lesson 3** (presented with RM Lesson 20) *George at the Zoo;* themes bravery, misbehavior; setting, characters, plot, fiction, nonfiction
Formal Assessment Reading Strand Language Arts Strand		**Reading Mastery Lesson 10 – Test 1:** individual fluency checkout, mastery test **Language Lesson 10 – Test 1:** writing parallel sentences, left/right, all/some/none, story, marking the test, test feedback, test remedies	**Reading Mastery Lesson 15 –** individual fluency checkout	**Reading Mastery Lesson 20 – Test 2:** individual fluency checkout, mastery test **Language Lesson 20 – Test 2:** writing parallel sentences, directions, story, marking the test, test feedback, test remedies

Strand Component	Lessons 21-25	Lessons 26-30	Lessons 31-35	Lessons 36-40
Core Lesson Connections	**A. Vocabulary** *New Vocabulary* – 21.A1, 22.A1, 23.A1, 24.A1 **B. Comprehension Strategies** *Comprehension Monitoring* – 21.B3 **C. Fluency** – 21.C, 22.C, 23.C, 24.C, 25.C	**A. Vocabulary** *New Vocabulary* – 26.A1, 27.A1, 28.A1, 29.A1 **B. Comprehension Strategies** **C. Fluency** – 26.C, 27.C, 28.C, 29.C, 30.C **D. Writing/Language Arts** – 30 D 1	**A. Vocabulary** *New Vocabulary* – 31.A1, 32.A1, 33.A1, 34.A1 **B. Comprehension Strategies** *Comprehension Monitoring* – 31.B2, 32.B2, 33.B2, 34.B2 **C. Fluency** – 31.C, 32.C, 33.C, 34.C, 35.C	**A. Vocabulary** *New Vocabulary* – 36.A1, 37.A1, 38.A1, 39.A1 **B. Comprehension Strategies** *Determine Text Type* – 38.B1, 38.B2 *Comprehension Monitoring* – 36.B3, 37.B2, 38.B3 **C. Fluency** – 36.C, 37.C, 38.C, 39.C, 40.C **D. Writing/Language Arts** – 40 D 1
Reading Strand *Reading Mastery*	**Presentation Book A** **Vocabulary** – 21.1, 21.2, 22.1, 22.2, 23.1, 23.2, 24.1, 24.2, 25.1–25.3 **Decoding/Word Analysis** – 21.1, 21.2, 22.1, 22.2, 23.1, 23.2, 24.1, 24.2	**Presentation Book A** **Vocabulary** – 26.1, 26.2, 27.1, 27.2, 28.1, 28.2, 29.1–29.3 **Decoding/Word Analysis** – 26.1, 26.2, 27.1, 27.2, 28.1, 28.2, 29.1–29.3	**Presentation Book A** **Vocabulary** – 31.1, 31.2, 32.1, 32.2, 33.1–33.3, 34.1, 34.2, 35.1, 35.2 **Decoding/Word Analysis** – 31.2, 31.1, 32.2, 33.1–33.3, 34.1, 34.2, 35.1, 35.2	**Presentation Book A** **Vocabulary** – 36.1, 36.2, 37.1–37.3, 38.1, 38.2, 39.1, 39.2 **Decoding/Word Analysis** – 36.1, 36.2, 37.1–37.3, 38.1, 38.2, 39.1, 39.2

F3

Strand Component	Lessons 21-25	Lessons 26-30	Lessons 31-35	Lessons 36-40
Reading Strand *Reading Mastery* (continued)	**Story Reading/ Comprehension –** 21.3, 21.4, 21.6, 22.3, 22.4, 23.3, 23.4, 23.6, 24.3, 24.4, 24.6, 25.4, 25.5, 25.7 **Fluency** **Paired Practice –** 21.5, 22.5, 23.5, 24.5 **Study Skills** **Informal Assessment** **Workcheck** **Formal Assessment** **Spelling –** 21, 22, 23, 24, 25	**Story Reading/ Comprehension –** 26.3, 26.4, 26.6, 27.3, 27.5, 28.3, 28.4, 28.6, 29.4, 29.5, 29.7 **Fluency** **Paired Practice –** 26.5, 27.4, 28.5, 29.6 **Study Skills –** 26.6 **Informal Assessment** **Workcheck –** 26, 27, 28, 29 **Formal Assessment –** 30.2, 30.3 **Spelling –** 26, 27, 28, 29	**Story Reading/ Comprehension –** 31.3, 31.4, 31.6, 32.3, 32.4, 32.6, 33.4, 33.5, 33.7, 34.3, 34.5, 35.3, 35.4, 35.6 **Fluency** **Paired Practice –** 31.5, 32.5, 33.6, 34.4 **Study Skills –** 31.6, 32.6 **Informal Assessment** **Workcheck –** 31, 32, 33, 34, 35 **Formal Assessment** **Spelling –** 31, 32, 33, 34, 35	**Story Reading/ Comprehension –** 36.3, 36.4, 374, 37.5, 38.3, 38.4, 39.3, 39.4 **Fluency** **Paired Practice –** 36.5, 37.6, 38.5, 39.6 **Study Skills –** 39.5 **Informal Assessment** **Workcheck –** 36, 37, 38, 39 **Formal Assessment –** 40.2, 40.3 **Spelling –** 36, 37, 38, 39
Language Arts Strand *Reading Mastery*	**Vocabulary** *To, from –* 22.2, 23.1, 25.1 **Comprehension** *Classification –* 22.3, 23.3 *Subclass –* 24.2 *Deduction –* 22.4, 25.3 *Listening Comprehension –* 22.4, 23.4, 24.3, 25.2 **Grammar/Usage/ Mechanics** *Correcting Word Usage Errors –* 24.4 **Writing/Composition/ Speaking** *Story Sentences –* 21.1 *Sentences –* 22.1, 23.5, 24.1 **Study Skills** *Maps –* 23.2, 25.1	**Vocabulary** *To, from –* 27.1, 30.2 **Comprehension** *Sequencing –* 27.2, 28.1 *Classification, subclass –* 27.3 *Deduction –* 28.2, 29.1, 30.2 *Listening Comprehension –* 27.4, 29.3, 30.3 **Grammar/Usage/ Mechanics** **Writing/Composition/ Speaking** *Story Sentences –* 26.1 *Fictional Story –* 27.5, 28.3 *Story Presentation –* 28.3 *Writing Deductions –* 29.1 *Sentences –* 30.1 **Study Skills** *Maps –* 27.1, 29.2, 29.4, 30.2	**Vocabulary** **Comprehension** *Classification –* 32.3, 33.3, 34.1, 35.3 *Listening Comprehension –* 32.4, 33.4, 34.4, 35.4 *Sequencing –* 34.3 **Grammar/Usage/ Mechanics** *Pronoun Referents –* 34.5, 35.5 **Writing/Composition/ Speaking** *Story Sentences –* 31.1 *Sentences –* 34.6 **Study Skills** *Alphabetical Order –* 32.1, 33.1, 35.1 *Maps –* 32.2, 32.5, 33.2, 34.2, 35.2	**Vocabulary** **Comprehension** *Following Written Directions –* 36.3, 37.2 *Listening Comprehension –* 36.4, 37.5, 38.4, 39.4, 40.3 *Deduction –* 37.3, 38.4, 39.2, 39.5 *Sequencing –* 40.2 *Classification –* 40.2 **Grammar/Usage/ Mechanics** *Pronoun Referents –* 36.5, 37.4, 38.3, 39.3 **Writing/Composition/ Speaking** *Story Sentences –* 37.1 *Sentences –* 40.1 **Study Skills** *Alphabetical Order –* 36.1, 38.1, 39.1 *Maps –* 36.2, 36.3, 38.2, 40.2
Literature Strand *Reading Mastery*		**Literature Lessons 4-1 and 4-2** (presented with RM Lesson 30) **Lesson 4-1** *A House with a Star Inside;* theme riddles; retelling, setting, characters, plot **Lesson 4-2** *Remember;* themes changes, memories		**Literature Lesson 5** (presented with RM Lesson 40) *Pop's Truck* themes old friends, recycling setting, characters, plot, retelling, fiction, nonfiction, stories, plays, poems
Formal Assessment Reading Strand Language Arts Strand	**Reading Mastery Lesson 25 –** individual fluency checkout	**Reading Mastery Lesson 30 – Test 3:** fact game, individual fluency checkout, mastery test, marking the test, test remedies		**Reading Mastery Lesson 40 – Test 4:** fact game, individual fluency checkout, mastery test, marking the test, test remedies

F4

Strand Component	Lessons 21-25	Lessons 26-30	Lessons 31-35	Lessons 36-40
Formal Assessment (continued)		**Language Lesson 30 – Test 3:** writing parallel sentences, map, deduction writing, story, marking the test, test feedback, test remedies		**Language Lesson 40 – Test 4:** writing parallel sentences, map, temporal sequencing, classification, story, marking the test, test feedback, test remedies

Strand Component	Lessons 41-45	Lessons 46-50	Lessons 51-55	Lessons 56-60
Core Lesson Connections	**A.** Vocabulary *New Vocabulary* – 41.A1, 42.A1, 43.A1, 44.A1 **B.** Comprehension Strategies *Generate Questions* – 42.B2, 43.B3, 44.B3 **C.** Fluency – 41.C, 42.C, 43.C, 44.C, 45.C	**A.** Vocabulary *New Vocabulary* – 46.A1, 47.A1, 48.A1, 49.A1 **B.** Comprehension Strategies *Generate Questions* – 46.B2, 47.B2, 48.B2, 49.B2 **C.** Fluency – 46.C, 47.C, 48.C, 49.C, 50.C **D.** Writing/Language Arts – 50 D 1	**A.** Vocabulary *New Vocabulary* – 51.A1, 52.A1, 53.A1, 54.A1 **B.** Comprehension Strategies *Comprehension Monitoring* – 51.B1, 52.B1, 53.B3, 54.B2 **C.** Fluency – 51.C, 52.C, 53.C, 54.C, 55.C	**A.** Vocabulary *New Vocabulary* – 56.A1, 57.A2, 58.A1, 59.A1 **B.** Comprehension Strategies *Determine Text Type* – 57.B2 *Comprehension Monitoring* – 56.B1, 56.B2, 57.B1, 58.B2, 59.B2, 59.B3 **C.** Fluency – 56.C, 57.C, 58.C, 59.C, 60.C **D.** Writing/Language Arts – 60 D 1
Reading Strand *Reading Mastery*	**Presentation Book A** **Vocabulary** – 41.1–41.3, 42.1, 42.2, 43.1, 43.2, 44.1, 44.2, 45.1–45.3 **Decoding/Word Analysis** – 41.1–41.3, 42.1, 42.2, 43.1, 43.2, 44.1, 44.2, 45.1–45.3 **Story Reading/ Comprehension** – 41.4, 41.5, 42.3, 42.4, 43.3, 43.4, 44.3, 45.4, 45.5 **Fluency** *Paired Practice* – 41.6, 42.5, 44.5 **Study Skills** – 43.4, 44.4 **Informal Assessment** **Workcheck** – 41, 42, 43, 44, 45 **Formal Assessment** **Spelling** – 41, 42, 43, 44, 45	**Presentation Book A** **Vocabulary** – 46.1, 46.2, 47.1, 47.2, 48.1–48.3, 49.1, 49.2 **Decoding/Word Analysis** – 46.1, 46.2, 47.1, 47.2, 48.1–48.3, 49.1, 49.2 **Story Reading/ Comprehension** – 46.3, 46.5, 47.3, 47.5, 48.4, 48.5, 49.3 **Fluency** *Paired Practice* – 46.6, 47.7, 48.7, 49.4 **Study Skills** – 46.4, 47.6, 48.4, 48.6 **Informal Assessment** **Workcheck** – 46, 47, 48, 49 **Formal Assessment** – 50.2, 50.3 **Spelling** – 46, 47, 48, 49	**Presentation Book B** **Vocabulary** – 51.1, 51.2, 52.1–52.3, 53.1, 53.2, 54.1, 54.2, 55.1–55.3 **Decoding/Word Analysis** – 51.1, 51.2, 52.1–52.3, 53.1, 53.2, 54.1, 54.2, 55.1–55.3 **Story Reading/ Comprehension** – 51.3, 51.4, 52.4, 53.3–53.5, 54.3, 55.4–55.6 **Fluency** *Paired Practice* – 51.6, 52.5, 54.4 **Study Skills** – 51.5 **Informal Assessment** **Workcheck** – 51, 52, 53, 54 **Formal Assessment** **Spelling** – 51, 52, 53, 54	**Presentation Book B** **Vocabulary** – 56.1, 56.2, 57.1, 57.2, 58.1–58.3, 59.1, 59.2 **Decoding/Word Analysis** – 56.1, 56.2, 57.1, 57.2, 58.1–58.3, 59.1, 59.2 **Story Reading/ Comprehension** – 56.3, 56.4, 57.3, 57.4, 58.4, 58.5, 59.3 **Fluency** *Paired Practice* – 56.5, 57.5, 58.6, 59.4 **Study Skills** **Informal Assessment** **Workcheck** – 56, 57, 58, 59 **Formal Assessment** – 60.2, 60.3 **Spelling** – 56, 57, 58, 59
Language Arts Strand *Reading Mastery*	**Vocabulary** **Comprehension** *Listening Comprehension* – 41.4, 42.3, 43.3, 44.3, 45.3 *Recalling Details* – 41.5, 42.4 *Deduction* – 44.2, 45.4	**Vocabulary** **Comprehension** *Listening Comprehension* – 46.4, 47.4, 48.3, 49.2, 50.3 *Sequencing* – 46.5	**Vocabulary** **Comprehension** *Sequencing* – 51.2, 52.1, 53.2 *Listening Comprehension* – 51.4, 52.2, 53.4, 54.4, 55.4 *Deduction* – 51.5, 52.3, 53.5, 55.3 *Recalling Details* – 53.5 *Character Extrapolation* – 55.5	**Vocabulary** **Comprehension** *Deduction* – 56.1, 57.5, 60.2 *Main Idea* – 56.2, 57.1, 57.2, 58.1, 59.1, 60.1 *Listening Comprehension* – 56.3, 57.3, 59.2

F5

Strand Component	Lessons 41-45	Lessons 46-50	Lessons 51-55	Lessons 56-60
Language Arts Strand *Reading Mastery* (continued)	**Grammar/Usage/ Mechanics** *Pronoun Referents* – 41.3, 42.3, 43.4, 45.3 **Writing/Composition/ Speaking** *Sentences* – 41.4, 42.1, 44.1, 45.1, 45.2 *Story Sentences* – 43.1 **Study Skills** *Maps* – 41.2, 43.2	**Grammar/Usage/ Mechanics** *Pronoun Referents* – 47.3 *Correcting Word Usage Errors* – 48.4, 49.3 **Writing/Composition/ Speaking** *Story Sentences* – 46.1, 46.3, 49.4 *Sentences* – 47.2, 48.1, 48.2, 49.1, 50.1 *Dramatic Activity* – 47.5 **Study Skills** *Maps* – 46.2, 47.1, 50.2	**Grammar/Usage/ Mechanics** *Pronoun Referents* – 51.3, 54.3 **Writing/Composition/ Speaking** *Sentences* – 51.1, 51.2, 52.1, 53.2 *Deductive Sentences* – 51.5, 52.3, 53.3 *Letter Writing* – 53.1, 54.1, 55.1 *Dramatic Activity* – 54.5 **Study Skills** *Maps* – 54.2, 55.2	**Grammar/Usage/ Mechanics** *Pronoun Referents* – 56.4 *Correcting Word Usage Errors* – 60.2 **Writing/Composition/ Speaking** *Sentences* – 57.2, 58.1, 59.1, 60.1 *Write an ending to a story* – 57.4, 58.2, 59.2, 60.3 **Study Skills**
Literature Strand *Reading Mastery*		**Literature Lesson 6** – (presented with RM Lesson 50) *Trixie;* themes handicaps, individual differences; retelling, setting, characters, plot, author's purpose, comparing stories		**Literature Lesson 7** – (presented with RM Lesson 60) *The Three Wishes* themes comparing ourselves with others, greed setting, characters, plot, retelling
Formal Assessment Reading Strand Language Arts Strand	**Reading Mastery Lesson 45** – individual fluency checkout	**Reading Mastery Lesson 50 – Test 5:** fact game, individual fluency checkout, mastery test, marking the test, test remedies **Language Lesson 50 – Test 5:** sentence construction, map, story, marking the test, test feedback, test remedies	**Reading Mastery Lesson 55** – individual fluency checkout	**Reading Mastery Lesson 60 – Test 6:** fact game, individual fluency checkout, mastery test, marking the test, test remedies **Language Lesson 60 – Test 6:** writing sentences, writing talk, story construction, marking the test, test feedback, test remedies

Strand Component	Lessons 61-65	Lessons 66-70	Lessons 71-75	Lessons 76-80
Core Lesson Connections	**A. Vocabulary** *New Vocabulary* – 61.A1, 62.A1, 63.A1, 64.A1 **B. Comprehension Strategies** *Determine Text Type* – 62.B1 **C. Fluency** – 61.C, 62.C, 63.C, 64.C, 65.C	**A. Vocabulary** *New Vocabulary* – 66.A1, 67.A1, 68.A1, 69.A1 **B. Comprehension Strategies** *Comprehension Monitoring* – 67.B1 **C. Fluency** – 66.C, 67.C, 68.C, 69.C, 70.C **D. Writing/Language Arts** – 70 D 1	**A. Vocabulary** *New Vocabulary* – 71.A1, 72.A1, 73.A1, 74.A1 **B. Comprehension Strategies** **C. Fluency** – 71.C, 72.C, 73.C, 74.C, 75.C	**A. Vocabulary** *New Vocabulary* – 76.A1, 77.A1, 78.A1, 79.A1 **B. Comprehension Strategies** **C. Fluency** – 76.C, 77.C, 78.C, 79.C, 80.C **D. Writing/Language Arts** – 80 D 1
Reading Strand *Reading Mastery*	**Presentation Book B** **Vocabulary** – 61.1, 61.2, 62.1–62.3, 63.1, 63.2, 64.1, 64.2, 65–65.3 **Decoding/Word Analysis** – 61.1, 61.2, 62.1–62.3, 63.1, 63.2, 64.1, 64.2, 65.1–65.3	**Presentation Book B** **Vocabulary** – 66.1, 66.2, 67.1, 67.2, 68.1–68.3, 69.1, 69.2 **Decoding/Word Analysis** – 66.1, 66.2, 67.1, 67.2, 68.1–68.3, 69.1, 69.2	**Presentation Book B** **Vocabulary** – 71.1, 71.2, 72.1–72.3, 73.1, 73.2, 74.1, 74.2, 75.1, 75.2 **Decoding/Word Analysis** – 71.1, 71.2, 72.1–72.3, 73.1, 73.2, 74.1, 74.2, 75.1, 75.2	**Presentation Book B** **Vocabulary** – 76.1–76.3, 77.1, 77.2, 78.1, 78.2, 79.1, 79.2 **Decoding/Word Analysis** – 76.1–76.3, 77.1, 77.2, 78.1, 78.2, 79.1, 79.2

Strand Component	Lessons 61-65	Lessons 66-70	Lessons 71-75	Lessons 76-80
Reading Strand *Reading Mastery* (continued)	**Story Reading/ Comprehension** – 61.3, 61.4, 62.4, 62.5, 63.3, 63.4, 64.3, 64.4, 65.4, 65.5 **Fluency** *Paired Practice* – 61.5, 62.6, 63.5, 64.5 **Study Skills** – 64.4, 65.4 **Informal Assessment** **Workcheck** – 61, 62, 63, 64, 65 **Formal Assessment** **Spelling** – 61, 62, 63, 64, 65	**Story Reading/ Comprehension** – 66.3, 66.4, 67.3, 68.4, 69.3 **Fluency** *Paired Practice* – 66.5, 67.4, 68.5, 69.4 **Study Skills** **Informal Assessment** **Workcheck** – 66, 67, 68, 69 **Formal Assessment** – 70.2, 70.3 **Spelling** – 66, 67, 68, 69	**Story Reading/ Comprehension** – 71.3, 71.4, 72.4, 73.3, 73.4, 74.3, 75.3, 75.4 **Fluency** *Paired Practice* – 71.5, 72.5, 73.5, 74.4 **Study Skills** **Informal Assessment** **Workcheck** – 71, 72, 73, 74, 75 **Formal Assessment** **Spelling** – 71, 72, 73, 74, 75	**Story Reading/ Comprehension** – 76.4, 77.3, 78.3, 79.3, 79.4 **Fluency** *Paired Practice* – 76.5, 77.4, 78.4, 79.5 **Study Skills** – 79.6 **Informal Assessment** **Workcheck** – 76, 77, 78, 79 **Formal Assessment** – 80.2, 80.3 **Spelling** – 76, 77, 78, 79
Language Arts Strand *Reading Mastery*	**Vocabulary** *After* – 63.1 **Comprehension** *Listening Comprehension* - 61.3, 62.4, 63.3, 64.2, 65.2 *Sequencing* – 63.1 *Main Idea* – 64.1, 65.1 *Recalling Details* – 64.3, 65.3 **Grammar/Usage/ Mechanics** *Pronoun Referents* – 61.4, 62.5 **Writing/Composition/ Speaking** *Sentences* – 61.2, 62.1, 63.2, 64.1, 65.1 *Letter Writing* – 64.4, 65.4 **Study Skills** *Maps* – 61.1, 62.2, 62.3, 63.4, 64.3	**Vocabulary** *Suffix –ed* – 69.2, 70.2 **Comprehension** *Main Idea* – 66.1, 67.2, 68.6, 69.5 *Deductions* – 66.5, 67.6, 68.4, 69.3, 70.4 **Grammar/Usage/ Mechanics** *Subject of Sentence* – 66.2, 67.3, 67.5, 68.3, 68.5, 69.2, 69.3 *Capitalization* – 66.3, 68.4, 69.3, 69.5 *Sentence Punctuation* – 66.3 *Punctuation* – 69.5 *Predicate of Sentence* – 70.4 **Writing/Composition/ Speaking** **Study Skills**	**Vocabulary** **Comprehension** *Deduction* – 71.5, 73.5 *Main Idea* – 71.6, 71.7, 72.5, 72.6, 73.7, 74.5, 75.2, 75.3 **Grammar/Usage/ Mechanics** *Irregular Verbs* – 71.2, 73.6, 75.3 *Verb Tense* – 71.3, 72.3, 73.4, 74.3, 75.3 *Subject/Predicate* – 71.4, 72.2, 73.2, 74.4, 75.3 *Pronouns* – 72.4, 73.3, 74.2 **Writing/Composition/ Speaking** *Editing* – 71.3, 72.3, 73.4, 74.3, 75.2 **Study Skills**	**Vocabulary** **Comprehension** *Main Idea* – 76.6, 76.7, 77.6, 77.7, 78.6, 78.7, 79.6, 79.7, 80.6 *Deductions* – 77.5 *Classification* – 80.5 **Grammar/Usage/ Mechanics** *Irregular Verbs* – 76.2, 77.3, 78.5, 79.5 *Subject/Predicate* – 76.3, 77.2, 78.3, 79.3, 80.4 *Pronouns* – 76.4, 77.4, 78.4, 79.2, 80.2 *Verb Tense* – 76.5, 78.2, 79.4, 80.3 **Writing/Composition/ Speaking** *Editing* – 76.5, 78.2, 79.4, 80.3 *Paragraph Copying* – 80.6
Literature Strand *Reading Mastery*		**Literature Lesson 8** (presented with RM Lesson 70) **Lesson 8:** *Tom's Friend* theme: freedom retelling, setting, characters, plot, author's purpose		**Literature Lesson 9-1 and 9-2** (presented with RM Lesson 80) **Lesson 9-1:** "The Case of Natty Nat" theme: self-contradiction **Lesson 9-2:** "Swap" Theme: changes don't always lead to change
Formal Assessment Reading Strand Language Arts Strand	**Reading Mastery Lesson 65** – individual fluency checkout	**Reading Mastery Lesson 70 – Test 7:** fact game, individual fluency checkout, mastery test, marking the test, test remedies **Language Lesson 70 – Test 7:** feedback, suffixes, irregular verbs, deductions, predicate, sentence completion, marking the test, test feedback, test remedies	**Reading Mastery Lesson 75** – individual fluency checkout **Language Lesson 75 – Test 8:** feedback, main idea, reporting, irregular verbs, subject/predicate, editing sentences, storytelling, marking the test, test feedback, test remedies	**Reading Mastery Lesson 80 – Test 8:** fact game, individual fluency checkout, mastery test, marking the test, test remedies

F7

Strand Component	Lessons 81-85	Lessons 86-90	Lessons 91-95	Lessons 96-100
Core Lesson Connections	**A.** Vocabulary *New Vocabulary* – 81.A1, 82.A1, 83.A1, 84.A1 **B.** Comprehension Strategies **C.** Fluency – 81.C, 82.C, 83.C, 84.C, 85.C	**A.** Vocabulary *New Vocabulary* – 86.A1, 87.A1, 88.A1, 89.A **B.** Comprehension Strategies **C.** Fluency – 86.C, 87.C, 88.C, 89.C, 90.C **D.** Writing/Language Arts – 90 D 1	**A.** Vocabulary *New Vocabulary* – 91.A1, 92.A1, 93.A1, 94.A1 **B.** Comprehension Strategies *Comprehension Monitoring* – 94.B3 *Identify Cause–and–Effect Relationships* – 91.B1, 92.B1, 93.B2, 94.B1 **C.** Fluency – 91.C, 92.C, 93.C, 94.C, 95.C	**A.** Vocabulary *New Vocabulary* – 96.A1, 97.A2, 98.A1, 99.A1 **B.** Comprehension Strategies *Identify Cause–and–Effect Relationships* – 96.B1, 97.B2, 98.B2, 99.B2 **C.** Fluency – 96.C, 97.C, 98.C, 99.C, 100.C **D.** Writing/Language Arts – 100 D 1
Reading Strand *Reading Mastery*	**Presentation Book B** **Vocabulary** – 81.1–81.3, 82.1, 82.2, 83.1, 83.2, 84.1, 84.2, 85.1, 85.2 **Decoding/Word Analysis** – 81.1–81.3, 82.1, 82.2, 83.1, 83.2, 84.1, 84.2, 85.1, 85.2 **Story Reading/ Comprehension** – 81.4, 81.5, 82.4, 83.4, 84.3, 84.4, 85.4, 85.5 **Fluency** *Paired Practice* – 81.6, 82.5, 83.5, 84.5 *Study Skills* – 82.3, 83.3, 85.3 **Informal Assessment** **Workcheck** – 81, 82, 83, 84, 85 **Formal Assessment** **Spelling** – 81, 82, 83, 84, 85	**Presentation Book B** **Vocabulary** – 86.1, 86.2, 87.1–87.3, 88.1, 88.2, 89.1, 89.2 **Decoding/Word Analysis** – 86.1, 86.2, 87.1–87.3, 88.1, 88.2, 89.1, 89.2 **Story Reading/ Comprehension** – 86.3, 87.4, 88.3, 89.3, 89.4 **Fluency** *Paired Practice* – 86.4, 87.5, 88.4, 89.5 *Study Skills* **Informal Assessment** **Workcheck** – 86, 87, 88, 89 **Formal Assessment** – 90.2, 90.3 **Spelling** – 86, 87, 88, 89	**Presentation Book B** **Vocabulary** – 91.1–91.3, 92.1, 92.2, 93.1, 93.2, 94.1, 94.2, 95.1–95.3 **Decoding/Word Analysis** – 91.1–91.3, 92.1, 92.2, 93.1, 93.2, 94.1, 94.2, 95.1–95.3 **Story Reading/ Comprehension** – 91.4, 91.5, 92.3, 93.3, 93.4, 94.3, 94.4, 95.4–95.6 **Fluency** *Paired Practice* – 91.6, 92.4, 93.5, 94.5 *Study Skills* **Informal Assessment** **Workcheck** – 91, 92, 93, 94, 95 **Formal Assessment** **Spelling** – 91, 92, 93, 94, 95	**Presentation Book B** **Vocabulary** – 96.1, 96.2, 97.1, 97.2, 98.1, 99.1 **Decoding/Word Analysis** – 96.1, 96.2, 97.1, 97.2, 98.1, 99.1 **Story Reading/ Comprehension** – 96.3, 97.3, 97.4, 98.2, 99.3 **Fluency** *Paired Practice* – 96.4, 97.5, 98.3, 99.4 *Study Skills* – 99.2 **Informal Assessment** **Workcheck** – 96, 97, 98, 99 **Formal Assessment** – 100.2, 100.3 **Spelling** – 96, 97, 98, 99
Language Arts Strand *Reading Mastery*	**Vocabulary** **Comprehension** *Classification* – 81.6, 82.4, 83.4, 84.5 *Main Idea* – 81.7, 82.6, 82.7, 83.4, 83.6, 84.5, 85.3 **Grammar/Usage/ Mechanics** *Verb Tense* – 81.2, 83.3, 84.4 *Subject/Predicate* – 81.3, 84.2 *Pronouns* – 81.4, 82.2, 85.3 *Capitalization* – 81.5, 82.3, 82.5, 83.2, 84.3, 84.6, 85.2, 85.3 *Punctuation* – 81.5, 82.3, 82.5, 83.2, 84.3, 84.6, 85.2, 85.3	**Vocabulary** **Comprehension** *Main Idea* – 86.5, 87.6, 88.5, 88.7, 89.5, 89.7, 90.7 **Grammar/Usage/ Mechanics** *Capitalization* – 86.2, 86.6, 87.2, 87.7, 88.3, 88.6, 89.2, 89.6, 90.2, 90.6 *Punctuation* – 86.2, 86.6, 87.2, 87.7, 88.3, 88.6, 89.2, 89.6, 90.2, 90.6 *Subject/Predicate* – 86.3, 89.3, 90.5 *Verb Tense* – 86.4, 87.4, 88.4, 90.4 *Irregular Verbs* – 86.4, 87.5, 88.4, 90.4 *Subject* – 87.3, 88.2	**Vocabulary** *Prepositions* – 95.2 **Comprehension** *Main Idea* – 92.6, 93.6, 94.5, 95.2, 95.4 **Grammar/Usage/ Mechanics** *Capitalization* – 91.2, 93.2, 93.7, 94.2, 94.4, 94.7, 95.4 *Punctuation* – 91.2, 93.2, 93.7, 94.2, 94.6, 95.4 *Verb Tense* – 91.3, 92.3, 93.5, 94.6, 95.3 *Irregular Verbs* – 91.3, 92.3, 93.5, 94.6, 95.3 *Pronouns* – 91.4, 92.4, 93.4, 94.3, 95.4	**Vocabulary** *Prepositions* – 96.4 **Comprehension** *Main Idea* – 96.4, 97.5 **Grammar/Usage/ Mechanics** *Capitalization* – 96.1, 96.2, 97.2, 97.4, 98.2, 98.4, 99.3, 99.5, 100.2 *Punctuation* – 96.2, 97.4, 98.4, 99.3 *Run-on Sentences* – 96.2, 97.4 *Verb Tense* – 96.3, 98.6, 100.4 *Irregular Verbs* – 96.3, 98.6, 100.4 *Subject/Predicate* – 96.5, 97.6, 98.5, 99.2, 100.5 *Pronouns* – 97.3, 98.3, 99.4, 100.3

F8

Strand Component	Lessons 81-85	Lessons 86-90	Lessons 91-95	Lessons 96-100
Language Arts Strand *Reading Mastery* (continued)	**Writing/Composition/ Speaking** *Editing* – 81.2, 82.3, 83.2, 83.3, 84.3, 84.4, 85.3 *Paragraph Copying* – 81.5, 82.5, 83.5, 84.6, 85.2 **Study Skills**	**Writing/Composition/ Speaking** *Editing* – 86.2, 87.2, 87.4, 88.3, 89.2, 90.2 *Paragraph Writing* – 86.6, 87.7, 88.6, 89.6, 90.6 **Study Skills**	**Writing/Composition/ Speaking** *Editing* – 91.2, 93.2, 94.2, 95.4 *Paragraph Writing* – 91.5, 92.7, 93.7, 94.7 *Sentences* – 91.7, 92.5 **Study Skills**	**Writing/Composition/ Speaking** *Editing* – 96.2, 97.4, 97.5, 98.4, 99.3, 100.3 *Paragraph Writing* – 96.6, 97.5 *Revising for Clarity* – 98.7, 99.6, 99.7, 100.6, 100.7 **Study Skills**
Literature Strand *Reading Mastery*		**Literature Lessons 10-1 and 10-2** (presented with RM Lesson 90) **Lesson 10-1:** *The Thirsty Crows* theme: persistence retelling, setting, characters, plot, fables **Lesson 10-2:** "Rabbit" theme: pets		**Literature Lesson 11** (presented with RM Lesson 100): Moonwalker theme: imagination
Formal Assessment Reading Strand Language Arts Strand	**Reading Mastery Lesson 85** – individual fluency checkout **Language Lesson 85 – Test 9:** Feedback, paragraph writing, editing, clarity, pronoun, storytelling, marking the test, test feedback, test remedies	**Reading Mastery Lesson 90 – Test 9:** fact game, individual fluency checkout, mastery test, marking the test, test remedies	**Reading Mastery Lesson 95** – individual fluency checkout **Language Lesson 95 – Test 10:** feedback, clarity, irregular verbs, subject/ predicate, paragraph editing, pronouns, clarity, marking the test, test feedback, test remedies	**Reading Mastery Lesson 100 – Test 10:** fact game, individual fluency checkout, mastery test, marking the test, test remedies

Strand Component	Lessons 101-105	Lessons 106-110	Lessons 111-115	Lessons 116-120
Core Lesson Connections	**A. Vocabulary** *New Vocabulary* – 101.A1, 102.A1, 103.A1, 104.A1 **B. Comprehension Strategies** *Choose a Comprehension Strategy* – 101.B2 *Comprehension Monitoring* – 102.B3, 103. B2 **C. Fluency** – 101.C, 102.C, 103.C, 104.C, 105.C	**A. Vocabulary** *New Vocabulary* – 106.A1, 107.A1, 108.A1, 109.A1 **B. Comprehension Strategies** *Identify Cause–and–Effect Relationships* – 106.B2 *Generate Questions* – 109. B2 *Choose a Comprehension Strategy* – 109.B3 **C. Fluency** – 106.C, 107.C, 108.C, 109.C, 110.C **D. Writing/Language Arts** – 110 D 1	**A. Vocabulary** *New Vocabulary* – 111.A1, 112.A1, 113.A1, 114.A1 **B. Comprehension Strategies** **C. Fluency** – 111.C, 112.C, 113.C, 114.C, 115.C	**A. Vocabulary** *New Vocabulary* – 116.A1, 117.A1, 118.A1, 119.A1 **B. Comprehension Strategies** *Identify Cause–and–Effect Relationships* – 119.B1 *Comprehension Monitoring* – 118.B1 **C. Fluency** – 116.C, 117.C, 118.C, 119.C, 120.C **D. Writing/Language Arts** – 120 D 1
Reading Strand *Reading Mastery*	**Presentation Book C** **Vocabulary –** 101.1–101.3, 102.1, 102.2, 103.1, 103.2, 104.1, 105.1 **Decoding/Word Analysis** – 101.1–101.3, 102.1, 102.2, 103.1, 103.2, 104.1, 105.1	**Presentation Book C** **Vocabulary –** 106.1, 107.1–107.3, 108.1, 108.2, 109.1, 109.2 **Decoding/Word Analysis** – 106.1, 107.1–107.3, 108.1, 108.2, 109.1, 109.2	**Presentation Book C** **Vocabulary –** 111.1–111.3, 112.1, 112.2, 113.1, 113.1, 114.1, 115.1–115.3 **Decoding/Word Analysis** – 111.1–111.3, 112.1, 112.2, 113.1, 113.2, 114.1, 115.1–115.3	**Presentation Book C** **Vocabulary –** 116.1, 116.2, 117.1, 117.2, 118.1–118.3, 119.1, 119.2 **Decoding/Word Analysis** – 116.1, 116.2, 117.1, 117.2, 118.1–118.3, 119.1, 119.2

F9

Strand Component	Lessons 101-105	Lessons 106-110	Lessons 111-115	Lessons 116-120
Reading Strand *Reading Mastery* (continued)	**Story Reading/ Comprehension** – 101.4, 102.3, 103.3, 104.2, 105.2, 105.3 **Fluency** *Paired Practice* – 101.5, 102.4, 103.4, 104.3 **Informal Assessment** **Workcheck** – 101, 102, 103, 104, 105 **Formal Assessment** **Spelling** – 101, 102, 103, 104, 105	**Story Reading/ Comprehension** – 106.2, 107.4, 107.5, 108.3, 108.4, 109.3, 109.4 **Fluency** *Paired Practice* – 106.3, 107.6, 108.5, 109.5 *Study Skills* – 107.4 **Informal Assessment** **Workcheck** – 106, 107, 108, 109 **Formal Assessment** – 110.2, 110.3 **Spelling** – 106, 107, 108, 109	**Story Reading/ Comprehension** – 111.4, 111.5, 112.3, 113.3, 113.5, 114.2, 114.3, 115.4–115.6 **Fluency** *Paired Practice* – 111.6, 112.4, 113.6, 114.4 *Study Skills* – 111.4, 113.3, 113.4 **Informal Assessment** **Workcheck** – 111, 112, 113, 114, 115 **Formal Assessment** **Spelling** – 111, 112, 113, 114, 115	**Story Reading/ Comprehension** – 116.3, 116.4, 117.3, 117.5, 118.4, 118.5, 118.7, 119.3, 119.4 **Fluency** *Paired Practice* – 116.5, 117.4, 118.6, 119.5 **Informal Assessment** **Workcheck** – 116, 117, 118, 119 **Formal Assessment** – 120.2, 120.3 **Spelling** – 116, 117, 118, 119
Language Arts Strand *Reading Mastery*	**Vocabulary** **Comprehension** *Supporting Facts* – 103.5 *Main Idea* – 104.5 **Grammar/Usage/ Mechanics** *Capitalization* – 101.2, 101.5, 102.2, 103.3, 104.2, 105.4 *Verb Tense* – 101.3, 102.5, 103.4 *Irregular Verbs* – 101.3, 102.5, 103.4 *Pronouns* – 101.4, 102.4, 104.4, 105.4 *Punctuation* – 101.5, 104.2 *Subject/Predicate* – 103.2, 105.4 *Run-on Sentences* – 104.3, 105.2 *Predicates* – 105.3 **Writing/Composition/ Speaking** *Editing* – 101.2, 102.2, 103.3, 104.2, 104.3, 105.2 *Revising for Clarity* – 101.4, 102.4, 103.6, 104.4 *Paragraph Writing* – 101.5, 102.6, 103.7, 104.6 *Sentences* – 104.5 **Study Skills**	**Vocabulary** **Comprehension** *Main Ideas* – 108.5, 109.5, 110.5 **Grammar/Usage/ Mechanics** *Pronouns* – 106.1, 107.5, 108.4, 108.5 *Run-on Sentences* – 106.2, 107.3, 108.3, 109.2, 110.2 *Verbs* – 106.3, 106.4, 109.3, 110.3 *Capitalization* – 106.5 *Subject/Predicate* – 107.2, 108.2 *Verb Tense* – 107.4, 109.3 *Irregular Verbs* – 107.4 *Possessives* – 109.4, 110.4 *Compound Predicate* – 110.6 **Writing/Composition/ Speaking** *Editing* – 106.2, 106.5, 107.3, 108.3 *Paragraph Writing* – 106.6, 107.6, 108.6, 109.6, 110.7 *Sentences* – 109.5, 110.5 **Study Skills**		
Literature Strand *Reading Mastery*		**Literature Lesson 12** (presented with RM Lesson 110): *See the Rabbits - Part 1* theme: misunderstanding	**Literature Lesson 13** (presented with RM Lesson 115): *See the Rabbits – Part 2* Theme: misunderstanding retelling, setting, characters, plot	**Literature Lesson 14** (presented with RM Lesson 120): *The Proud Crow* theme: vanity play
Formal Assessment Reading Strand Language Arts Strand	**Reading Mastery Lesson 105** – individual fluency checkout **Language Lesson 105 – Test 11:** feedback, run-on sentences, predicate, capitalizing, pronouns, subject/predicate, marking the test, test feedback, test remedies	**Reading Mastery Lesson 110 – Test 11:** fact game, individual fluency checkout, mastery test, marking the test, test remedies	**Reading Mastery Lesson 115** – individual fluency checkout	**Reading Mastery Lesson 120 – Test 12:** fact game, individual fluency checkout, mastery test, marking the test, test remedies

F10

Strand Component	Lessons 121-125	Lessons 126-130	Lessons 131-135	Lessons 136-140
Core Lesson Connections	**A. Vocabulary** *New Vocabulary* – 121.A1, 122.A1, 123.A1, 124.A1 **B. Comprehension Strategies** *Comprehension Monitoring* – 121.B2, 123.B2, 123.B3 *Generate Questions* – 122.B2 **C. Fluency** – 121.C, 122.C, 123.C, 124.C, 125.C	**A. Vocabulary** *New Vocabulary* – 126.A1, 127.A1, 128.A1, 129.A1 **B. Comprehension Strategies** *Generate Questions* – 129.B2 **C. Fluency** – 126.C, 127.C, 128.C, 129.C, 139.C **D. Writing/Language Arts** – 130 D 1	**A. Vocabulary** *New Vocabulary* – 131.A1, 132.A1, 133.A1, 134.A1 **B. Comprehension Strategies** *Identify Cause–and–Effect Relationships* – 132.B2 *Comprehension Monitoring* – 132.B1, 132.B2, 134.B1 *Generate Questions* – 133.B1 **C. Fluency** – 131.C, 132.C, 133.C, 134.C, 135.C	**A. Vocabulary** *New Vocabulary* – 136.A1, 137.A2, 138.A1, 139.A **B. Comprehension Strategies** *Comprehension Monitoring* – 137.B1 **C Fluency** – 136.C, 137.C, 138.C, 139.C, 140.C **D. Writing/Language Arts** – 140 D 1
Reading Strand *Reading Mastery*	**Presentation Book C** **Vocabulary** – 121.1, 121.2, 122.1–122.3, 123.1, 123.2, 124.1, 124.2, 125.1, 125.2 **Decoding/Word Analysis** – 121.1, 121.2, 122.1–122.3, 123.1, 123.2, 124.1, 124.2, 125.1, 125.2 **Story Reading/ Comprehension** – 121.3, 121.4, 122.4, 123.3, 123.4, 124.3, 124.4, 125.3, 125.4, 125.5 **Fluency** *Paired Practice* – 121.5, 122.5, 123.5, 124.5 **Informal Assessment Workcheck** – 121, 122, 123, 124, 125 **Formal Assessment** **Spelling** – 121, 122, 123, 124, 125	**Presentation Book C** **Vocabulary** – 126.1, 126.2, 127.1–127.3, 128.1, 128.2, 129.1, 129.2 **Decoding/Word Analysis** – 126.1, 126.2, 127.1–127.3, 128.1, 128.2, 129.1, 129.2 **Story Reading/ Comprehension** – 126.3, 127.4, 127.5, 128.3, 129.3 **Fluency** *Paired Practice* – 126.4, 127.6, 128.4, 129.4 **Informal Assessment Workcheck** – 126, 127, 128, 129 **Formal Assessment** – 130.2, 130.3 **Spelling** – 126, 127, 128, 129	**Presentation Book C** **Vocabulary** – 131.1–131.3, 132.1, 132.2, 133.1, 133.2, 134.1, 134.2, 135.1, 134.2 **Decoding/Word Analysis** – 131.1–131.3, 132.1, 132.2, 133.1, 133.2, 134.1, 134.2, 135.1, 134.2 **Story Reading/ Comprehension** – 131.4, 131.5, 132.3–132.5, 133.3, 133.4, 134.3, 134.4, 135.5 **Fluency** *Paired Practice* – 131.6, 132.6, 133.5, 134.5 *Study Skills* – 132.4, 135.3 **Informal Assessment Workcheck** – 131, 132, 133, 134, 135 **Formal Assessment** **Spelling** – 131, 132, 133, 134, 135	**Presentation Book C** **Vocabulary** – 136.1, 136.2, 137.1, 137.2, 138.1–138.3, 139.1, 139.2 **Decoding/Word Analysis** – 136.1, 136.2, 137.1, 137.2, 138.1–138.3, 139.1, 139.2 **Story Reading/ Comprehension** – 136.3, 136.4, 137.3, 137.4, 138.4, 138.5, 139.3, 139.4 **Fluency** *Paired Practice* – 136.5, 137.5, 138.6, 139.6 *Study Skills* – 139.5 **Informal Assessment Workcheck** – 136, 137, 138, 139 **Formal Assessment** – 140.2, 140.3 **Spelling** – 136, 137, 138, 139
Language Arts Strand *Reading Mastery*				
Literature Strand *Reading Mastery*		**Literature Lesson 15** (presented with RM Lesson 130): *The Fox and the Crow* theme: vanity setting, characters, plot compare/contrast, literature preferences		**Literature Lesson 16** (presented with RM Lesson 140): *The Magic Teakettle* themes: good fortune, appearances, keeping promises setting, characters, plot, retelling, play
Formal Assessment **Reading Strand** **Language Arts Strand**	**Reading Mastery Lesson 125** – individual fluency checkout	**Reading Mastery Lesson 130 – Test 13:** fact game, individual fluency checkout, mastery test, marking the test, test remedies		**Reading Mastery Lesson 140 – Test 14:** fact game, individual fluency checkout, mastery test, marking the test, test remedies

F11

Strand Component	Lessons 141-145			
Core Lesson Connections	**A.** Vocabulary *New Vocabulary* – 141.A1, 142.A1, 143.A1, 144.A1 **B.** Comprehension Strategies **C.** Fluency – 141.C, 142.C, 143.C, 144.C, 145.C			
Reading Strand *Reading Mastery*	**Presentation Book C** **Vocabulary** – 141.1, 141.2, 142.1, 142.2, 143.1, 143.2, 144.1, 144.2, 145.1 **Decoding/Word Analysis** – 141.1, 141.2, 142.1, 143.1, 143.2, 144.1, 144.2, 145.1 **Story Reading/ Comprehension** – 141.3, 141.4, 142.3, 142.4, 143.3, 143.4, 144.3, 144.4, 145.2–145.4 **Fluency** *Paired Practice* – 141.5, 142.5, 143.5, 144.5 **Informal Assessment Workcheck** – 141, 142, 143, 144, 145 **Formal Assessment** – 145.1 **Spelling** – 141, 142, 143, 144, 145			
Language Arts Strand *Reading Mastery*				
Literature Strand *Reading Mastery*				
Formal Assessment **Reading Strand** **Language Arts Strand**	**Reading Mastery Lesson 145 –** individual fluency checkout **Lesson 145 –** end of program test			

F12

Appendix G

English Language Arts Standards  GRADE 2

GRADE 2 STANDARDS	PAGE REFERENCES
Reading Standards for Literature: Key Ideas and Details	
RL.2.1	Ask and answer such questions as *who, what, where, when, why,* and *how* to demonstrate understanding of key details in a text.	**Reading Presentation Book A:** (Lesson.Exercise) 1.2, 1.4, 2.2, 2.4, 3.2, 3.4, 4.4, 4.6, 5.3, 5.5, 6.3, 6.4, 7.4, 7.5, 8.3, 8.4, 9.3, 9.4, 11.4, 11.5, 12.3, 12.4, 13.3, 13.4, 14.4, 14.5, 15.3, 15.4, 16.3, 16.4, 17.4, 17.5, 18.3, 18.4, 19.3, 19.4, 21.3, 21.4, 22.3, 22.4, 23.3, 23.4, 24.3, 24.4, 25.4, 25.5, 26.3, 26.4, 27.3, 28.3, 28.4, 29.4, 29.5, 30.1, 31.3, 31.4, 32.3, 32.4, 33.4, 33.5, 34.3, 35.3, 35.4, 36.3, 36.4, 37.4, 37.5, 38.3, 38.4, 39.3, 39.4, 40.1, 41.4, 41.5, 42.3, 42.4, 43.3, 43.4, 44.3, 44.4, 45.4, 45.5, 46.4, 46.5, 47.4, 47.5, 48.4, 48.5, 49.3, 50.1 **Reading Presentation Book B:** (Lesson.Exercise) 51.3, 51.4, 52.4, 53.3, 53.5, 54.3, 55.4, 55.5, 56.3, 56.4, 57.3, 57.4, 58.4, 58.5, 59.3, 60.1, 61.3, 61.4, 62.4, 62.5, 63.3, 63.4, 64.3, 64.4, 65.4, 66.3, 66.4, 67.3, 68.4, 69.3, 70.1, 71.3, 71.4, 72.4, 73.3, 73.4, 74.3, 75.3, 76.4, 77.3, 78.3, 79.4, 80.1, 81.4, 81.5, 82.3, 82.4, 83.3, 83.4, 84.3, 84.4, 85.3, 85.4, 86.3, 87.4, 88.3, 89.3, 89.4, 90.1, 91.4, 91.5, 92.3, 93.3, 93.4, 94.3, 94.4, 95.4, 95.5, 96.3, 97.3, 97.4, 98.2, 99.2, 99.3, 100.1 **Reading Presentation Book C:** (Lesson.Exercise) 101.4, 102.3, 103.3, 104.2, 105.2, 106.2, 107.4, 107.5, 108.3, 108.4, 109.3, 109.4, 110.1, 111.4, 111.5, 112.3, 113.3, 113.5, 114.2, 114.3, 115.4, 115.5, 116.3, 116.4, 117.3, 118.4, 119.3, 119.4, 120.1, 121.3, 121.4, 122.4, 123.3, 123.4, 124.3, 124.4, 125.3, 125.4, 126.3, 127.4, 127.5, 128.3, 129.3, 130.1, 131.4, 131.5, 132.3, 132.5, 133.3, 133.4, 134.3, 135.4, 136.3, 136.4, 137.3, 137.4, 138.4, 138.5, 139.3, 139.4, 140.1, 141.3, 141.4, 142.3, 142.4, 143.3, 143.4, 144.3, 144.4, 145.2, 145.3 **Language Presentation Book A:** (Lesson.Exercise) 1.7, 1.8, 2.6, 2.7, 3.5, 3.6, 4.4, 4.5, 5.6, 5.7, 6.4, 8.7, 9.7, 11.5, 15.4, 16.4, 17.3, 19.3, 22.5, 24.3, 25.2, 29.3, 32.4, 34.4, 35.4, 38.4, 39.4, 42.4, 48.3, 49.2, 53.4, 55.4, 56.3, 61.3, 63.3, 64.2, 65.2 **Core Language Presentation Book B:** (Lesson.Exercise) 66.6, 67.8, 68.7, 69.7, 70.7, 71.8, 82.7, 73.8, 74.6, 75.3, 76.8, 77.8, 78.8, 79.8, 80.8, 81.8, 92.3, 83.7, 84.7, 85.3 **Lesson Connections:** (Lesson.Part.Activity) 2.B.1, 3.B.1, 4.B.1, 5.B.1, 6.B.1, 7.B.1, 8.B.1, 9.B.1, 10.B.1, 11.B.1, 11.B.2, 12.B.1, 12.B.2, 13.B.1, 13.B.2, 14.B.1, 14.B.2, 15.B.1, 16.B.1, 17.B.1, 19.B.1, 20.B.1, 21.B.1, 21.B.2, 22.B.1, 22.B.2, 22.B.3, 23.B.1, 23.B.2, 24.B.2, 24.B.3, 25.B.1, 26.B.1, 26.B.2, 27.B.1, 27.B.2, 28.B.1, 29.B.1, 30.B.1, 39.B.1, 40.B.1, 45.B.1, 46.B.1, 49.B.1, 58.B.1, 59.B.1, 63.B.1, 64.B.1, 65.B.1, 69.B.1, 75.B.1, 79.B.2, 91.B.1, 92.B.1, 93.B.2, 94.B.1, 96.B.1, 96.B.2, 97.B.2, 98.B.2, 99.B.2, 100.B.1, 104.B.2, 105.B.2, 106.B.2, 108.B.2, 115.B.1, 119.B.1, 120.B.1, 124.B.2, 129.B.2, 133.B.1, 136.B.2, 141.B.1 **Literature Anthology/Guide:** Lessons 1, 2, 3, 4, 5, 6, 7, 8, 9, 10, 11, 12, 13, 14, 15, 16
RL.2.2	Recount stories, including fables and folktales from diverse cultures, and determine their central message, lesson, or moral.	**Reading Presentation Book B:** (Lesson.Exercise) 63.4 **Reading Textbook B:** Lessons 63.C **Core Lesson Connections:** (Lesson.Part.Activity) 22.B.3, 23.B.3, 24.B.4, 26.B.3, 27.B.3, 28.B.2, 29.B.2, 39.B.2, 59.B.1, 61.B.1, 69.B.2, 76.B.1, 77.B.2, 78.B.2, 79.B.3, 91.B.2, 92.B.2, 93.B.3, 94.B.2, 97.B.1, 98.B.1, 99.B.1, 104.B.3, 121.B.1, 124.B.3, 131.B.1, 133.B.2, 136.B.3, 141.B.2 **Literature Anthology/Guide:** Lessons 2, 3, 4, 5, 6, 7, 8, 9, 10, 11, 12, 13, 14, 15, 16

G3

GRADE 2 STANDARDS		PAGE REFERENCES
RL.2.3	Describe how characters in a story respond to major events and challenges.	**Reading Presentation Book A:** (Lesson.Exercise) 4.6, 6.4, 22.4, 26.4, 27.3, 29.5, 35.4 **Reading Presentation Book B:** (Lesson.Exercise) 54.3, 62.5, 68.4, 71.4, 74.3, 78.3, 79.4, 81.5, 84.4, 91.5, 92.3, 95.5, 96.3, 97.4, 99.3 **Reading Presentation Book C:** (Lesson.Exercise) 102.3, 104.2, 109.4, 111.5, 116.4, 122.4, 129.3, 141.4 **Reading Textbook A:** Lessons 4.D, 6.C, 22.D, 26.C, 27.B, 29.D, 35.C **Reading Textbook B:** Lessons 54.B, 62.C, 68.B, 71.C, 74.B, 78.B, 79.C, 81.C, 84.C, 91.C, 92.B, 95.C, 96.B, 97.C, 99.B **Reading Textbook C:** Lessons 102.B, 104.B, 109.C, 111.C, 116.D, 122.B, 129.B, 141.C **Language Presentation Book A:** (Lesson.Exercise) 55.5 **Language Workbook:** Lessons 55 **Core Lesson Connections:** (Lesson.Part.Activity) 2.B.1, 3.B.1, 4.B.1, 5.B.1, 6.B.1, 7.B.1, 8.B.1, 9.B.1, 10.B.1, 11.B.1, 12.B.1, 13.B.1, 14.B.1, 15.B.1, 16.B.1, 17.B.1, 19.B.1, 21.B.1, 23.B.1, 24.B.2, 24.B.3, 26.B.1, 27.B.1, 28.B.1, 29.B.1, 39.B.1, 45.B.1, 46.B.1, 49.B.1, 58.B.1, 59.B.1, 63.B.1, 64.B.1, 68.B.1, 69.B.1, 70.B.1, 79.B.2, 96.B.2, 104.B.2, 105.B.2, 107.B.3, 108.B.2, 124.B.2, 136.B.2, 140.B.1, 141.B.1 **Literature Anthology/Guide:** Lessons 2, 3, 4, 5, 6, 7, 8, 9, 10, 11, 12, 13, 14, 15, 16
Reading Standards for Literature: Craft and Structure		
RL.2.4	Describe how words and phrases (e.g., regular beats, alliteration, rhymes, repeated lines) supply rhythm and meaning in a story, poem, or song.	**Reading Presentation Book B:** (Lesson.Exercise) 53.4 **Literature Anthology/Guide:** Lessons 4.2, 9.2, 10.2, 11

GRADE 2 STANDARDS		PAGE REFERENCES
RL.2.5	Describe the overall structure of a story, including describing how the beginning introduces the story and the ending concludes the action.	**Reading Presentation Book A:** (Lesson.Exercise) 1.2, 1.4, 2.2, 2.4, 3.2, 3.4, 4.4, 4.6, 5.3, 5.5, 6.3, 6.4, 7.4, 7.5, 8.3, 8.4, 9.3, 9.4, 11.4, 11.5, 12.3, 12.4, 13.3, 13.4, 14.4, 14.5, 15.3, 15.4, 16.3, 16.4, 17.4, 17.5, 18.3, 18.4, 19.3, 19.4, 21.3, 21.4, 22.3, 22.4, 24.3, 24.4, 25.4, 25.5, 26.3, 26.4, 27.3, 28.3, 28.4, 29.4, 29.5, 31.3, 31.4, 32.3, 32.4, 33.4, 33.5, 34.3, 35.3, 35.4, 36.3, 36.4, 37.4, 37.5, 38.3, 38.4, 39.3, 39.4, 41.4, 41.5, 42.3, 42.4, 43.3, 43.4, 44.3, 44.4, 45.4, 45.5, 46.3, 46.5, 47.3, 47.5, 48.4, 48.5, 49.3 **Reading Presentation Book B:** (Lesson.Exercise) 51.3, 51.4, 52.4, 53.3, 53.5, 54.3, 55.4, 55.5, 56.3, 56.4, 57.3, 57.4, 58.4, 58.5, 59.3, 61.3, 61.4, 62.4, 62.5, 63.3, 63.4, 64.3, 64.4, 65.4, 66.3, 66.4, 67.3, 68.4, 69.3, 71.3, 71.4, 72.4, 73.3, 73.4, 74.3, 75.3, 76.4, 77.3, 78.3, 79.3, 79.4, 81.4, 81.5, 82.4, 83.4, 84.3, 84.4, 85.4, 86.3, 87.4, 88.3, 89.3, 89.4, 91.4, 91.5, 92.3, 93.3, 93.4, 94.3, 94.4, 95.4, 95.5, 96.3, 97.3, 97.4, 98.2, 99.3 **Reading Presentation Book C:** (Lesson.Exercise) 101.4, 102.3, 103.3, 104.2, 105.2, 106.2, 107.4, 107.5, 108.3, 108.4, 109.4, 111.4, 111.5, 112.3, 113.3, 113.5, 114.2, 114.3, 115.4, 115.5, 116.3, 116.4, 117.3, 118.4, 118.5, 119.3, 119.4, 121.3, 121.4, 122.43, 123.3, 123.4, 124.3, 124.4, 125.3, 125.4, 126.3, 127.4, 127.5, 128.3, 129.3, 131.4, 131.5, 132.3, 132.5, 133.3, 133.4, 134.3, 134.4, 135.4, 136.3, 136.4, 137.3, 137.4, 138.4, 138.5, 139.3, 139.4, 141.3, 141.4, 142.3, 142.4, 143.3, 143.4, 144.3, 144.4, 145.2, 145.3 **Reading Textbook 1:** Lessons 1–50 **Reading Textbook 2:** Lessons 51–100 **Reading Textbook 3:** Lessons 101–145 **Core Lesson Connections:** (Lesson.Part.Activity) 2.B.2, 3.B.2, 4.B.2, 6.B.2, 11.B.2, 12.B.2, 13.B.2, 14.B.2, 16.B.1, 17.B.1, 18.B.1, 19.B.1, 21.B.1, 22.B.1, 23.B.1, 24.B.2, 26.B.1, 27.B.1, 28.B.1, 29.B.1, 38.B.1, 39.B.1, 57.B.2, 62.B.2, 69.B.1, 71.B.2, 72.B.1, 72.B.3, 73.B.1, 73.B.3, 74.B.1, 74.B.2, 76.B.2, 77.B.1, 77.B.3, 78.B.1, 78.B.3, 79.B.1, 81.B.2, 82.B.1, 83.B.2, 84.B.1, 92.B.3, 93.B.1, 96.B.2, 97.B.3, 104.B.2, 106.B.1, 107.B.1, 111.B.1, 113.B.1, 116.B.1, 116.B.2, 121.B.3, 122.B.1, 122.B.3, 123.B.1, 128.B.1, 131.B.1, 137.B.2, 138.B.1, 144.B.1, 144.B3 **Literature Anthology/Literature Guide:** Lessons 2, 3, 4, 5, 6, 7, 8, 9, 10, 11, 12, 13, 14, 15, 16
RL.2.6	Acknowledge differences in the points of view of characters, including by speaking in a different voice for each character when reading dialogue aloud.	**Core Lesson Connections:** (Lesson.Part.Activity) 7.B.2, 8.B.2, 9.B.2, 11.B.3, 12.B.3, 13.B.3, 14.B.3, 16.B.2, 17.B.2, 21.B.3, 56.B.1, 59.B.3, 61.B.1, 102.B.3, 124.B.2, 136.B.2, 141.B.1 **Literature Anthology/Literature Guide:** Lessons 14, 16

G5

GRADE 2 STANDARDS	PAGE REFERENCES
Reading Standards for Literature: Integration of Knowledge and Ideas	

RL.2.7	Use information gained from the illustrations and words in a print or digital text to demonstrate understanding of its characters, setting, or plot.	**Reading Presentation Book A:** (Lesson.Exercise) 4.4, 5.5, 12.4, 16.4, 17.5, 19.3, 22.4, 29.5, 31.4, 36.4, 38.3, 41.5, 43.3, 45.5 **Reading Presentation Book B:** (Lesson.Exercise) 51.4, 54.3, 57.3, 58.5, 59.3, 61.4, 62.5, 63.3, 65.4, 66.4, 67.3, 68.4, 71.3, 72.4, 73.4, 74.3, 78.3, 82.4, 84.4, 89.4, 92.3, 93.3, 93.4, 94.3, 94.4, 96.3, 98.2, 99.3 **Reading Presentation Book C:** (Lesson.Exercise) 103.3, 104.2, 106.2, 107.5, 111.5, 113.5, 116.4, 118.5, 119.3, 119.4, 121.3, 121.4, 122.3, 129.3, 131.5, 133.4, 134.4, 136.4, 137.4, 138.5, 139.4, 141.4, 142.4, 143.4, 144.4, 145.3 **Reading Textbook A:** Lessons 4..B, 5.B, 12.C, 16.C, 17.D, 19.B, 22.D, 24.D, 29.D, 31.C, 36.C, 38.B, 41.D, 43.B, 45.C **Reading Textbook B:** Lessons 51.C, 54.B, 57.B, 58.C, 59.B, 61.C, 62.C, 63.B, 65.B, 66.C, 67.B, 68.B, 71.B, 72.B, 73.C, 74.B, 78.B, 82.B, 84.C, 89.C, 92.B, 93.B, 93.C, 94.B, 94.C, 96.B, 98.B, 99.B **Reading Textbook B:** Lessons 103.B, 104.B, 106.B, 107.C, 111.C, 113.C, 116.D, 119.B, 119.C, 121.B, 121.C, 122.B, 129.B, 131.C, 133.C, 134.C, 136.C, 137.C, 138.C, 139.D, 141.C, 142.C, 143.C, 144.C, 145.C **Language Presentation Book A:** (Lesson.Exercise) 1.8, 2.8, 3.6, 4.5, 5.7, 8.7, 9.7, 11.6, 15.5, 24.4, 27.4, 32.5, 41.5, 42.4, 44.4, 53.5, 64.3, 65.3 **Language Presentation Book B:** (Lesson.Exercise) 76.6, 77.6, 79.6, 82.6 **Language Textbook:** (Lesson.Exercise) 76.E, 77.E, 79.E, 82.E **Language Workbook:** (Lesson.Exercise) 1.D, 2.F, 3.E, 4.D, 5.D, 8.E, 9.E, 11.C, 15.D, 24.C, 27.D, 32.D, 41.D, 42.C, 44.C, 53.D, 64.B, 65.B **Core Lesson Connections:** (Lesson.Part.Activity) 24.B.1, 71.B.2, 72.B.3, 74.B.3, 76.B.2, 77.B.3, 78.B.3, 81.B.2, 83.B.1, 92.B.3, 106.B.3, 121.B.3, 122.B.3, 137.B.2 **Literature Anthology/Guide:** Lessons 2, 3, 4, 5, 6, 7, 8, 9, 110, 11, 12, 13, 14, 15, 16
RL.2.8	*(Not applicable to literature)*	
RL.2.9	Compare and contrast two or more versions of the same story (e.g., Cinderella stories) by different authors or from different cultures.	**Literature Guide:** Lessons 9, 15

GRADE 2 STANDARDS	PAGE REFERENCES

Reading Standards for Literature: Range of Reading and Level of Text Complexity

| RL.2.10 | By the end of the year, read and comprehend literature, including stories and poetry, in the grades 2–3 text complexity band proficiently, with scaffolding as needed at the high end of the range. | **Reading Presentation Book A:** (Lesson.Exercise) 1.4, 2.2, 3.2, 4.4, 5.3, 6.3, 7.4, 8.3, 9.3, 11.4, 12.3, 13.3, 14.4, 15.3, 16.3, 17.4, 18.3, 19.3, 21.3, 22.3, 23.3, 24.3, 25.4, 26.3, 28.3, 29.4, 31.3, 32.3, 33.4, 35.3, 36.3, 37.4, 38.3, 39.3, 41.4, 42.3, 43.3, 44.3, 45.4, 46.3, 47.3, 48.4, 49.3
 Reading Presentation Book B: (Lesson.Exercise) 51.3, 53.3, 53.5, 55.4, 57.3, 58.4, 61.3, 62.4, 63.3, 64.3, 64.4, 65.4, 66.3, 67.3, 68.4, 71.3, 73.3, 79.3, 81.4, 83.4, 84.3, 85.4, 86.3, 87.4, 88.3, 89.3, 91.4, 93.3, 94.3, 95.4, 97.3
 Reading Presentation Book C: (Lesson.Exercise) 101.4, 102.3, 103.3, 104.2, 105.2, 106.2, 107.5, 108.4, 111.4, 111.5, 112.3, 113.3, 11.5, 114.2, 114.3, 115.5, 116.3, 116.4, 117.3, 118.4, 118.5, 119.3, 119.4, 121.4, 122.4, 123.3, 123.4, 124.4, 125.4, 126.3, 127.4, 127.5, 128.3, 129.3, 131.4, 131.5, 132.3, 132.5, 133.4, 134.3, 134.4, 135.4, 136.3, 136.4, 137.3, 137.4, 138.5, 139.3, 139.4, 141.4, 142.4, 143.4, 144.4, 145.3
 Reading Textbook A: Lessons 1.D, 2.B, 3.B, 4.B, 5.B, 6.B, 7.B, 8.B, 9.B, 11.B, 12.B, 13.B, 14.B, 15.B, 16.B, 17.B, 17.C, 18.B, 18.C, 19.B, 19.C, 21.B, 21.C, 22.B, 22.C, 23.B, 24.B, 25.B, 26.B, 27.B, 28.B, 29.B, 31.B, 32.B, 33.B, 35.B, 36.B, 37.B, 38.B, 39.B, 41.B, 41.C, 42.B, 43.B, 44.B, 45.B, 46.B, 47.B, 48.B, 48.C, 49.B
 Reading Textbook B: Lessons 51.B, 53.B, 53.C, 53.D, 55.B, 57.B, 58.B, 61.B, 62.B, 63.B, 64.B, 64.C, 65.B, 66.B, 67.B, 68.B, 71.B, 73.B, 79.B, 81.B, 83.B, 84.B, 85.B, 86.B, 87.B, 88.B, 89.B, 91.B, 93.B, 94.B, 95.B, 97.B
 Reading Textbook C: Lessons 101.B, 102.B, 103.B, 104.B, 105.B, 106.B, 107.C, 108.C, 111.B, 111.C, 112.B, 113.B, 113.C, 114.B, 114.C, 115.C, 116.B, 116.C, 116.D, 117.B, 118.B, 118.C, 119.B, 119.C, 121.C, 122.B, 123.B, 123.C, 124.C, 125.C, 126.B, 127.B, 127.C, 128.B, 128.C, 129.B, 131.B, 131.C, 132.B, 132.C, 132.D, 133.C, 134.B, 134.C, 135.B, 136.B, 136.C, 137.B, 137.C, 138.C, 139.C, 139.D, 141.C, 142.C, 143.C, 144.C, 145.C
 Language Presentation Book A: (Lesson.Exercise) 1.8, 2.8, 3.6, 4.5, 5.7, 8.7, 9.7, 11.6, 14.6, 41.5, 42.4, 44.4, 53.5, 65.3
 Language Workbook: Lessons 1.D, 2.F, 3.E, 4.D, 5.D, 8.E, 9.E, 11.C, 14.D, 41.D, 42.C, 44.C, 53.D, 65.B
 Core Lesson Connections: (Lesson.Part.Activity) 2.B.1, 3.B.1, 4.B.1, 6.B.1, 7.B.1, 7.B.3, 8.B.1, 9.B.1, 11.B.1, 12.B.1, 13.B.1, 14.B.1, 16.B.1, 17.B.1, 18.B.2, 19.B.1, 19.B.2, 21.B.1, 21.B.2, 21.B.3, 22.B.1, 22.B.2, 23.B.1, 23.B.2, 24.B.2, 24.B.3, 26.B.1, 26.B.2, 27.B.1, 27.B.2, 28.B.1, 29.B.2, 33.B.2, 34.B.1, 36.B.3, 37.B.2, 38.B.3, 39.B.1, 44.B.2, 46.B.1, 46.B.2, 47.B.3, 49.B.1, 51.B.1, 52.B.1, 53.B.3, 56.B.1, 57.B.1, 58.B.1, 58.B.2, 59.B.1, 59.B.2, 59.B.3, 63.B.1, 64.B.1, 66.B.1, 67.B., 68.B.1, 69.B.1, 72.B.1, 73.B.1, 74.B.1, 76.B.1, 77.B.1, 78.B.1, 79.B.1, 79.B.3, 82.B.1, 84.B.1, 91.B.2, 92.B.2, 93.B.1, 94.B.2, 96.B.2, 97.B.1, 98.B.1, 99.B.1, 99.B.3, 103.B.1, 104.B.1, 104.B.2, 107.B.1, 107.B.2, 107.B.3, 108.B.1, 108.B.2,, 109.B.1, 118.B.1, 118.B.2, 121.B.1, 122.B.1, 123.B.1, 124.B.2, 131.B.1, 133.B.2, 136.B.2, 136.B.3, 128.B.1, 138.B.2, 129.B.1, 141.B.1
 Literature Anthology/Guide: Lessons 2, 3, 4, 5, 6, 7, 8, 9, 110, 11, 12, 13, 14, 15, 16 |

G7

GRADE 2 STANDARDS		PAGE REFERENCES
Reading Standards for Informational Text: Key Ideas and Details		
RI.2.1	Ask and answer such questions as *who, what, where, when, why*, and *how* to demonstrate understanding of key details in a text.	**Reading Presentation Book A:** (Lesson.Exercise) 1.2, 2.2, 3.2, 8.3, 9.3, 11.4, 12.3, 14.4, 15.3, 16.3, 18.3, 19.3, 21.3, 21.4, 22.3, 23.3, 24.3, 26.3, 27.4, 29.4, 29.5, 32.4, 35.3, 36.3, 36.4, 37.4, 38.3, 38.4, 39.3, 41.4, 42.3, 42.4, 43.3, 44.3, 44.4, 45.4, 45.5, 48.4, 49.3 **Reading Presentation Book B:** (Lesson.Exercise) 51.3, 51.4, 52.4, 53.3, 53.5, 54.3, 55.5, 56.3, 57.3, 57.4, 58.4, 61.3, 61.4, 62.4, 62.5, 63.3, 64.3, 64.4, 66.3, 71.3, 73.3, 79.4, 82.3, 83.3, 83.4, 85.3, 87.4, 88.3, 89.3, 91.4, 94.3, 98.3, 99.2 **Reading Presentation Book C:** (Lesson.Exercise) 101.4, 101.5, 108.4, 109.3, 109.4, 111.4, 112.3, 113.3, 114.2, 115.4, 116.3, 118.4, 119.3, 121.3, 123.3, 124.3, 124.5, 125.3, 127.4, 128.3, 131.4, 131.5, 132.3, 132.5, 133.3, 134.3, 136.3, 136.4, 138.4, 138.5, 139.3, 139.4, 141.3, 142.3, 143.3, 144.3, 144.4, 145.2 **Reading Textbook A:** Lessons 1.B., 2.B, 3.B, 8.B, 9.B, 11.B, 12.B, 14.C, 15.B, 16.B, 18.B, 18.C, 19.C, 21.B, 21.D, 22.C, 23.B, 24.B, 26.B, 27.C, 29.C, 29.D, 32.C, 35.B, 36.B, 36.C, 37.B, 38.B, 38.C, 39.B, 41.B, 42.B, 42.C, 43.B, 44.B, 44.C, 45.B, 45.C, 48.B, 49.B **Reading Textbook B:** Lessons 51.B, 51.C, 52.B, 53.B, 53.C, 53.D, 54.B, 55.B, 56.B, 57.B, 57.C, 58.B, 61.B, 61.C, 62.B, 62.C, 63.B, 64.B, 64.C, 66.B, 71.B, 73.B, 79.C, 83.B, 87.B, 88.B, 89.B, 91.B, 94.B, 98.B **Reading Textbook C:** Lessons 101.B, 101.C, 108.C, 109.C, 112.B, 113.B, 114.B, 115.B, 116.B, 116.C, 118.B, 119.B, 121.B, 123.B, 124.B, 124.C, 125.B, 127.B, 128.B, 128.C, 128.D, 131.B, 131.C, 132.B, 132.C, 132.D, 133.B, 134.B, 136.B, 136.C, 138.B, 138.C, 139.B, 139.C, 139.D, 141.B, 142.B, 143.B, 144.B, 144.C, 1454.B **Core Lesson Connections:** (Lesson.Part.Activity) 31.B.1, 32.B.1, 33.B.1, 34.B.1, 35.B.1, 36.B.1, 36.B.2, 37.B.1, 41.B.1, 41.B.2, 42.B.1, 44.B.2, 43.B.1, 43.B.2, 43.B.3, 44.B.1, 46.B.2, 47.B.1, 47.B.2, 47.B.3, 48.B.1, 48.B.2, 53.B.1, 53.B.2, 54.B.1, 83.B.1, 84.B.2, 86.B.1, 86.B.2, 87.B.1, 87.B.2, 88.B.1, 88.B.2, 89.B.1, 89.B.2, 111.B.3, 111.B.4, 112.B.2, 112.B.3, 114.B.2, 114.B.3, 117.B.2, 126.B.2, 126.B.3, 127.B.2, 129.B.2, 142.B.2, 142.B.3, 143.B.2 **Research Projects**

G8

GRADE 2 STANDARDS		PAGE REFERENCES
RI.2.2	Identify the main topic of a multiparagraph text as well as the focus of specific paragraphs within the text.	**Reading Presentation Book A:** (Lesson.Exercise) 1.2, 2.2, 3.2, 8.3, 9.3, 11.4, 12.3, 14.4, 15.3, 16.3, 18.3, 19.3, 21.3, 21.4, 22.3, 23.3, 24.3, 26.3, 27.4, 29.4, 29.5, 32.4, 35.3, 36.3, 36.4, 37.4, 38.3, 38.4, 39.3, 41.4, 42.3, 42.4, 43.3, 44.3, 44.4, 45.4, 45.5, 48.4, 49.3 **Reading Presentation Book B:** (Lesson.Exercise) 51.3, 51.4, 52.4, 53.3, 53.5, 54.3, 55.5, 56.3, 57.3, 57.4, 58.4, 61.3, 61.4, 62.4, 62.5, 63.3, 64.3, 64.4, 66.3, 71.3, 73.3, 79.4, 82.3, 83.3, 83.4, 85.3, 87.4, 88.3, 89.3, 91.4, 94.3, 98.3, 99.2 **Reading Presentation Book C:** (Lesson.Exercise) 101.4, 101.5, 108.4, 109.3, 109.4, 111.4, 112.3, 113.3, 114.2, 115.4, 116.3, 118.4, 119.3, 121.3, 123.3, 124.3, 124.5, 125.3, 127.4, 128.3, 131.4, 131.5, 132.3, 132.5, 133.3, 134.3, 136.3, 136.4, 138.4, 138.5, 139.3, 139.4, 141.3, 142.3, 143.3, 144.3, 144.4, 145.2 **Reading Textbook A:** Lessons 1.B., 2.B, 3.B, 8.B, 9.B, 11.B, 12.B, 14.C, 15.B, 16.B, 18.B, 18.C, 19.C, 21.B, 21.D, 22.C, 23.B, 24.B, 26.B, 27.C, 29.C, 29.D, 32.C, 35.B, 36.B, 36.C, 37.B, 38.B, 38.C, 39.B, 41.B, 42.B, 42.C, 43.B, 44.B, 44.C, 45.B, 45.C, 48.B, 49.B **Reading Textbook B:** Lessons 51.B, 51.C, 52.B, 53.B, 53.C, 53.D, 54.B, 55.B, 56.B, 57.B, 57.C, 58.B, 61.B, 61.C, 62.B, 62.C, 63.B, 64.B, 64.C, 66.B, 71.B, 73.B, 79.C, 83.B, 87.B, 88.B, 89.B, 91.B, 94.B, 98.B **Reading Textbook C:** Lessons 101.B, 101.C, 108.C, 109.C, 112.B, 113.B, 114.B, 115.B, 116.B, 116.C, 118.B, 119.B, 121.B, 123.B, 124.B, 124.C, 125.B, 127.B, 128.B, 128.C, 128.D, 131.B, 131.C, 132.B, 132.C, 132.D, 133.B, 134.B, 136.B, 136.C, 138.B, 138.C, 139.B, 139.C, 139.D, 141.B, 142.B, 143.B, 144.B, 144.C, 1454.B **Core Lesson Connections:** (Lesson.Part.Activity) 33.B.1, 34.B.1, 37.B.1, 42.B.1, 44.B.1, 48.B.1, 54.B.1, 83.B.1, 94.B.2, 87.B.1, 87.B.2, 88.B.1, 88.B.2, 89.B.1, 89.B.2, 112.B.2, 112.B.3, 113.B.3, 113.B.4, 114.B.2, 114.B.3, 127.B.2, 143.B.2 **Research Projects**
RI.2.3	Describe the connection between a series of historical events, scientific ideas or concepts, or steps in technical procedures in a text.	**Core Lesson Connections:** (Lesson.Part.Activity) 116.B.3, 117.B.1, 129.B.1

G9

GRADE 2 STANDARDS		PAGE REFERENCES
Reading Standards for Informational Text: Craft and Structure		
RI.2.4	Determine the meaning of words and phrases in a text relevant to a *grade 2 topic or subject area*.	**Reading Presentation Book A:** (Lesson.Exercise) 1.1, 2.1, 3.1, 4.1–3, 5.1, 5.2, 6.1, 6.2, 7.1–3, 8.1, 8.2, 9.1, 9.2, 11.1–3, 12.1, 12.2, 13.1, 13.2, 14.1–3, 15.1, 15.2, 16.1, 16.2, 17.1–3, 18.1, 18.2, 19.1, 19.2, 21.1, 21.2, 22.1, 22.2, 23.1, 23.2, 24.1, 24.2, 25.1–3, 26.1, 26.2, 27.1, 27.2, 28.1, 28.2, 29.1–3, 31.1, 31.2, 32.1, 32.2, 33.1–3, 34.1, 34.2, 35.1, 35.2, 36.1, 36.2, 37.1–3, 38.1, 38.2, 39.1, 39.2, 41.1–3, 42.1, 42.2, 43.1, 43.2, 44.1, 44.2, 45.1–3, 2, 46.1, 46.2, 47.1, 47.2, 48.1–3, 49.1, 49.2
		Reading Presentation Book B: (Lesson.Exercise) 51.1, 51.2, 52.1–3, 53.1, 53.2, 54.1, 54.2, 55.1–3, 56.1, 56.2, 57.1, 57.2, 58.1–3, 59.1, 59.2, 61.1, 61.2, 62.1–3, 63.1, 63.2, 64.1, 64.2, 65.1–3, 66.1, 66.2, 67.1, 67.1–3, 68.1, 68.2, 69.1, 69.2, 71.1, 71.3, 72.1–3, 73.1, 73.2, 74.1, 74.2, 75.1, 75.2, , 76.1–3, 77.1, 77.2, 78.1, 78.2, 79.1, 79.2, 81.1–3, 82.1, 82.2, 83.1, 83.2, 84.1, 84.2, 85.1, 85.2, 86.1, 86.2, 87.1–3, 88.1, 88.2, 89.1, 89.2, 91.1–3, 92.1, 92.2, 93.1, 93.2, 94.1, 94.2, 95.1–3, 96.1, 96.2, 97.1, 97.2, 98.1, 99.1
		Reading Presentation Book C: (Lesson.Exercise) 101.1–3, 102.1, 102.2, 103.1, 103.2, 04.1, 105.1, 106.1, 107.1–3, 108.1, 108.2, 109.1, 109.2, 111.1–3, 112.1, 112.2, 113.1, 113.2, 114.1, 115.1–3, 116.1, 116.2, 117.1, 117.2, 118.1–3, 119.1, 119.2, 121.1, 121.2, 122.1–3, 1123.1, 123.2, 124.1, 124.2, 125.1, 125.2, 126.1, 126.2, 127.1–3, 128.1, 128.2, 129.1, 129.2, 131.1–3, 132.1, 132.2, 133.1, 133.2, 134.1, 134.2, 135.1, 135.2, 136.1, 136.2, 137.1, 137.2, 138.1–3, 139.1, 139.2, 141.1, 141.2, 142.1, 142.2, 143.1, 143.2, 144.1, 144.2, 145.1
		Core Lesson Connections: (Lesson.Part.Activity) 1.A.2, 2.A.1, 2.A.2, 3.A.1, 3.A.2, 4.A.1, 4.A.2, 5.A.1, 6.A.1, 6.A.2, 7.A.1, 7.A.2, 8.A.1, 8.A.2, 9.A.1, 9.A.2, 10.A.1, 11.A.1, 11.A.2, 12.A.1, 12.A.2, 13.A.1, 13.A.1, 14.A.1, 15.A.1, 16.A.1, 16.A.2, 17.A.1, 17.A.2, 17.A.3, 18.A.1, 18.A.2, 19.A.1, 19.A.2, 20.A.1, 22.A.2, 21.A.1, 21.A.2, 22.A.1, 22.A.2, 23.A.1, 23.A.2, 24.A.1, 24.A.2, 25.A.1, 25.A.2, 26.A.1, 26.A.2, 27.A.1, 27.A.2, 28.A.1, 28.A.2, 29.A.1, 29.A.2, 30.A.1, 30.A.2, 31.A.1, 31.A.2, 32.A.1, 32.A.2, 33.A.1, 33.A.2, 34.A.1, 34.A.2, 35.A.1, 35.A.2, 36.A.1, 36.A.2, 37.A.1, 37.A.2, 38.A.1, 38.A.2, 39.A.1, 39.A.2, 40.A.1, 40.A.2, 41.A.1, 41.A.2, 42.A.1, 42.A.2, 43.A.1, 43.A.2, 44.A.1, 44.A.2, 45.A.1, 45.A.2, 46.A.1, 46.A.2, 47.A.1, 47.A.2, 48.A.1, 48.A.2, 49.A.1, 49.A.2, 50.A.1, 50.A.2, 51.A.1, 51.A.2, 52.A.1, 52.A.2, 53.A.1, 53.A.2, 54.A.1, 54.A.2, 55.A.1, 55.A.2, 56.A.1, 56.A.2, 57.A.1, 57.A.2, 58.A.1, 58.A.2, 59.A.1, 59.A.2, 60.A.1, 60.A.2, 61.A.1, 61.A.2, 62.A.1, 62.A.2, 63.A.1, 63.A.2, 64.A.1, 64.A.2, 65.A.1, 65.A.2, 66.A.1, 66.A.2, 67.A.1, 67.A.2, 68.A.1, 68.A.2, 69.A.1, 69.A.2, 70.A.1, 70.A.2, 71.A.1, 71.A.2, 72.A.1, 72.A.2, 73.A.1, 73.A.2, 74.A.1, 74.A.2, 75.A.1, 75.A.2, 76.A.1, 76.A.2, 77.A.1, 77.A.2, 78.A.1, 78.A.2, 79.A.1, 79.A.2, 80.A.1, 80.A.2, 81.A.1, 81.A.2, 82.A.1, 82.A.2, 83.A.1, 83.A.2, 84.A.1, 84.A.2, 85.A.1, 85.A.2, 86.A.1, 86.A.2, 87.A.1, 87.A.2, 88.A.1, 88.A.2, 89.A.1, 89.A.2, 90.A.1, 90.A.2, 91.A.1, 91.A.2, 92.A.1, 92.A.2, 93.A.1, 93.A.2, 94.A.1, 94.A.2, 95.A.1, 95.A.2, 96.A.1, 96.A.2, 97.A.1, 97.A.2, 98.A.1, 98.A.2, 99.A.1, 99.A.2, 100.A.1, 100.A.2, 101.A.1, 101.A.2, 102.A.1, 102.A.2, 103.A.1, 103.A.2, 104.A.1, 104.A.2, 105.A.1, 105.A.2, 106.A.1, 106.A.2, 107.A.1, 107.A.2, 108.A.1, 108.A.2, 109.A.1, 109.A.2, 110.A.1, 109.A.2, 110.A.1, 110.A.2, 111.A.1, 111.A.2, 112.A.1, 112.A.2, 113.A.1, 113.A.2, 114.A.1, 114.A.2, 115.A.1, 115.A.2, 116.A.1, 116.A.2, 117.A.1, 117.A.2, 118.A.1, 118.A.2, 119.A.1, 119.A.2, 120.A.1, 120.A.2, 121.A.1, 121.A.2, 122.A.1, 122.A.2, 123.A.1, 123.A.2, 124.A.1, 124.A.2, 125.A.1, 125.A.2, 126.A.1, 126.A.2, 127.A.1, 127.A.2, 128.A.1, 128.A.2, 129.A.1, 129.A.2, 130.A.1, 130.A.2, 131.A.1–3, 132.A.1–3, 133.A.1–3, 134.A.1–3, 135.A.1, 135.A.2, 136.A.1–3, 137.A.1–3, 138.A.1–3, 139.A.1–3, 140.A.1, 140.A.2, 141.A.1–3, 142.A.1–3, 143.A.1–3, 144.A.1–3, 145.A.1, 145.A.2 **Research Projects**

G10

	GRADE 2 STANDARDS	PAGE REFERENCES
RI.2.5	Know and use various text features (e.g., captions, bold print, subheadings, glossaries, indexes, electronic menus, icons) to locate key facts or information in a text efficiently.	**Reading Presentation Book B:** (Lesson.Exercise) 78 Special Project, 81 Special Project **Reading Presentation Book C:** (Lesson.Exercise) 122 Special Project **Reading Textbook B:** Lessons 78 Special Project, 81 Special Project **Reading Textbook C:** Lessons 122 Special Project **Core Lesson Connections:** (Lesson.Part.Activity) 38.B.1, 116.B.2, 128.B.1, 144.B.1 **Research Projects**
RI.2.6	Identify the main purpose of a text, including what the author wants to answer, explain, or describe.	**Reading Presentation Book B:** (Lesson.Exercise) 51.3, 51.4, 53.3, 54.3, 56.4, 61.3, 66.3, 73.4 **Reading Presentation Book C:** (Lesson.Exercise) 101.4, 116.4 **Reading Textbook B:** Lessons 51.B, 51.C, 53.C, 54.B, 56.C, 61.B, 66.B, 73.C **Reading Textbook C:** Lessons 101.B, 116.D **Core Lesson Connections:** (Lesson.Part.Activity) 2.B.2, 3.B.2, 4.B.2, 6.B.2, 18.B.1, 57.B.2, 62.B.2, 111.B.1, 113.B.1, 116.B.1, 144.B.3 **Literature Anthology/Guide:** Lessons 6, 7, 8, 10, 12, 13, 14, 15, 16
	**Reading Standards for Informational Text: Integration of Knowledge and Ideas**	
RI.2.7	Explain how specific images (e.g., a diagram showing how a machine works) contribute to and clarify a text.	**Reading Presentation Book A:** (Lesson.Exercise) 4.4, 12.4, 15.4, 16.4, 19.3, 22.4, 23.3, 29.5, 31.4, 33.4, 35.3, 36.3, 36.4, 37.4, 38.3, 38.4, 41.5, 43.3, 44.3, 45.4, 46.3, 46.5, 47.3 **Reading Presentation Book B:** (Lesson.Exercise) 51.4, 52.4, 53.3, 54.3, 55.4, 56.4, 57.3, 58.4, 61.3, 61.4, 63.3, 64.3, 64.4, 65.4, 66.3, 69.3, 71.3, 72.4, 73.4, 78.3, 81.4, 82.4, 83.4, 85.4, 86.3, 87.4, 91.4, 93.3, 94.3, 95.4, 96.3 **Reading Presentation Book C:** (Lesson.Exercise) 103.2, 104.2, 106.2, 107.4, 107.5, 108.3, 109.4, 111.4, 113.3, 113.5, 114.2, 115.4, 116.3, 116.4, 118.5, 119.3, 121.3, 121.4, 122.4, 125.4, 128.3, 129.3, 132.3, 134.4, 136.4, 137.3, 138.4, 139.3, 139.4, 141.3, 141.4, 142.3, 142.4, 143.3, 144.4, 145.2 **Reading Textbook A:** Lessons 4.B, 12.C, 15.C, 16.C, 19.B, 22.D, 23.B, 29.D, 31.C, 33.B, 35.B, 36.B, 36.C, 37.B, 38.B, 38.C, 41.D, 43.B, 44.B, 45.B, 46.B, 46.C, 47.B **Reading Textbook B:** Lessons 51.C, 52.B, 53.B, 53.C, 54.B, 55.B, 56.C, 57.B, 58.B, 61.B, 61.C, 63.B, 64.B, 64.C, 65.B, 66.B, 69.B, 71.B, 72.B, 73.C, 78.B, 81.B, 82.B, 83.B, 85.B, 86.B, 87.B, 91.B, 93.B, 94.B, 95.B, 96.B **Reading Textbook C:** Lessons 103.B, 104.B, 106.B, 107.B, 107.C, 108.B, 109.C, 111.C, 113.B, 113.C, 114.B, 115.B, 116.C, 116.D, 118.C, 119.B, 121.B, 121.C, 122.B, 125.C, 128.D, 129.B, 132.C, 134.C, 136.C, 137.B, 138.B, 139.B, 139.C, 139.D, 141.B, 141.C, 142.B, 142.C, 143.B, 144.C, 145.B **Activities Across the Curriculum:** Activities 10, 13, 15, 16, 18, 32 **Research Projects**
RI.2.8	Describe how reasons support specific points the author makes in a text.	**Reading Presentation Book B:** (Lesson.Exercise) 51.3, 51.4, 53.3, 54.3, 56.4, 61.3, 66.3, 73.4 **Reading Presentation Book C:** (Lesson.Exercise) 101.4, 116.4 **Reading Textbook B:** Lessons 51.B, 51.C, 53.C, 54.B, 56.C, 61.B, 66.B, 73.C **Reading Textbook C:** Lessons 101.B, 116.D

GRADE 2 STANDARDS		PAGE REFERENCES
RI.2.9	Compare and contrast the most important points presented by two texts on the same topic.	**Reading Presentation Book B:** (Lesson.Exercise) 78 Special Project, 81 Special Project **Reading Presentation Book C:** (Lesson.Exercise) 122 Special Project, 143 Special Project, 144 Special Project **Reading Textbook B:** Lessons 78 Special Project, 81 Special Project **Reading Textbook C:** Lessons 122 Special Project, 143 Special Project, 144 Special Project **Core Lesson Connections:** (Lesson.Part.Activity) 64.B.1, 66.B.1, 81.B.1, 82.B.2, 108.B.2, 116.B.3, 117.B.1, 129.B.1 **Activities Across the Curriculum:** Activities 12, 18 **Research Projects**
	**Reading Standards for Informational Text: Range of Reading and Level of Text Complexity**	
RI.2.10	By the end of year, read and comprehend informational texts, including history/social studies, science, and technical texts, in the grades 2–3 text complexity band proficiently, with scaffolding as needed at the high end of the range.	**Reading Presentation Book A:** (Lesson.Exercise) 1.2, 2.2, 3.2, 8.3, 9.3, 11.4, 12.3, 14.4, 15.3, 16.3, 18.3, 19.3, 21.3, 21.4, 22.3, 23.3, 24.3, 26.3, 27.4, 29.4, 29.5, 32.4, 35.3, 36.3, 36.4, 37.4, 38.3, 38.4, 39.3, 41.4, 42.3, 42.4, 43.3, 44.3, 44.4, 45.4, 45.5, 48.4, 49.3 **Reading Presentation Book B:** (Lesson.Exercise) 51.3, 51.4, 52.4, 53.3, 53.5, 54.3, 55.5, 56.3, 57.3, 57.4, 58.4, 61.3, 61.4, 62.4, 62.5, 63.3, 64.3, 64.4, 66.3, 71.3, 73.3, 79.4, 82.3, 83.3, 83.4, 85.3, 87.4, 88.3, 89.3, 91.4, 94.3, 98.3, 99.2 **Reading Presentation Book C:** (Lesson.Exercise) 101.4, 101.5, 108.4, 109.3, 109.4, 111.4, 112.3, 113.3, 114.2, 115.4, 116.3, 118.4, 119.3, 121.3, 123.3, 124.3, 124.5, 125.3, 127.4, 128.3, 131.4, 131.5, 132.3, 132.5, 133.3, 134.3, 136.3, 136.4, 138.4, 138.5, 139.3, 139.4, 141.3, 142.3, 143.3, 144.3, 144.4, 145.2 **Reading Textbook A:** Lessons 1.B., 2.B, 3.B, 8.B, 9.B, 11.B, 12.B, 14.C, 15.B, 16.B, 18.B, 18.C, 19.C, 21.B, 21.D, 22.C, 23.B, 24.B, 26.B, 27.C, 29.C, 29.D, 32.C, 35.B, 36.B, 36.C, 37.B, 38.B, 38.C, 39.B, 41.B, 42.B, 42.C, 43.B, 44.B, 44.C, 45.B, 45.C, 48.B, 49.B **Reading Textbook B:** Lessons 51.B, 51.C, 52.B, 53.B, 53.C, 53.D, 54.B, 55.B, 56.B, 57.B, 57.C, 58.B, 61.B, 61.C, 62.B, 62.C, 63.B, 64.B, 64.C, 66.B, 71.B, 73.B, 79.C, 83.B, 87.B, 88.B, 89.B, 91.B, 94.B, 98.B **Reading Textbook C:** Lessons 101.B, 101.C, 108.C, 109.C, 112.B, 113.B, 114.B, 115.B, 116.B, 116.C, 118.B, 119.B, 121.B, 123.B, 124.B, 124.C, 125.B, 127.B, 128.B, 128.C, 128.D, 131.B, 131.C, 132.B, 132.C, 132.D, 133.B, 134.B, 136.B, 136.C, 138.B, 138.C, 139.B, 139.C, 139.D, 141.B, 142.B, 143.B, 144.B, 144.C, 145.B **Core Lesson Connections:** (Lesson.Part.Activity) 18.B.2, 19.B.2, 31.B.1, 32.B.1, 32.B.2, 33.B.1, 34.B.1, 36.B.1, 36.B.2,, 27.B.1, 37.B.2, 41.B.1, 41.B.2, 42.B.1, 42.B.2, 43.B.1, 43.B.2, 43.B.3, 44.B.1, 44.B.2, 46.B.2, 47.B.1, 47.B.2, 47.B.3, 48.B.1, 48.B.2, 51.B.1, 53.B.1, 53.B.2, 54.B.1, 54.B.2, 57.B.2, 62.B.1, 62.B.2,, 66.B.1, 66.B.2, 67.B.1, 81.B.1, 82.B.2, 83.B.1, 84.B.2, 86.B.1, 86.B.2, 87.B.1, 87.B.2,, 88.B.1, 88.B.2, 89.B.1, 89.B.2, 111.B.1, 111.B.3, 111.B.4, 112.B.2, 112.B.3, 113.B.3, 113.B.4, 114.B.2, 114.B.3, 116.B.1, 116.B.2, 117.B.1, 117.B.2, 126.B.2, 126.B.3, 127.B.2, 128.B.1, 129.B.1, 142.B.2, 142.B.3, 143.B.2, 144.B.1 **Research Projects**
	**Reading Standards for Foundational Skills: Print Concepts**	
RF.2.1	*(Not applicable to Grade 2)*	
	**Reading Standards for Foundational Skills: Phonological Awareness**	
RF.2.2	*(Not applicable to Grade 2)*	

GRADE 2 STANDARDS	PAGE REFERENCES
Reading Standards for Foundational Skills: Phonics and Word Recognition	
RF.2.3	Know and apply grade-level phonics and word analysis skills in decoding words.	
RF.2.3a	Distinguish long and short vowels when reading regularly spelled one-syllable words.	**Reading Presentation Book A:** (Lesson.Exercise) 1.1, 1.2, 1.4, 2.1, 2.2, 2.4, 3.1, 3.2, 3.4, 4.1–4, 4.6, 5.1–3, 5.5, 6.1–5, 7.1–6, 8.1–5, 9.1–5, 10.1, 11.1–6, 12.1–5, 13.1–5, 14.1–6, 15.4, 15.6, 16.1–5, 17.1–6, 18.1–5, 19.1–5, 20.1, 21.1–5, 22.1–5, 23.1–5, 24.1–5, 25.1–6, 26.1–5, 27.1–4, 28.1–5, 29.1–6, 30.2, 31.1–5, 32.1–5, 33.1–6, 34.1–5, 35.1–4, 36.1–5, 37.1–6, 38.1–5, 39.1, 39.4–6, 40.2, 41.1–6, 42.1–5, 43.1–5, 44.1–5, 45.1–6, 46.1–3, 46.5, 46.6, 47.1–3, 47.5, 47.7, 48.1–5, 48.7, 49.1–4, 50.2

		Reading Presentation Book B: (Lesson.Exercise) 51.1–4, 51.6, 52.1–5, 53.1–5, 54.1–4, 55.1–6, 56.1–5, 57.1–5, 58.1–6, 59.1–4, 60.2, 61.1–5, 62.1–6, 63.1–5, 64.1–5, 65.1–5, 66.1–5, 67.1–4, 68.1–5, 69.1–4, 70.1, 71.1–5, 72.1–5, 73.1–5, 74.1–4, 75.1–4, 76.1–5, 77.1–4, 78.1–4, 79.1–5, 80.2, 81.1–6, 82.1–5, 83.1–5, 84.1–5, 85.1–5, 86.1–4, 87.1–7, 88.1–4, 89.1–5, 90.2, 91.1–6, 92.1–4, 93.1–5, 94.1–5, 95.1–6, 96.1–4, 97.1–5, 98.1–3, 99.1–4, 100.2
		Reading Presentation Book C: (Lesson.Exercise) 101.1–5, 102.1–4, 103.1–4, 104.1–3, 105.1–3, 106.1–3, 107.1–6, 108.1–5, 109.1–5, 110.2, 111.1–6, 112.1–4, 113.1–3, 113.5, 113.6, 114.1–4, 115.1–6, 116.1–6, 117.1–4, 118.1–6, 119.1–5, 120.2, 121.1–5, 122.1–5, 123.1–5, 124.1–5, 125.1–5, 126.1–4, 127.1–6, 128.1–4, 129.1–4, 130.2, 131.1–6, 132.1–3, 132.5, 132.6, 133.1–5, 134.1–5, 135.1, 135.2, 135.4, 135.5, 136.1–5, 137.1–5, 138.1–6, 139.1–4, 139.6, 140.2, 141.1–5, 142.1–5, 143.1–5, 144.1–5, 145.1–4
		Reading Textbook A: (Lesson.Exercise) 1.A, 1.B, 1.D, 2.A, 2.B, 2.D, 3.D, 4.A, 4.B, 4.D, 5.A, 5.B, 5.D, 6.A–C, 7.A–C, 8.A–C, 9.A–C, 11.A–C, 12.A–C, 13.A–D, 14.A–D, 15.A–C, 16.A–C, 17.A–D, 18.A–D, 19.A–D, 21.A–D, 22.A–D, 23.A–C, 24.A–C, 25.A–C, 26.A–C, 27.A, 27.B, 28.A–C, 29.A–D, 31.A–C, 32.A–C, 33.A–C, 34.A, 34.C, 35.A–C, 36.A–C, 37.A–C, 38.A–C, 39.A–C, 41.A–D, 42.A–C, 43.A–C, 44.A–C, 45.A–C, 46.A–C, 47.A–C, 48.A–D, 49.A, 49.B
		Reading Textbook B: (Lesson.Exercise) 51.A–C, 52.A, 52.B, 53.A–E, 54.A, 54.B, 55.A–C, 56.A–C, 57.A–C, 58.A–C, 59.A, 59.B, 61.A–C, 62.A–C, 63.A–C, 64.A–C, 65.A, 65.B, 66.A–C, 67.A, 67.B, 68.A, 68.B, 69.A, 69.B, 71.A–C, 72.A, 72.B, 73.A–C, 74.A, 74.B, 75.A, 75.B, 76.A, 76.B, 77.A, 77.B, 78.A, 78.B, 79.A–C, 81.A–C, 82.A, 82.B, 83.A, 83.B, 84.A–C, 85.A, 85.B, 86.A, 86.B, 87.A, 87.B, 88.A, 88.B, 89.A–C, 91.A–C, 92.A, 92.B, 93.A–C, 94.A–C, 95.A–C, 96.A, 96.B, 97.A–C, 98.A, 98.B, 99.A, 99.B
		Reading Textbook C: (Lesson.Exercise) 101.A, 101.B, 102.A, 102.B, 103.A, 103.B, 104.A, 104.B, 105.A, 105.B, 106.A, 106.B, 107.A–C, 108.A–C, 109.A–C, 111.A–C, 112.A, 112.B, 113.A–C, 114.A–C, 115.A–C, 116.A–D, 117.A, 117.B, 118.A–C, 119.A–C, 121.A–C, 122.A, 122.B, 123.A–C, 124.A–C, 125.A–C, 126.A, 126.B, 127.A–C, 128.A–D, 129.A, 129.B, 131.A–C, 132.A–D, 133.A–C, 134.A–C, 135.A, 135.B, 136.A–C, 137.A–C, 138.A–C, 139.A–D, 141.A–C, 142.A–C, 143.A–C, 144.A–C, 145.A–C
		Spelling Teacher Presentation Book: Lessons 1.2, 2.2, 3.2, 4.2, 6.2, 7.2, 8.2, 9.2, 10.2, 11.2, 12.2, 13.2, 15.1, 16.1, 16.2, 17.2, 18.1, 18.2, 19.2, 20.2, 21.1, 21.2, 22.1, 22.2, 24.1, 24.2, 25.2, 26.2, 27.2, 28.1, 28.2, 29.2, 30.2, 37.1, 38.1, 39.1, 39.2, 40.1, 42.1, 43.1, 44.2, 45.2, 47.2, 49.2, 50.2, 52.2, 53.2, 54.2, 55.2, 56.2, 57.2, 61.2, 64.2, 71.2, 72.2, 73.1, 74.1, 75.1, 76.1, 78.1, 79.1, 81.1, 82.1, 83.1, 84.1, 85.1, 89.1, 93.2, 101.2, 102.2, 103.2, 107.1
		Research Projects

G13

	GRADE 2 STANDARDS	PAGE REFERENCES
RF.2.3b	Know spelling-sound correspondences for additional common vowel teams.	**Reading Presentation Book A:** (Lesson.Exercise) 35 Special Project **Reading Presentation Book B:** (Lesson.Exercise) 63 Special Project 2, 78 Special Project, 81 Special Project **Reading Presentation Book C:** (Lesson.Exercise) 122 Special Project, 143 Special Project, 144 Special Project **Reading Textbook B:** Lessons 63 Special Project 2, 78 Special Project, 81 Special Project **Reading Textbook C:** Lessons 122 Special Project, 143 Special Project, 144 Special Project **Language Presentation Book B:** (Lesson.Exercise) 69.2, 70.2, 70.3, 71.2, 76.2, 77.3, 78.5, 79.5, 87.5, 88.4, 92.3, 93.5, 94.6, 102.5, 103.4, 109.5, 110.4 **Language Textbook:** (Lesson.Exercise) 78, 79, 102 **Language Workbook:** Lessons 69, 70, 71, 76, 77, 87, 88, 92, 93, 94, 103, 109, 110 **Spelling Teacher Presentation Book:** Lessons 13.1, 14.1, 17.1, 19.1, 20.1, 29.1, 30.1, 45.1, 46.1, 47.1, 48.1, 58.1, 60.1, 62.1, 63.1, 64.1, 65.1, 66.1, 69.1, 70.1, 71.1, 72.1 **Research Projects**
RF.2.3c	Decode regularly spelled two-syllable words with long vowels.	**Reading Presentation Book A:** (Lesson.Exercise) 1.2, 2.2, 2.4, 3.2, 3.4, 4.4, 4.6, 5.5, 6.3, 6.5, 6.6, 7.6, 8.3, 8.5, 8.6, 9.5, 11.2, 11.4, 11.6, 11.7, 12.5, 13.3, 13.5, 14.6, 15.2, 16.3, 16.5, 17.4, 17.6, 18.5, 19.3, 19.5, 21.2, 21.3, 21.5, 22.2, 22.3, 22.4, 22.5, 23.2, 23.3, 23.5, 24.2, 24.3, 24.5, 25.2, 25.4, 25.6, 25.7, 26.3, 26.5, 27.2, 27.3, 27.4, 28.2, 28.3, 28.5, 29.2, 29.4, 29.5, 29.6, 31.2, 31.3, 31.5, 32.2, 32.3, 32.4, 32.5, 33.2, 33.4, 33.6, 34.2, 34.4, 35.2, 35.3, 36.4, 36.5, 37.6, 38.3, 38.5, 39.2, 39.3, 39.4, 39.6, 41.2, 41.4, 41.6, 42.2, 42.3, 42.4, 42.5, 43.2, 43.3, 43.5, 44.2, 44.3, 44.5, 45.4, 46.3, 46.6, 47.2, 47.3, 47.5, 47.7, 48.2, 48.4, 48.7, 49.2, 49.3, 49.4 **Reading Presentation Book B:** (Lesson.Exercise) 51.3, 51.6, 52.5, 53.3, 53.5, 54.4, 55.4, 56.3, 56.5, 57.3, 57.5, 58.6, 59.4, 61.3, 61.5, 62.6, 63.3, 63.5, 64.3, 64.5, 66.3, 66.5, 67.4, 68.5, 69.4, 70.1, 71.3, 71.5, 72.5, 73.3, 73.5, 74.4, 76.5, 77.4, 78.4, 79.3, 79.6, 81.4, 81.6, 82.5, 83.5, 84.3, 84.5, 86.4, 87.5, 88.4, 89.3, 89.5, 91.4, 91.6, 92.4, 93.3, 93.5, 94.3, 94.5, 95.4, 96.4, 97.3, 97.5, 98.3 **Reading Presentation Book C:** (Lesson.Exercise) 101.5, 102.4, 103.4, 104.3, 106.3, 107.4, 107.6, 108.3, 108.5, 109.5, 111.4, 111.6, 112.4, 113.3, 113.6, 114.2, 114.4, 115.4, 116.3, 116.5, 117.4, 118.4, 118.6, 119.3, 119.5, 121.3, 121.5, 122.3, 122.5, 123.3, 123.5, 124.3, 124.5, 125.3, 126.4, 127.4, 127.6, 128.3, 128.4, 129.4, 131.4, 131.6, 132.3, 132.6, 133.5, 134.3, 134.5, 136.3, 136.5, 137.3, 137.5, 138.4, 138.6, 139.3, 139.6, 141.3, 141.5, 142.3, 142.5, 143.3, 143.5, 144.3, 144.5, 145.2 **Reading Textbook A:** (Lesson.Exercise) 1.B, 1.D, 2.B, 2.D, 3.B, 3.D, 4.B, 4.D, 5.B, 5.D, 6.B, 6.C, 7.B, 7.C, 8.B, 8.D, 9.B, 9.C, 11.B, 11.C, 12.B, 12.C, 13.B–D, 14.B–D, 15.B, 15.C, 16.B, 16.C, 17.B–D, 18.B, 18.D, 19.B, 19.D, 21.B, 21.D, 22.B–D, 23.B, 23.C, 24.B, 24.C, 25.B, 25.C, 26.B, 26.C, 27.B, 28.B, 28.C, 29.B–D, 31.B, 231.C, 32.B, 32.C, 33.B, 33.C, 34.B, 35.B, 35.C, 36.B, 36.C, 37.B, 37.C, 38.B, 38.C, 39.B, 39.C, 41.B–D, 42.B, 42.C, 43.B, 43.C, 44.B, 44.C, 45.B, 45.C, 46.B, 46.C, 47.B, 47.C, 48.B–D, 49.B **Reading Textbook B:** (Lesson.Exercise) 51.B, 51.C, 51.D, 52.B, 53.B, 53.C, 53.D, 54.B, 55.B, 55.C, 56.B, 56.B, 57.B, 57.C, 58.B, 58.C, 59.B, 61.B, 61.C, 62.B, 62.C, 63.B, 63.C, 64.B, 64.C, 65.B, 66.B, 66.C, 67.B, 68.B, 69.B, 71.B, 71.C, 72.B, 73.B, 73.C, 74.B, 75B., 76.B, 77.B, 78.B, 79.B, 79.C, 81.B, 81.C, 82.B, 83.B, 84.B, 84.C, 85.B, 86.B, 87.B, 88.B, 89.B, 89.C, 91.B, 91.C, 92.B, 93.B, 93.C, 94.B, 94.C, 95.B, 95.C, 96.B, 97.B, 97.C, 98.B, 99.B **Reading Textbook C:** (Lesson.Exercise) 101.B, 102.B, 103.B, 104.B, 105.B, 106.B, 107.B, 107.C, 108.B, 108.C, 109.B, 109.C, 111.B, 111.C, 112.B, 113.B, 113.C, 114.B, 115.B, 115.C, 116.B, 116.C, 116.D, 117.B, 118.B, 118.C, 119.B, 119.C, 121.B, 122.B, 123.C, 124.B, 124.C, 125.B, 125.C, 126.B, 127.B, 127.C, 128.B, 128.C, 128.D, 129.B, 131.B, 131.C, 132.B, 132.D, 133.B, 133.C, 134.B, 134.C, 135.B, 136.B, 136.C, 137.B, 137.C, 137.D, 138.B, 138.C, 139.B, 139.C, 139.D, 141.B, 141.C, 142.B, 142.C, 143.B, 143.C, 144.B, 144.C, 145.B, 145.C

GRADE 2 STANDARDS		PAGE REFERENCES
RF.2.3d	Decode words with common prefixes and suffixes.	**Reading Presentation Book A:** (Lesson.Exercise) 1.1, 3.1, 4.1, 11.2, 15.2, 16.2, 18.2, 19.2, 21.2, 22.2, 23.2, 24.2, 28.2, 31.2, 32.2, 33.2, 34.2, 35.2, 37.2, 41.2, 42.2, 43.2, 44.2, 45.2, 46.2, 47.2, 48.2, 49.2 **Reading Presentation Book B:** (Lesson.Exercise) 51.2, 52.2, 53.2, 55.2, 56.2, 57.2, 59.2, 61.2, 62.2, 63.2, 64.2, 65.2, 67.2, 68.2, 69.2, 71.2, 72.2, 73.2, 74.2, 75.2, 76.2, 77.2, 78.2, 81.2, 83.2, 84.2, 86.2, 91.2, 92.2, 93.2, 95.2, 96.2, 97.2, 98.2, 99.2 **Reading Presentation Book C:** (Lesson.Exercise) 101.2, 102.2, 103.2, 104.1, 105.1, 106.1, 107.2, 108.2, 111.2, 112.2, 113.2, 114.1, 115.2, 117.2, 118.2, 121.2, 122.2, 123.2, 124.2, 127.2, 129.2, 131.2, 132.2, 133.2, 134.2, 137.2, 141.2, 143.2, 144.2, 145.2 **Reading Textbook A:** Lessons 1.A, 3.A, 4.A, 11.A, 15.A, 16.A, 18.A, 19.A, 21.A, 22.A, 23.A, 24.A, 28.A, 31.A, 32.A, 33.A, 34.A, 35.A, 37.A, 41.A, 42.A, 43.A, 44.A, 45.A, 46.A, 47.A, 48.A, 49.A **Reading Textbook B:** Lessons 51.A, 52.A, 53.A, 55.A, 56.A, 57.A, 59.A, 61.A, 62.A, 63.A, 64.A, 65.A, 67.A, 68.A, 69.A, 71.A, 72.A, 73.A, 74.A, 75.A, 76.A, 77.A, 78.A, 81.A, 82.A, 83.A, 84.A, 86.A, 91.A, 92.A, 93.A, 95.A, 96.A, 97.A, 98.A, 99.A **Reading Textbook C:** Lessons 101.1A, 102.A, 103.A, 104.A, 105.A, 106.A, 107.A, 108.A, 109.A, 111.A, 112.A, 113.A, 114.A, 115.A, 117.A, 118.A, 121.A, 122.A, 123.A, 124.A, 127.A, 129.A, 131.A, 132.A, 133.A, 134.A, 137.A, 141.A, 143.A, 144.A, 145.A **Language Presentation Book B:** (Lesson.Exercise) 69.2, 70.2 **Language Workbook:** (Lesson.Exercise) 69.A, 70.A **Core Lesson Connections:** (Lesson.Part.Activity) 17.A.1, 17.A.2, 18.B.2, 57.A.1, 57.A.2, 58.A.2, 97.A.1, 97.A.2, 98.A.2, 137.A.1, 137.A.2, 138.A.3 **Spelling Teacher Presentation Book:** Lessons 25.1, 26.1, 27.1, 28.3, 34.2, 35.2, 36.2, 38.2, 43.2, 46.2, 48.2, 53.2, 54.2, 56.2, 58.2, 63.2, 66.2, 67.2, 69.2, 73.2, 83.2, 87.1, 87.2, 88.1, 88.2, 89.1, 89.2, 90.1, 92.1, 92.2, 93.1, 94.1, 94.3, 96.1, 96.2, 97.1, 97.2, 98.1, 99.1, 99.2, 99.3, 100.1, 100.2, 101.1, 101.2, 102.1, 102.3, 103.1, 103.2, 105.1, 106.1, 106.3, 108.1, 108.3, 109.1, 110.1, 111.1, 111.2, 111.3, 112.1, 112.3, 114.1, 114.3, 115.1, 115.3, 116.1, 116.3, 117.1, 117.3, 118.1, 118.3, 119.1, 119.3, 120.1, 121.1, 123.1, 123.3, 124.1, 124.3, 125.1, 126.1, 127.1, 128.1, 129.1, 129.3, 130.1, 130.3, 132.1, 132.3, 133.1, 133.3, 134.1, 134.3, 135.1, 136.1, 136.3, 137.1, 137.3, 138.1, 138.2, 139.1, 139.2, 141.1, 141.2, 142.1, 142.2, 143.1, 143.2, 144.1
RF.2.3e	Identify words with inconsistent but common spelling-sound correspondences.	**Reading Presentation Book A:** (Lesson.Exercise) 35 Special Project **Reading Presentation Book B:** (Lesson.Exercise) 63 Special Project 2, 78 Special Project, 81 Special Project **Reading Presentation Book C:** (Lesson.Exercise) 122 Special Project, 143 Special Project, 144 Special Project **Reading Textbook B:** Lessons 63 Special Project 2, 78 Special Project, 81 Special Project **Reading Textbook C:** Lessons 122 Special Project, 143 Special Project, 144 Special Project **Language Presentation Book B:** (Lesson.Exercise) 69.2, 70.2, 70.3, 71.2, 76.2, 77.3, 78.5, 79.5, 87.5, 88.4, 92.3, 93.5, 94.6, 102.5, 103.4, 109.5, 110.4 **Language Textbook:** (Lesson.Exercise) 78, 79, 102 **Language Workbook:** Lessons 69–71, 76, 77, 87, 88, 92 –94, 103, 109, 110 **Activities Across the Curriculum:** Activities 5, 37, 38 **Spelling Teacher Presentation Book:** Lessons 1–145

G15

GRADE 2 STANDARDS		PAGE REFERENCES
RF.2.3f	Recognize and read grade-appropriate irregularly spelled words.	**Reading Presentation Book A:** (Lesson.Exercise) 1.1, 2.1, 3.1, 4.2, 5.2, 6.2, 7.2, 8.2, 9.2, 11.2, 12.2, 13.2, 14.2, 15.2, 16.2, 17.2, 18.2, 19.2, 21.2, 22.2, 23.2, 24.2, 25.2, 26.2, 27.2, 28.2, 29.2, 31.2, 32.2, 33.2, 34.2, 35.2, 36.2, 37.2, 38.2, 39.2, 41.2, 42.2, 43.2, 44.2, 45.2, 46.2, 47.2, 48.2, 49.2 **Reading Presentation Book B:** (Lesson.Exercise) 51.2, 52.2, 53.2, 54.2, 55.2, 56.2, 57.2, 58.2, 59.2, 61.2, 62.2, 63.2, 64.2, 65., 66.2, 67.2, 68.2, 69.2, 71.2, 72.2, 73.2, 74.2, 75.2, 76.2, 77.2, 78.2, 79.2, 81.2, 82.2, 83.2, 84.2, 85.2, 86.2, 87.2, 88.2, 89.2, 91.2, 92.2, 93.2, 94.2, 95.2, 96.2, 97.2, 98.1, 99.1 **Reading Presentation Book C:** (Lesson.Exercise) 101.2, 102.2, 103.2, 04.1, 105.1, 106.1, 107.2, 108.2, 109.2, 111.2, 112.2, 113.2, 114.1, 115.2, 116.2, 117.2, 118.2, 119.2, 121.2, 122.2, 123.2, 124.2, 125.2, 126.2, 127.2, 128.2, 129.2, 131.2, 132.2, 133.2, 134.2, 135.2, 136.2, 137.2, 138.2, 139.2, 141.2, 142.2, 143.2, 144.2, 145.1 **Core Lesson Connections:** (Lesson.Part.Activity) 1.A.2, 2.A.1, 2.A.2, 3.A.1, 3.A.2, 4.A.1, 4.A.2, 5.A.1, 6.A.1, 6.A.2, 7.A.1, 7.A.2, 8.A.1, 8.A.2, 9.A.1, 9.A.2, 10.A.1, 11.A.1, 11.A.2, 12.A.1, 12.A.2, 13.A.1, 13.A.1, 14.A.1, 15.A.1, 16.A.1, 16.A.2, 17.A.1, 17.A.2, 17.A.3, 18.A.1, 18.A.2, 19.A.1, 19.A.2, 20.A.1, 22.A.2, 21.A.1, 21.A.2, 22.A.1, 22.A.2, 23.A.1, 23.A.2, 24.A.1, 24.A.2, 25.A.1, 25.A.2, 26.A,1, 26.A.2, 27.A.1, 27.A.2, 28.A.1, 28.A.2, 29.A.1, 29.A.2, 30.A.1, 30.A.2, 31.A.1, 31.A.2, 32.A.1, 32.A.2, 33.A.1, 33.A.2, 34.A.1, 34.A.2, 35.A.1, 35.A.2, 36.A.1, 36.A.2, 37.A.1, 37.A.2, 38.A.1, 38.A.2, 39.A.1, 39.A.2, 40.A.1, 40.A.2, 41.A.1, 41.A.2, 42.A.1, 42.A.2, 43.A.1, 43.A.2, 44.A.1, 44.A.2, 45.A.1, 45.A.2, 46.A.1, 46.A.2, 47.A.1, 47.A.2, 48.A.1, 48.A.2, 49.A.1, 49.A.2, 50.A.1, 50.A.2, 51.A.1, 51.A.2, 52.A.1, 52.A.2, 53.A.1, 53.A.2, 54.A.1, 54.A.2, 55.A.1, 55.A.2, 56.A.1, 56.A.2, 57.A.1, 57.A.2, 58.A.1, 58.A.2, 59.A.1, 59.A.2, 60.A.1, 60.A.2, 61.A.1, 61.A.2, 62.A.1, 62.A.2, 63.A.1, 63.A.2, 64.A.1, 64.A.2, 65.A.1, 65.A.2, 66.A.1, 66.A.2, 67.A.1, 67.A.2, 68.A.1, 68.A.2, 69.A.1, 69.A.2, 70.A.1, 70.A.2, 71.A.1, 71.A.2, 72.A.1, 72.A.2, 73.A.1, 73.A.2, 74.A.1, 74.A.2, 75.A.1, 75.A.2, 76.A.1, 76.A.2, 77.A.1, 77.A.2, 78.A.1, 78.A.2, 79.A.1, 79.A.2, 80.A.1, 80.A.2, 81.A.1, 81.A.2, 82.A.1, 82.A.2, 83.A.1, 83.A.2, 84.A.1, 84.A.2, 85.A.1, 85.A.2, 86.A.1, 86.A.2, 87.A.1, 87.A.2, 88.A.1, 88.A.2, 89.A.1, 89.A.2, 90.A.1, 90.A.2, 91.A.1, 91.A.2, 92.A.1, 92.A.2, 93.A.1, 93.A.2, 94.A.1, 94.A.2, 95.A.1, 95.A.2, 96.A.1, 96.A.2, 97.A.1, 97.A.2, 98.A.1, 98.A.2, 99.A.1, 99.A.2, 100.A.1, 100.A.2, 101.A.1, 101.A.2, 102.A.1, 102.A.2, 103.A.1, 103.A.2, 104.A.1, 104.A.2, 105.A.1, 105.A.2, 106.A.1, 106.A.2, 107.A.1, 107.A.2, 108.A.1, 108.A.2, 109.A.1, 109.A.2, 110.A.1, 109.A.2, 110.A.1, 110.A.2, 111.A.1, 111.A.2, 112.A.1, 112.A.2, 113.A.1, 113.A.2, 114.A.1, 114.A.2, 115.A.1, 115.A.2, 116.A.1, 116.A.2, 117.A.1, 117.A.2, 118.A.1, 118.A.2, 119.A.1, 119.A.2, 120.A.1, 120.A.2, 121.A.1, 121.A.2, 122.A.1, 122.A.2, 123.A.1, 123.A.2, 124.A.1, 124.A.2, 125.A.1, 125.A.2, 126.A.1, 126.A.2, 127.A.1, 127.A.2, 128.A.1, 128.A.2, 129.A.1, 129.A.2, 130.A.1, 130.A.2, 131.A.1–3, 132.A.1–3, 133.A.1–3, 134.A.1–3, 135.A.1, 135.A.2, 136.A.1–3, 137.A.1–3, 138.A.1–3, 139.A.1–3, 140.A.1, 140.A.2, 141.A.1–3, 142.A.1–3, 143.A.1–3, 144.A.1–3, 145.A.1, 145.A.2 **Student Practice CD**
Reading Standards for Foundational Skills: Fluency		
RF.2.4	Read with sufficient accuracy and fluency to support comprehension.	

GRADE 2 STANDARDS		PAGE REFERENCES
RF.2.4a	Read grade-level text with purpose and understanding.	**Reading Presentation Book A:** (Lesson.Exercise) 1.2, 1.4, 2.2, 2.4, 3.2, 3.4, 4.4, 4.6, 5.3, 5.5, 6.3, 6.4, 7.4, 7.5, 8.3, 8.4, 9.3, 9.4, 10.1, 11.4, 11.5, 12.3, 12.4, 13.3, 13.4, 14.4, 14.5, 15.3, 15.4, 15.6, 16.3, 16.4, 17.4, 17.5, 18.3, 18.4, 19.3, 19.4, 20.1, 21.3, 21.4, 22.3, 22.4, 23.3, 23.4, 24.3, 24.4, 25.4, 25.5, 25.6, 26.3, 26.4, 27.3, 28.3, 28.4, 29.4, 29.5, 30.2, 31.3, 31.4, 32.3, 32.4, 33.4, 33.5, 34.3, 35.3, 35.4, 35.6, 36.3, 36.4, 37.4, 37.5, 38.3, 38.4, 39.3, 39.4, 40.1, 41.4, 41.5, 42.3, 42.4, 43.3, 43.4, 44.3, 44.4, 45.4, 45.5, 45.6, 46.4, 46.5, 47.4, 47.5, 48.4, 48.5, 49.3, 50.2 **Reading Presentation Book B:** (Lesson.Exercise) 51.3, 51.4, 52.4, 53.3, 53.5, 54.3, 55.4, 55.5, 55.6, 56.3, 56.4, 57.3, 57.4, 58.4, 58.5, 59.3, 60.2, 61.3, 61.4, 62.4, 62.5, 63.3, 63.4, 64.3, 64.4, 65.4, 65.5, 66.3, 66.4, 67.3, 68.4, 69.3, 70.2, 71.3, 71.4, 72.4, 73.3, 73.4, 74.3, 75.3, 75.4, 76.4, 77.3, 78.3, 79.4, 80.2, 81.4, 81.5, 82.3, 82.4, 83.3, 83.4, 84.3, 84.4, 85.3, 85.4, 85.5, 86.3, 87.4, 88.3, 89.3, 89.4, 90.2, 91.4, 91.5, 92.3, 93.3, 93.4, 94.3, 94.4, 95.4, 95.5, 95.6, 96.3, 97.3, 97.4, 98.2, 99.2, 99.3, 100.2 **Reading Presentation Book C:** (Lesson.Exercise) 101.4, 102.3, 103.3, 104.2, 105.2, 105.3, 106.2, 107.4, 107.5, 108.3, 108.4, 109.3, 109.4, 110.2, 111.4, 111.5, 112.3, 113.3, 113.5, 114.2, 114.3, 115.4, 115.5, 115.6, 116.3, 116.4, 117.3, 118.4, 119.3, 119.4, 120.2, 121.3, 121.4, 122.4, 123.3, 123.4, 124.3, 124.4, 125.3, 125.4, 125.5, 126.3, 127.4, 127.5, 128.3, 129.3, 130.2, 131.4, 131.5, 132.3, 132.5, 133.3, 133.4, 134.3, 135.4, 135.5, 136.3, 136.4, 137.3, 137.4, 138.4, 138.5, 139.3, 139.4, 140.2, 141.3, 141.4, 142.3, 142.4, 143.3, 143.4, 144.3, 144.4, 145.2, 145.3, 145.4 **Literature Anthology/Guide:** Lessons 2, 3, 4, 5, 6, 7, 8, 9, 10, 11, 12, 13, 14, 15, 16
RF.2.4b	Read grade-level text orally with accuracy, appropriate rate, and expression.	**Reading Presentation Book A:** (Lesson.Exercise) 1.2, 1.4, 2.2, 2.4, 3.2, 3.4, 4.4, 4.6, 5.3, 5.5, 6.3, 6.4, 7.4, 7.5, 8.3, 8.4, 9.3, 9.4, 10.1, 11.4, 11.5, 12.3, 12.4, 13.3, 13.4, 14.4, 14.5, 15.3, 15.4, 15.6, 16.3, 16.4, 17.4, 17.5, 18.3, 18.4, 19.3, 19.4, 20.1, 21.3, 21.4, 22.3, 22.4, 23.3, 23.4, 24.3, 24.4, 25.4, 25.5, 25.6, 26.3, 26.4, 27.3, 28.3, 28.4, 29.4, 29.5, 30.2, 31.3, 31.4, 32.3, 32.4, 33.4, 33.5, 34.3, 35.3, 35.4, 35.6, 36.3, 36.4, 37.4, 37.5, 38.3, 38.4, 39.3, 39.4, 40.1, 41.4, 41.5, 42.3, 42.4, 43.3, 43.4, 44.3, 44.4, 45.4, 45.5, 45.6, 46.4, 46.5, 47.4, 47.5, 48.4, 48.5, 49.3, 50.2 **Reading Presentation Book B:** (Lesson.Exercise) 51.3, 51.4, 52.4, 53.3, 53.5, 54.3, 55.4, 55.5, 55.6, 56.3, 56.4, 57.3, 57.4, 58.4, 58.5, 59.3, 60.2, 61.3, 61.4, 62.4, 62.5, 63.3, 63.4, 64.3, 64.4, 65.4, 65.5, 66.3, 66.4, 67.3, 68.4, 69.3, 70.2, 71.3, 71.4, 72.4, 73.3, 73.4, 74.3, 75.3, 75.4, 76.4, 77.3, 78.3, 79.4, 80.2, 81.4, 81.5, 82.3, 82.4, 83.3, 83.4, 84.3, 84.4, 85.3, 85.4, 85.5, 86.3, 87.4, 88.3, 89.3, 89.4, 90.2, 91.4, 91.5, 92.3, 93.3, 93.4, 94.3, 94.4, 95.4, 95.5, 95.6, 96.3, 97.3, 97.4, 98.2, 99.2, 99.3, 100.2 **Reading Presentation Book C:** (Lesson.Exercise) 101.4, 102.3, 103.3, 104.2, 105.2, 105.3, 106.2, 107.4, 107.5, 108.3, 108.4, 109.3, 109.4, 110.2, 111.4, 111.5, 112.3, 113.3, 113.5, 114.2, 114.3, 115.4, 115.5, 115.6, 116.3, 116.4, 117.3, 118.4, 119.3, 119.4, 120.2, 121.3, 121.4, 122.4, 123.3, 123.4, 124.3, 124.4, 125.3, 125.4, 125.5, 126.3, 127.4, 127.5, 128.3, 129.3, 130.2, 131.4, 131.5, 132.3, 132.5, 133.3, 133.4, 134.3, 135.4, 135.5, 136.3, 136.4, 137.3, 137.4, 138.4, 138.5, 139.3, 139.4, 140.2, 141.3, 141.4, 142.3, 142.4, 143.3, 143.4, 144.3, 144.4, 145.2, 145.3, 145.4 **Literature Anthology/Guide:** Lessons 2, 3, 4, 5, 6, 7, 8, 9, 10, 11, 12, 13, 14, 15, 16

GRADE 2 STANDARDS		PAGE REFERENCES
RF.2.4c	Use context to confirm or self-correct word recognition and understanding, rereading as necessary.	**Reading Presentation Book A:** (Lesson.Exercise) 11.7, 13.6, 14.4, 15.2, 15.5, 16.6, 17.4, 17.7, 18.6, 19.6, 21.1, 21.2, 21.6, 22.1, 22.2, 22.6, 23.1, 23.2, 23.6, 24.1, 24.6, 25.1, 25.3, 25.7, 26.1, 26.2, 26.6, 27.1, 27.2, 28.1, 28.2, 28.6, 29.1, 29.2, 29.3, 29.7, 31.1, 31.2, 31.6, 32.1, 32.2, 32.6, 33.1, 33.2, 33.3, 33.7, 34.1, 34.5, 35.1, 35.2, 35.6, 36.1, 37.4, 39.1, 39.2, 41.1, 41.2, 41.3, 42.1, 42.2, 43.1, 43.2, 44.1, 45.4, 47.1, 47.2, 48.1, 48.2, 48.3, 49.1, 49.2 **Reading Presentation Book B:** (Lesson.Exercise) 51.1, 51.2, 52.1, 52.3, 53.1, 54.1, 55.1, 55.3, 56.1, 57.1, 58.1, 58.3, 59.1, 61.1, 62.1, 63.1, 64.1, 65.1, 65.3, 66.1, 67.1, 68.1, 68.3, 69.1, 71.1, 72.1, 72.3, 73.1, 74.1, 75.1, 76.1, 76.3, 77.1, 78.1, 79.1, 81.1, 81.3, 86.1, 87.1, 87.3, 88.1, 89.1, 92.1, 93.1, 94.1, 95.1, 95.3, 96.1, 97.1 **Reading Presentation Book C:** (Lesson.Exercise) 101.1, 101.3, 102.1, 103.1, 107.1, 107.3, 108.1, 109.1, 111.1, 111.3, 112.1, 113.1, 115.1, 115.3, 116.1, 117.1, 118.3, 119.1, 121.1, 122.1, 123.123.5, 1, 124.1, 125.1, 126.1, 127.1, 127.3, 127 Special Project, 128.1, 129.1, 131.1, 131.3, 132.1, 133.1, 134.1, 135.1, 136.1, 137.1, 138.1, 138.3, 139.1, 141.1, 142.1, 143.1, 144.1 **Student Practice CD** **Literature Anthology/Literature Guide:** Lessons 2, 3, 4, 5, 6, 7, 8, 9, 10, 11, 12, 13, 14, 15, 16
Writing Standards: Text Types and Purposes		
W.2.1	Write opinion pieces in which they introduce the topic or book they are writing about, state an opinion, supply reasons that support the opinion, use linking words (e.g., *because, and, also*) to connect opinion and reasons, and provide a concluding statement or section.	**Language Presentation Book A:** (Lesson.Exercise) 64.4 **Language Workbook:** (Lesson.Exercise) 64.C **Core Lesson Connections:** (Lesson.Part.Activity) 120.B.1 **Activities Across the Curriculum:** Activities 1, 22 **Literature Anthology/Literature Guide:** Lesson 5
W.2.2	Write informative/explanatory texts in which they introduce a topic, use facts and definitions to develop points, and provide a concluding statement or section.	**Reading Presentation Book A:** (Lesson.Exercise) 23 Special Project, 35 Special Project **Reading Presentation Book B:** (Lesson.Exercise) 61 Special Project, 63 Special Project 2, 78 Special Project, 81 Special Project **Reading Presentation Book C:** (Lesson.Exercise) 106 Special Project, 122 Special Project, 127 Special Project, 143 Special Project, 144 Special Project, 145 Special Project **Reading Textbook B:** (Lesson.Exercise) 78 Special Project, 81 Special Project **Reading Textbook C:** (Lesson.Exercise) 122 Special Project, 143 Special Project, 144 Special Project , 145 Special Project 1 **Activities Across the Curriculum:** Activities 3, 7, 9, 12, 20, 23, 27, 28, 33 **Research Projects** **Literature Anthology/Literature Guide:** Lessons 3, 4.2, 5, 6, 10.2, 15
W.2.3	Write narratives in which they recount a well-elaborated event or short sequence of events, include details to describe actions, thoughts, and feelings, use temporal words to signal event order, and provide a sense of closure.	**Language Presentation Book A:** (Lesson.Exercise) 27.5, 28.3, 59.2 **Language Presentation Book B:** (Lesson.Exercise) 84.6, 85.2, 86.6, 87.7, 88.6, 89.6, 90.6, 91.5, 92.7, 93.7, 94.7, 96.6, 97.5, 98.7, 99.6, 99.7, 100.6, 100.7, 101.5, 102.6, 103.7, 104.6, 106.6, 107.6, 108.6, 109.6, 110.5, 110.7 **Language Textbook:** (Lesson.Exercise) 84.E, 85.A, 86.E, 87.F, 88.E, 89.E, 90.E, 91.D, 92.F, 93.F, 94.F, 96.F, 97.D, 98.F, 99.E, 99.F, 100.E, 100.F, 101.D, 102.E, 103.F, 104.E, 106.E, 107.E, 108.E, 109.E, 110.D, 110.F **Language Workbook:** (Lesson.Exercise) 27.D, 28.D, 59.B, 99.E, 100.E **Activities Across the Curriculum:** Activities 19, 31, 34 **Literature Anthology/Literature Guide:** Lessons 4.1, 4.2, 5, 7, 8, 9.1, 10.1, 11, 12

GRADE 2 STANDARDS		PAGE REFERENCES
Writing Standards: Production and Distribution of Writing		
W.2.4	*(Begins in Grade 3)*	
W.2.5	With guidance and support from adults and peers, focus on a topic and strengthen writing as needed by revising and editing.	**Reading Presentation Book A:** (Lesson.Exercise) 35 Special Project **Reading Presentation Book B:** (Lesson.Exercise) 63 Special Project, 78 Special Project, 81 Special Project **Reading Presentation Book C:** (Lesson.Exercise) 122 Special Project, 143 Special Project, 144 Special Project **Reading Textbook B:** Lessons 63 Special Project, 78 Special Project, 81 Special Project **Reading Textbook :** Lessons 122 Special Project, 143 Special Project, 144 Special Project **Language Presentation Book A:** (Lesson.Exercise) 6.6, 7.5, 8.4, 12.6, 13.6, 15.3, 24.4, 34.5, 35.5, 36.5, 37.4, 38.3, 39.3, 41.3, 42.2, 43.4, 45.3, 47.3, 48.4, 49.3, 51.3, 54.3, 56.4, 57.4, 61.4, 62.5 **Language Presentation Book B:** (Lesson.Exercise) 97.5, 98.7, 99.6, 100.6, 101.4, 102.4, 103.5, 104.5, 106.1, 107.5, 108.4 **Language Textbook:** (Lesson.Exercise) 97–104 **Language Workbook:** Lessons 106, 107, 108 **Activities Across the Curriculum:** Activities 1, 3, 7, 9, 12, 19, 31, 33 **Research Projects** **Literature Anthology/Guide:** Lessons 3, 4, 5, 6, 7, 8, 9, 10, 11, 13, 15
W.2.6	With guidance and support from adults, use a variety of digital tools to produce and publish writing, including in collaboration with peers.	**Reading Presentation Book B:** (Lesson.Exercise) 78 Special Project, 81 Special Project **Reading Presentation Book C:** (Lesson.Exercise) 122 Special Project **Reading Textbook B:** Lessons 78 Special Project, 81 Special Project **Reading Textbook C:** Lessons 122 Special Project **Research Projects**
Writing Standards: Research to Build and Present Knowledge		
W.2.7	Participate in shared research and writing projects (e.g., read a number of books on a single topic to produce a report; record science observations).	**Reading Presentation Book B:** (Lesson.Exercise) 78 Special Project, 81 Special Project **Reading Presentation Book C:** (Lesson.Exercise) 122 Special Project, 143 Special Project, 144 Special Project, 145 Special Project 1 **Reading Textbook B:** Lessons 78 Special Project, 81 Special Project **Reading Textbook C:** Lessons 122 Special Project, 143 Special Project, 144 Special Project, 145 Special Project 1 **Research Projects:** Projects 1, 2, 3, 4, 5 **Literature Anthology/Guide:** Lessons 4, 10
W.2.8	Recall information from experiences or gather information from provided sources to answer a question.	**Reading Presentation Book B:** (Lesson.Exercise) 78 Special Project, 81 Special Project **Reading Presentation Book C:** (Lesson.Exercise) 122 Special Project, 143 Special Project, 144 Special Project, 145 Special Project 1 **Reading Textbook B:** Lessons 78 Special Project, 81 Special Project **Reading Textbook C:** Lessons 122 Special Project, 143 Special Project, 144 Special Project, 145 Special Project 1 **Research Projects:** Projects 1, 2, 3, 4, 5 **Literature Anthology/Guide:** Lessons 4.2, 10.2
W.2.9	*(Begins in Grade 4)*	

G19

GRADE 2 STANDARDS		PAGE REFERENCES
Writing Standards: Range of Writing		
W.2.10	*(Begins in Grade 3)*	
Speaking & Listening Standards: Comprehension and Collaboration		
SL.2.1	Participate in collaborative conversations with diverse partners about *grade 2 topics and texts* with peers and adults in small and larger groups.	
SL.2.1a	Follow agreed-upon rules for discussions (e.g., gaining the floor in respectful ways, listening to others with care, speaking one at a time about the topics and texts under discussion).	**Reading Presentation Book A:** (Lesson.Exercise) 1.2, 1.4, 2.2, 2.4, 3.2, 3.4, 4.4, 4.6, 5.3, 5.5, 6.3, 6.4, 7.4, 7.5, 8.3, 8.4, 9.3, 9.4, 11.4, 11.5, 12.3, 12.4, 13.3, 13.4, 14.4, 14.5, 15.3, 15.4, 16.3, 16.4, 17.4, 17.5, 18.3, 18.4, 19.3, 19.4, 21.3, 21.4, 22.3, 22.4, 23.3, 23.4, 24.3, 24.4, 25.4, 25.5, 26.3, 26.4, 27.3, 28.3, 28.4, 29.4, 29.5, 30.1, 31.3, 31.4, 32.3, 32.4, 33.4, 33.5, 34.3, 35.3, 35.4, 36.3, 36.4, 37.4, 37.5, 38.3, 38.4, 39.3, 39.4, 40.1, 41.4, 41.5, 42.3, 42.4, 43.3, 43.4, 44.3, 44.4, 45.4, 45.5, 46.4, 46.5, 47.4, 47.5, 48.4, 48.5, 49.3, 50.1 **Reading Presentation Book B:** (Lesson.Exercise) 51.3, 51.4, 52.4, 53.3, 53.5, 54.3, 55.4, 55.5, 56.3, 56.4, 57.3, 57.4, 58.4, 58.5, 59.3, 60.1, 61.3, 61.4, 62.4, 62.5, 63.3, 63.4, 64.3, 64.4, 65.4, 66.3, 66.4, 67.3, 68.4, 69.3, 70.1, 71.3, 71.4, 72.4, 73.3, 73.4, 74.3, 75.3, 76.4, 77.3, 78.3, 79.4, 80.1, 81.4, 81.5, 82.3, 82.4, 83.3, 83.4, 84.3, 84.4, 85.3, 85.4, 86.3, 87.4, 88.3, 89.3, 89.4, 90.1, 91.4, 91.5, 92.3, 93.3, 93.4, 94.3, 94.4, 95.4, 95.5, 96.3, 97.3, 97.4, 98.2, 99.2, 99.3, 100.1 **Reading Presentation Book C:** (Lesson.Exercise) 101.4, 102.3, 103.3, 104.2, 105.2, 106.2, 107.4, 107.5, 108.3, 108.4, 109.3, 109.4, 110.1, 111.4, 111.5, 112.3, 113.3, 113.5, 114.2, 114.3, 115.4, 115.5, 116.3, 116.4, 117.3, 118.4, 119.3, 119.4, 120.1, 121.3, 121.4, 122.4, 123.3, 123.4, 124.3, 124.4, 125.3, 125.4, 126.3, 127.4, 127.5, 128.3, 129.3, 130.1, 131.4, 131.5, 132.3, 132.5, 133.3, 133.4, 134.3, 135.4, 136.3, 136.4, 137.3, 137.4, 138.4, 138.5, 139.3, 139.4, 140.1, 141.3, 141.4, 142.3, 142.4, 143.3, 143.4, 144.3, 144.4, 145.2, 145.3 **Language Presentation Book A:** (Lesson.Exercise) 1.7, 2.6, 3.5, 4.4, 5.6, 6.4, 7.4, 8.6, 9.6, 11.5, 12.5, 13.5, 14.5, 15.4, 16.4, 17.3, 18.3, 19.3, 22.5, 23.4, 24.3, 25.2, 27.4, 29.3, 32.4, 33.4, 34.4, 35.4, 36.4, 37.5, 38.4, 39.4, 41.4, 42.3, 43.3, 44.3, 45.5, 46.4, 47.4, 48.3, 49.2, 51.4, 52.2, 53.4, 54.4, 55.4, 56.3, 57.3, 58.2, 61.3, 62.4, 63.3, 64.2, 65.2 **Language Presentation Book B:** (Lesson.Exercise) 66.6, 67.7, 68.7, 69.7, 70.7, 71.8, 72.7, 73.8, 74.6, 75.3, 76.8, 77.8, 78.8, 79.8, 80.8, 81.8, 82.8, 83.7, 84.7, 85.3 **Research Projects** **Literature Anthology/Guide:** Lessons 1, 2, 3, 4, 5, 6, 7, 8, 9, 10, 11, 12, 13, 14, 15, 16

GRADE 2 STANDARDS		PAGE REFERENCES
SL.2.1b	Build on others' talk in conversations by linking their comments to the remarks of others.	**Reading Presentation Book A:** (Lesson.Exercise) 23 Special Project, 35 Special Project **Reading Presentation Book B:** (Lesson.Exercise) 63 Special Project 2, 78 Special Project, 81 Special Project **Reading Presentation Book C:** (Lesson.Exercise) 106 Special Project, 145 Special Project 2 **Reading Textbook B:** Lessons 78 Special Project, 81 Special Project **Reading Textbook B:** Lessons 106 Special Project **Language Presentation Book A:** (Lesson.Exercise) 27.5, 28.3, 47.5, 54.5, 58.3, 59.2 **Core Lesson Connections:** (Lesson.Part.Activity) 5.B.1, 10.B.1, 15.B.1, 20.B.1, 25.B.1, 30.B.1, 35.B.1, 40.B.1, 45.B.1, 5 0.B.1, 55.B.1, 60.B.1, 65.B.1, 70.B.1, 70.B.1, 75.B.1, 80.B.1, 85.B.1, 90.B.1, 95.B.1, 100.B.1, 105.B.1, 110.B.1, 115.B.1, 120.B.1, 125.B.1, 130.B.1, 135.B.1, 140.B.1, 145.B.1 **Research Projects** **Literature Anthology/Guide:** Lessons 2, 3, 4, 5, 6, 7, 8, 9, 10, 11, 12, 13, 14, 15, 16
SL.2.1c	Ask for clarification and further explanation as needed about the topics and texts under discussion.	**Reading Presentation Book A:** (Lesson.Exercise) 35 Special Project **Reading Presentation Book B:** (Lesson.Exercise) 78 Special Project, 81 Special Project **Reading Presentation Book C:** (Lesson.Exercise) 106 Special Project, 122 Special Project, 145 Special Project 2 **Reading Textbook B:** Lessons 78 Special Project, 81 Special Project **Reading Textbook B:** Lessons 106 Special Project, 122 Special Project **Language Presentation Book A:** (Lesson.Exercise) 27.5, 28.3, 47.5, 54.5, 58.3, 59.2 **Core Lesson Connections:** (Lesson.Part.Activity) 5.B.1, 10.B.1, 15.B.1, 20.B.1, 25.B.1, 30.B.1, 35.B.1, 40.B.1, 45.B.1, 5 0.B.1, 55.B.1, 60.B.1, 65.B.1, 70.B.1, 70.B.1, 75.B.1, 80.B.1, 85.B.1, 90.B.1, 95.B.1, 100.B.1, 105.B.1, 110.B.1, 115.B.1, 120.B.1, 125.B.1, 130.B.1, 135.B.1, 140.B.1, 145.B.1 **Research Projects** **Literature Anthology/Guide:** Lessons 2, 3, 4, 5, 6, 7, 8, 9, 10, 11, 12, 13, 14, 15, 16

GRADE 2 STANDARDS		PAGE REFERENCES
SL.2.2	Recount or describe key ideas or details from a text read aloud or information presented orally or through other media.	**Reading Presentation Book A:** (Lesson.Exercise) 1.2, 2.2, 3.2, 8.3, 9.3, 11.4, 12.3, 14.4, 15.3, 16.3, 18.3, 19.3, 21.3, 21.4, 22.3, 23.3, 24.3, 26.3, 27.4, 29.4, 29.5, 32.4, 35.3, 36.3, 36.4, 37.4, 38.3, 38.4, 39.3, 41.4, 42.3, 42.4, 43.3, 44.3, 44.4, 45.4, 45.5, 48.4, 49.3 **Reading Presentation Book B:** (Lesson.Exercise) 51.3, 51.4, 52.4, 53.3, 53.5, 54.3, 55.5, 56.3, 57.3, 57.4, 58.4, 61.3, 61.4, 62.4, 62.5, 63.3, 64.3, 64.4, 66.3, 71.3, 73.3, 79.4, 82.3, 83.3, 83.4, 85.3, 87.4, 88.3, 89.3, 91.4, 94.3, 98.3, 99.2 **Reading Presentation Book C:** (Lesson.Exercise) 101.4, 101.5, 108.4, 109.3, 109.4, 111.4, 112.3, 113.3, 114.2, 115.4, 116.3, 118.4, 119.3, 121.3, 123.3, 124.3, 124.5, 125.3, 127.4, 128.3, 131.4, 131.5, 132.3, 132.5, 133.3, 134.3, 136.3, 136.4, 138.4, 138.5, 139.3, 139.4, 141.3, 142.3, 143.3, 144.3, 144.4, 145.2 **Reading Textbook A:** Lessons 1.B., 2.B, 3.B, 8.B, 9.B, 11.B, 12.B, 14.C, 15.B, 16.B, 18.B, 18.C, 19.C, 21.B, 21.D, 22.C, 23.B, 24.B, 26.B, 27.C, 29.C, 29.D, 32.C, 35.B, 36.B, 36.C, 37.B, 38.B, 38.C, 39.B, 41.B, 42.B, 42.C, 43.B, 44.B, 44.C, 45.B, 45.C, 48.B, 49.B **Reading Textbook B:** Lessons 51.B, 51.C, 52.B, 53.B, 53.C, 53.D, 54.B, 55.B, 56.B, 57.B, 57.C, 58.B, 61.B, 61.C, 62.B, 62.C, 63.B, 64.B, 64.C, 66.B, 71.B, 73.B, 79.C, 83.B, 87.B, 88.B, 89.B, 91.B, 94.B, 98.B **Reading Textbook C:** Lessons 101.B, 101.C, 108.C, 109.C, 112.B, 113.B, 114.B, 115.B, 116.B, 116.C, 118.B, 119.B, 121.B, 123.B, 124.B, 124.C, 125.B, 127.B, 128.B, 128.C, 128.D, 131.B, 131.C, 132.B, 132.C, 132.D, 133.B, 134.B, 136.B, 136.C, 138.B, 138.C, 139.B, 139.C, 139.D, 141.B, 142.B, 143.B, 144.B, 144.C, 1454.B **Core Lesson Connections:** (Lesson.Part.Activity) 33.B.1, 34.B.1, 37.B.1, 42.B.1, 44.B.1, 48.B.1, 54.B.1, 87.B.1, 87.B., 88.B.1, 88.B.2, 89.B.1, 89.B.2, 112.B.2, 112.B.3, 114.B.2, 114.B.3, 127.B.2, 143.B.2 **Activities Across the Curriculum:** Activities 9, 12, 15, 17, 18, 30 **Research Projects** **Literature Anthology/Guide:** Lessons 2, 3, 4, 5, 6, 7, 8, 9, 10, 11, 12, 13, 14, 15, 16
SL.2.3	Ask and answer questions about what a speaker says in order to clarify comprehension, gather additional information, or deepen understanding of a topic or issue.	**Reading Presentation Book B:** (Lesson.Exercise) 67 Special Project **Reading Presentation Book C:** (Lesson.Exercise) 106 Special Project, 145 Special Project 2 **Language Presentation Book A:** (Lesson.Exercise) 27.5, 28.3, 47.5, 54.5, 58.3, 59.2 **Core Lesson Connections:** (Lesson.Part.Activity) 61.B.1, 131.B.1 **Research Projects** **Literature Anthology/Guide:** Lessons 2, 3, 4, 5, 6, 7, 8, 9, 10, 11, 12, 13, 14, 15, 16
Speaking & Listening Standards: Presentation of Knowledge and Ideas		
SL.2.4	Tell a story or recount an experience with appropriate facts and relevant, descriptive details, speaking audibly in coherent sentences.	**Reading Presentation Book C:** (Lesson.Exercise) 143 Special Project, 144 Special Project **Reading Textbook C:** Lessons 143 Special Project, 144 Special Project **Core Lesson Connections:** (Lesson.Part.Activity) 22.B.3, 23.B.3, 24.B.4, 26.B.3, 27.B.3, 28.B.2, 29.B.2, 39.B.2, 59.B.1, 61.B.1, 69.B.2, 97.B.1, 104.B.3, 124.B.3, 131.B.1, 136.B.3, 141.B.2 **Research Projects** **Literature Anthology/Guide:** Lessons 2, 3, 4, 5, 6, 7, 8, 9, 10, 11, 12, 13, 14, 15, 16
SL.2.5	Create audio recordings of stories or poems; add drawings or other visual displays to stories or recounts of experiences when appropriate to clarify ideas, thoughts, and feelings.	**Activities Across the Curriculum:** Activities 2, 14, 19, 22, 24, 26, 29 **Research Projects** **Literature Anthology/Guide:** Lessons 2, 3, 4.2, 10.1, 11

GRADE 2 STANDARDS		PAGE REFERENCES
SL.2.6	Produce complete sentences when appropriate to task and situation in order to provide requested detail or clarification.	**Reading Presentation Book A:** (Lesson.Exercise) 1.2, 1.4, 2.2, 2.4, 3.2, 3.4, 4.4, 4.6, 5.3, 5.5, 6.3–5, 7.4–6, 8.3–5, 9.3–5, 10.1, 11.4–6, 12.3–5, 13.3–5, 14.4–6, 15.3, 15.4, 15.6, 16.3–5, 17.4–6, 18.3–5, 19.3–5, 20.1, 21.3–5, 22.3–5, 23.3–5, 24.3–5, 25.4–6, 27.3, 27.4, 28.3–5, 29.4–6, 30.2, 31.3–5, 32.3–5, 33.4–6, 34.4–6, 35.3–5, 36.3–5, 37.4–7, 38.3–5, 39.3, 39.4, 39.6, 40.2, 41.4–6, 42.3–5, 43.3–5, 44.3–5, 45.4–6, 46.4, 46.5, 46.6, 47.3, 47.5, 47.7, 48.4, 48.5, 48.7, 49.3, 49.4, 50.2 **Reading Presentation Book B:** (Lesson.Exercise) 51.3, 51.4, 51.6, 52.3–5, 53.3–5, 54.3, 54.4, 55.4–6, 56.3–5, 57.3–5, 58.4–6, 59.3, 59.4, 60.2, 61.3–5, 62.4–6, 63.3–5, 64.3–5, 65.4, 65.5, 66.3–5, 67.3, 67.4, 68.4, 68.5, 69.3, 69.4, 70.2, 71.3–5, 72.4, 72.5, 73.3–5, 74.3, 74.4, 75.3, 75.4, 76.4, 76.5, 77.3, 77.4, 78.3, 78.4, 79.3–5, 80.2, 81.4–6, 82.4, 82.5, 83.4, 83.5, 84.3–5, 85.4, 85.5, 86.3, 86.4, 87.4, 87.5, 88.3, 88.4, 89.3–5, 90.2, 91.4–6, 92.3, 92.4, 93.3–5, 94.3–5, 95.4–6, 96.3, 96.4, 97.3–5, 98.2, 98.3, 99.3, 99.4, 100.2 **Reading Presentation Book C:** (Lesson.Exercise) 101.4, 101.5, 102.3, 102.4, 103.3, 103.4, 104.2, 104.3, 105.2, 105.3, 106.2, 106.3, 107.4, 107.5, 108.3–7, 109.4, 109.5, 110.2, 111.4–6, 112.3, 112.4, 113.3, 113.5, 113.6, 114.2–4, 115.4–6, 116.3–5, 117.3, 117.4, 118.4–6, 119.3–5, 120.2, 121.3–5, 122.4, 122.5, 123.3–5, 124.3–5, 125.3–5, 126.3, 126.4, 127.4–6, 128.3, 128.4, 129.3, 129.4, 130.2, 131.4–6, 132.3, 132.5, 132.6, 133.3–5, 134.3–5, 135.4, 135.5, 136.3–5, 137.3–5, 138.4–6, 139.3, 139.4, 139.6, 140.2, 141.3–5, 142.3–5, 143.3–5, 144.3–5, 145.2–4 **Reading Textbook A:** (Lesson.Exercise) 1.B, 1.D, 2.B, 2.D, 3.B, 3.D, 4.B, 4.D, 5.B, 5.D, 6.B, 6.C, 7.B, 7.C, 8.B, 8.D, 9.B, 9.C, 11.B, 11.C, 12.B, 12.C, 13.B–D, 14.B–D, 15.B, 15.C, 16.B, 16.C, 17.B–D, 18.B, 18.D, 19.B, 19.D, 21.B, 21.D, 22.B–D, 23.B, 23.C, 24.B, 24.C, 25.B, 25.C, 26.B, 26.C, 27.B, 28.B, 28.C, 29.B–D, 31.B, 231.C, 32.B, 32.C, 33.B, 33.C, 34.B, 35.B, 35.C, 36.B, 36.C, 37.B, 37.C, 38.B, 38.C, 39.B, 39.C, 41.B–D, 42.B, 42.C, 43.B, 43.C, 44.B, 44.C, 45.B, 45.C, 46.B, 46.C, 47.B, 47.C, 48.B–D, 49.B **Reading Textbook B:** (Lesson.Exercise) 51.B, 51.C, 52.B, 53.B–E, 54.B, 55.B, 55.C, 56.B, 56.C, 57.B, 57.C, 58.B, 58.C, 59.B, 61.B, 61.C, 62.B, 62.C, 63.B, 63.C, 64.B, 64.C, 65.B, 66.B, 66.C, 67.B, 68.B, 69.B, 71.B, 71.C, 72.B, 73.B, 73.C, 74.B, 75.B, 76.B, 77.B, 78.B, 79.B, 79.C, 81.B, 81.C, 82.B, 83.B, 84.B, 84.C, 85.B, 86.B, 87.B, 88.B, 89.B, 89.C, 91.B, 91.C, 92.B, 93.B, 93.C, 94.B, 94.C, 95.B, 95.C, 96.B, 97.B, 97.C, 98.B, 99.B **Reading Textbook C:** (Lesson.Exercise) 101.B, 102.B, 103.B, 104.B, 105.B, 106.B, 107.B, 107.C, 108.B, 108.C, 109.B, 109.C, 111.B, 111.C, 112.B, 113.B, 113.C, 114.B, 114.C, 115.B, 115.C, 116.B–D, 117.B, 118.B, 118.C, 119.B, 119.C, 121.B **Research Projects**
Language Standards: Conventions of Standard English		
L.2.1	Demonstrate command of the conventions of standard English grammar and usage when writing or speaking.	
L.2.1a	Use collective nouns (e.g., *group*).	**Core Lesson Connections:** (Lesson.Part.Activity) 10.D.1, 20.D.1, 30.D.1, 40.D.1, 50.D.1, 60.D.1, 70.D.1, 80.D.1, 90.D.1, 100.D.1, 110.D.1, 120.D.1, 130.D.1, 140.D.1
L.2.1b	Form and use frequently occurring irregular plural nouns (e.g., *feet, children, teeth, mice, fish*).	**Reading Presentation Book A:** (Lesson.Exercise) 1.1, 49.2 **Reading Presentation Book B:** (Lesson.Exercise) 53.2, 55.2, 56.2, 57.2, 64.2, 65.2, 71.2, 84.2, 86.2 **Reading Presentation Book C:** (Lesson.Exercise) 101.2 **Reading Textbook A:** (Lesson.Exercise) 1.A, 49.A **Reading Textbook B:** (Lesson.Exercise) 53.A, 55.A, 56.A, 57.A, 64.A, 65.A, 71.A, 84.A, 86.A **Reading Textbook B:** (Lesson.Exercise) 101.A

GRADE 2 STANDARDS		PAGE REFERENCES
L.2.1c	Use reflexive pronouns (e.g., *myself, ourselves*).	**Core Lesson Connections:** (Lesson.Part.Activity) 10.D.1, 20.D.1, 30.D.1, 40.D.1, 50.D.1, 60.D.1, 70.D.1, 80.D.1, 90.D.1, 100.D.1, 110.D.1, 120.D.1, 130.D.1, 140.D.1
L.2.1d	Form and use the past tense of frequently occurring irregular verbs (e.g., *sat, hid, told*).	**Language Presentation Book B:** (Lesson.Exercise) 69.2, 70.2, 70.3, 71.2, 71.3, 72.3, 73.4, 73.6, 74.3, 76.2, 77.3, 78.2, 78.5, 79.4, 79.5, 80.3, 81.2, 83.3, 84.4, 86.4, 87.4, 87.5, 88.4, 90.4, 91.3, 92.3, 93.5, 94.6, 95.3, 96.3, 98.6, 100.4, 102.5, 103.4, 105.3, 106.3, 106.4, 107.2, 107.4, 108.2, 109.3, 110.3 **Language Textbook:** (Lesson.Exercise) 76.E, 78.D, 79.D, 102.D **Language Workbook:** (Lesson.Exercise) 69.A, 70.A, 70.B, 71.A, 71.B, 72.B, 73.C, 74.B, 76.A, 77.B, 78.A, 79.C, 80.B, 81.A, 83.B, 84.C, 86.C, 87.C, 87.D, 88.C, 90.C, 91.B, 92.B, 93.D, 94.E, 95.B, 96.C, 98.E, 100.C, 103.C, 106.C, 107.A, 107.C, 108.A, 109.B, 110.B
L.2.1e	Use adjectives and adverbs, and choose between them depending on what is to be modified.	**Reading Presentation Book A:** (Lesson.Exercise) 35 Special Project **Reading Presentation Book B:** (Lesson.Exercise) 61 Special Project **Reading Presentation Book C:** (Lesson.Exercise) 122 Special Project **Reading Textbook C:** Lessons 122 Special Project **Activities Across the Curriculum:** Activities 1, 9, 33
L.2.1f	Produce, expand, and rearrange complete simple and compound sentences (e.g., *The boy watched the movie; The little boy watched the movie; The action movie was watched by the little boy*).	**Reading Presentation Book A:** (Lesson.Exercise) 35 Special Project **Reading Presentation Book B:** (Lesson.Exercise) 63 Special Project, 67 Special Project, 78 Special Project, 81 Special Project **Reading Presentation Book C:** (Lesson.Exercise) 143 Special Project, 144 Special Project **Reading Textbook B:** Lessons 63 Special Project, 67 Special Project, 78 Special Project, 81 Special Project **Reading Textbook C:** Lessons 143 Special Project, 144 Special Project **Activities Across the Curriculum:** Activities 1, 3, 7, 9, 12, 19, 28, 31, 33, 34 **Research Projects** **Literature Anthology/Guide:** Lessons 3, 4, 5, 6, 7, 8, 9, 10, 11, 12, 13, 15
L.2.2	Demonstrate command of the conventions of standard English capitalization, punctuation, and spelling when writing.	
L.2.2a	Capitalize holidays, product names, and geographic names.	**Reading Presentation Book A:** (Lesson.Exercise) 23 Special Project **Reading Presentation Book B:** (Lesson.Exercise) 53 Special Project **Reading Textbook A:** Lessons 23 Special Project **Reading Textbook B:** Lessons 53 Special Project **Activities Across the Curriculum:** Activities 8, 10, 13, 18, 32 **Research Projects**
L.2.2b	Use commas in greetings and closings of letters.	**Language Presentation Book A:** (Lesson.Exercise) 53.1, 54.1, 55.1, 64.4, 65.4 **Language Workbook:** (Lesson.Exercise) 53.A, 54.A, 55.A, 64.C, 65.C
L.2.2c	Use an apostrophe to form contractions and frequently occurring possessives.	**Reading Presentation Book C:** (Lesson.Exercise) 127.4, 127.5 **Reading Textbook C:** Lessons 127.B, 127.C **Workbook C:** Lesson 127 **Language Presentation Book B:** (Lesson.Exercise) 109.4, 110.4 **Language Workbook:** (Lesson.Exercise) 109.C, 110.C **Activities Across the Curriculum:** Activity 38 **Student Practice CD**

GRADE 2 STANDARDS		PAGE REFERENCES
L.2.2d	Generalize learned spelling patterns when writing words (e.g., *cage →* *badge; boy → boil*).	**Reading Presentation Book A:** (Lesson.Exercise) 35 Special Project **Reading Presentation Book B:** (Lesson.Exercise) 63 Special Project 2, 78 Special Project, 81 Special Project **Reading Presentation Book C:** (Lesson.Exercise) 122 Special Project, 143 Special Project, 144 Special Project **Reading Textbook B:** Lessons 63 Special Project 2, 78 Special Project, 81 Special Project **Reading Textbook C:** Lessons 122 Special Project, 143 Special Project, 144 Special Project **Language Presentation Book B:** (Lesson.Exercise) 69.2, 70.2, 70.3, 71.2, 76.2, 77.3, 78.5, 79.5, 87.5, 88.4, 92.3, 93.5, 94.6, 102.5, 103.4, 109.5, 110.4 **Language Textbook:** (Lesson.Exercise) 78, 79, 102 **Language Workbook:** Lessons 69–71, 76, 77, 87, 88, 92 –94, 103, 109, 110 **Spelling Teacher Presentation Book:** Lessons 13.2, 15.1, 15.2, 16.2, 17.1, 17.2, 18.2, 19.1, 20.1, 20.2, 24.2, 25.2, 26.2, 27.2, 28.2, 29.2, 30.1, 30.2, 31.2, 33.2, 39.2, 44.1, 45.1, 46.1, 47.1, 48.1, 49.1, 89.1, 90.1, 91.1, 92.1, 93.1, 94.1, 95.1, 96.1, 97.1, 98.1, 99.1, 100.1, 101.1, 102.1, 103.1, 109.1, 110.1, 111.1, 112.1, 113.1, 114.1, 115.1, 116.1, 117.1, 119.1, 120.1, 121.1, 123.1, 124.1, 125.1, 126.1, 127.1, 128.1, 129.1, 130.1, 132.1, 133.1, 134.1, 136.1, 137.1, 138.1, 138.2, 139.1, 139.2, 141.1, 141.2, 142.1, 142.2, 143.1, 143.2
L.2.2e	Consult reference materials, including beginning dictionaries, as needed to check and correct spellings.	**Reading Presentation Book B:** (Lesson.Exercise) 81, Special Project **Reading Textbook B:** Lesson 81 Special Project **Core Lesson Connections:** (Lesson.Part.Activity) 131.A.2, 132.A.2, 133.A.2, 134.A.2, 136.A.2, 138.A.2, 139.A.2, 131.A.1, 142.A.1, 143.A.1, 144.A.1 **Research Projects**
Language Standards: Knowledge of Language		
L.2.3	Use knowledge of language and its conventions when writing, speaking, reading, or listening.	
L.2.3a	Compare formal and informal uses of English.	**Reading Presentation Book A:** (Lesson.Exercise) 35 Special Project **Reading Presentation Book B:** (Lesson.Exercise) 63 Special Project, 67 Special Project, 78 Special Project, 81 Special Project **Reading Presentation Book C:** (Lesson.Exercise) 106 Special Project, 122 Special Project, 143 Special Project, 144 Special Project, 145 Special Project 2 **Reading Textbook B:** Lessons 63 Special Project, 67 Special Project, 78 Special Project, 81 Special Project **Reading Textbook C:** Lessons 122 Special Project, 143 Special Project, 144 Special Project **Language Presentation Book B:** (Lesson.Exercise) 70.3, 71.2, 71.3, 72.3, 72.4, 73.3, 73.4, 73.6, 74.2, 74.3, 75.4, 76.2, 76.4, 77.3, 77.4, 78.2, 78.4, 78.5, 79.2, 79.4, 79.5, 80.2, 80.3, 81.2, 81.4, 82.2, 82.3, 83.2, 83.3, 84.3, 84.4, 85.4, 86.2, 86.4, 87.2, 87.4, 87.5, 88.3, 88.4, 89.2, 89.4, 90.2, 90.4, 91.2–4, 92.3, 92.4, 93.2, 93.4, 93.4, 94.2–4, 94.6, 95.3, 95.4, 96.1–3, 97.2–4, 98.2–4, 98.6, 99.3–5, 100.24, 101.2, 101.3, 1–2.2, 102.3, 102.5, 103.3, 103.4, 104.2, 104.3, 105.2–4, 106.1–5, 107.2–4, 108.2, 108.3, 109.2–4, 110.2–4 **Core Lesson Connections:** (Lesson.Part.Activity) 5.B.1, 10.B.1, 15.B.1, 20.B.1, 25.B.1, 30.B.1, 35.B.1, 40.B.1, 45.B.1, 50.B.1, 55.B.1, 60.B.1, 65.B.1, 70.B.1, 75.B.1, 80.B.1, 85.B.1, 90.B.1, 95.B.1, 100.B.1, 105.B.1, 110.B.1, 115.B.1, 120.B.1, 125.B.1, 130.B.1, 135.B.1, 140.B.1, 145.B.1 **Research Projects** **Literature Anthology/Guide:** Lessons 12, 13

G25

GRADE 2 STANDARDS		PAGE REFERENCES
Language Standards: Vocabulary Acquisition and Use		
L.2.4	Determine or clarify the meaning of unknown and multiple-meaning words and phrases based on grade 2 reading and content, choosing flexibly from an array of strategies.	
L.2.4a	Use sentence-level context as a clue to the meaning of a word or phrase.	**Reading Presentation Book A:** (Lesson.Exercise) 11.7, 13.6, 14.4, 15.2, 15.5, 16.6, 17.4, 17.7, 18.6, 19.6, 21.1, 21.2, 21.6, 22.1, 22.2, 22.6, 23.1, 23.2, 23.6, 24.1, 24.6, 25.1, 25.3, 25.7, 26.1, 26.2, 26.6, 27.1, 27.2, 28.1, 28.2, 28.6, 29.1, 29.2, 29.3, 29.7, 31.1, 31.2, 31.6, 32.1, 32.2, 32.6, 33.1, 33.2, 33.3, 33.7, 34.1, 34.5, 35.1, 35.2, 35.6, 36.1, 37.4, 39.1, 39.2, 41.1, 41.2, 41.3, 42.1, 42.2, 43.1, 43.2, 44.1, 45.4, 47.1, 47.2, 48.1, 48.2, 48.3, 49.1, 49.2 **Reading Presentation Book B:** (Lesson.Exercise) 51.1, 51.2, 52.1, 52.3, 53.1, 54.1, 55.1, 55.3, 56.1, 57.1, 58.1, 58.3, 59.1, 61.1, 62.1, 63.1, 64.1, 65.1, 65.3, 66.1, 67.1, 68.1, 68.3, 69.1, 71.1, 72.1, 72.3, 73.1, 74.1, 75.1, 76.1, 76.3, 77.1, 78.1, 79.1, 81.1, 81.3, 86.1, 87.1, 87.3, 88.1, 89.1, 92.1, 93.1, 94.1, 95.1, 95.3, 96.1, 97.1 **Reading Presentation Book C:** (Lesson.Exercise) 101.1, 101.3, 102.1, 103.1, 107.1, 107.3, 108.1, 109.1, 111.1, 111.3, 112.1, 113.1, 115.1, 115.3, 116.1, 117.1, 118.3, 119.1, 121.1, 122.1, 123.123.5, 1, 124.1, 125.1, 126.1, 127.1, 127.3, 127 Special Project, 128.1, 129.1, 131.1, 131.3, 132.1, 133.1, 134.1, 135.1, 136.1, 137.1, 138.1, 138.3, 139.1, 141.1, 142.1, 143.1, 144.1 **Reading Textbook A:** Lessons 11.D, 13.E, 14.B, 14.C, 14.E, 15.D, 16.D, 17.C, 17.E, 18.E, 19.E, 21.E, 22.E, 23.D, 24.E, 25.E, 26.E, 27.E, 28.E, 29.E, 31.E, 32.E, 33.E, 34.E, 35.E, 36.E, 37.E, 38.E, 39.E, 41.E, 42.E, 43.E, 44.E, 45.E, 46.E, 47.E, 48.E, 49.E **Research Projects** **Student Practice CD** **Literature Anthology/Literature Guide:** Lessons 2, 3, 4, 5, 6, 7, 8, 9, 10, 11, 12, 13, 14, 15, 16
L.2.4b	Determine the meaning of the new word formed when a known prefix is added to a known word (e.g., *happy/ unhappy, tell/retell*).	**Reading Presentation Book A:** (Lesson.Exercise) 5.2, 19.2, 21.2, 29.2, 45.2 **Reading Presentation Book C:** (Lesson.Exercise) 107.2, 108.2, 111.2, 112.2, 121.1, 122.2 **Reading Textbook A:** (Lesson.Exercise) 5.A, 19.A, 21.A, 29.A, 45.A **Reading Textbook C:** (Lesson.Exercise) 104.A, 108.A **Language Presentation Book B:** (Lesson.Exercise) 69.2, 70.2 **Language Workbook:** (Lesson.Exercise) 69.A, 70.A **Core Lesson Connections:** (Lesson.Part.Activity) 17.A.1, 17.A.2, 18.B.2 **Spelling Teacher Presentation Book:** Lessons 96.2, 97.2, 99.2, 100.2, 105.1, 106.1

G26

GRADE 2 STANDARDS		PAGE REFERENCES
L.2.4c	Use a known root word as a clue to the meaning of an unknown word with the same root (e.g., *addition, additional*).	**Reading Presentation Book A:** (Lesson.Exercise) 5.2, 19.2, 21.2, 29.2, 45.2 **Reading Presentation Book C:** (Lesson.Exercise) 107.2, 108.2, 111.2, 112.2, 121.1, 122.2 **Reading Textbook A:** (Lesson.Exercise) 5.A, 19.A, 21.A, 29.A, 45.A **Reading Textbook C:** (Lesson.Exercise) 104.A, 108.A **Language Presentation Book B:** (Lesson.Exercise) 69.2, 70.2 **Language Workbook:** (Lesson.Exercise) 69.A, 70.A **Core Lesson Connections:** (Lesson.Part.Activity) 17.A.1, 17.A.2, 18.B.2 **Spelling Teacher Presentation Book:** Lessons 25.1, 26.1, 27.1, 28.3, 34.2, 35.2, 36.2, 38.2, 43.2, 46.2, 48.2, 53.2, 54.2, 56.2, 58.2, 63.2, 66.2, 67.2, 69.2, 73.2, 83.2, 87.1, 87.2, 88.1, 88.2, 89.1, 89.2, 90.1, 92.1, 92.2, 93.1, 94.1, 94.3, 96.1, 96.2, 97.1, 97.2, 98.1, 99.1, 99.2, 99.3, 100.1, 100.2, 101.1, 101.2, 102.1, 102.3, 103.1, 103.2, 105.1, 106.1, 106.3, 108.1, 108.3, 109.1, 110.1, 111.1, 111.2, 111.3, 112.1, 112.3, 114.1, 114.3, 115.1, 115.3, 116.1, 116.3, 117.1, 117.3, 118.1, 118.3, 119.1, 119.3, 120.1, 121.1, 123.1, 123.3, 124.1, 124.3, 125.1, 126.1, 127.1, 128.1, 129.1, 129.3, 130.1, 130.3, 132.1, 132.3, 133.1, 133.3, 134.1, 134.3, 135.1, 136.1, 136.3, 137.1, 137.3, 138.1, 138.2, 139.1, 139.2, 141.1, 141.2, 142.1, 142.2, 143.1, 143.2, 144.1
L.2.4d	Use knowledge of the meaning of individual words to predict the meaning of compound words (e.g., *birdhouse, lighthouse, housefly; bookshelf, notebook, bookmark*).	**Reading Presentation Book A:** (Lesson.Exercise) 6.2, 21.2, 25.2, 26.2, 27.2, 29.2, 32.2, 38.2, 41.2, 42.2 **Reading Presentation Book B:** (Lesson.Exercise) 52.2, 54.2, 56.2, 61.2, 67.2, 68.2, 69.2, 85.2, 86.2, 92.2, 97.2, 98.2 **Reading Presentation Book C:** (Lesson.Exercise) 107.2, 118.2, 131.2 **Reading Textbook A:** Lessons 6.A, 21.A, 25.A, 26.A, 27.A, 29.A, 32.A, 38.A, 41.A, 42.A **Reading Textbook B:** Lessons 52.A, 54.A, 56.A, 61.A, 67.A, 68.A, 69.A, 85.A, 86.A, 92.A, 97.A, 98.A **Reading Textbook C:** Lessons 107.A, 118.A, 131.A **Activities Across the Curriculum:** Activity 5 **Spelling Teacher Presentation Book:** Lessons 114.2, 115.2, 116.2, 117.2, 118.2, 119.2, 121.2, 123.2, 124.2, 126.2, 137.2
L.2.4e	Use glossaries and beginning dictionaries, both print and digital, to determine or clarify the meaning of words and phrases.	**Reading Presentation Book B:** (Lesson.Exercise) 81, Special Project **Reading Textbook B:** Lesson 81 Special Project **Core Lesson Connections:** (Lesson.Part.Activity) 131.A.2, 132.A.2, 133.A.2, 134.A.2, 136.A.2, 138.A.2, 139.A.2, 131.A.1, 142.A.1, 143.A.1, 144.A.1 **Research Projects**
L.2.5	Demonstrate understanding of figurative language, word relationships and nuances in word meanings.	

G27

GRADE 2 STANDARDS		PAGE REFERENCES
L.2.5a	Identify real-life connections between words and their use (e.g., *describe foods that are spicy or juicy*).	**Reading Presentation Book A:** (Lesson.Exercise) 1.1, 2.1, 3.1, 4.1–3, 5.1, 5.2, 6.1, 6.2, 7.1–3, 8.1, 8.2, 9.1, 9.2, 11.1–3, 12.1, 12.2, 13.1, 13.2, 14.1–3, 15.1, 15.2, 16.1, 16.2, 17.1–3, 18.1, 18.2, 19.1, 19.2, 21.1, 21.2, 22.1, 22.2, 23.1, 23.2, 24.1, 24.2, 25.1–3, 26.1, 26.2, 27.1, 27.2, 28.1, 28.2, 29.1–3, 31.1, 31.2, 32.1, 32.2, 33.1–3, 34.1, 34.2, 35.1, 35.2, 36.1, 36.2, 37.1–3, 38.1, 38.2, 39.1, 39.2, 41.1–3, 42.1, 42.2, 43.1, 43.2, 44.1, 44.2, 45.1–3, 2, 46.1, 46.2, 47.1, 47.2, 48.1–3, 49.1, 49.2 **Reading Presentation Book B:** (Lesson.Exercise) 51.1, 51.2, 52.1–3, 53.1, 53.2, 54.1, 54.2, 55.1–3, 56.1, 56.2, 57.1, 57.2, 58.1–3, 59.1, 59.2, 61.1, 61.2, 62.1–3, 63.1, 63.2, 64.1, 64.2, 65.1–3, 66.1, 66.2, 67.1, 67.1–3, 68.1, 68.2, 69.1, 69.2, 71.1, 71.3, 72.1–3, 73.1, 73.2, 74.1, 74.2, 75.1, 75.2, , 76.1–3, 77.1, 77.2, 78.1, 78.2, 79.1, 79.2, 81.1–3, 82.1, 82.2, 83.1, 83.2, 84.1, 84.2, 85.1, 85.2, 86.1, 86.2, 87.1–3, 88.1, 88.2, 89.1, 89.2, 91.1–3, 92.1, 92.2, 93.1, 93.2, 94.1, 94.2, 95.1–3, 96.1, 96.2, 97.1, 97.2, 98.1, 99.1 **Reading Presentation Book C:** (Lesson.Exercise) 101.1–3, 102.1, 102.2, 103.1, 103.2, 04.1, 105.1, 106.1, 107.1–3, 108.1, 108.2, 109.1, 109.2, 111.1–3, 112.1, 112.2, 113.1, 113.2, 114.1, 115.1–3, 116.1, 116.2, 117.1, 117.2, 118.1–3, 119.1, 119.2, 121.1, 121.2, 122.1–3, 1123.1, 123.2, 124.1, 124.2, 125.1, 125.2, 126.1, 126.2, 127.1–3, 128.1, 128.2, 129.1, 129.2, 131.1–3, 132.1, 132.2, 133.1, 133.2, 134.1, 134.2, 135.1, 135.2, 136.1, 136.2, 137.1, 137.2, 138.1–3, 139.1, 139.2, 141.1, 141.2, 142.1, 142.2, 143.1, 143.2, 144.1, 144.2, 145.1 **Reading Textbook A:** Lessons 1–9, 11–19, 21–29, 31–39, 41–49 **Reading Textbook B:** Lessons 51–59, 61–69, 71–79, 81–89, 91–99 **Reading Textbook B:** Lessons 101–109, 111–119, 121–129, 131–139, 141–145 **Core Lesson Connections:** (Lesson.Part.Activity) 1.A.2, 2.A.1, 2.A.2, 3.A.1, 3.A.2, 4.A.1, 4.A.2, 5.A.1, 6.A.1, 6.A.2, 7.A.1, 7.A.2, 8.A.1, 8.A.2, 9.A.1, 9.A.2, 10.A.1, 11.A.1, 11.A.2, 12.A.1, 12.A.2, 13.A.1, 13.A.1, 14.A.1, 15.A.1, 16.A.1, 16.A.2, 17.A.1, 17.A.2, 17.A.3, 18.A.1, 18.A.2, 19.A.1, 19.A.2, 20.A.1, 22.A.2, 21.A.1, 21.A.2, 22.A.1, 22.A.2, 23.A.1, 23.A.2, 24.A.1, 24.A.2, 25.A.1, 25.A.2, 26.A,1, 26.A.2, 27.A.1, 27.A.2, 28.A.1, 28.A.2, 29.A.1, 29.A.2, 30.A.1, 30.A.2, 31.A.1, 31.A.2, 32.A.1, 32.A.2, 33.A.1, 33.A.2, 34.A.1, 34.A.2, 35.A.1, 35.A.2, 36.A.1, 36.A.2, 37.A.1, 37.A.2, 38.A.1, 38.A.2, 39.A.1, 39.A.2, 40.A.1, 40.A.2, 41.A.1, 41.A.2, 42.A.1, 42.A.2, 43.A.1, 43.A.2, 44.A.1, 44.A.2, 45.A.1, 45.A.2, 46.A.1, 46.A.2, 47.A.1, 47.A.2, 48.A.1, 48.A.2, 49.A.1, 49.A.2, 50.A.1, 50.A.2, 51.A.1, 51.A.2, 52.A.1, 52.A.2, 53.A.1, 53.A.2, 54.A.1, 54.A.2, 55.A.1, 55.A.2, 56.A.1, 56.A.2, 57.A.1, 57.A.2, 58.A.1, 58.A.2, 59.A.1, 59.A.2, 60.A.1, 60.A.2, 61.A.1, 61.A.2, 62.A.1, 62.A.2, 63.A.1, 63.A.2, 64.A.1, 64.A.2, 65.A.1, 65.A.2, 66.A.1, 66.A.2, 67.A.1, 67.A.2, 68.A.1, 68.A.2, 69.A.1, 69.A.2, 70.A.1, 70.A.2, 71.A.1, 71.A.2, 72.A.1, 72.A.2, 73.A.1, 73.A.2, 74.A.1, 74.A.2, 75.A.1, 75.A.2, 76.A.1, 76.A.2, 77.A.1, 77.A.2, 78.A.1, 78.A.2, 79.A.1, 79.A.2, 80.A.1, 80.A.2, 81.A.1, 81.A.2, 82.A.1, 82.A.2, 83.A.1, 83.A.2, 84.A.1, 84.A.2, 85.A.1, 85.A.2, 86.A.1, 86.A.2, 87.A.1, 87.A.2, 88.A.1, 88.A.2, 89.A.1, 89.A.2, 90.A.1, 90.A.2, 91.A.1, 91.A.2, 92.A.1, 92.A.2, 93.A.1, 93.A.2, 94.A.1, 94.A.2, 95.A.1, 95.A.2, 96.A.1, 96.A.2, 97.A.1, 97.A.2, 98.A.1, 98.A.2, 99.A.1, 99.A.2, 100.A.1, 100.A.2, 101.A.1, 101.A.2, 102.A.1, 102.A.2, 103.A.1, 103.A.2, 104.A.1, 104.A.2, 105.A.1, 105.A.2, 106.A.1, 106.A.2, 107.A.1, 107.A.2, 108.A.1, 108.A.2, 109.A.1, 109.A.2, 110.A.1, 109.A.2, 110.A.1, 110.A.2, 111.A.1, 111.A.2, 112.A.1, 112.A.2, 113.A.1, 113.A.2, 114.A.1, 114.A.2, 115.A.1, 115.A.2, 116.A.1, 116.A.2, 117.A.1, 117.A.2, 118.A.1, 118.A.2, 119.A.1, 119.A.2, 120.A.1, 120.A.2, 121.A.1, 121.A.2, 122.A.1, 122.A.2, 123.A.1, 123.A.2, 124.A.1, 124.A.2, 125.A.1, 125.A.2, 126.A.1, 126.A.2, 127.A.1, 127.A.2, 128.A.1, 128.A.2, 129.A.1, 129.A.2, 130.A.1, 130.A.2, 131.A.1–3, 132.A.1–3, 133.A.1–3, 134.A.1–3, 135.A.1, 135.A.2, 136.A.1–3, 137.A.1–3, 138.A.1–3, 139.A.1–3, 140.A.1, 140.A.2, 141.A.1–3, 142.A.1–3, 143.A.1–3, 144.A.1–3, 145.A.1, 145.A.2

G28

GRADE 2 STANDARDS		PAGE REFERENCES
L.2.5b	Distinguish shades of meaning among closely related verbs (e.g., *toss, throw, hurl*) and closely related adjectives (e.g., *thin, slender, skinny, scrawny*).	**Core Lesson Connections:** (Lesson.Part.Activity) 5.A.2, 10.A.2, 15.A.3, 20.A.3, 25.A.3, 30.A.3, 35.A.3, 40.A.3, 45.A.3, 50.A.3, 55.A.3, 60.A.3, 65.A.3, 70.A.3, 75.A.3, 80.A.3, 85.A.3, 90.A.3, 95.A.3, 100.A.3, 105.A.3, 110.A.3, 115.A.3, 120.A.3, 125.A.3, 130.A.3, 135.A.3, 140.A.3, 145.A.3
L.2.6	Use words and phrases acquired through conversations, reading and being read to, and responding to texts, including using adjectives and adverbs to describe (e.g., *When other kids are happy that makes me happy*).	**Reading Presentation Book A:** (Lesson.Exercise) 1.1, 1.2, 1.4, 2.1, 2.2, 2.4, 3.1, 3.2, 3.4, 4.1–4, 4.6, 5.1–3, 5.5, 6.1–5, 7.1–6, 8.1–5, 9.1–5, 11.1–6, 12.1–5, 13.1–5, 14.1–6, 15.4, 15.6, 16.1–5, 17.1–6, 18.1–5, 19.1–5, 21.1–5, 22.1–5, 23.1–5, 24.1–5, 25.1–6, 26.1–5, 27.1–4, 28.1–5, 29.1–6, 31.1–5, 32.1–5, 33.1–6, 34.1–5, 35.1–4, 36.1–5, 37.1–6, 38.1–5, 39.1, 39.4–6, 41.1–6, 42.1–5, 43.1–5, 44.1–5, 45.1–6, 46.1–3, 46.5, 46.6, 47.1–3, 47.5, 47.7, 48.1–5, 48.7, 49.1–4, 50.2 **Reading Presentation Book B:** (Lesson.Exercise) 51.1–4, 51.6, 52.1–5, 53.1–5, 54.1–4, 55.1–6, 56.1–5, 57.1–5, 58.1–6, 59.1–4, 61.1–5, 62.1–6, 63.1–5, 64.1–5, 65.1–5, 66.1–5, 67.1–4, 68.1–5, 69.1–4, 71.1–5, 72.1–5, 73.1–5, 74.1–4, 75.1–4, 76.1–5, 77.1–4, 78.1–4, 79.1–5, 81.1–6, 82.1–5, 83.1–5, 84.1–5, 85.1–5, 86.1–4, 87.1–7, 88.1–4, 89.1–5, 91.1–6, 92.1–4, 93.1–5, 94.1–5, 95.1–6, 96.1–4, 97.1–5, 98.1–3, 99.1–4 **Reading Presentation Book C:** (Lesson.Exercise) 101.1–5, 102.1–4, 103.1–4, 104.1–3, 105.1–3, 106.1–3, 107.1–6, 108.1–5, 109.1–5, 111.1–6, 112.1–4, 113.1–3, 113.5, 113.6, 114.1–4, 115.1–6, 116.1–6, 117.1–4, 118.1–6, 119.1–5, 121.1–5, 122.1–5, 123.1–5, 124.1–5, 125.1–5, 126.1–4, 127.1–6, 128.1–4, 129.1–4, 131.1–6, 132.1–3, 132.5, 132.6, 133.1–5, 134.1–5, 135.1, 135.2, 135.4, 135.5, 136.1–5, 137.1–5, 138.1–6, 139.1–4, 139.6, 141.1–5, 142.1–5, 143.1–5, 144.1–5, 145.1–4 **Reading Textbook A:** (Lesson.Exercise) 1.A, 1.B, 1.D, 2.A, 2.B, 2.D, 3.D, 4.A, 4.B, 4.D, 5.A, 5.B, 5.D, 6.A–C, 7.A–C, 8.A–C, 9.A–C, 11.A–C, 12.A–C, 13.A–D, 14.A–D, 15.A–C, 16.A–C, 17.A–D, 18.A–D, 19.A–D, 21.A–D, 22.A–D, 23.A–C, 24.A–C, 25.A–C, 26.A–C, 27.A, 27.B, 28.A–C, 29.A–D, 31.A–C, 32.A–C, 33.A–C, 34.A, 34.C, 35.A–C, 36.A–C, 37.A–C, 38.A–C, 39.A–C, 41.A–D, 42.A–C, 43.A–C, 44.A–C, 45.A–C, 46.A–C, 47.A–C, 48.A–D, 49.A, 49.B **Reading Textbook B:** (Lesson.Exercise) 51.A–C, 52.A, 52.B, 53.A–E, 54.A, 54.B, 55.A–C, 56.A–C, 57.A–C, 58.A–C, 59.A, 59.B, 61.A–C, 62.A–C, 63.A–C, 64.A–C, 65.A, 65.B, 66.A–C, 67.A, 67.B, 68.A, 68.B, 69.A, 69.B, 71.A–C, 72.A, 72.B, 73.A–C, 74.A, 74.B, 75.A, 75.B, 76.A, 76.B, 77.A, 77.B, 78.A, 78.B, 79.A–C, 81.A–C, 82.A, 82.B, 83.A, 83.B, 84.A–C, 85.A, 85.B, 86.A, 86.B, 87.A, 87.B, 88.A, 88.B, 89.A–C, 91.A–C, 92.A, 92.B, 93.A–C, 94.A–C, 95.A–C, 96.A, 96.B, 97.A–C, 98.A, 98.B, 99.A, 99.B **Reading Textbook C:** (Lesson.Exercise) 101.A, 101.B, 102.A, 102.B, 103.A, 103.B, 104.A, 104.B, 105.A, 105.B, 106.A, 106.B, 107.A–C, 108.A–C, 109.A–C, 111.A–C, 112.A, 112.B, 113.A–C, 114.A–C, 115.A–C, 116.A–D, 117.A, 117.B, 118.A–C, 119.A–C, 121.A–C, 122.A, 122.B, 123.A–C, 124.A–C, 125.A–C, 126.A, 126.B, 127.A–C, 128.A–D, 129.A, 129.B, 131.A–C, 132.A–D, 133.A–C, 134.A–C, 135.A, 135.B, 136.A–C, 137.A–C, 138.A–C, 139.A–D, 141.A–C, 142.A–C, 143.A–C, 144.A–C, 145.A–C **Language Presentation Book A:** (Lesson.Exercise) 1.2–4, 2.2, 2.3, 3.1, 3.2, 4.2, 5.2, 5.3, 5.5, 6.1, 7.1, 8.1, 9.1, 9.4, 10.2, 11.1, 11.4, 12.1, 12.2, 13.1, 13.2, 14.2, 14.3, 16.2, 16.4, 17.4, 20.2, 22.2, 23.1 **Language Presentation Book B:** (Lesson.Exercise) 70.3, 71.2, 73.6, 76.2, 77.3, 78.5, 79.5, 86.4, 87.5, 88.4, 90.4, 91.3, 92.3, 93.5, 94.6, 95.3, 96.3, 98.6, 100.4, 101.3, 102.5, 103.4, 107.4 **Language Textbook:** (Lesson.Exercise) 70.B, 71.A, 76.A, 77.B, 86.C, 87.D, 88.C, 90.C, 91.B, 92.B, 93.D, 94.E, 95.B, 96.C, 98.E, 100.C, 101.B, 103.C, 107.C **Language Workbook:** (Lesson.Exercise) 1.A, 2.A, 2.B, 3.A, 3.B, 4.B, 5.B, 9.C, 10.B, 10.C, 12.A, 13.A, 14.B, 17.D, 20.B, 73.E, 78.D, 79.D, 102.D

GRADE 2 STANDARDS	PAGE REFERENCES
	Core Lesson Connections: (Lesson.Part.Activity) 1.A.2, 2.A.1, 2.A.2, 3.A.1, 3.A.2, 4.A.1, 4.A.2, 5.A.1, 6.A.1, 6.A.2, 7.A.1, 7.A.2, 8.A.1, 8.A.2, 9.A.1, 9.A.2, 10.A.1, 11.A.1, 11.A.2, 12.A.1, 12.A.2, 13.A.1, 13.A.1, 14.A.1, 15.A.1, 16.A.1, 16.A.2, 17.A.1, 17.A.2, 17.A.3, 18.A.1, 18.A.2, 19.A.1, 19.A.2, 20.A.1, 22.A.2, 21.A.1, 21.A.2, 22.A.1, 22.A.2, 23.A.1, 23.A.2, 24.A.1, 24.A.2, 25.A.1, 25.A.2, 26.A,1, 26.A.2, 27.A.1, 27.A.2, 28.A.1, 28.A.2, 29.A.1, 29.A.2, 30.A.1, 30.A.2, 31.A.1, 31.A.2, 32.A.1, 32.A.2, 33.A.1, 33.A.2, 34.A.1, 34.A.2, 35.A.1, 35.A.2, 36.A.1, 36.A.2, 37.A.1, 37.A.2, 38.A.1, 38.A.2, 39.A.1, 39.A.2, 40.A.1, 40.A.2, 41.A.1, 41.A.2, 42.A.1, 42.A.2, 43.A.1, 43.A.2, 44.A.1, 44.A.2, 45.A.1, 45.A.2, 46.A.1, 46.A.2, 47.A.1, 47.A.2, 48.A.1, 48.A.2, 49.A.1, 49.A.2, 50.A.1, 50.A.2, 51.A.1, 51.A.2, 52.A.1, 52.A.2, 53.A.1, 53.A.2, 54.A.1, 54.A.2, 55.A.1, 55.A.2, 56.A.1, 56.A.2, 57.A.1, 57.A.2, 58.A.1, 58.A.2, 59.A.1, 59.A.2, 60.A.1, 60.A.2, 61.A.1, 61.A.2, 62.A.1, 62.A.2, 63.A.1, 63.A.2, 64.A.1, 64.A.2, 65.A.1, 65.A.2, 66.A.1, 66.A.2, 67.A.1, 67.A.2, 68.A.1, 68.A.2, 69.A.1, 69.A.2, 70.A.1, 70.A.2, 71.A.1, 71.A.2, 72.A.1, 72.A.2, 73.A.1, 73.A.2, 74.A.1, 74.A.2, 75.A.1, 75.A.2, 76.A.1, 76.A.2, 77.A.1, 77.A.2, 78.A.1, 78.A.2, 79.A.1, 79.A.2, 80.A.1, 80.A.2, 81.A.1, 81.A.2, 82.A.1, 82.A.2, 83.A.1, 83.A.2, 84.A.1, 84.A.2, 85.A.1, 85.A.2, 86.A.1, 86.A.2, 87.A.1, 87.A.2, 88.A.1, 88.A.2, 89.A.1, 89.A.2, 90.A.1, 90.A.2, 91.A.1, 91.A.2, 92.A.1, 92.A.2, 93.A.1, 93.A.2, 94.A.1, 94.A.2, 95.A.1, 95.A.2, 96.A.1, 96.A.2, 97.A.1, 97.A.2, 98.A.1, 98.A.2, 99.A.1, 99.A.2, 100.A.1, 100.A.2, 101.A.1, 101.A.2, 102.A.1, 102.A.2, 103.A.1, 103.A.2, 104.A.1, 104.A.2, 105.A.1, 105.A.2, 106.A.1, 106.A.2, 107.A.1, 107.A.2, 108.A.1, 108.A.2, 109.A.1, 109.A.2, 110.A.1, 109.A.2, 110.A.1, 110.A.2, 111.A.1, 111.A.2, 112.A.1, 112.A.2, 113.A.1, 113.A.2, 114.A.1, 114.A.2, 115.A.1, 115.A.2, 116.A.1, 116.A.2, 117.A.1, 117.A.2, 118.A.1, 118.A.2, 119.A.1, 119.A.2, 120.A.1, 120.A.2, 121.A.1, 121.A.2, 122.A.1, 122.A.2, 123.A.1, 123.A.2, 124.A.1, 124.A.2, 125.A.1, 125.A.2, 126.A.1, 126.A.2, 127.A.1, 127.A.2, 128.A.1, 128.A.2, 129.A.1, 129.A.2, 130.A.1, 130.A.2, 131.A.1–3, 132.A.1–3, 133.A.1–3, 134.A.1–3, 135.A.1, 135.A.2, 136.A.1–3, 137.A.1–3, 138.A.1–3, 139.A.1–3, 140.A.1, 140.A.2, 141.A.1–3, 142.A.1–3, 143.A.1–3, 144.A.1–3, 145.A.1, 145.A.2 **Activities Across the Curriculum:** Activities 4, 5, 6, 11, 17, 27, 37, 38 **Research Projects** **Literature Anthology/Guide:** Lessons 2, 3, 4, 5, 6, 7, 8, 9, 10, 11, 12, 13, 14, 15, 16